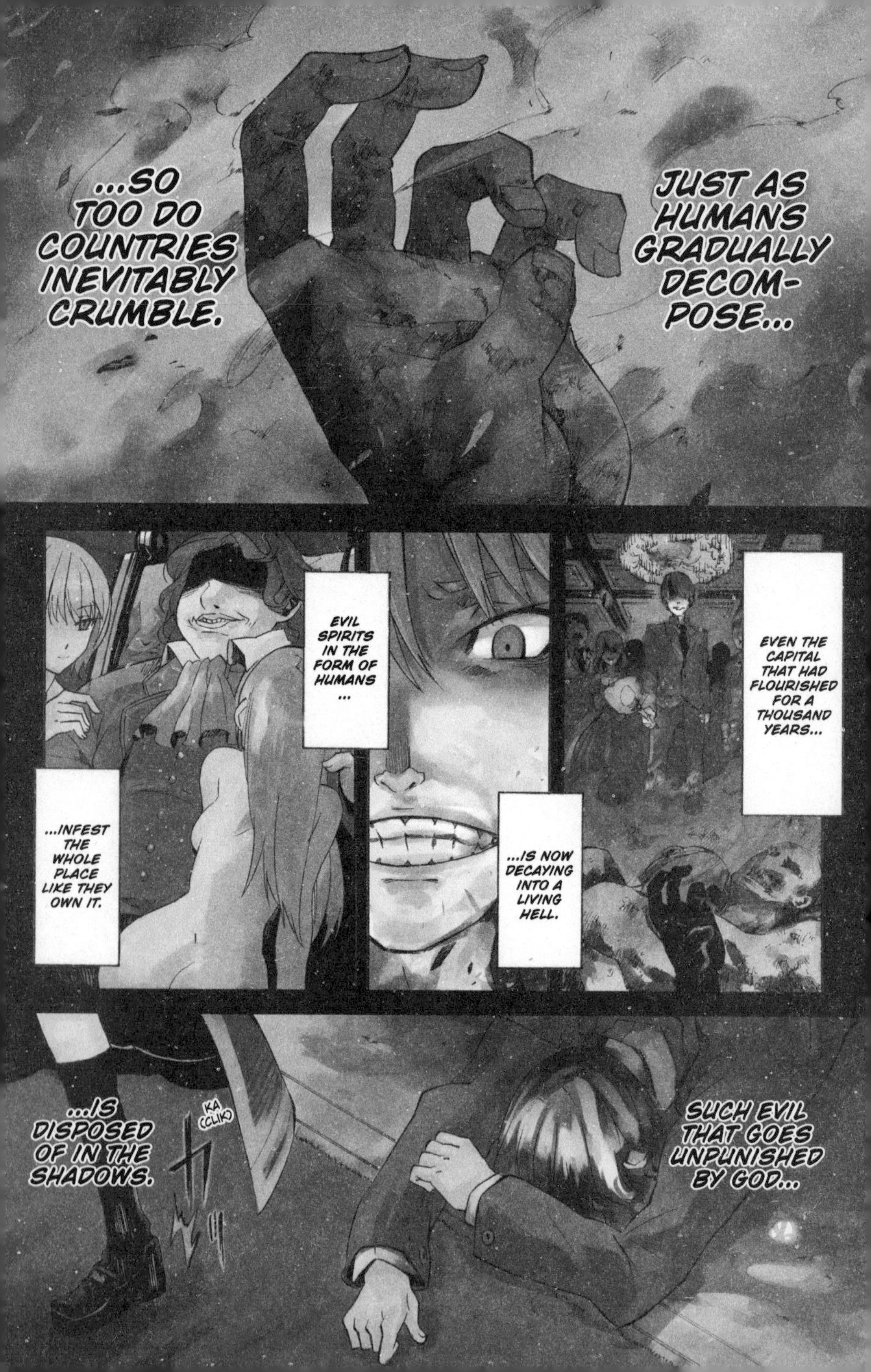
JUST AS HUMANS GRADUALLY DECOMPOSE...
...SO TOO DO COUNTRIES INEVITABLY CRUMBLE.
EVEN THE CAPITAL THAT HAD FLOURISHED FOR A THOUSAND YEARS...
...IS NOW DECAYING INTO A LIVING HELL.
EVIL SPIRITS IN THE FORM OF HUMANS...
...INFEST THE WHOLE PLACE LIKE THEY OWN IT.
SUCH EVIL THAT GOES UNPUNISHED BY GOD...
KA (CLIK)
...IS DISPOSED OF IN THE SHADOWS.

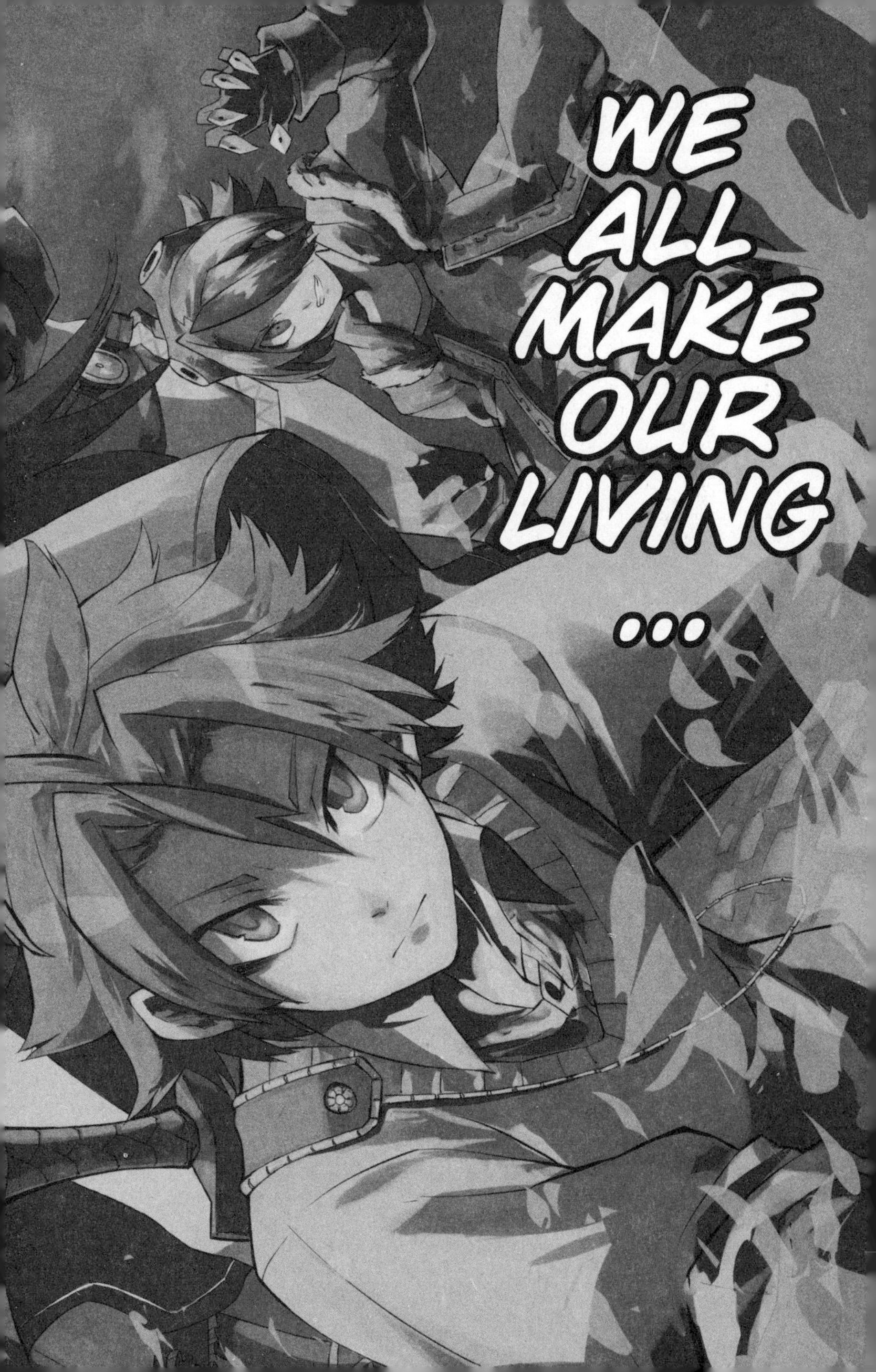
WE ALL MAKE OUR LIVING
...

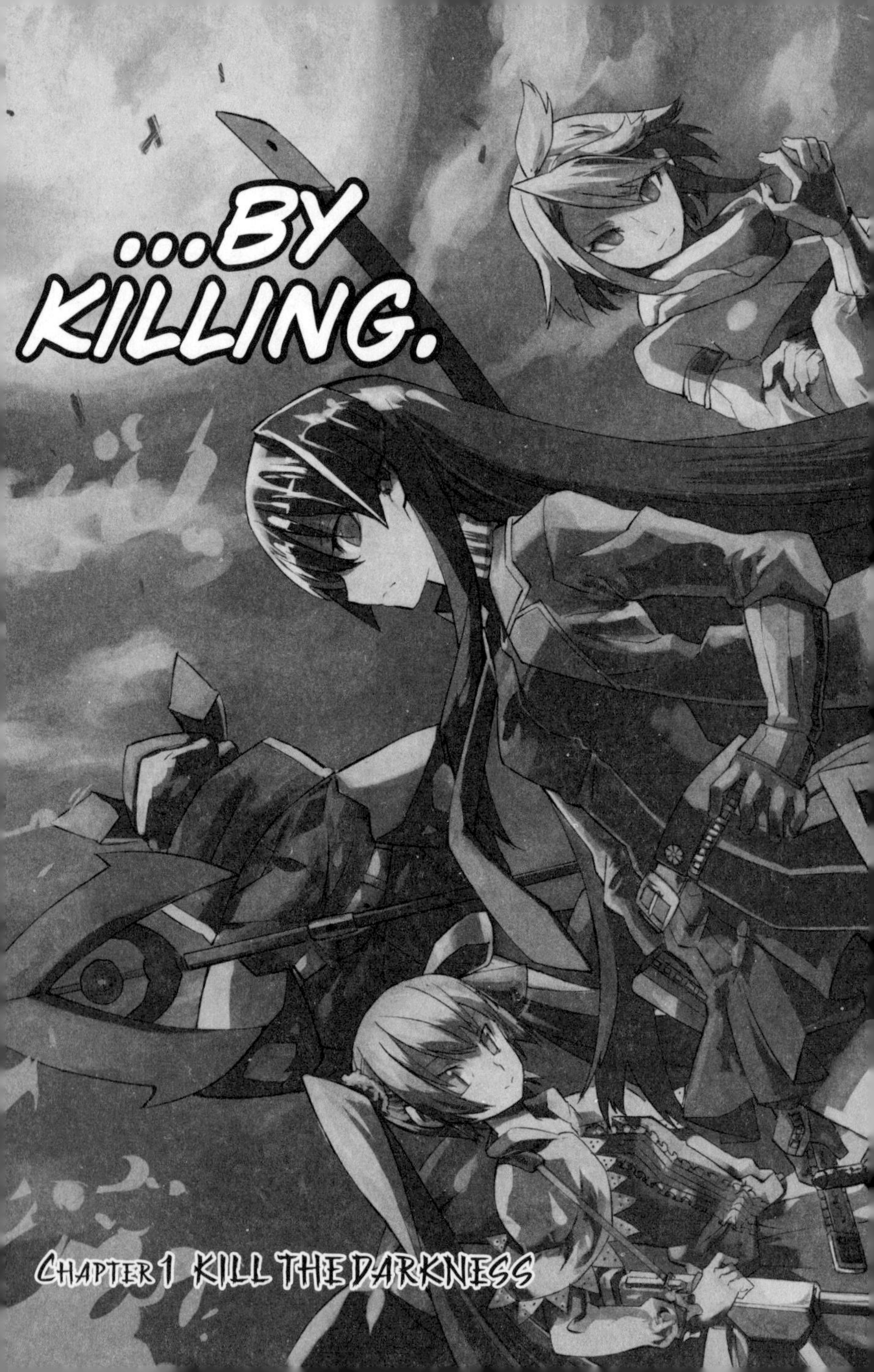
...BY KILLING.
CHAPTER 1 KILL THE DARKNESS

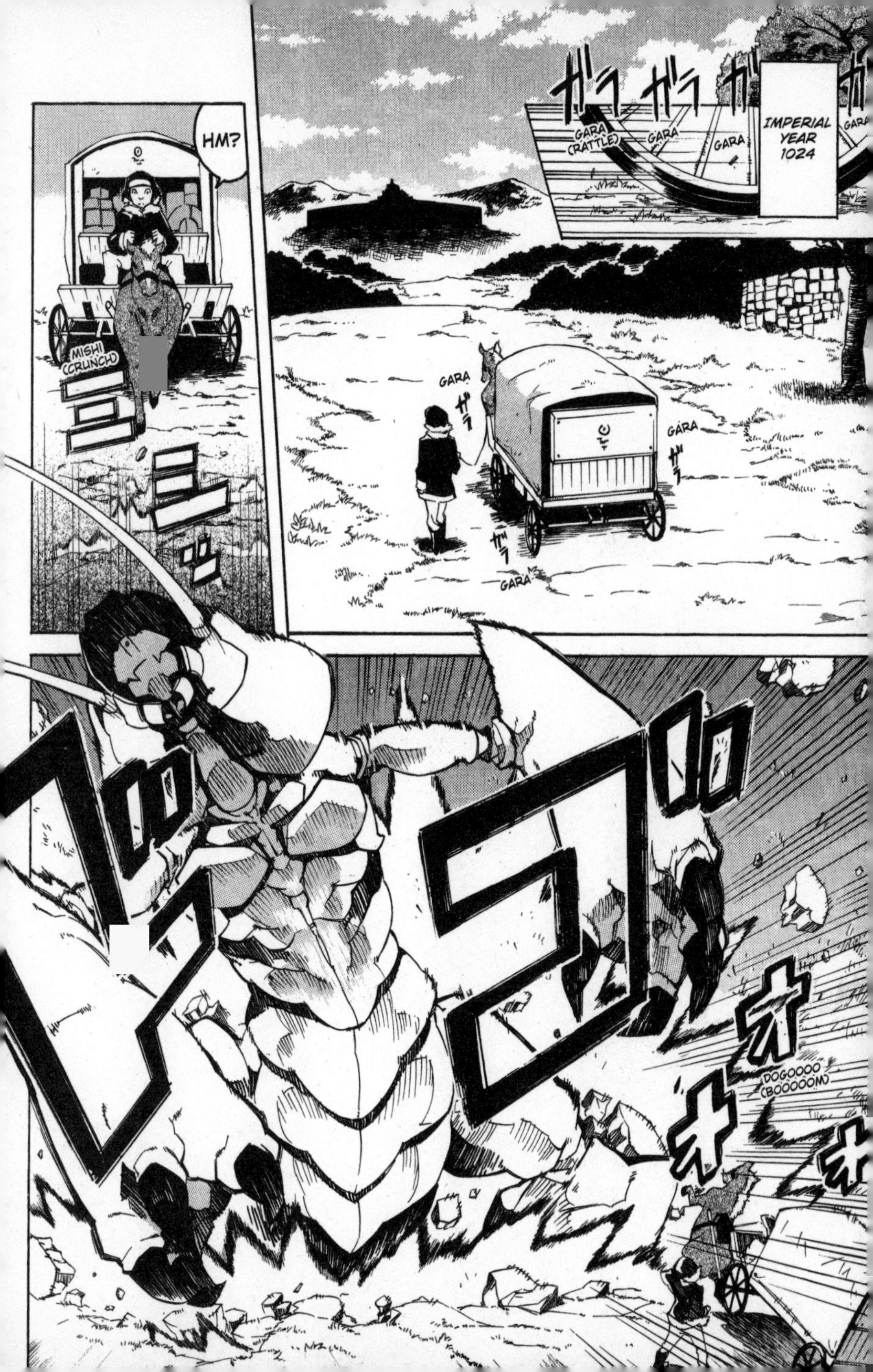
IMPERIAL YEAR 1024
GARA
GARA
GARA
GARA (RATTLE)
GARA
GARA
GARA
HM?
MISHI (CRUNCH)
DOGOOOO (BOOOOOM)

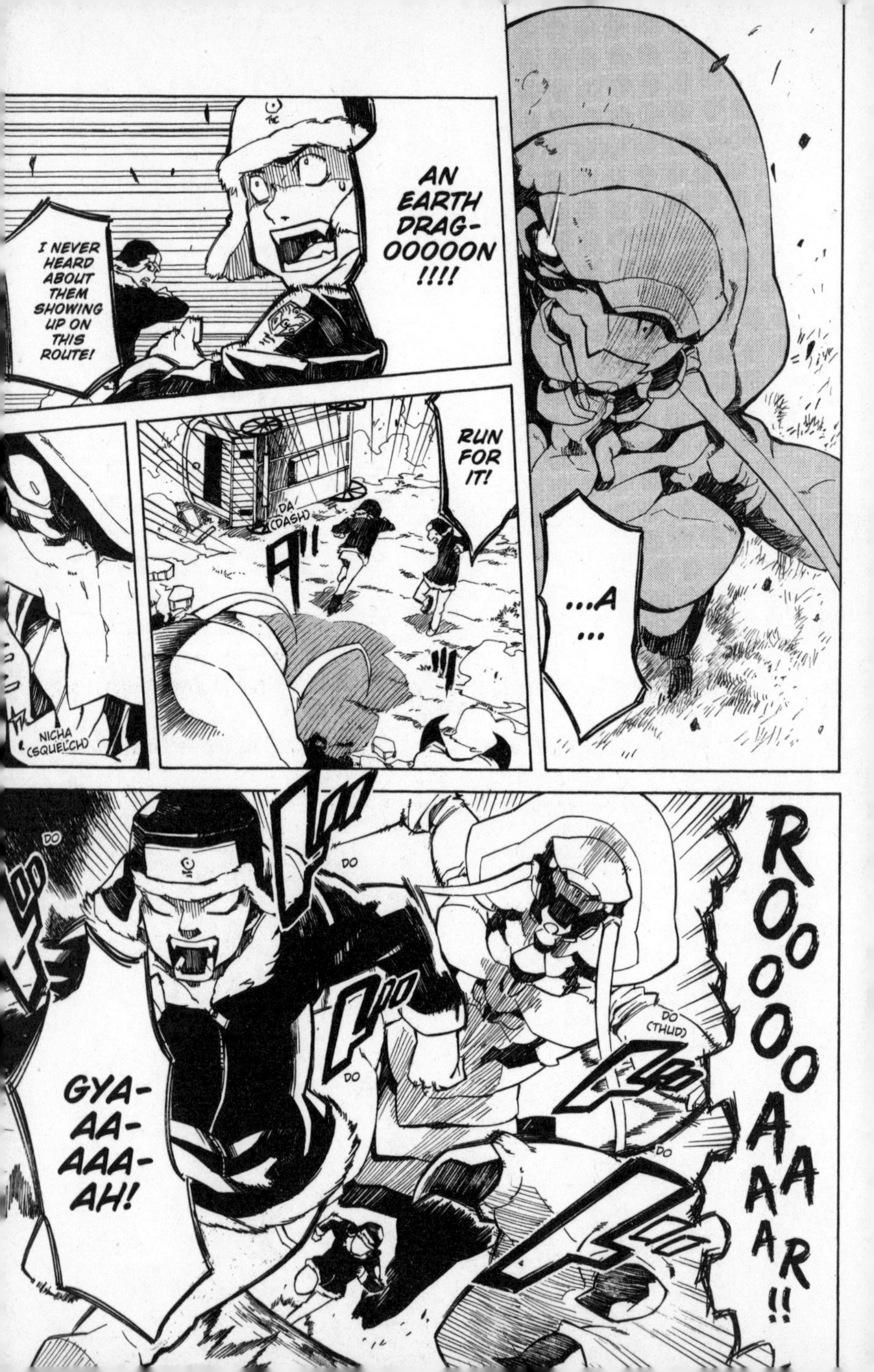
...A ...
AN EARTH DRAG-OOOOON!!!!
I NEVER HEARD ABOUT THEM SHOWING UP ON THIS ROUTE!
RUN FOR IT!
DA (DASH)
NICHA (SQUELCH)
ROOOOOAAAAR!!
DO (THUD)
DO
DO
DO
GYA-AA-AAA-AH!
DO

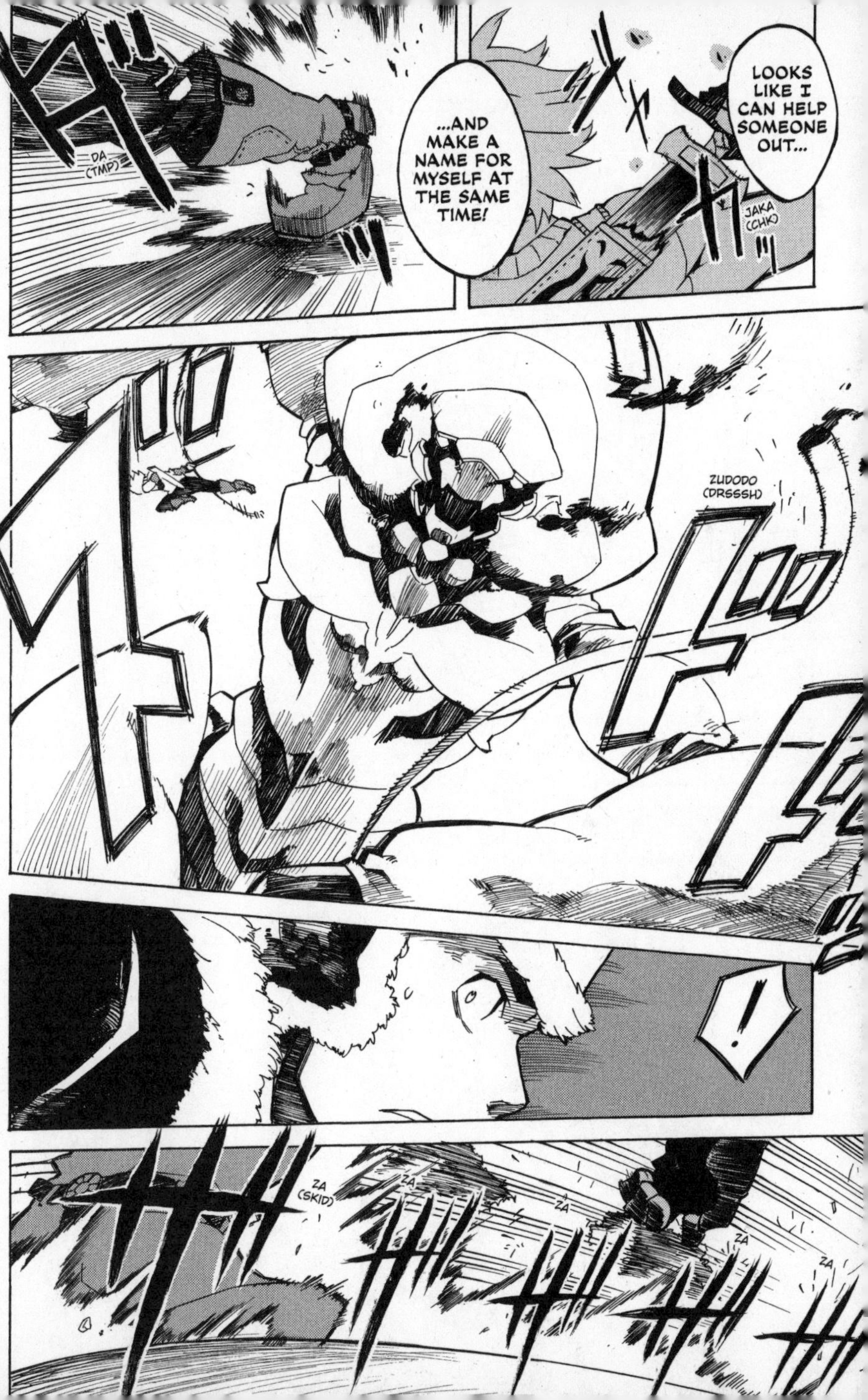
LOOKS LIKE I CAN HELP SOMEONE OUT...
JAKA (CHK)
...AND MAKE A NAME FOR MYSELF AT THE SAME TIME!
DA (TMP)
ZUDODO (DRSSSH)
!
ZA (SKID)
ZA
ZA
ZA
ZA

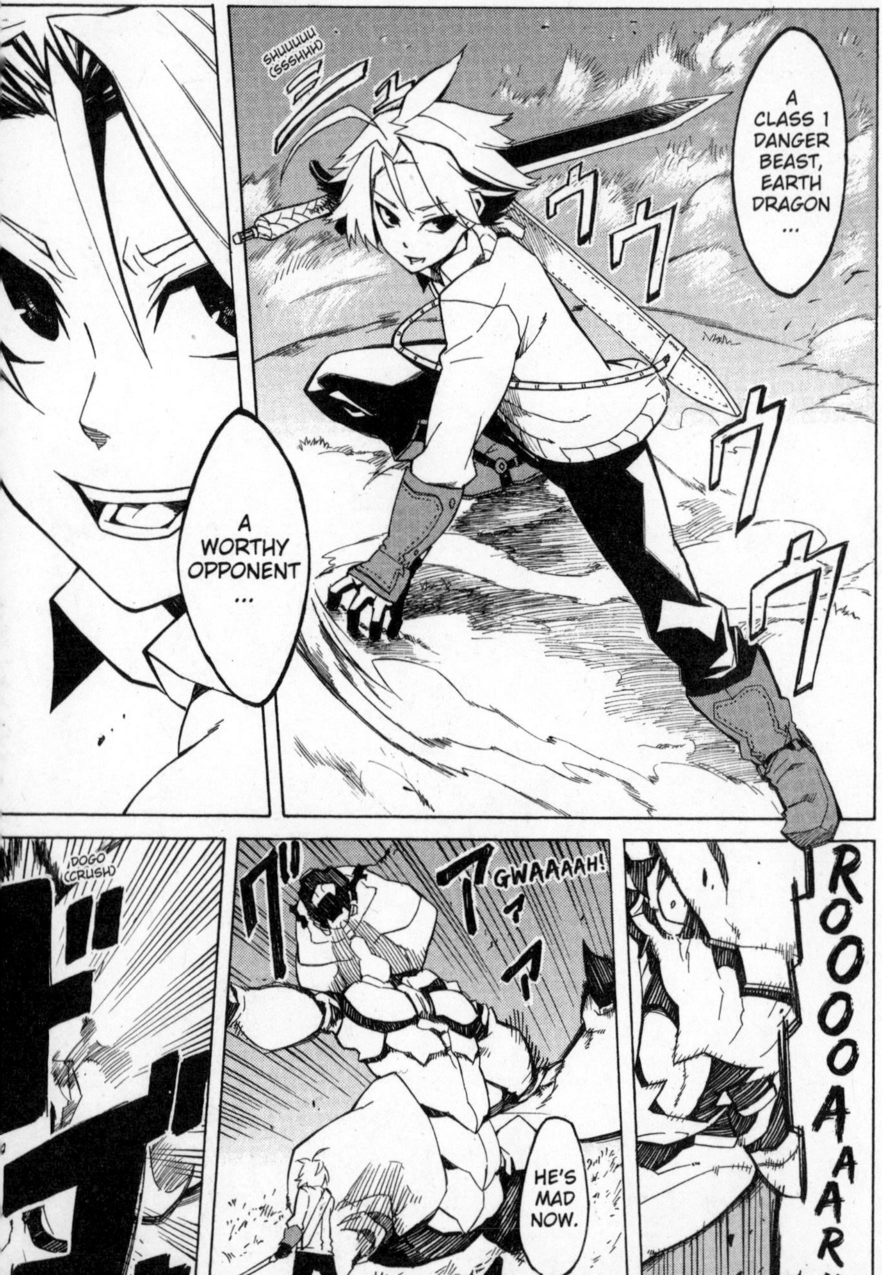
A CLASS 1 DANGER BEAST, EARTH DRAGON ...
SHUUUUU (SSSSHHH)
A WORTHY OPPONENT ...
ROOOOAAAR!!
GWAAAAH!
HE'S MAD NOW.
DOGO (CRUSH)

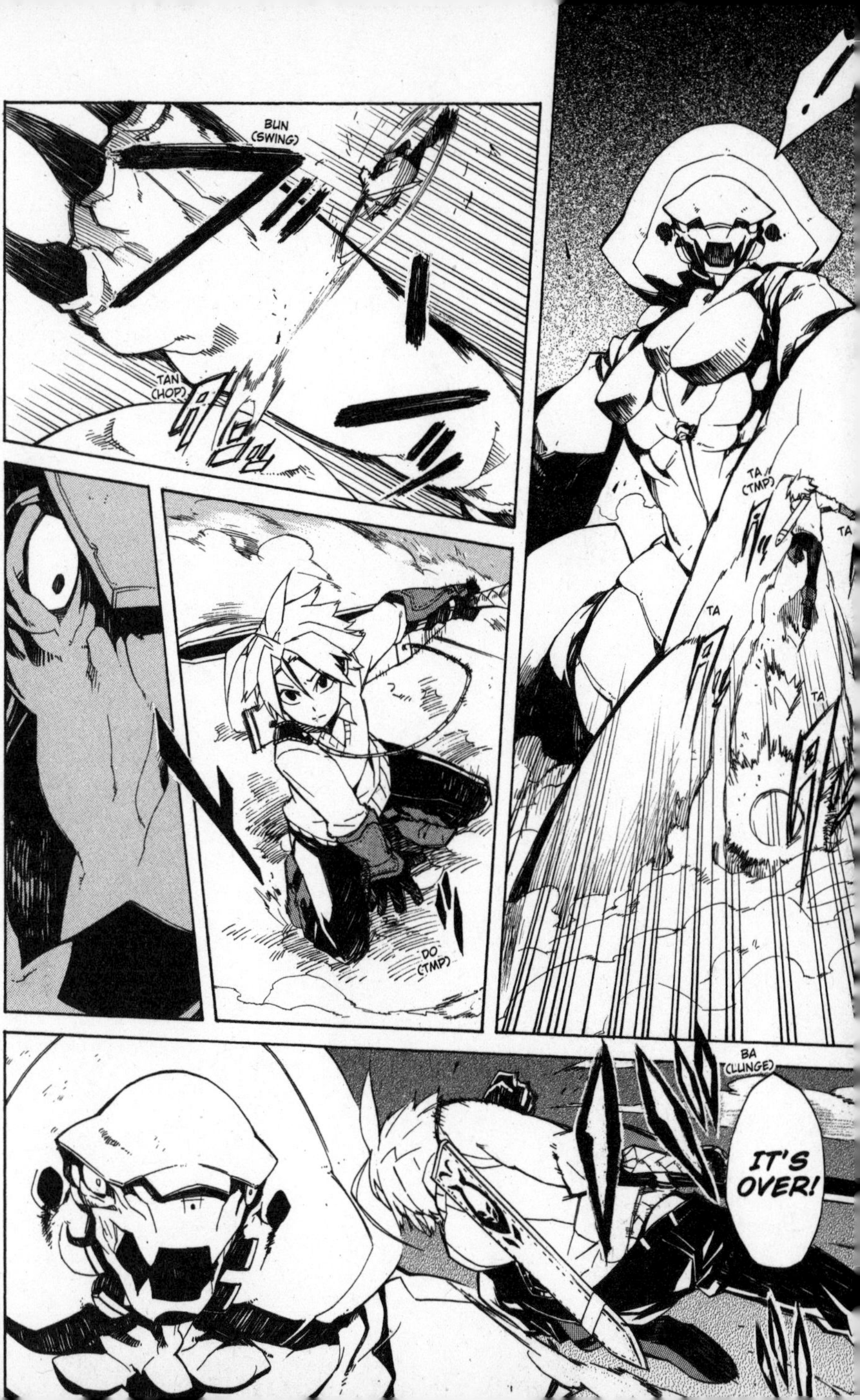
!
TA (TMP)
TA
TA
TA
BUN (SWING)
TAN (HOP)
DO (TMP)
BA (LUNGE)
IT'S OVER!

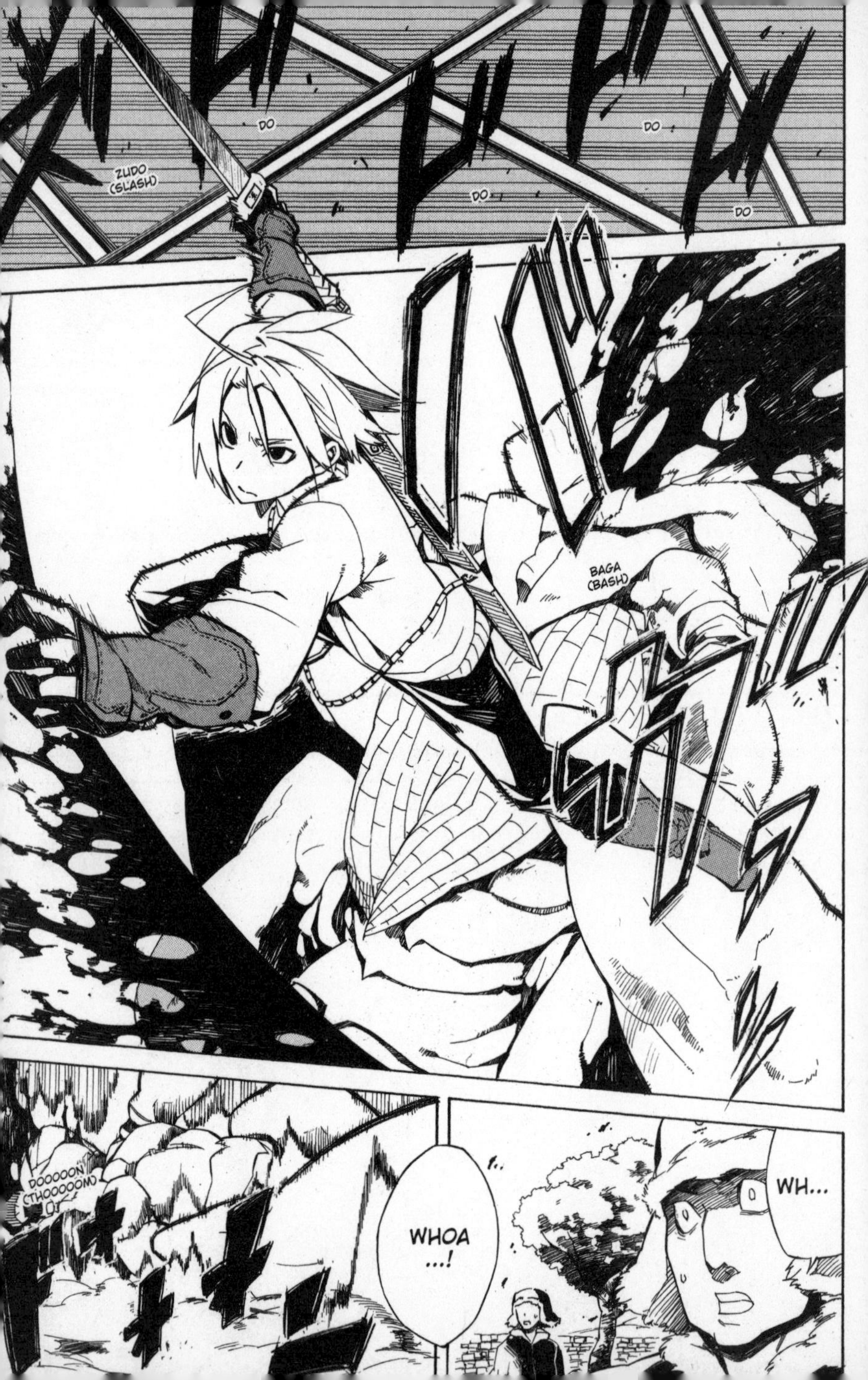
DO
DO
DO
DO
ZUDO (SLASH)
BAGA (BASH)
WH...
WHOA ...!
DOOOOON (THOOOOOM)

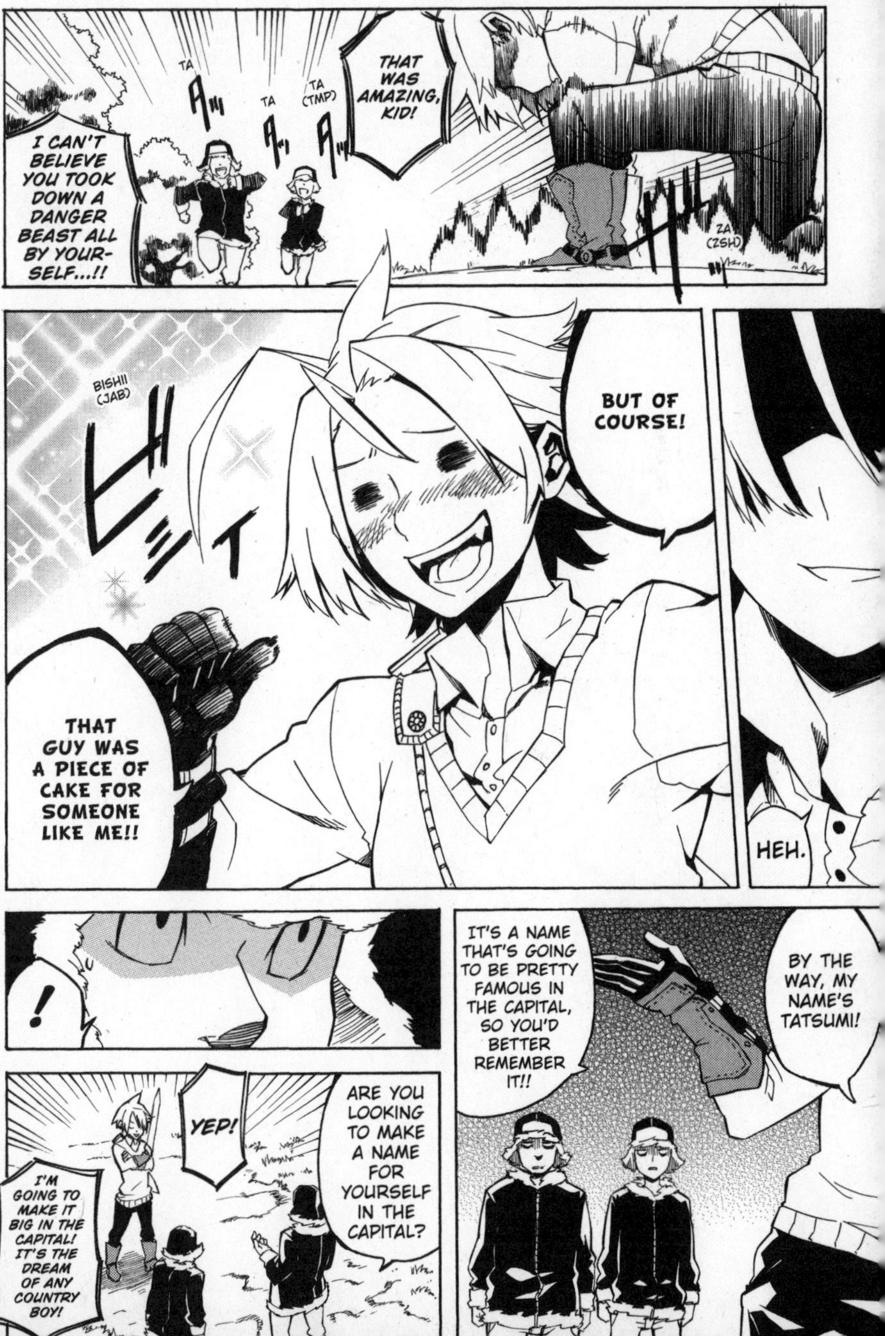
THAT WAS AMAZING, KID!
ZA (ZSH)
TA (TMP)
TA
TA
I CAN'T BELIEVE YOU TOOK DOWN A DANGER BEAST ALL BY YOURSELF...!!
HEH.
BUT OF COURSE!
BISHII (JAB)
THAT GUY WAS A PIECE OF CAKE FOR SOMEONE LIKE ME!!
BY THE WAY, MY NAME'S TATSUMI!
IT'S A NAME THAT'S GOING TO BE PRETTY FAMOUS IN THE CAPITAL, SO YOU'D BETTER REMEMBER IT!!
!
ARE YOU LOOKING TO MAKE A NAME FOR YOURSELF IN THE CAPITAL?
YEP!
I'M GOING TO MAKE IT BIG IN THE CAPITAL! IT'S THE DREAM OF ANY COUNTRY BOY!

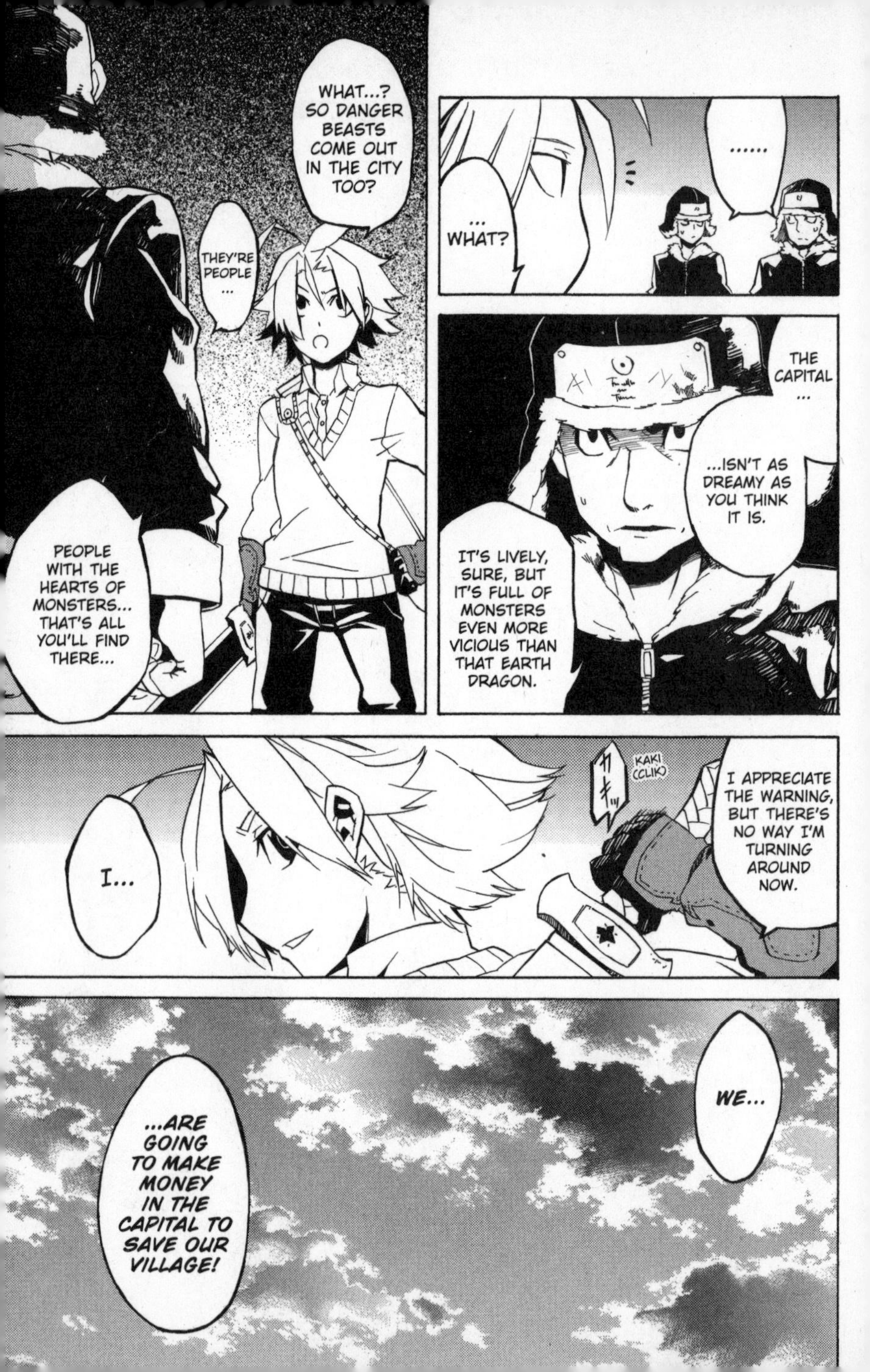
......
... WHAT?
THE CAPITAL ...
...ISN'T AS DREAMY AS YOU THINK IT IS.
IT'S LIVELY, SURE, BUT IT'S FULL OF MONSTERS EVEN MORE VICIOUS THAN THAT EARTH DRAGON.
WHAT...? SO DANGER BEASTS COME OUT IN THE CITY TOO?
THEY'RE PEOPLE ...
PEOPLE WITH THE HEARTS OF MONSTERS... THAT'S ALL YOU'LL FIND THERE...
KAKI (CLIK)
I APPRECIATE THE WARNING, BUT THERE'S NO WAY I'M TURNING AROUND NOW.
I...
WE...
...ARE GOING TO MAKE MONEY IN THE CAPITAL TO SAVE OUR VILLAGE!

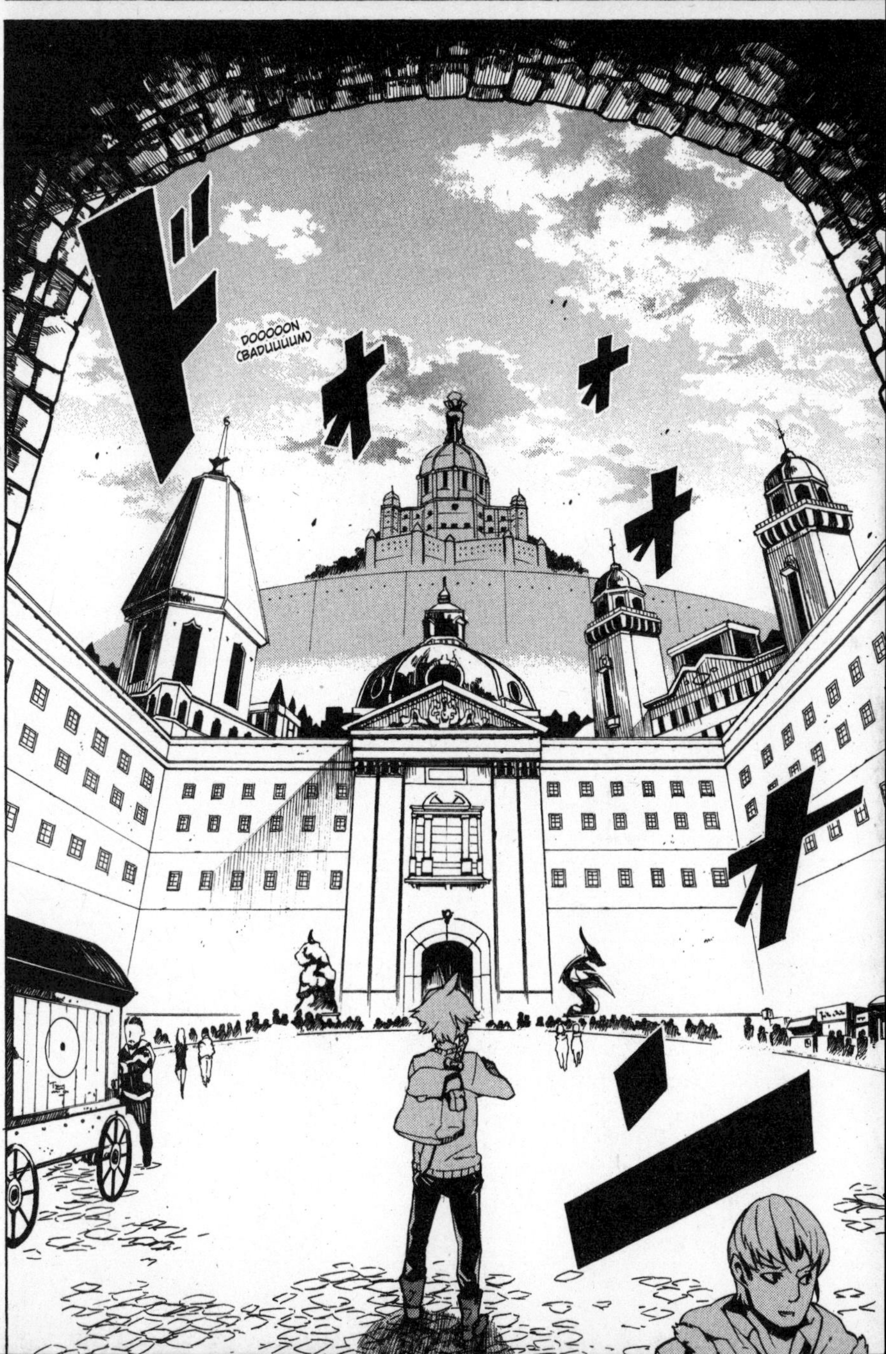
ドォォォォーン
DOOOOON
(BADUUUUUM)

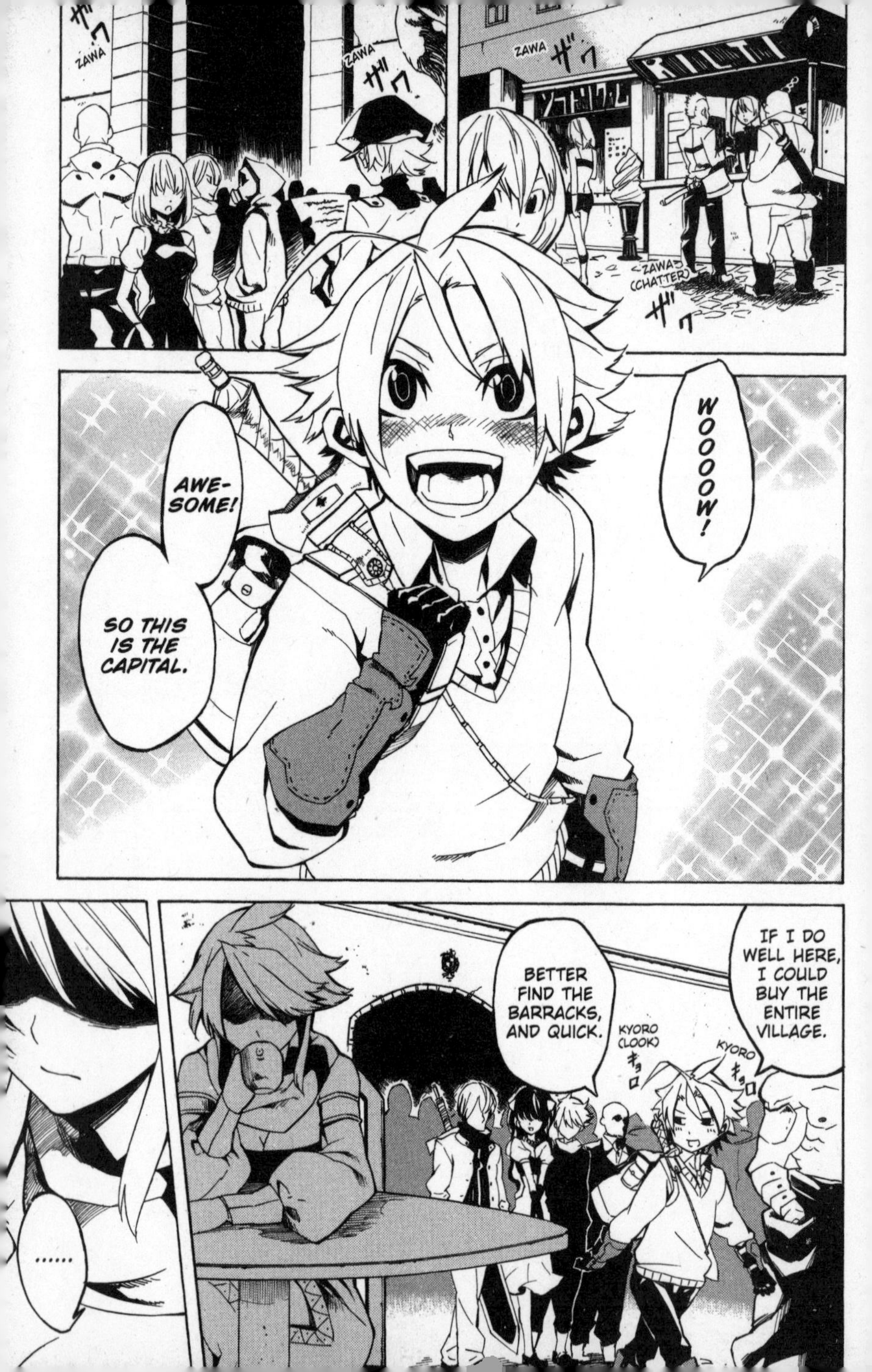
ZAWA ザワ
ZAWA ザワ
ZAWA ザワ
ZAWA (CHATTER) ザワ
WOOOOOW!
AWE-SOME!
SO THIS IS THE CAPITAL.
IF I DO WELL HERE, I COULD BUY THE ENTIRE VILLAGE.
KYORO キョロ
BETTER FIND THE BARRACKS, AND QUICK.
KYORO (LOOK) キョロ
......

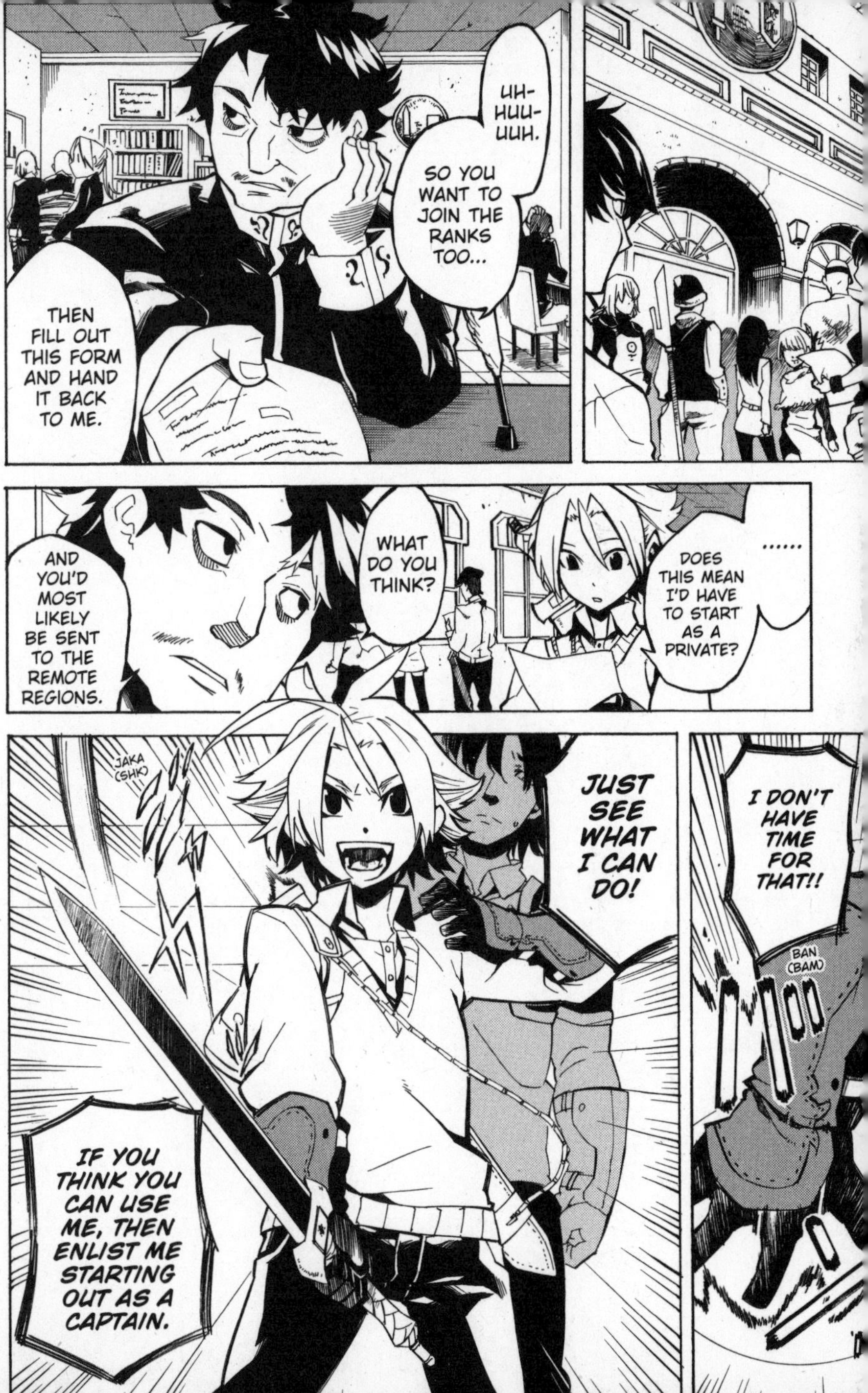
UH-HUUU-UUH.
SO YOU WANT TO JOIN THE RANKS TOO...
THEN FILL OUT THIS FORM AND HAND IT BACK TO ME.
......
DOES THIS MEAN I'D HAVE TO START AS A PRIVATE?
WHAT DO YOU THINK?
AND YOU'D MOST LIKELY BE SENT TO THE REMOTE REGIONS.
I DON'T HAVE TIME FOR THAT!!
BAN (BAM)
JUST SEE WHAT I CAN DO!
JAKA (SHK)
IF YOU THINK YOU CAN USE ME, THEN ENLIST ME STARTING OUT AS A CAPTAIN.

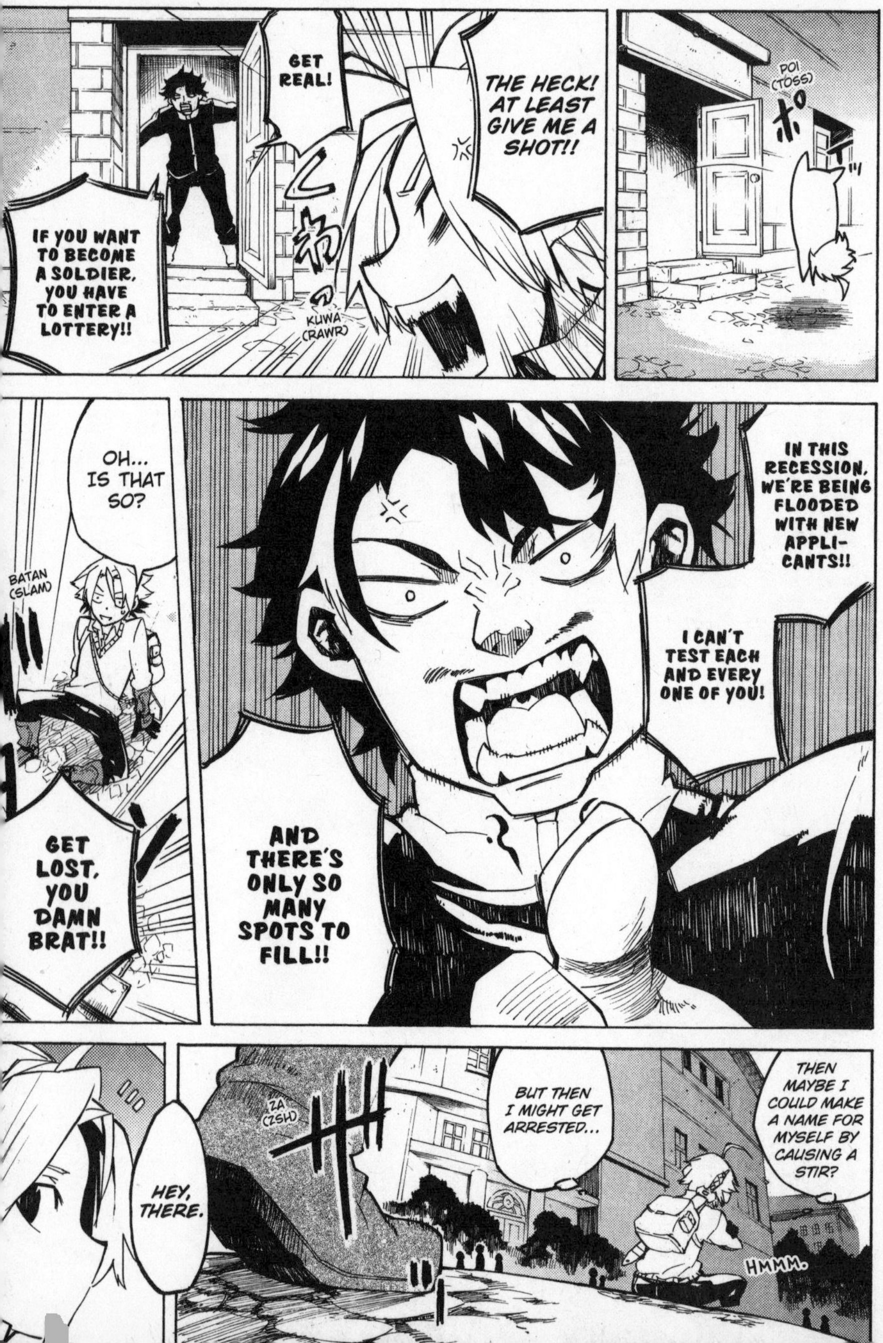
POI
(TOSS)
THE HECK! AT LEAST GIVE ME A SHOT!!
GET REAL!
KUWA
(RAWR)
IF YOU WANT TO BECOME A SOLDIER, YOU HAVE TO ENTER A LOTTERY!!
IN THIS RECESSION, WE'RE BEING FLOODED WITH NEW APPLI- CANTS!!
I CAN'T TEST EACH AND EVERY ONE OF YOU!
AND THERE'S ONLY SO MANY SPOTS TO FILL!!
GET LOST, YOU DAMN BRAT!!
OH... IS THAT SO?
BATAN
(SLAM)
THEN MAYBE I COULD MAKE A NAME FOR MYSELF BY CAUSING A STIR?
HMMM.
BUT THEN I MIGHT GET ARRESTED...
ZA
(ZSH)
HEY, THERE.

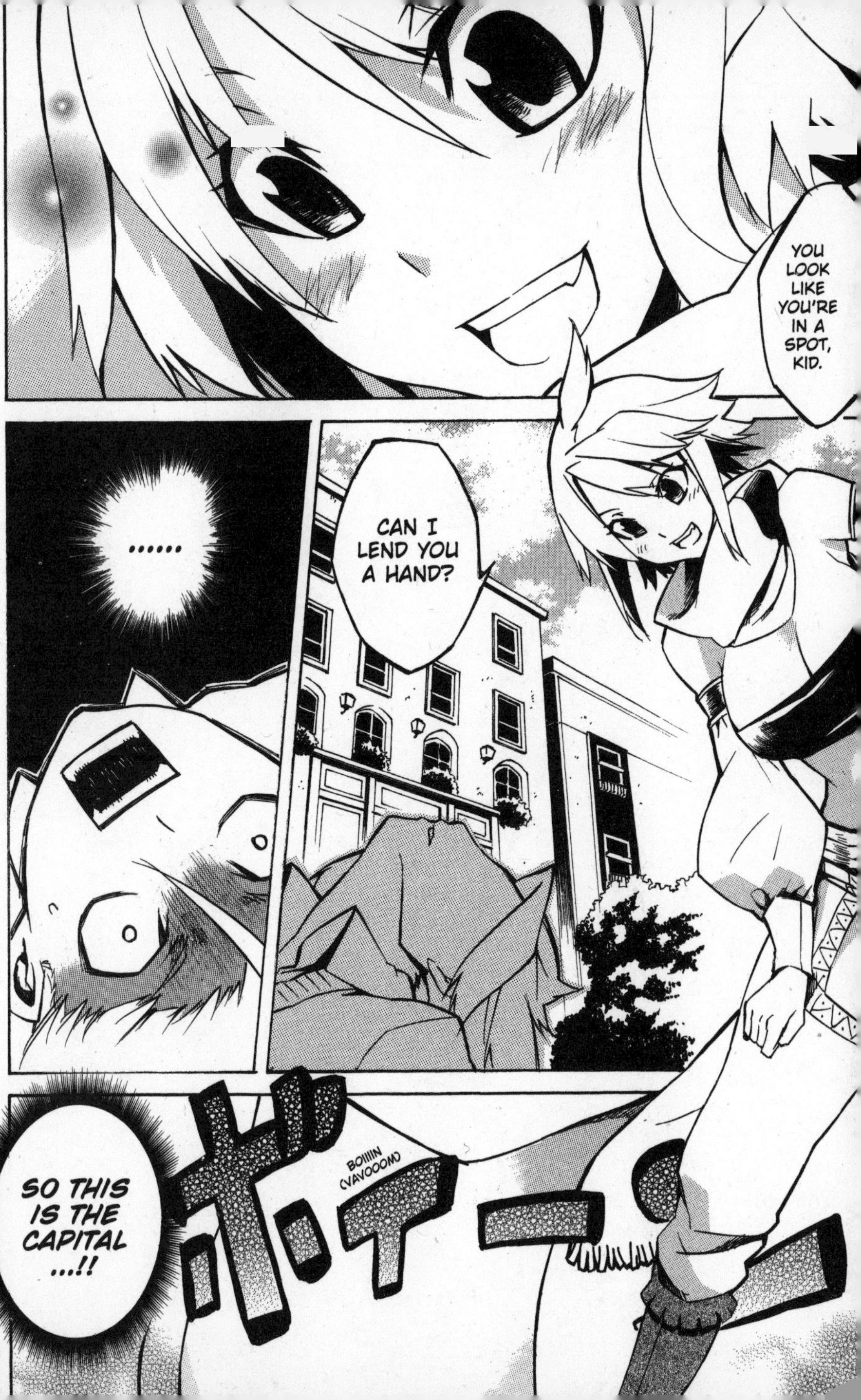
YOU LOOK LIKE YOU'RE IN A SPOT, KID.
CAN I LEND YOU A HAND?
......
BOIIIIN (VAVOOOM)
SO THIS IS THE CAPITAL ...!!

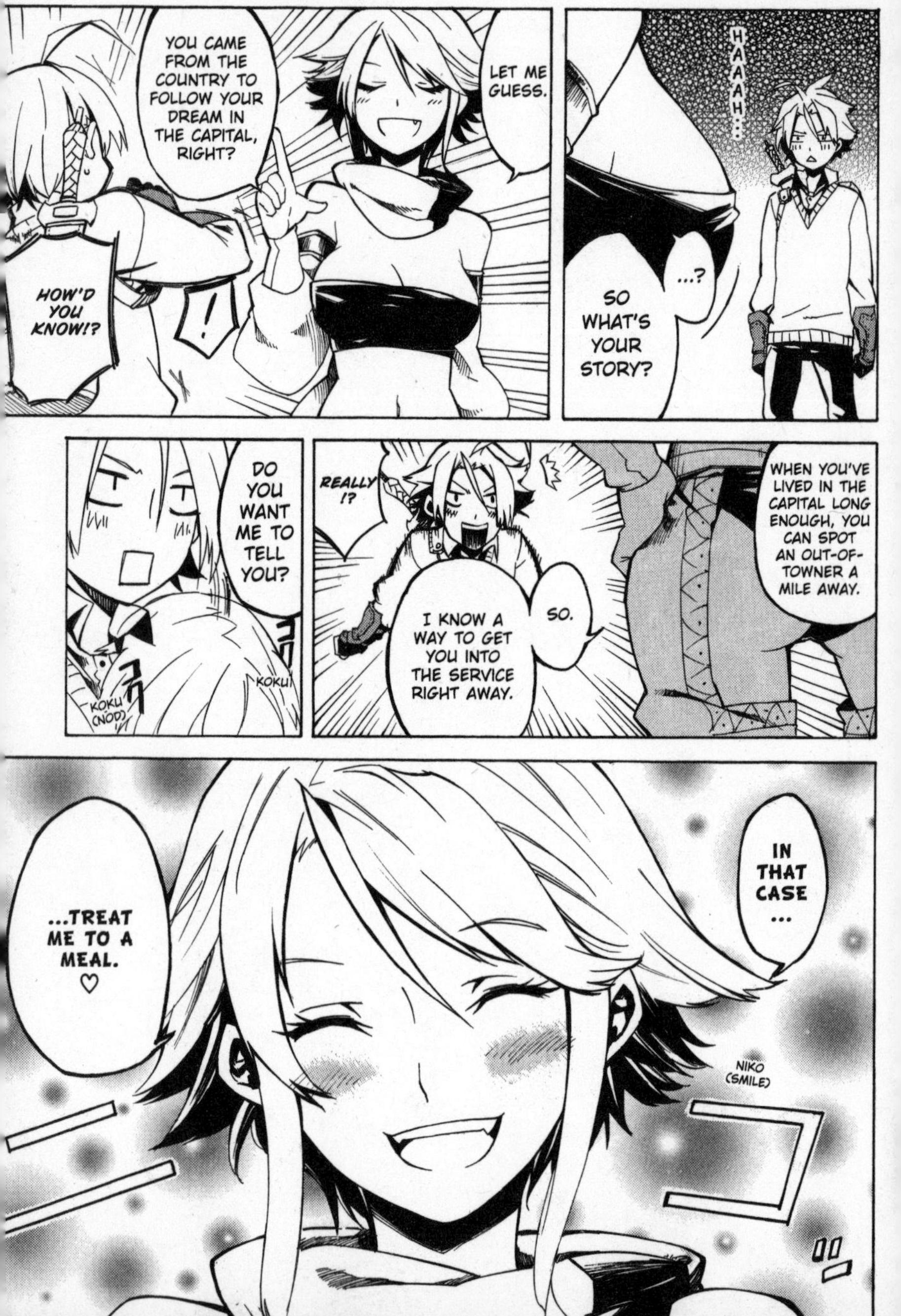
HAAAAH...
...?
SO WHAT'S YOUR STORY?
LET ME GUESS.
YOU CAME FROM THE COUNTRY TO FOLLOW YOUR DREAM IN THE CAPITAL, RIGHT?
!
HOW'D YOU KNOW!?
WHEN YOU'VE LIVED IN THE CAPITAL LONG ENOUGH, YOU CAN SPOT AN OUT-OF-TOWNER A MILE AWAY.
SO.
I KNOW A WAY TO GET YOU INTO THE SERVICE RIGHT AWAY.
REALLY!?
DO YOU WANT ME TO TELL YOU?
KOKU
KOKU (NOD)
IN THAT CASE...
...TREAT ME TO A MEAL. ♡
NIKO (SMILE)

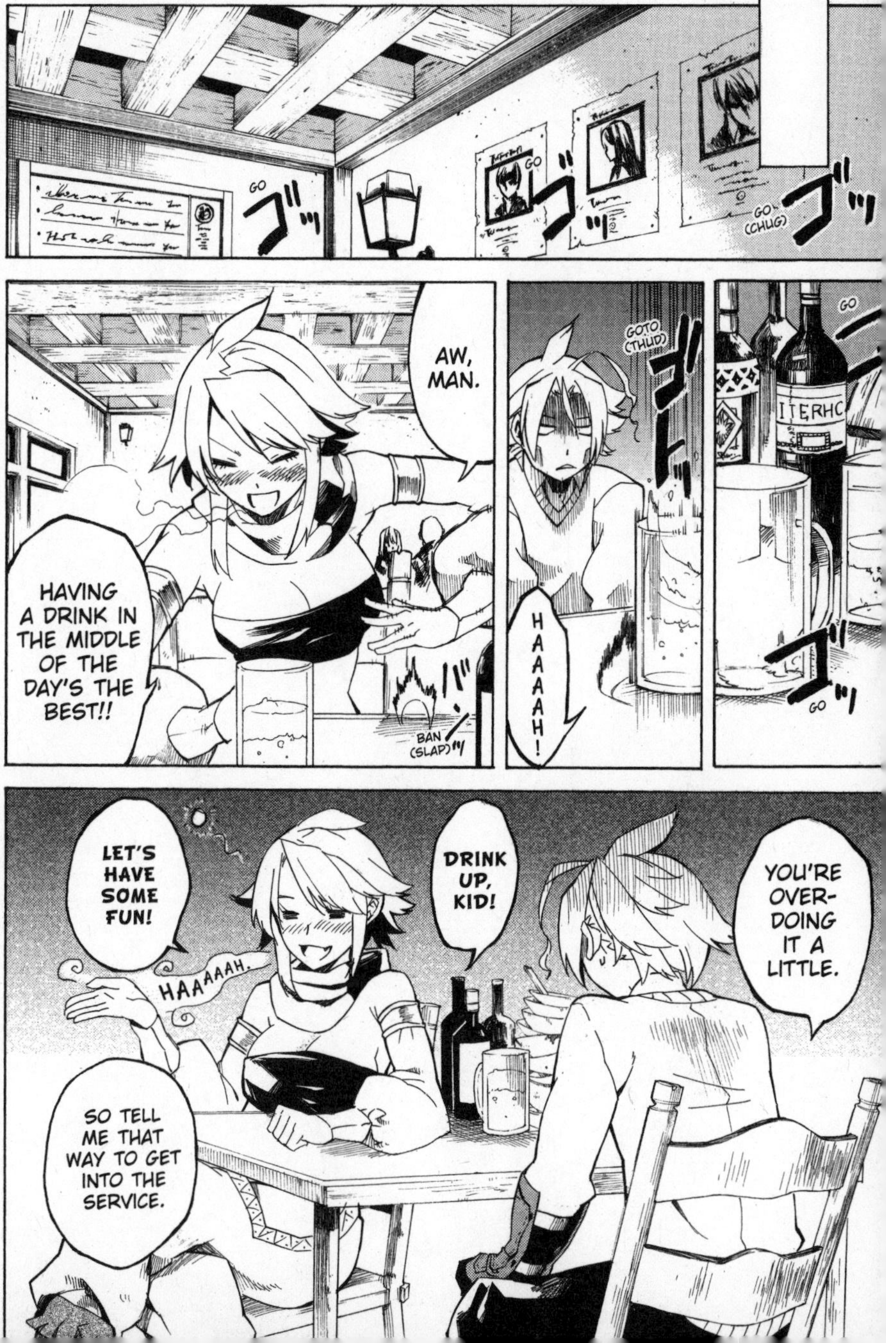
GO (CHUG)
GO
GO
GO
ITERHC
GO
GOTO (THUD)
HAAAAAH!
AW, MAN.
HAVING A DRINK IN THE MIDDLE OF THE DAY'S THE BEST!!
BAN (SLAP)
YOU'RE OVER-DOING IT A LITTLE.
DRINK UP, KID!
LET'S HAVE SOME FUN!
HAAAAAH.
SO TELL ME THAT WAY TO GET INTO THE SERVICE.

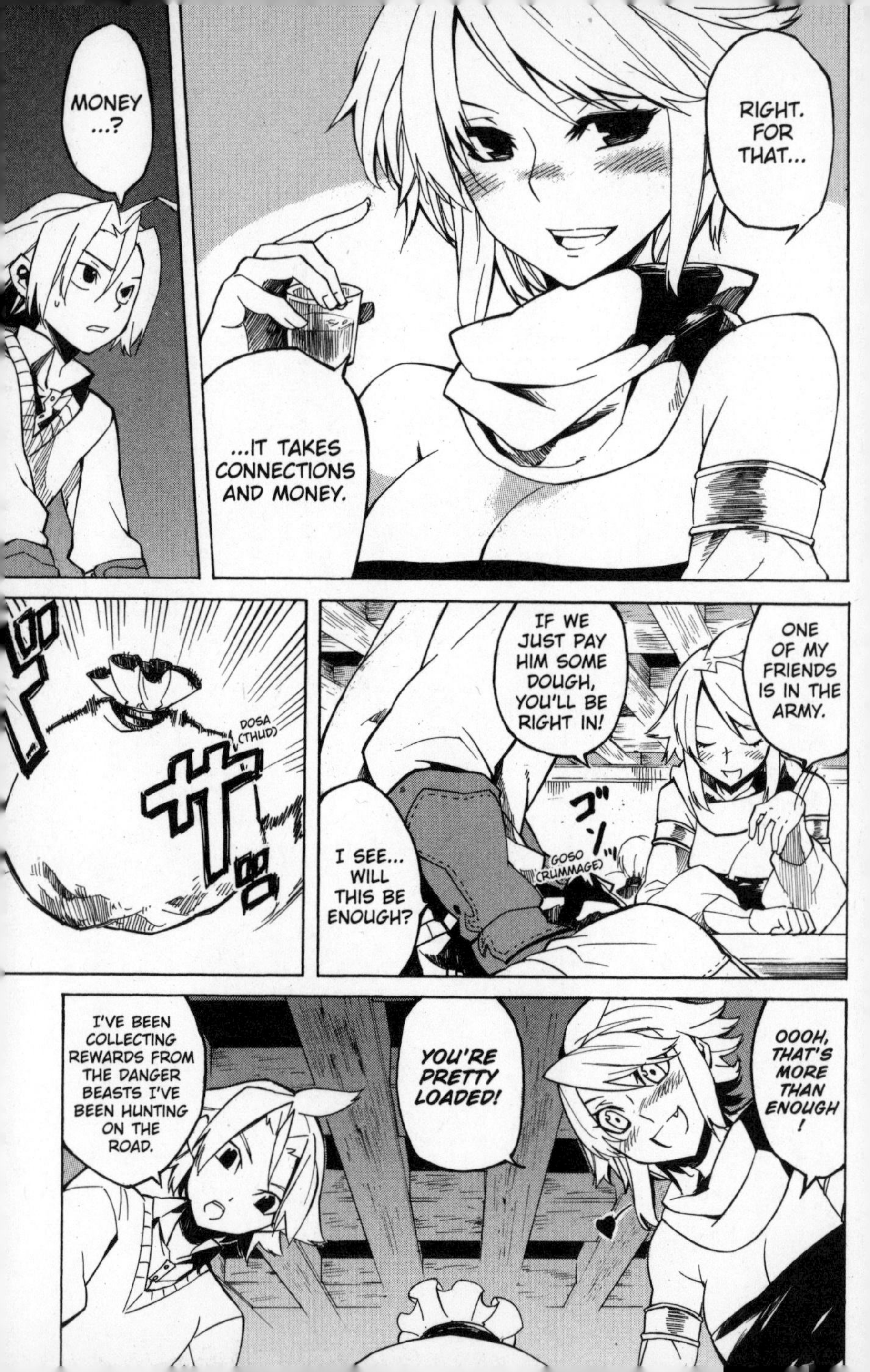
RIGHT. FOR THAT...
...IT TAKES CONNECTIONS AND MONEY.
MONEY ...?
ONE OF MY FRIENDS IS IN THE ARMY.
IF WE JUST PAY HIM SOME DOUGH, YOU'LL BE RIGHT IN!
GOSO (RUMMAGE)
I SEE... WILL THIS BE ENOUGH?
DOSA (THUD)
OOOH, THAT'S MORE THAN ENOUGH!
YOU'RE PRETTY LOADED!
I'VE BEEN COLLECTING REWARDS FROM THE DANGER BEASTS I'VE BEEN HUNTING ON THE ROAD.

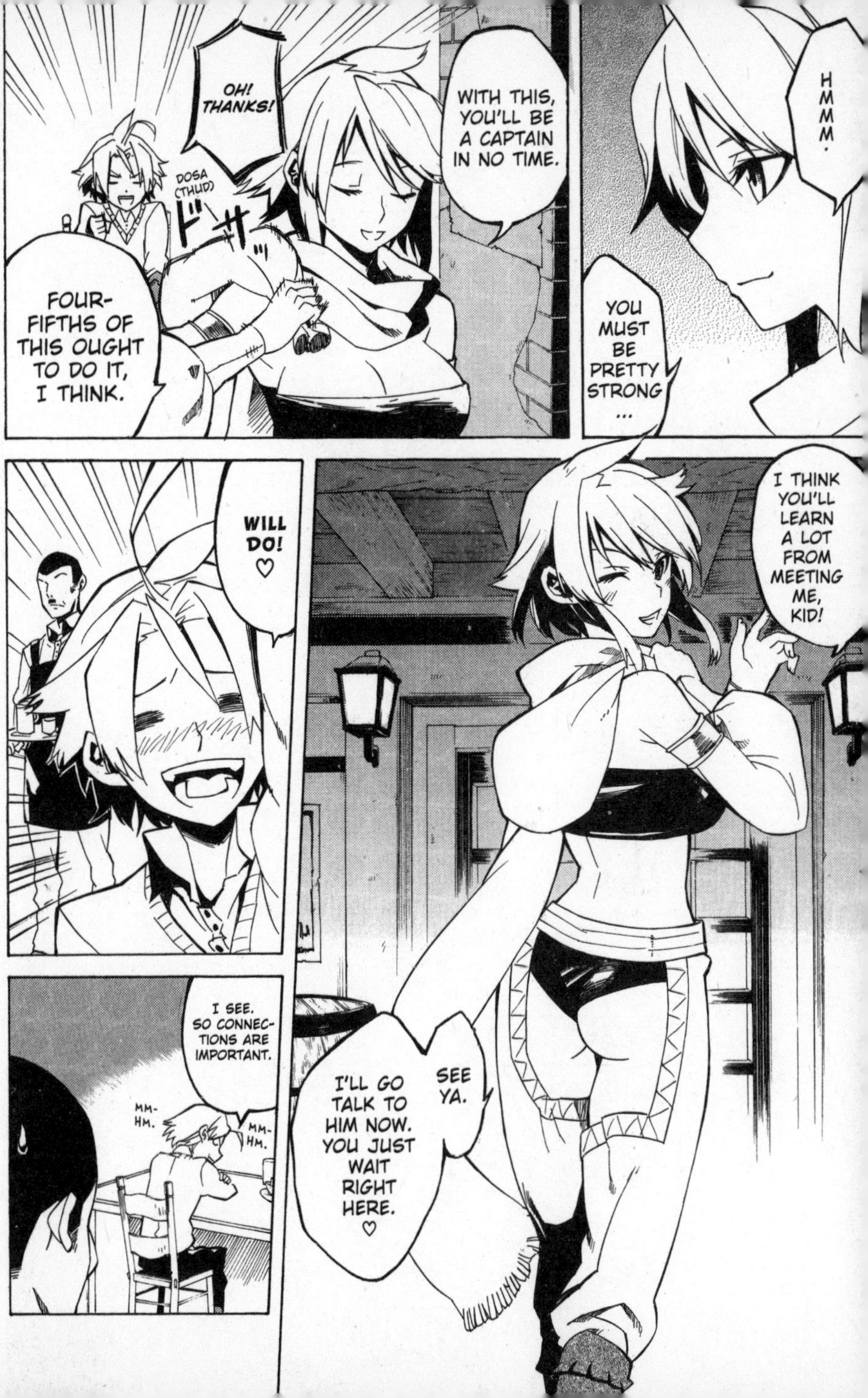
HMMM.
YOU MUST BE PRETTY STRONG...
WITH THIS, YOU'LL BE A CAPTAIN IN NO TIME.
OH! THANKS!
DOSA (THUD)
FOUR-FIFTHS OF THIS OUGHT TO DO IT, I THINK.
I THINK YOU'LL LEARN A LOT FROM MEETING ME, KID!
SEE YA.
I'LL GO TALK TO HIM NOW. YOU JUST WAIT RIGHT HERE. ♡
WILL DO! ♡
I SEE. SO CONNECTIONS ARE IMPORTANT.
MM-HM.
MM-HM.

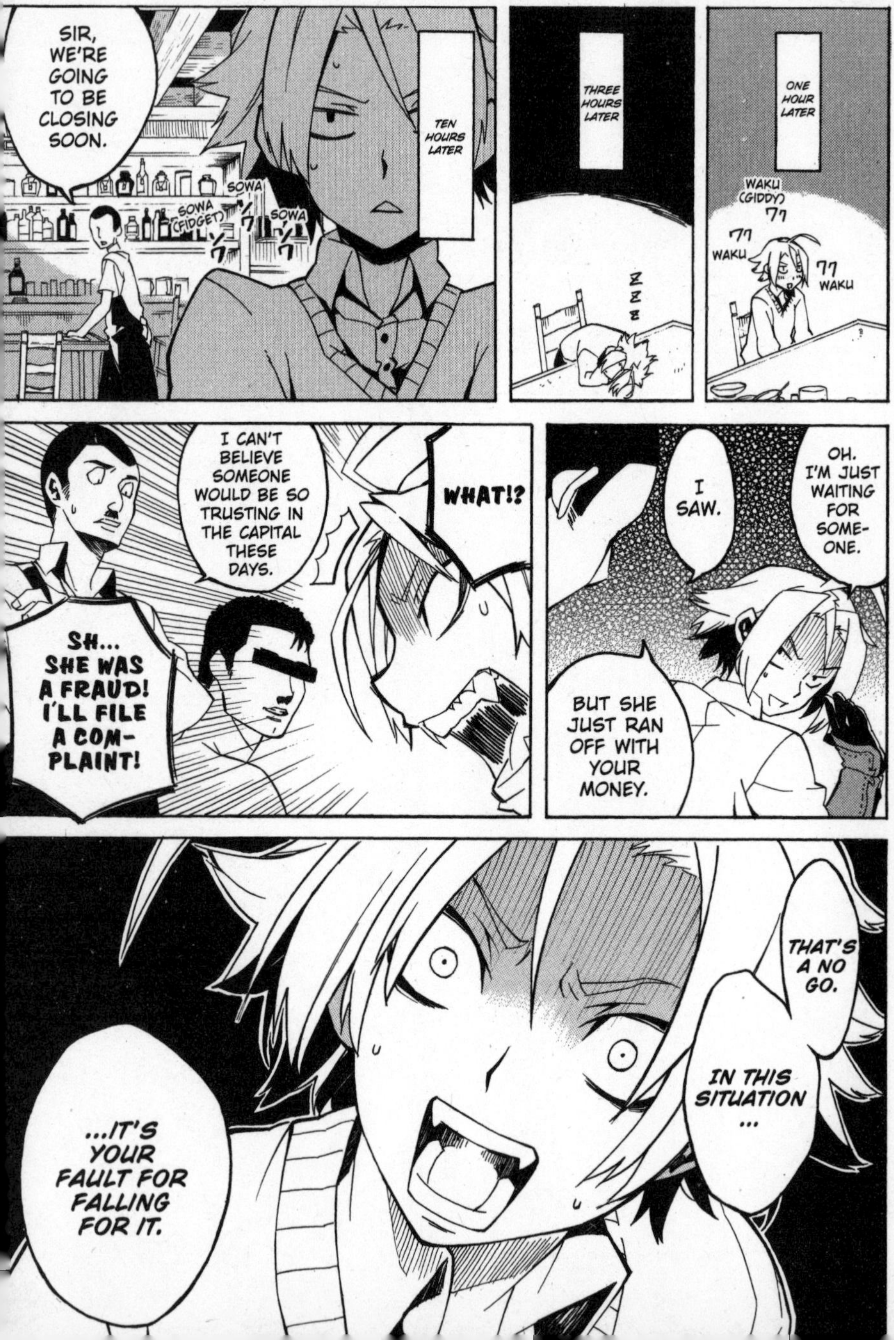
ONE HOUR LATER
WAKU (GIDDY)
ワク
ワク
WAKU
ワク
WAKU
THREE HOURS LATER
Z Z Z
TEN HOURS LATER
SIR, WE'RE GOING TO BE CLOSING SOON.
SOWA
ソワ
SOWA (FIDGET)
ソワ
SOWA
ソワ
OH. I'M JUST WAITING FOR SOME-ONE.
I SAW.
BUT SHE JUST RAN OFF WITH YOUR MONEY.
WHAT!?
I CAN'T BELIEVE SOMEONE WOULD BE SO TRUSTING IN THE CAPITAL THESE DAYS.
SH... SHE WAS A FRAUD! I'LL FILE A COM-PLAINT!
THAT'S A NO GO.
IN THIS SITUATION...
...IT'S YOUR FAULT FOR FALLING FOR IT.

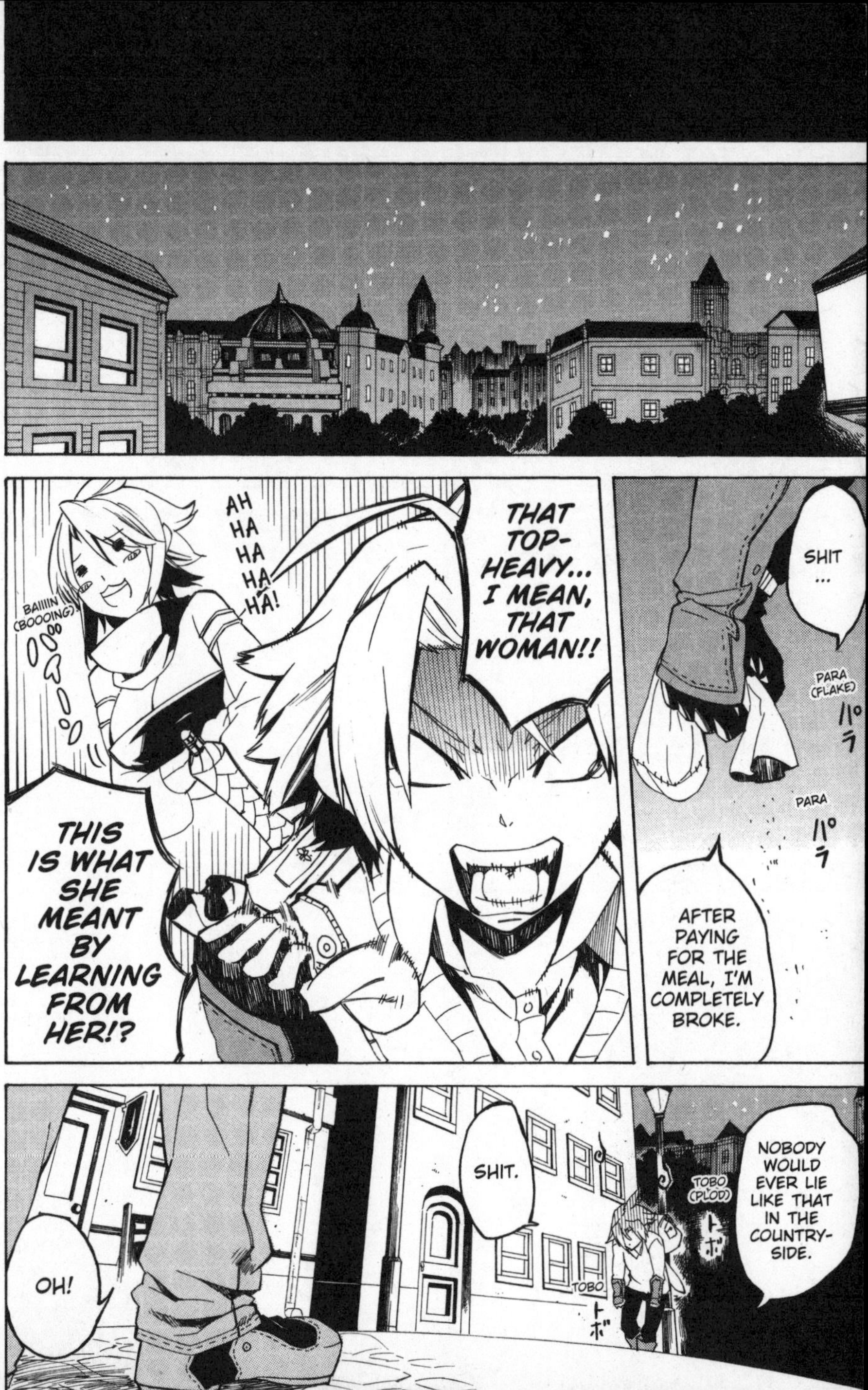
SHIT ...
PARA (FLAKE)
パラ
PARA
パラ
AFTER PAYING FOR THE MEAL, I'M COMPLETELY BROKE.
THAT TOP-HEAVY... I MEAN, THAT WOMAN!!
AH HA HA HA HA!
BAIIIN (BOOOING)
THIS IS WHAT SHE MEANT BY LEARNING FROM HER!?
NOBODY WOULD EVER LIE LIKE THAT IN THE COUNTRY-SIDE.
TOBO (PLOD)
トボ
SHIT.
TOBO
トボ
OH!

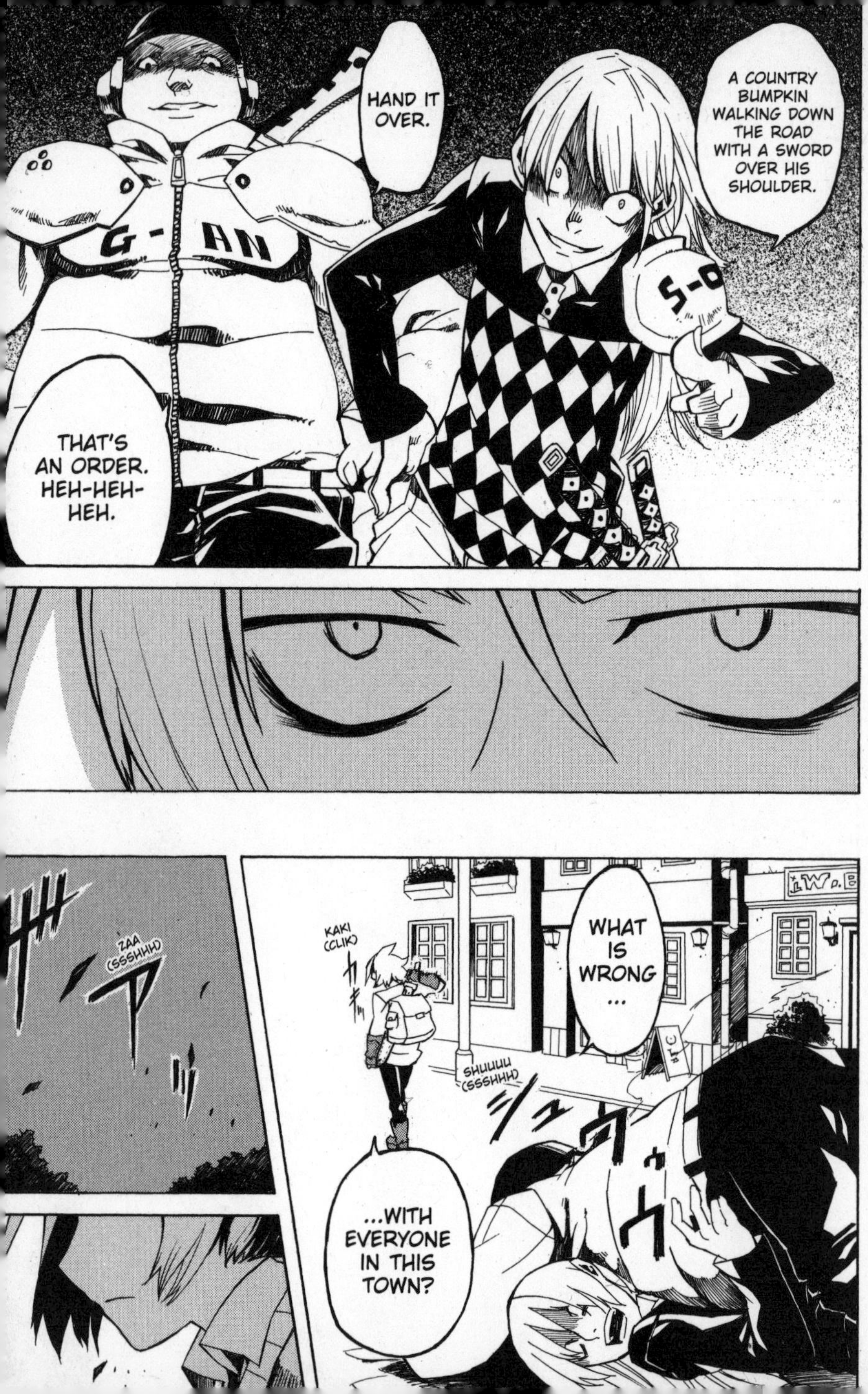
A COUNTRY BUMPKIN WALKING DOWN THE ROAD WITH A SWORD OVER HIS SHOULDER.
HAND IT OVER.
THAT'S AN ORDER. HEH-HEH-HEH.
WHAT IS WRONG ...
KAKI (CLIK)
SHUUUU (SSSHHH)
...WITH EVERYONE IN THIS TOWN?
ZAA (SSSHHH)

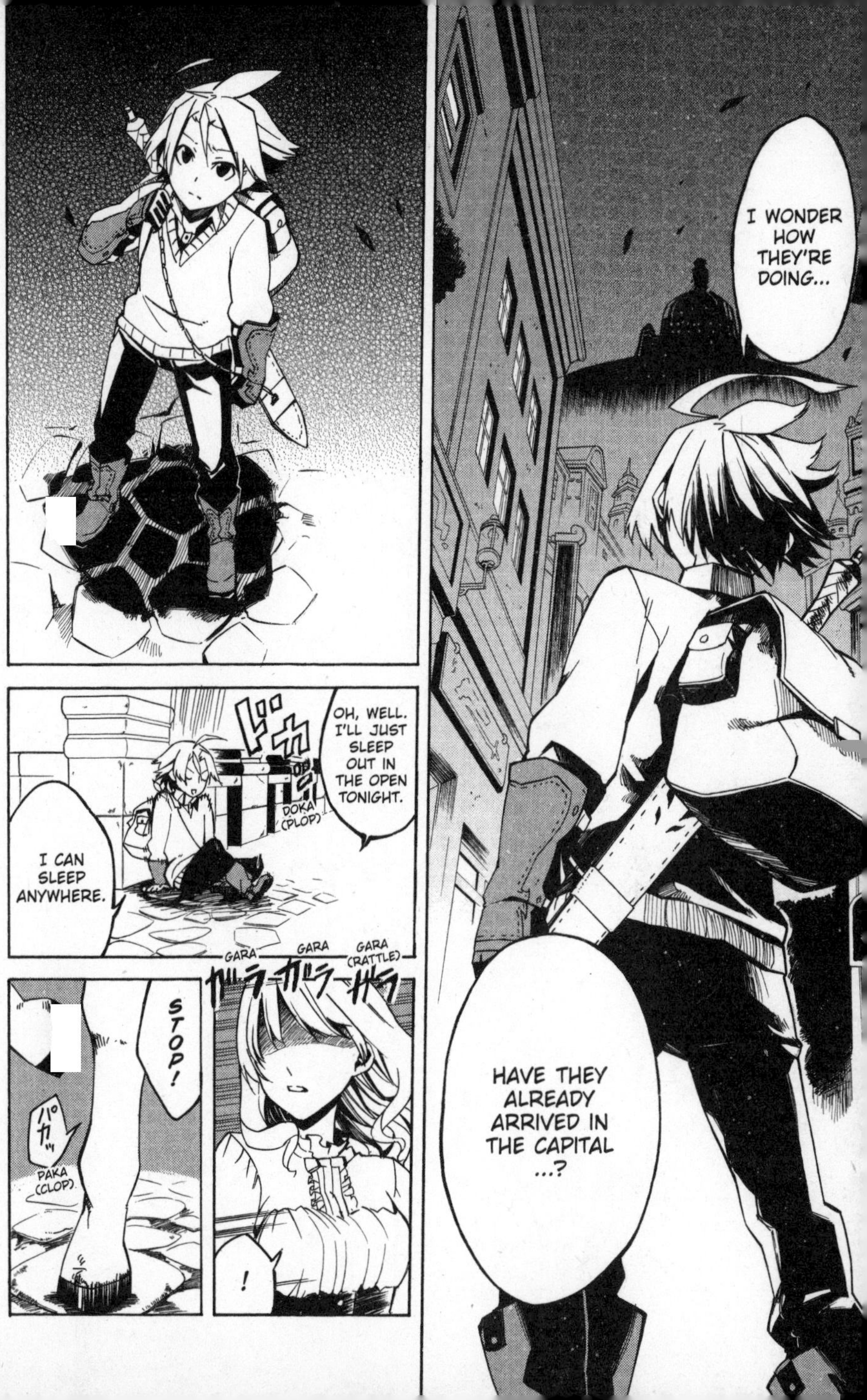
I WONDER HOW THEY'RE DOING...
HAVE THEY ALREADY ARRIVED IN THE CAPITAL ...?
OH, WELL. I'LL JUST SLEEP OUT IN THE OPEN TONIGHT.
ドカッ
DOKA (PLOP)
I CAN SLEEP ANYWHERE.
ガラ ガラ ガラ
GARA GARA GARA (RATTLE)
!
STOP!
パカッ
PAKA (CLOP)

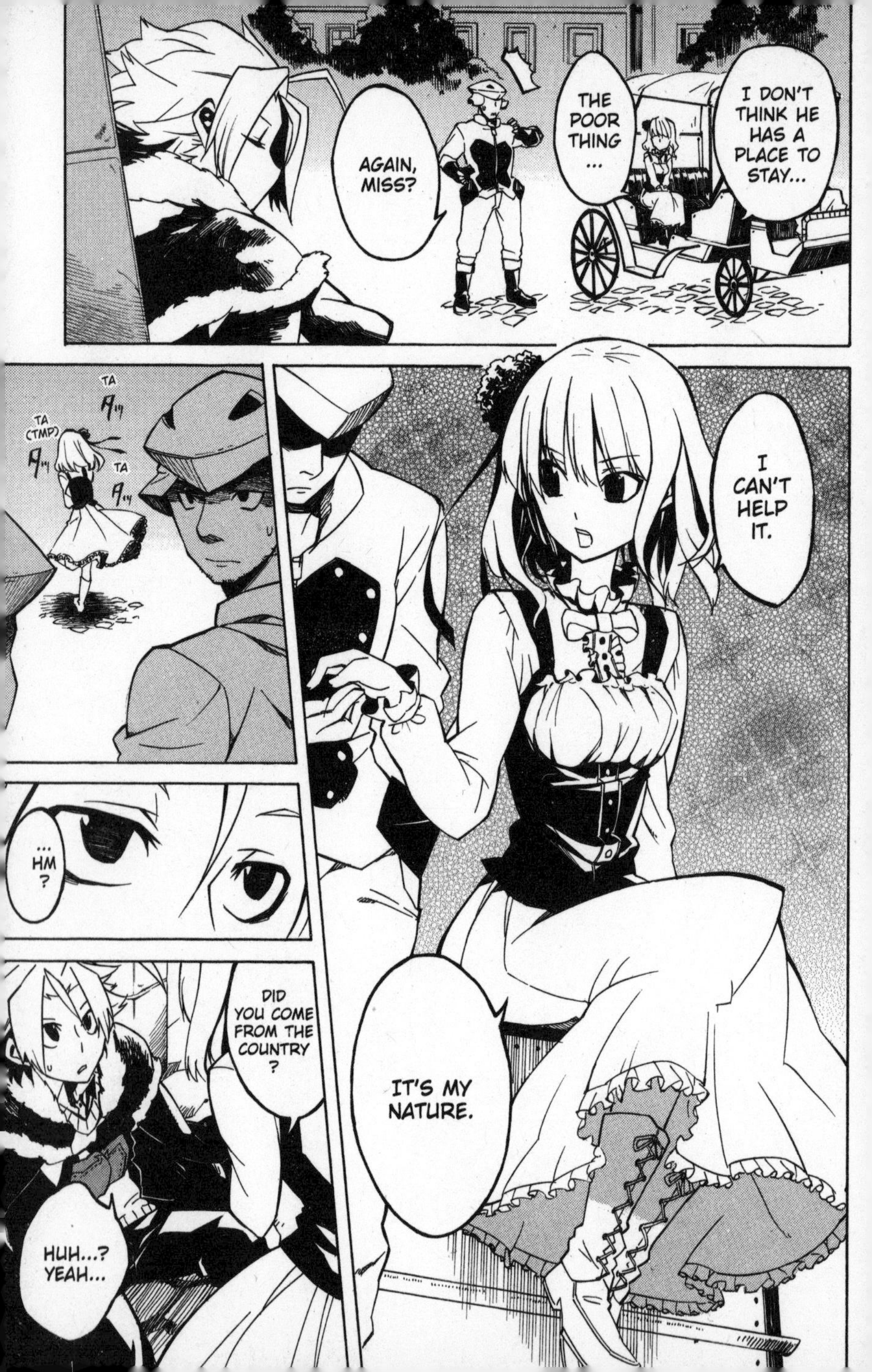
I DON'T THINK HE HAS A PLACE TO STAY...
THE POOR THING...
AGAIN, MISS?
I CAN'T HELP IT.
IT'S MY NATURE.
TA
TA (TMP)
TA
... HM?
DID YOU COME FROM THE COUNTRY?
HUH...? YEAH...

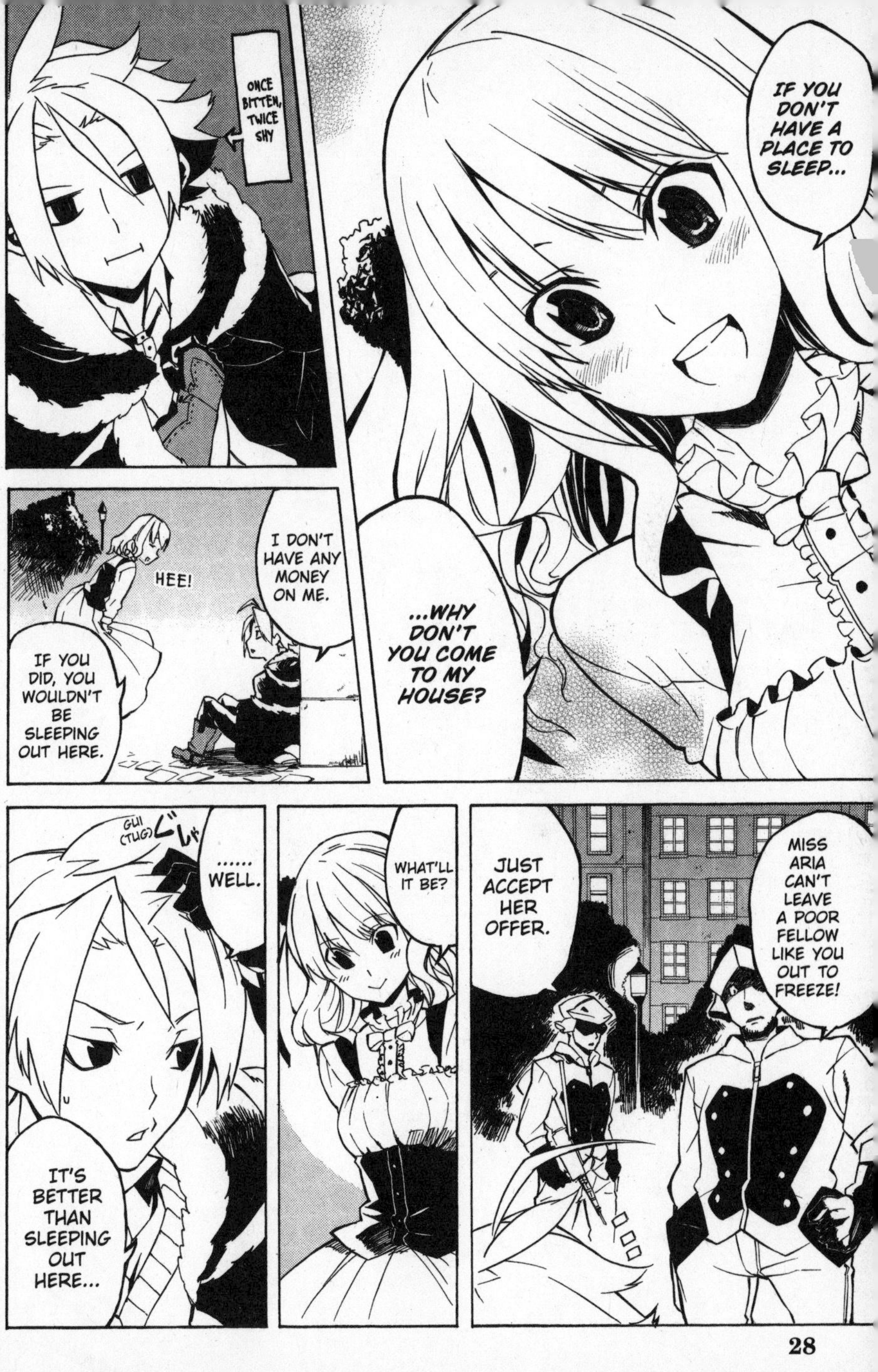
IF YOU DON'T HAVE A PLACE TO SLEEP...
...WHY DON'T YOU COME TO MY HOUSE?
ONCE BITTEN, TWICE SHY
I DON'T HAVE ANY MONEY ON ME.
HEE!
IF YOU DID, YOU WOULDN'T BE SLEEPING OUT HERE.
MISS ARIA CAN'T LEAVE A POOR FELLOW LIKE YOU OUT TO FREEZE!
JUST ACCEPT HER OFFER.
WHAT'LL IT BE?
GUI (TUG)
...... WELL.
IT'S BETTER THAN SLEEPING OUT HERE...

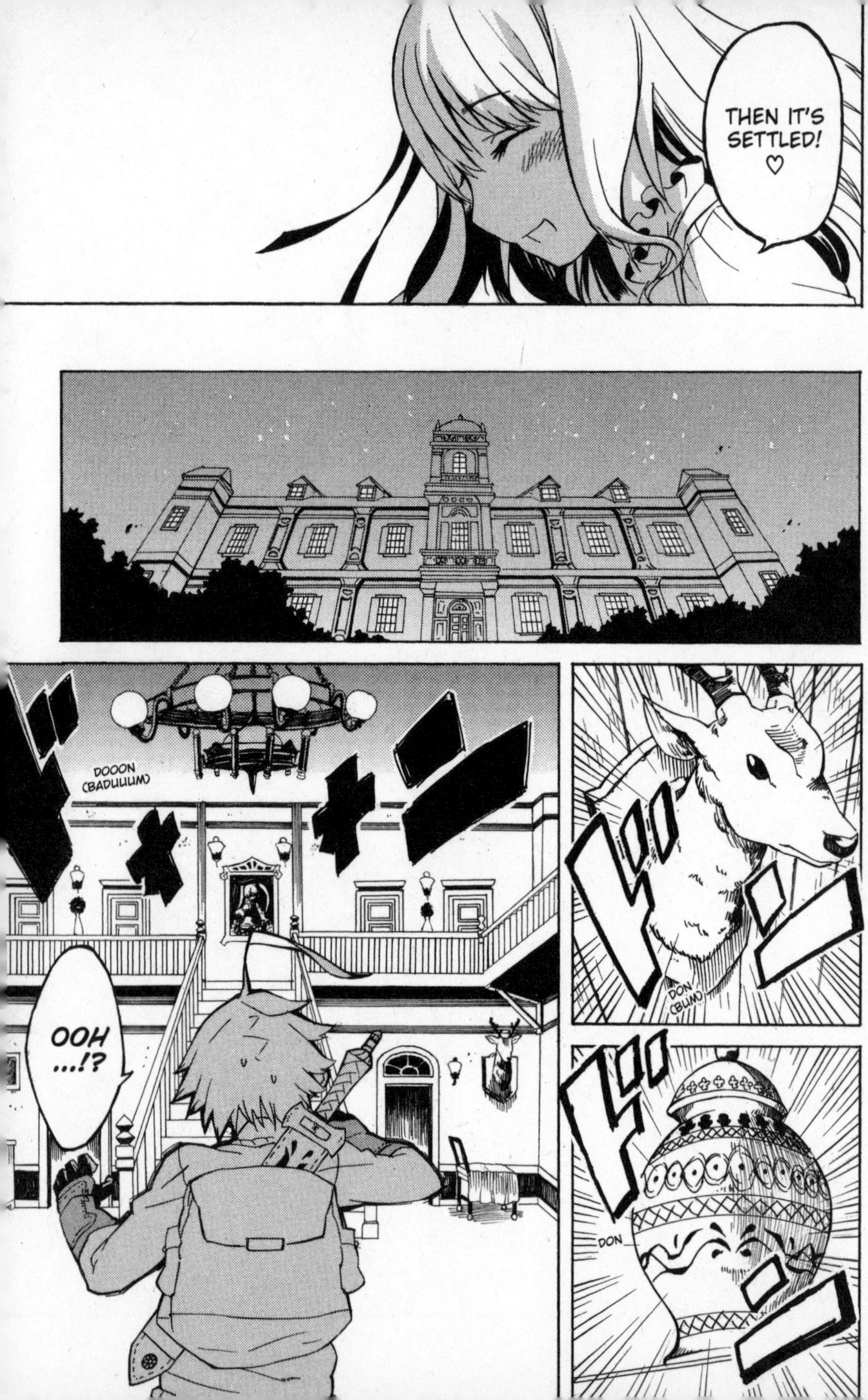
THEN IT'S SETTLED! ♡
DON (BLUM)
DON
DOOON (BADUUUM)
OOH ...!?

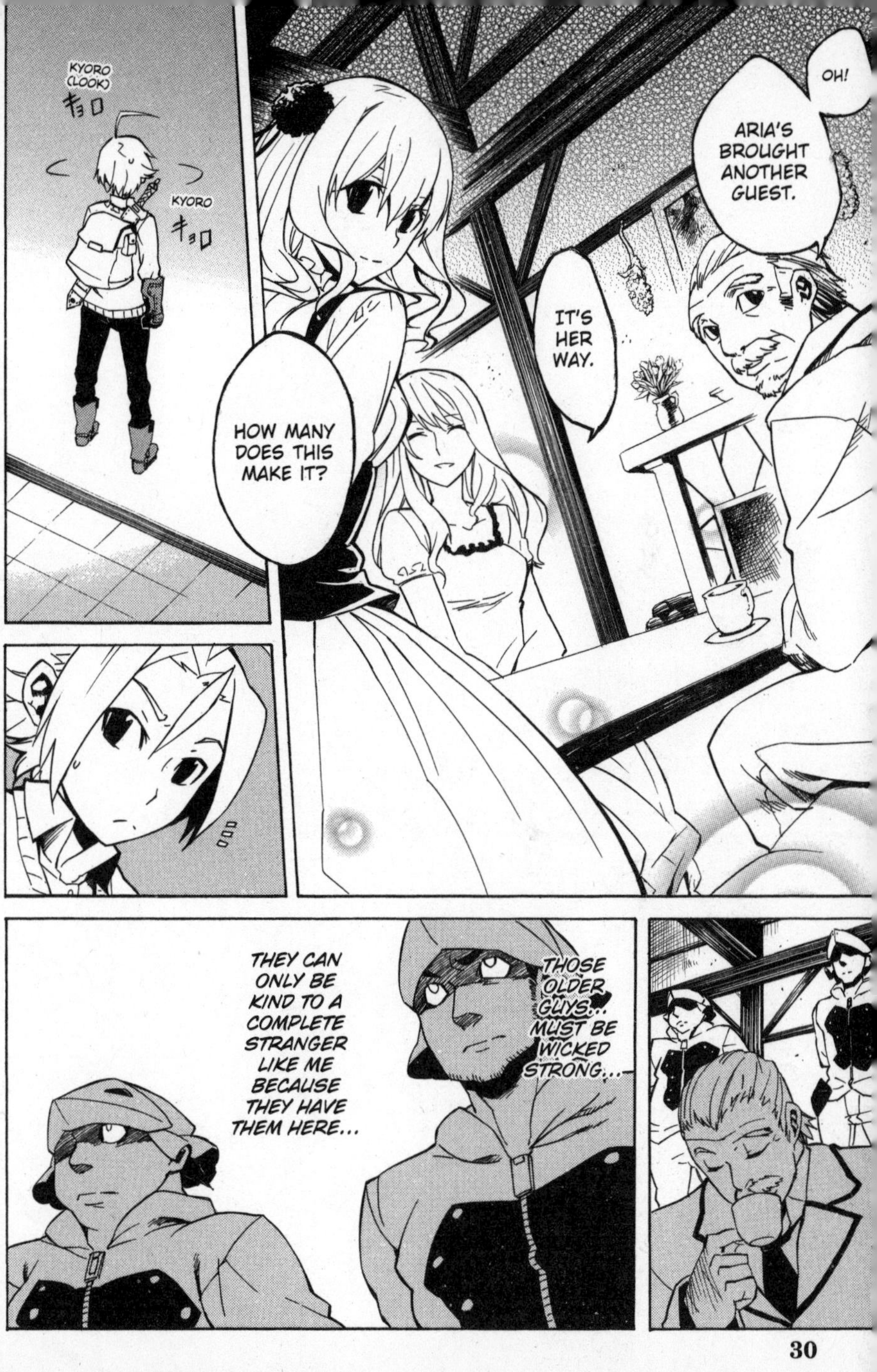
OH!
ARIA'S BROUGHT ANOTHER GUEST.
IT'S HER WAY.
HOW MANY DOES THIS MAKE IT?
KYORO (LOOK)
キョロ
KYORO
キョロ
THOSE OLDER GUYS... MUST BE WICKED STRONG...
THEY CAN ONLY BE KIND TO A COMPLETE STRANGER LIKE ME BECAUSE THEY HAVE THEM HERE...

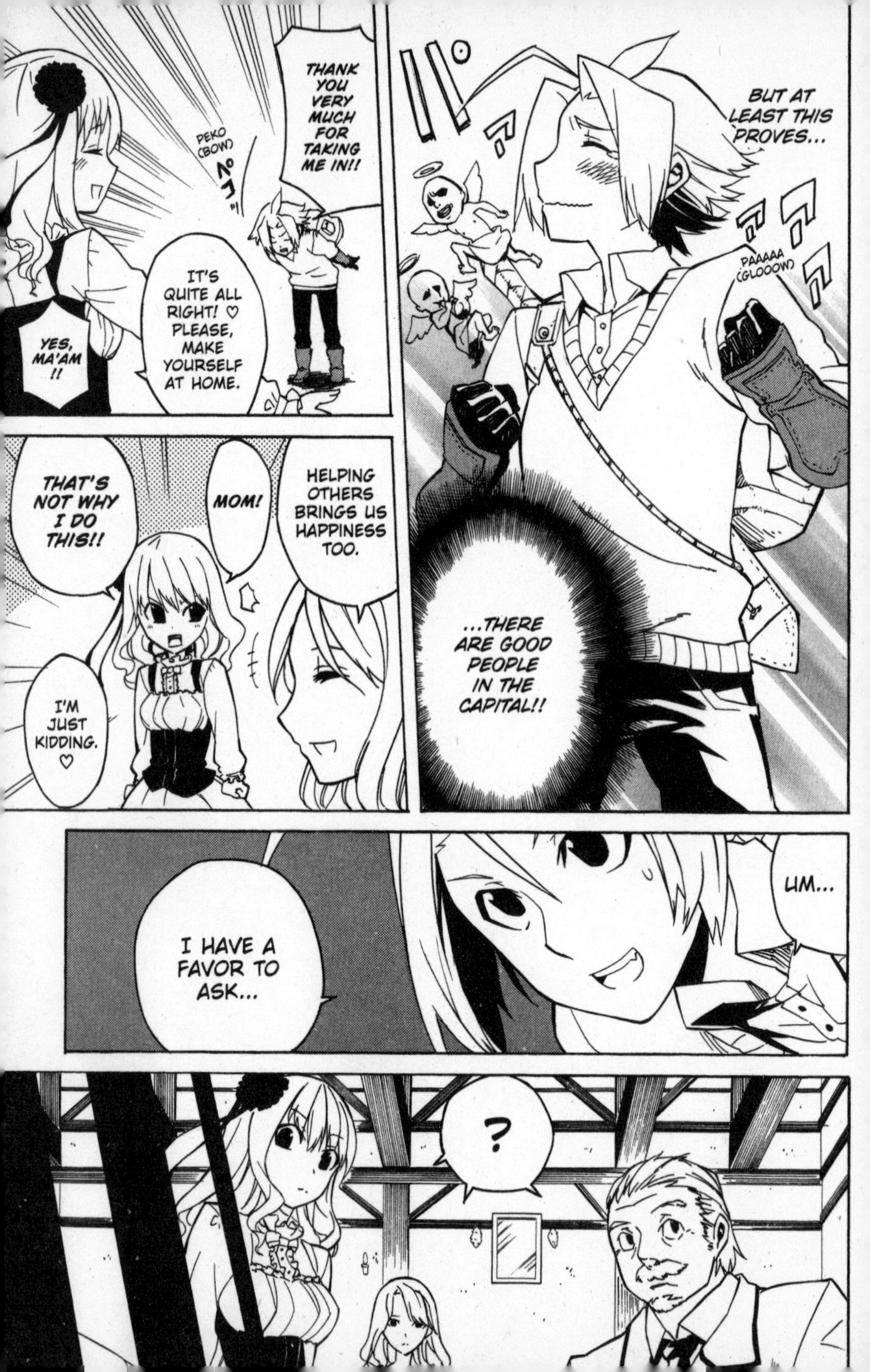
BUT AT LEAST THIS PROVES...
PAAAAA (GLOOOW)
...THERE ARE GOOD PEOPLE IN THE CAPITAL!!
THANK YOU VERY MUCH FOR TAKING ME IN!!
PEKO (BOW)
IT'S QUITE ALL RIGHT! ♡ PLEASE, MAKE YOURSELF AT HOME.
YES, MA'AM !!
HELPING OTHERS BRINGS US HAPPINESS TOO.
MOM!
THAT'S NOT WHY I DO THIS!!
I'M JUST KIDDING. ♡
UM...
I HAVE A FAVOR TO ASK...
?

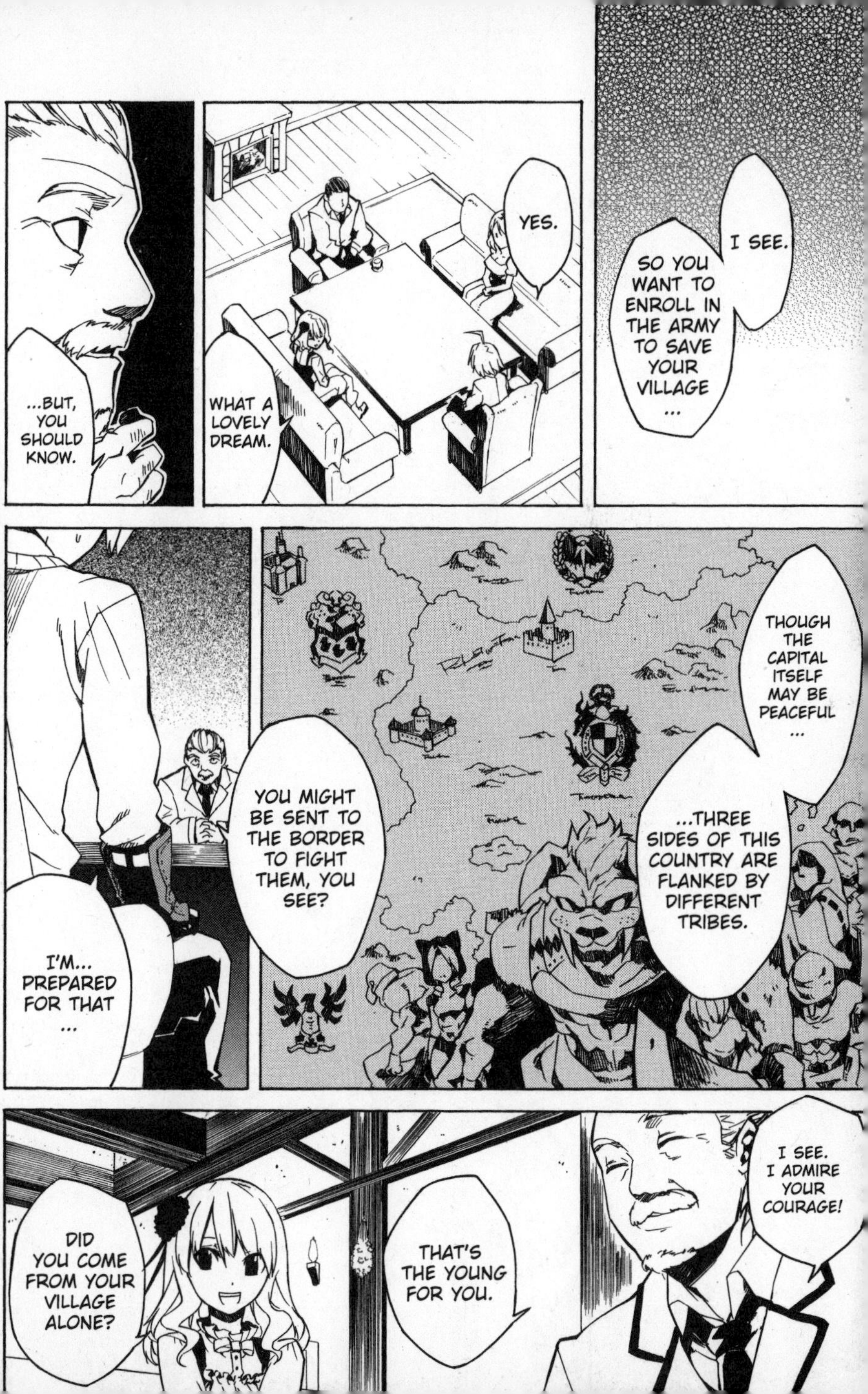
I SEE.
SO YOU WANT TO ENROLL IN THE ARMY TO SAVE YOUR VILLAGE ...
YES.
WHAT A LOVELY DREAM.
...BUT, YOU SHOULD KNOW.
THOUGH THE CAPITAL ITSELF MAY BE PEACEFUL ...
...THREE SIDES OF THIS COUNTRY ARE FLANKED BY DIFFERENT TRIBES.
YOU MIGHT BE SENT TO THE BORDER TO FIGHT THEM, YOU SEE?
I'M... PREPARED FOR THAT ...
I SEE. I ADMIRE YOUR COURAGE!
THAT'S THE YOUNG FOR YOU.
DID YOU COME FROM YOUR VILLAGE ALONE?

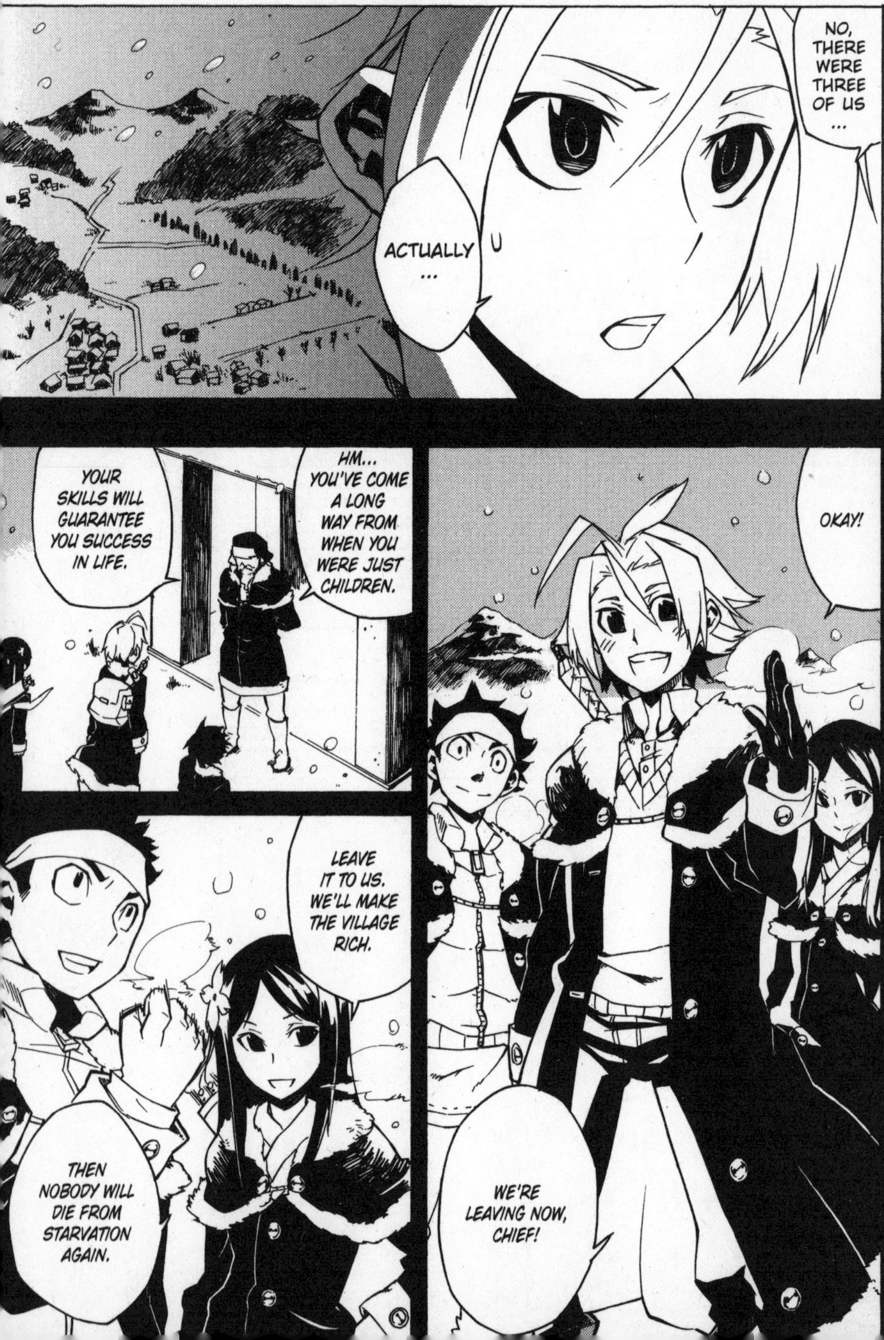
NO, THERE WERE THREE OF US ...
ACTUALLY ...
OKAY!
WE'RE LEAVING NOW, CHIEF!
HM... YOU'VE COME A LONG WAY FROM WHEN YOU WERE JUST CHILDREN.
YOUR SKILLS WILL GUARANTEE YOU SUCCESS IN LIFE.
LEAVE IT TO US. WE'LL MAKE THE VILLAGE RICH.
THEN NOBODY WILL DIE FROM STARVATION AGAIN.

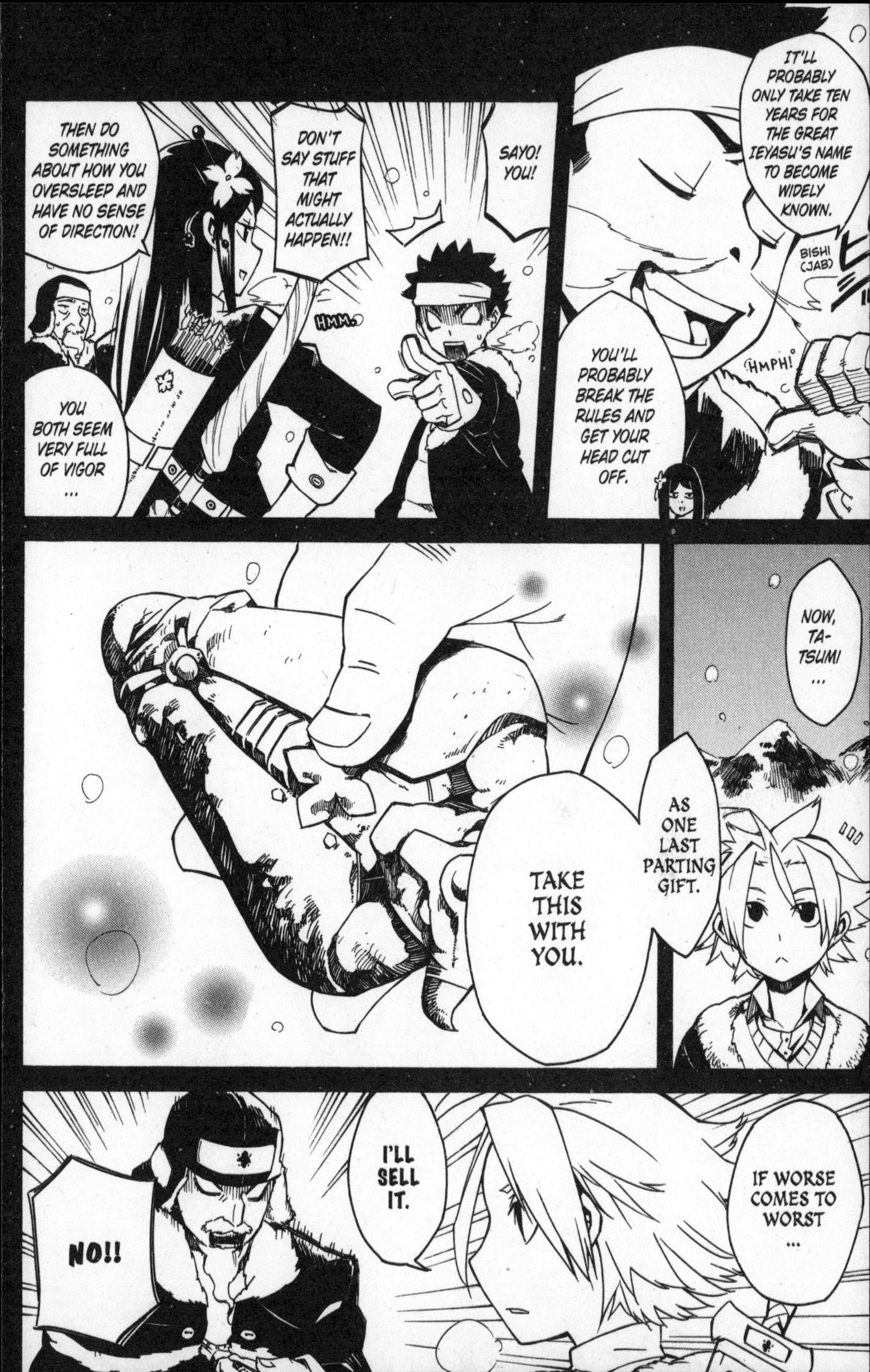
IT'LL PROBABLY ONLY TAKE TEN YEARS FOR THE GREAT IEYASU'S NAME TO BECOME WIDELY KNOWN.
BISHI (JAB)
HMPH!
YOU'LL PROBABLY BREAK THE RULES AND GET YOUR HEAD CUT OFF.
SAYO! YOU!
DON'T SAY STUFF THAT MIGHT ACTUALLY HAPPEN!!
HMM.
THEN DO SOMETHING ABOUT HOW YOU OVERSLEEP AND HAVE NO SENSE OF DIRECTION!
YOU BOTH SEEM VERY FULL OF VIGOR ...
NOW, TA-TSUMI ...
AS ONE LAST PARTING GIFT.
TAKE THIS WITH YOU.
IF WORSE COMES TO WORST ...
I'LL SELL IT.
NO!!

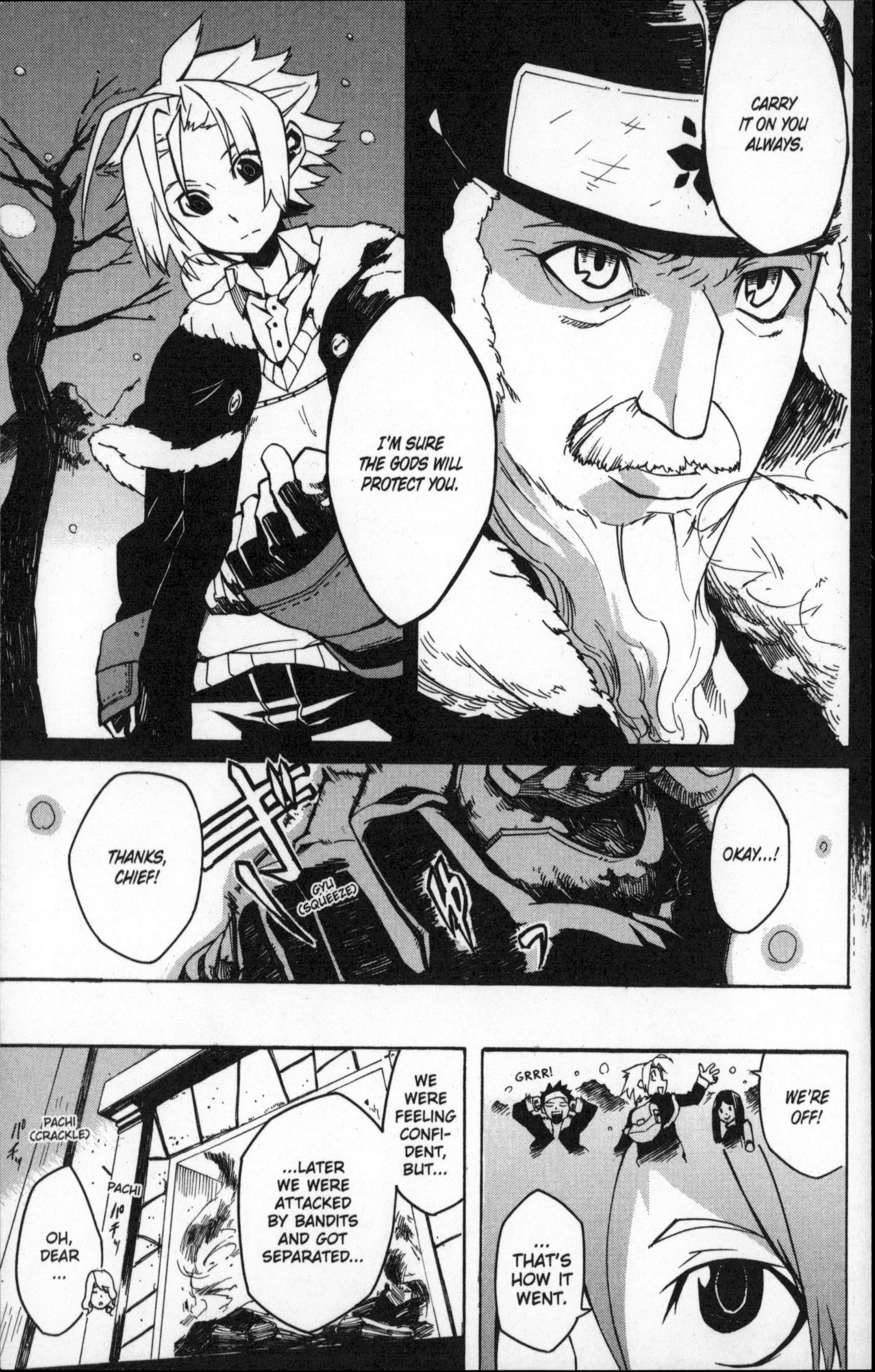

CARRY IT ON YOU ALWAYS.
I'M SURE THE GODS WILL PROTECT YOU.
OKAY...!
GYU (SQUEEZE)
THANKS, CHIEF!
WE'RE OFF!
GRRR!
... THAT'S HOW IT WENT.
WE WERE FEELING CONFI-DENT, BUT...
...LATER WE WERE ATTACKED BY BANDITS AND GOT SEPARATED...
PACHI (CRACKLE)
PACHI
OH, DEAR ...

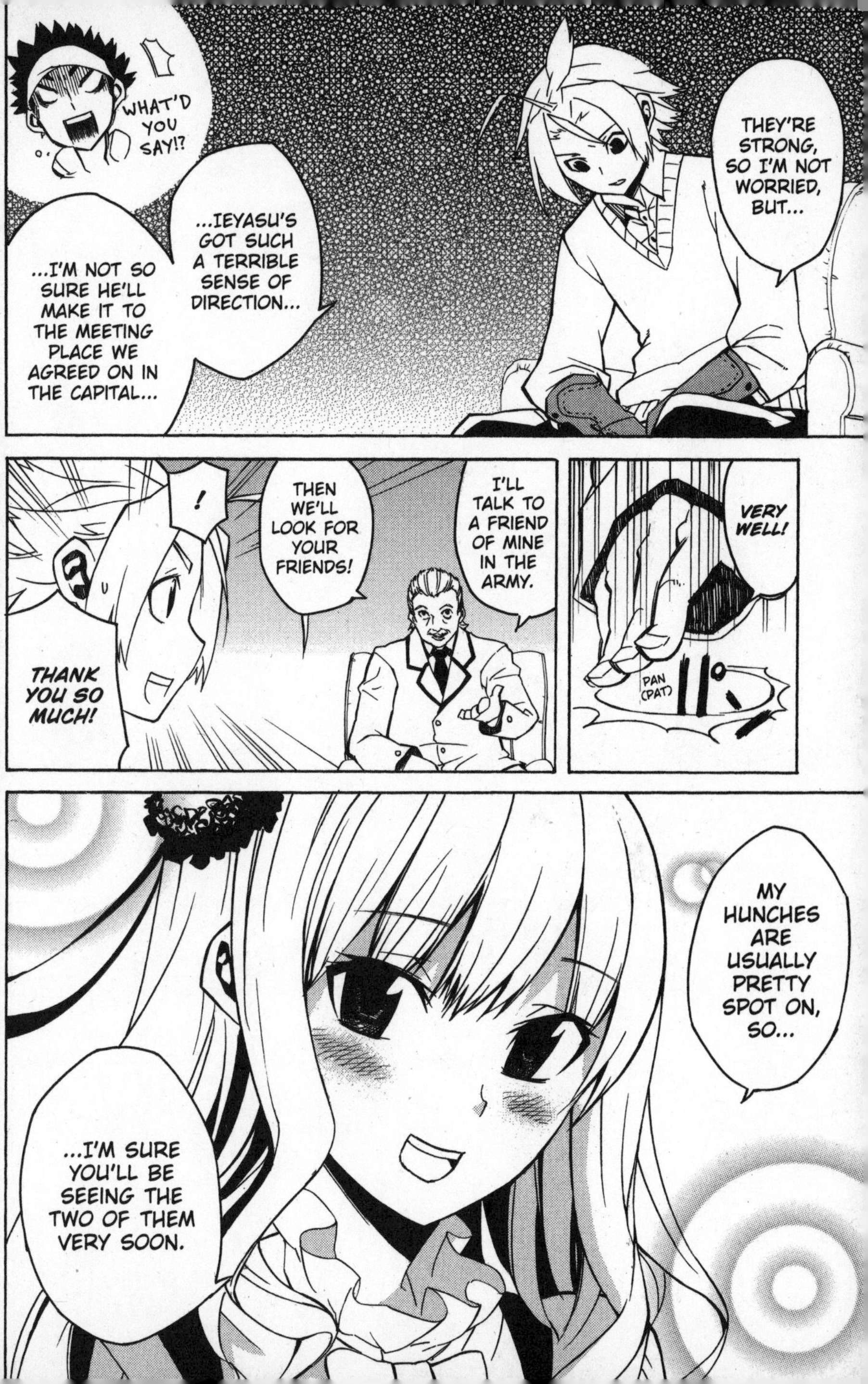
THEY'RE STRONG, SO I'M NOT WORRIED, BUT...
...IEYASU'S GOT SUCH A TERRIBLE SENSE OF DIRECTION...
...I'M NOT SO SURE HE'LL MAKE IT TO THE MEETING PLACE WE AGREED ON IN THE CAPITAL...
WHAT'D YOU SAY!?
VERY WELL!
PAN (PAT)
I'LL TALK TO A FRIEND OF MINE IN THE ARMY.
THEN WE'LL LOOK FOR YOUR FRIENDS!
!
THANK YOU SO MUCH!
MY HUNCHES ARE USUALLY PRETTY SPOT ON, SO...
...I'M SURE YOU'LL BE SEEING THE TWO OF THEM VERY SOON.

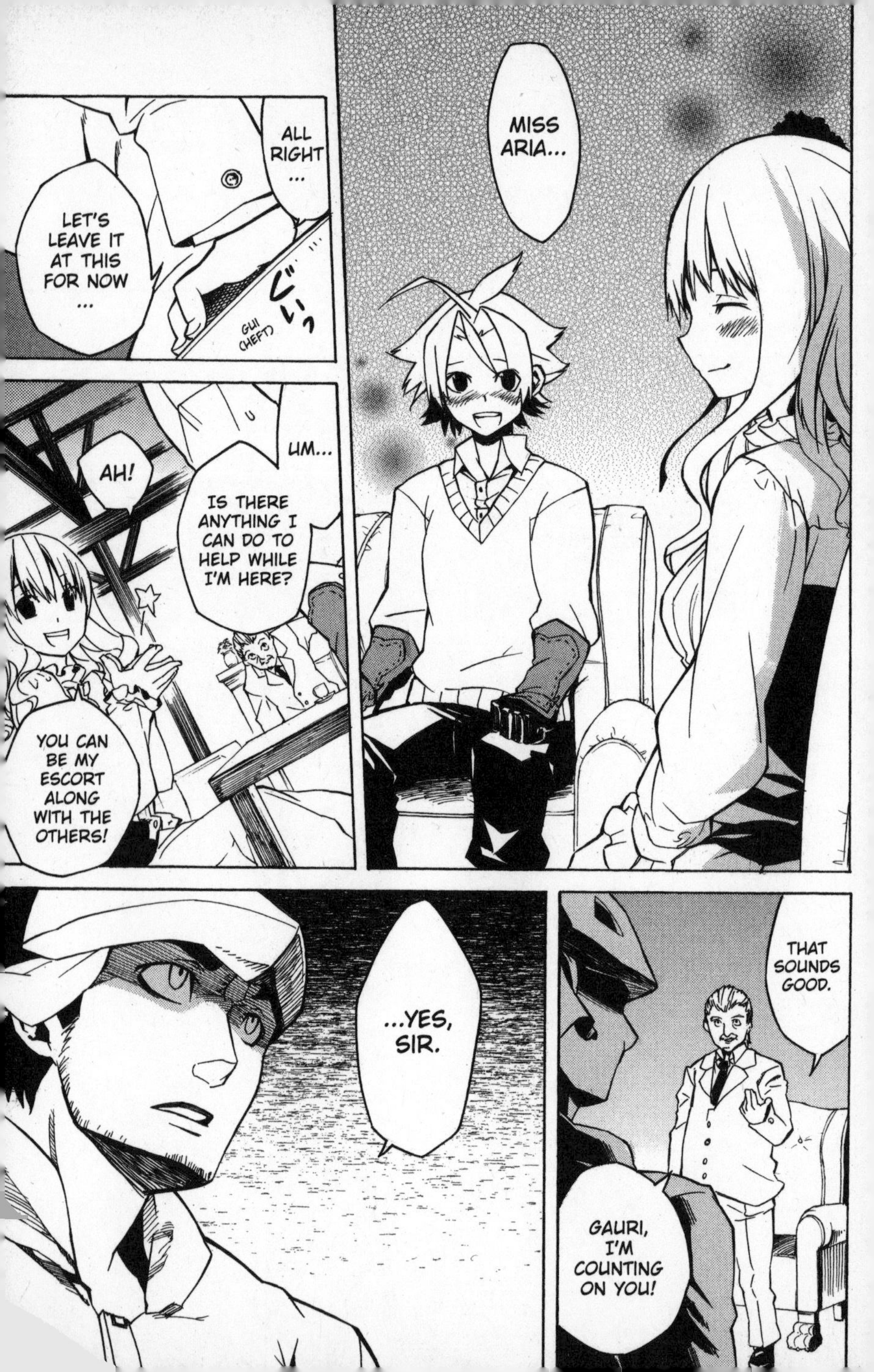
MISS ARIA...
ALL RIGHT...
LET'S LEAVE IT AT THIS FOR NOW...
ぐいっ
GUI (HEFT)
UM...
IS THERE ANYTHING I CAN DO TO HELP WHILE I'M HERE?
AH!
YOU CAN BE MY ESCORT ALONG WITH THE OTHERS!
THAT SOUNDS GOOD.
GAURI, I'M COUNTING ON YOU!
...YES, SIR.

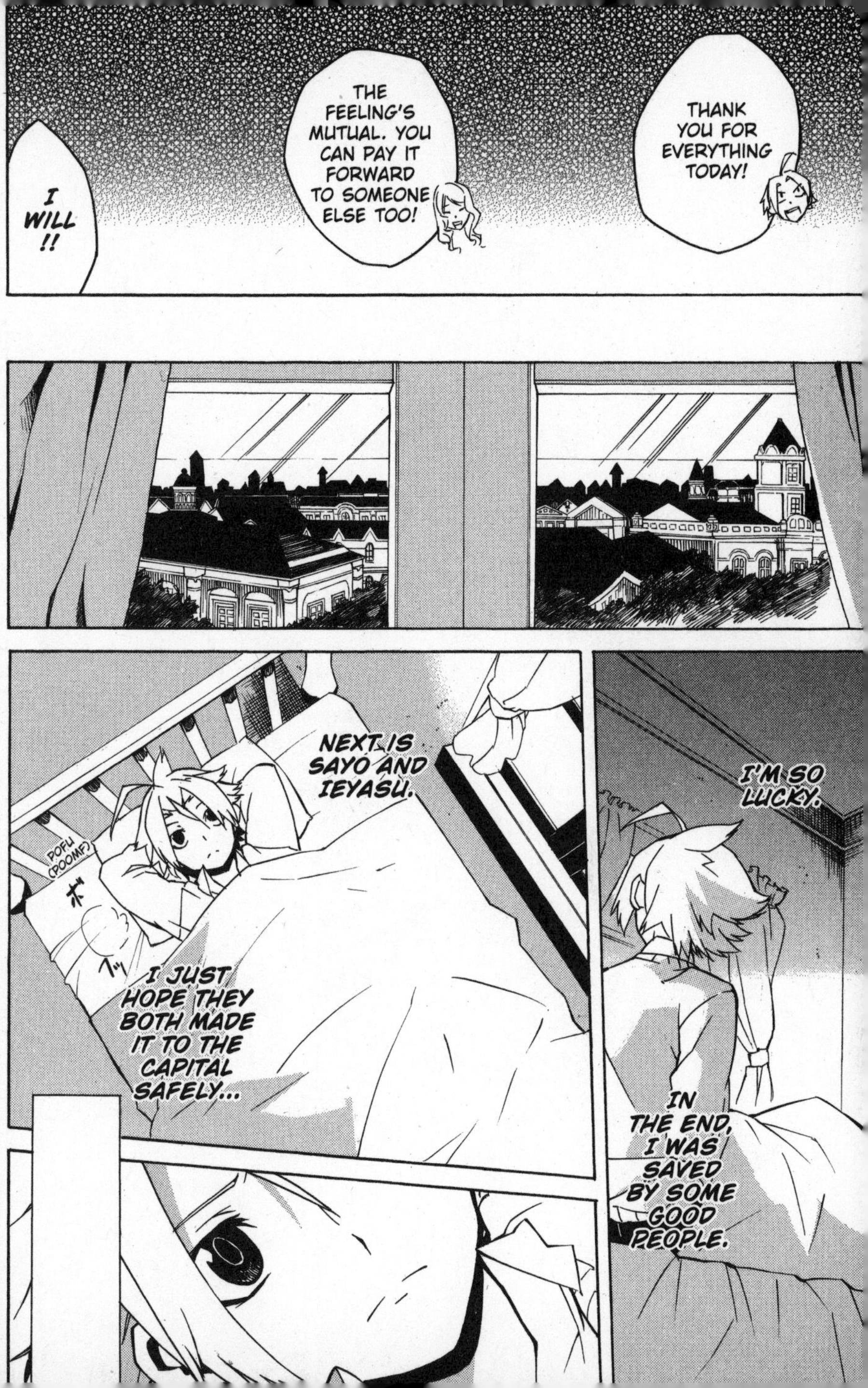
THANK YOU FOR EVERYTHING TODAY!
THE FEELING'S MUTUAL. YOU CAN PAY IT FORWARD TO SOMEONE ELSE TOO!
I WILL!!
I'M SO LUCKY.
IN THE END, I WAS SAVED BY SOME GOOD PEOPLE.
NEXT IS SAYO AND IEYASU.
POFU (POOMF)
I JUST HOPE THEY BOTH MADE IT TO THE CAPITAL SAFELY...

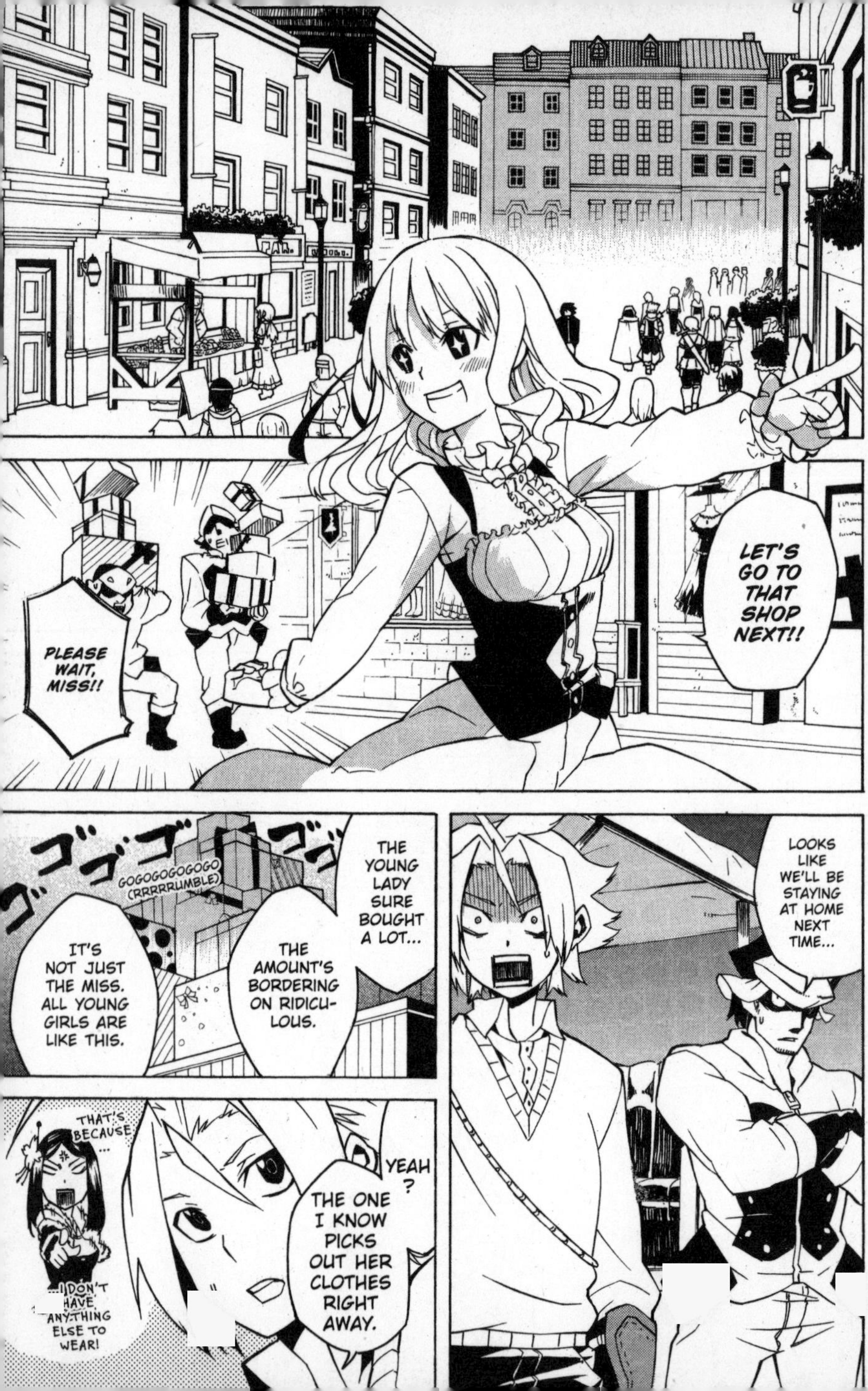
LET'S GO TO THAT SHOP NEXT!!
PLEASE WAIT, MISS!!
LOOKS LIKE WE'LL BE STAYING AT HOME NEXT TIME...
THE YOUNG LADY SURE BOUGHT A LOT...
GOGOGOGOGOGO (RRRRRUMBLE)
THE AMOUNT'S BORDERING ON RIDICU-LOUS.
IT'S NOT JUST THE MISS. ALL YOUNG GIRLS ARE LIKE THIS.
YEAH?
THE ONE I KNOW PICKS OUT HER CLOTHES RIGHT AWAY.
THAT'S BECAUSE...
...I DON'T HAVE ANYTHING ELSE TO WEAR!

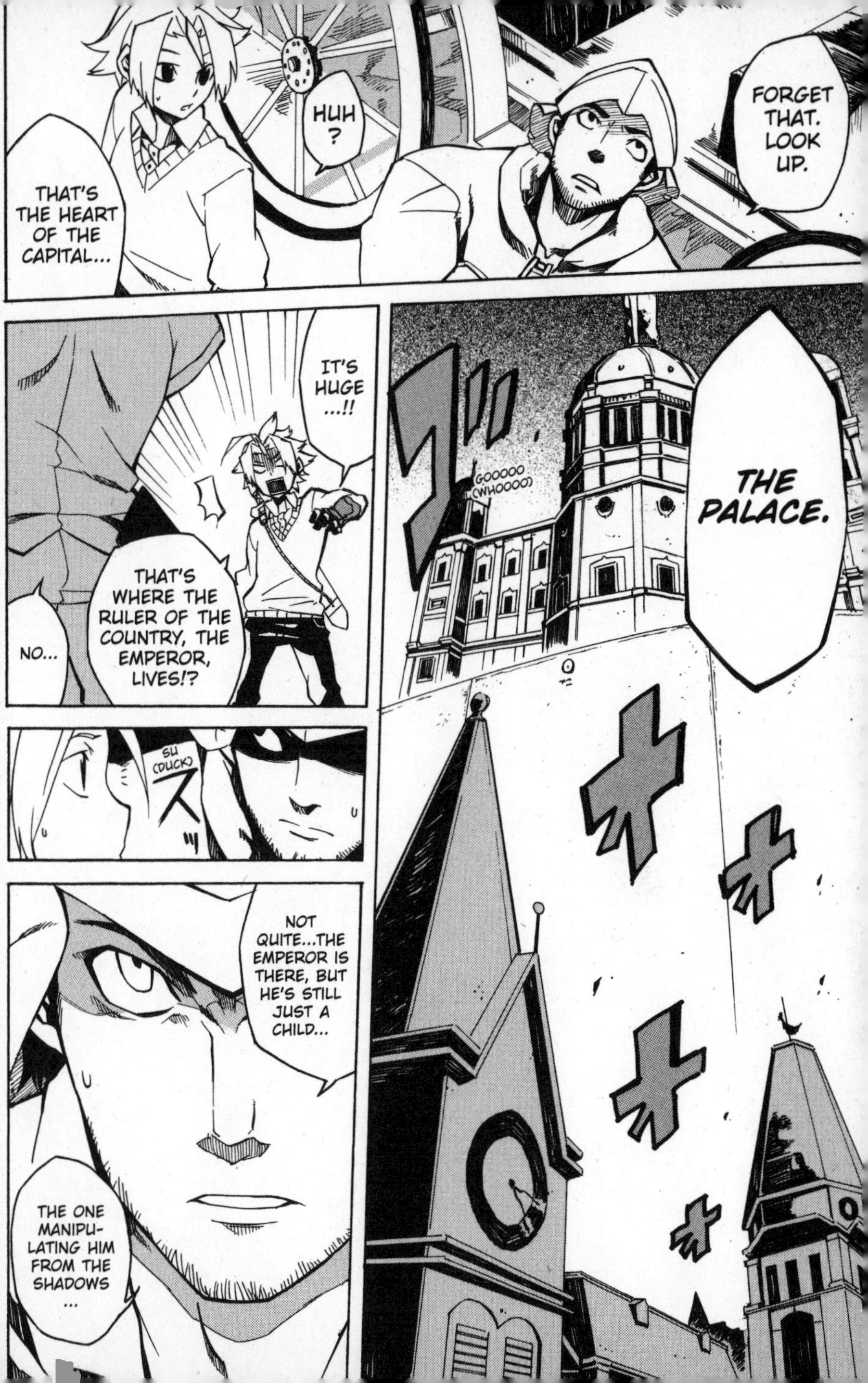
FORGET THAT. LOOK UP.
HUH?
THAT'S THE HEART OF THE CAPITAL...
THE PALACE.
GOOOOO (WHOOOO)
IT'S HUGE...!!
THAT'S WHERE THE RULER OF THE COUNTRY, THE EMPEROR, LIVES!?
NO...
SU (DUCK)
NOT QUITE...THE EMPEROR IS THERE, BUT HE'S STILL JUST A CHILD...
THE ONE MANIPU-LATING HIM FROM THE SHADOWS...

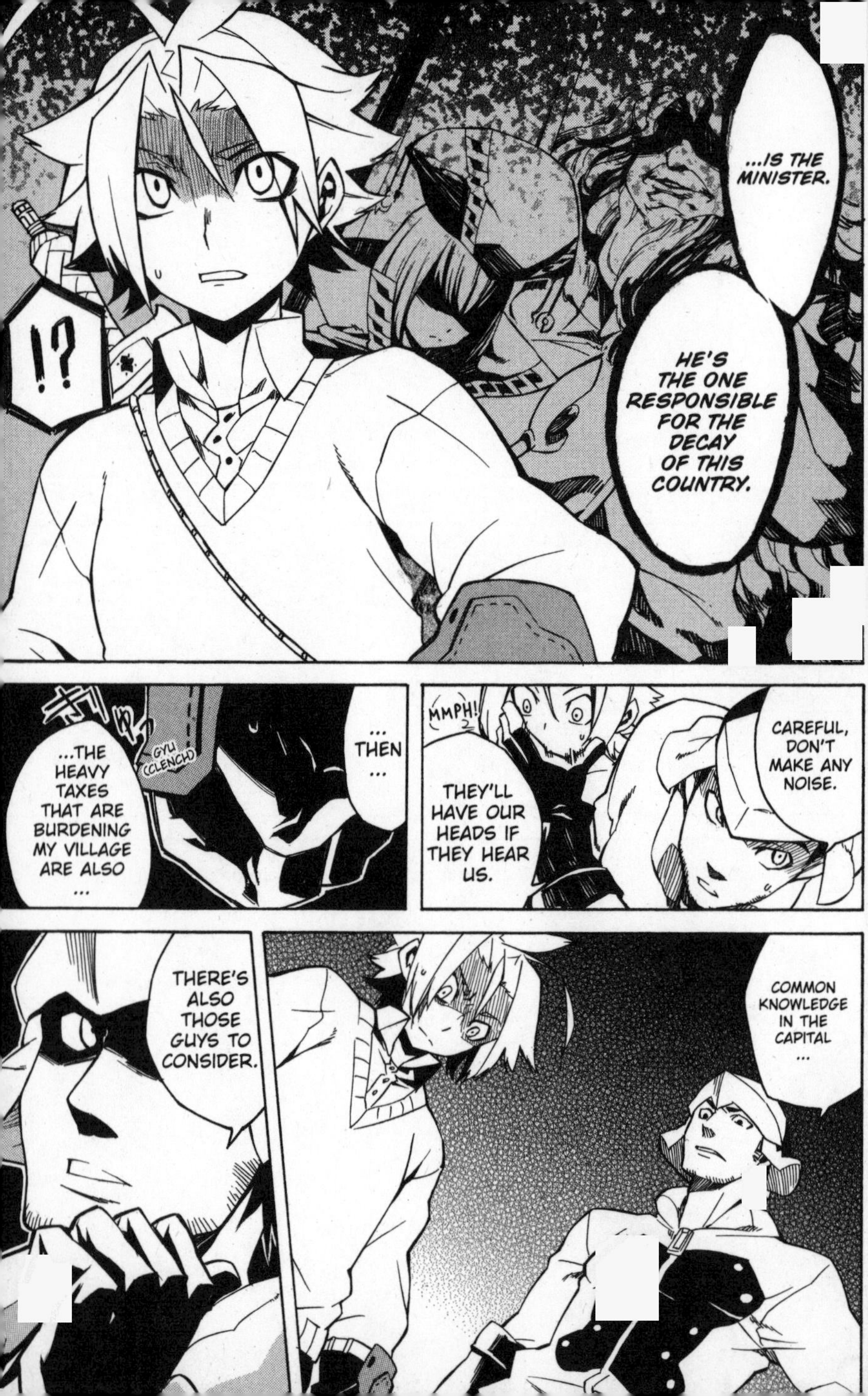
...IS THE MINISTER.
HE'S THE ONE RESPONSIBLE FOR THE DECAY OF THIS COUNTRY.
!?
CAREFUL, DON'T MAKE ANY NOISE.
MMPH!
THEY'LL HAVE OUR HEADS IF THEY HEAR US.
... THEN ...
GYU (CLENCH)
...THE HEAVY TAXES THAT ARE BURDENING MY VILLAGE ARE ALSO ...
COMMON KNOWLEDGE IN THE CAPITAL ...
THERE'S ALSO THOSE GUYS TO CONSIDER.

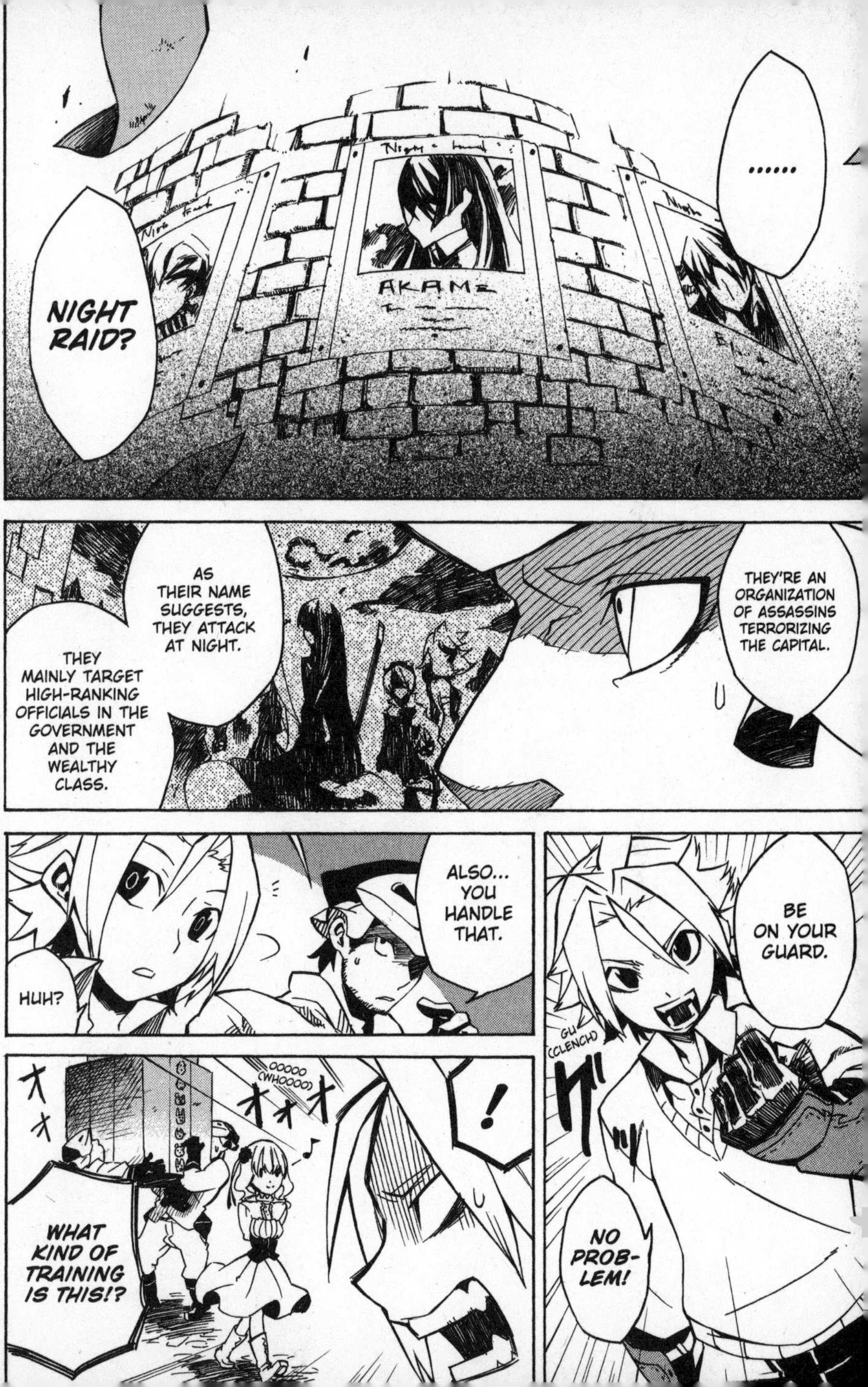
......
AKAME
NIGHT RAID?
THEY'RE AN ORGANIZATION OF ASSASSINS TERRORIZING THE CAPITAL.
AS THEIR NAME SUGGESTS, THEY ATTACK AT NIGHT.
THEY MAINLY TARGET HIGH-RANKING OFFICIALS IN THE GOVERNMENT AND THE WEALTHY CLASS.
BE ON YOUR GUARD.
GU (CLENCH)
NO PROB-LEM!
ALSO... YOU HANDLE THAT.
HUH?
!
OOOOO (WHOOOO)
WHAT KIND OF TRAINING IS THIS!?

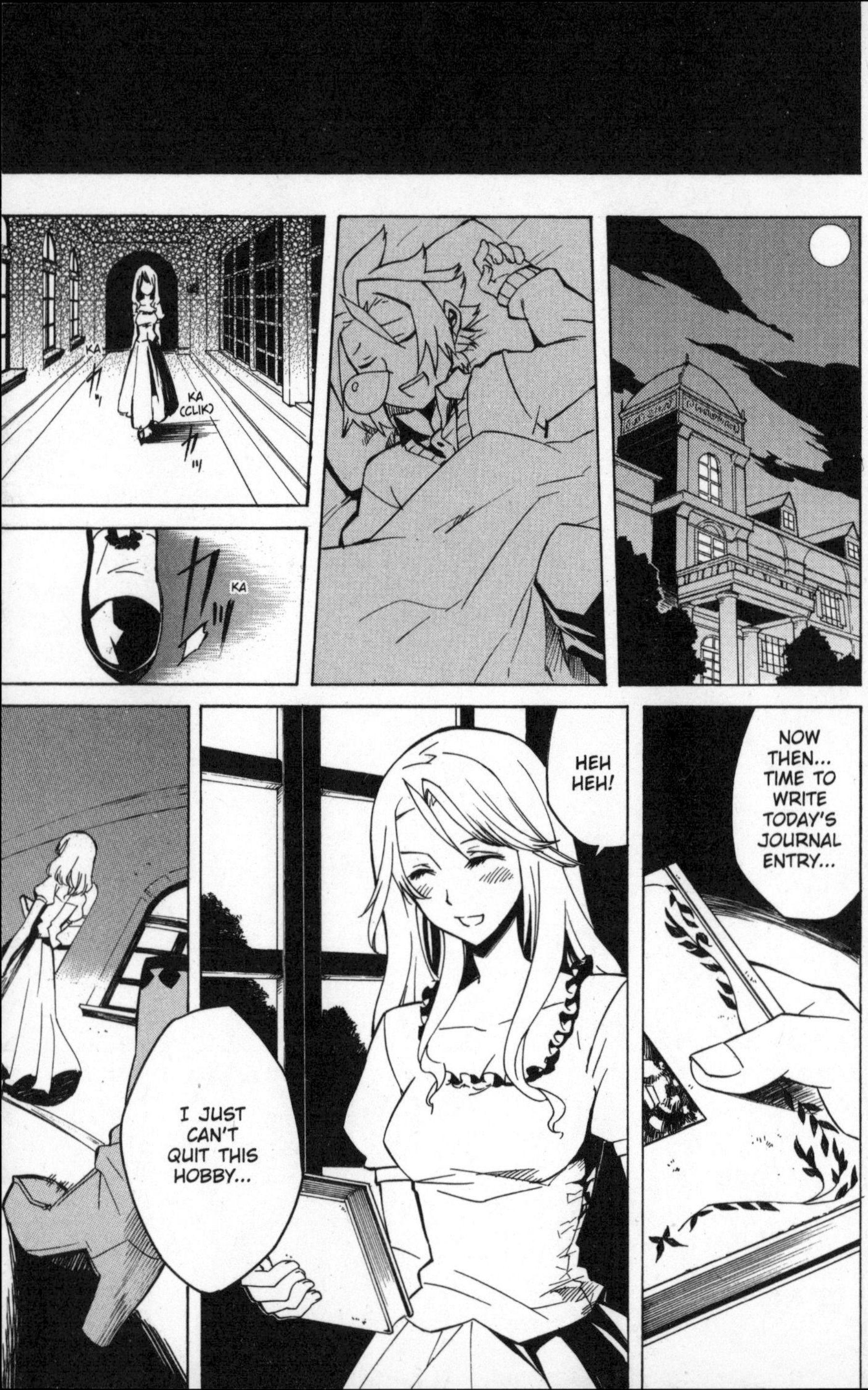
KA
KA (CLIK)
KA
NOW THEN... TIME TO WRITE TODAY'S JOURNAL ENTRY...
HEH HEH!
I JUST CAN'T QUIT THIS HOBBY...

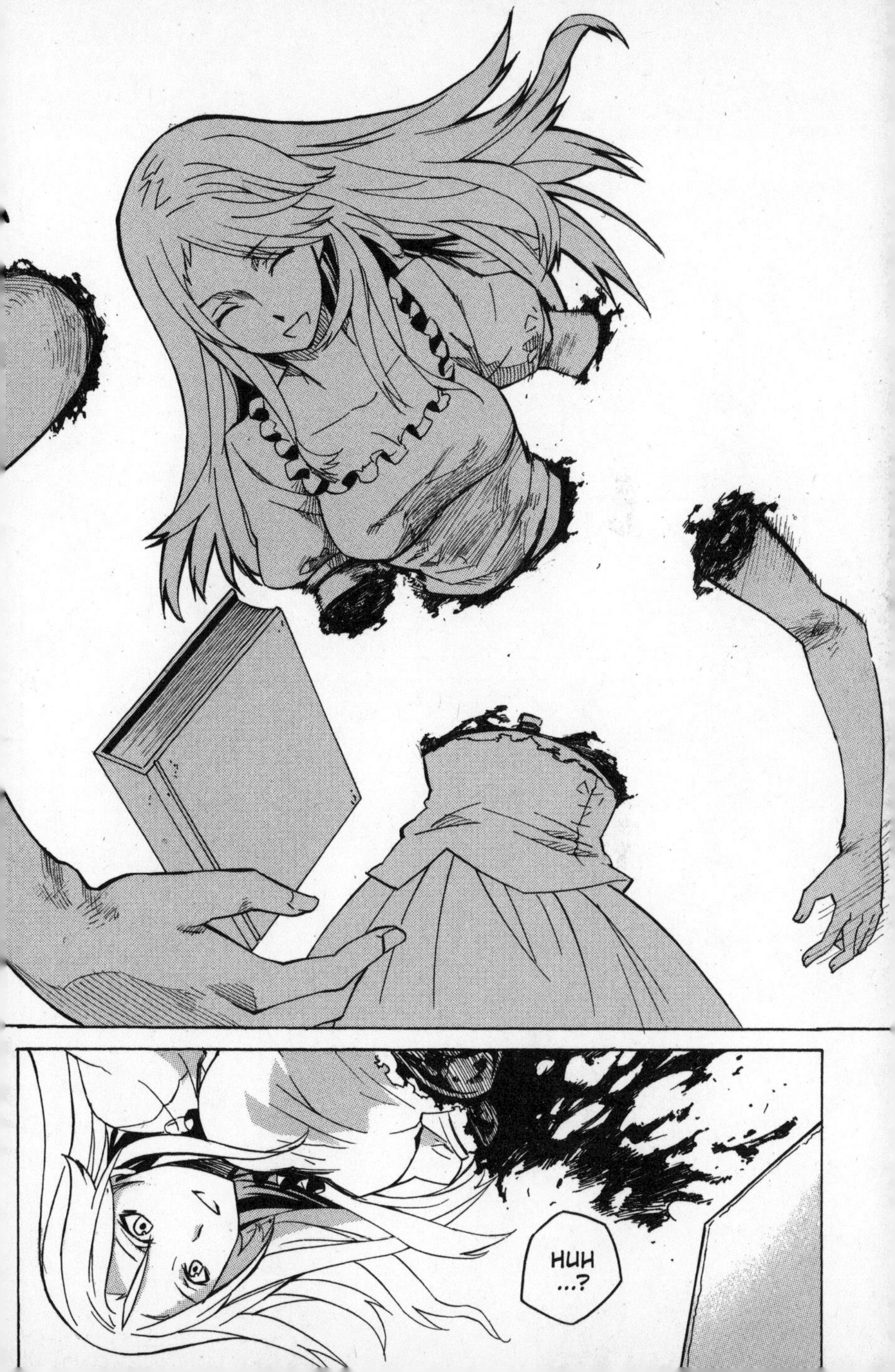
HUH ...?

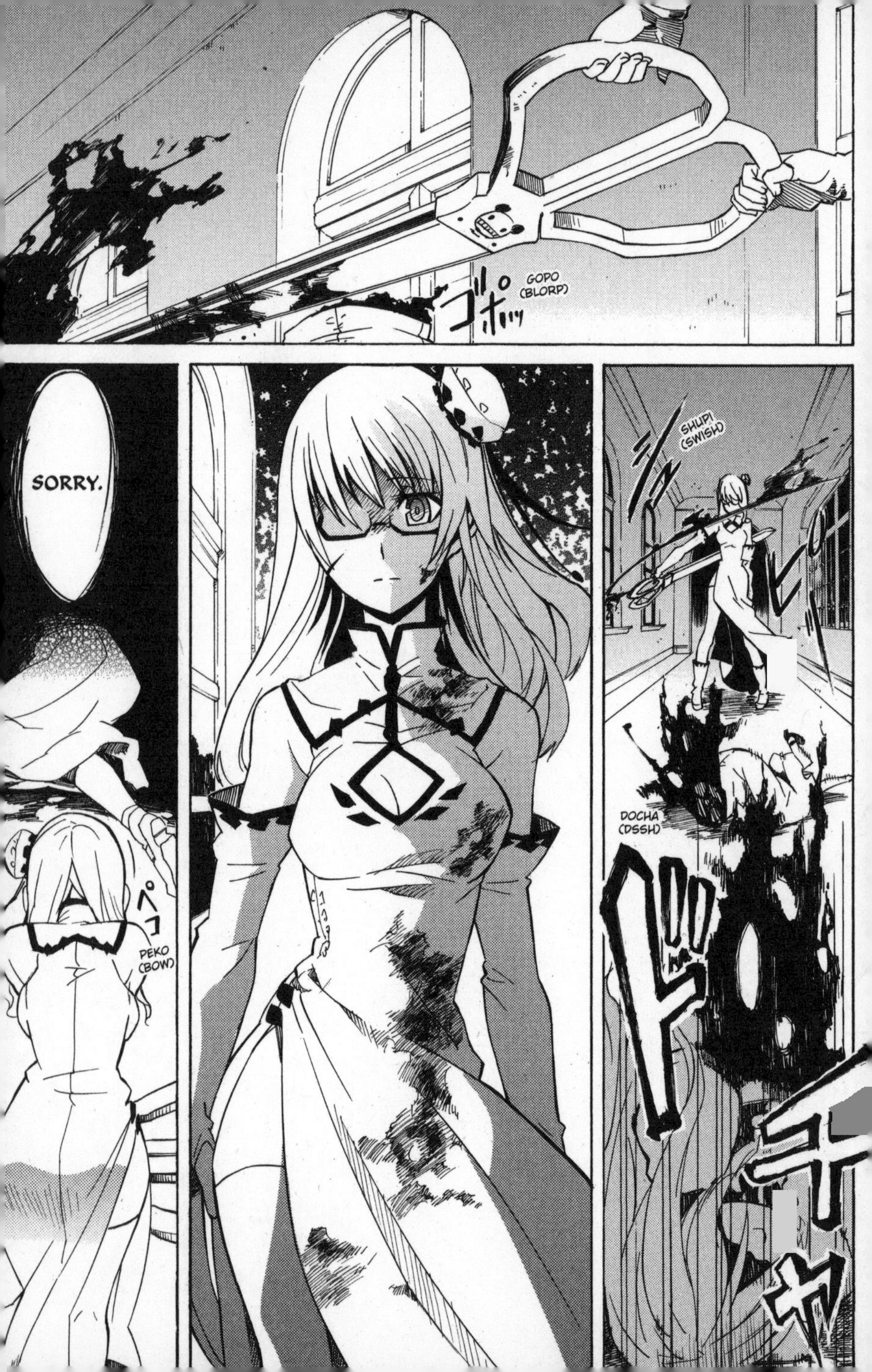
GOPO
(BLORP)
SHUP!
(SWISH)
DOCHA
(DSSH)
SORRY.
PEKO
(BOW)

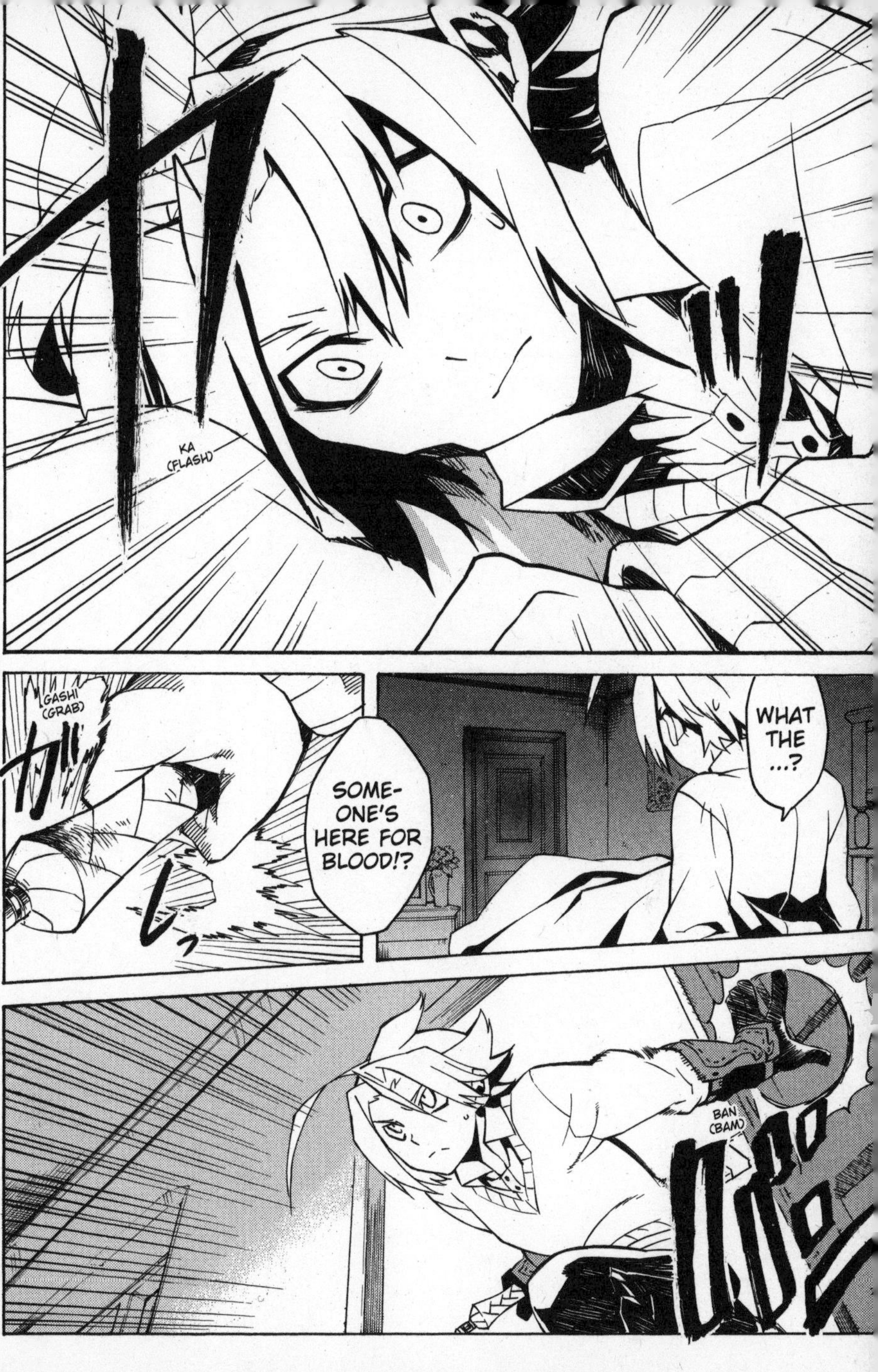
KA
(FLASH)
WHAT THE ...?
SOME-ONE'S HERE FOR BLOOD!?
GASHI
(GRAB)
BAN
(BAM)

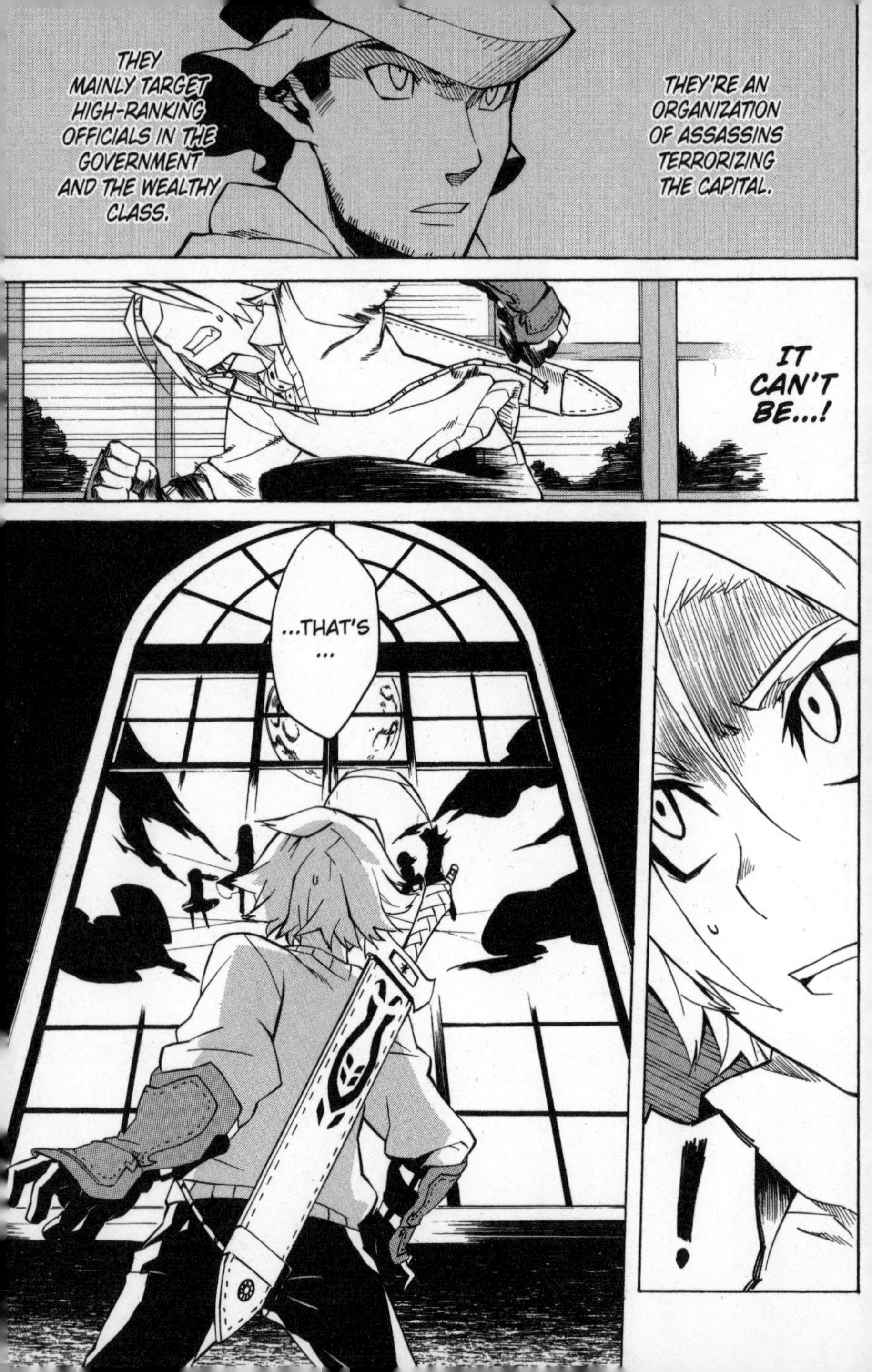
THEY'RE AN ORGANIZATION OF ASSASSINS TERRORIZING THE CAPITAL.
THEY MAINLY TARGET HIGH-RANKING OFFICIALS IN THE GOVERNMENT AND THE WEALTHY CLASS.
IT CAN'T BE...!
!
...THAT'S ...

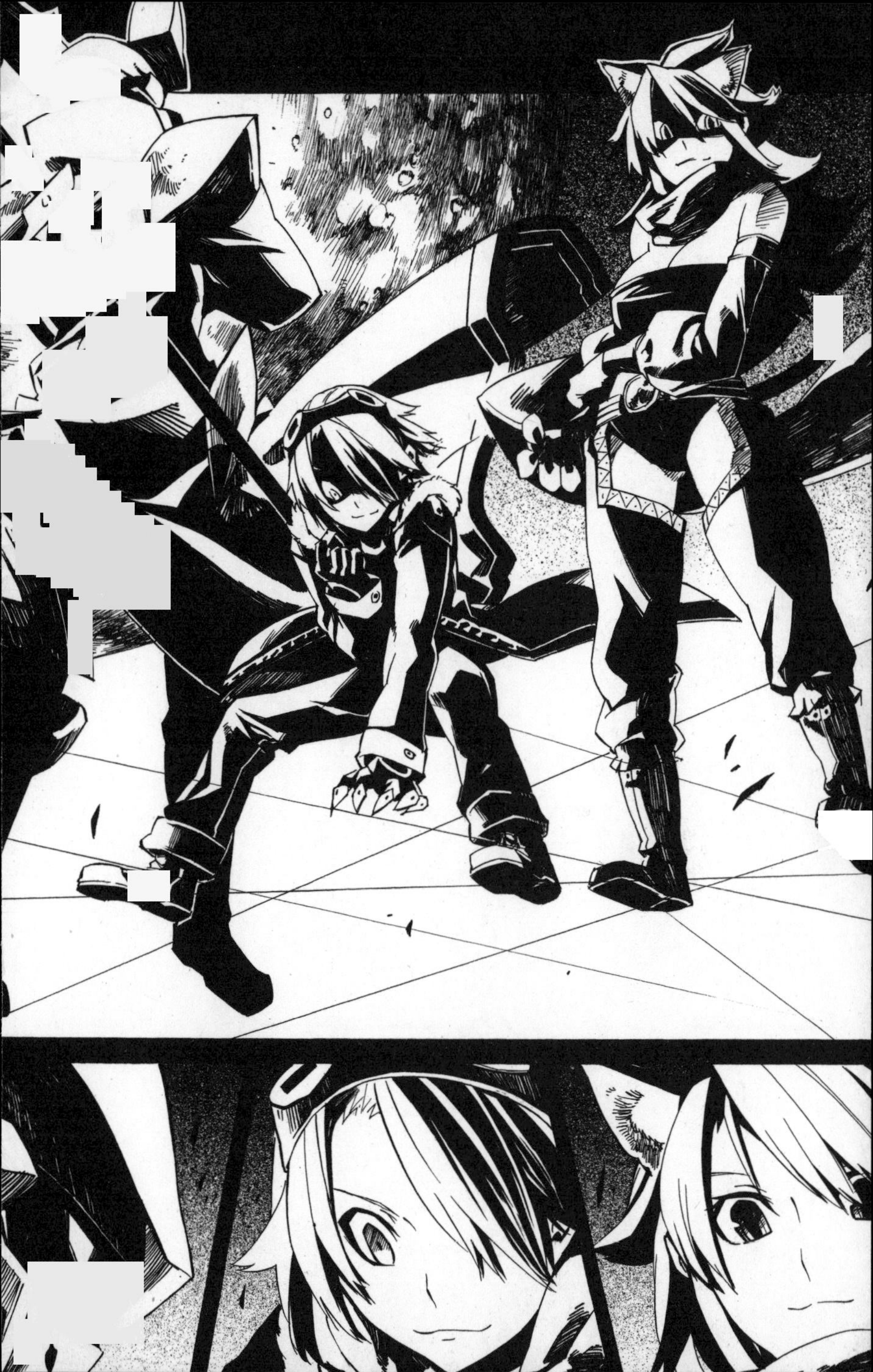

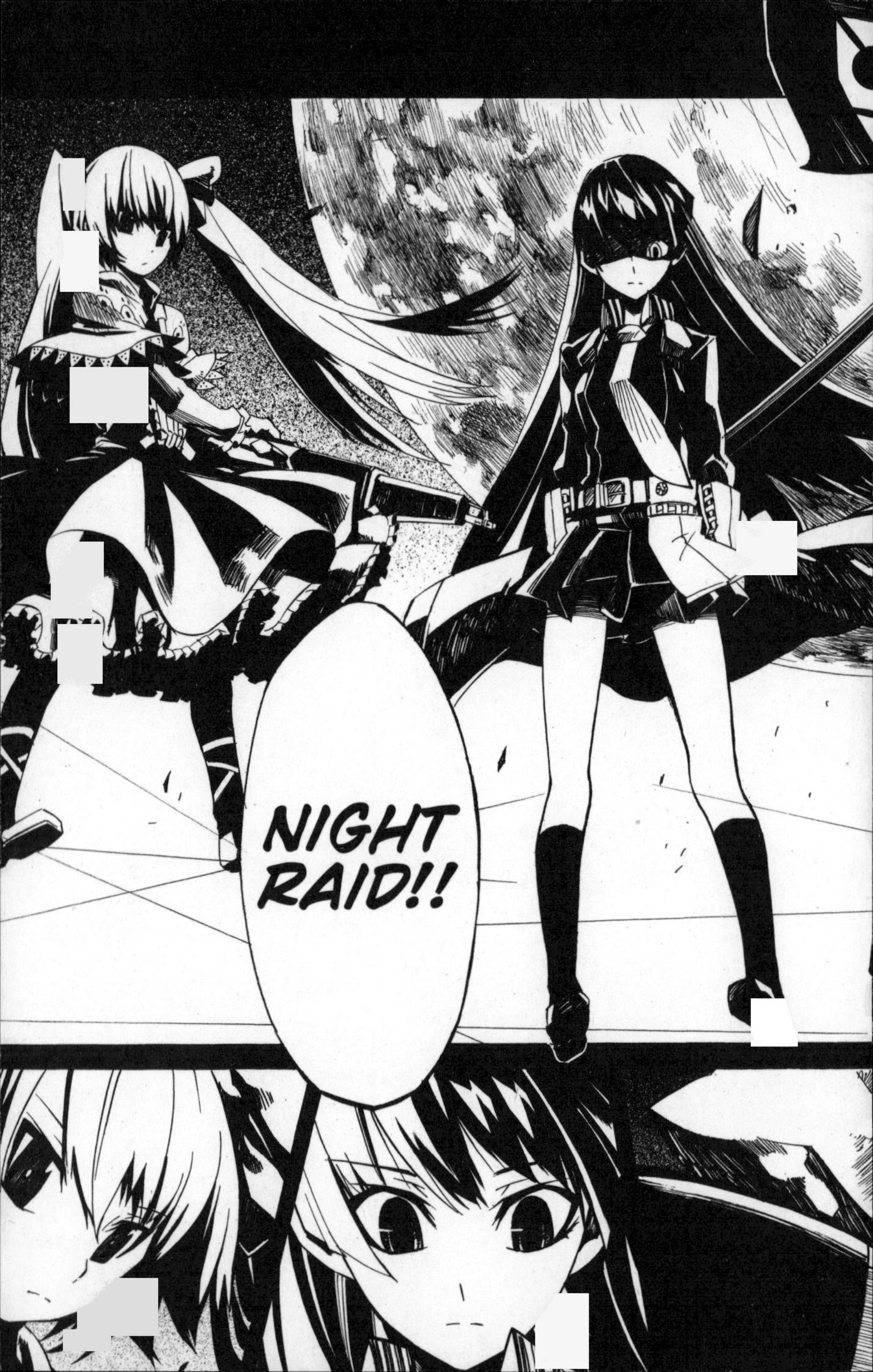
NIGHT RAID!!

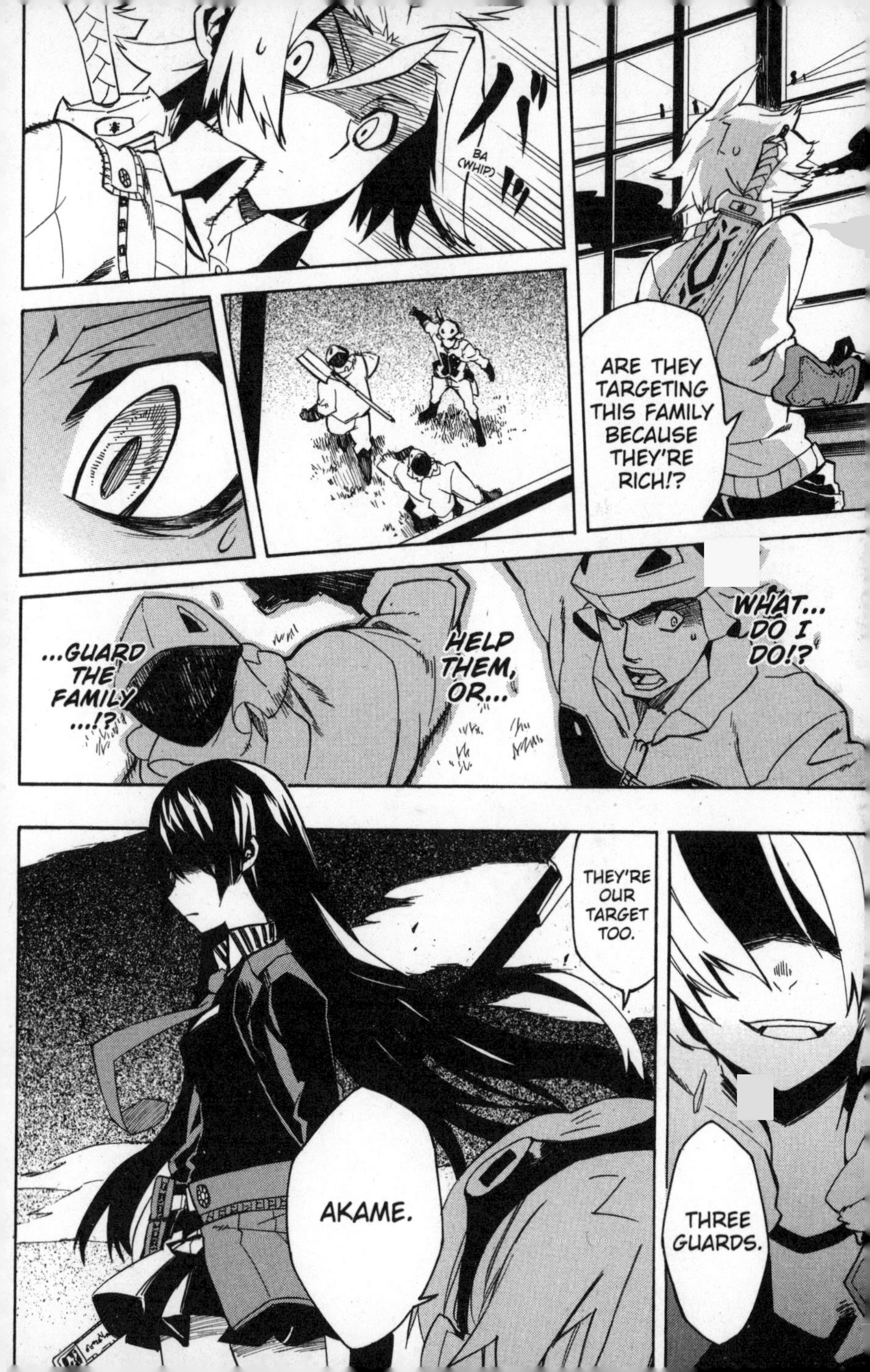
BA (WHIP)
ARE THEY TARGETING THIS FAMILY BECAUSE THEY'RE RICH!?
WHAT... DO I DO!?
HELP THEM, OR...
...GUARD THE FAMILY ...!?
THREE GUARDS.
THEY'RE OUR TARGET TOO.
AKAME.

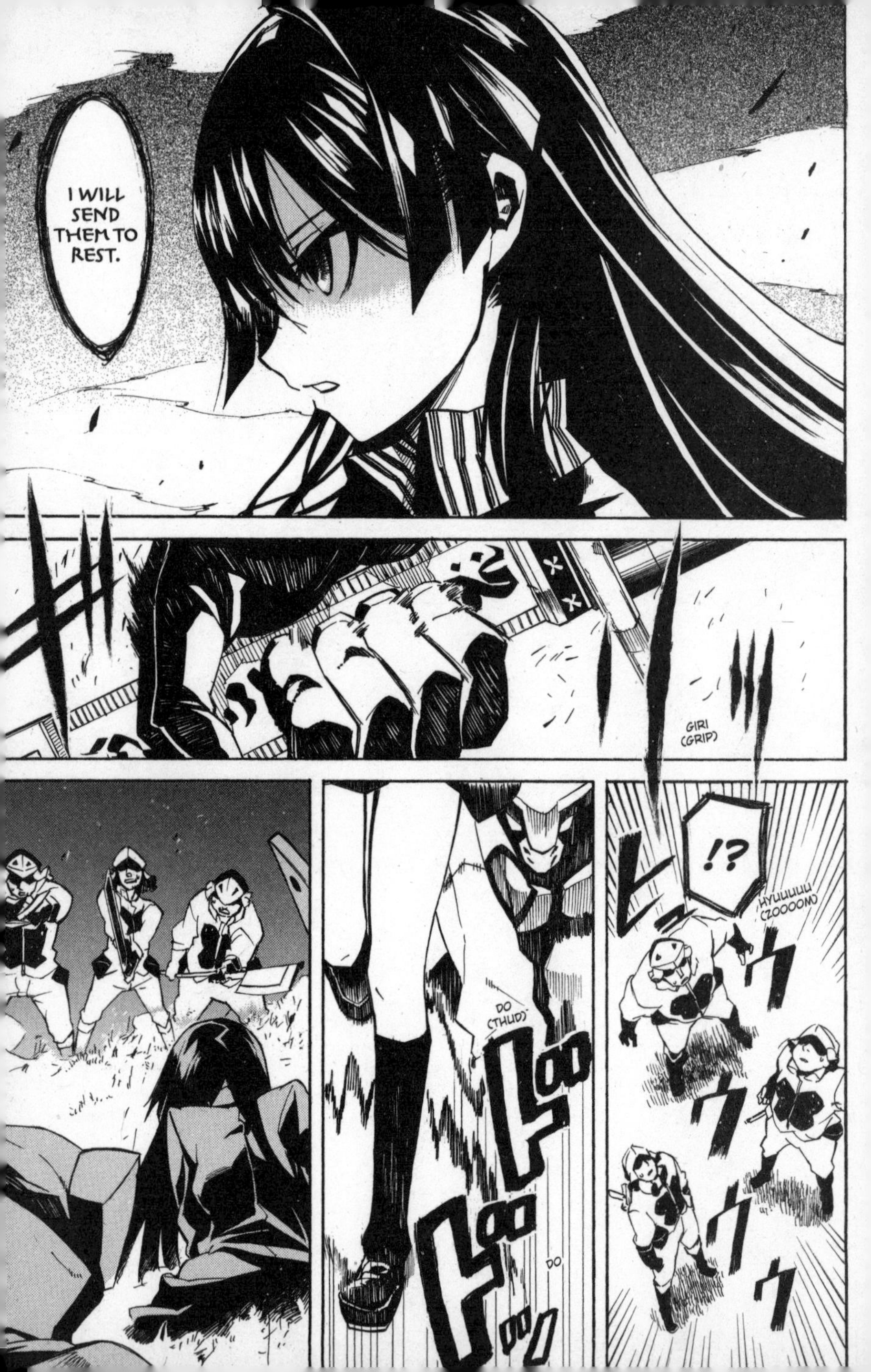
I WILL SEND THEM TO REST.
GIRI (GRIP)
!?
HYUUUUUU (ZOOOOM)
DO (THUD)
DO

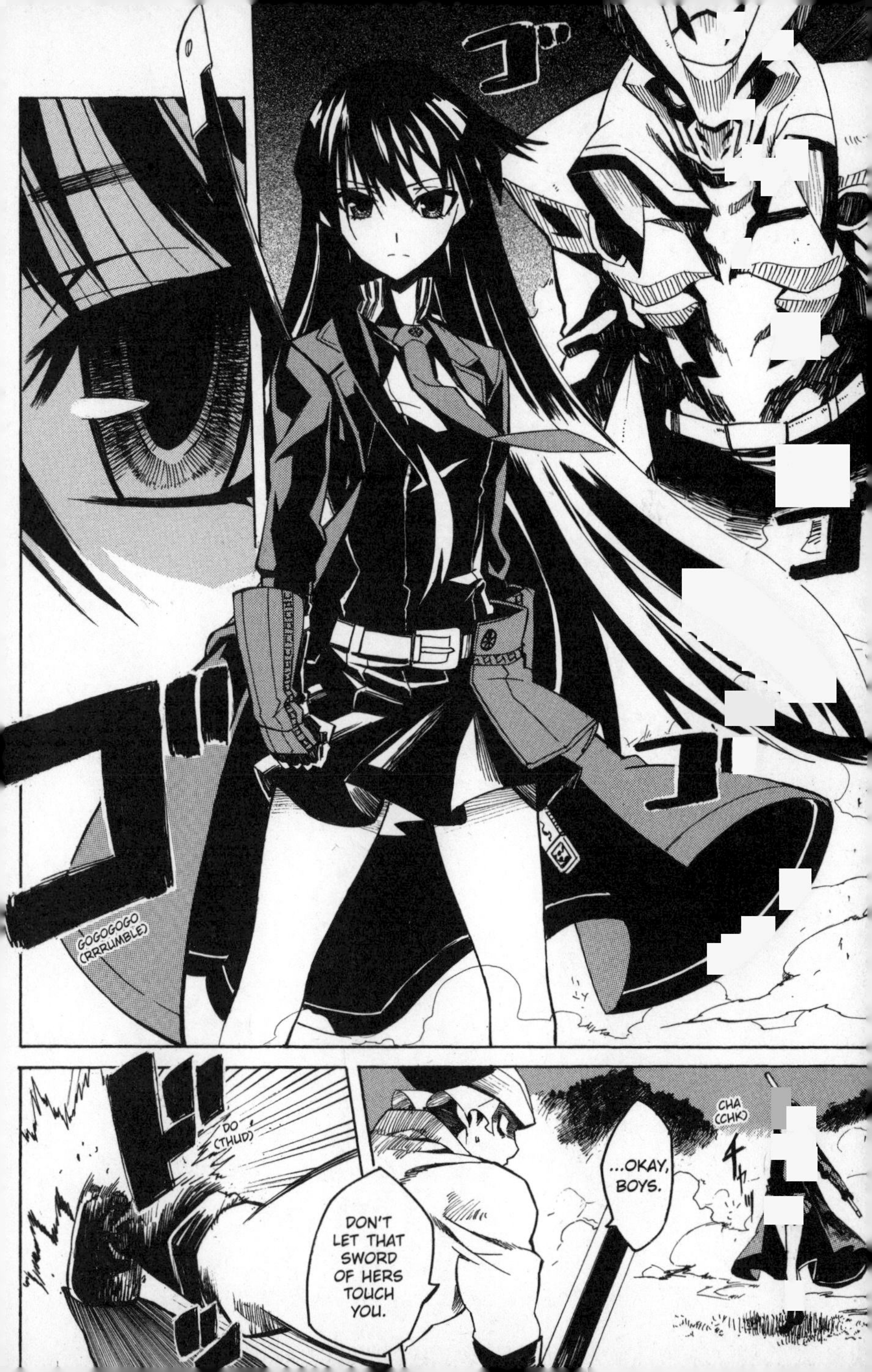
GOGOGOGO (RRRUMBLE)
CHA (CHK)
...OKAY, BOYS.
DON'T LET THAT SWORD OF HERS TOUCH YOU.
DO (THUD)

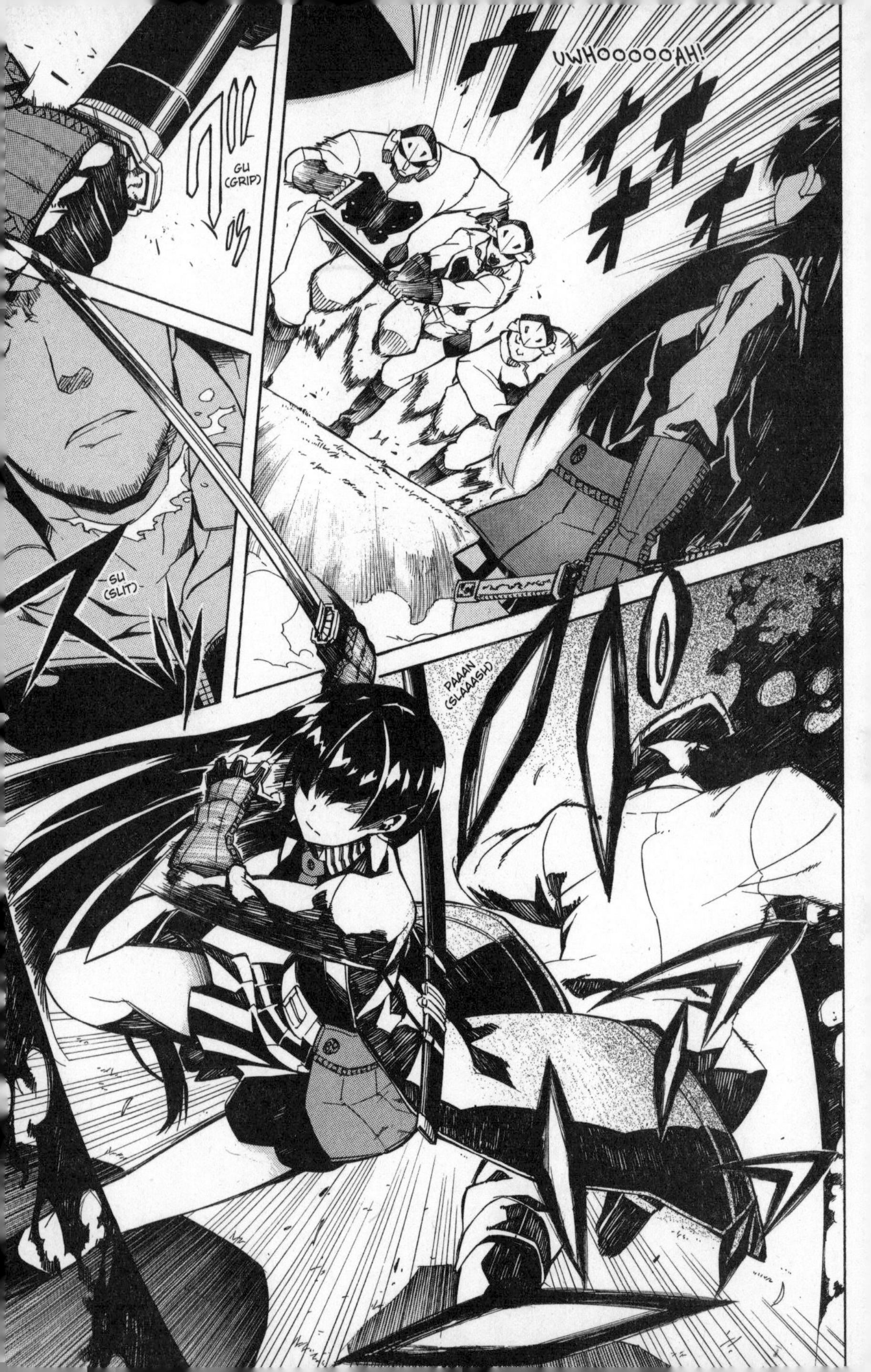
UWHOOOOOAH!
GU (GRIP)
SU (SLIT)
PAAAN (SLAAASH)

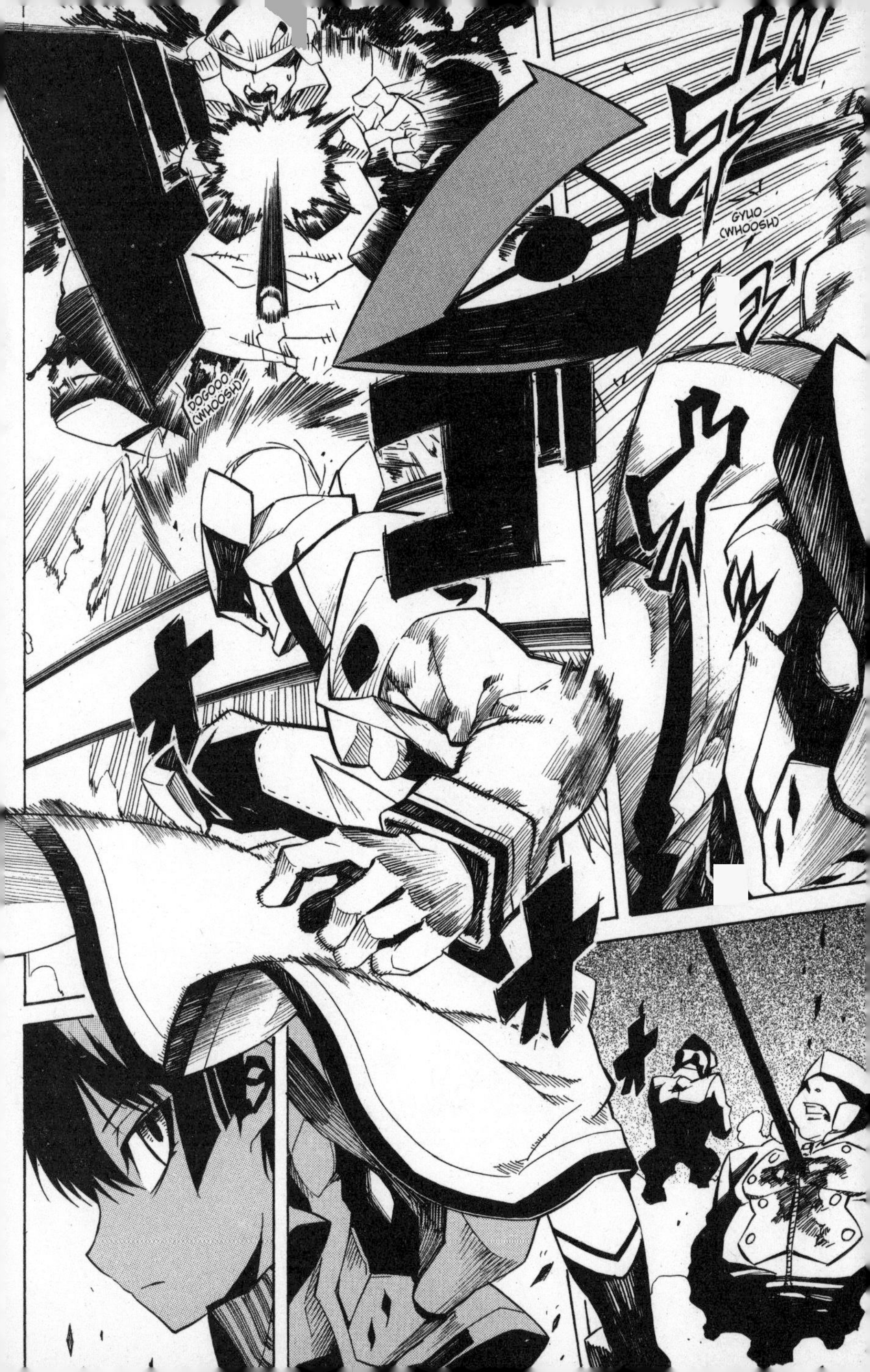
GYUO
(WHOOSH)
DOGOOO
(WHOOSH)

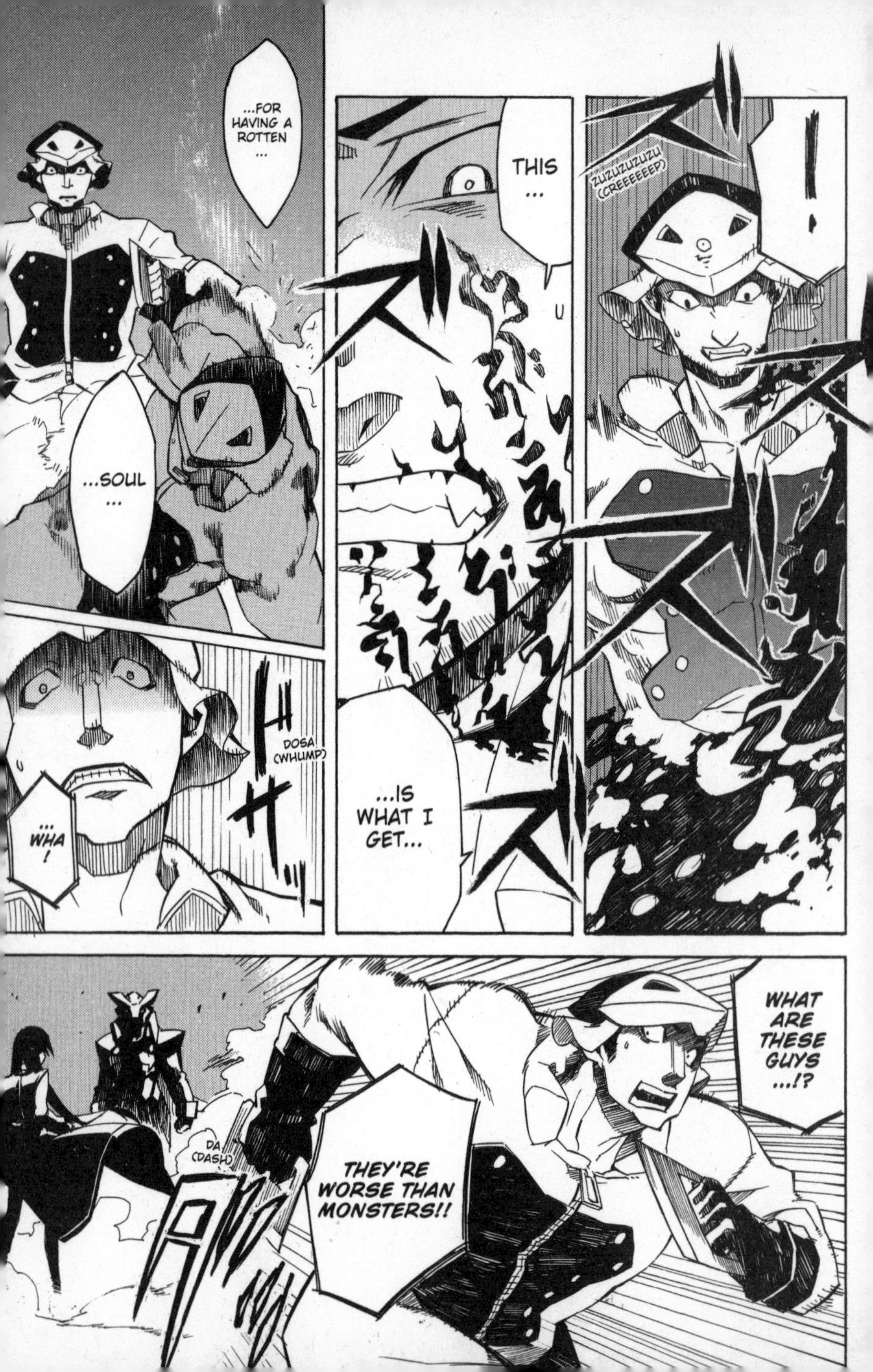
ZUZUZUZUZU (CREEEEEEP)
THIS ...
...IS WHAT I GET...
...FOR HAVING A ROTTEN ...
...SOUL ...
DOSA (WHUMP)
... WHA !
WHAT ARE THESE GUYS ...!?
THEY'RE WORSE THAN MONSTERS!!
DA (DASH)

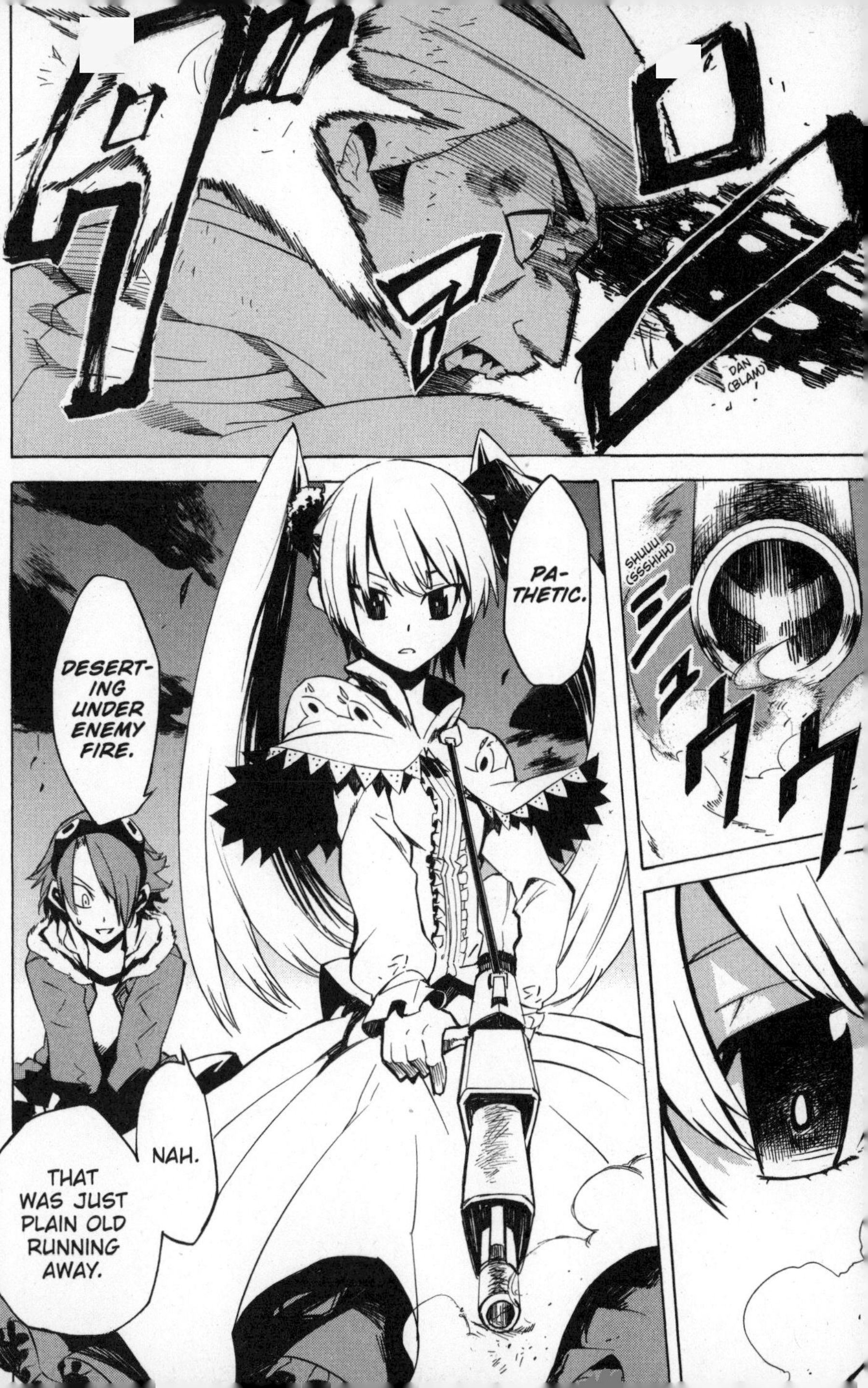
DAN (BLAM)
SHUUU (SSSHHH)
PA-THETIC.
DESERT-ING UNDER ENEMY FIRE.
NAH.
THAT WAS JUST PLAIN OLD RUNNING AWAY.

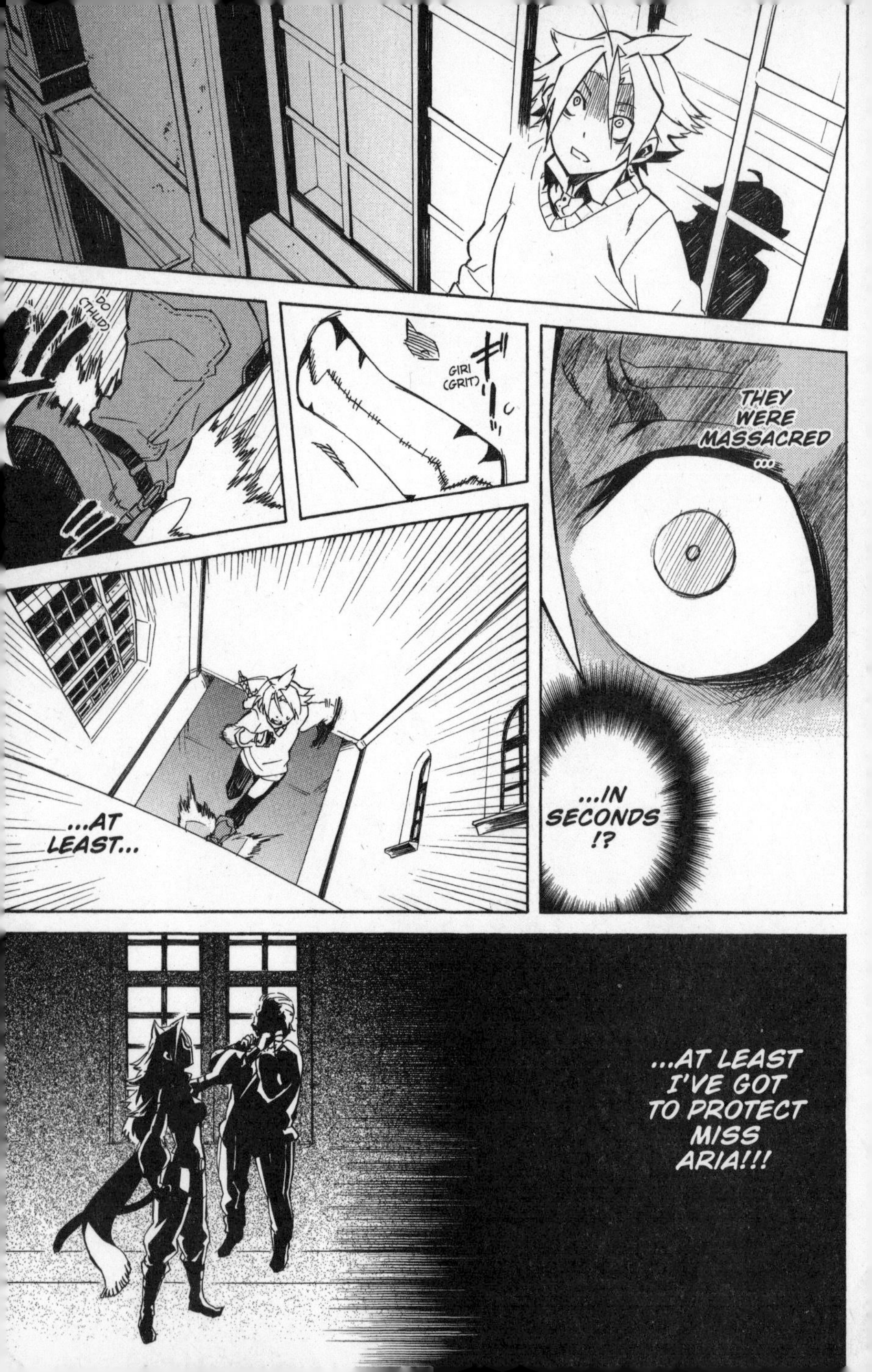
THEY WERE MASSACRED ...
...IN SECONDS !?
GIRI (GRIT)
DO (THUD)
...AT LEAST...
...AT LEAST I'VE GOT TO PROTECT MISS ARIA!!!

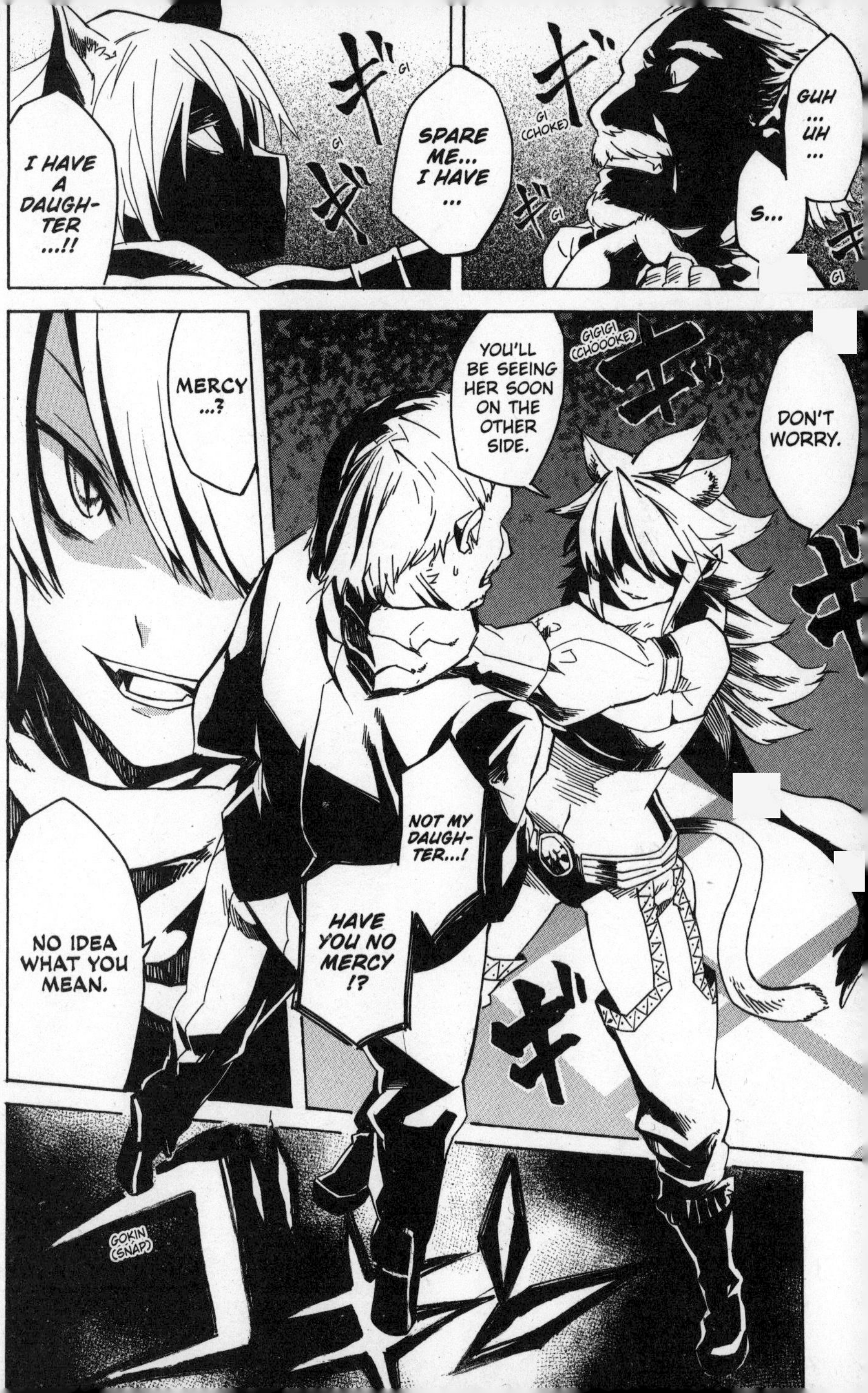
GUH ... UH ... S...
GI
GI (CHOKE)
GI
GI
SPARE ME... I HAVE ...
GI
I HAVE A DAUGHTER ...!!
DON'T WORRY.
GIGIGI (CHOOOKE)
YOU'LL BE SEEING HER SOON ON THE OTHER SIDE.
NOT MY DAUGHTER...!
HAVE YOU NO MERCY !?
MERCY ...?
NO IDEA WHAT YOU MEAN.
GOKIN (SNAP)

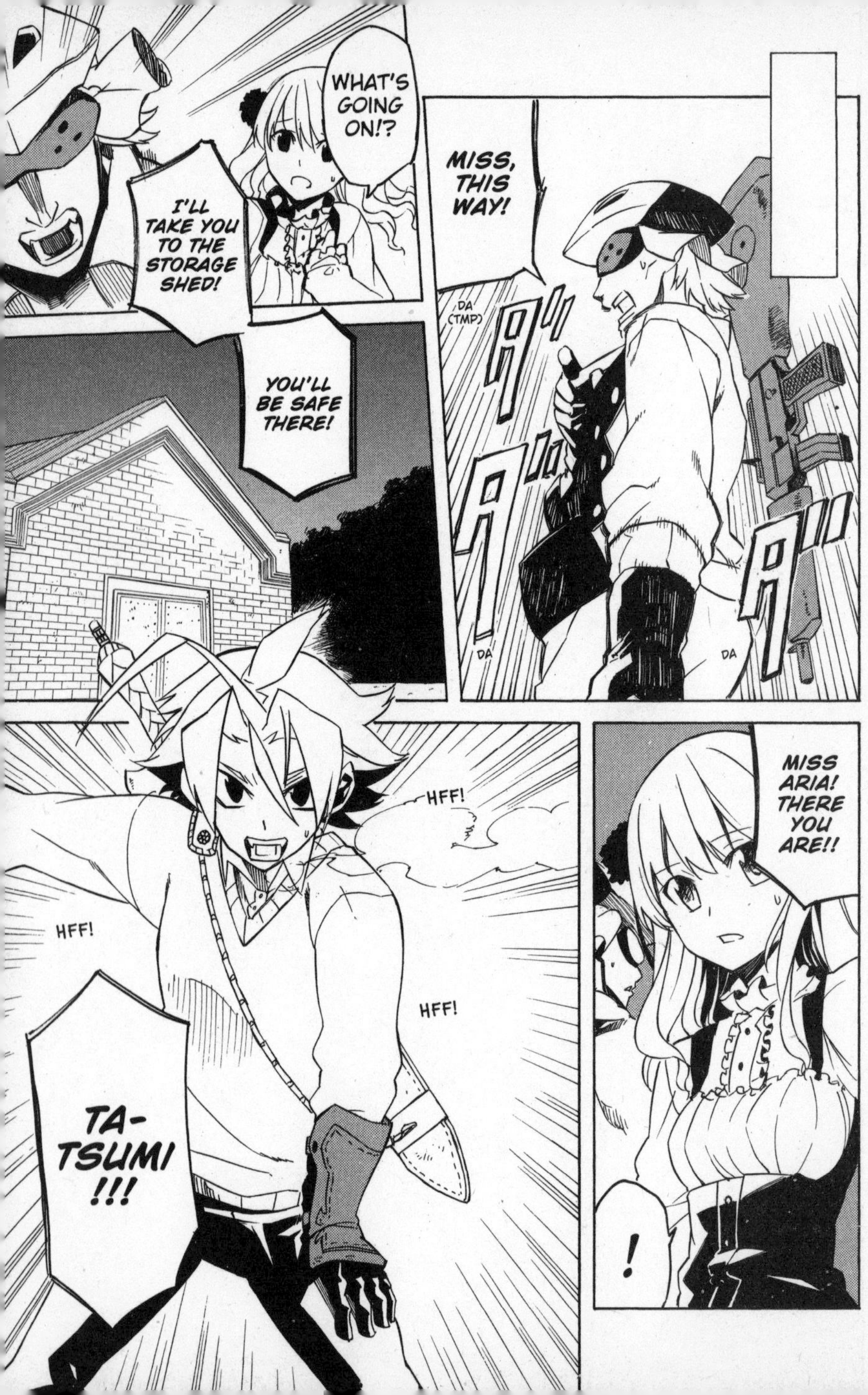
MISS, THIS WAY!
DA (TMP)
DA
DA
WHAT'S GOING ON!?
I'LL TAKE YOU TO THE STORAGE SHED!
YOU'LL BE SAFE THERE!
MISS ARIA! THERE YOU ARE!!
!
HFF!
HFF!
HFF!
TA-TSUMI!!!

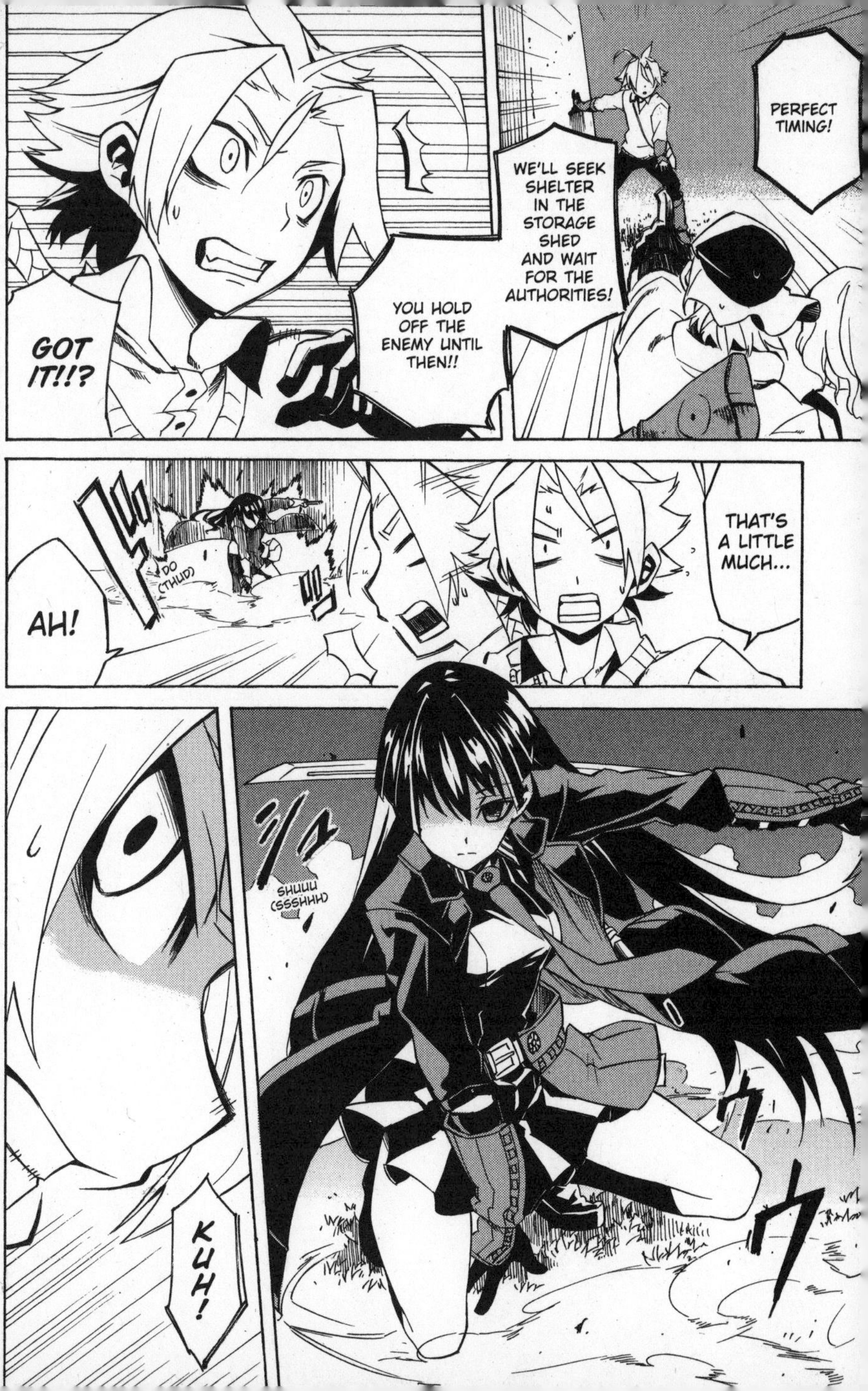
PERFECT TIMING!
WE'LL SEEK SHELTER IN THE STORAGE SHED AND WAIT FOR THE AUTHORITIES!
YOU HOLD OFF THE ENEMY UNTIL THEN!!
GOT IT!!?
THAT'S A LITTLE MUCH...
DO (THUD)
AH!
SHUUU (SSSHHH)
KUH!

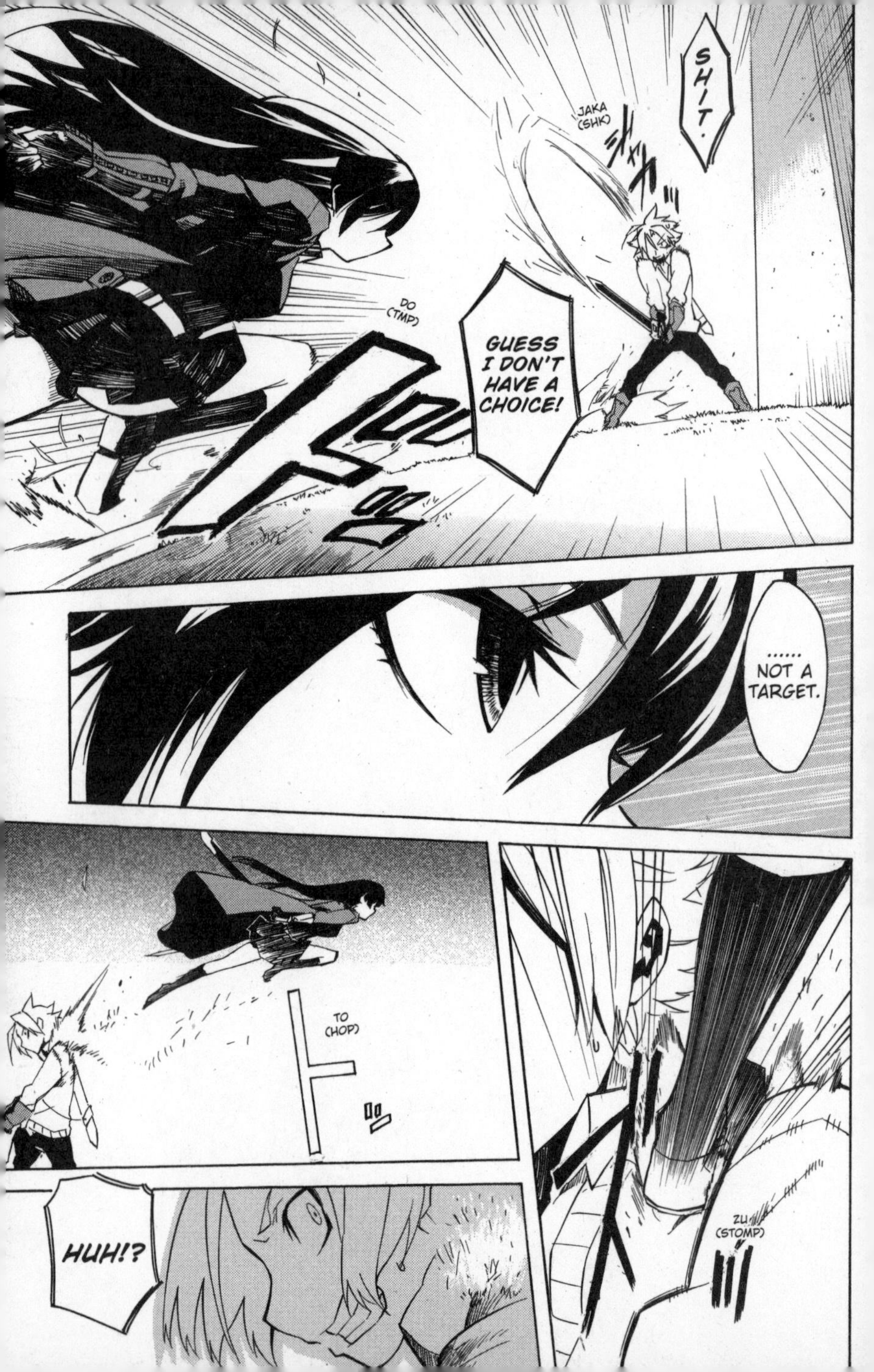
SHIT.
JAKA (SHK)
GUESS I DON'T HAVE A CHOICE!
DO (TMP)
...... NOT A TARGET.
ZU (STOMP)
TO (HOP)
HUH!?

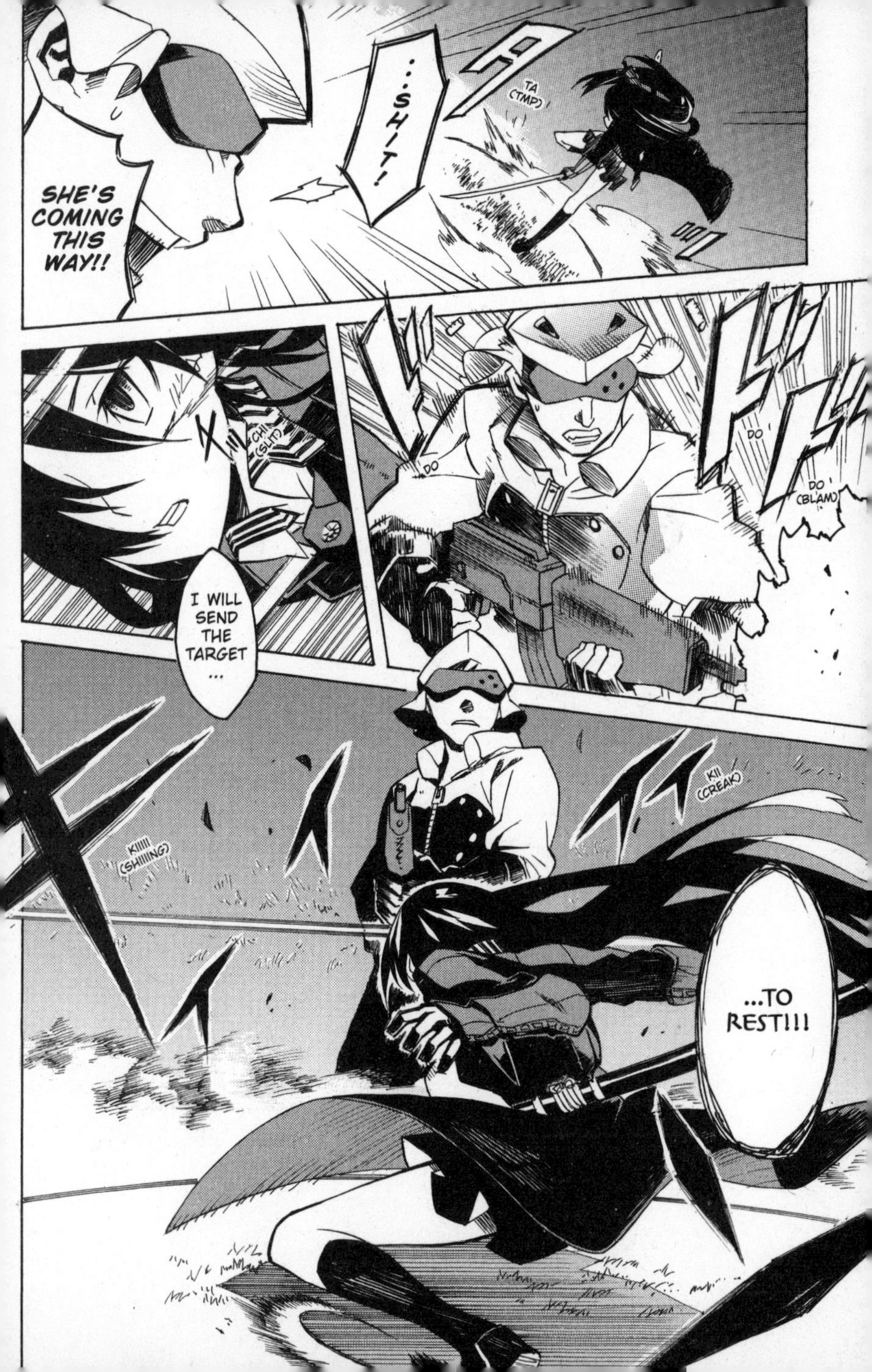
TA (TMP)
...SHIT!
SHE'S COMING THIS WAY!!
DO
DO (BLAM)
DO
CHI (GLIT)
I WILL SEND THE TARGET ...
KII (CREAK)
...TO REST!!!
KIIII (SHIIING)

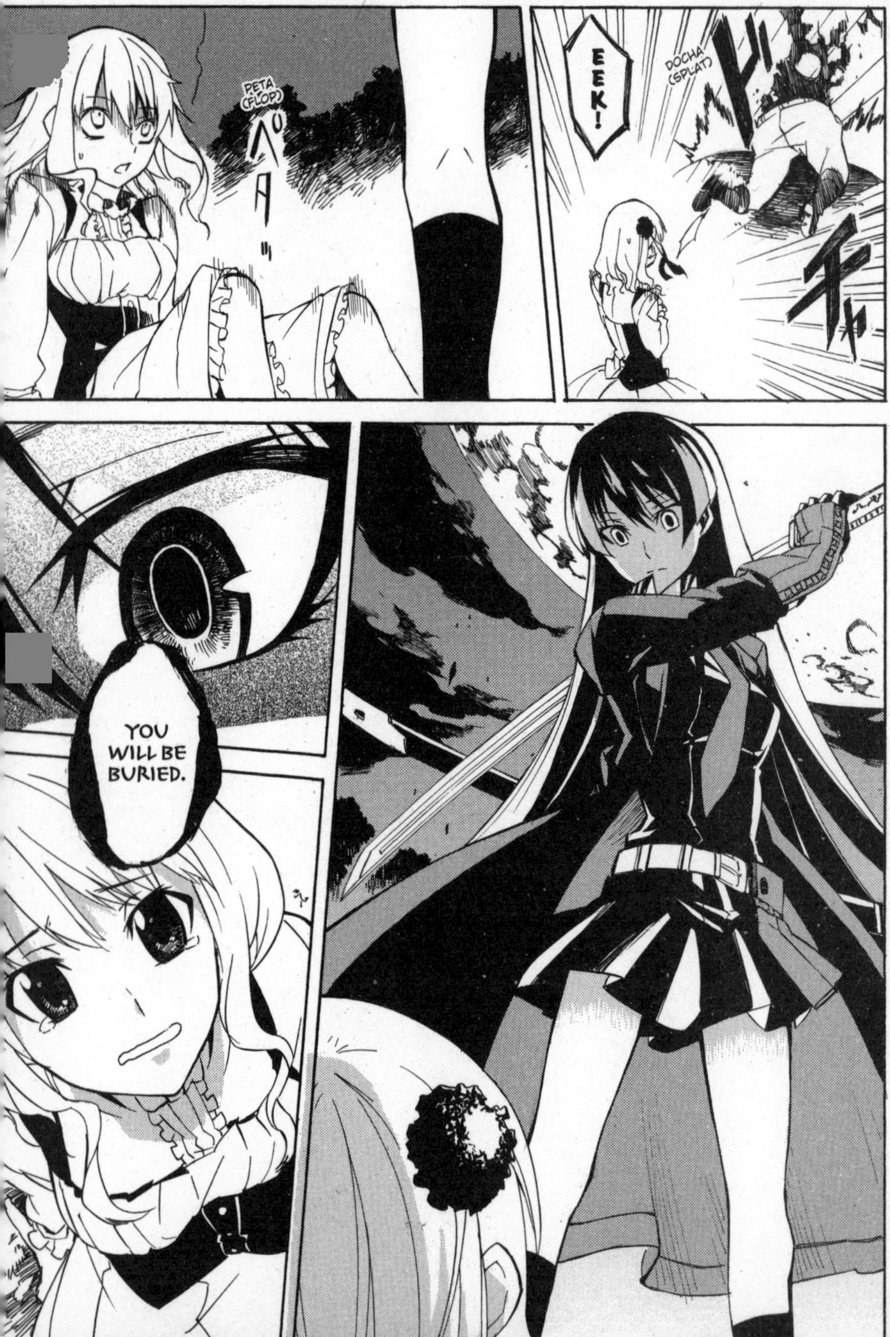
EEK!
DOCHA (SPLAT)
PETA (FLOP)
YOU WILL BE BURIED.

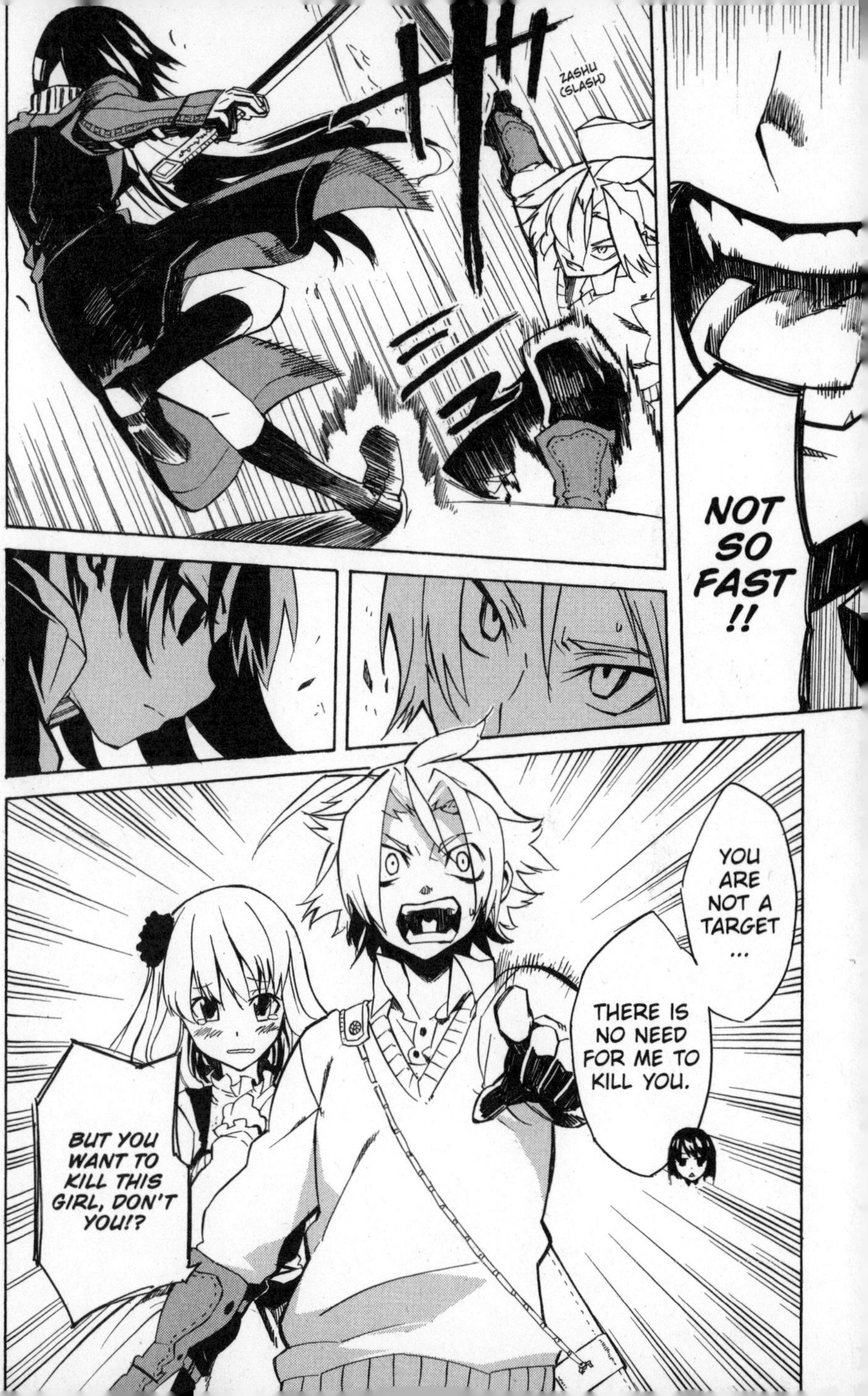
NOT SO FAST!!
ZASHU (SLASH)
YOU ARE NOT A TARGET...
THERE IS NO NEED FOR ME TO KILL YOU.
BUT YOU WANT TO KILL THIS GIRL, DON'T YOU!?

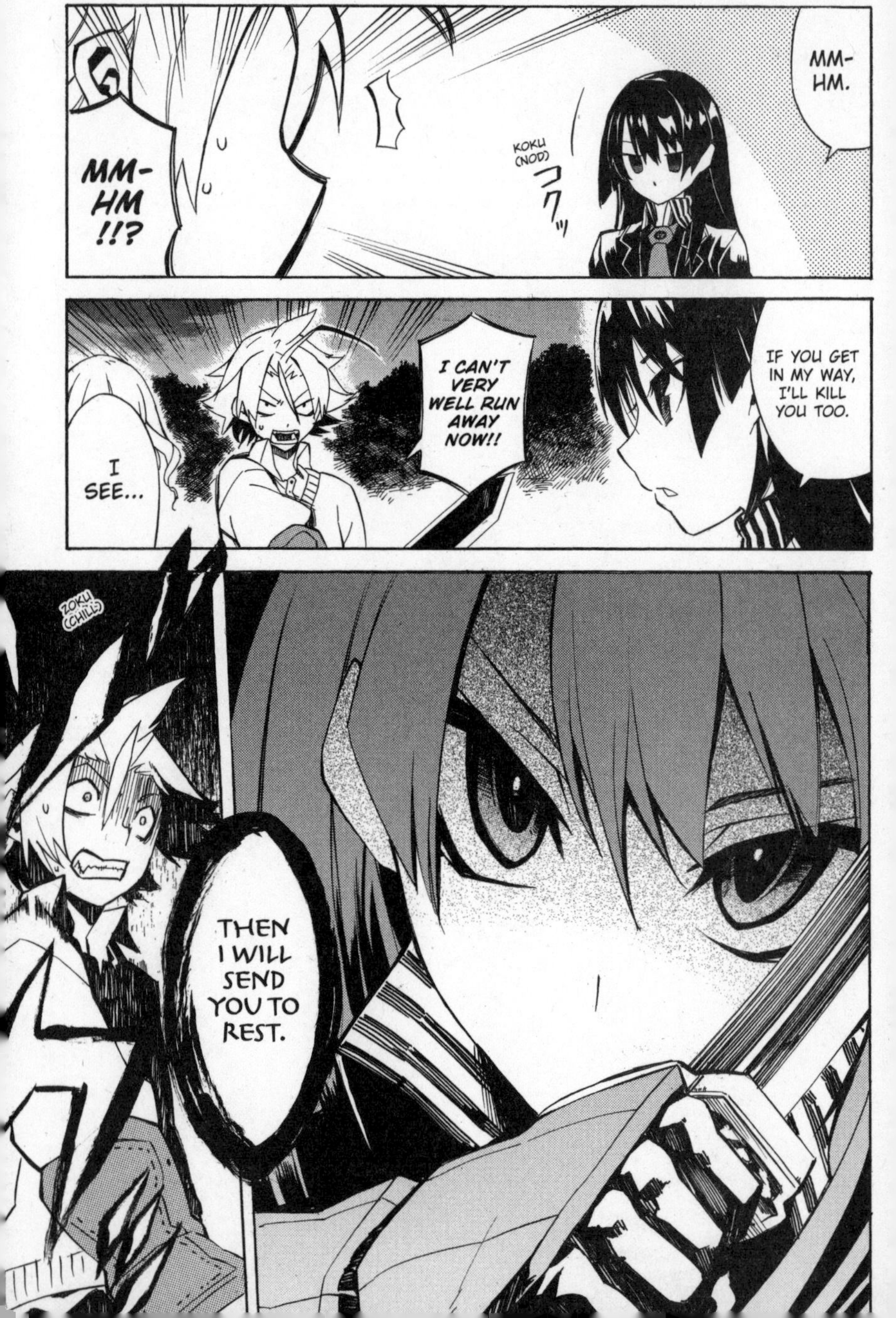
MM-HM.
KOKU (NOD)
MM-HM!!?
IF YOU GET IN MY WAY, I'LL KILL YOU TOO.
I CAN'T VERY WELL RUN AWAY NOW!!
I SEE...
ZOKU (CHILL)
THEN I WILL SEND YOU TO REST.

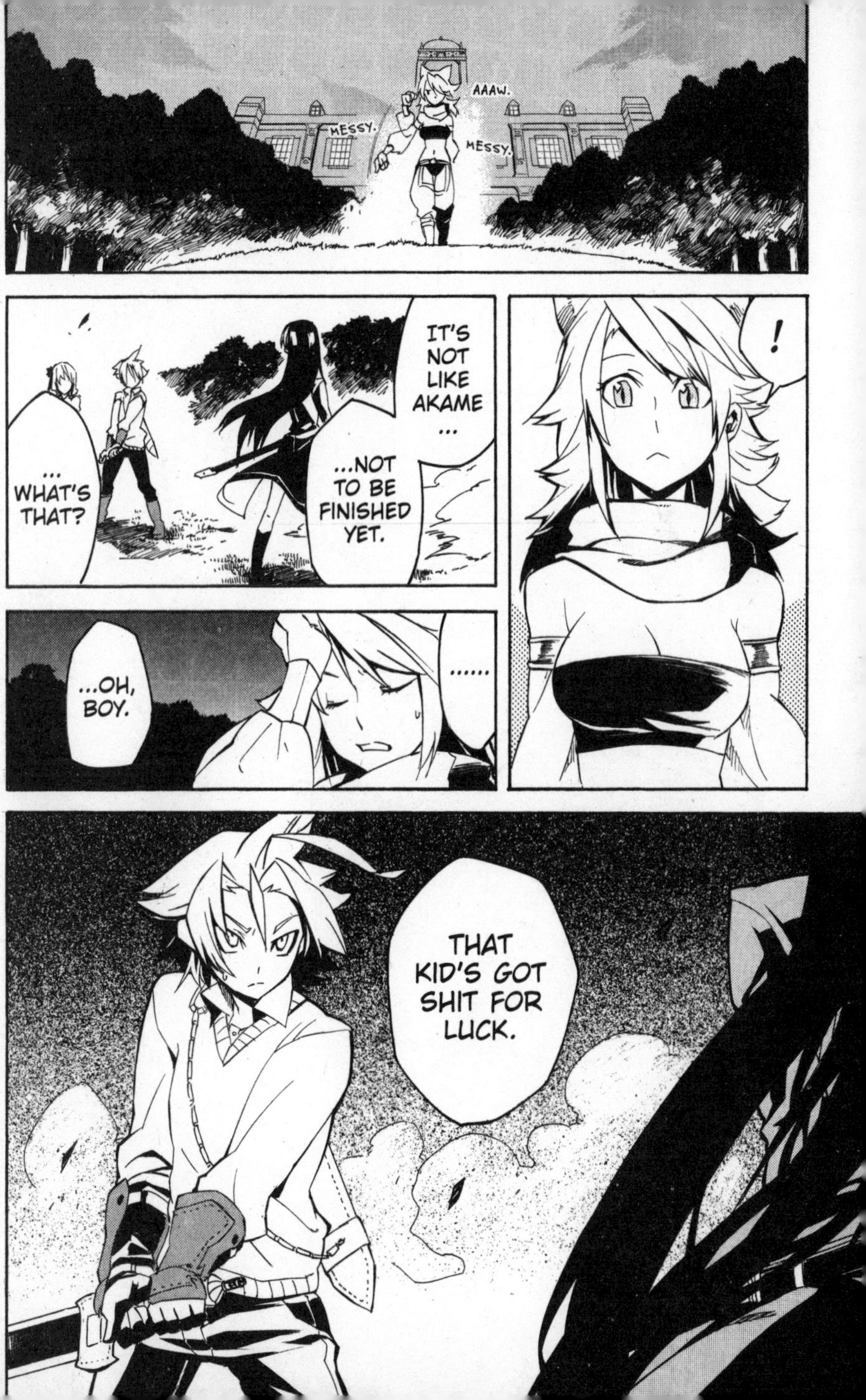
AAAW.
MESSY.
MESSY.
!
IT'S NOT LIKE AKAME ...
...NOT TO BE FINISHED YET.
... WHAT'S THAT?
......
...OH, BOY.
THAT KID'S GOT SHIT FOR LUCK.

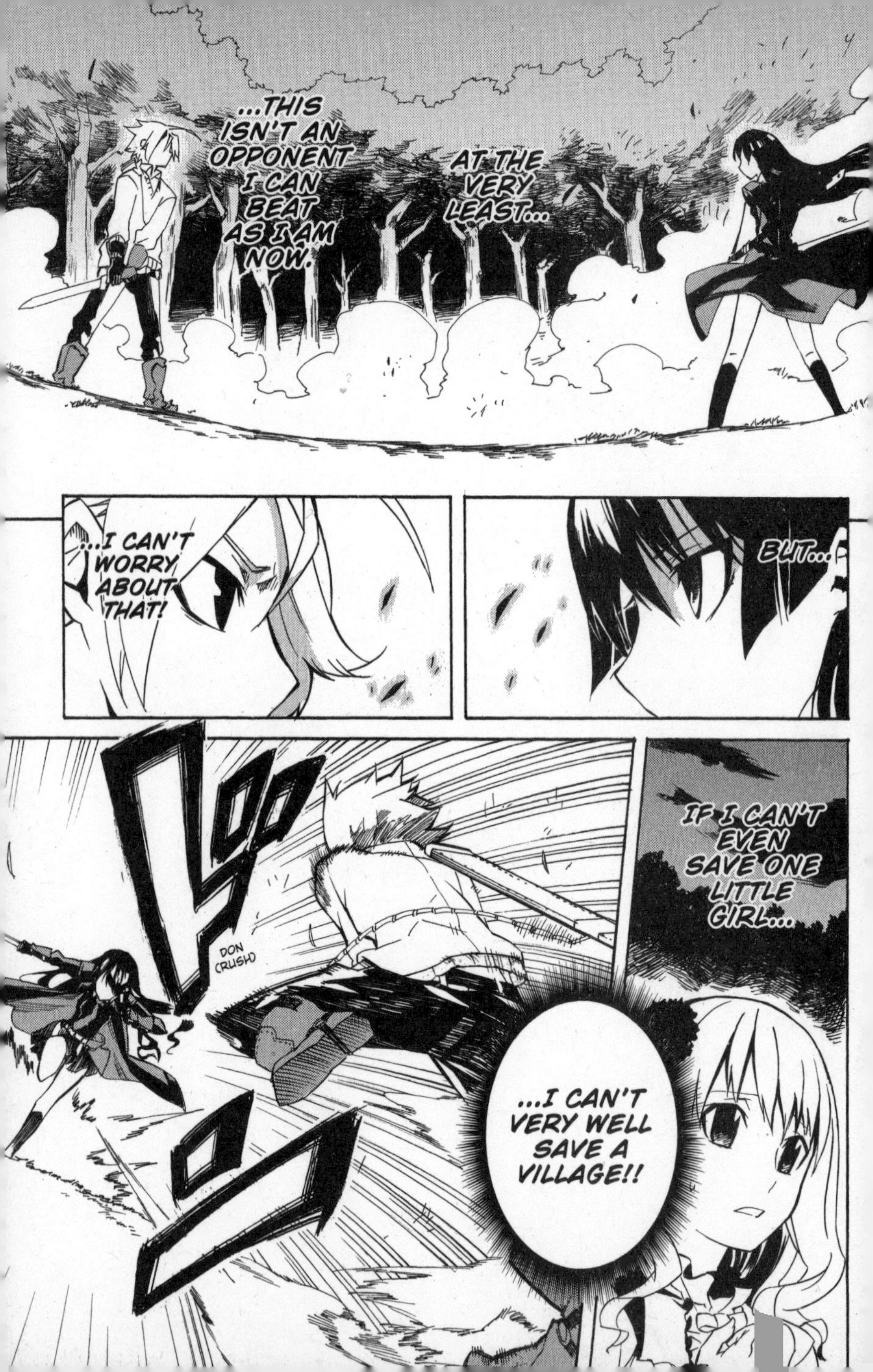
AT THE VERY LEAST...
...THIS ISN'T AN OPPONENT I CAN BEAT AS I AM NOW.
BUT...
...I CAN'T WORRY ABOUT THAT!
IF I CAN'T EVEN SAVE ONE LITTLE GIRL...
...I CAN'T VERY WELL SAVE A VILLAGE!!
DON (CRUSH)

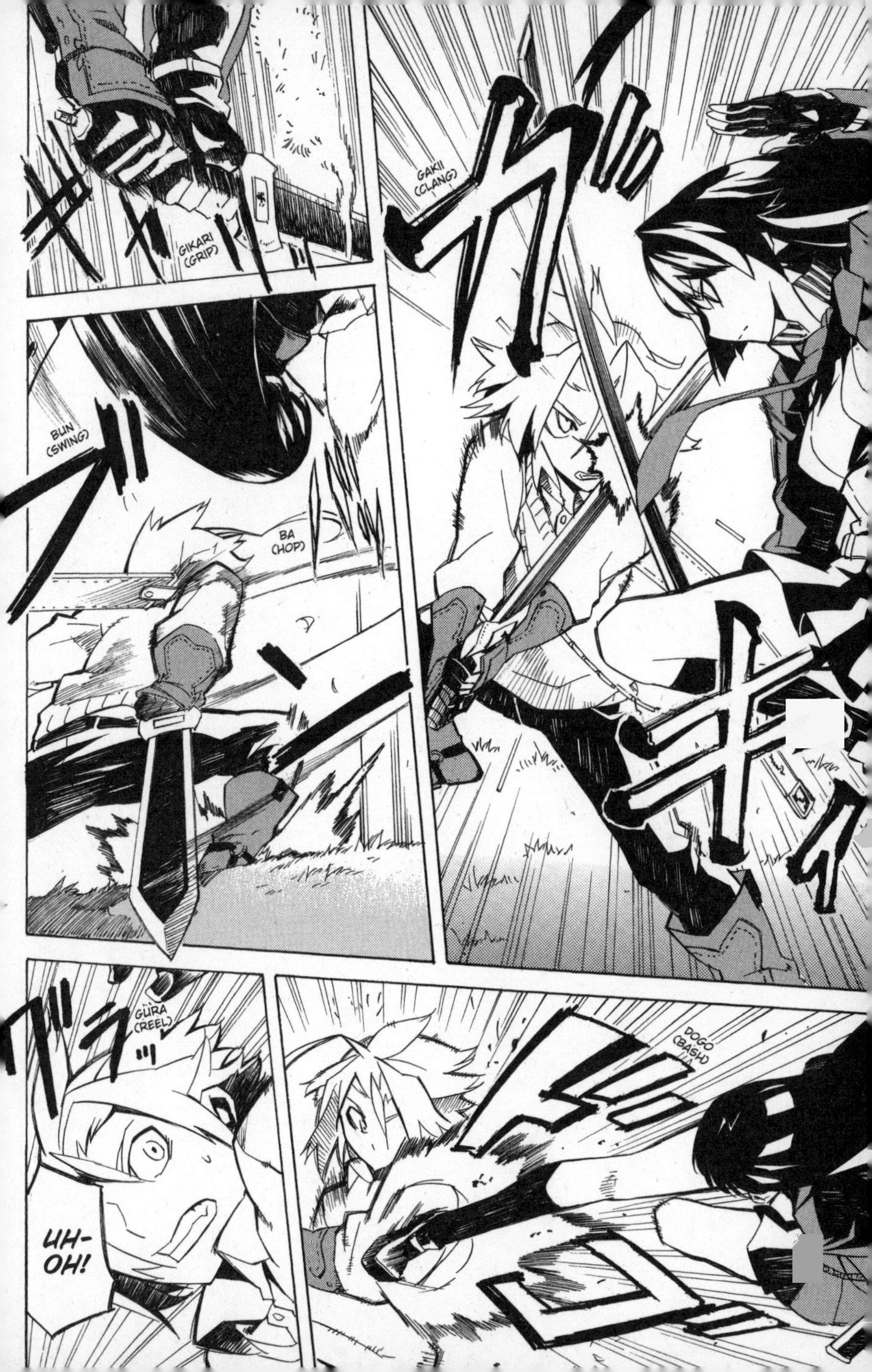
GAKII (CLANG)
GIKARI (GRIP)
BUN (SWING)
BA (HOP)
DOGO (BASH)
GŪRA (REEL)
UH-OH!

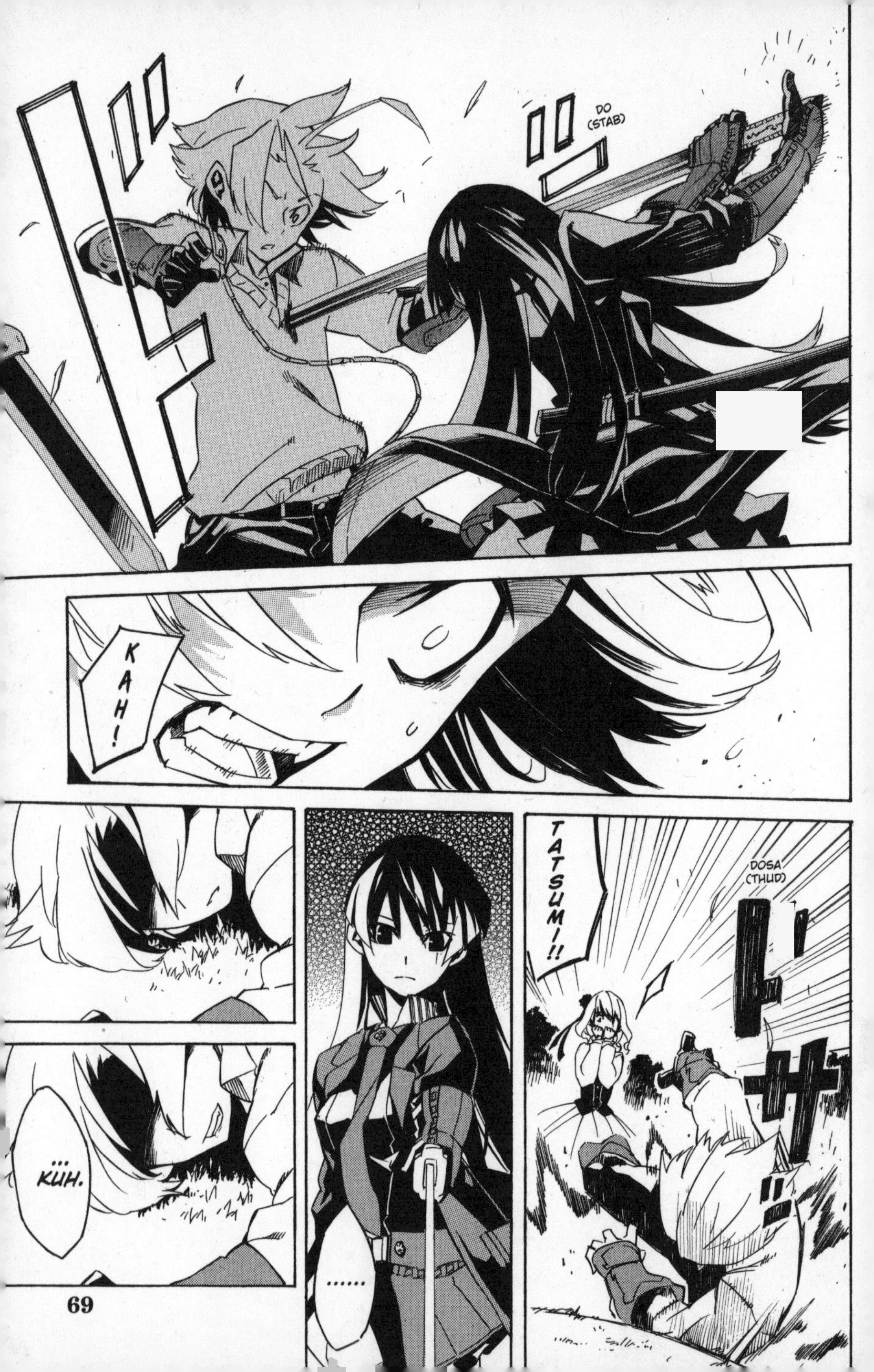
DO (STAB)
KAH!
TATSUMI!!
DOSA (THUD)
......
...KUH.

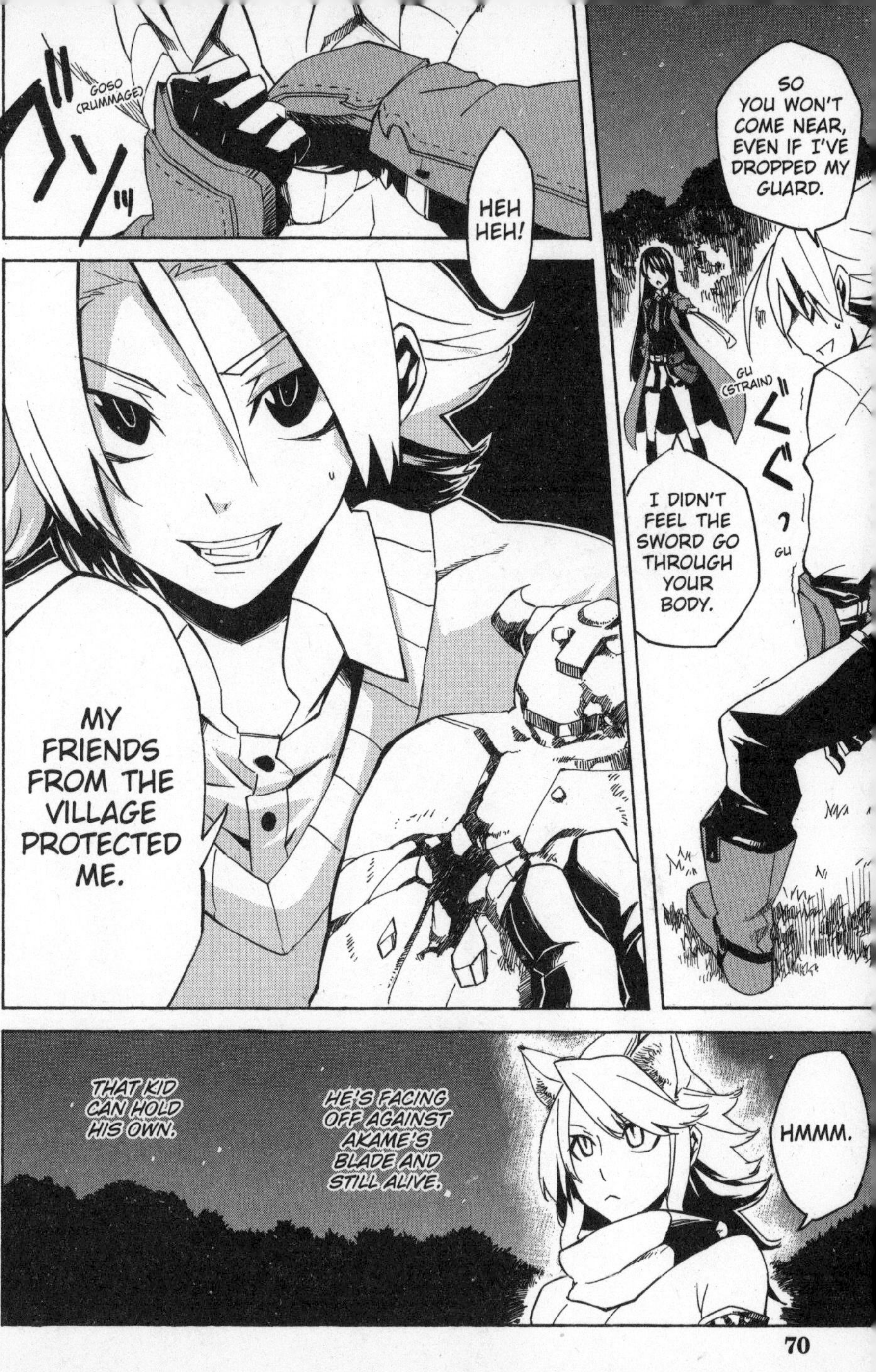
SO YOU WON'T COME NEAR, EVEN IF I'VE DROPPED MY GUARD.
GU (STRAIN)
I DIDN'T FEEL THE SWORD GO THROUGH YOUR BODY.
GU
HEH HEH!
GOSO (RUMMAGE)
MY FRIENDS FROM THE VILLAGE PROTECTED ME.
HMMM.
HE'S FACING OFF AGAINST AKAME'S BLADE AND STILL ALIVE.
THAT KID CAN HOLD HIS OWN.

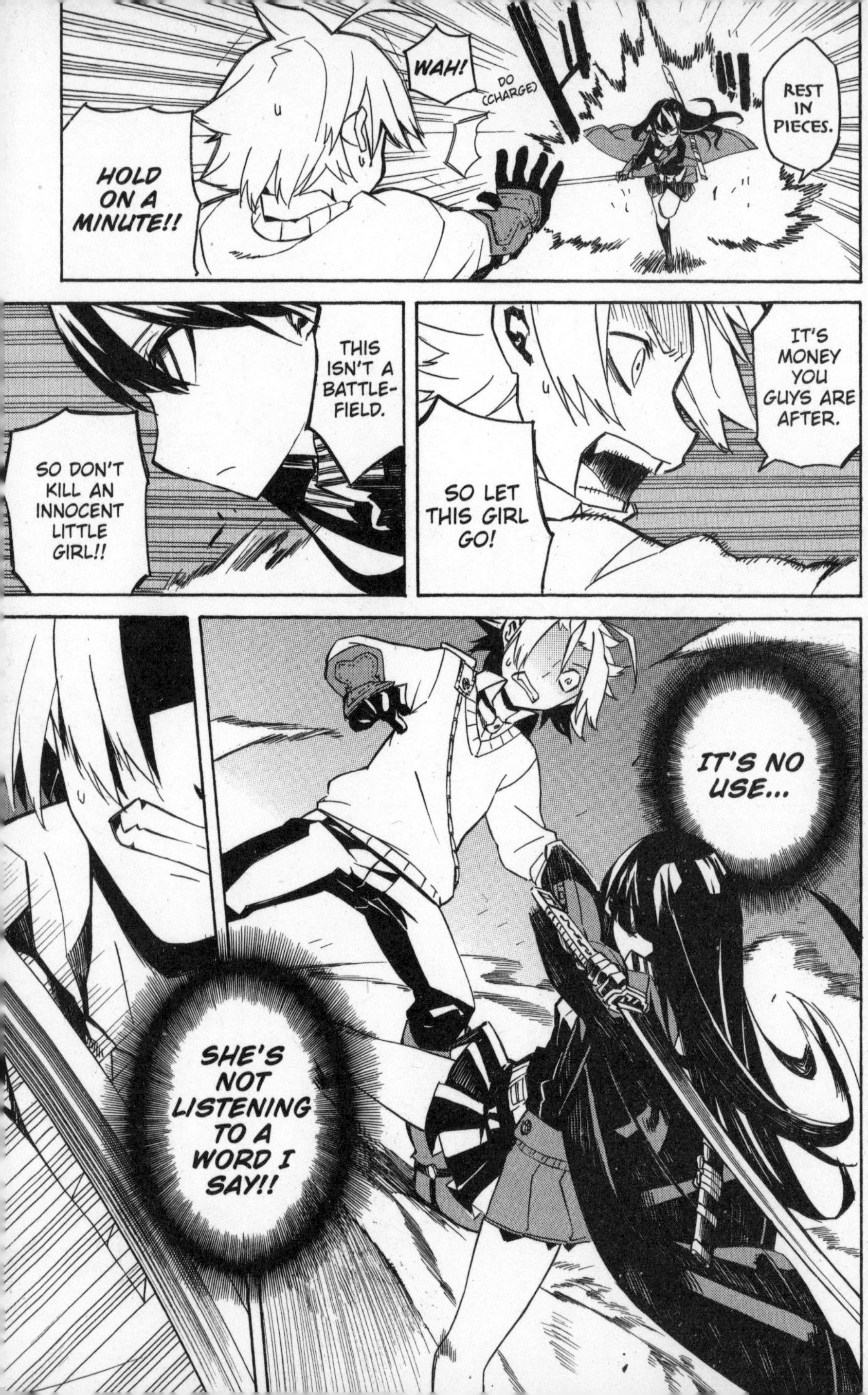
REST IN PIECES.
DO (CHARGE)
WAH!
HOLD ON A MINUTE!!
IT'S MONEY YOU GUYS ARE AFTER.
SO LET THIS GIRL GO!
THIS ISN'T A BATTLE-FIELD.
SO DON'T KILL AN INNOCENT LITTLE GIRL!!
IT'S NO USE...
SHE'S NOT LISTENING TO A WORD I SAY!!

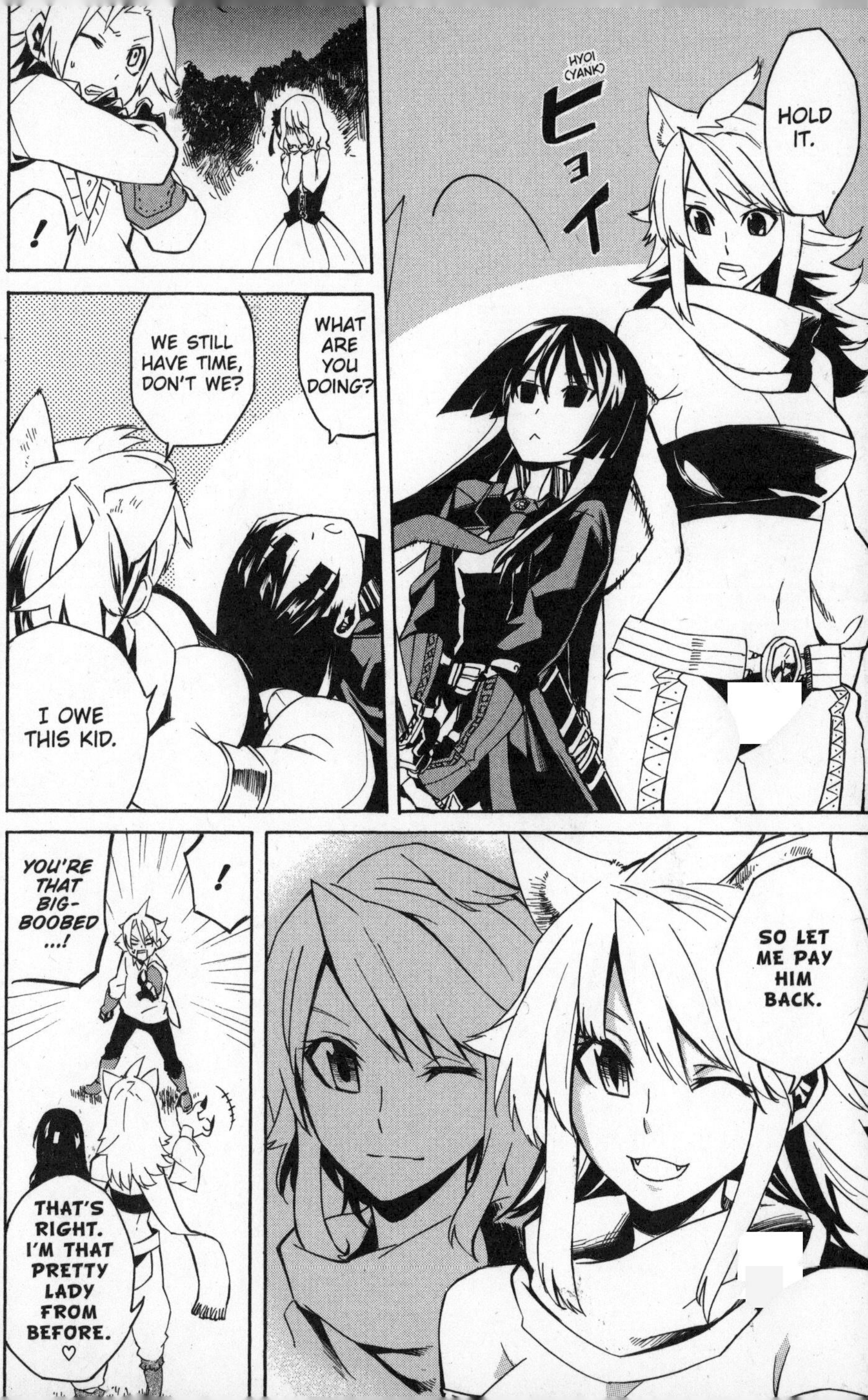
HOLD IT.
HYOI (YANK)
ヒョイ
!
WHAT ARE YOU DOING?
WE STILL HAVE TIME, DON'T WE?
I OWE THIS KID.
SO LET ME PAY HIM BACK.
!
YOU'RE THAT BIG-BOOBED ...!
THAT'S RIGHT. I'M THAT PRETTY LADY FROM BEFORE. ♡

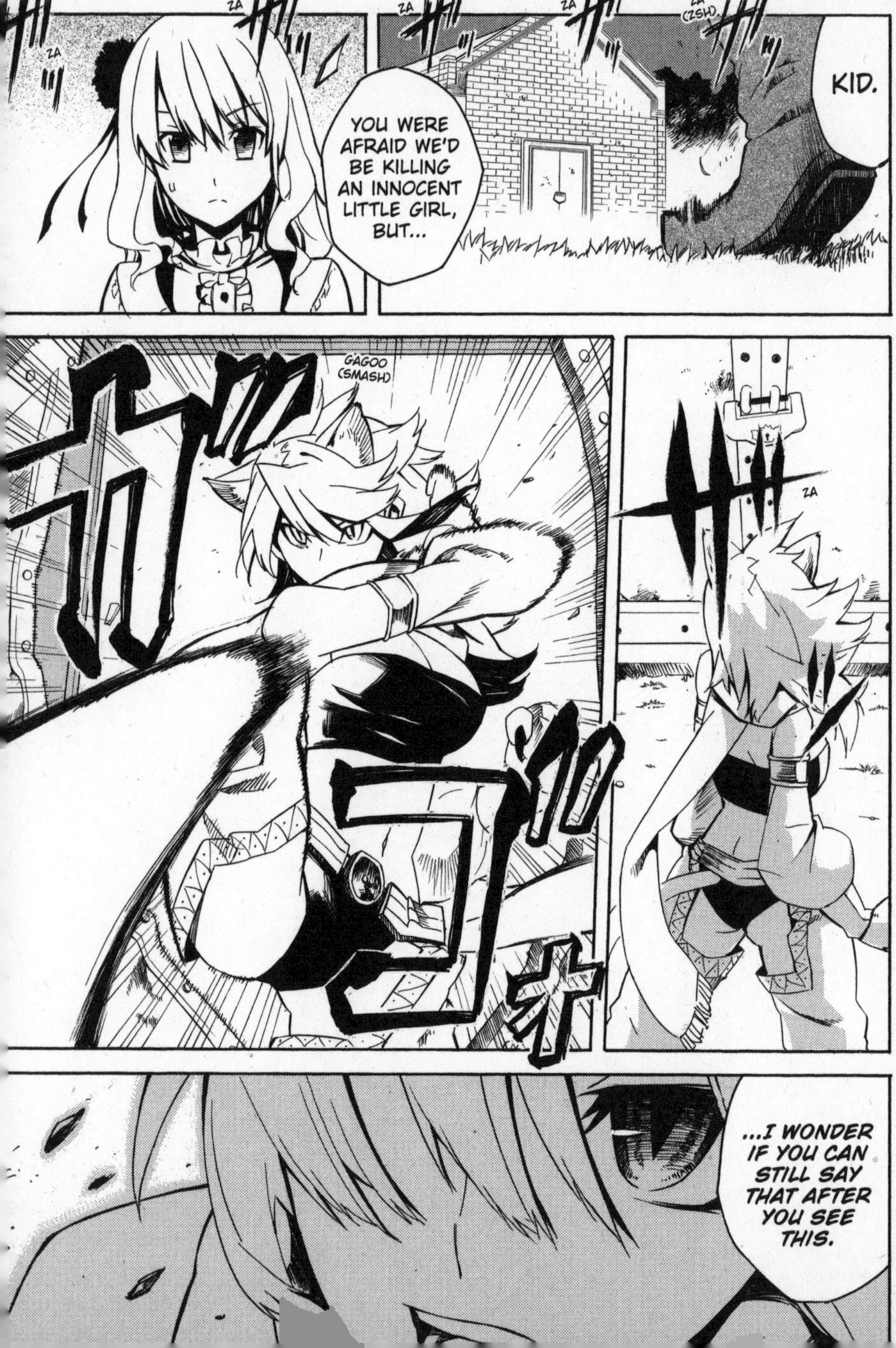
ZA (ZSH)
ZA
ZA
KID.
ZA
ZA
YOU WERE AFRAID WE'D BE KILLING AN INNOCENT LITTLE GIRL, BUT...
ZA
GAGOO (SMASH)
...I WONDER IF YOU CAN STILL SAY THAT AFTER YOU SEE THIS.

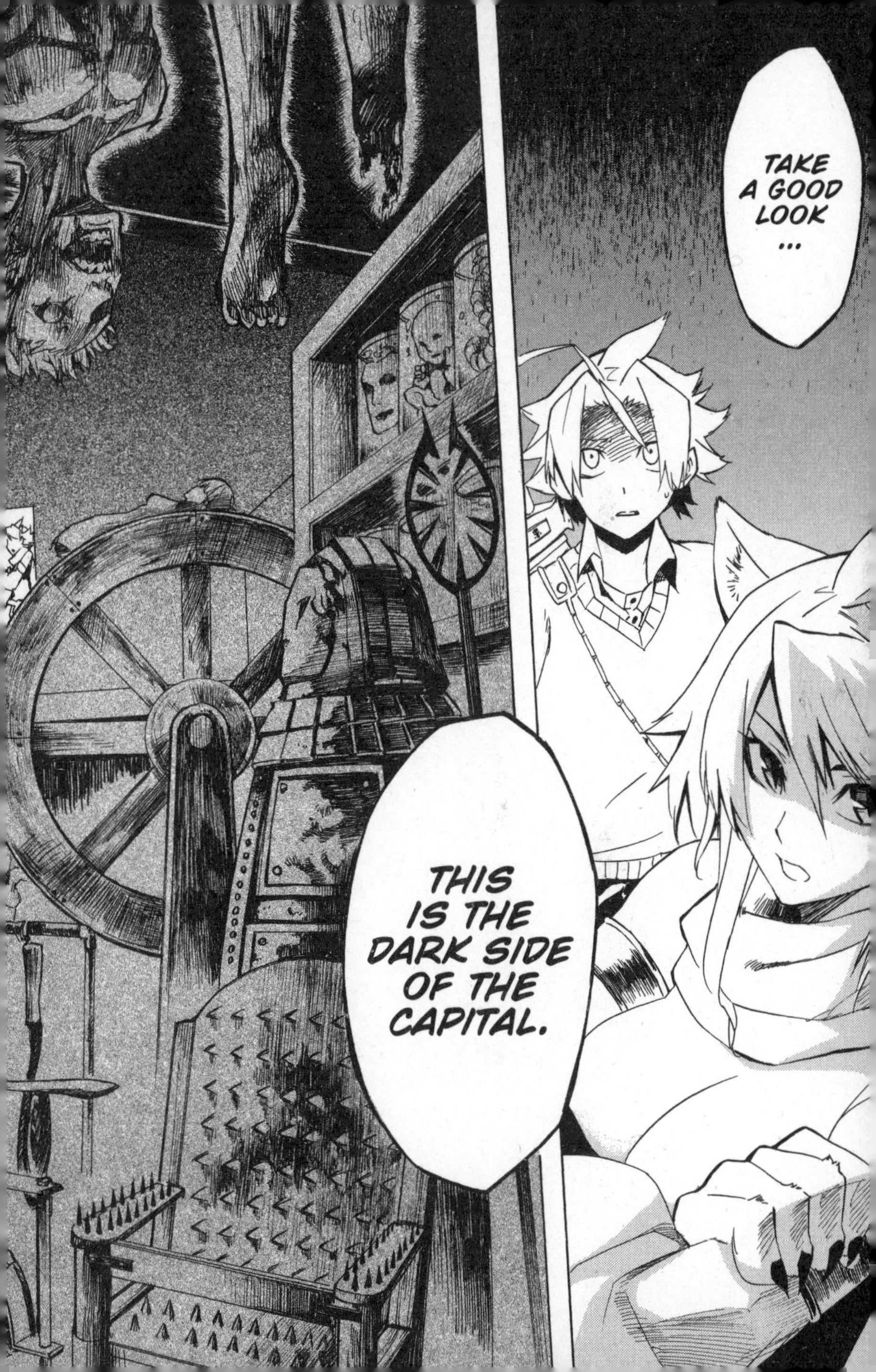
TAKE A GOOD LOOK ...
THIS IS THE DARK SIDE OF THE CAPITAL.

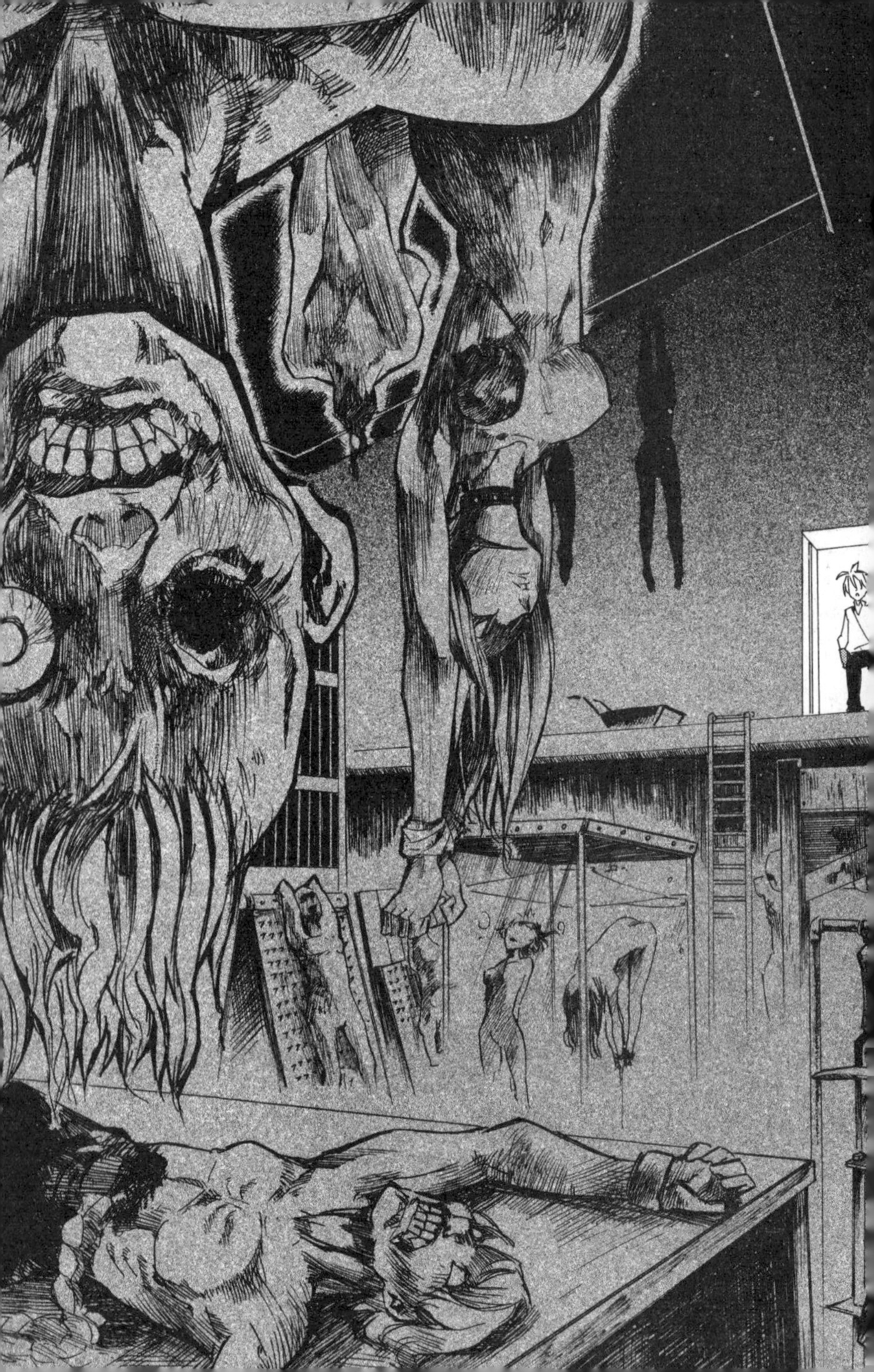

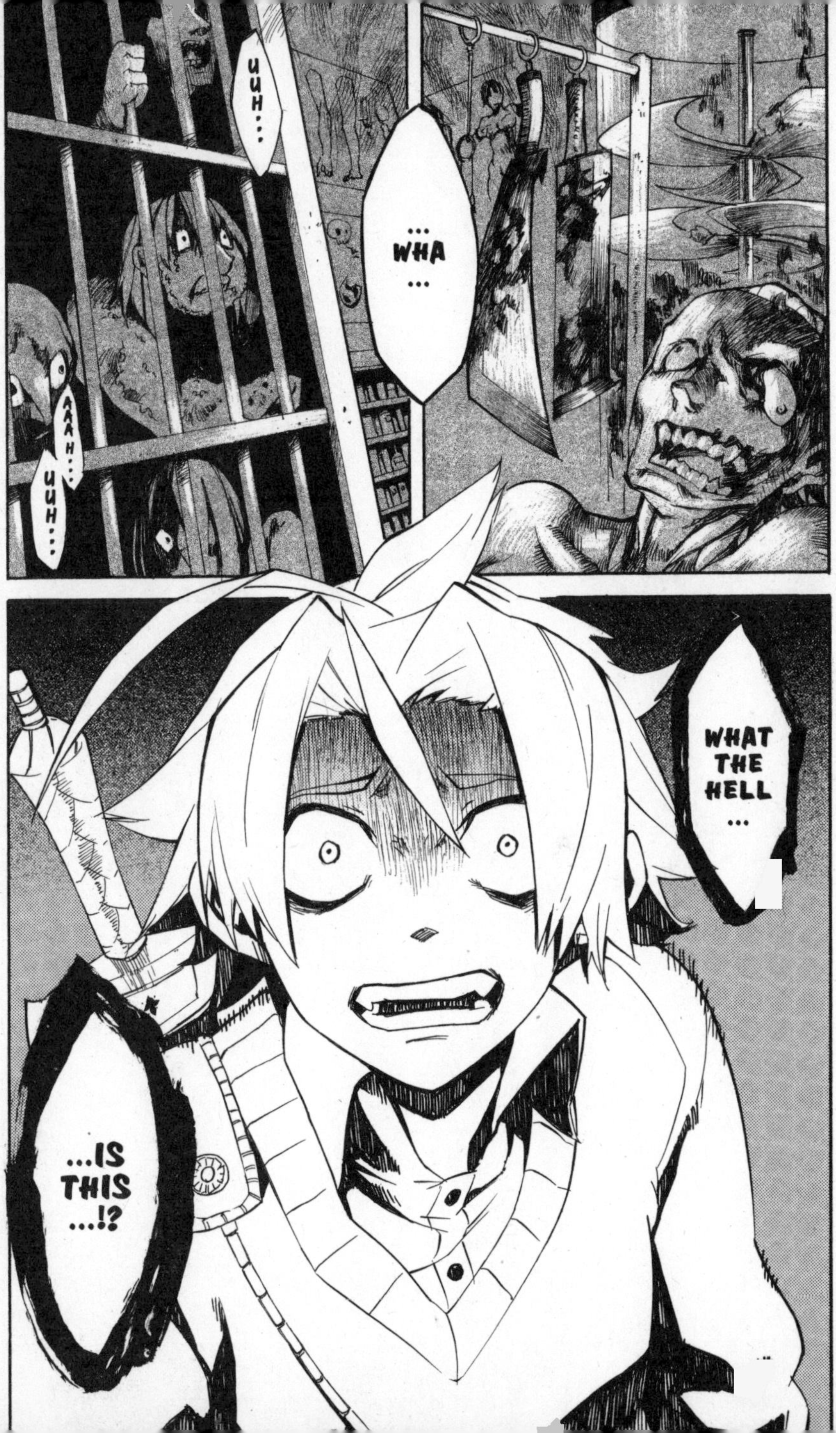
UUH...
...WHA...
AAAH...
UUH...
WHAT THE HELL...
...IS THIS...!?

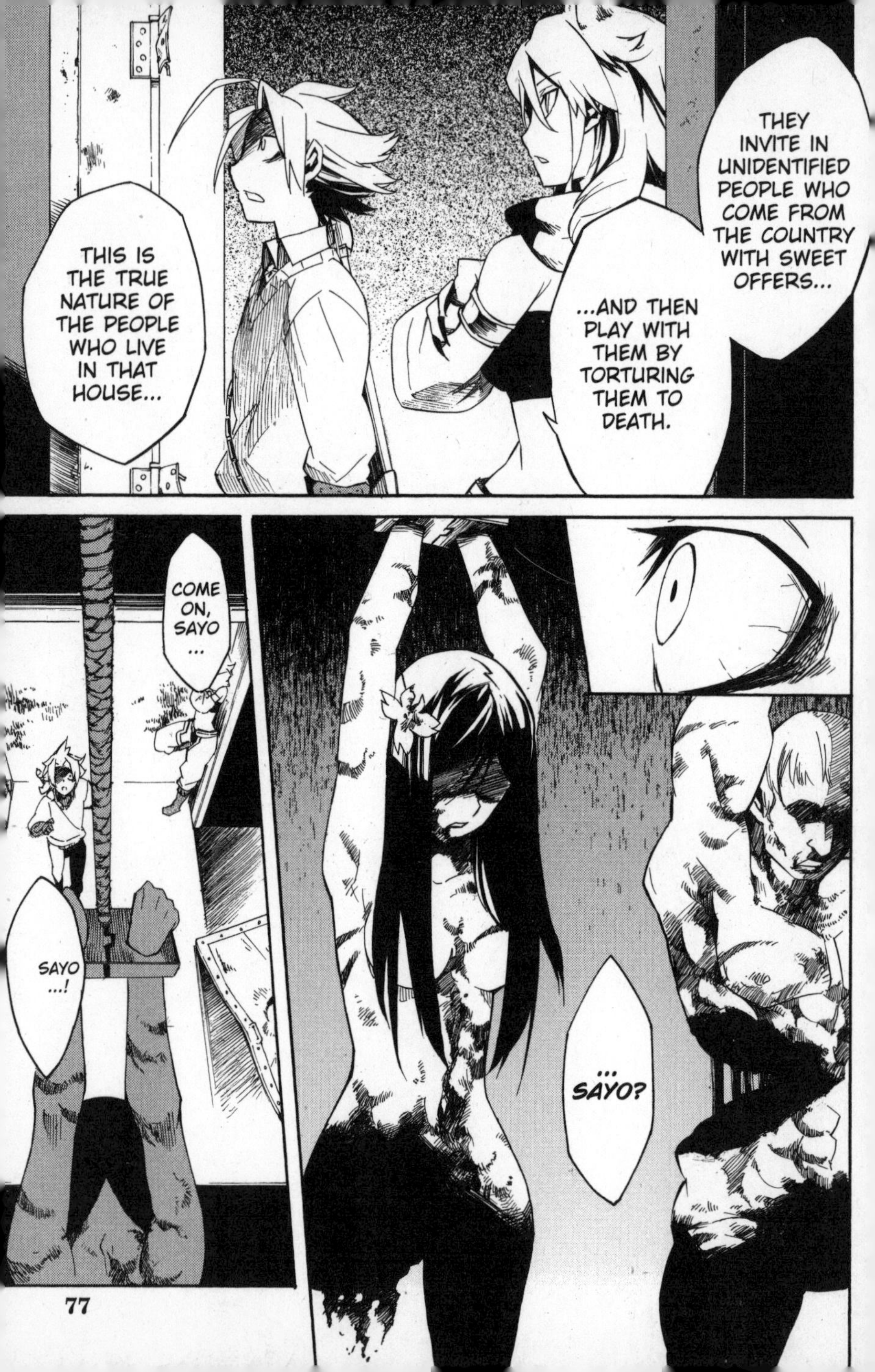
THEY INVITE IN UNIDENTIFIED PEOPLE WHO COME FROM THE COUNTRY WITH SWEET OFFERS...
...AND THEN PLAY WITH THEM BY TORTURING THEM TO DEATH.
THIS IS THE TRUE NATURE OF THE PEOPLE WHO LIVE IN THAT HOUSE...
...SAYO?
COME ON, SAYO...
SAYO...!

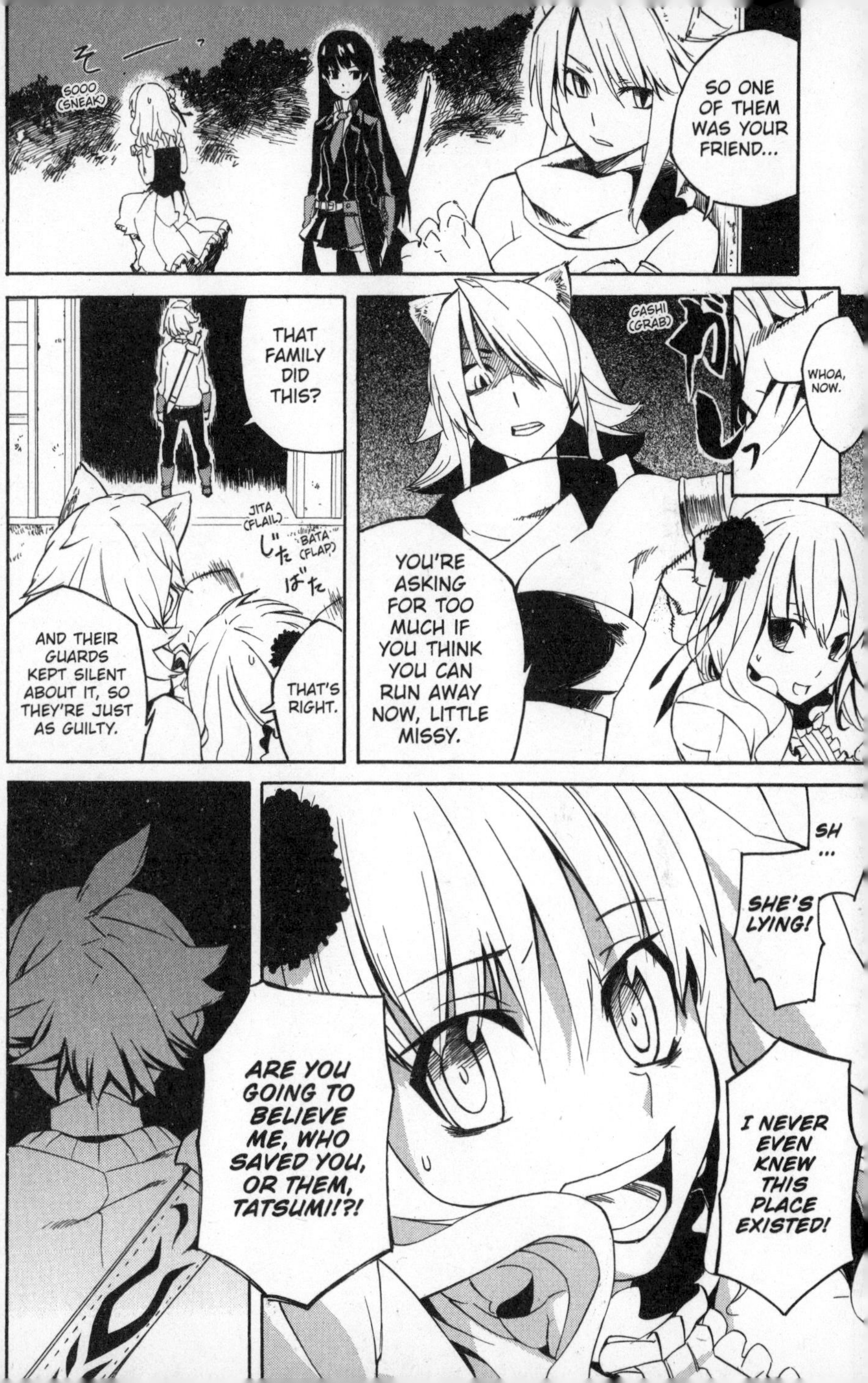
SO ONE OF THEM WAS YOUR FRIEND...
SOOO (SNEAK)
WHOA, NOW.
GASHI (GRAB)
YOU'RE ASKING FOR TOO MUCH IF YOU THINK YOU CAN RUN AWAY NOW, LITTLE MISSY.
THAT FAMILY DID THIS?
JITA (FLAIL) BATA (FLAP)
THAT'S RIGHT.
AND THEIR GUARDS KEPT SILENT ABOUT IT, SO THEY'RE JUST AS GUILTY.
SH...
SHE'S LYING!
I NEVER EVEN KNEW THIS PLACE EXISTED!
ARE YOU GOING TO BELIEVE ME, WHO SAVED YOU, OR THEM, TATSUMI!?!

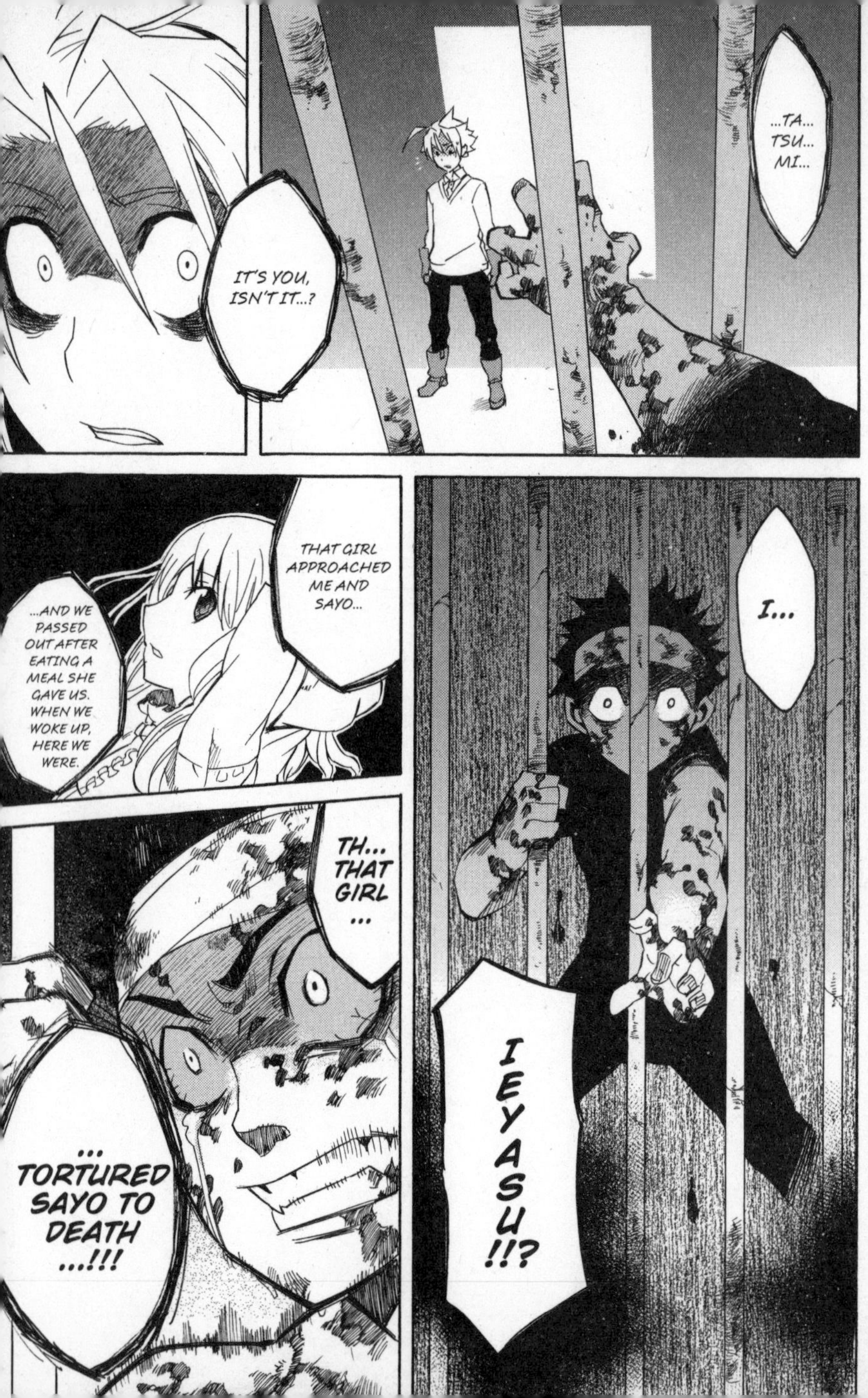
...TA... TSU... MI...
IT'S YOU, ISN'T IT...?
I...
IEYASU!!?
THAT GIRL APPROACHED ME AND SAYO...
...AND WE PASSED OUT AFTER EATING A MEAL SHE GAVE US. WHEN WE WOKE UP, HERE WE WERE.
TH... THAT GIRL ...
... TORTURED SAYO TO DEATH ...!!!

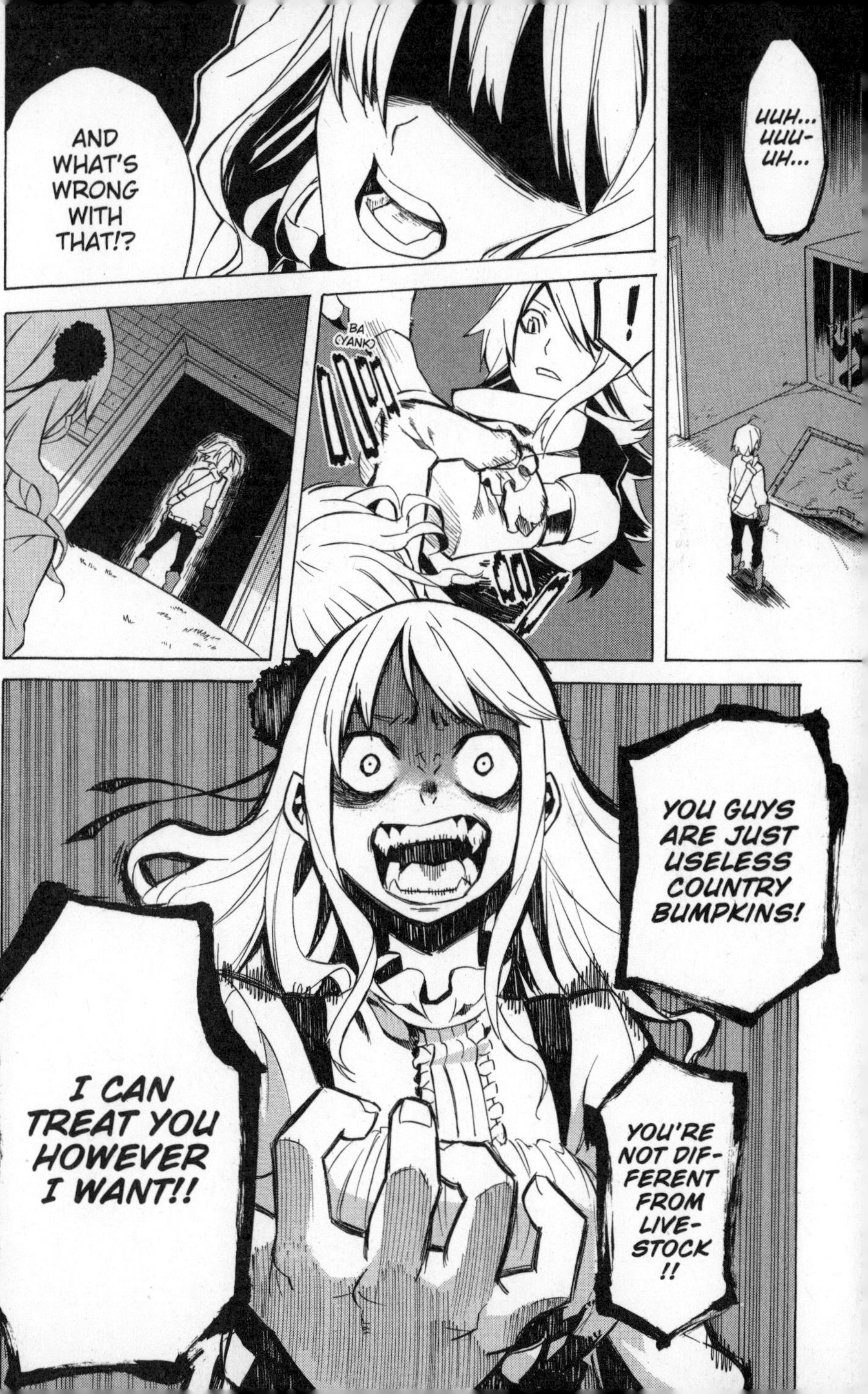
UUH... UUU-UH...
AND WHAT'S WRONG WITH THAT!?
BA (YANK)
!
YOU GUYS ARE JUST USELESS COUNTRY BUMPKINS!
YOU'RE NOT DIF-FERENT FROM LIVE-STOCK !!
I CAN TREAT YOU HOWEVER I WANT!!

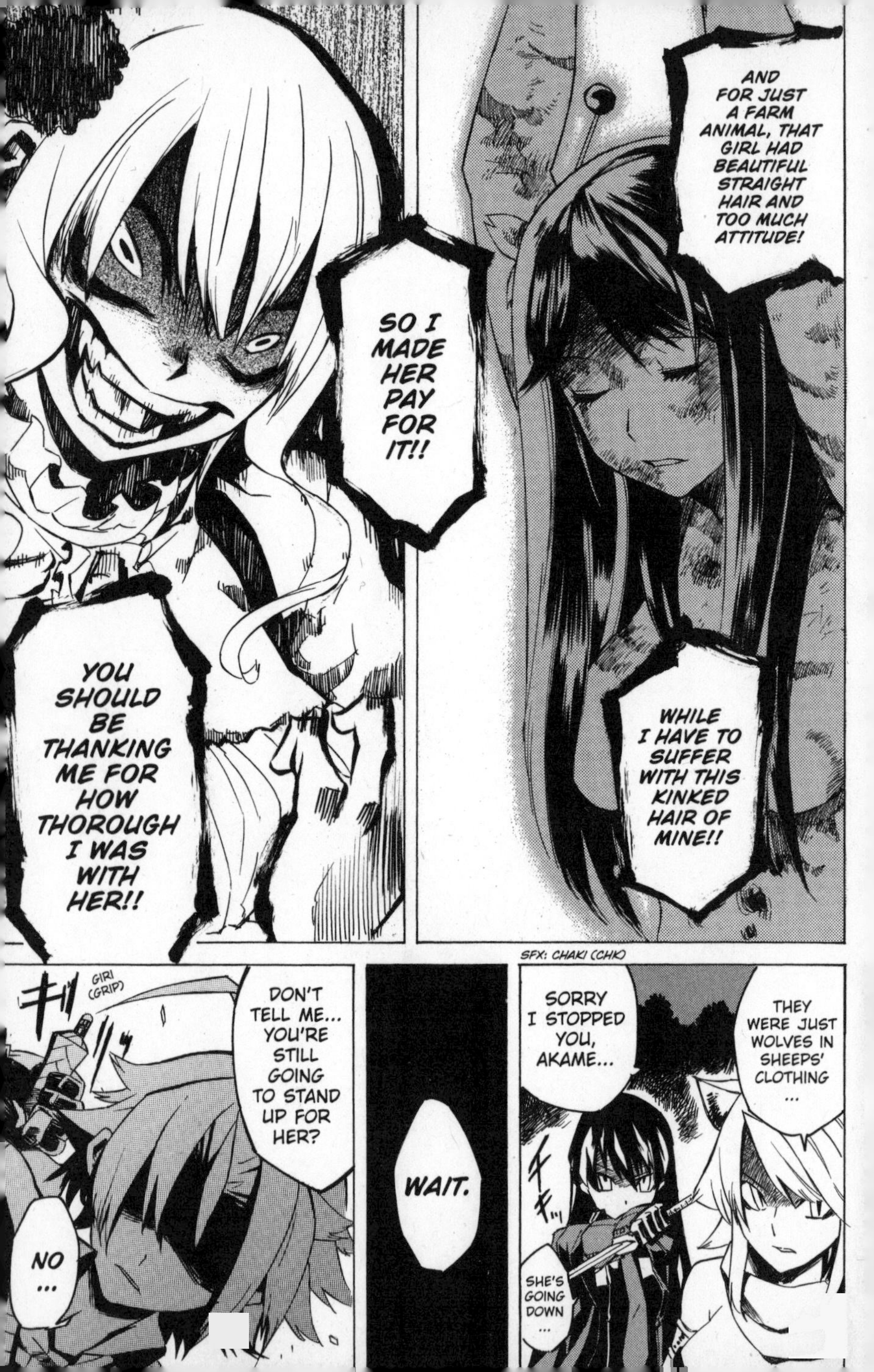
AND FOR JUST A FARM ANIMAL, THAT GIRL HAD BEAUTIFUL STRAIGHT HAIR AND TOO MUCH ATTITUDE!
WHILE I HAVE TO SUFFER WITH THIS KINKED HAIR OF MINE!!
SO I MADE HER PAY FOR IT!!
YOU SHOULD BE THANKING ME FOR HOW THOROUGH I WAS WITH HER!!
SFX: CHAKI (CHK)
THEY WERE JUST WOLVES IN SHEEPS' CLOTHING ...
SORRY I STOPPED YOU, AKAME...
SHE'S GOING DOWN ...
WAIT.
DON'T TELL ME... YOU'RE STILL GOING TO STAND UP FOR HER?
GIRI (GRIP)
NO ...

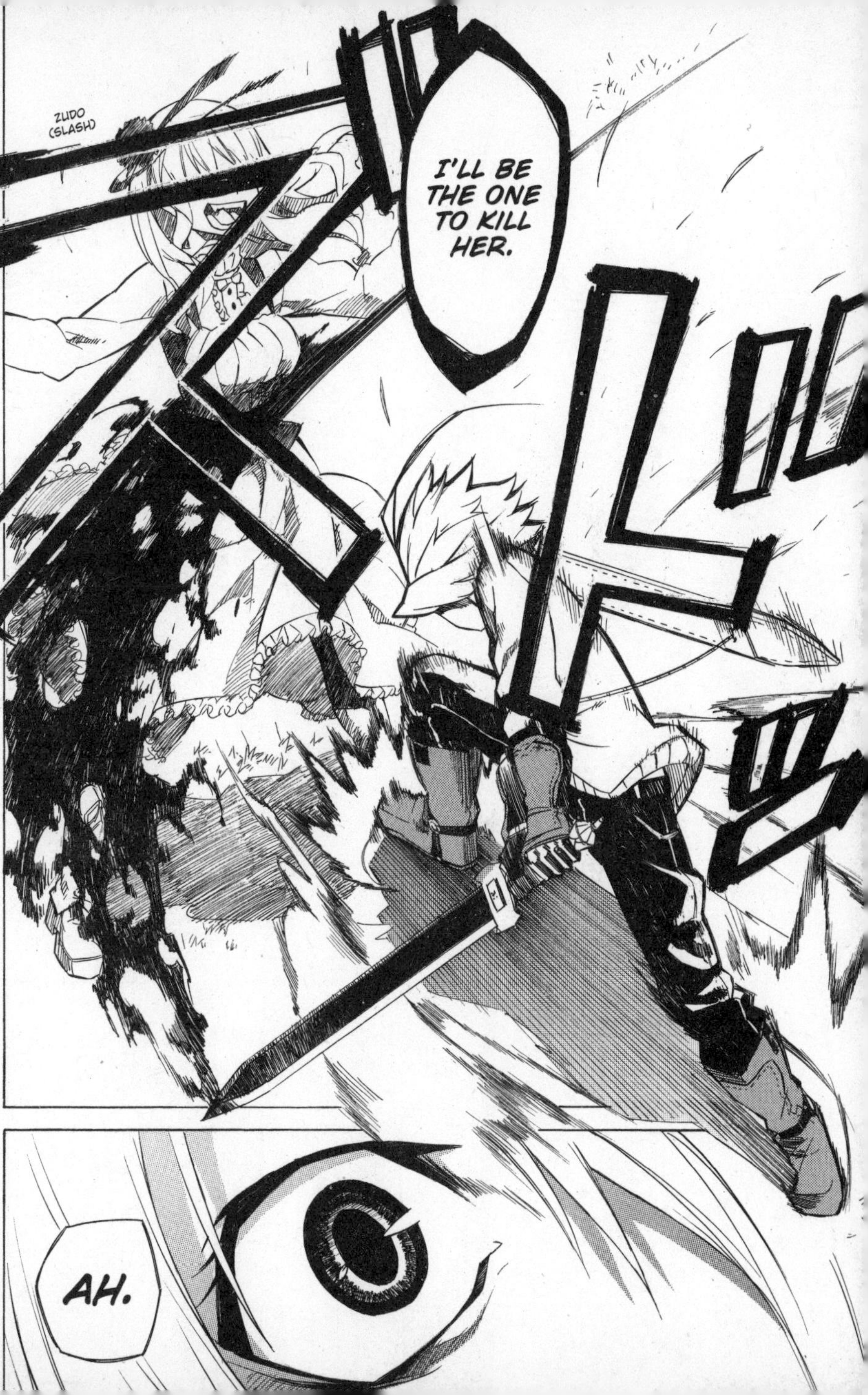
I'LL BE THE ONE TO KILL HER.
ZUDO (SLASH)
AH.

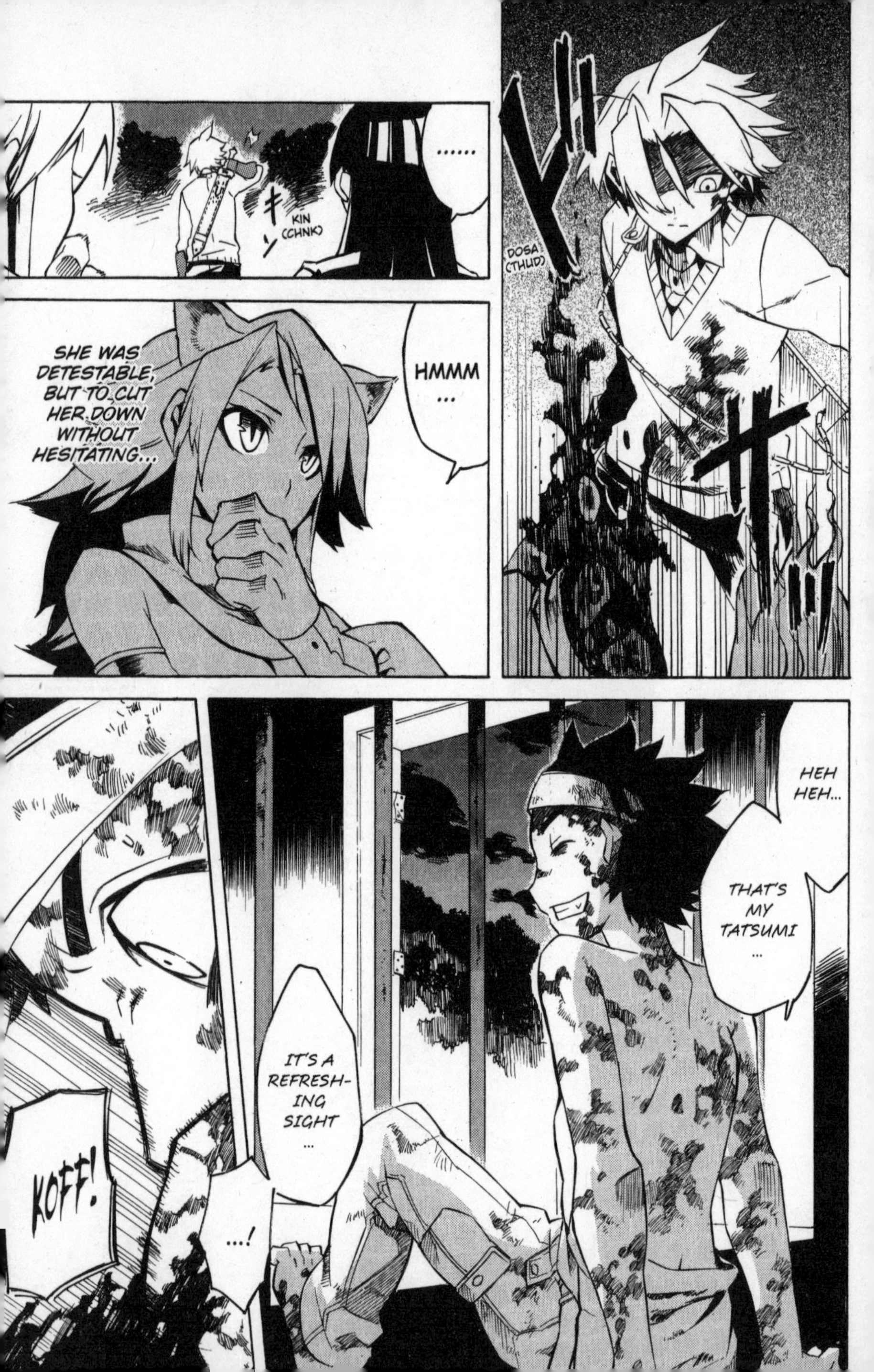
DOSA (THUD)
....
KIN (CHNK)
HMMM ...
SHE WAS DETESTABLE, BUT TO CUT HER DOWN WITHOUT HESITATING...
HEH HEH...
THAT'S MY TATSUMI ...
IT'S A REFRESHING SIGHT ...
KOFF!
...!

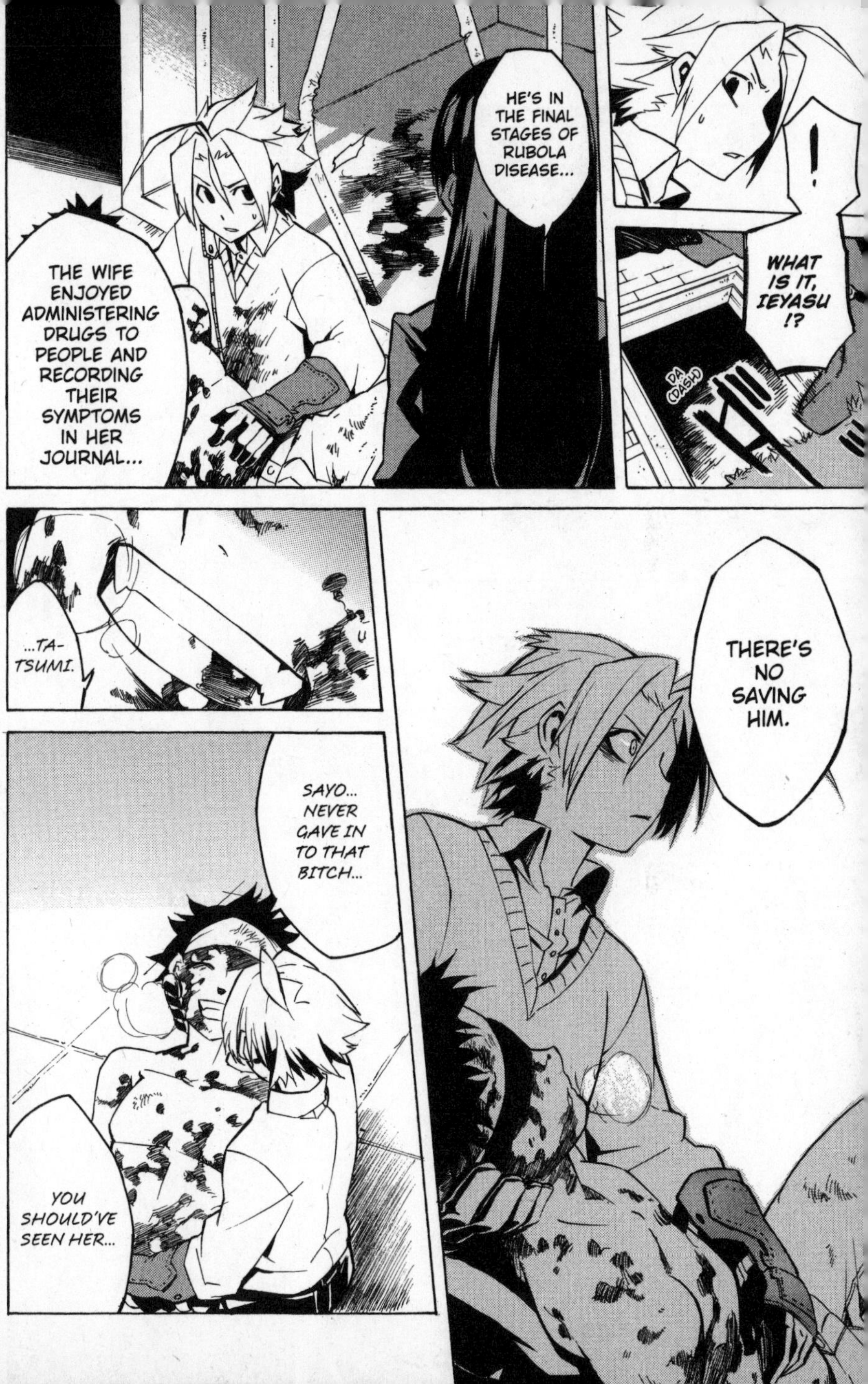
!
WHAT IS IT, IEYASU!?
DA (DASH)
HE'S IN THE FINAL STAGES OF RUBOLA DISEASE...
THE WIFE ENJOYED ADMINISTERING DRUGS TO PEOPLE AND RECORDING THEIR SYMPTOMS IN HER JOURNAL...
THERE'S NO SAVING HIM.
...TA-TSUMI.
SAYO... NEVER GAVE IN TO THAT BITCH...
YOU SHOULD'VE SEEN HER...

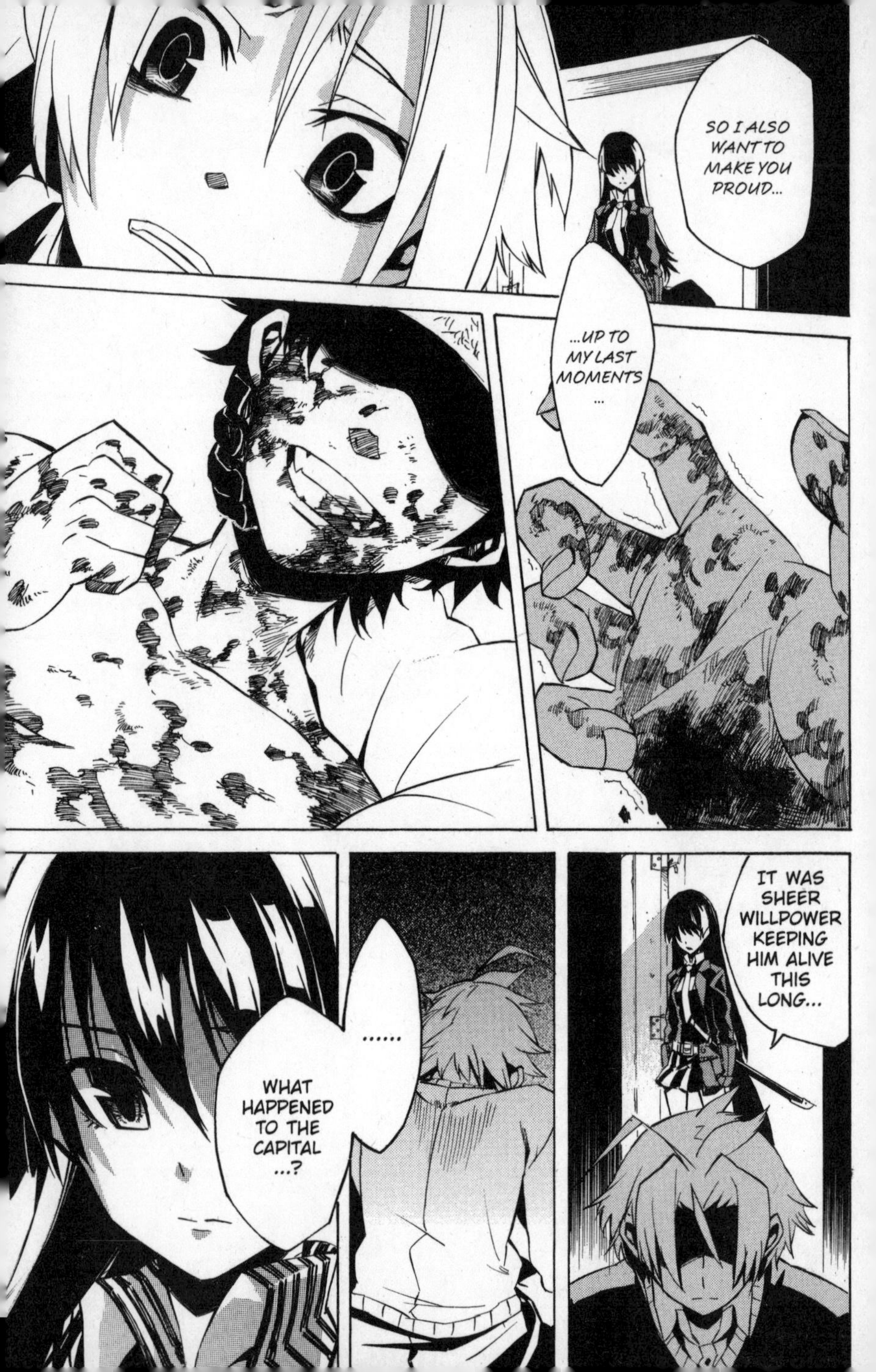
SO I ALSO WANT TO MAKE YOU PROUD...
...UP TO MY LAST MOMENTS ...
IT WAS SHEER WILLPOWER KEEPING HIM ALIVE THIS LONG...
......
WHAT HAPPENED TO THE CAPITAL ...?

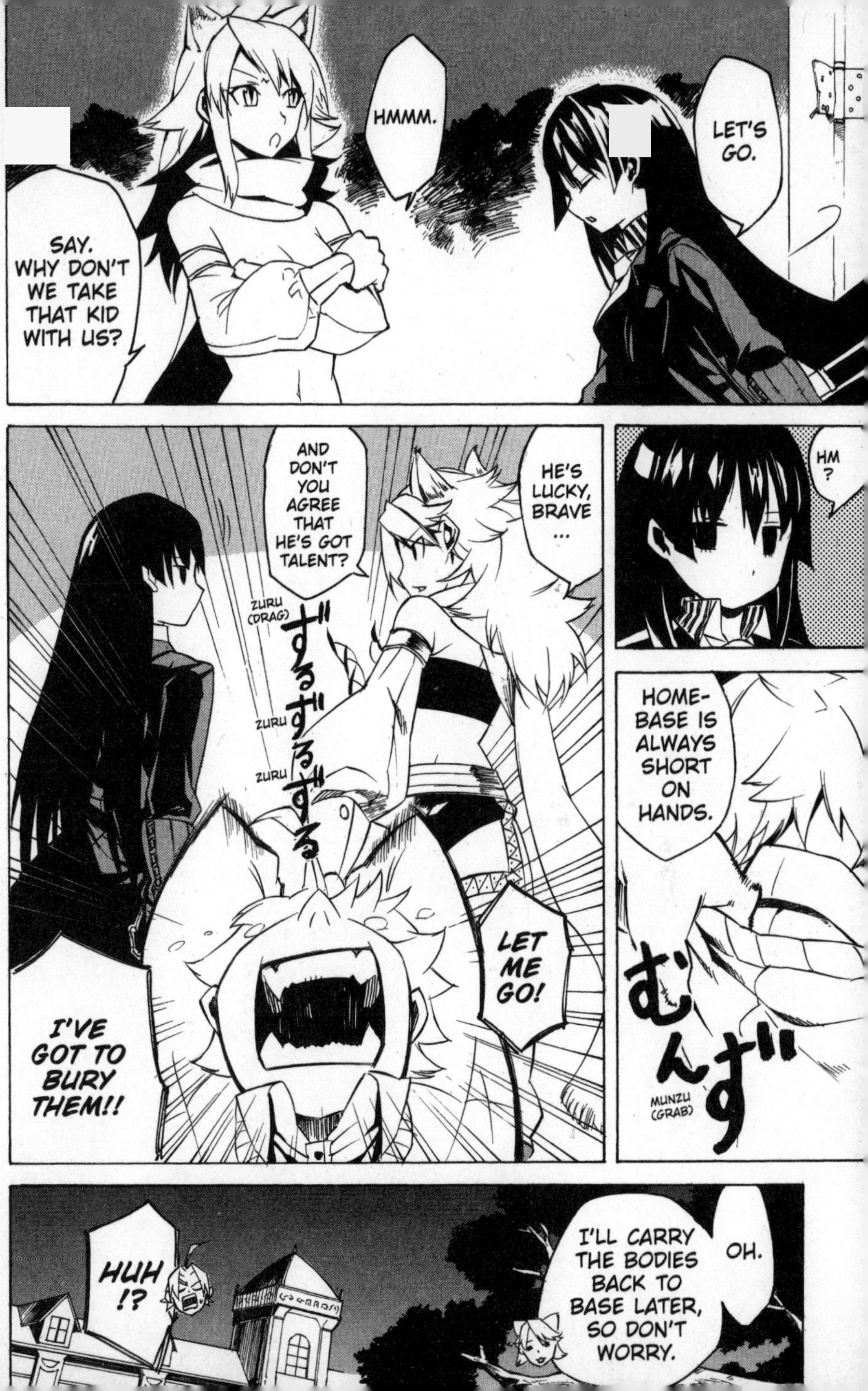
LET'S GO.
HMMM.
SAY. WHY DON'T WE TAKE THAT KID WITH US?
HM ?
HOME-BASE IS ALWAYS SHORT ON HANDS.
むんず
MUNZU (GRAB)
HE'S LUCKY, BRAVE ...
AND DON'T YOU AGREE THAT HE'S GOT TALENT?
ずる
ZURU (DRAG)
ずる
ZURU
ずる
ZURU
LET ME GO!
I'VE GOT TO BURY THEM!!
OH.
I'LL CARRY THE BODIES BACK TO BASE LATER, SO DON'T WORRY.
HUH !?

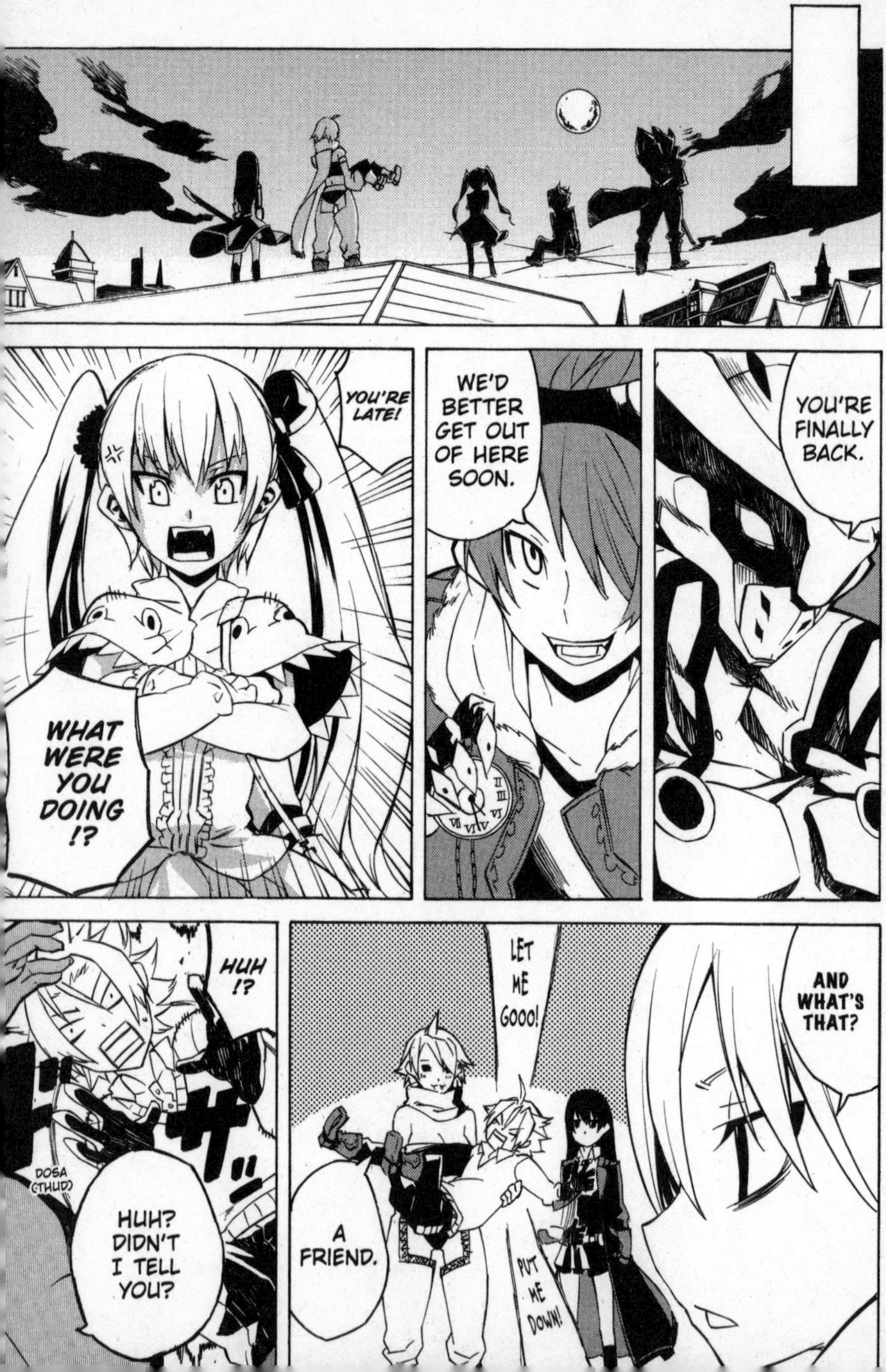
YOU'RE FINALLY BACK.
WE'D BETTER GET OUT OF HERE SOON.
YOU'RE LATE!
WHAT WERE YOU DOING!?
AND WHAT'S THAT?
LET ME GOOO!
A FRIEND.
PUT ME DOWN!
HUH!?
DOSA (THUD)
HUH? DIDN'T I TELL YOU?

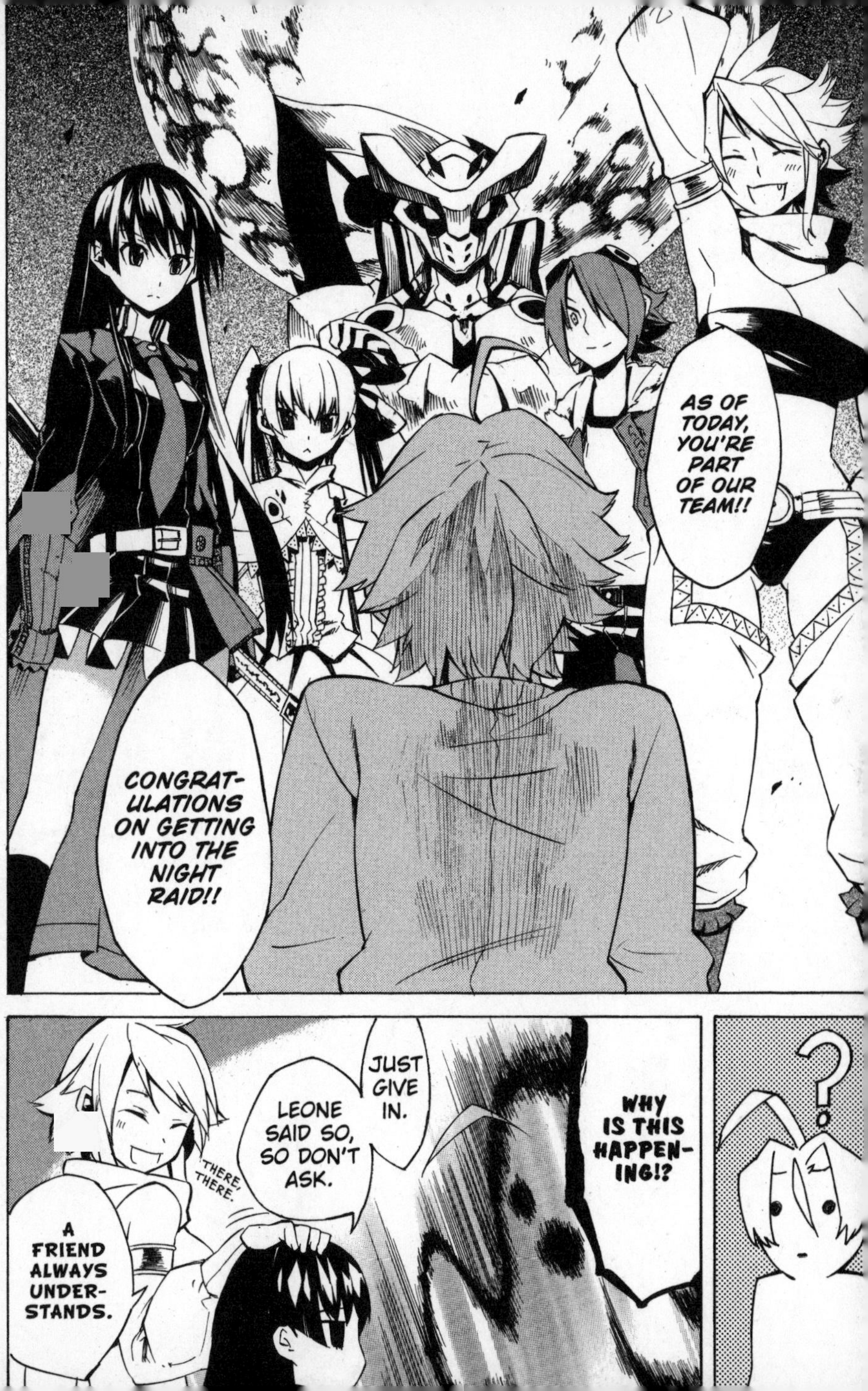
AS OF TODAY, YOU'RE PART OF OUR TEAM!!
CONGRATULATIONS ON GETTING INTO THE NIGHT RAID!!
?
WHY IS THIS HAPPENING!?
JUST GIVE IN.
LEONE SAID SO, SO DON'T ASK.
THERE, THERE.
A FRIEND ALWAYS UNDERSTANDS.

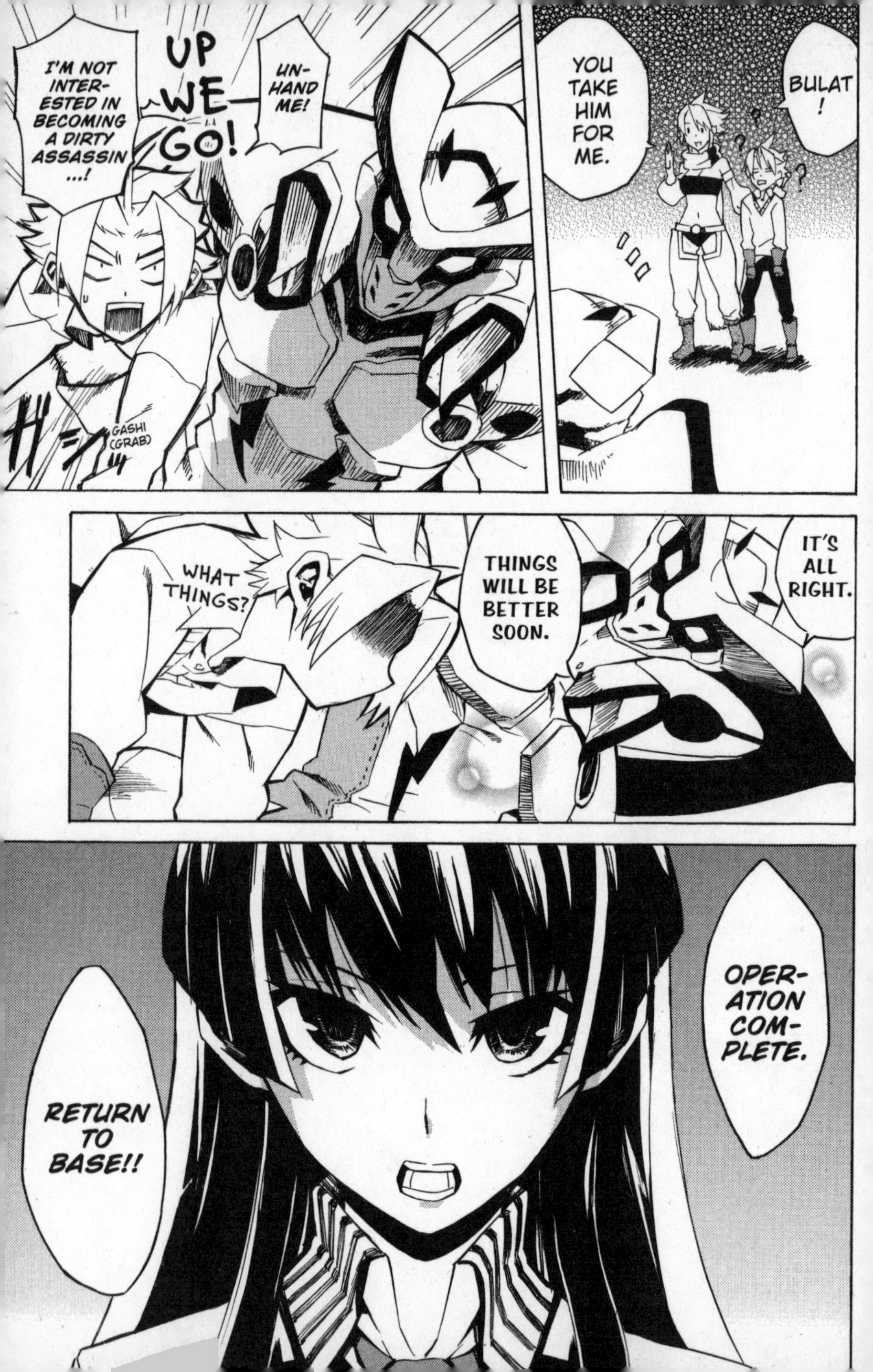
BULAT!
YOU TAKE HIM FOR ME.
UN-HAND ME!
UP WE GO!
I'M NOT INTER-ESTED IN BECOMING A DIRTY ASSASSIN ...!
GASHI (GRAB)
IT'S ALL RIGHT.
THINGS WILL BE BETTER SOON.
WHAT THINGS?
OPER-ATION COM-PLETE.
RETURN TO BASE!!

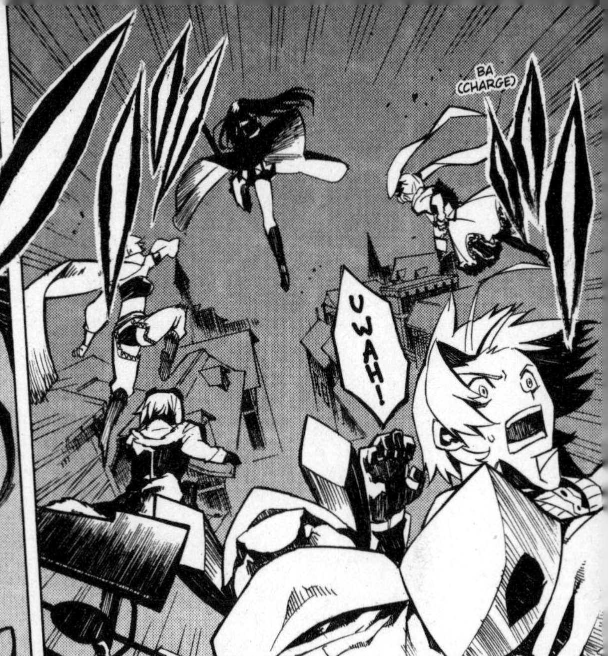
BA (CHARGE)
UWAH!
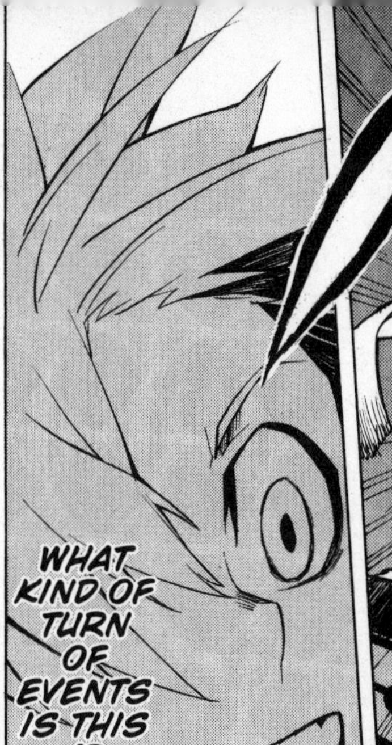
WHAT KIND OF TURN OF EVENTS IS THIS !?
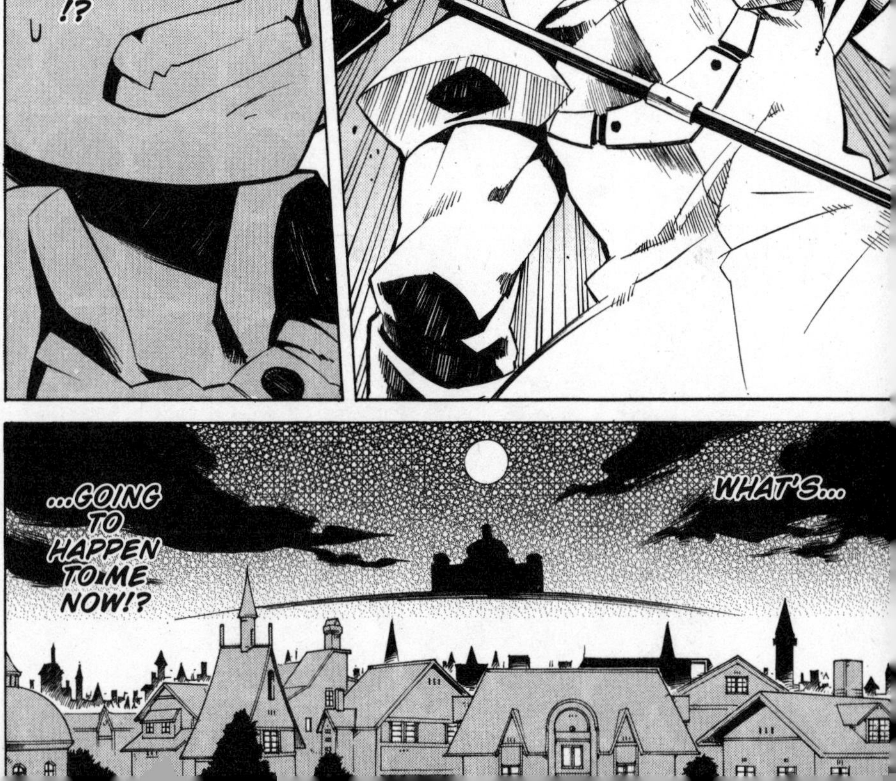
WHAT'S...
...GOING TO HAPPEN TO ME NOW!?

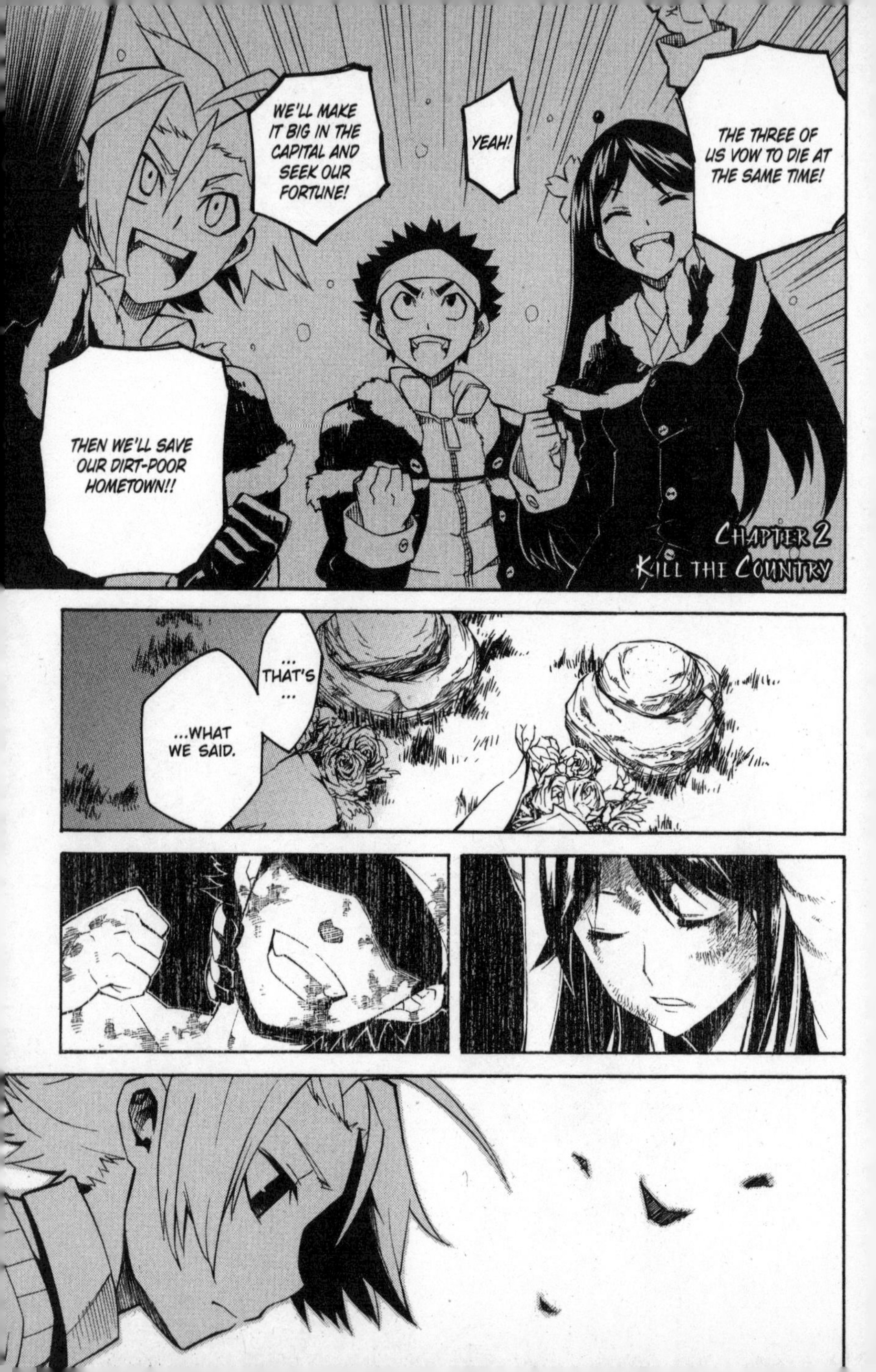
THE THREE OF US VOW TO DIE AT THE SAME TIME!
YEAH!
WE'LL MAKE IT BIG IN THE CAPITAL AND SEEK OUR FORTUNE!
THEN WE'LL SAVE OUR DIRT-POOR HOMETOWN!!
CHAPTER 2
KILL THE COUNTRY
... THAT'S ...
...WHAT WE SAID.

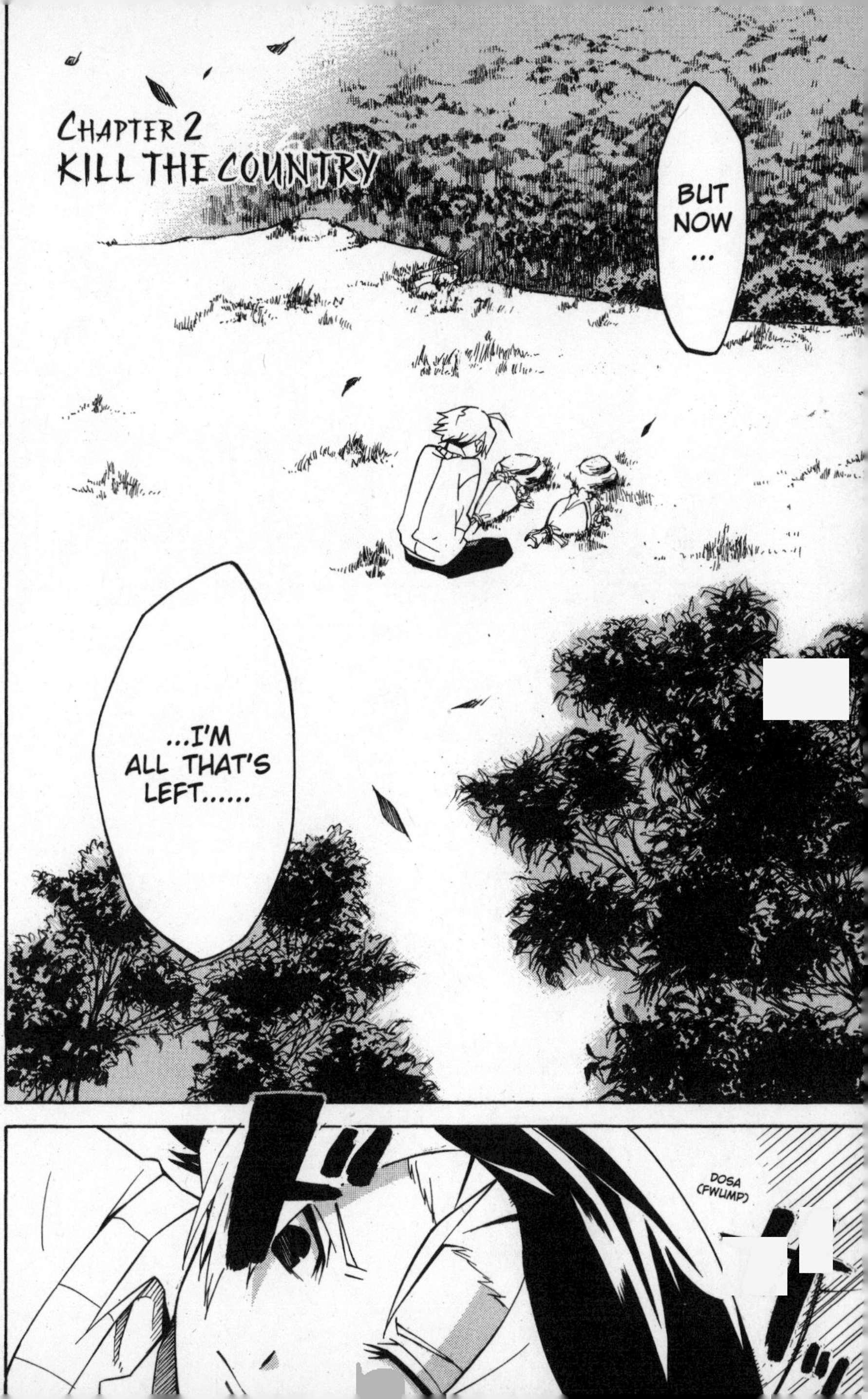
CHAPTER 2
KILL THE COUNTRY
BUT NOW ...
...I'M ALL THAT'S LEFT......
DOSA (FWUMP)

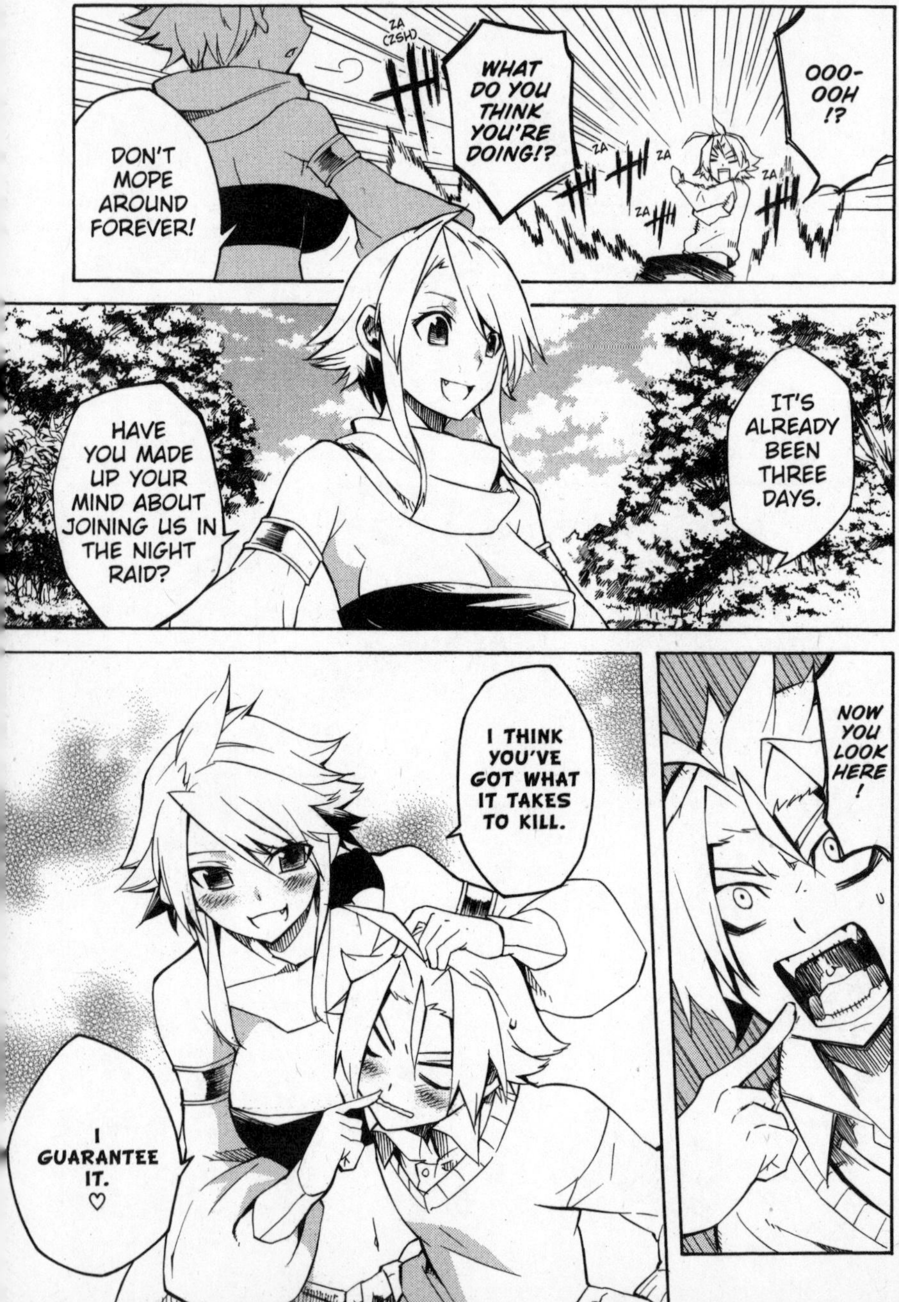
OOO-OOH!?
ZA ZA ZA ZA
WHAT DO YOU THINK YOU'RE DOING!?
ZA (ZSH)
DON'T MOPE AROUND FOREVER!
IT'S ALREADY BEEN THREE DAYS.
HAVE YOU MADE UP YOUR MIND ABOUT JOINING US IN THE NIGHT RAID?
NOW YOU LOOK HERE!
I THINK YOU'VE GOT WHAT IT TAKES TO KILL.
I GUARANTEE IT. ♡

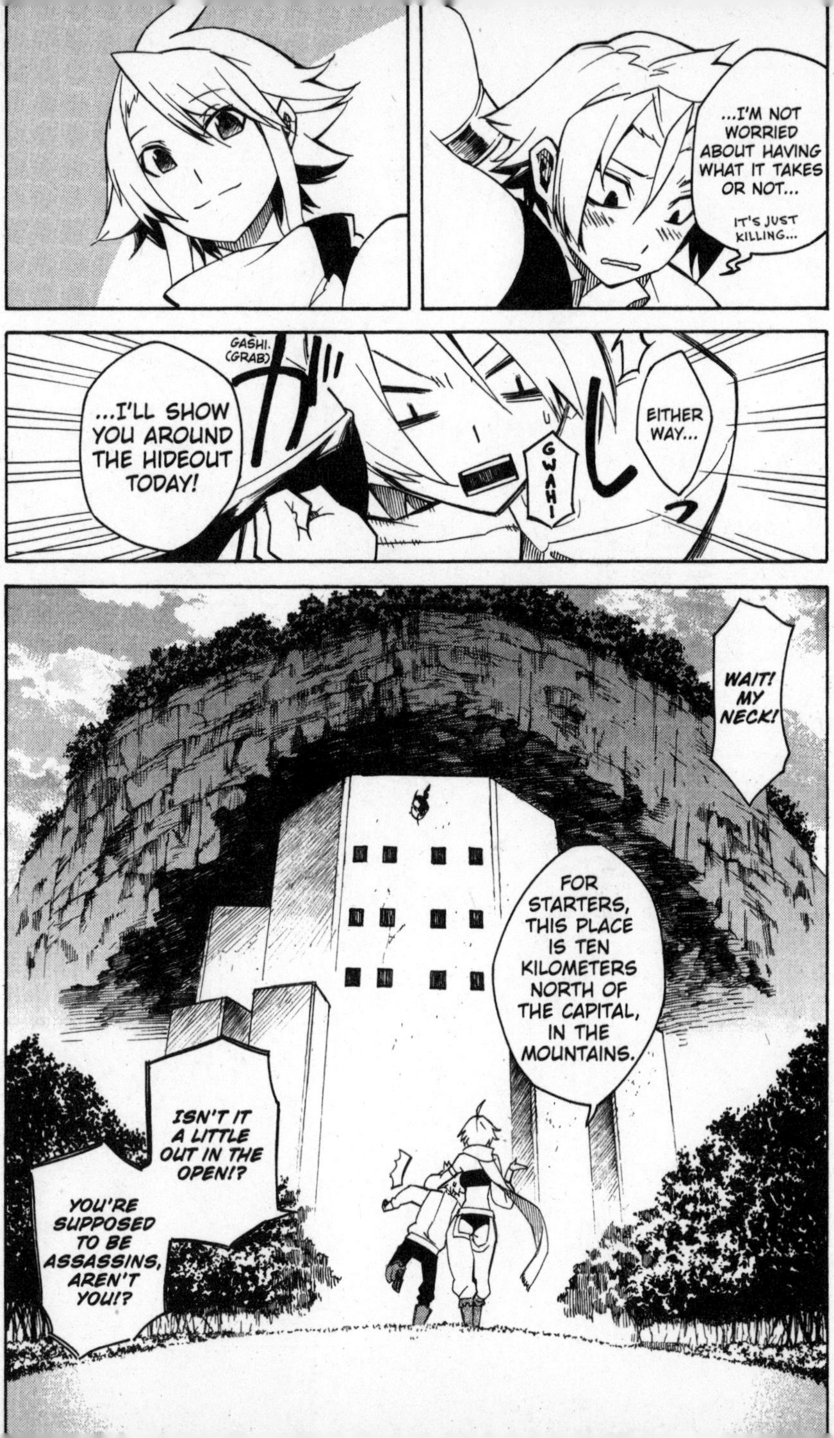
...I'M NOT WORRIED ABOUT HAVING WHAT IT TAKES OR NOT...
IT'S JUST KILLING...
EITHER WAY...
GWAHI
GASHI. (GRAB)
...I'LL SHOW YOU AROUND THE HIDEOUT TODAY!
WAIT! MY NECK!
FOR STARTERS, THIS PLACE IS TEN KILOMETERS NORTH OF THE CAPITAL, IN THE MOUNTAINS.
ISN'T IT A LITTLE OUT IN THE OPEN!?
YOU'RE SUPPOSED TO BE ASSASSINS, AREN'T YOU!?

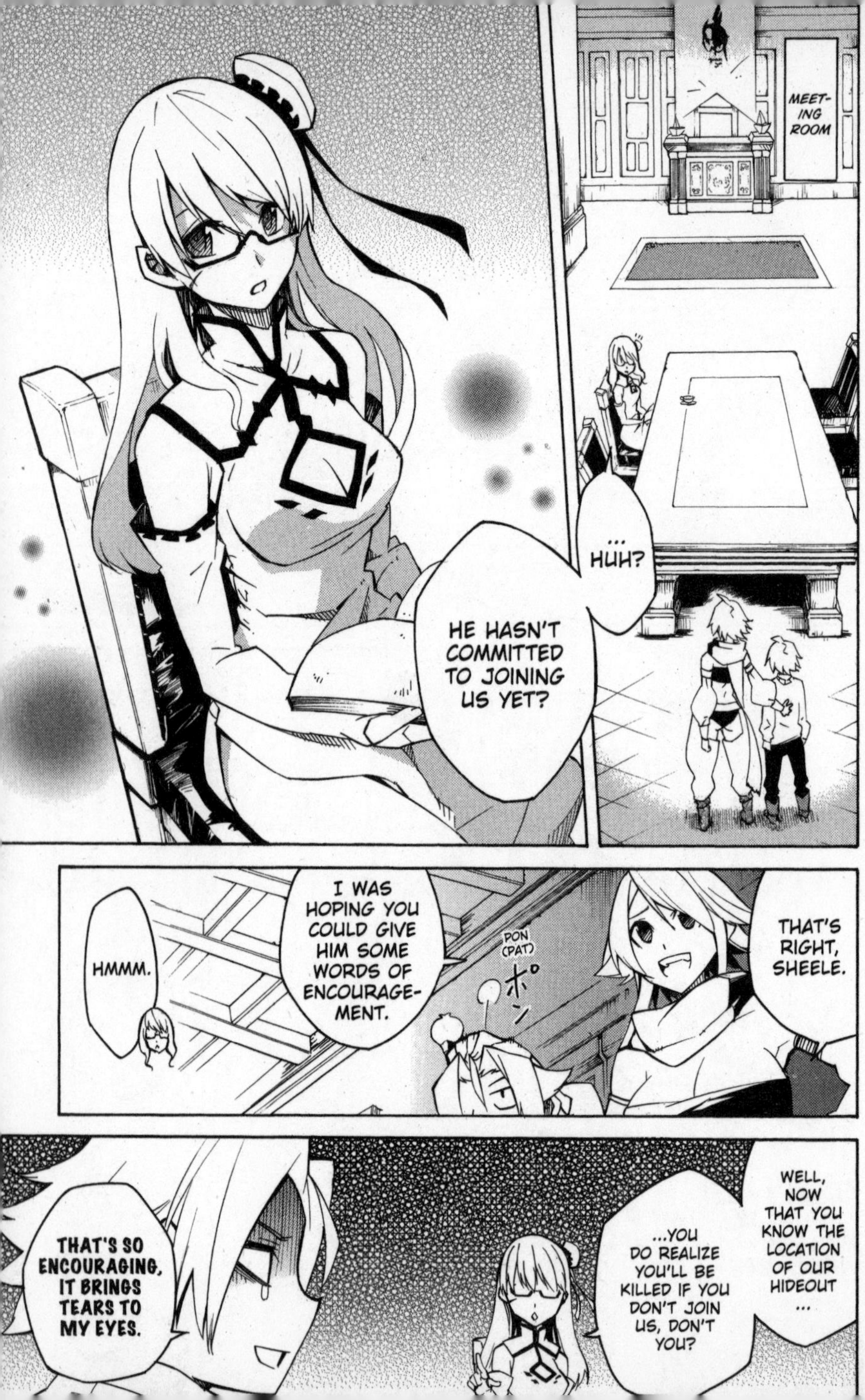
MEETING ROOM
... HUH?
HE HASN'T COMMITTED TO JOINING US YET?
THAT'S RIGHT, SHEELE.
PON (PAT)
I WAS HOPING YOU COULD GIVE HIM SOME WORDS OF ENCOURAGEMENT.
HMMM.
WELL, NOW THAT YOU KNOW THE LOCATION OF OUR HIDEOUT ...
...YOU DO REALIZE YOU'LL BE KILLED IF YOU DON'T JOIN US, DON'T YOU?
THAT'S SO ENCOURAGING, IT BRINGS TEARS TO MY EYES.

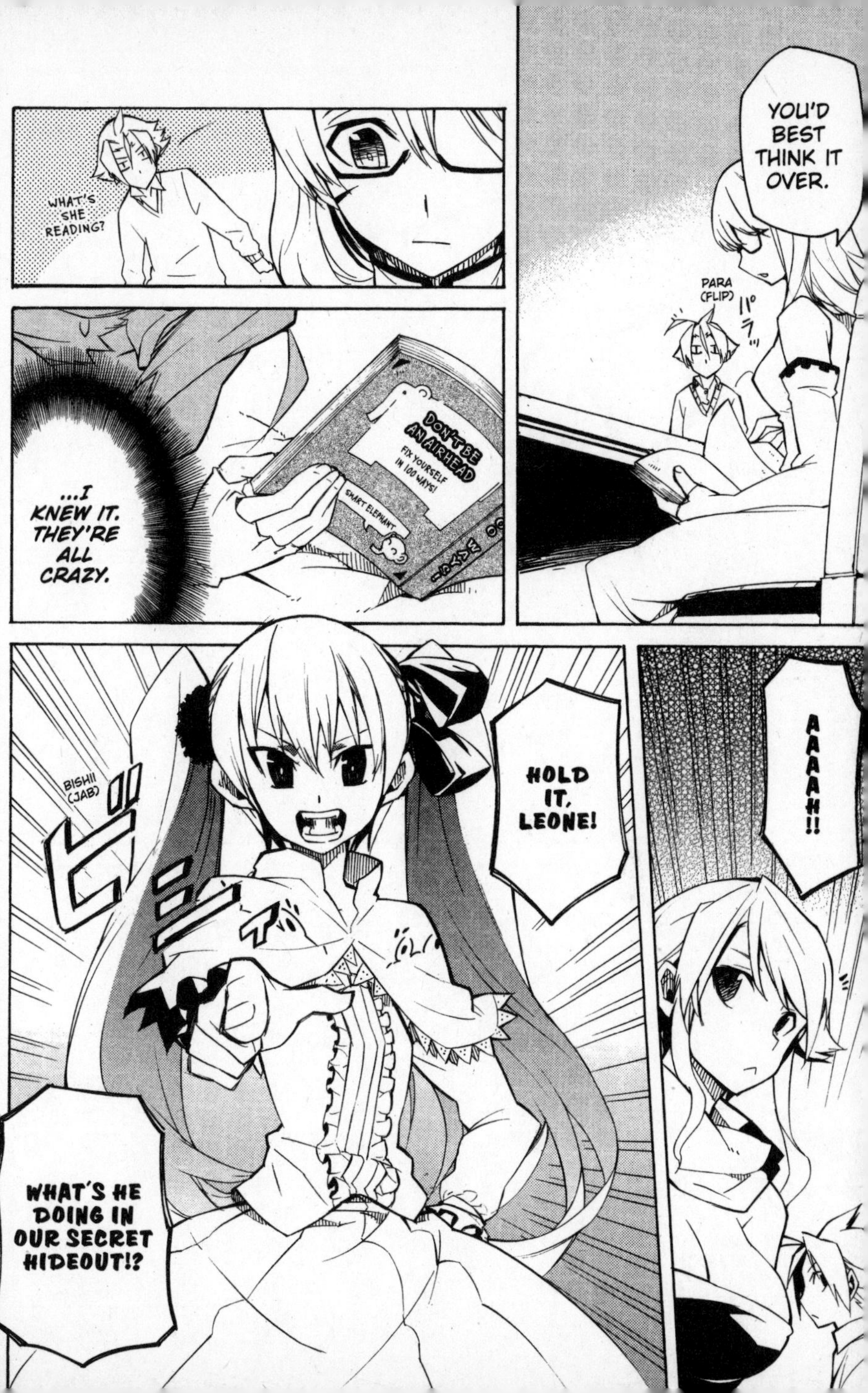
YOU'D BEST THINK IT OVER.
PARA (FLIP)
WHAT'S SHE READING?
DON'T BE AN AIRHEAD
FIX YOURSELF IN 100 WAYS!
SMART ELEPHANT
...I KNEW IT. THEY'RE ALL CRAZY.
AAAAAH!!
HOLD IT, LEONE!
BISHII (JAB)
WHAT'S HE DOING IN OUR SECRET HIDEOUT!?

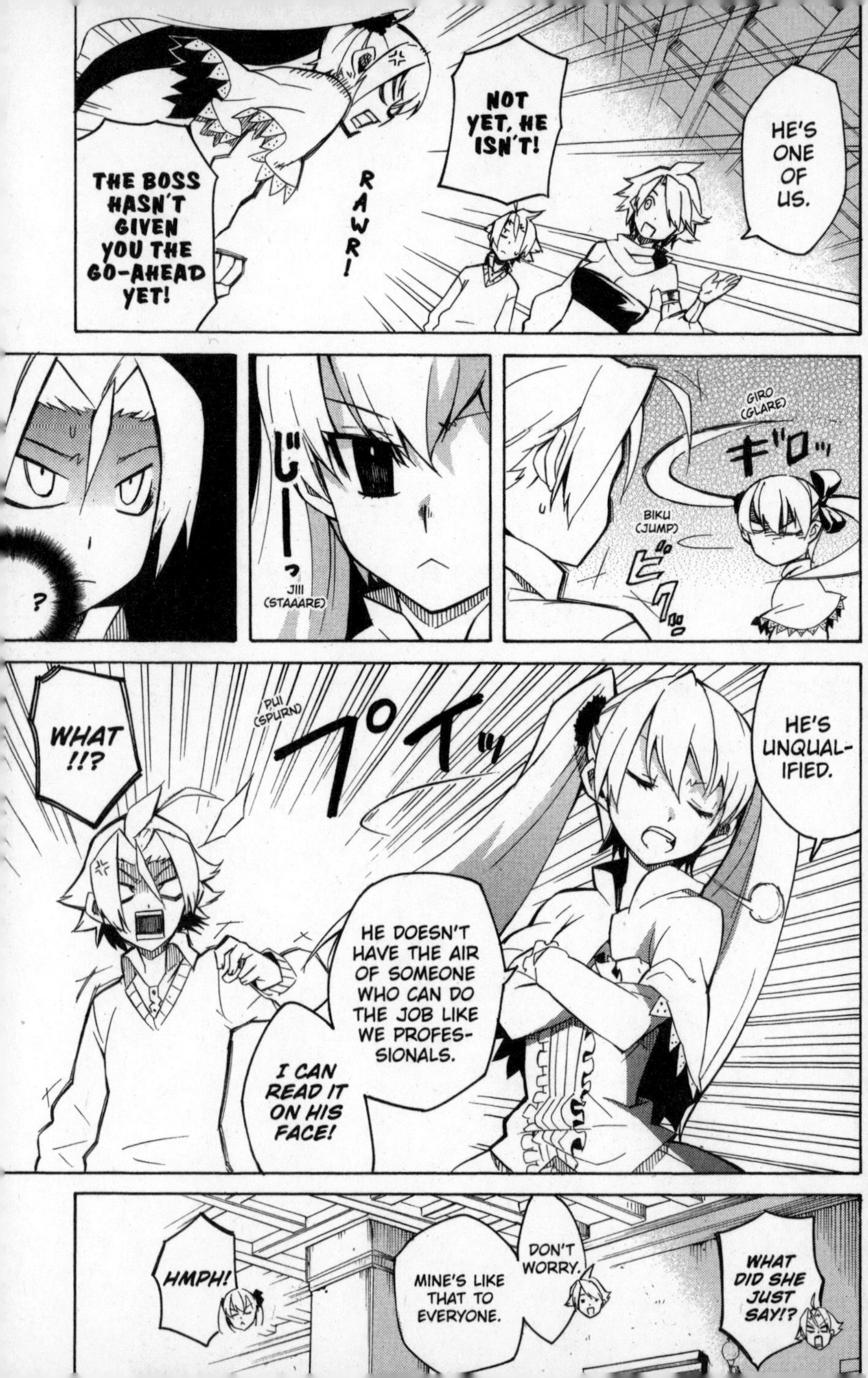
HE'S ONE OF US.
NOT YET, HE ISN'T!
RAWR!
THE BOSS HASN'T GIVEN YOU THE GO-AHEAD YET!
GIRO (GLARE)
ギロッ
BIKU (JUMP)
ビクッ
じーっ
JIII (STAAARE)
?
HE'S UNQUAL-IFIED.
PUI (SPURN)
プイッ
WHAT !!?
HE DOESN'T HAVE THE AIR OF SOMEONE WHO CAN DO THE JOB LIKE WE PROFES-SIONALS.
I CAN READ IT ON HIS FACE!
WHAT DID SHE JUST SAY!?
DON'T WORRY.
MINE'S LIKE THAT TO EVERYONE.
HMPH!

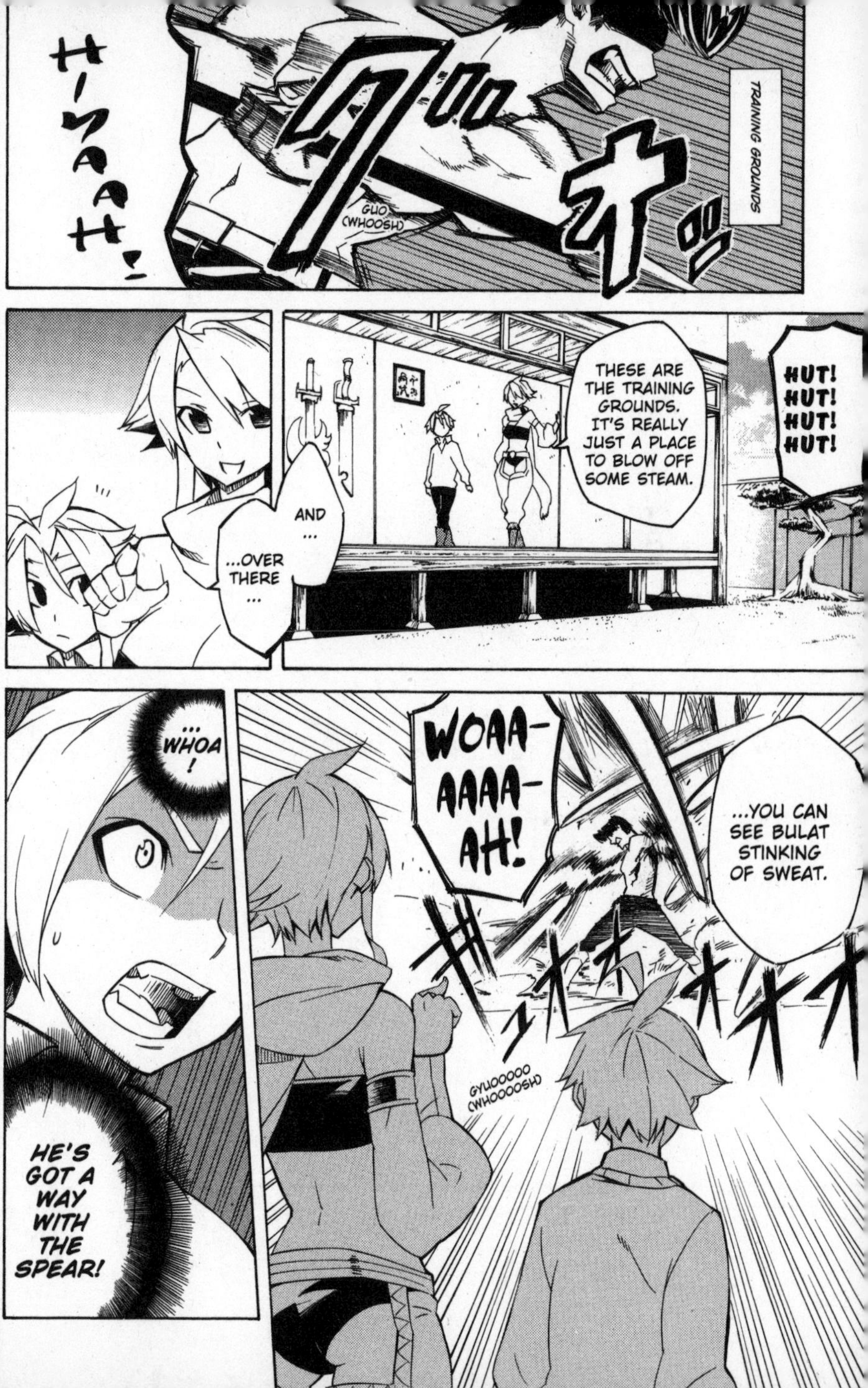
TRAINING GROUNDS
GUO (WHOOSH)
HIYAAAH!
HUT! HUT! HUT! HUT!
THESE ARE THE TRAINING GROUNDS. IT'S REALLY JUST A PLACE TO BLOW OFF SOME STEAM.
AND ...
...OVER THERE ...
...YOU CAN SEE BULAT STINKING OF SWEAT.
WOAAAAAAAH!
GYUOOOOO (WHOOOOSH)
...WHOA!
HE'S GOT A WAY WITH THE SPEAR!

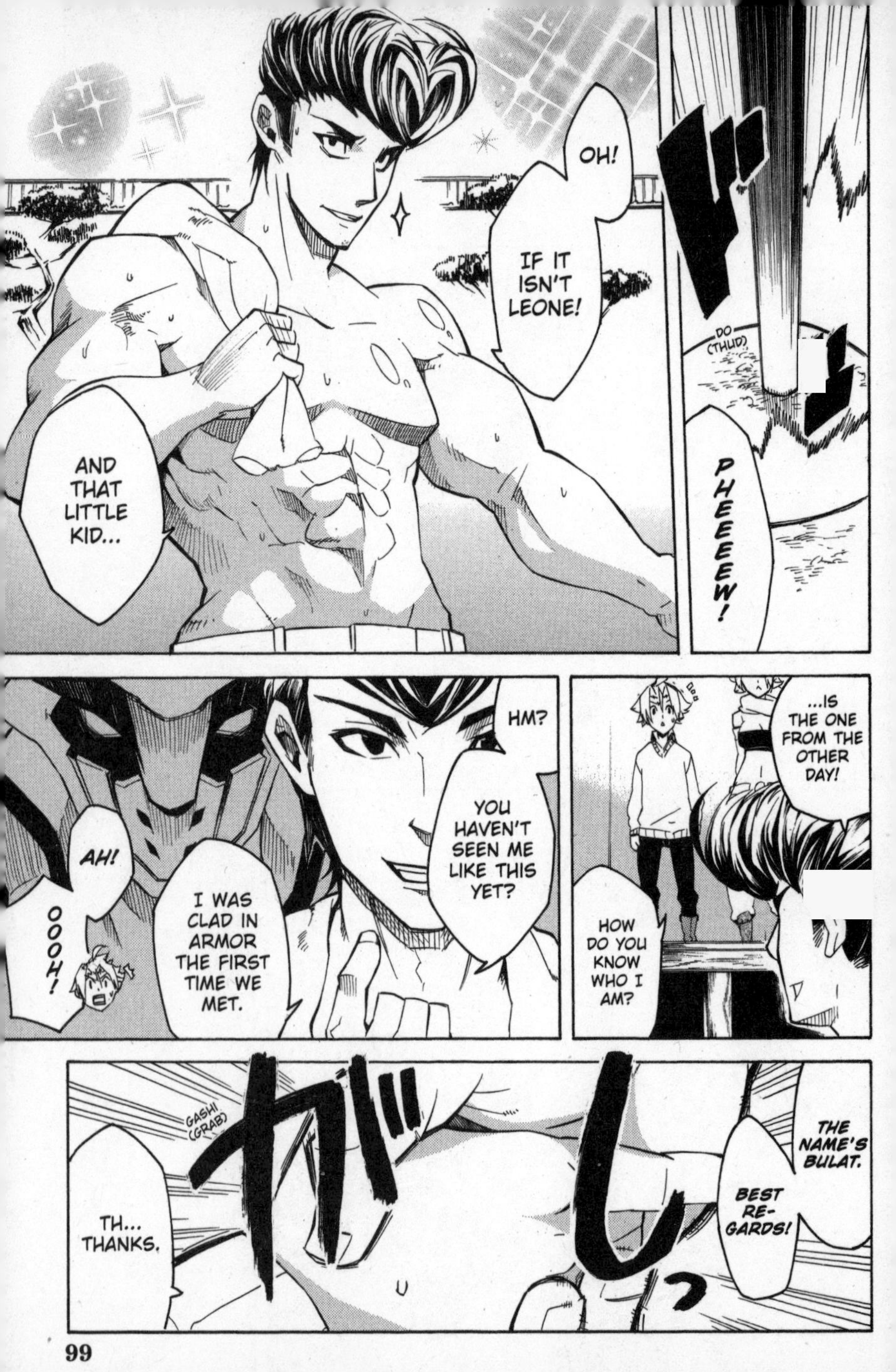
DO (THUD)
PHEEEEEW!
OH!
IF IT ISN'T LEONE!
AND THAT LITTLE KID...
...IS THE ONE FROM THE OTHER DAY!
HOW DO YOU KNOW WHO I AM?
HM?
YOU HAVEN'T SEEN ME LIKE THIS YET?
I WAS CLAD IN ARMOR THE FIRST TIME WE MET.
AH!
OOOH!
THE NAME'S BULAT.
BEST RE-GARDS!
GASHI (GRAB)
TH... THANKS.

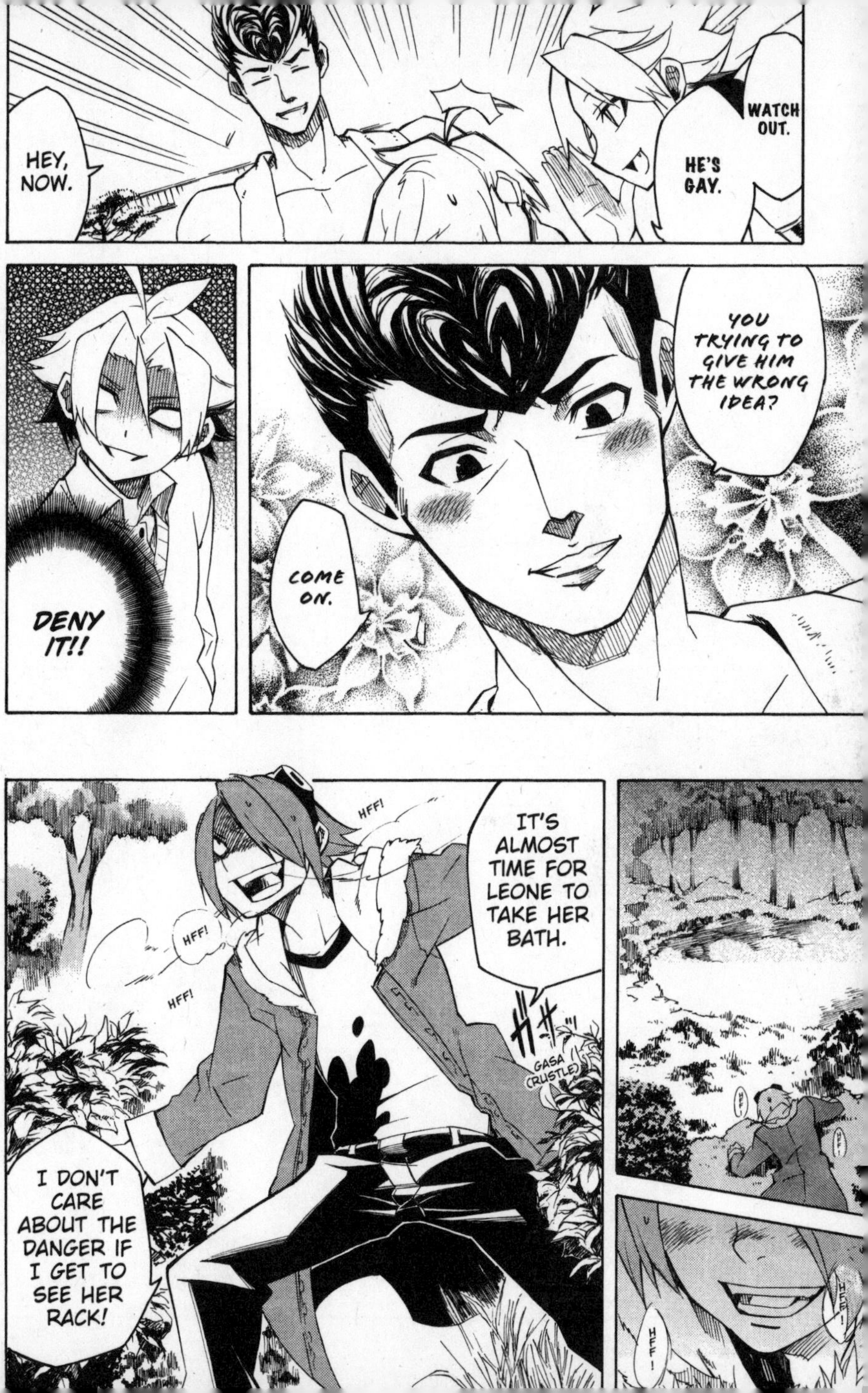
WATCH OUT.
HE'S GAY.
HEY, NOW.
YOU TRYING TO GIVE HIM THE WRONG IDEA?
COME ON.
DENY IT!!
HFF!
HFF!
HFF!
HFF!
IT'S ALMOST TIME FOR LEONE TO TAKE HER BATH.
HFF!
HFF!
HFF!
GASA (RUSTLE)
I DON'T CARE ABOUT THE DANGER IF I GET TO SEE HER RACK!

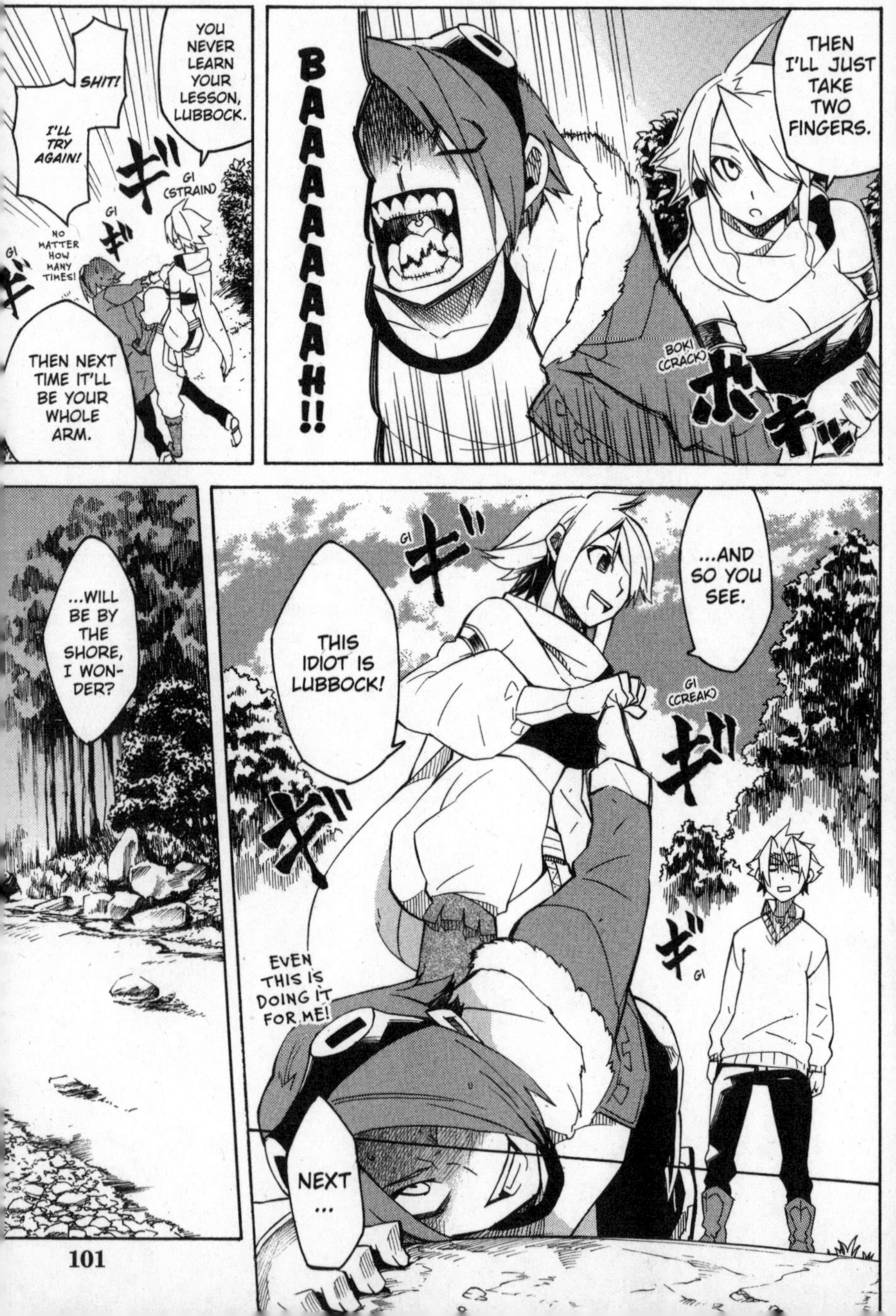
THEN I'LL JUST TAKE TWO FINGERS.
BOKI (CRACK)
BAAAAAAAAAH!!
YOU NEVER LEARN YOUR LESSON, LUBBOCK.
SHIT!
I'LL TRY AGAIN!
GI (STRAIN)
GI
NO MATTER HOW MANY TIMES!
GI
THEN NEXT TIME IT'LL BE YOUR WHOLE ARM.
...AND SO YOU SEE.
THIS IDIOT IS LUBBOCK!
GI
GI (CREAK)
GI
EVEN THIS IS DOING IT FOR ME!
NEXT ...
...WILL BE BY THE SHORE, I WONDER?

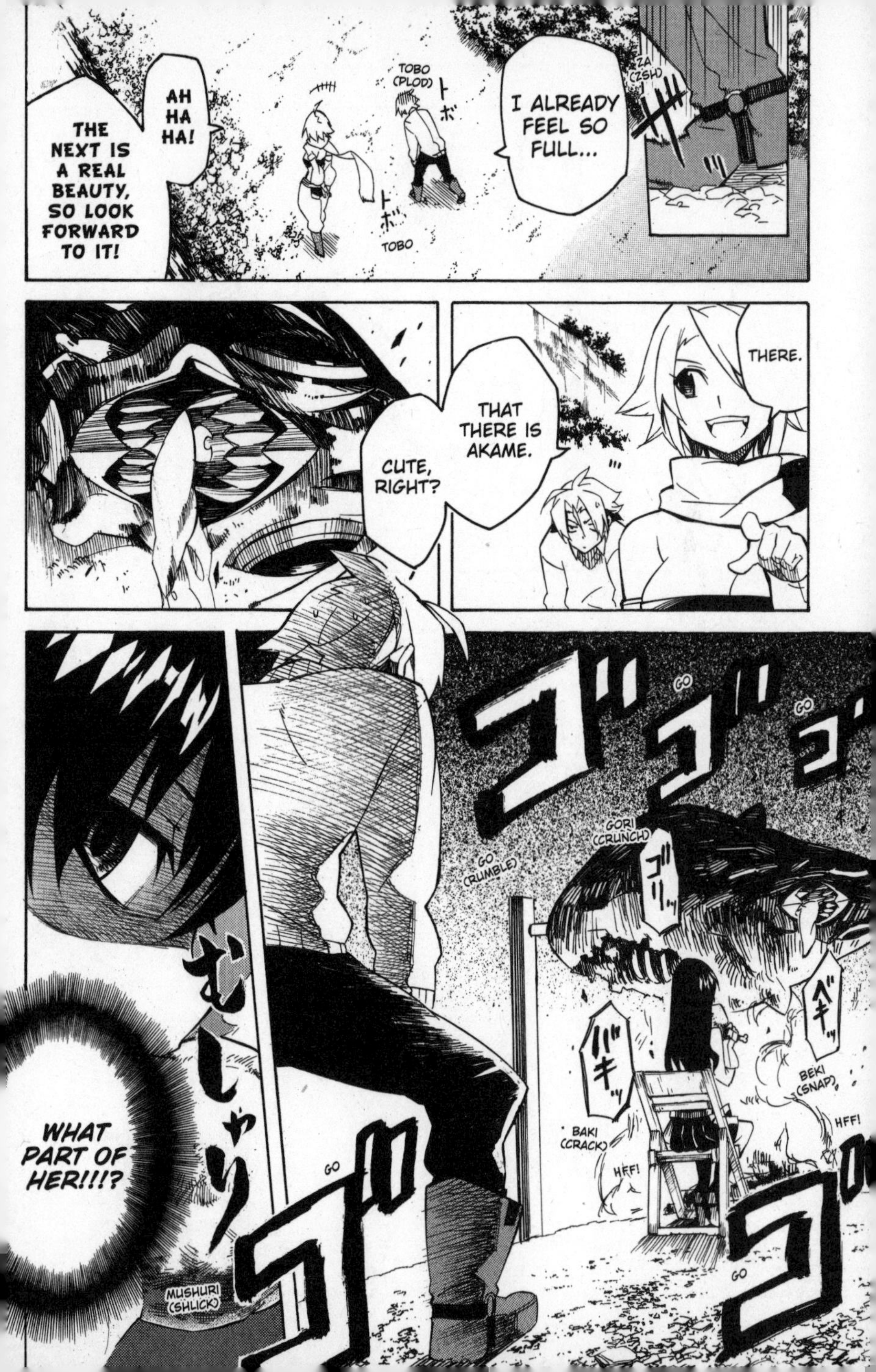
ZA (ZSH)
I ALREADY FEEL SO FULL...
TOBO (PLOD) トボ
トボ TOBO
AH HA HA!
THE NEXT IS A REAL BEAUTY, SO LOOK FORWARD TO IT!
THERE.
THAT THERE IS AKAME.
CUTE, RIGHT?
GO
GO
GORI (CRUNCH) ゴリッ
GO (RUMBLE)
ベキッ
BEKI (SNAP)
HFF!
バキッ
BAKI (CRACK)
HFF!
GO
GO
むしゃり
MUSHURI (SHLICK)
WHAT PART OF HER!!!?

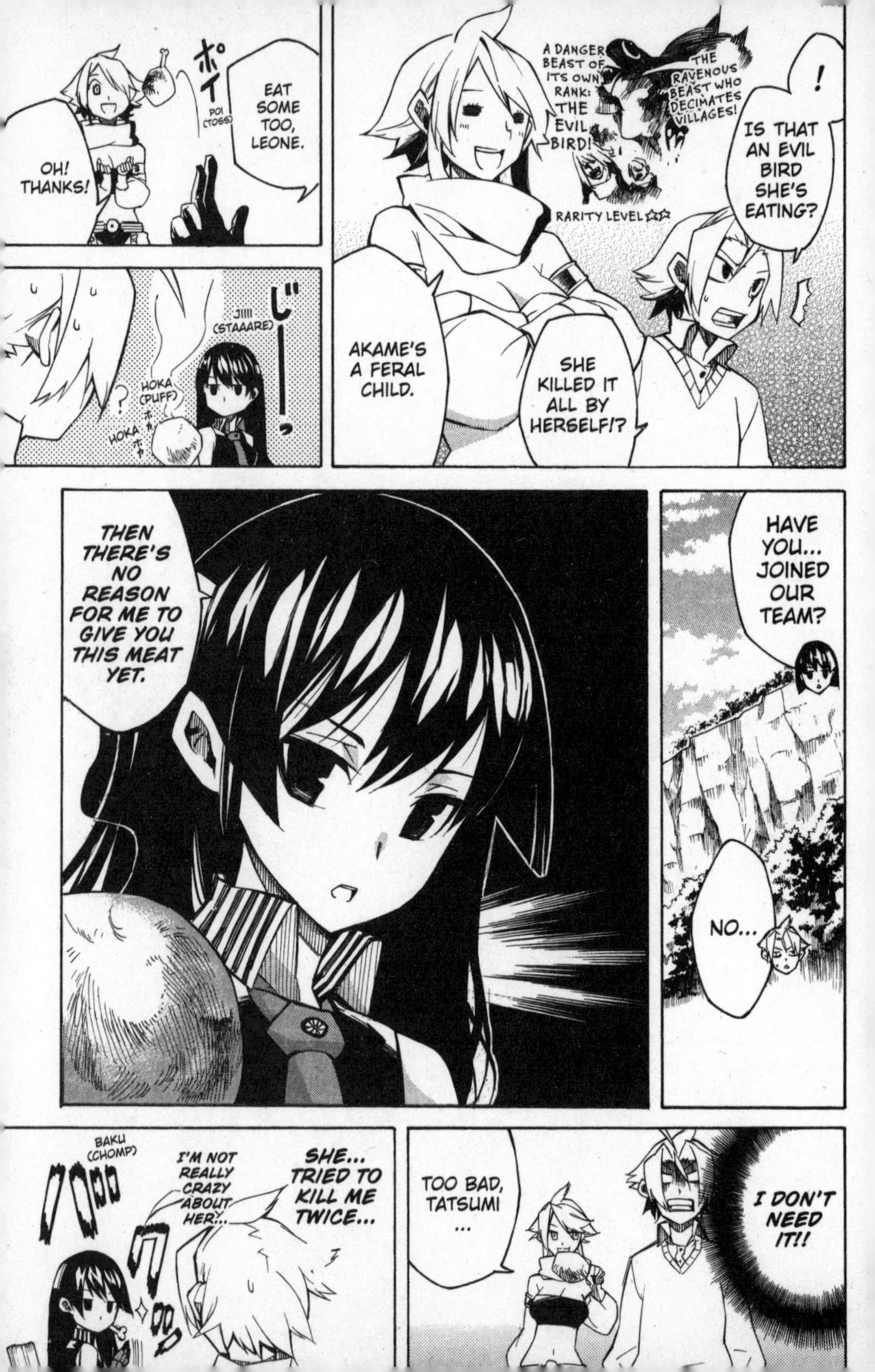
!
IS THAT AN EVIL BIRD SHE'S EATING?
THE RAVENOUS BEAST WHO DECIMATES VILLAGES!
A DANGER BEAST OF ITS OWN RANK: THE EVIL BIRD!
RARITY LEVEL ☆☆
SHE KILLED IT ALL BY HERSELF!?
AKAME'S A FERAL CHILD.
EAT SOME TOO, LEONE.
ポイ
POI (TOSS)
OH! THANKS!
じーっ
JIIII (STAAARE)
HOKA (PUFF)
HOKA
?
HAVE YOU... JOINED OUR TEAM?
NO...
THEN THERE'S NO REASON FOR ME TO GIVE YOU THIS MEAT YET.
I DON'T NEED IT!!
TOO BAD, TATSUMI ...
SHE... TRIED TO KILL ME TWICE...
I'M NOT REALLY CRAZY ABOUT HER...
BAKU (CHOMP)

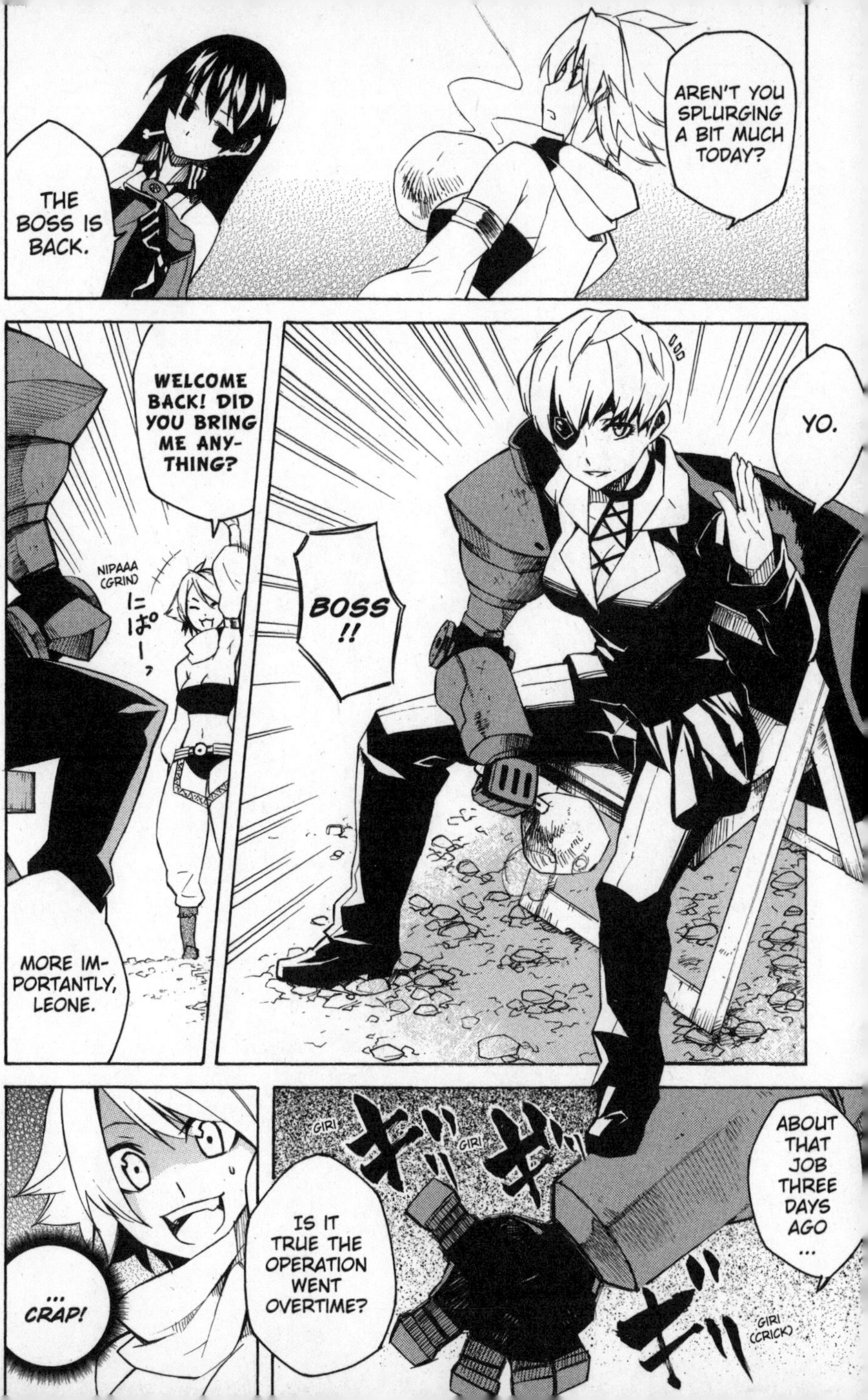
AREN'T YOU SPLURGING A BIT MUCH TODAY?
THE BOSS IS BACK.
YO.
BOSS!!
WELCOME BACK! DID YOU BRING ME ANY-THING?
NIPAAA (GRIN)
にぱー
MORE IM-PORTANTLY, LEONE.
ABOUT THAT JOB THREE DAYS AGO ...
GIRI
ギリ
GIRI
ギリ
IS IT TRUE THE OPERATION WENT OVERTIME?
GIRI (CRICK)
ギリ
... CRAP!

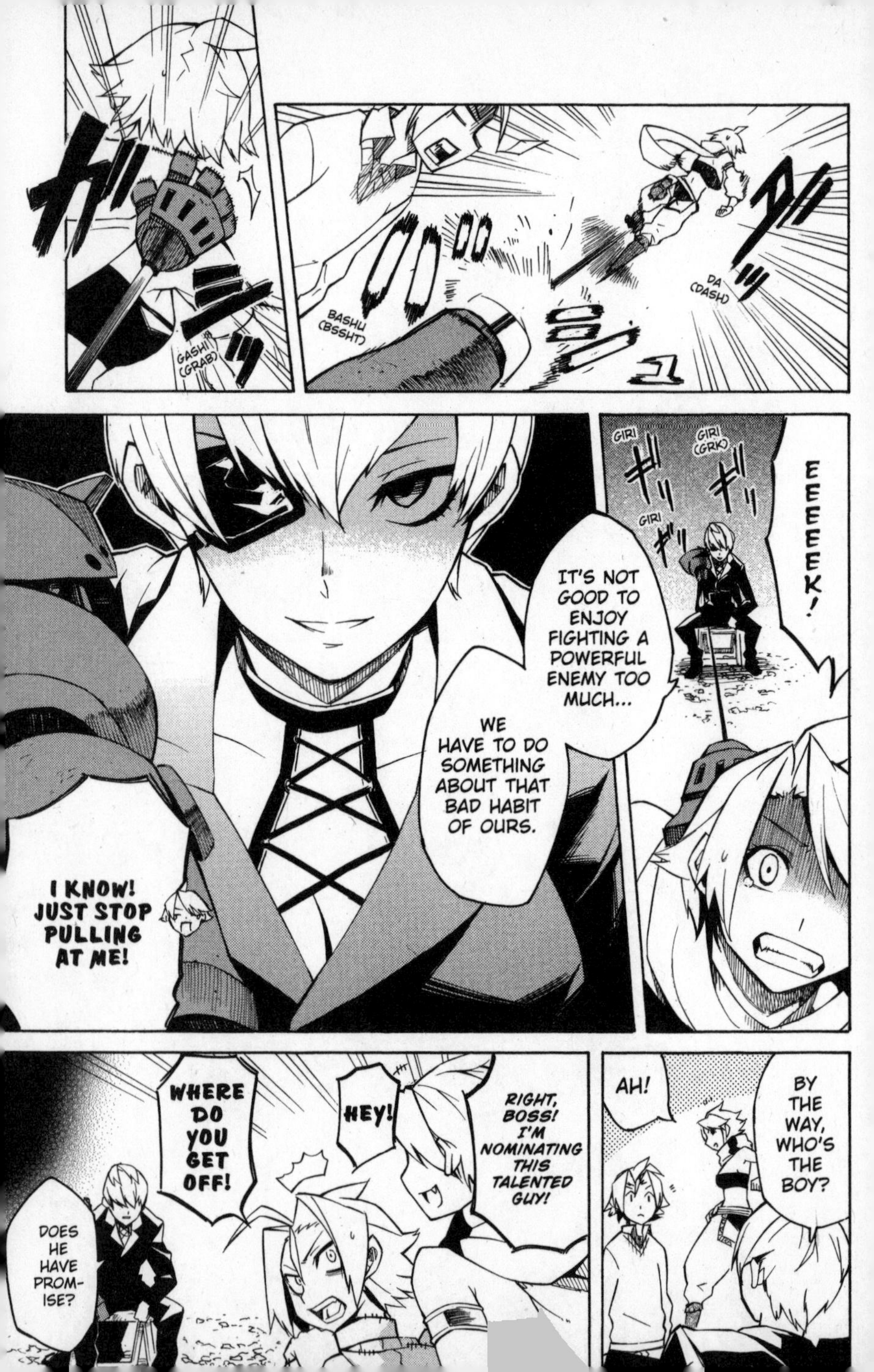
DA (DASH)
BASHU (BSSHT)
GASHI (GRAB)
EEEEEEK!
GIRI (GRK)
GIRI
GIRI
IT'S NOT GOOD TO ENJOY FIGHTING A POWERFUL ENEMY TOO MUCH...
WE HAVE TO DO SOMETHING ABOUT THAT BAD HABIT OF OURS.
I KNOW! JUST STOP PULLING AT ME!
BY THE WAY, WHO'S THE BOY?
AH!
RIGHT, BOSS! I'M NOMINATING THIS TALENTED GUY!
HEY!
WHERE DO YOU GET OFF!
DOES HE HAVE PROM-ISE?

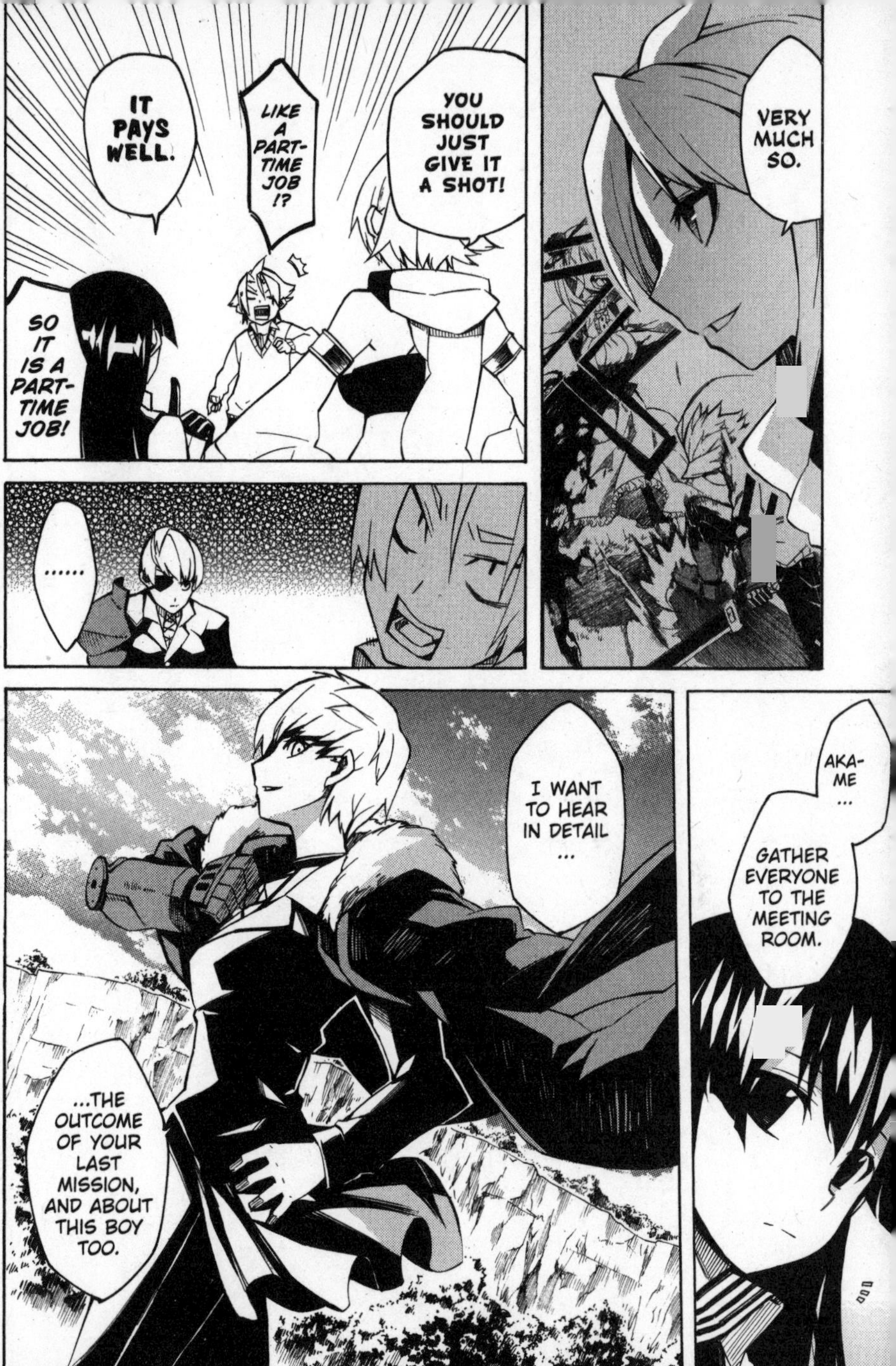
VERY MUCH SO.
YOU SHOULD JUST GIVE IT A SHOT!
LIKE A PART-TIME JOB !?
IT PAYS WELL.
SO IT IS A PART-TIME JOB!
......
AKA-ME ...
GATHER EVERYONE TO THE MEETING ROOM.
I WANT TO HEAR IN DETAIL ...
...THE OUTCOME OF YOUR LAST MISSION, AND ABOUT THIS BOY TOO.

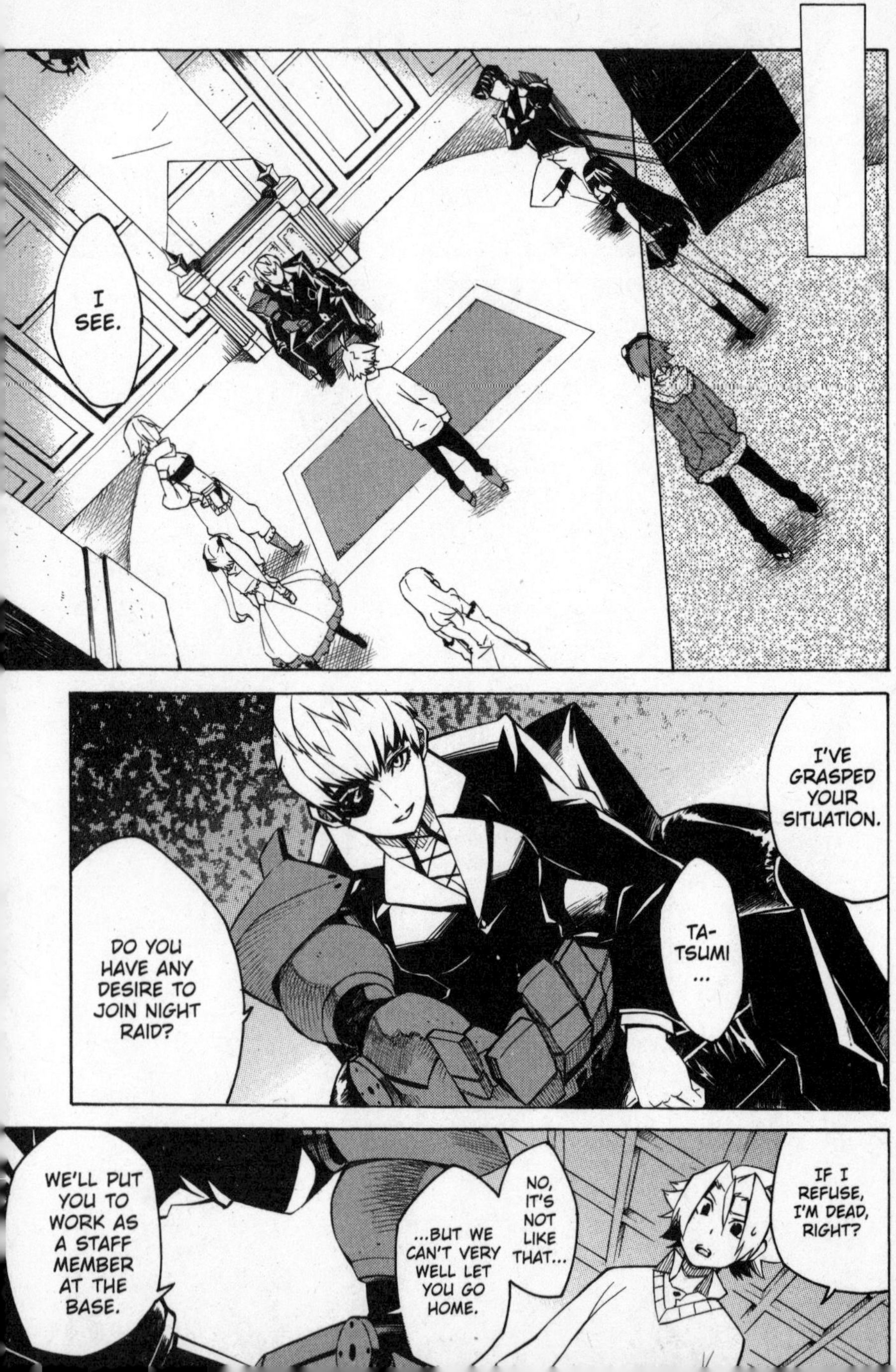
I SEE.
I'VE GRASPED YOUR SITUATION.
TA-TSUMI...
DO YOU HAVE ANY DESIRE TO JOIN NIGHT RAID?
IF I REFUSE, I'M DEAD, RIGHT?
NO, IT'S NOT LIKE THAT...
...BUT WE CAN'T VERY WELL LET YOU GO HOME.
WE'LL PUT YOU TO WORK AS A STAFF MEMBER AT THE BASE.

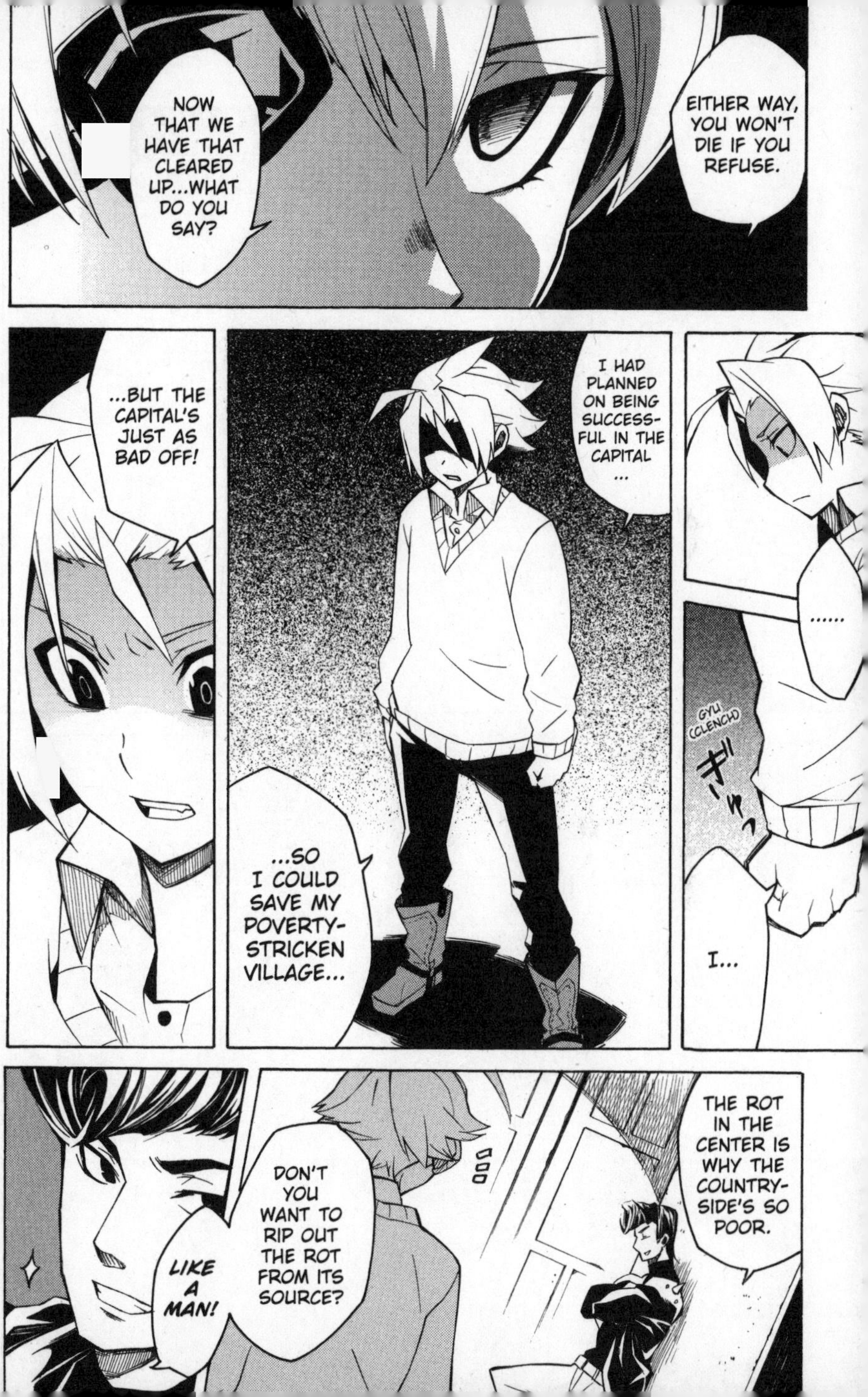
EITHER WAY, YOU WON'T DIE IF YOU REFUSE.
NOW THAT WE HAVE THAT CLEARED UP...WHAT DO YOU SAY?
......
GYU (CLENCH)
I...
I HAD PLANNED ON BEING SUCCESSFUL IN THE CAPITAL ...
...SO I COULD SAVE MY POVERTY-STRICKEN VILLAGE...
...BUT THE CAPITAL'S JUST AS BAD OFF!
THE ROT IN THE CENTER IS WHY THE COUNTRYSIDE'S SO POOR.
DON'T YOU WANT TO RIP OUT THE ROT FROM ITS SOURCE?
LIKE A MAN!

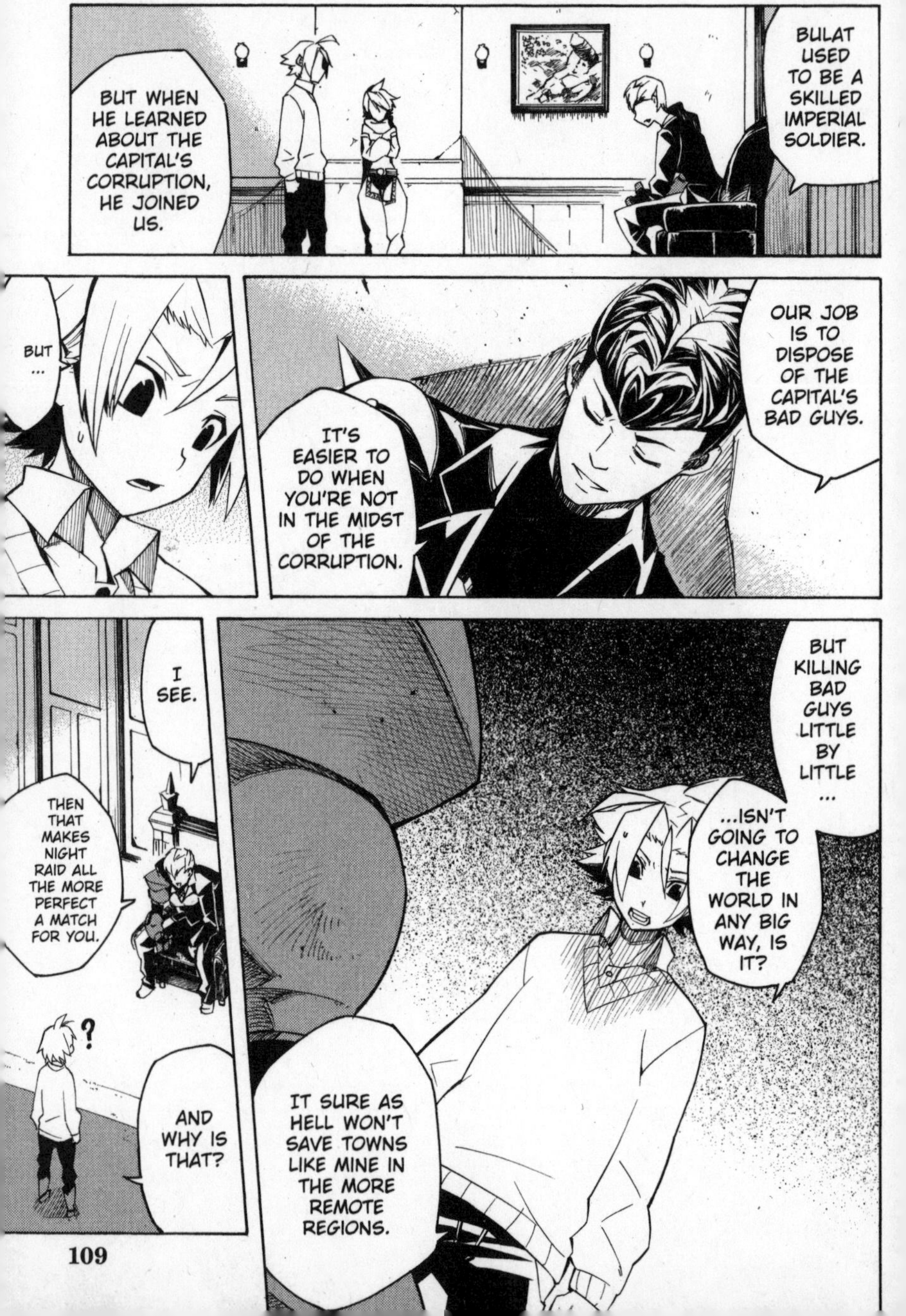
BULAT USED TO BE A SKILLED IMPERIAL SOLDIER.
BUT WHEN HE LEARNED ABOUT THE CAPITAL'S CORRUPTION, HE JOINED US.
OUR JOB IS TO DISPOSE OF THE CAPITAL'S BAD GUYS.
IT'S EASIER TO DO WHEN YOU'RE NOT IN THE MIDST OF THE CORRUPTION.
BUT ...
BUT KILLING BAD GUYS LITTLE BY LITTLE ...
...ISN'T GOING TO CHANGE THE WORLD IN ANY BIG WAY, IS IT?
IT SURE AS HELL WON'T SAVE TOWNS LIKE MINE IN THE MORE REMOTE REGIONS.
I SEE.
THEN THAT MAKES NIGHT RAID ALL THE MORE PERFECT A MATCH FOR YOU.
?
AND WHY IS THAT?

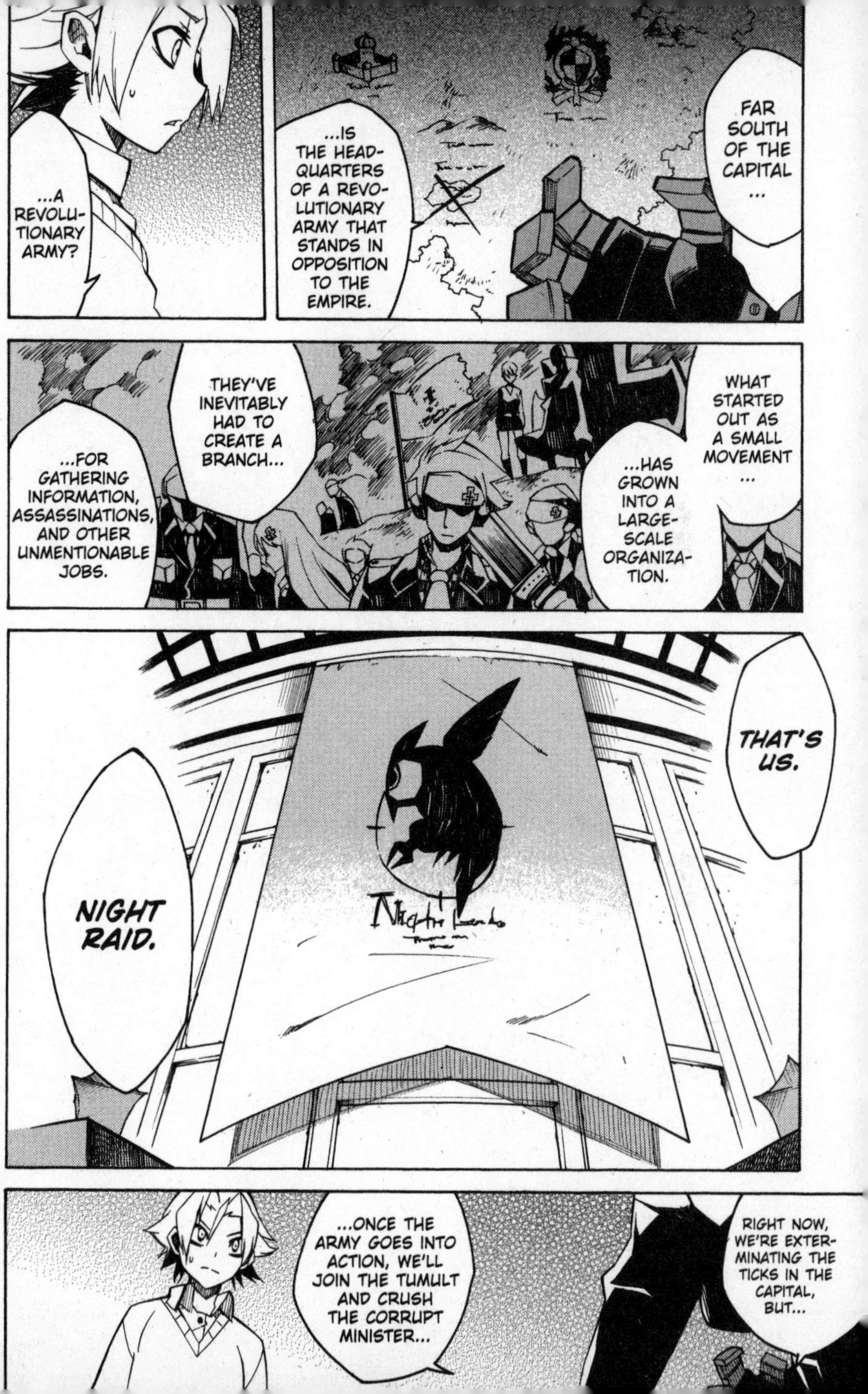

FAR SOUTH OF THE CAPITAL...
...IS THE HEADQUARTERS OF A REVOLUTIONARY ARMY THAT STANDS IN OPPOSITION TO THE EMPIRE.
...A REVOLUTIONARY ARMY?
WHAT STARTED OUT AS A SMALL MOVEMENT...
...HAS GROWN INTO A LARGE-SCALE ORGANIZATION.
THEY'VE INEVITABLY HAD TO CREATE A BRANCH...
...FOR GATHERING INFORMATION, ASSASSINATIONS, AND OTHER UNMENTIONABLE JOBS.
THAT'S US.
NIGHT RAID.
RIGHT NOW, WE'RE EXTERMINATING THE TICKS IN THE CAPITAL, BUT...
...ONCE THE ARMY GOES INTO ACTION, WE'LL JOIN THE TUMULT AND CRUSH THE CORRUPT MINISTER...

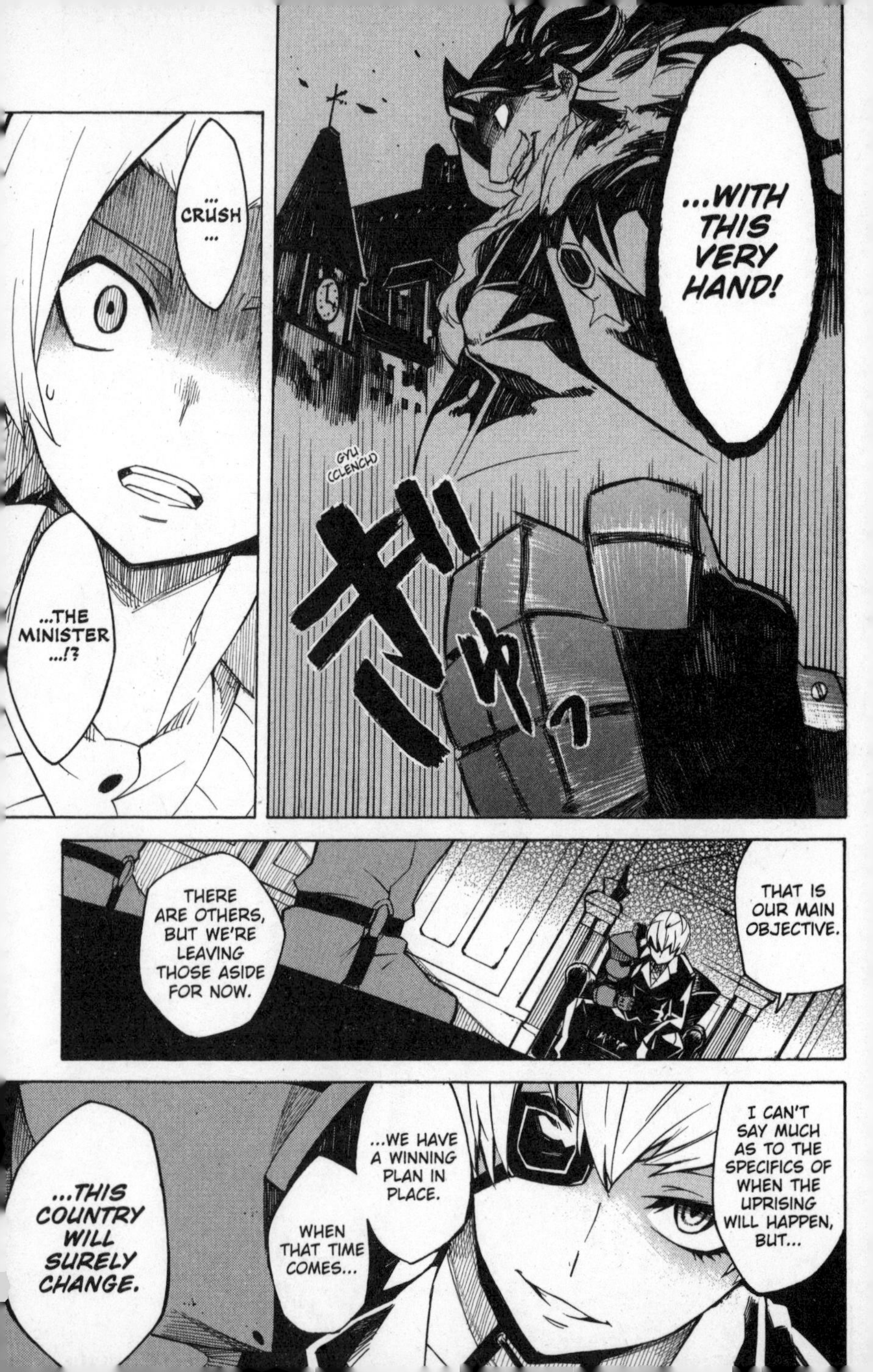
...WITH THIS VERY HAND!
GYU (CLENCH)
...CRUSH...
...THE MINISTER ...!?
THAT IS OUR MAIN OBJECTIVE.
THERE ARE OTHERS, BUT WE'RE LEAVING THOSE ASIDE FOR NOW.
I CAN'T SAY MUCH AS TO THE SPECIFICS OF WHEN THE UPRISING WILL HAPPEN, BUT...
...WE HAVE A WINNING PLAN IN PLACE.
WHEN THAT TIME COMES...
...THIS COUNTRY WILL SURELY CHANGE.

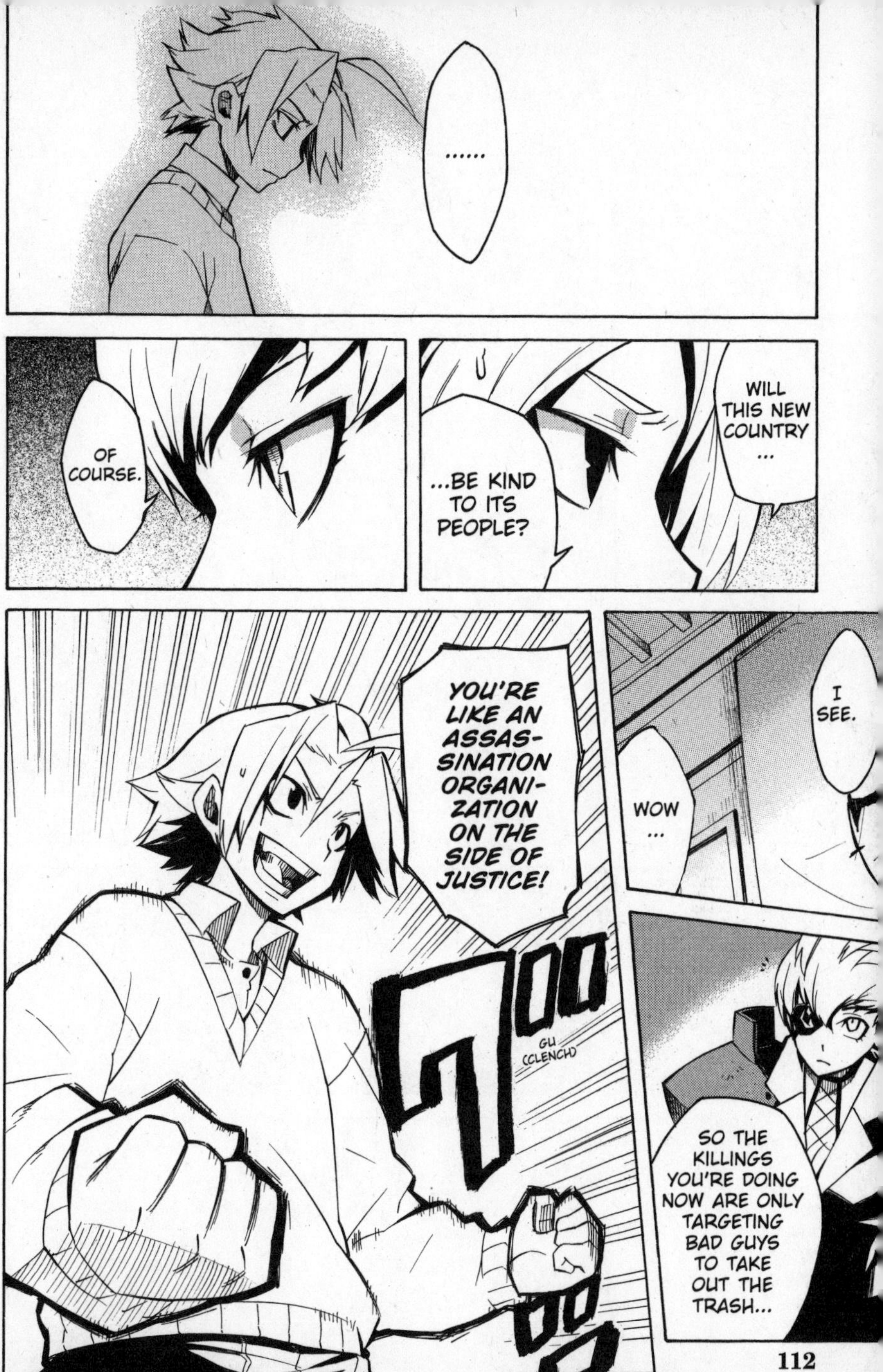
......
WILL THIS NEW COUNTRY ...
...BE KIND TO ITS PEOPLE?
OF COURSE.
I SEE.
WOW ...
SO THE KILLINGS YOU'RE DOING NOW ARE ONLY TARGETING BAD GUYS TO TAKE OUT THE TRASH...
YOU'RE LIKE AN ASSASSINATION ORGANIZATION ON THE SIDE OF JUSTICE!
GU (CLENCH)

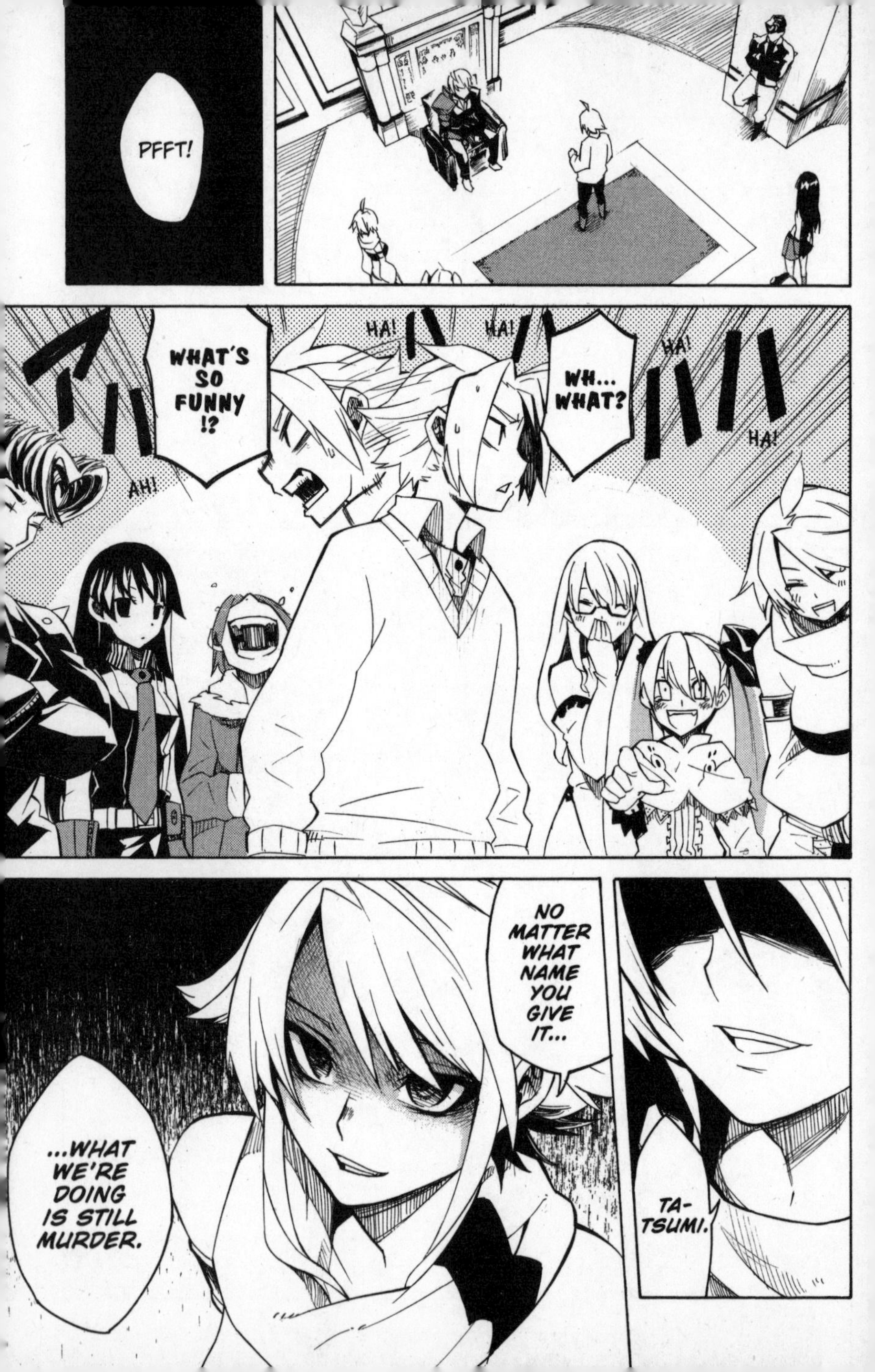
PFFT!
HA!
WH... WHAT?
HA!
HA!
HA!
WHAT'S SO FUNNY!?
AH!
TA-TSUMI.
NO MATTER WHAT NAME YOU GIVE IT...
...WHAT WE'RE DOING IS STILL MURDER.

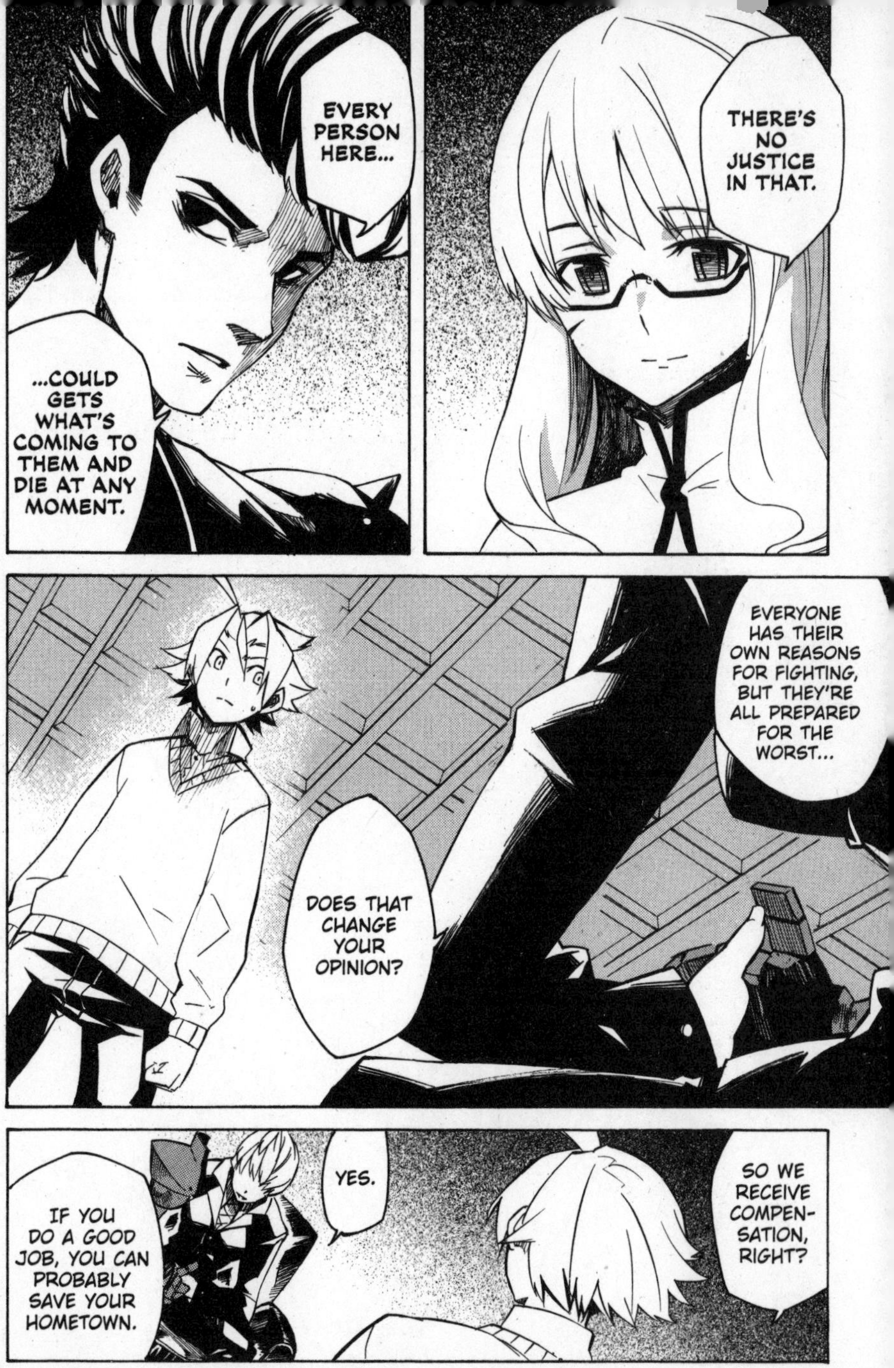
THERE'S NO JUSTICE IN THAT.
EVERY PERSON HERE...
...COULD GETS WHAT'S COMING TO THEM AND DIE AT ANY MOMENT.
EVERYONE HAS THEIR OWN REASONS FOR FIGHTING, BUT THEY'RE ALL PREPARED FOR THE WORST...
DOES THAT CHANGE YOUR OPINION?
SO WE RECEIVE COMPEN-SATION, RIGHT?
YES.
IF YOU DO A GOOD JOB, YOU CAN PROBABLY SAVE YOUR HOMETOWN.

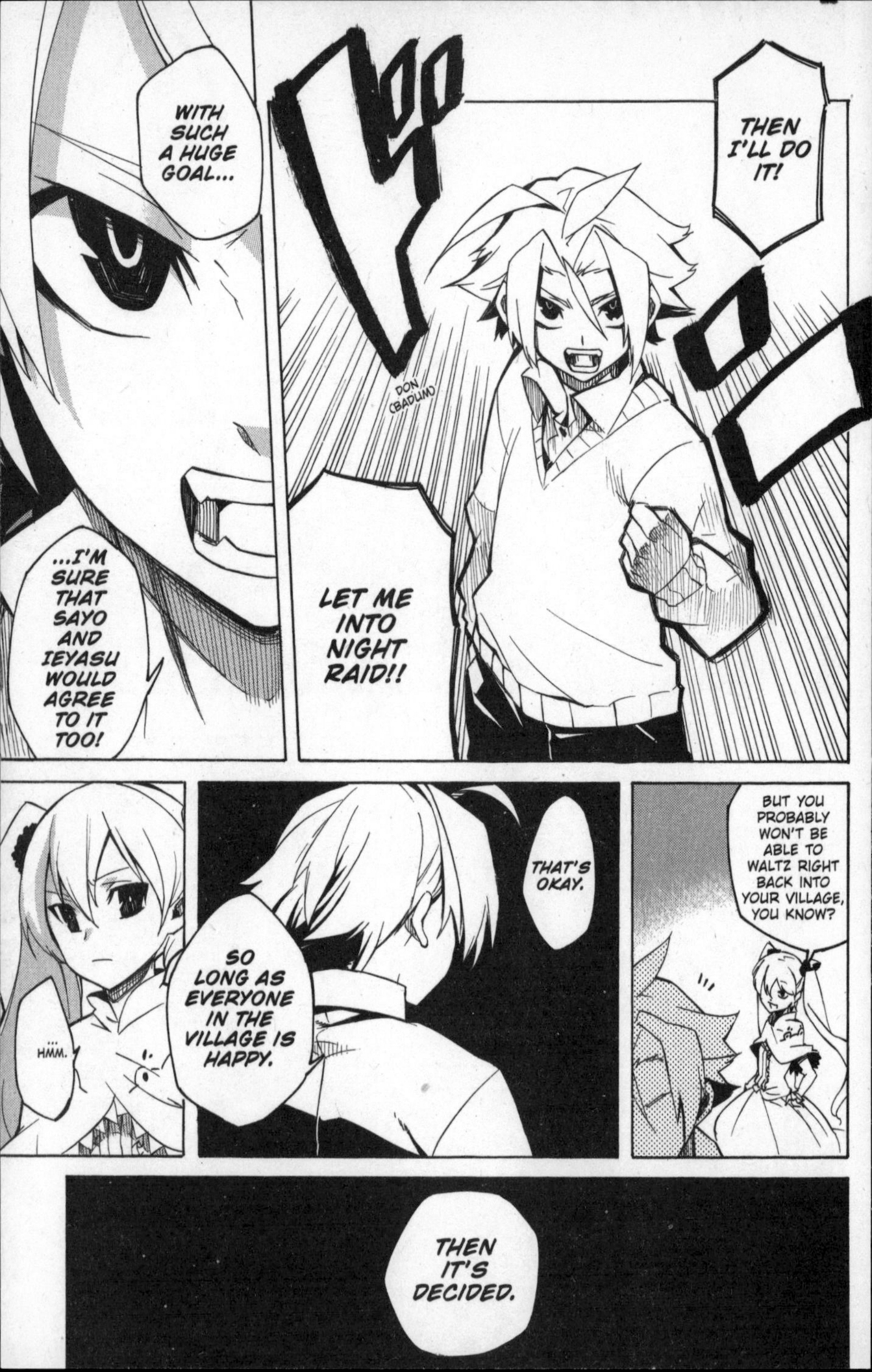
THEN I'LL DO IT!
DON (BADUM)
LET ME INTO NIGHT RAID!!
WITH SUCH A HUGE GOAL...
...I'M SURE THAT SAYO AND IEYASU WOULD AGREE TO IT TOO!
BUT YOU PROBABLY WON'T BE ABLE TO WALTZ RIGHT BACK INTO YOUR VILLAGE, YOU KNOW?
THAT'S OKAY.
SO LONG AS EVERYONE IN THE VILLAGE IS HAPPY.
...HMM.
THEN IT'S DECIDED.

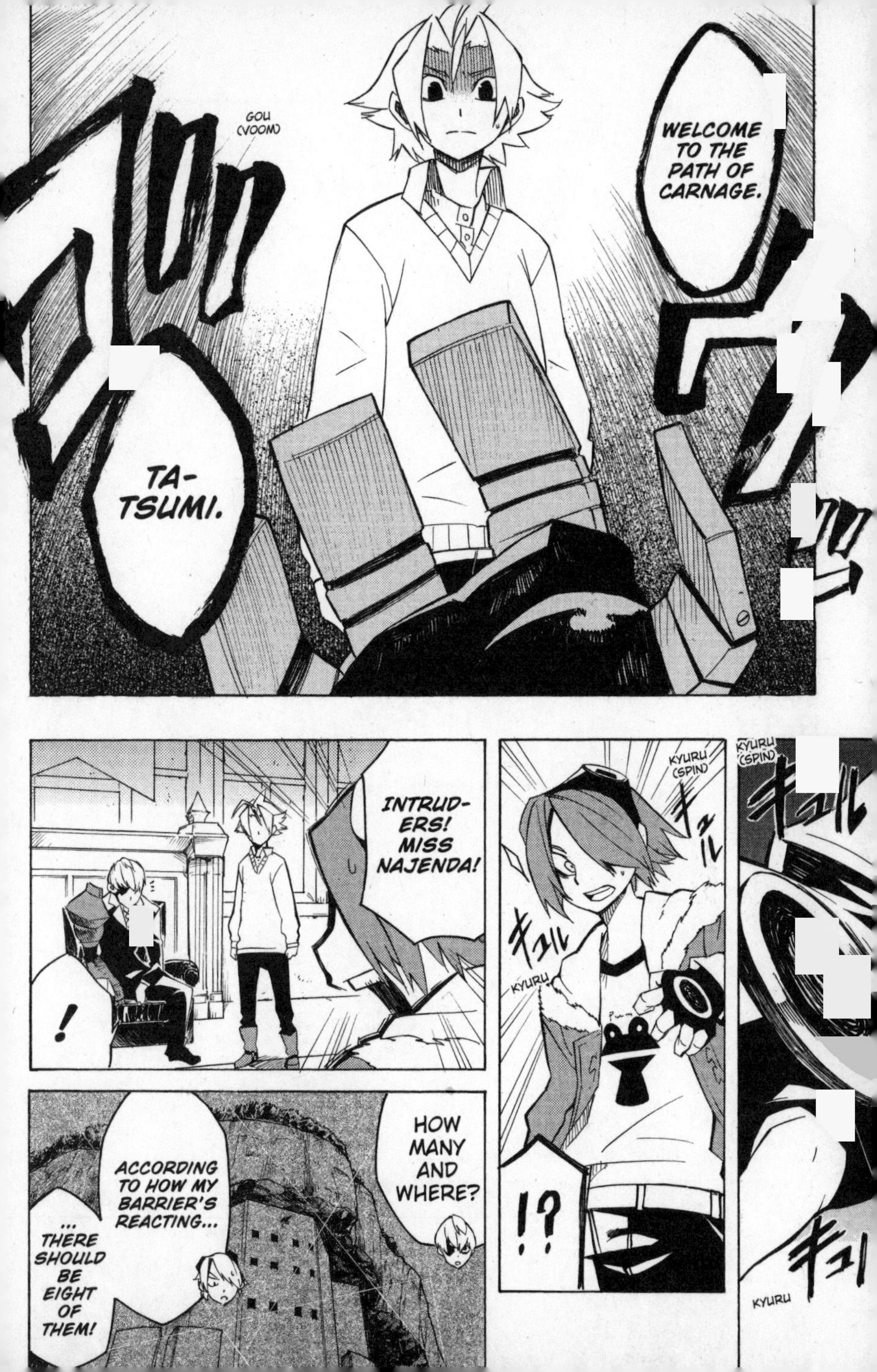
WELCOME TO THE PATH OF CARNAGE.
GOU (VOOM)
TA-TSUMI.
KYURU (SPIN)
KYURU
KYURU (SPIN)
KYURU
!?
INTRUD-ERS! MISS NAJENDA!
!
HOW MANY AND WHERE?
ACCORDING TO HOW MY BARRIER'S REACTING...
... THERE SHOULD BE EIGHT OF THEM!

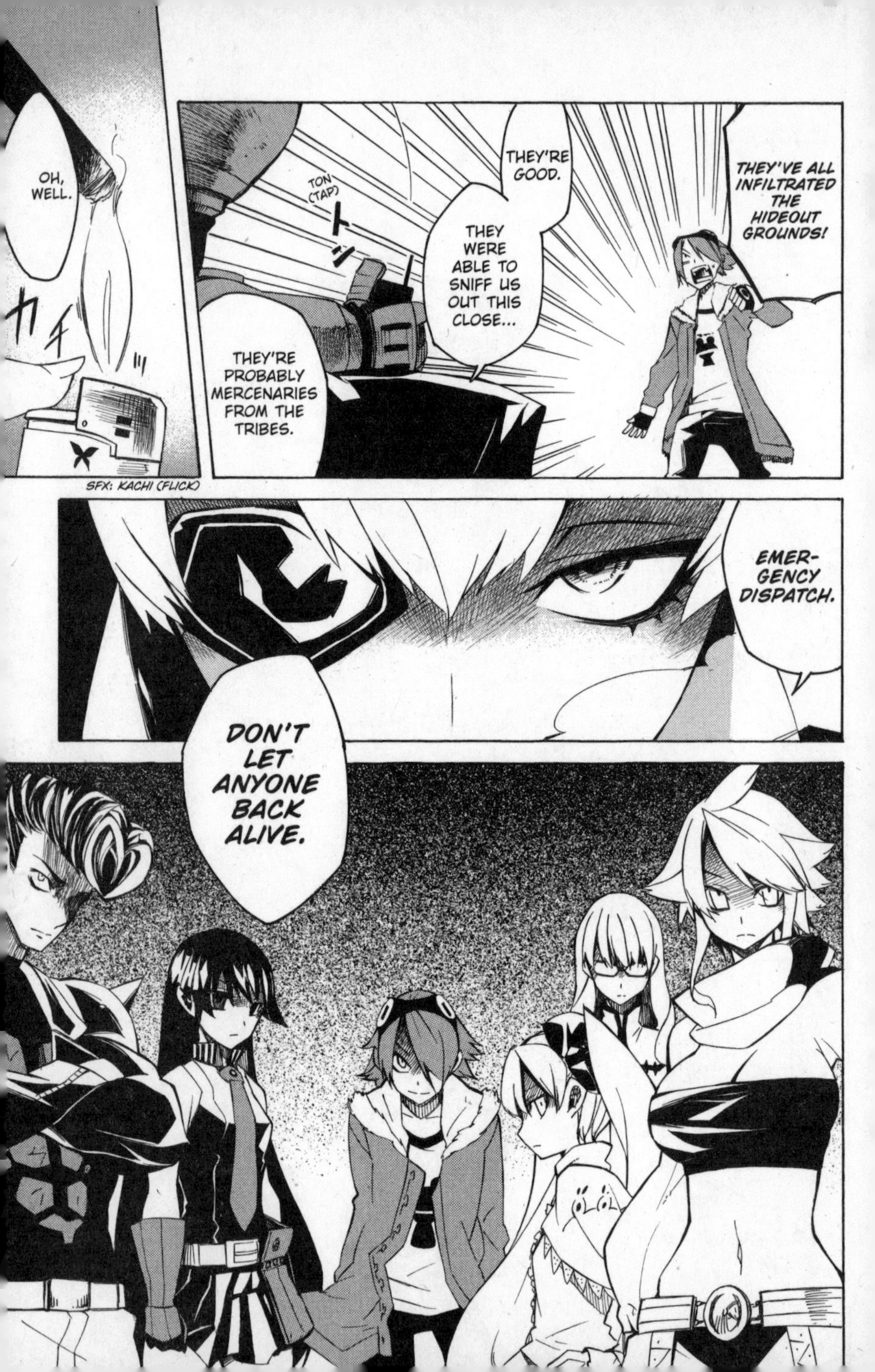
THEY'VE ALL INFILTRATED THE HIDEOUT GROUNDS!
THEY'RE GOOD.
THEY WERE ABLE TO SNIFF US OUT THIS CLOSE...
TON (TAP)
THEY'RE PROBABLY MERCENARIES FROM THE TRIBES.
OH, WELL.
SFX: KACHI (FLICK)
EMERGENCY DISPATCH.
DON'T LET ANYONE BACK ALIVE.

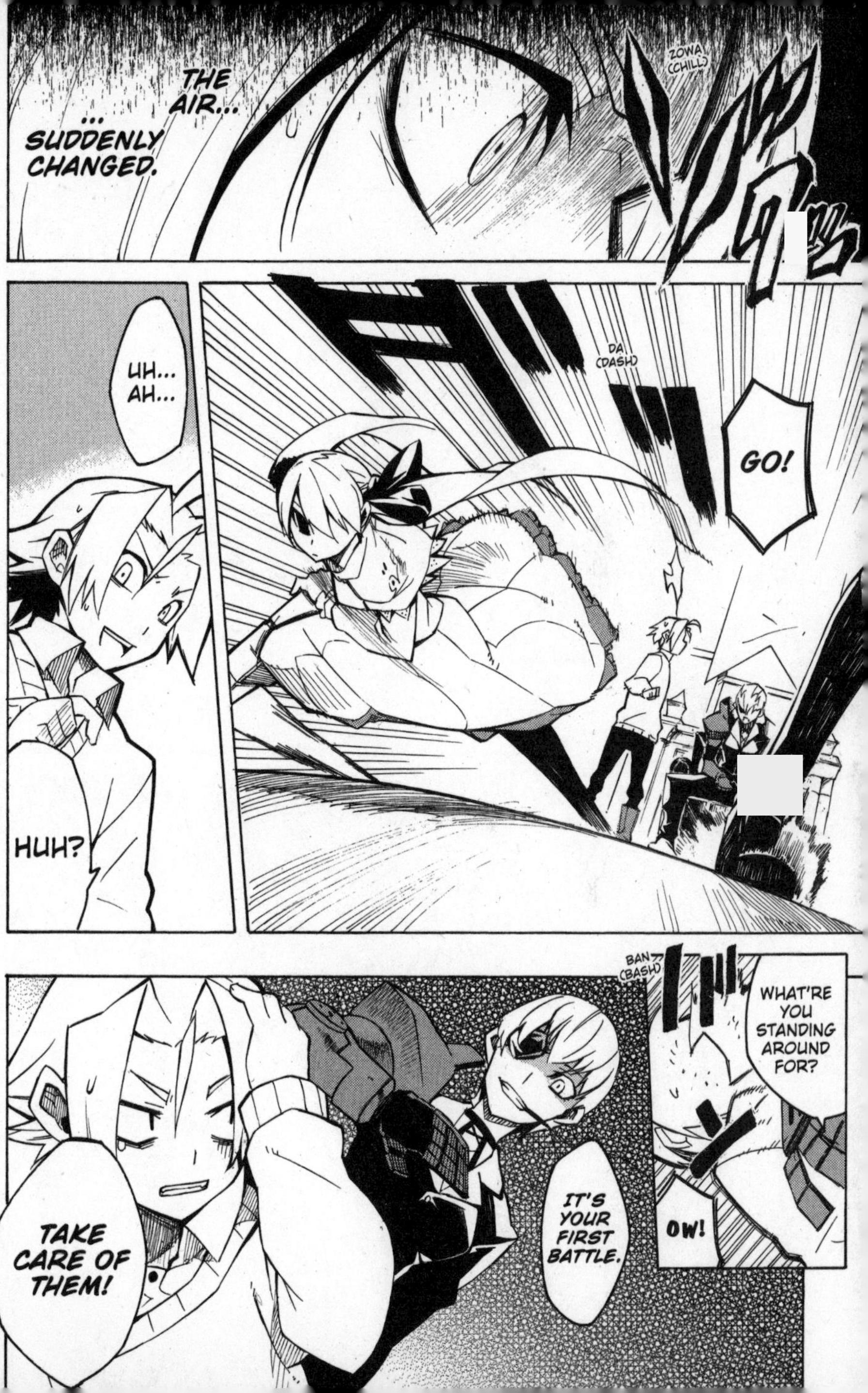
ZOWA (CHILL)
THE AIR...
... SUDDENLY CHANGED.
DA (DASH)
GO!
UH... AH...
HUH?
BAN (BASH)
WHAT'RE YOU STANDING AROUND FOR?
OW!
IT'S YOUR FIRST BATTLE.
TAKE CARE OF THEM!

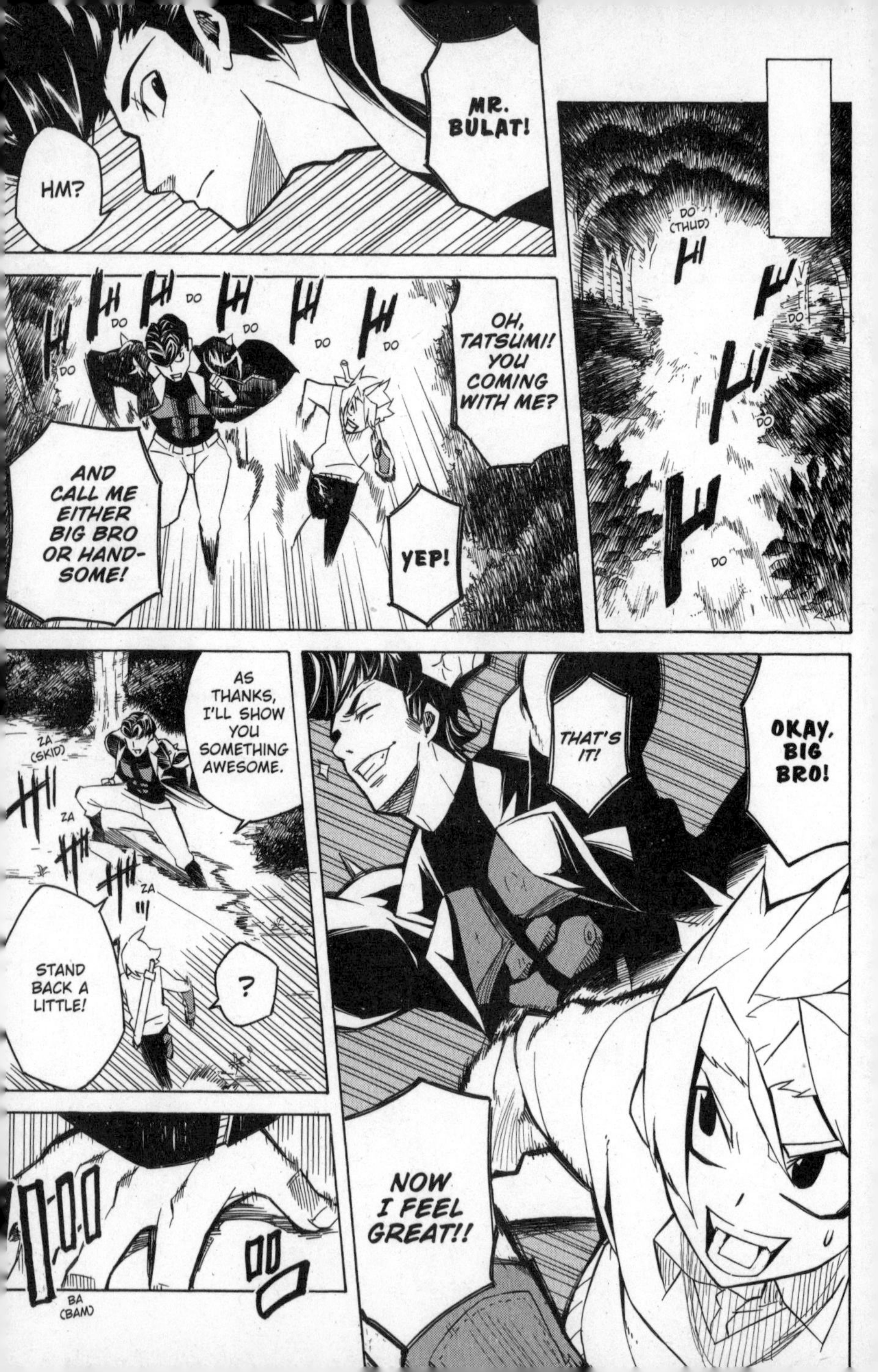
DO (THUD)
DO
DO
DO
MR. BULAT!
HM?
DO
DO
DO
DO
DO
DO
OH, TATSUMI! YOU COMING WITH ME?
YEP!
AND CALL ME EITHER BIG BRO OR HAND-SOME!
OKAY, BIG BRO!
THAT'S IT!
NOW I FEEL GREAT!!
AS THANKS, I'LL SHOW YOU SOMETHING AWESOME.
ZA (SKID)
ZA
ZA
STAND BACK A LITTLE!
?
BA (BAM)

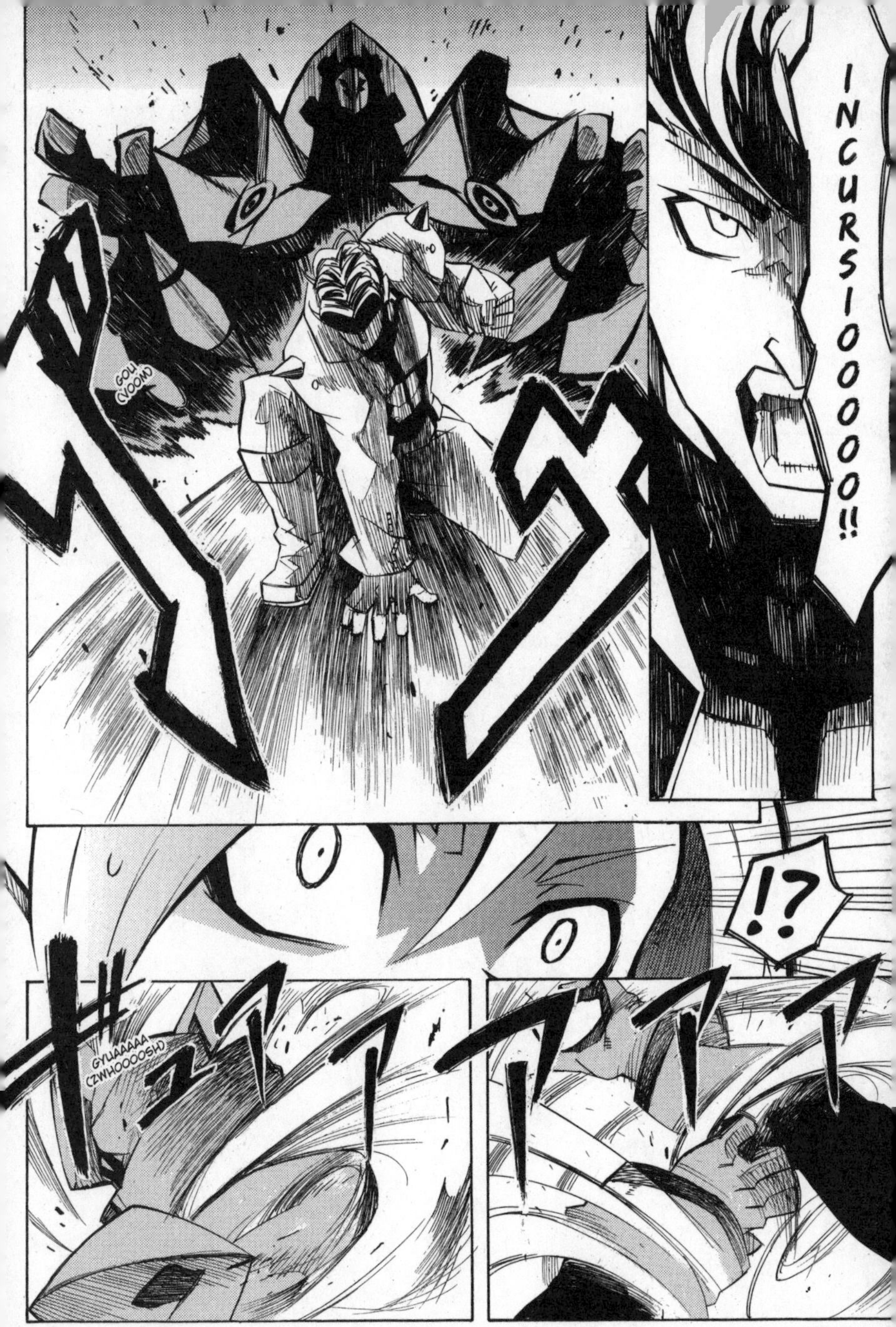
INCURSIOOOOOO!!
GOU (VOOM)
!?
GYUAAAAA (ZWHOOOOSH)

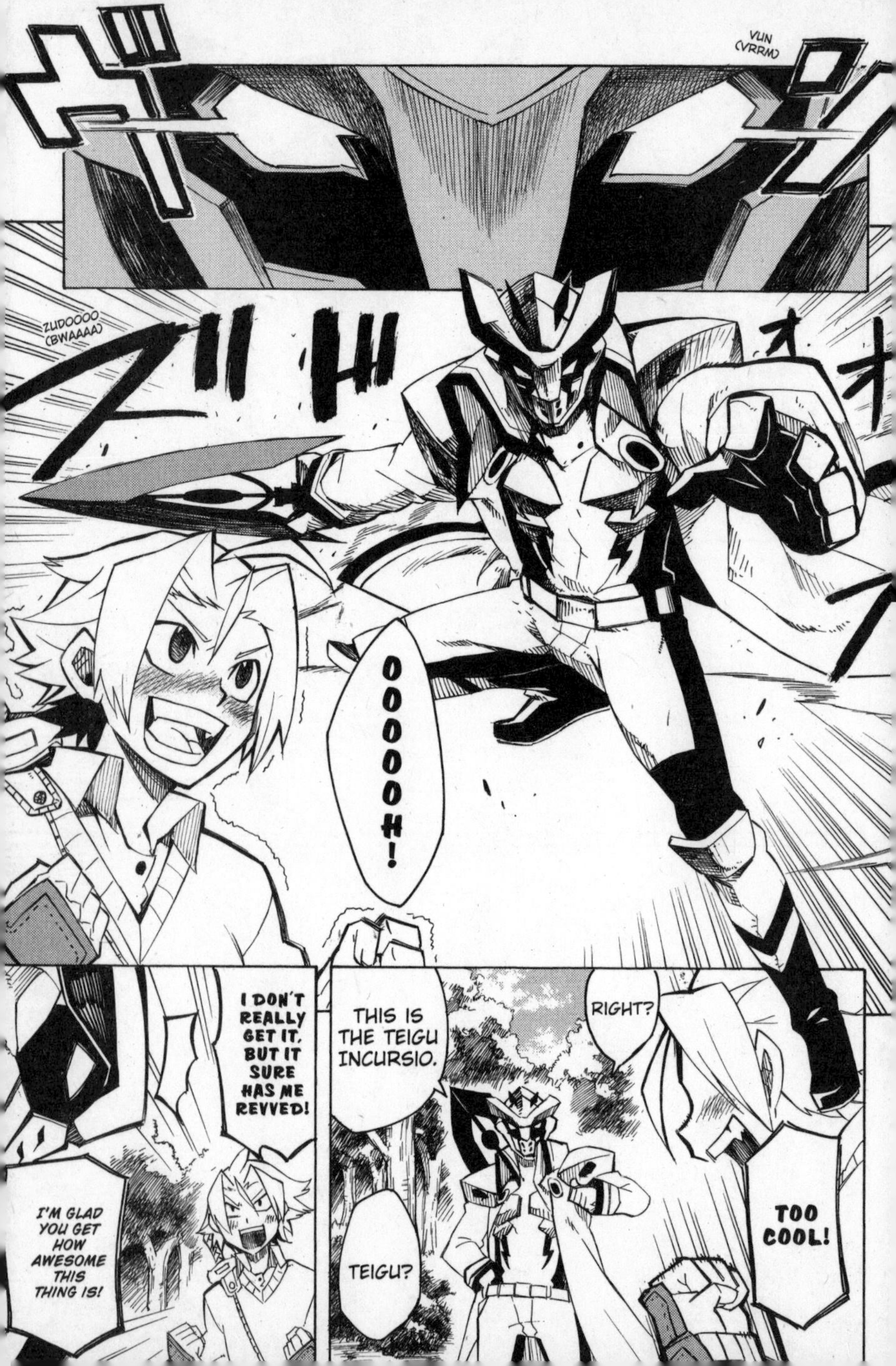
VUN (VRRM)
ZUDOOOO (BWAAAA)
OOOOOOH!
RIGHT?
THIS IS THE TEIGU INCURSIO.
TOO COOL!
TEIGU?
I DON'T REALLY GET IT, BUT IT SURE HAS ME REVVED!
I'M GLAD YOU GET HOW AWESOME THIS THING IS!

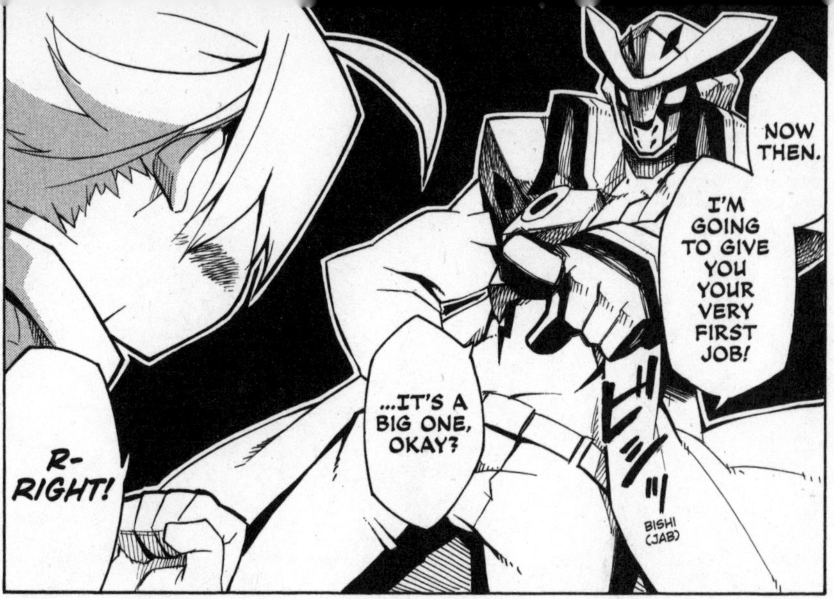
NOW THEN.
I'M GOING TO GIVE YOU YOUR VERY FIRST JOB!
BISHI (JAB)
...IT'S A BIG ONE, OKAY?
R-RIGHT!
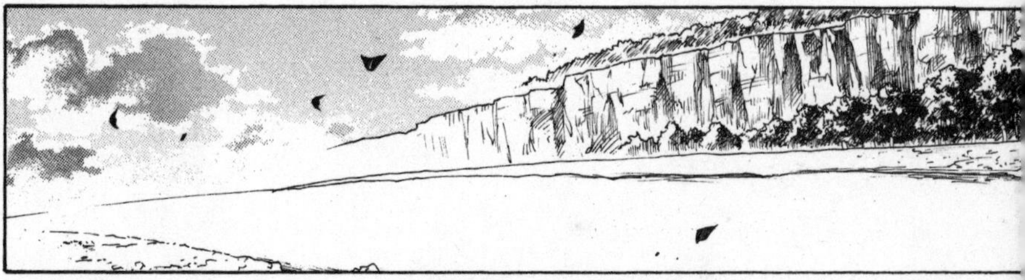
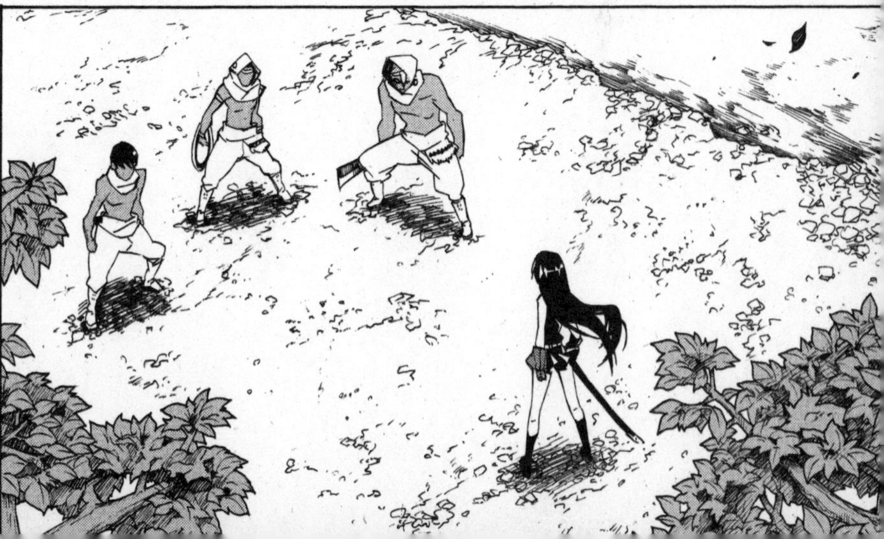

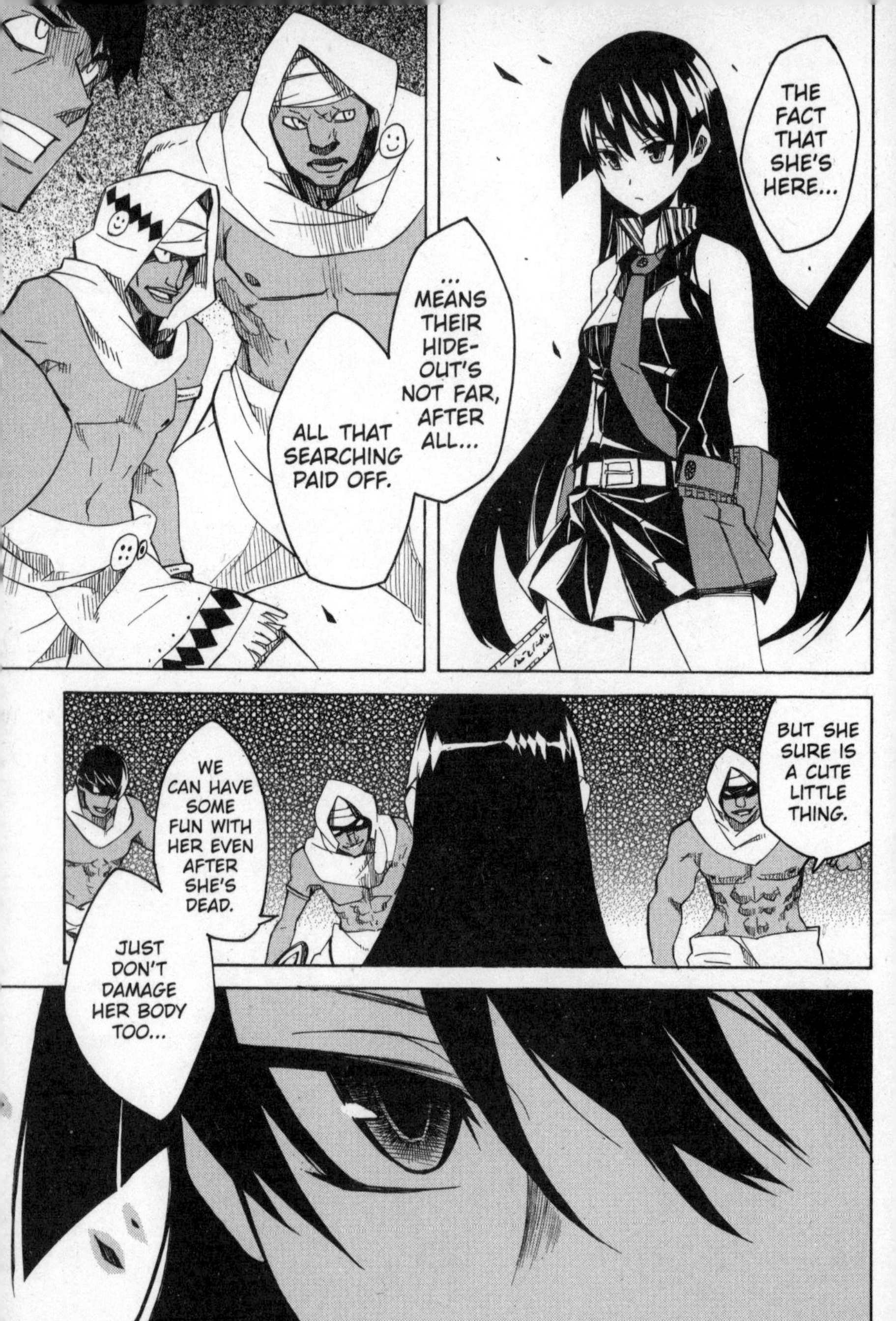
THE FACT THAT SHE'S HERE...
... MEANS THEIR HIDE-OUT'S NOT FAR, AFTER ALL...
ALL THAT SEARCHING PAID OFF.
BUT SHE SURE IS A CUTE LITTLE THING.
WE CAN HAVE SOME FUN WITH HER EVEN AFTER SHE'S DEAD.
JUST DON'T DAMAGE HER BODY TOO...

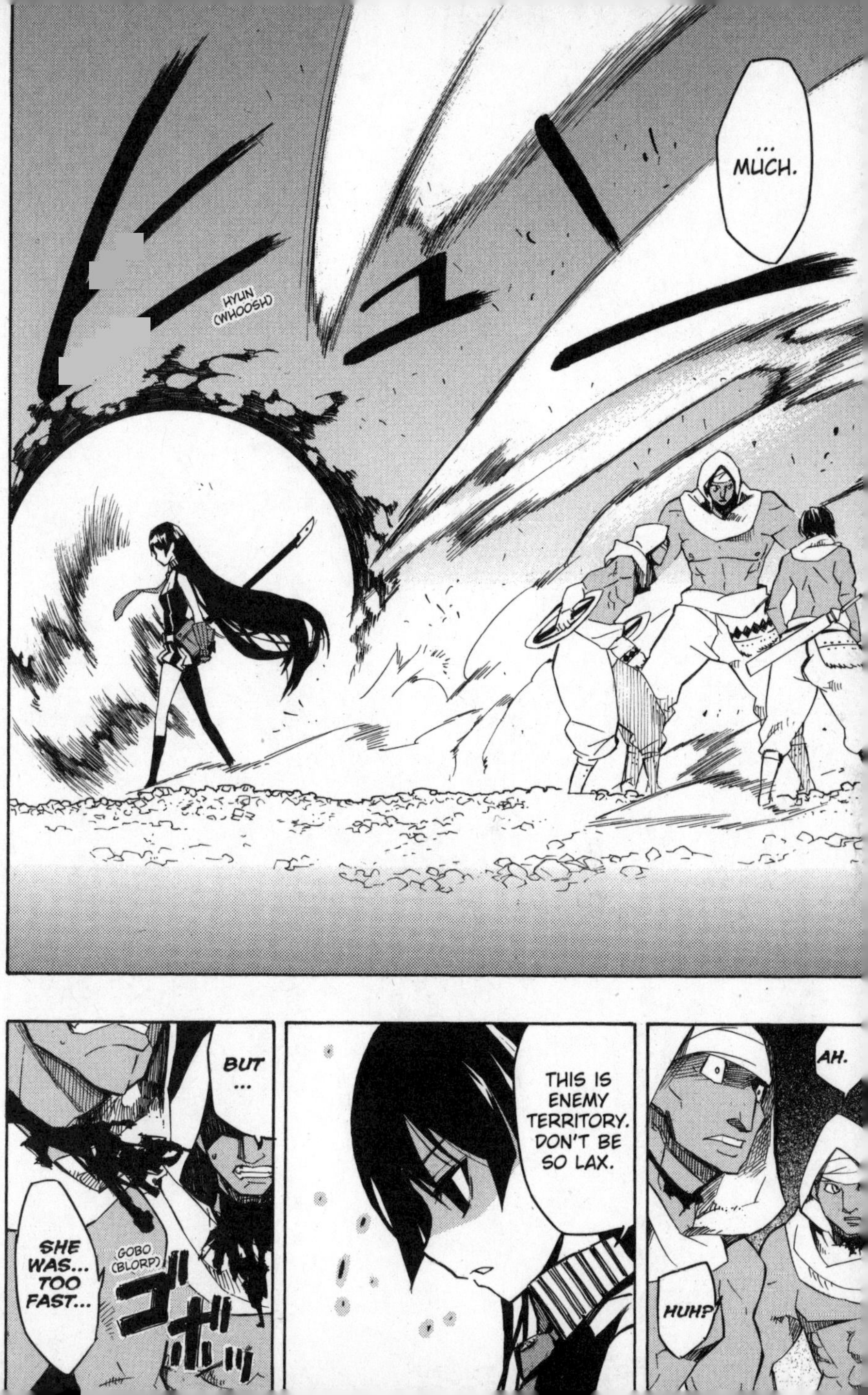

... MUCH.
HYUN (WHOOSH)
AH.
HUH?
THIS IS ENEMY TERRITORY. DON'T BE SO LAX.
BUT ...
SHE WAS... TOO FAST...
GOBO (BLORP)

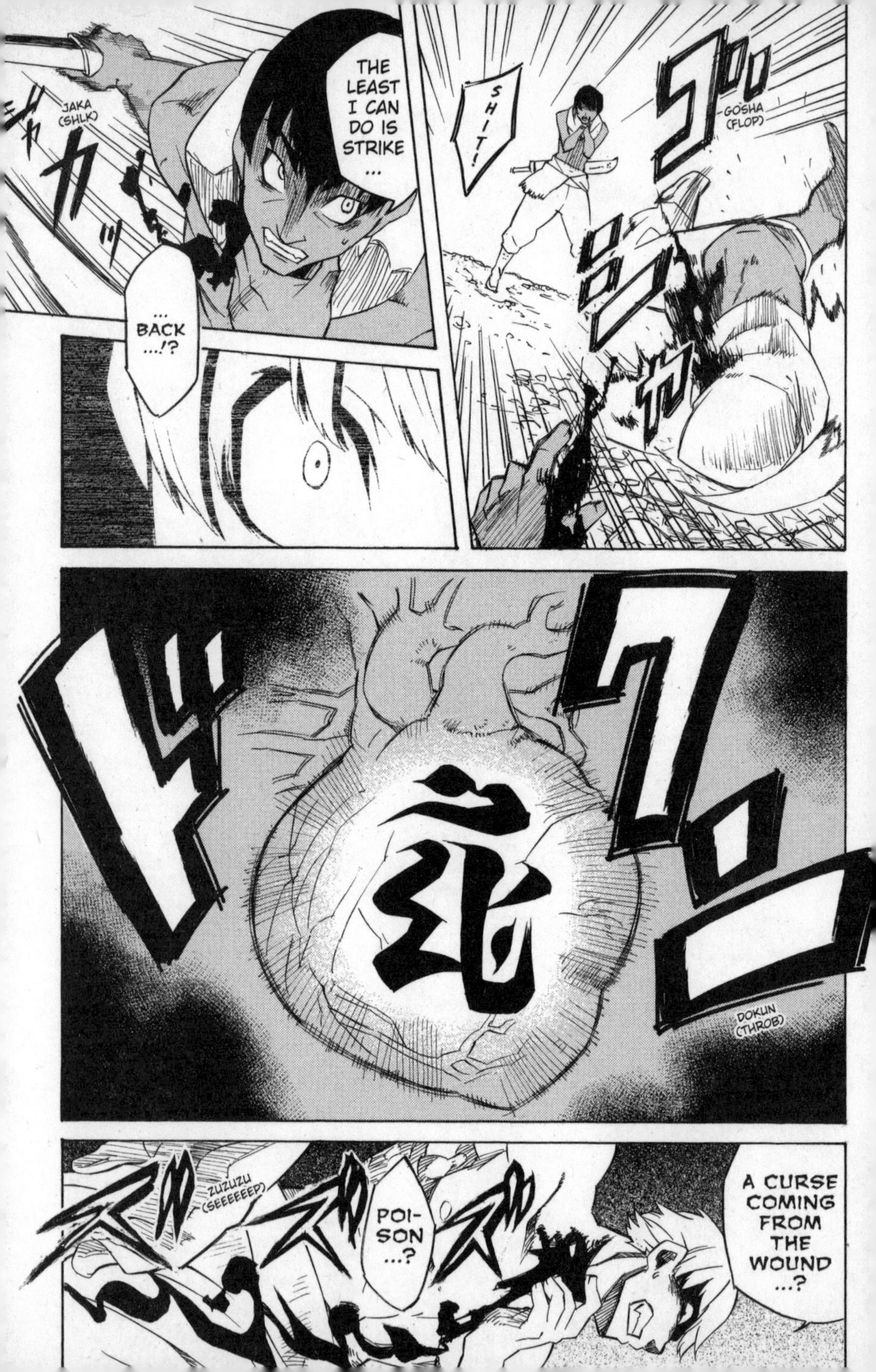
GOSHA (FLOP)
SHIT...!
THE LEAST I CAN DO IS STRIKE ...
JAKA (SHLK)
... BACK ...!?
DOKUN (THROB)
A CURSE COMING FROM THE WOUND ...?
POI-SON ...?
ZUZUZU (SEEEEEEP)

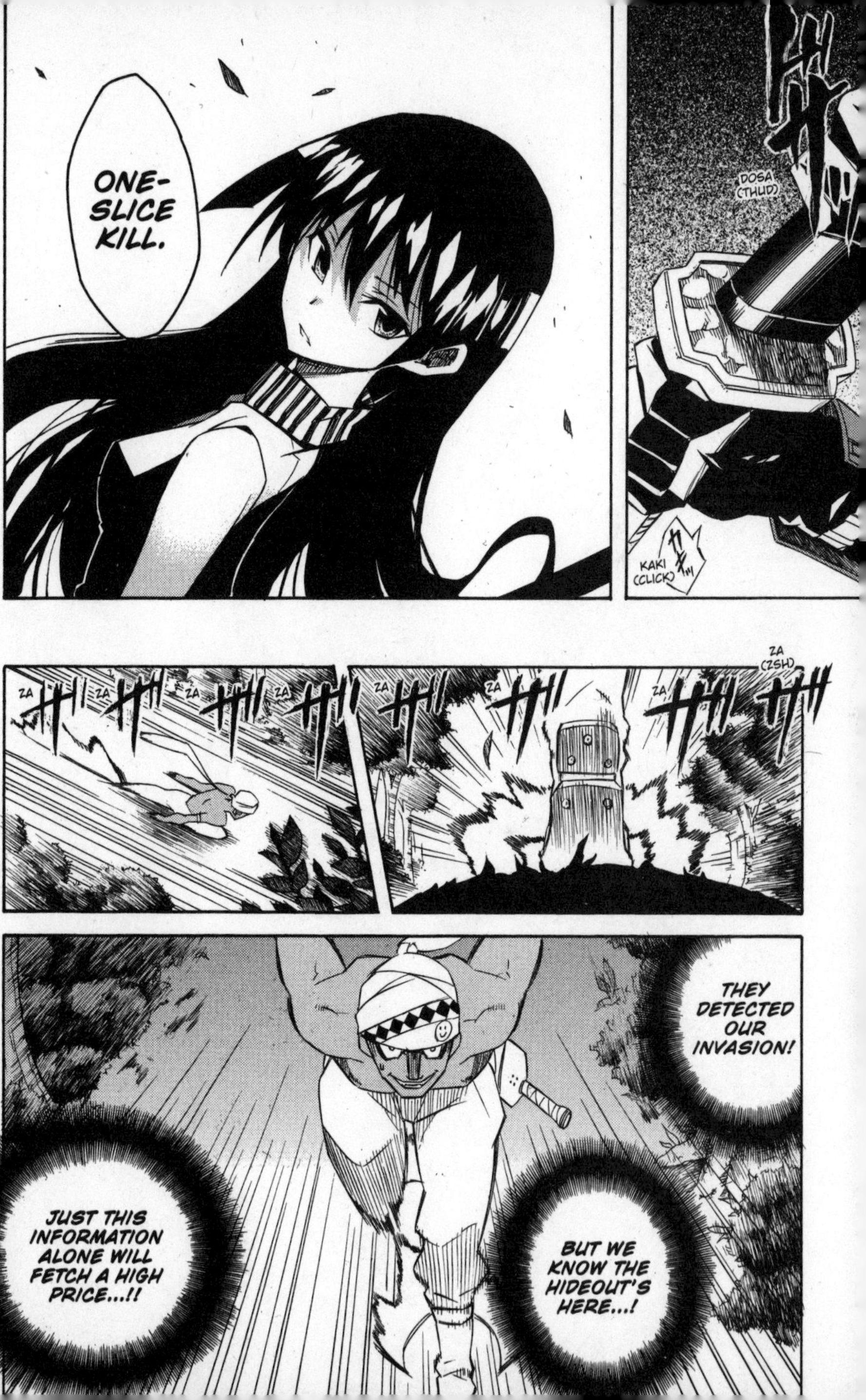
DOSA (THUD)
KAKI (CLICK)
ONE-SLICE KILL.
ZA (ZSH)
ZA
ZA
ZA
ZA
ZA
ZA
ZA
THEY DETECTED OUR INVASION!
BUT WE KNOW THE HIDEOUT'S HERE...!
JUST THIS INFORMATION ALONE WILL FETCH A HIGH PRICE...!!

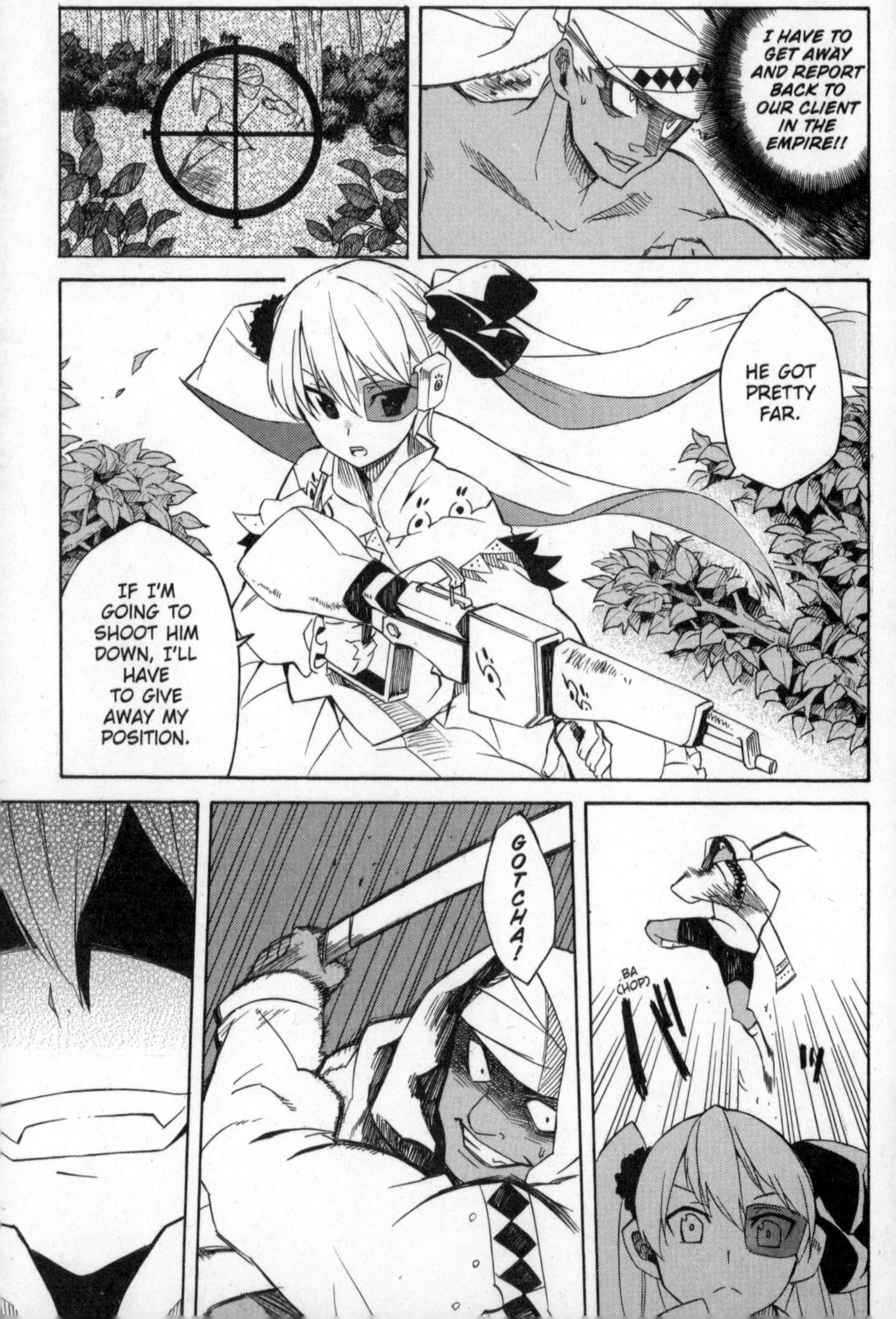
I HAVE TO GET AWAY AND REPORT BACK TO OUR CLIENT IN THE EMPIRE!!
HE GOT PRETTY FAR.
IF I'M GOING TO SHOOT HIM DOWN, I'LL HAVE TO GIVE AWAY MY POSITION.
BA (HOP)
GOTCHA!

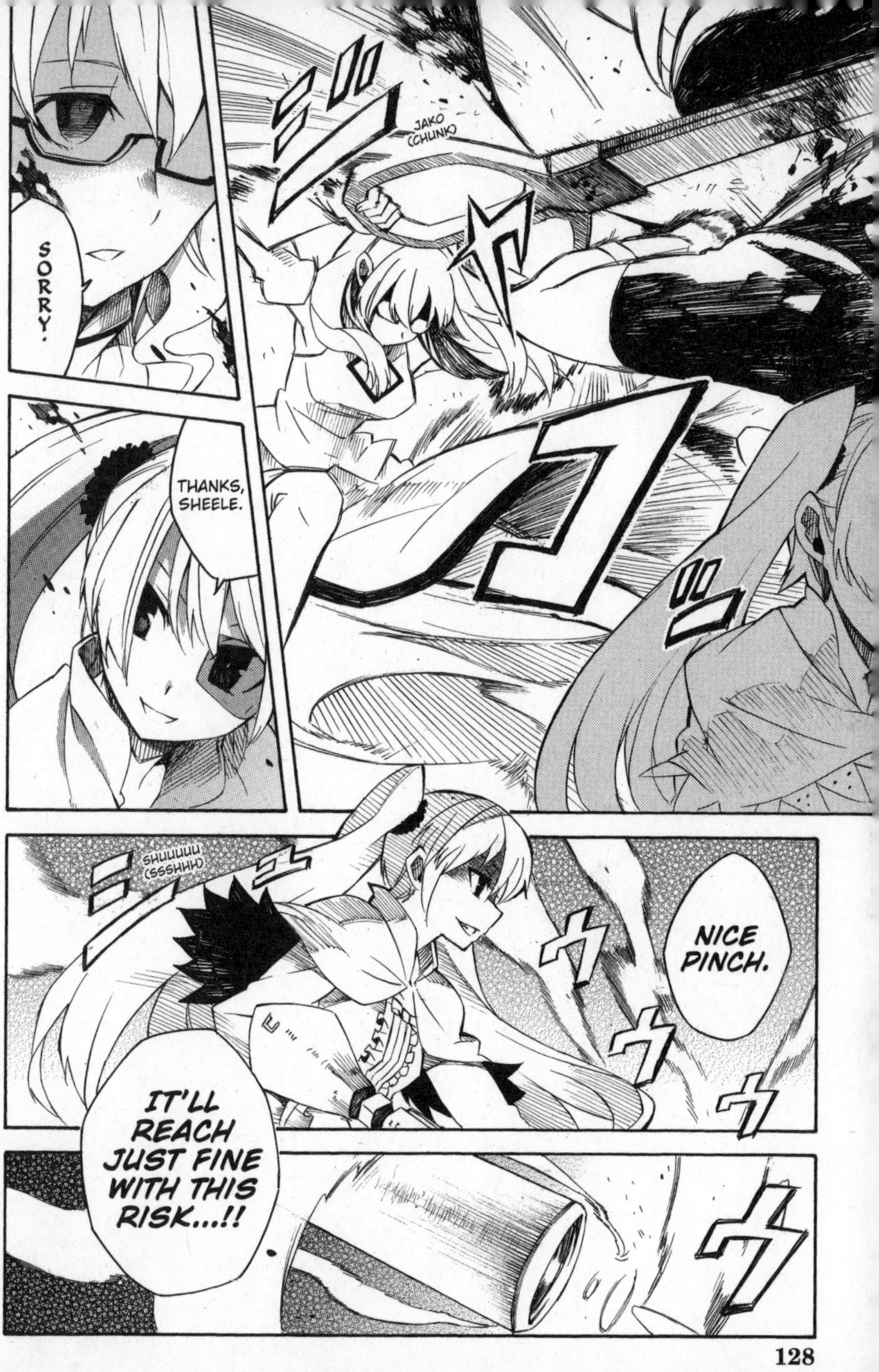

JAKO (CHUNK)
SORRY.
THANKS, SHEELE.
NICE PINCH.
SHUUUUUU (SSSSHHH)
IT'LL REACH JUST FINE WITH THIS RISK...!!

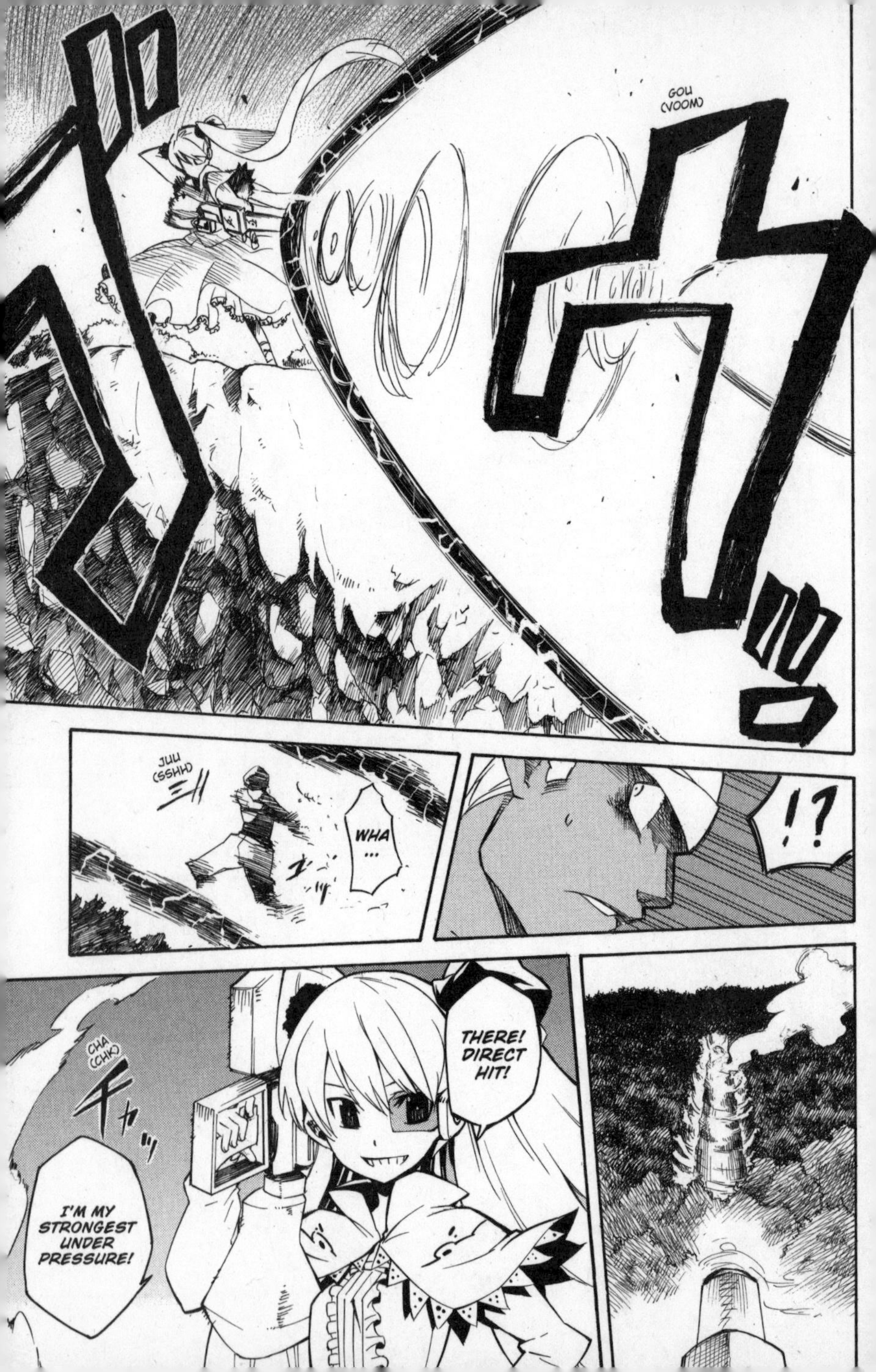
GOU (VOOM)
!?
JUU (SSHH)
WHA...
THERE! DIRECT HIT!
CHA (CHK)
I'M MY STRONGEST UNDER PRESSURE!

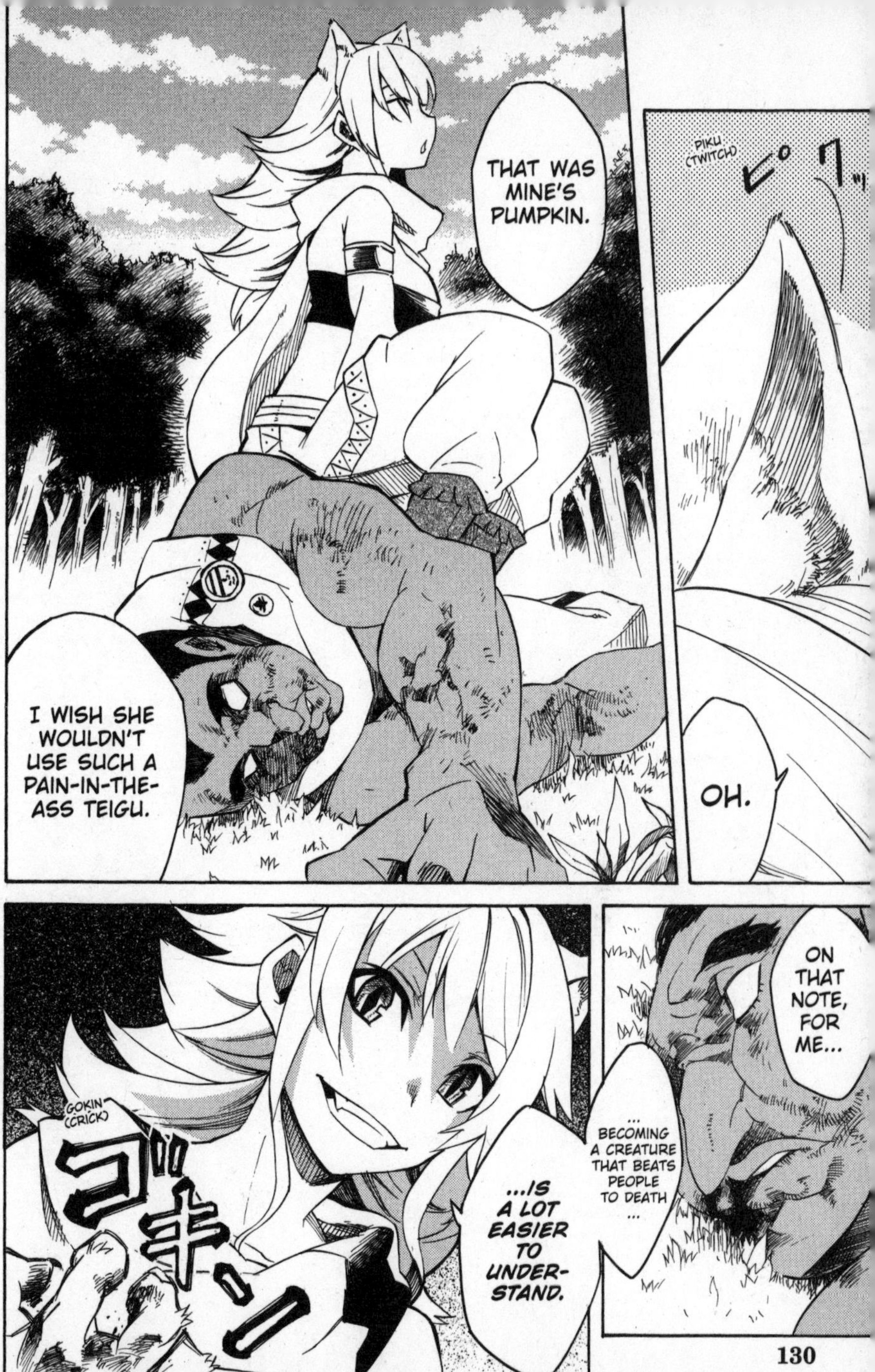
PIKU (TWITCH)
OH.
THAT WAS MINE'S PUMPKIN.
I WISH SHE WOULDN'T USE SUCH A PAIN-IN-THE-ASS TEIGU.
ON THAT NOTE, FOR ME...
...BECOMING A CREATURE THAT BEATS PEOPLE TO DEATH...
...IS A LOT EASIER TO UNDER-STAND.
GOKIN (CRICK)

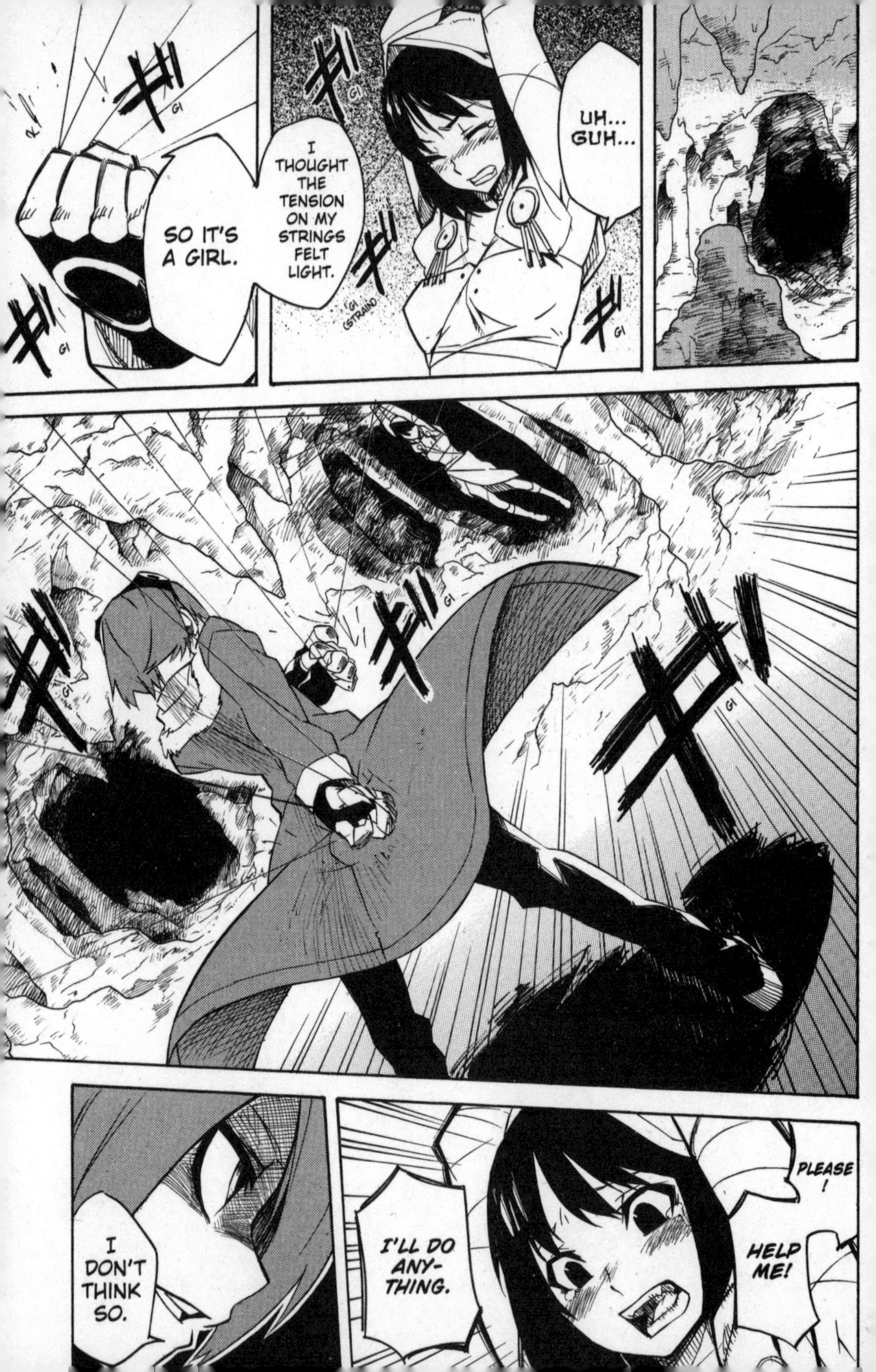
UH... GUH...
GI
I THOUGHT THE TENSION ON MY STRINGS FELT LIGHT.
GI (STRAIN)
GI
SO IT'S A GIRL.
GI
GI
GI
GI
GI
PLEASE!
HELP ME!
I'LL DO ANY-THING.
I DON'T THINK SO.

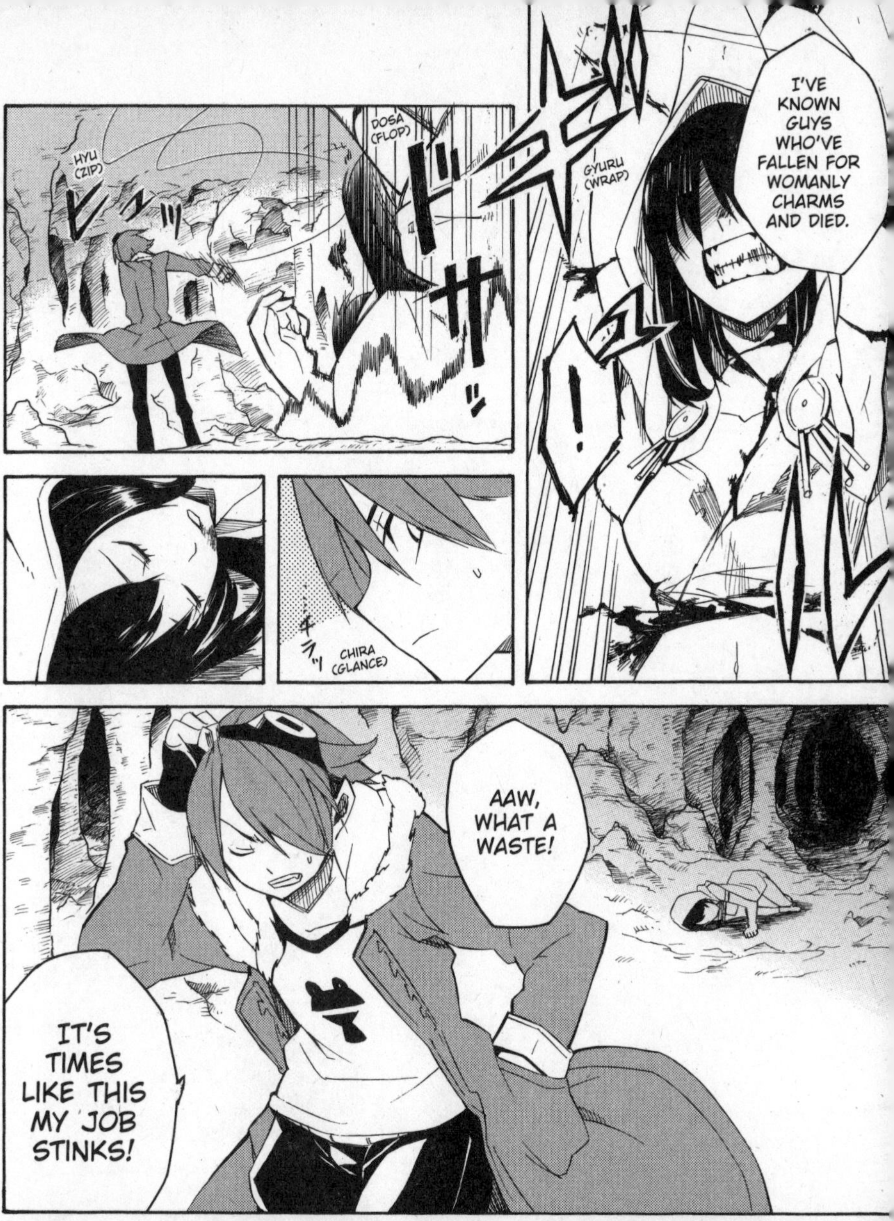
GYURU (WRAP)
I'VE KNOWN GUYS WHO'VE FALLEN FOR WOMANLY CHARMS AND DIED.
DOSA (FLOP)
HYU (ZIP)
CHIRA (GLANCE)
AAW, WHAT A WASTE!
IT'S TIMES LIKE THIS MY JOB STINKS!

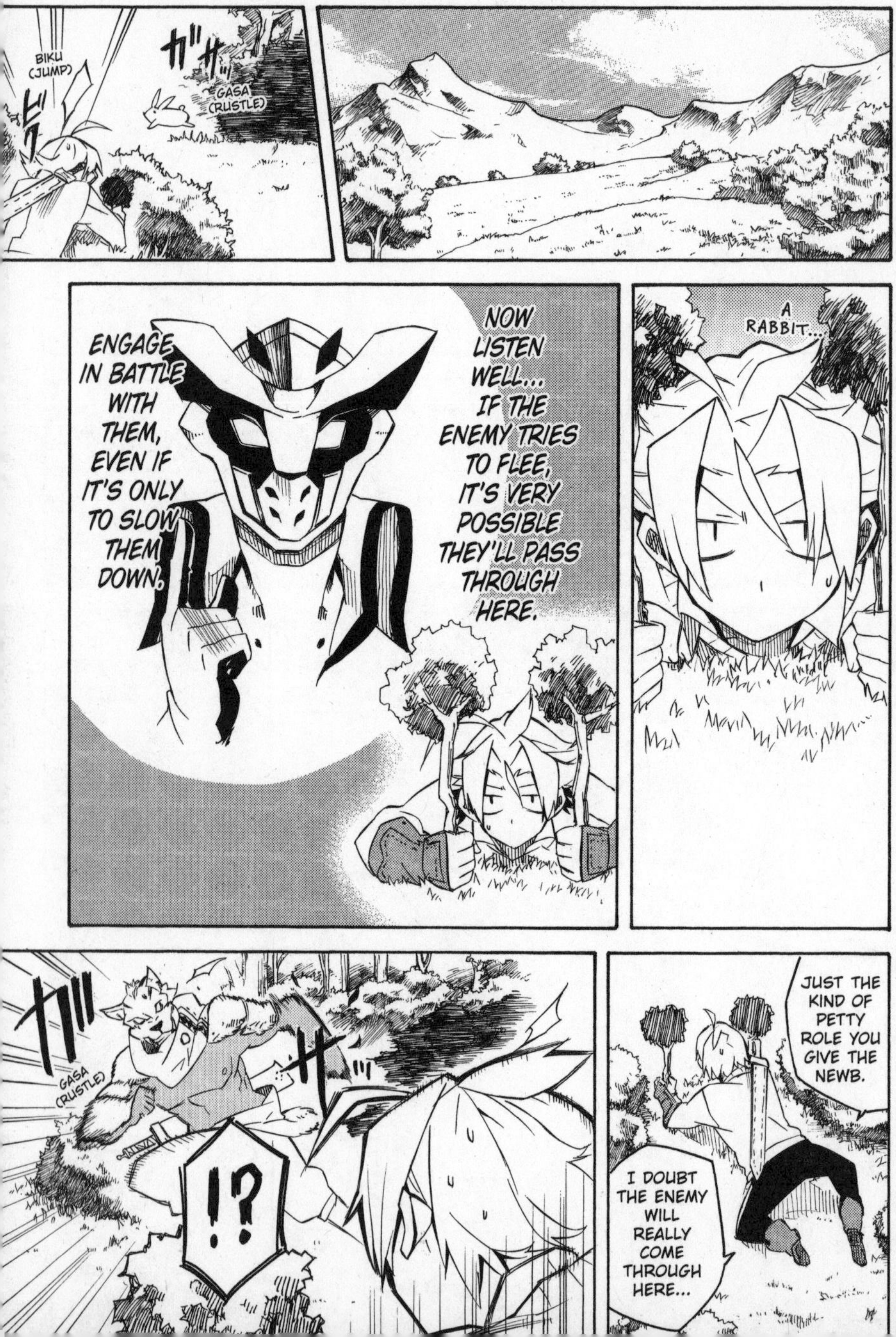
GASA (RUSTLE)
BIKU (JUMP)
A RABBIT...
NOW LISTEN WELL... IF THE ENEMY TRIES TO FLEE, IT'S VERY POSSIBLE THEY'LL PASS THROUGH HERE.
ENGAGE IN BATTLE WITH THEM, EVEN IF IT'S ONLY TO SLOW THEM DOWN.
JUST THE KIND OF PETTY ROLE YOU GIVE THE NEWB.
I DOUBT THE ENEMY WILL REALLY COME THROUGH HERE...
!?
GASA (RUSTLE)

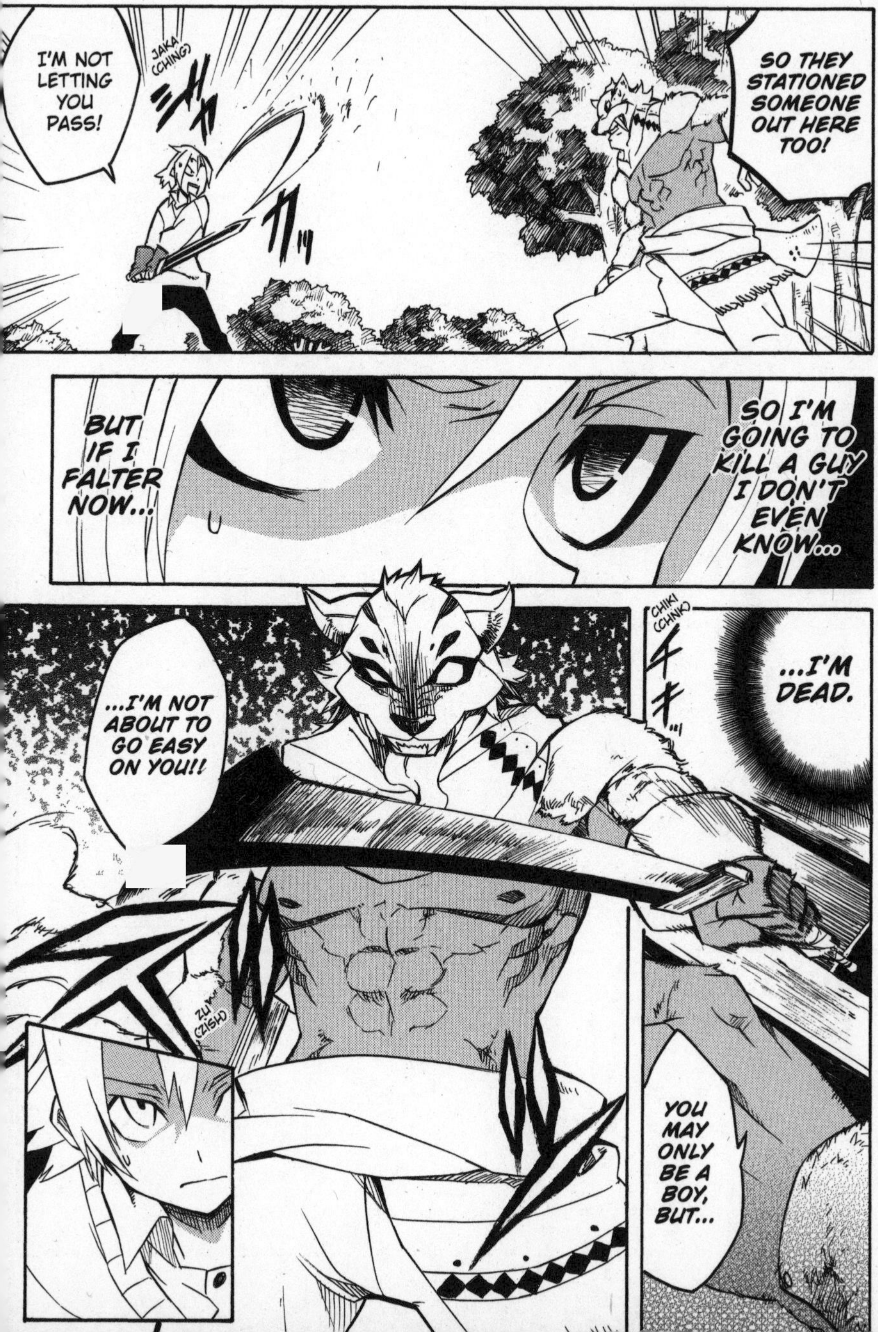
SO THEY STATIONED SOMEONE OUT HERE TOO!
JAKA (CHING)
I'M NOT LETTING YOU PASS!
SO I'M GOING TO KILL A GUY I DON'T EVEN KNOW...
BUT IF I FALTER NOW...
CHIKI (CHNK)
...I'M DEAD.
YOU MAY ONLY BE A BOY, BUT...
...I'M NOT ABOUT TO GO EASY ON YOU!!
ZU (ZISH)

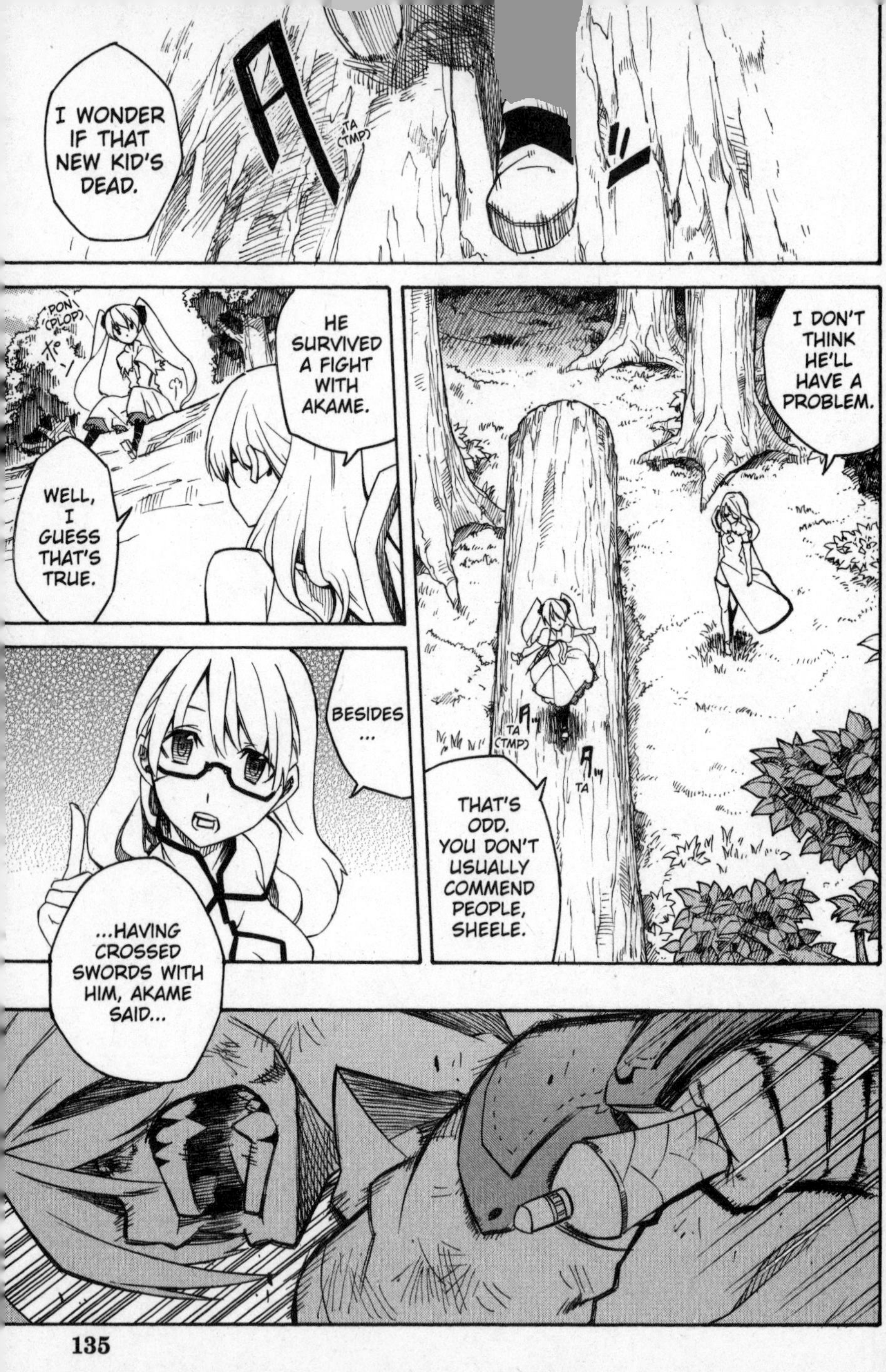
TA (TMP)
I WONDER IF THAT NEW KID'S DEAD.
I DON'T THINK HE'LL HAVE A PROBLEM.
TA (TMP)
TA
THAT'S ODD. YOU DON'T USUALLY COMMEND PEOPLE, SHEELE.
HE SURVIVED A FIGHT WITH AKAME.
PON (PLOP)
WELL, I GUESS THAT'S TRUE.
BESIDES ...
...HAVING CROSSED SWORDS WITH HIM, AKAME SAID...

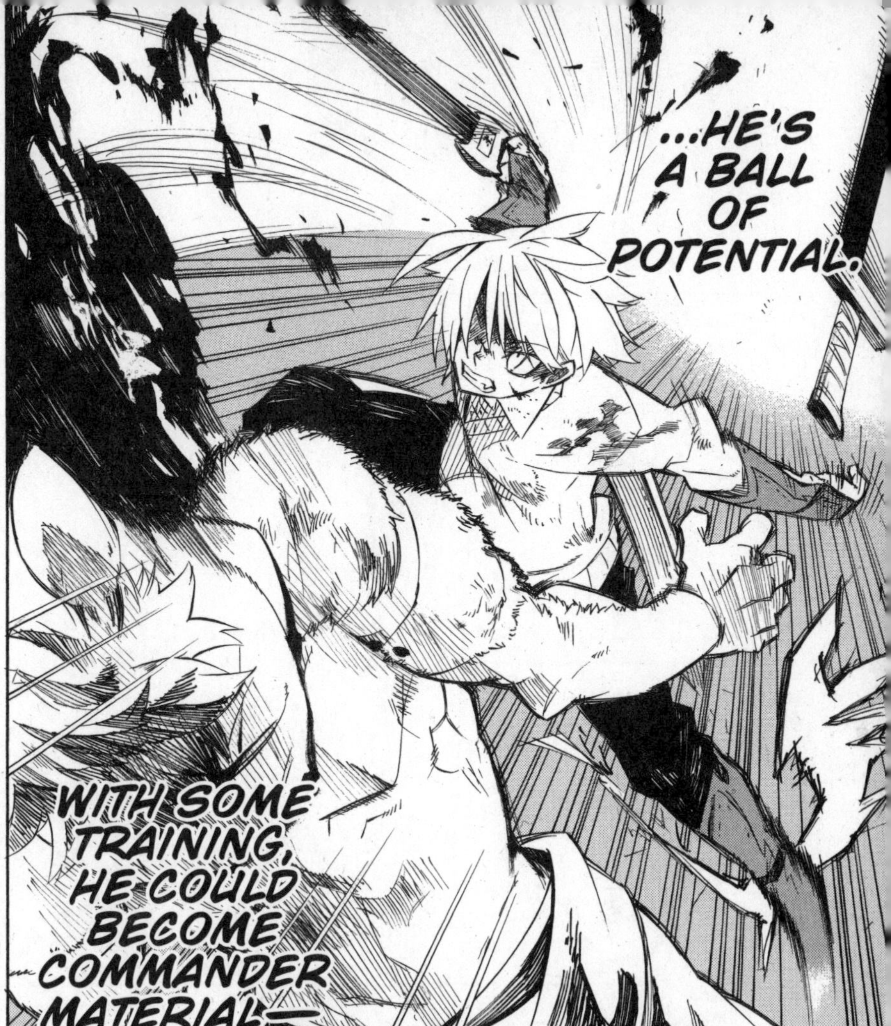
...HE'S A BALL OF POTENTIAL.
WITH SOME TRAINING, HE COULD BECOME COMMANDER MATERIAL—
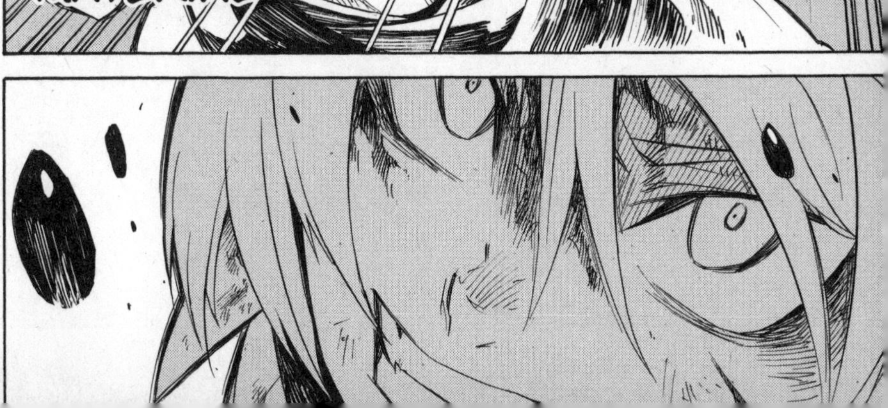

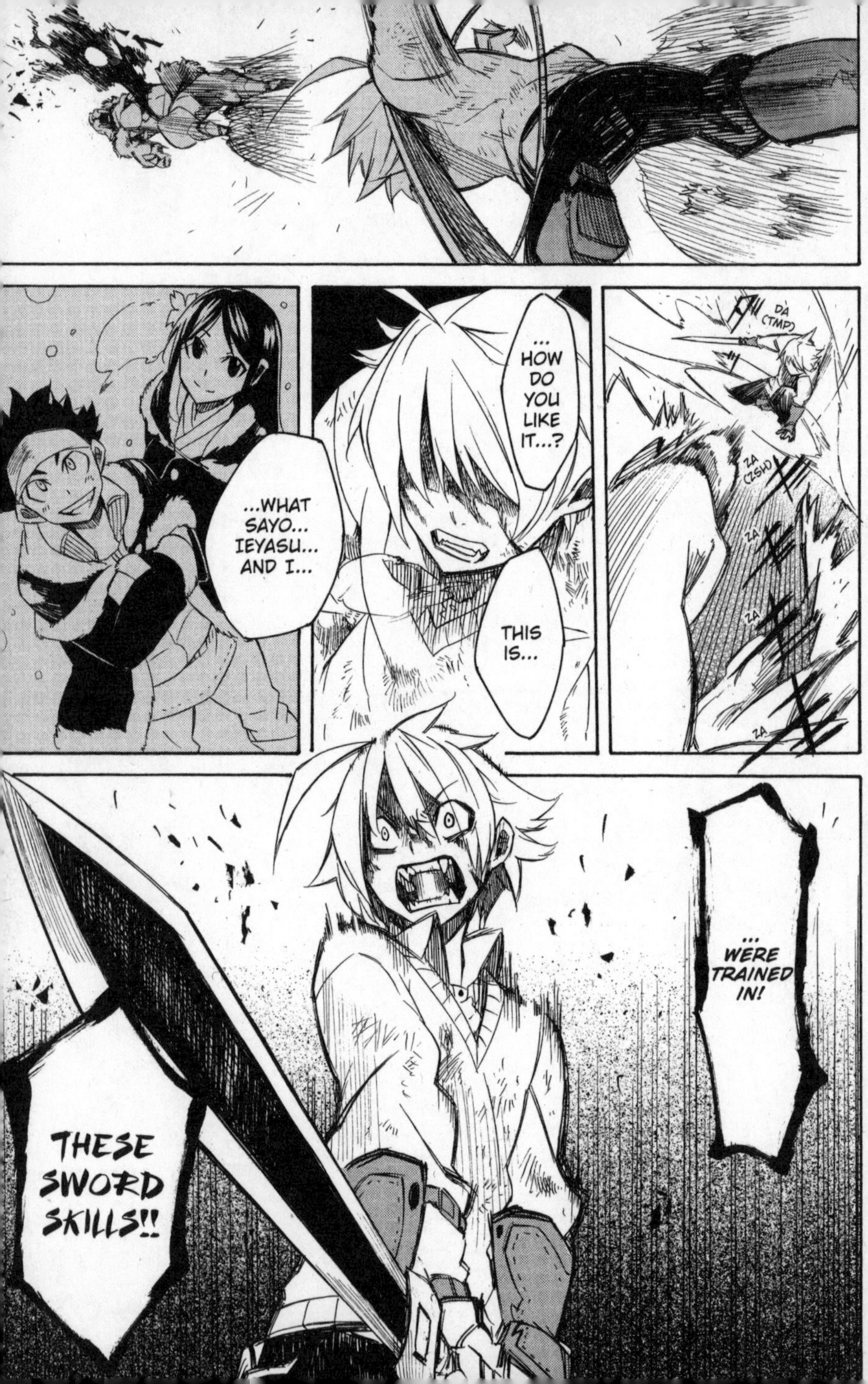
DA (TMP)
ZA (ZSW)
ZA
ZA
ZA
...HOW DO YOU LIKE IT...?
THIS IS...
...WHAT SAYO... IEYASU... AND I...
...WERE TRAINED IN!
THESE SWORD SKILLS!!

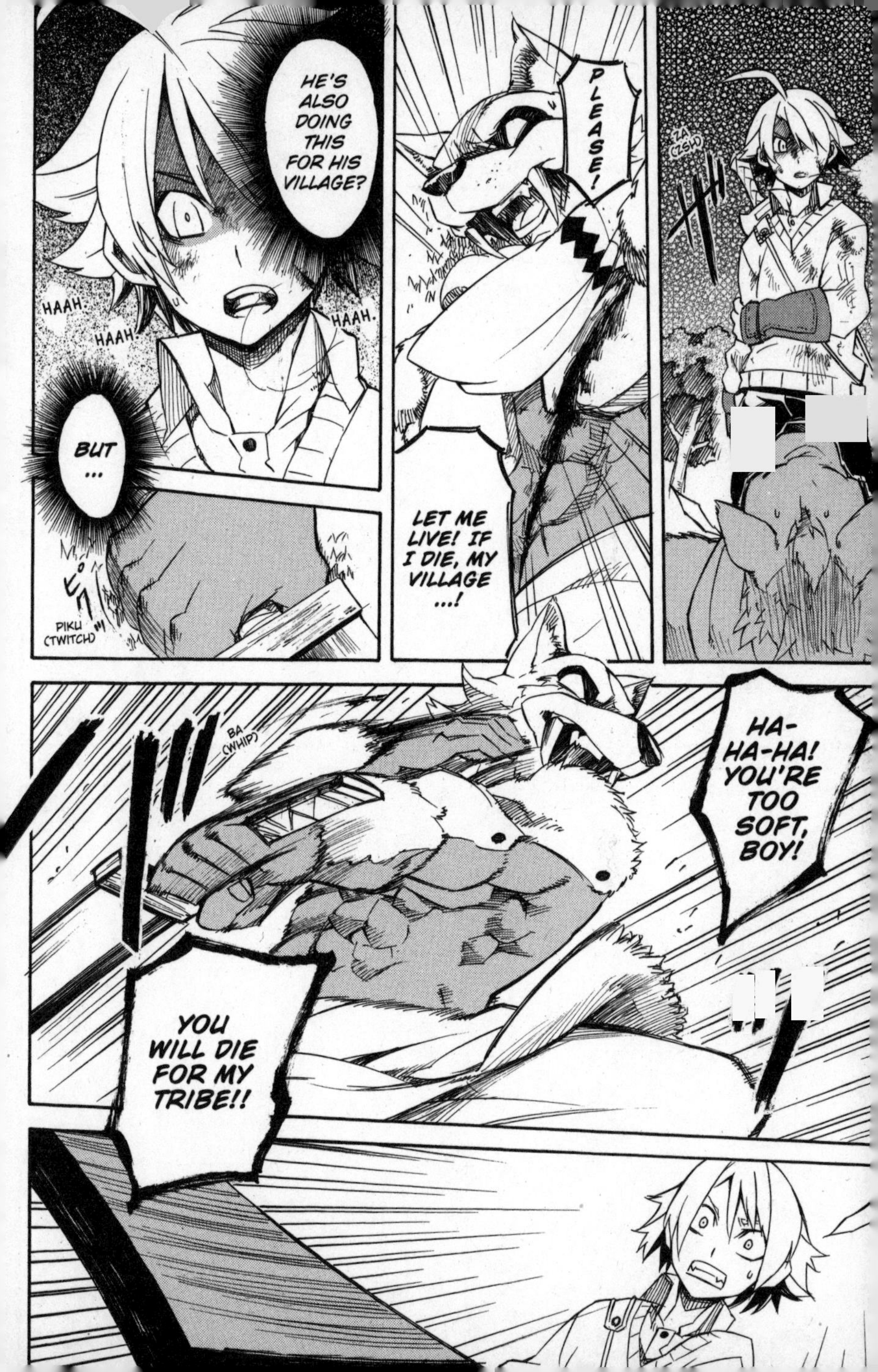
ZA (ZSH)
PLEASE!
LET ME LIVE! IF I DIE, MY VILLAGE ...!
HE'S ALSO DOING THIS FOR HIS VILLAGE?
HAAH.
HAAH.
HAAH.
BUT ...
PIKU (TWITCH)
HA-HA-HA! YOU'RE TOO SOFT, BOY!
BA (WHIP)
YOU WILL DIE FOR MY TRIBE!!

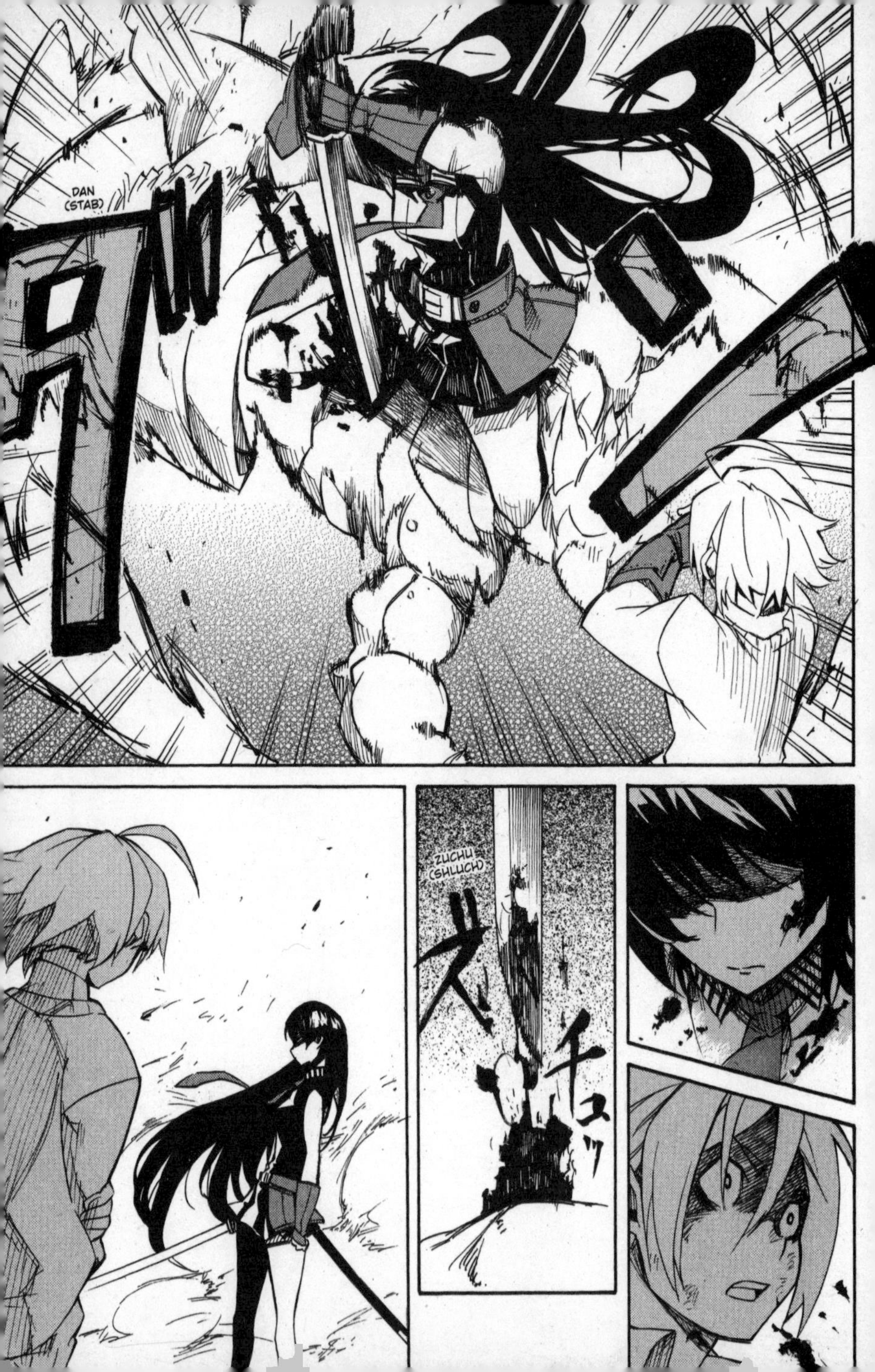
DAN
(STAB)
ZUCHU
(SHLUCH)

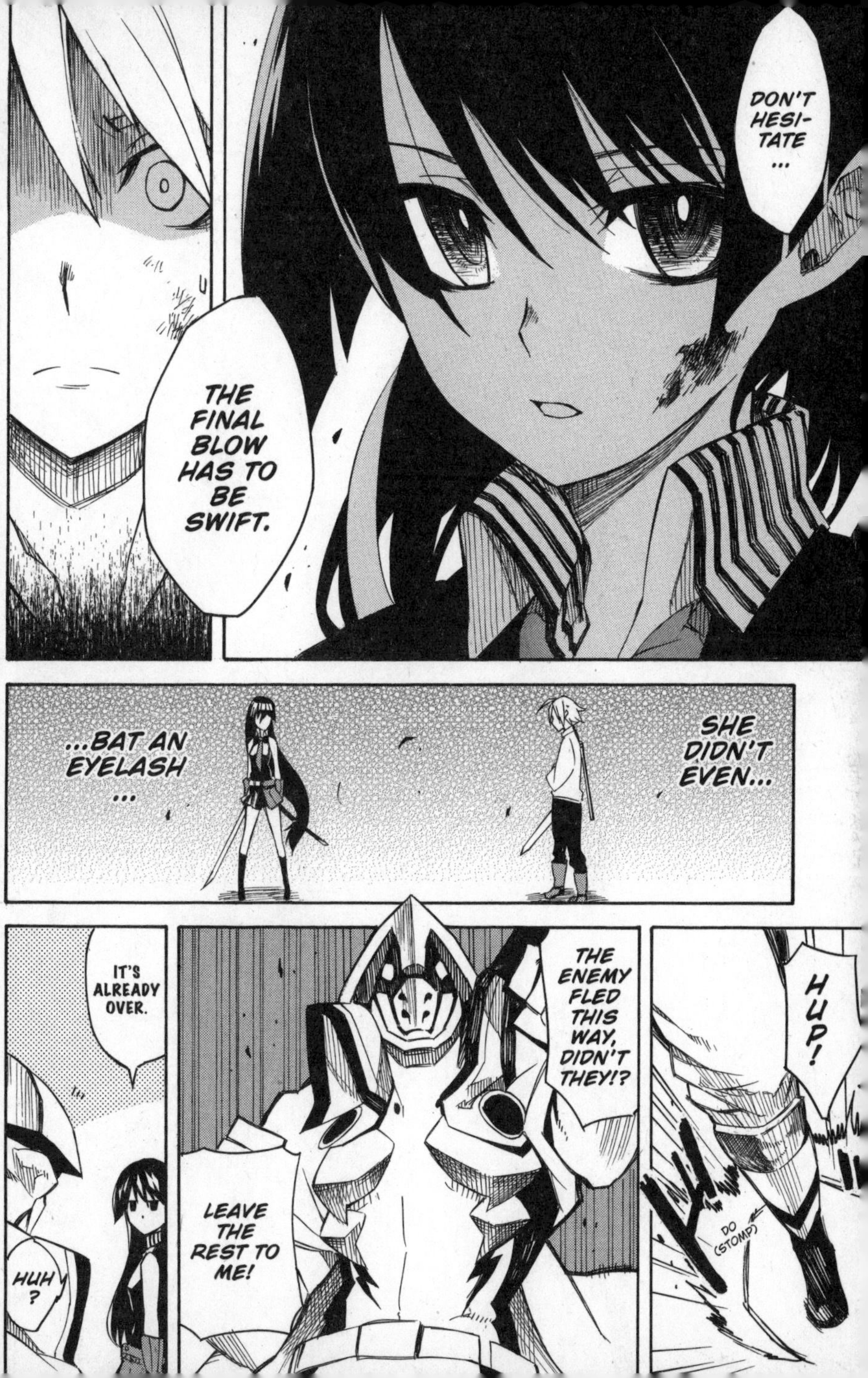
DON'T HESI-TATE ...
THE FINAL BLOW HAS TO BE SWIFT.
SHE DIDN'T EVEN...
...BAT AN EYELASH ...
HUP!
DO (STOMP)
THE ENEMY FLED THIS WAY, DIDN'T THEY!?
LEAVE THE REST TO ME!
IT'S ALREADY OVER.
HUH ?

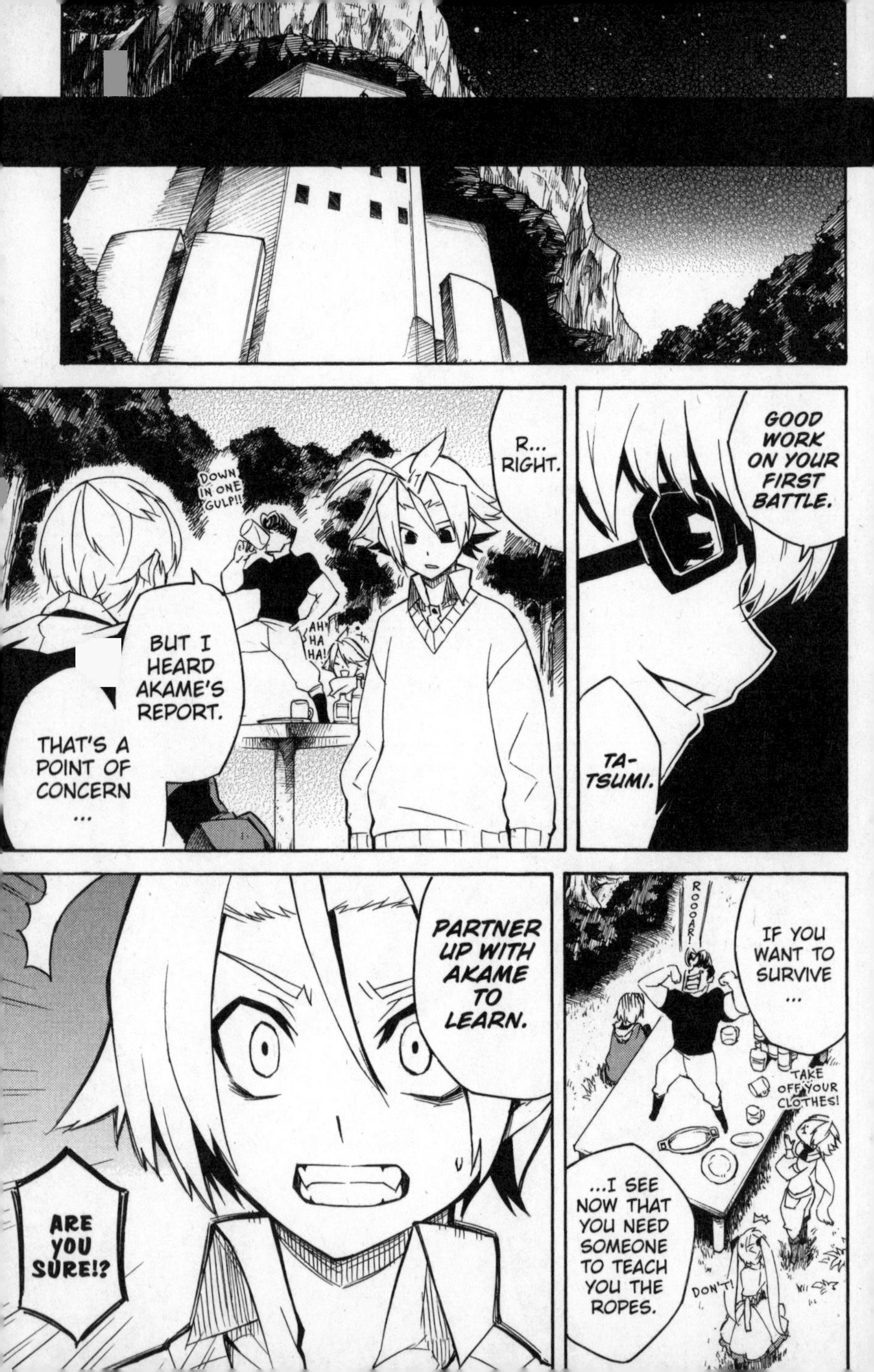
[redacted]
GOOD WORK ON YOUR FIRST BATTLE.
TA-TSUMI.
R... RIGHT.
DOWN IN ONE GULP!!
AH HA HA!
BUT I HEARD AKAME'S REPORT.
THAT'S A POINT OF CONCERN ...
IF YOU WANT TO SURVIVE ...
ROOOAR!
TAKE OFF YOUR CLOTHES!
...I SEE NOW THAT YOU NEED SOMEONE TO TEACH YOU THE ROPES.
DON'T!
PARTNER UP WITH AKAME TO LEARN.
ARE YOU SURE!?

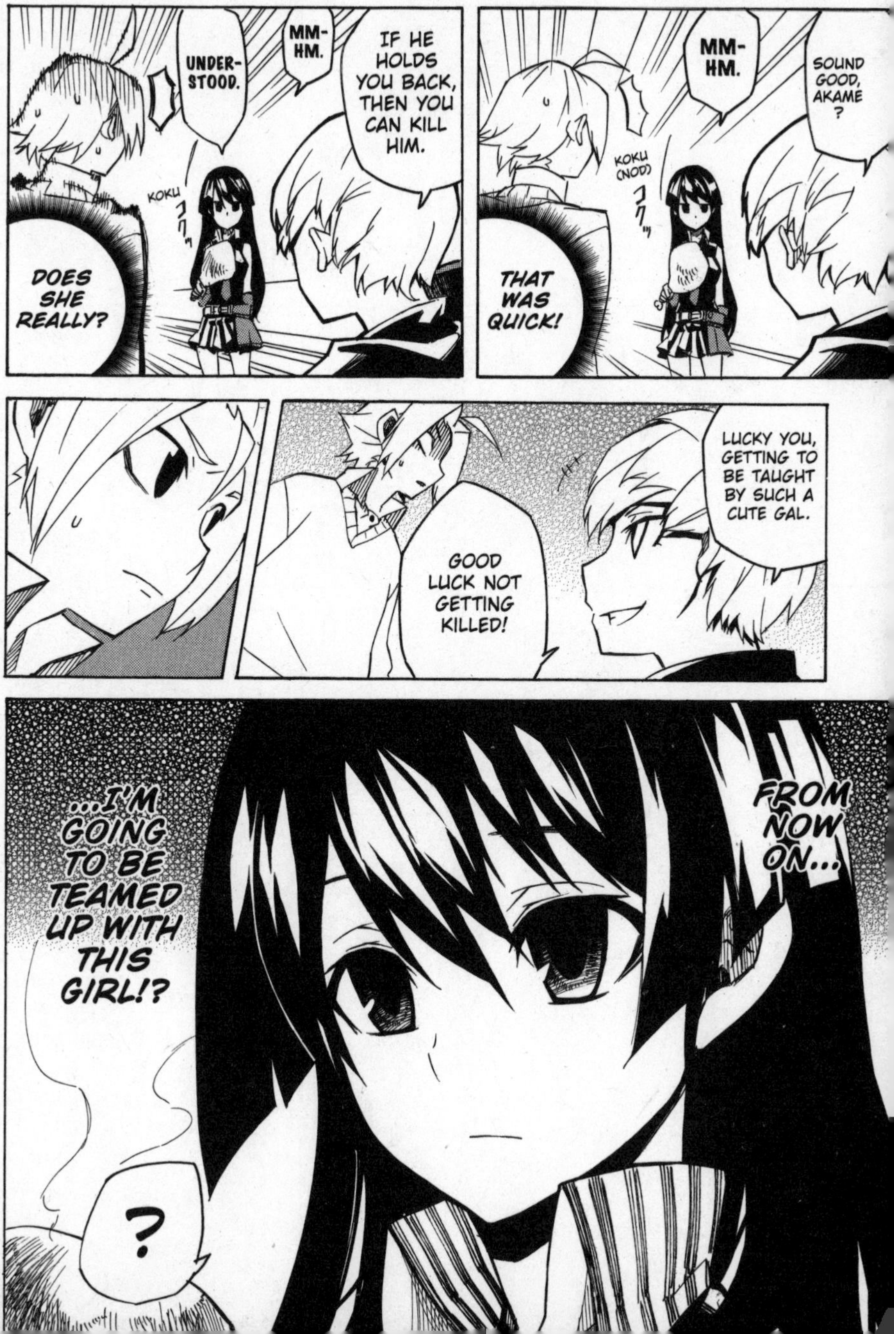
SOUND GOOD, AKAME?
MM-HM.
KOKU (NOD)
THAT WAS QUICK!
IF HE HOLDS YOU BACK, THEN YOU CAN KILL HIM.
MM-HM.
UNDER-STOOD.
KOKU
DOES SHE REALLY?
LUCKY YOU, GETTING TO BE TAUGHT BY SUCH A CUTE GAL.
GOOD LUCK NOT GETTING KILLED!
FROM NOW ON...
...I'M GOING TO BE TEAMED UP WITH THIS GIRL!?
?

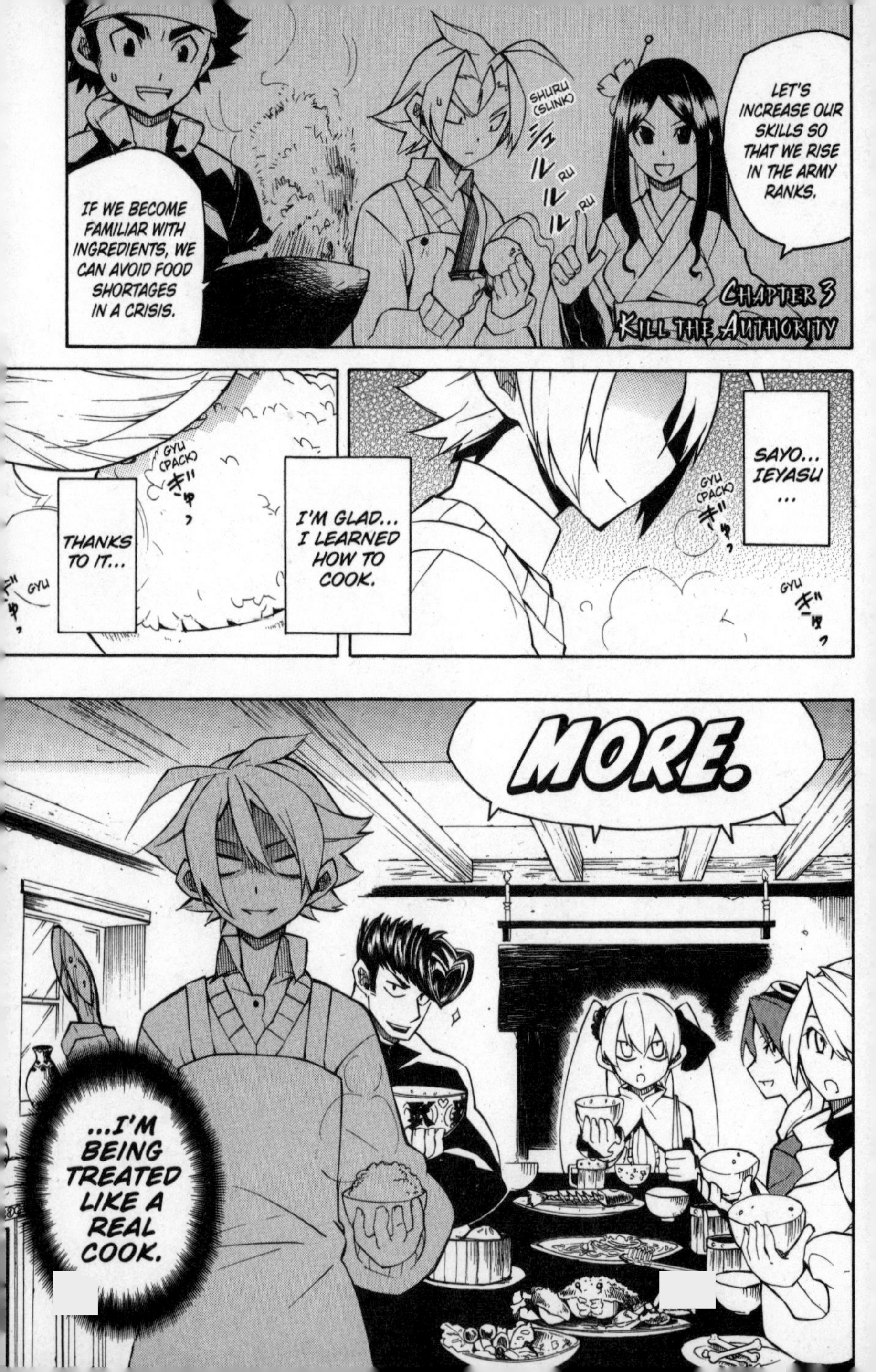
LET'S INCREASE OUR SKILLS SO THAT WE RISE IN THE ARMY RANKS.
SHURU (SLINK)
シュ
ル RU
ル RU
ル
CHAPTER 3
KILL THE AUTHORITY
IF WE BECOME FAMILIAR WITH INGREDIENTS, WE CAN AVOID FOOD SHORTAGES IN A CRISIS.
SAYO... IEYASU...
GYU (PACK)
ぎゅっ
GYU
ぎゅっ
I'M GLAD... I LEARNED HOW TO COOK.
GYU (PACK)
ぎゅっ
THANKS TO IT...
GYU
ぎゅっ
MORE.
...I'M BEING TREATED LIKE A REAL COOK.

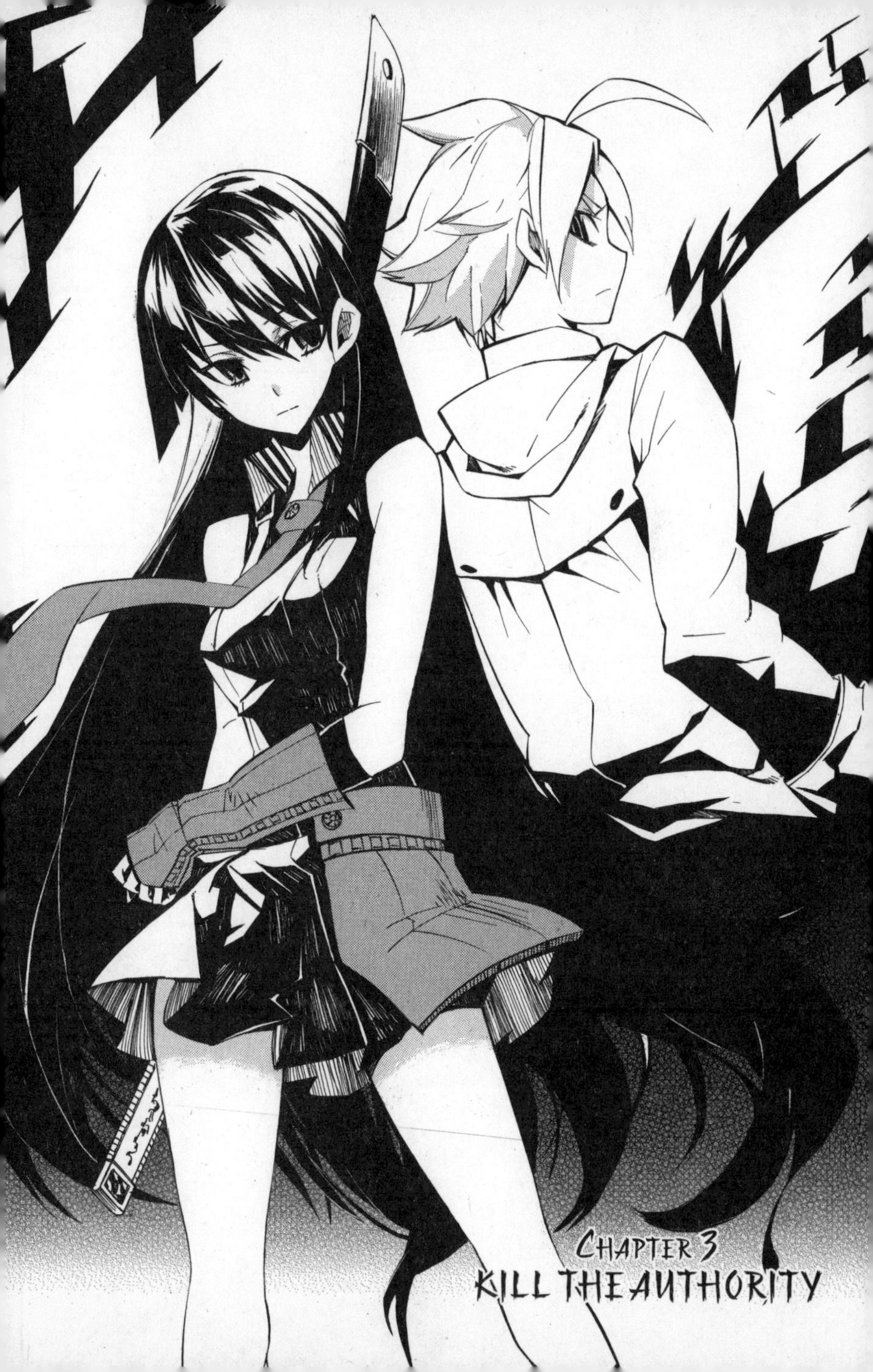
Chapter 3
Kill the Authority

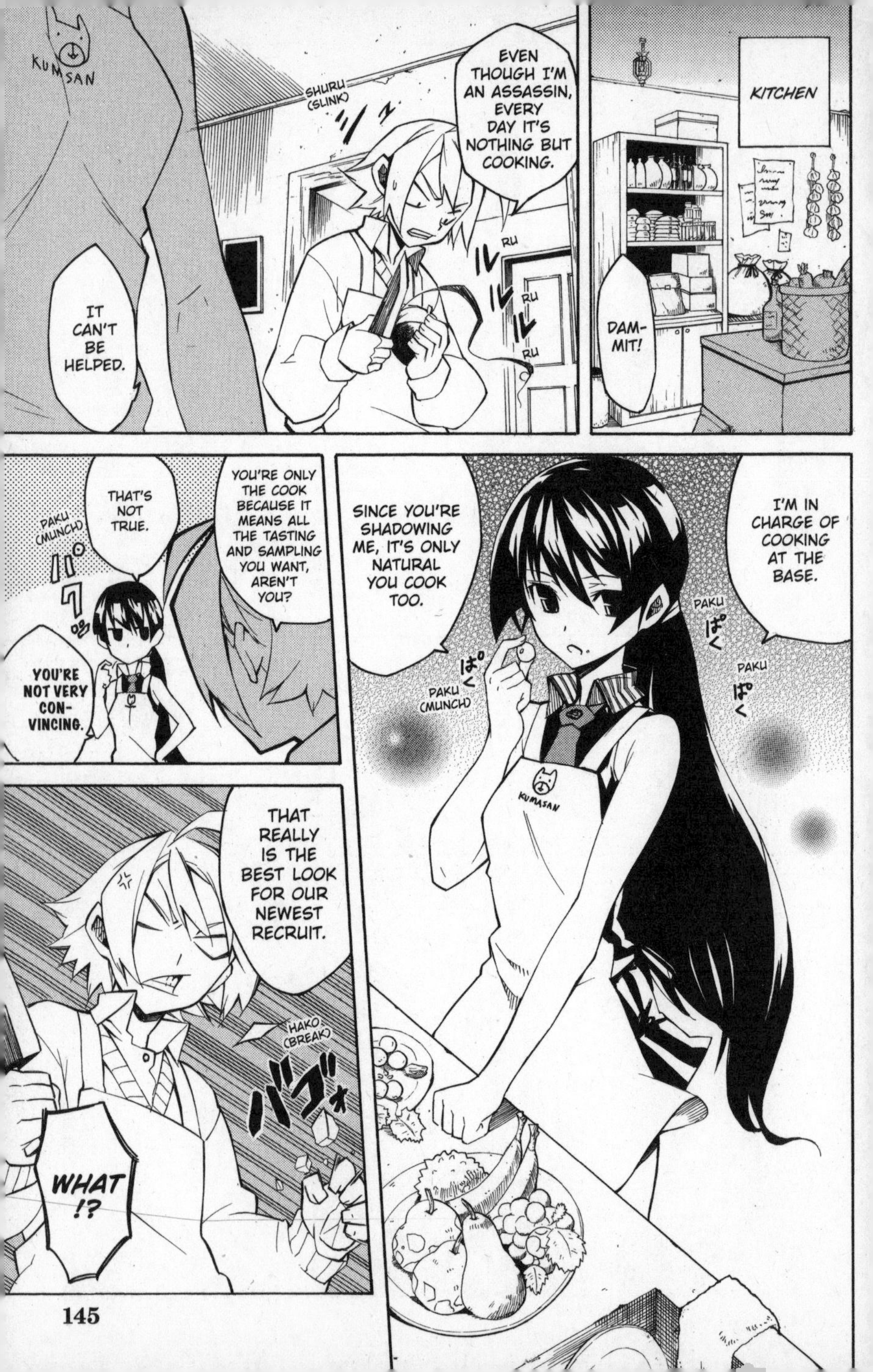

KITCHEN
DAM-MIT!
EVEN THOUGH I'M AN ASSASSIN, EVERY DAY IT'S NOTHING BUT COOKING.
SHURU (SLINK)
RU
RU
RU
KUMSAN
IT CAN'T BE HELPED.
I'M IN CHARGE OF COOKING AT THE BASE.
SINCE YOU'RE SHADOWING ME, IT'S ONLY NATURAL YOU COOK TOO.
PAKU
PAKU
PAKU (MUNCH)
KUMASAN
YOU'RE ONLY THE COOK BECAUSE IT MEANS ALL THE TASTING AND SAMPLING YOU WANT, AREN'T YOU?
THAT'S NOT TRUE.
PAKU (MUNCH)
YOU'RE NOT VERY CON-VINCING.
THAT REALLY IS THE BEST LOOK FOR OUR NEWEST RECRUIT.
HAKO (BREAK)
WHAT!?

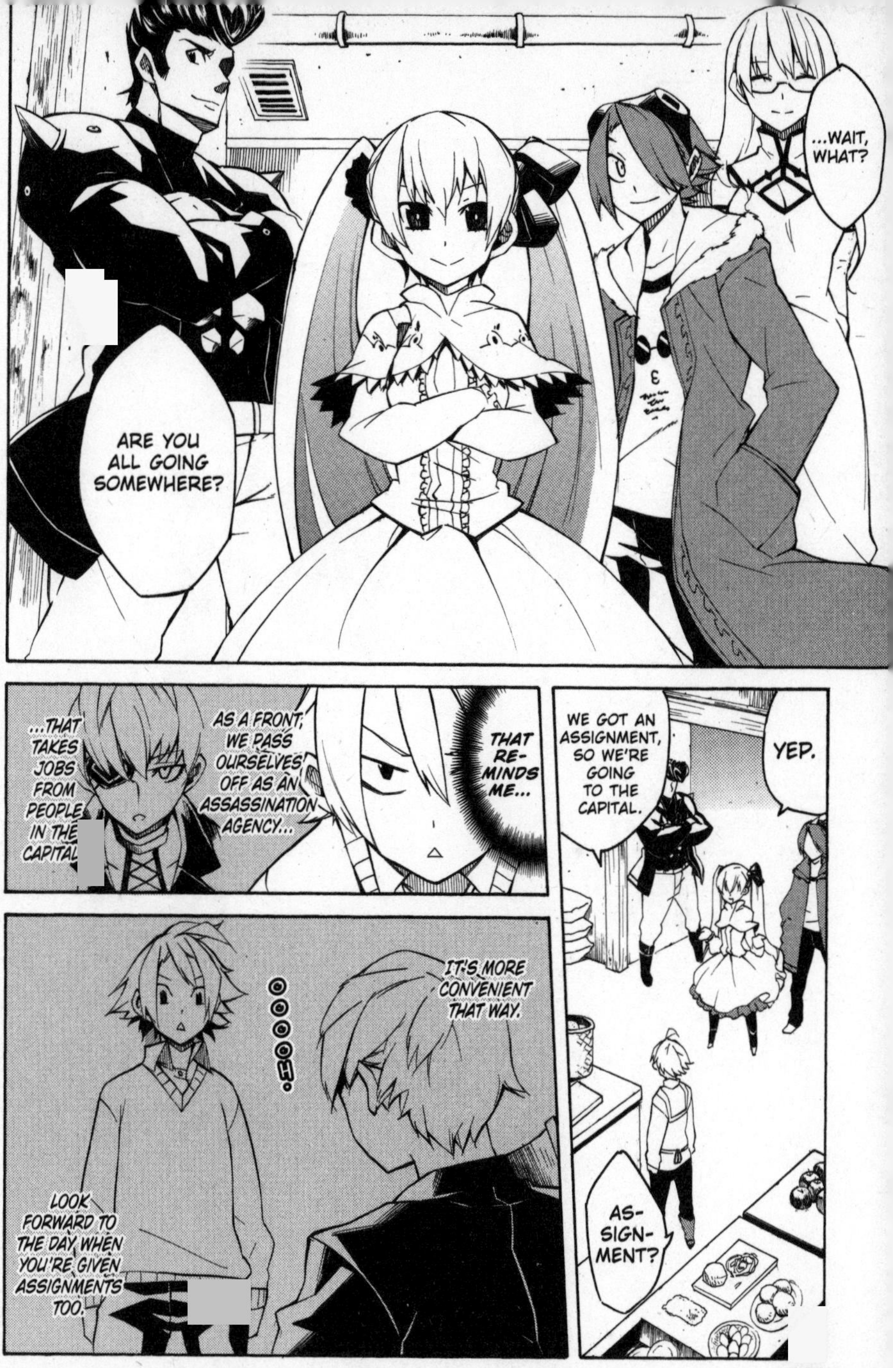
...WAIT, WHAT?
ARE YOU ALL GOING SOMEWHERE?
YEP.
WE GOT AN ASSIGNMENT, SO WE'RE GOING TO THE CAPITAL.
AS-SIGN-MENT?
THAT RE-MINDS ME...
AS A FRONT, WE PASS OURSELVES OFF AS AN ASSASSINATION AGENCY...
...THAT TAKES JOBS FROM PEOPLE IN THE CAPITAL.
IT'S MORE CONVENIENT THAT WAY.
OOOOOH.
LOOK FORWARD TO THE DAY WHEN YOU'RE GIVEN ASSIGNMENTS TOO.

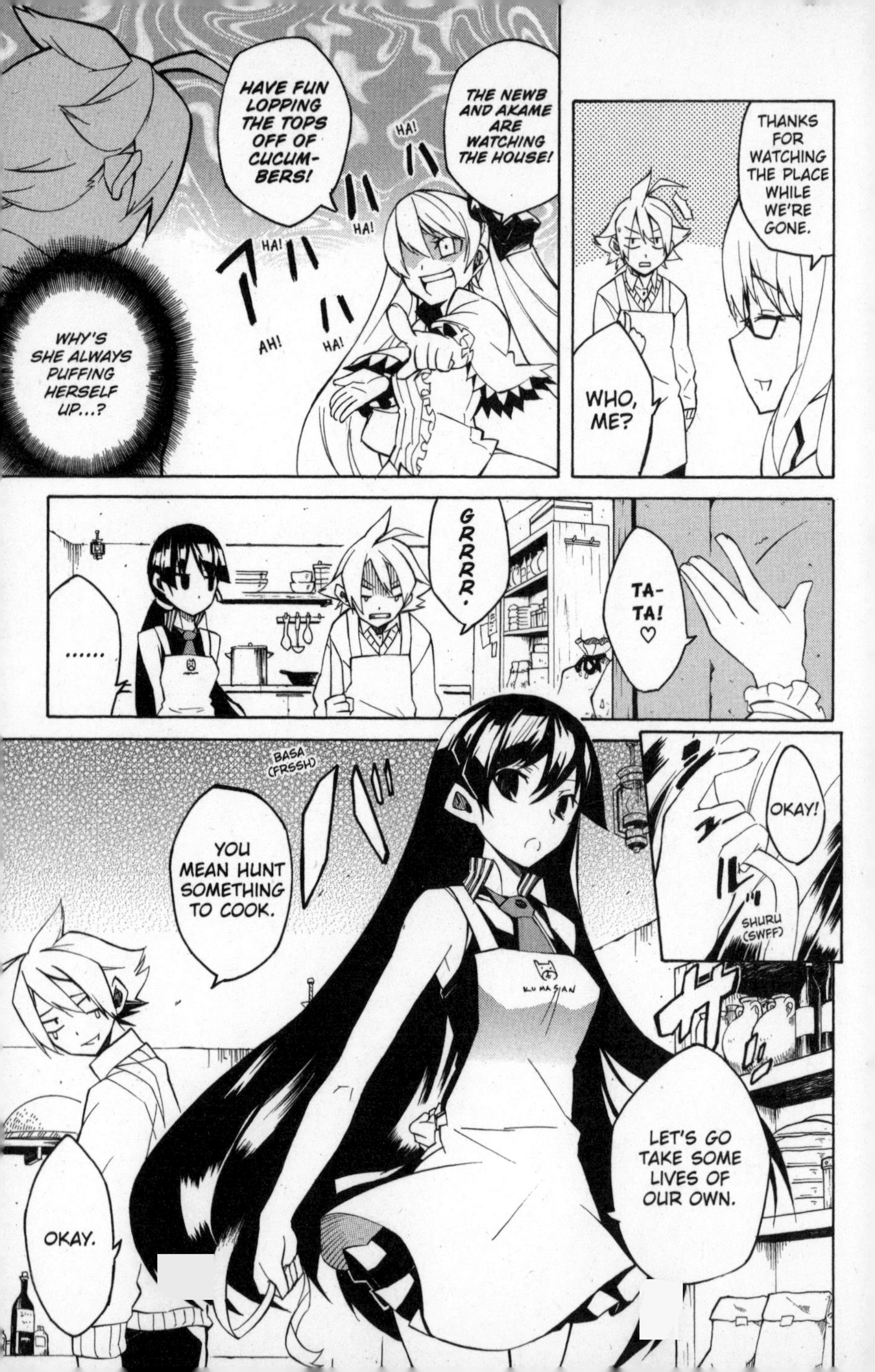
THANKS FOR WATCHING THE PLACE WHILE WE'RE GONE.
WHO, ME?
THE NEWB AND AKAME ARE WATCHING THE HOUSE!
HA!
HAVE FUN LOPPING THE TOPS OFF OF CUCUMBERS!
HA!
HA!
HA!
AH!
WHY'S SHE ALWAYS PUFFING HERSELF UP...?
TA-TA! ♡
GRRRR.
......
OKAY!
SHURU (SWFF)
BASA (FRSSH)
YOU MEAN HUNT SOMETHING TO COOK.
KUMASIAN
LET'S GO TAKE SOME LIVES OF OUR OWN.
OKAY.

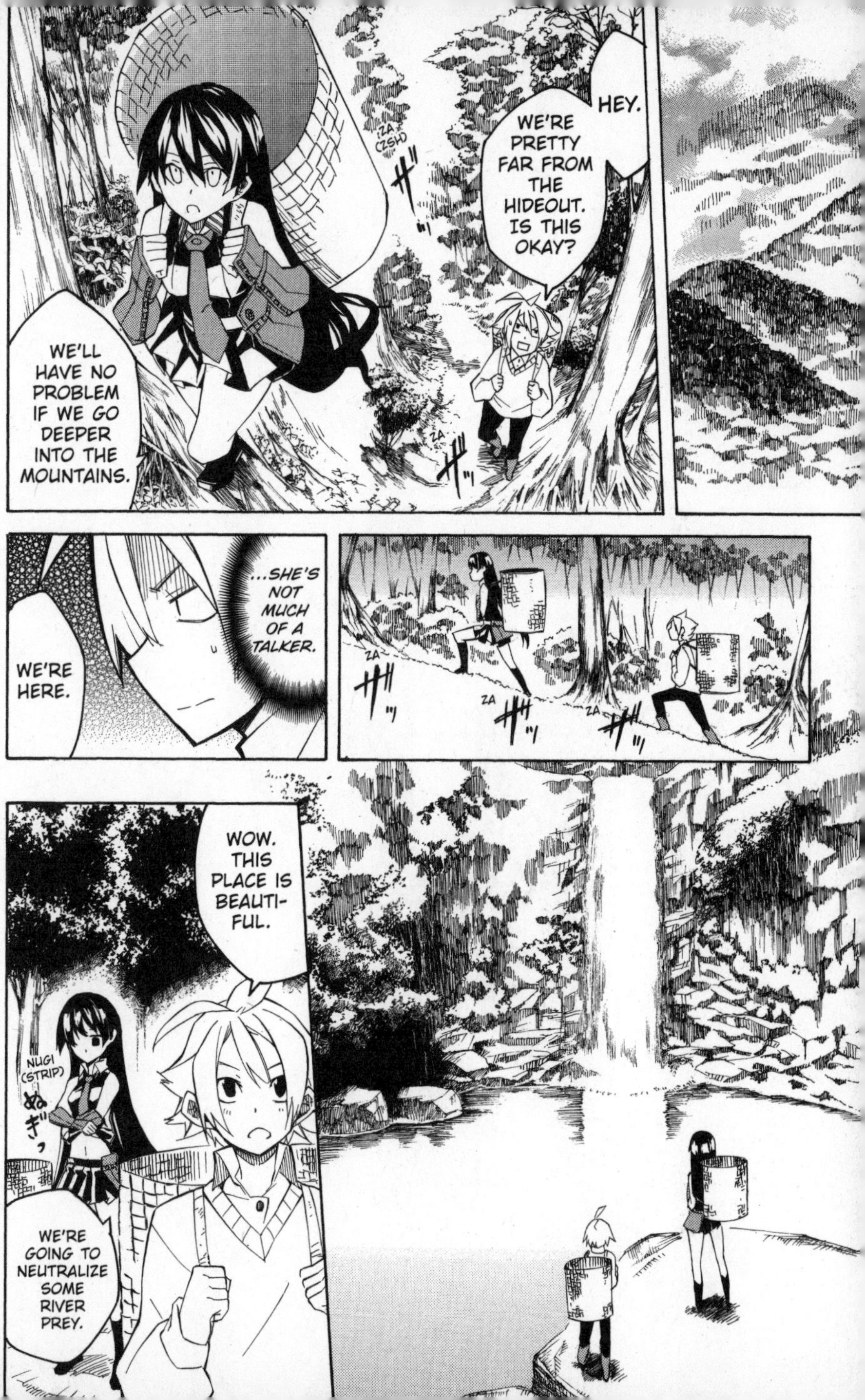
HEY.
WE'RE PRETTY FAR FROM THE HIDEOUT. IS THIS OKAY?
ZA (ZSH)
ZA
WE'LL HAVE NO PROBLEM IF WE GO DEEPER INTO THE MOUNTAINS.
ZA
ZA
ZA
...SHE'S NOT MUCH OF A TALKER.
WE'RE HERE.
WOW. THIS PLACE IS BEAUTI-FUL.
NUGI (STRIP)
ぬぎ
WE'RE GOING TO NEUTRALIZE SOME RIVER PREY.

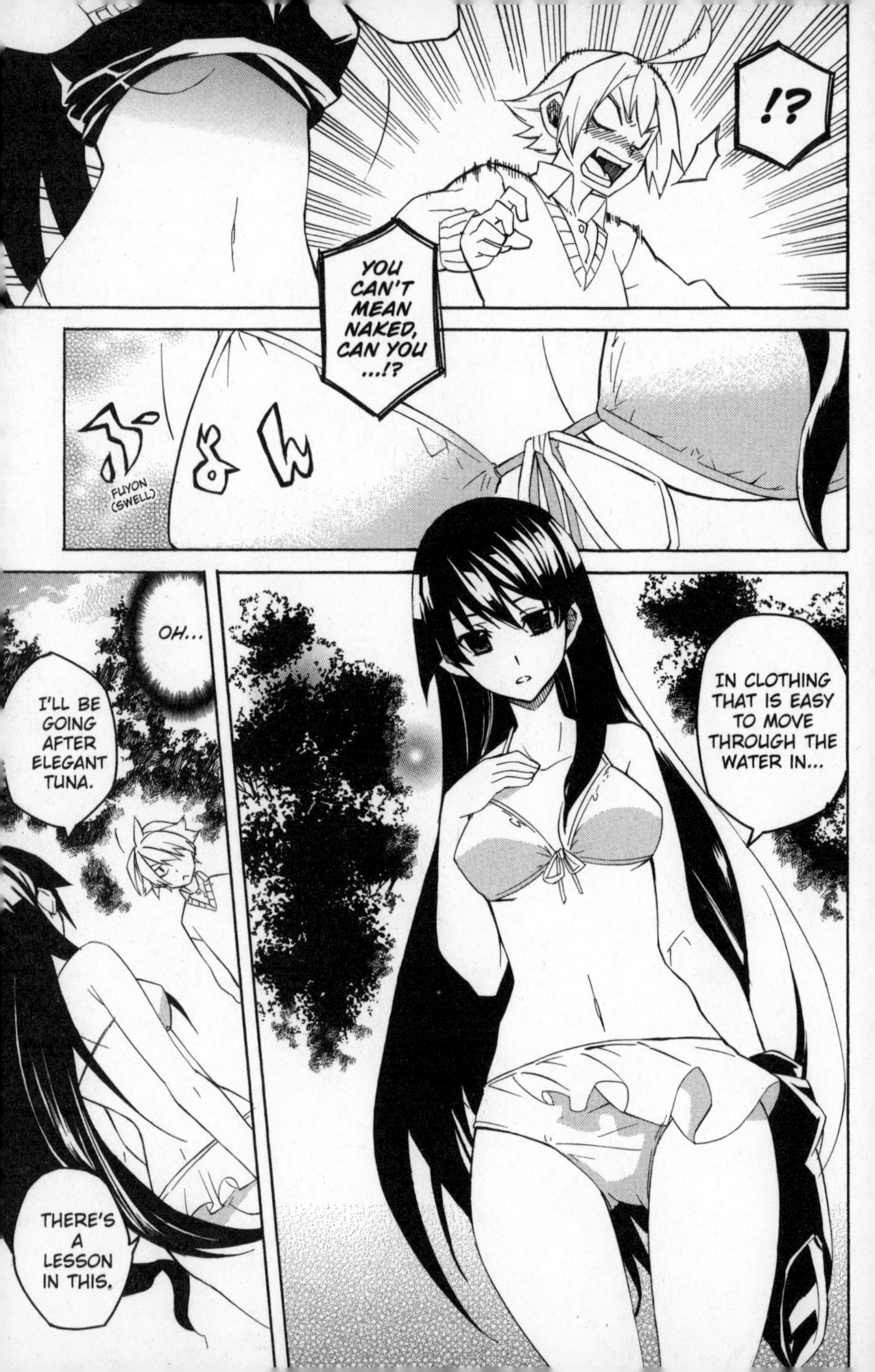
!?
YOU CAN'T MEAN NAKED, CAN YOU ...!?
ふよん
FUYON (SWELL)
IN CLOTHING THAT IS EASY TO MOVE THROUGH THE WATER IN...
OH...
I'LL BE GOING AFTER ELEGANT TUNA.
THERE'S A LESSON IN THIS.

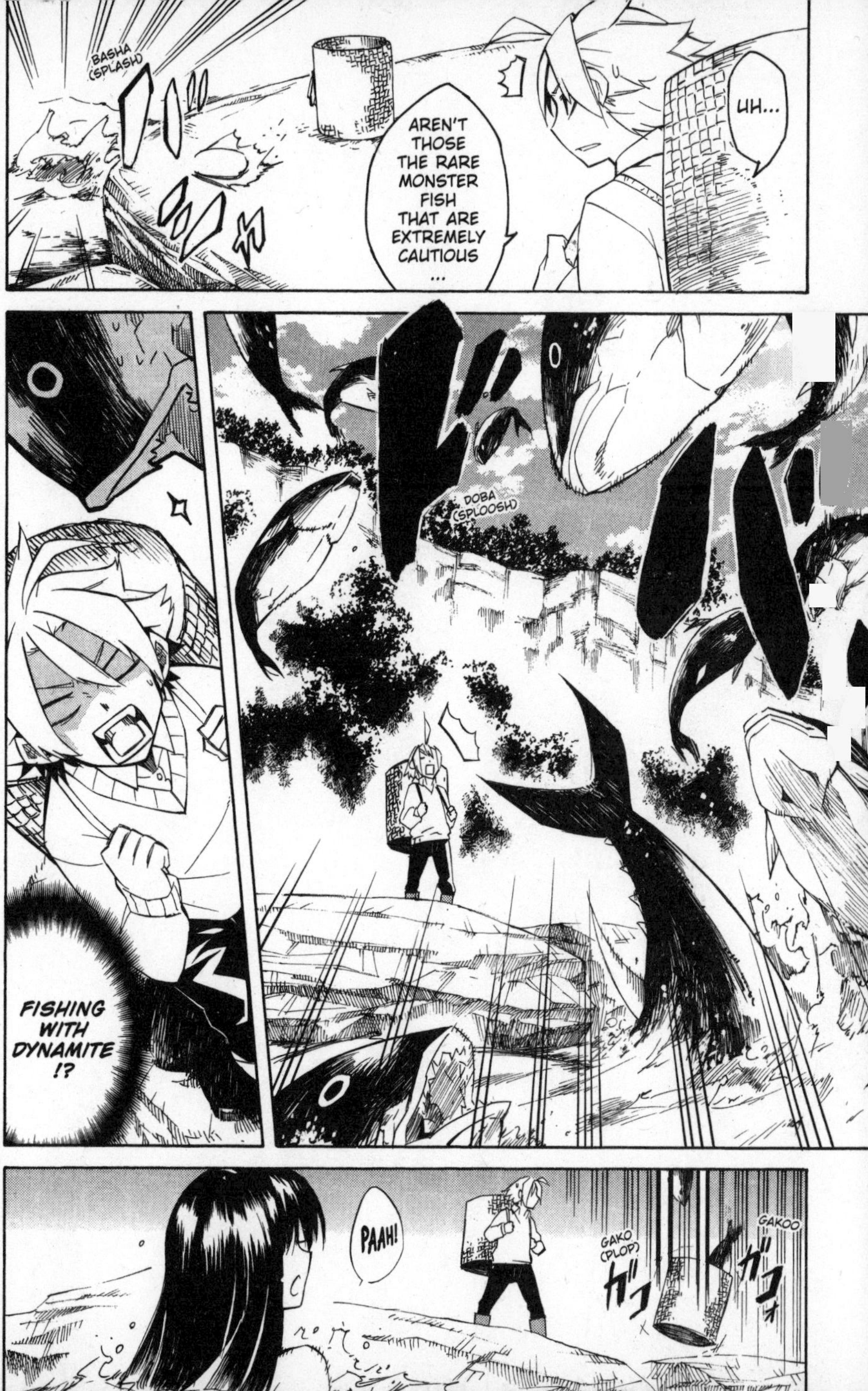
UH...
AREN'T THOSE THE RARE MONSTER FISH THAT ARE EXTREMELY CAUTIOUS ...
BASHA (SPLASH)
DOBA (SPLOOSH)
FISHING WITH DYNAMITE !?
GAKOO
GAKO (PLOP)
PAAH!

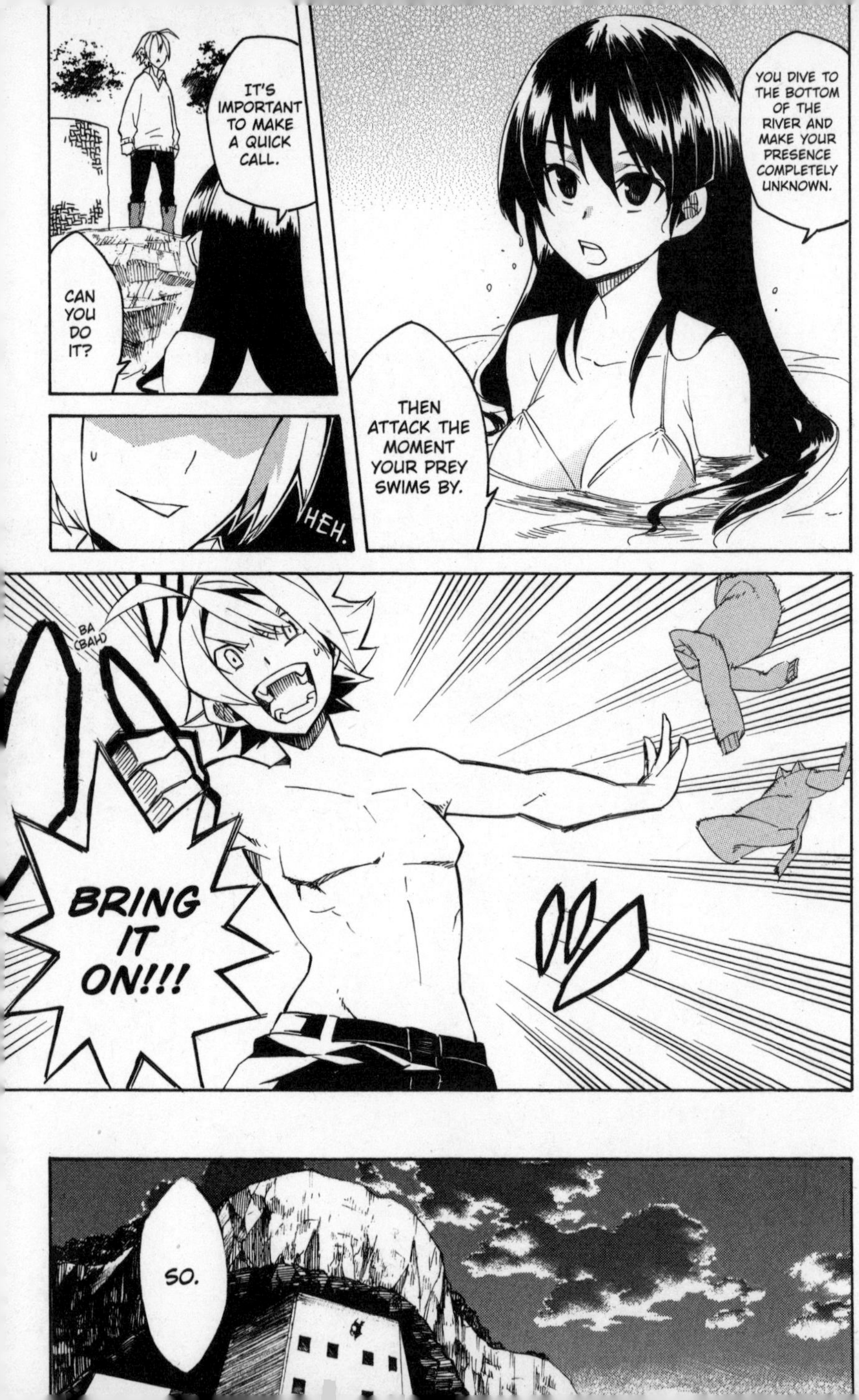
YOU DIVE TO THE BOTTOM OF THE RIVER AND MAKE YOUR PRESENCE COMPLETELY UNKNOWN.
THEN ATTACK THE MOMENT YOUR PREY SWIMS BY.
IT'S IMPORTANT TO MAKE A QUICK CALL.
CAN YOU DO IT?
HEH.
BA (BAH)
BRING IT ON!!!
SO.

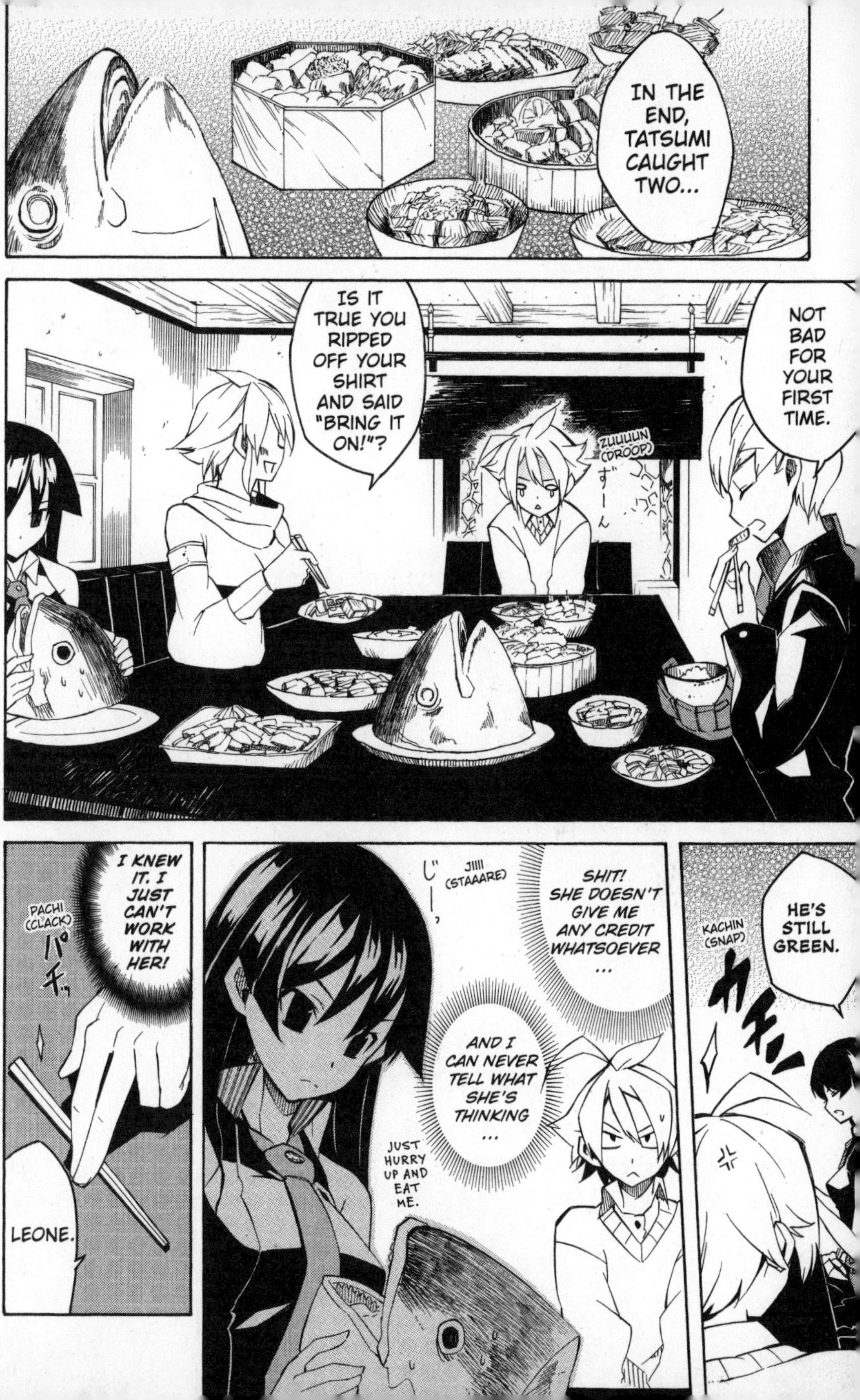
IN THE END, TATSUMI CAUGHT TWO...
NOT BAD FOR YOUR FIRST TIME.
IS IT TRUE YOU RIPPED OFF YOUR SHIRT AND SAID "BRING IT ON!"?
ZUUUUUN (DROOP)
HE'S STILL GREEN.
KACHIN (SNAP)
SHIT! SHE DOESN'T GIVE ME ANY CREDIT WHATSOEVER ...
JIIII (STAAARE)
AND I CAN NEVER TELL WHAT SHE'S THINKING ...
JUST HURRY UP AND EAT ME.
I KNEW IT. I JUST CAN'T WORK WITH HER!
PACHI (CLACK)
LEONE.

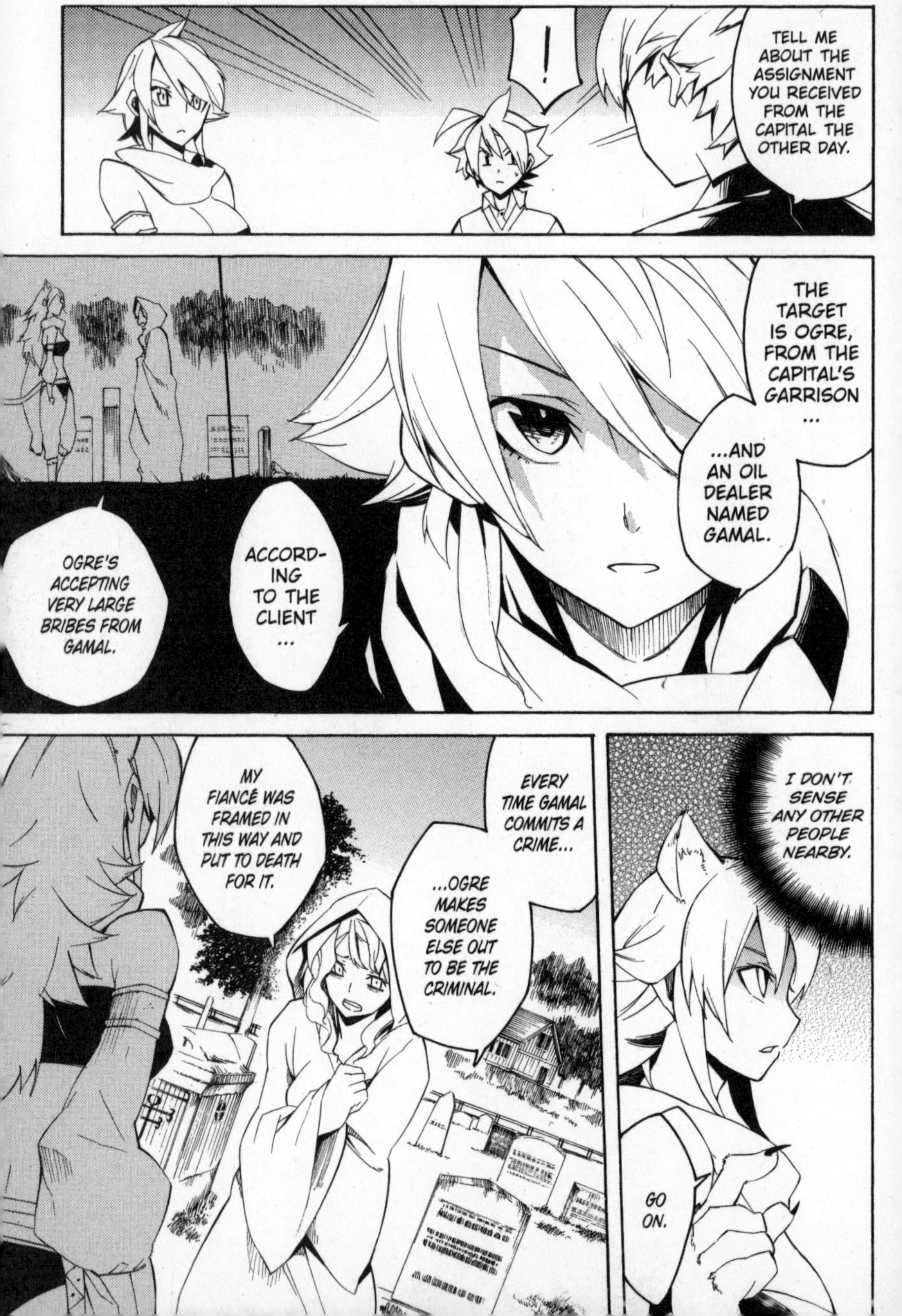
TELL ME ABOUT THE ASSIGNMENT YOU RECEIVED FROM THE CAPITAL THE OTHER DAY.
!
THE TARGET IS OGRE, FROM THE CAPITAL'S GARRISON...
...AND AN OIL DEALER NAMED GAMAL.
ACCORD-ING TO THE CLIENT...
OGRE'S ACCEPTING VERY LARGE BRIBES FROM GAMAL.
I DON'T SENSE ANY OTHER PEOPLE NEARBY.
GO ON.
EVERY TIME GAMAL COMMITS A CRIME...
...OGRE MAKES SOMEONE ELSE OUT TO BE THE CRIMINAL.
MY FIANCÉ WAS FRAMED IN THIS WAY AND PUT TO DEATH FOR IT.

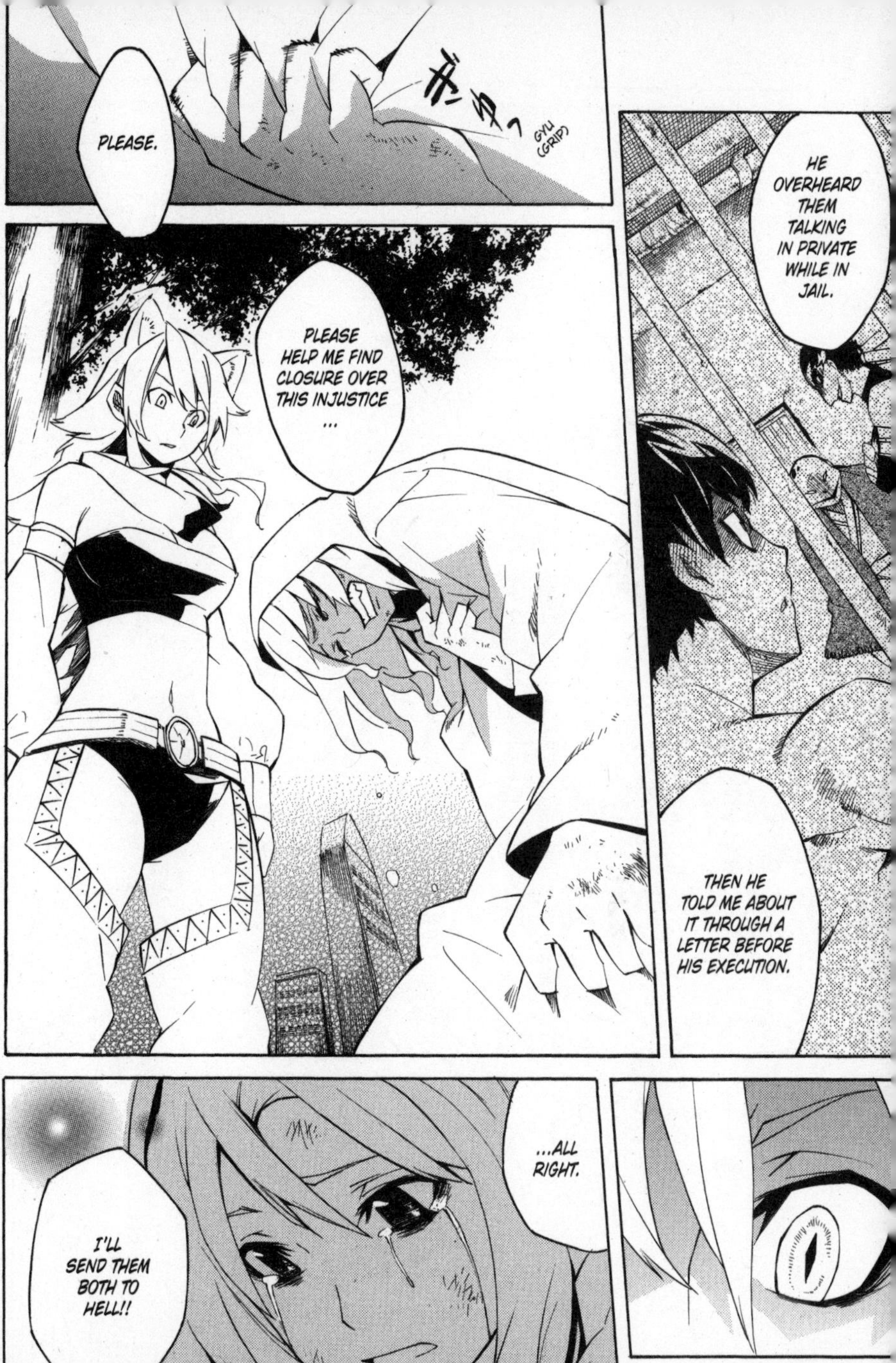
HE OVERHEARD THEM TALKING IN PRIVATE WHILE IN JAIL.
THEN HE TOLD ME ABOUT IT THROUGH A LETTER BEFORE HIS EXECUTION.
PLEASE.
ギュッ
GYU (GRIP)
PLEASE HELP ME FIND CLOSURE OVER THIS INJUSTICE ...
...ALL RIGHT.
I'LL SEND THEM BOTH TO HELL!!

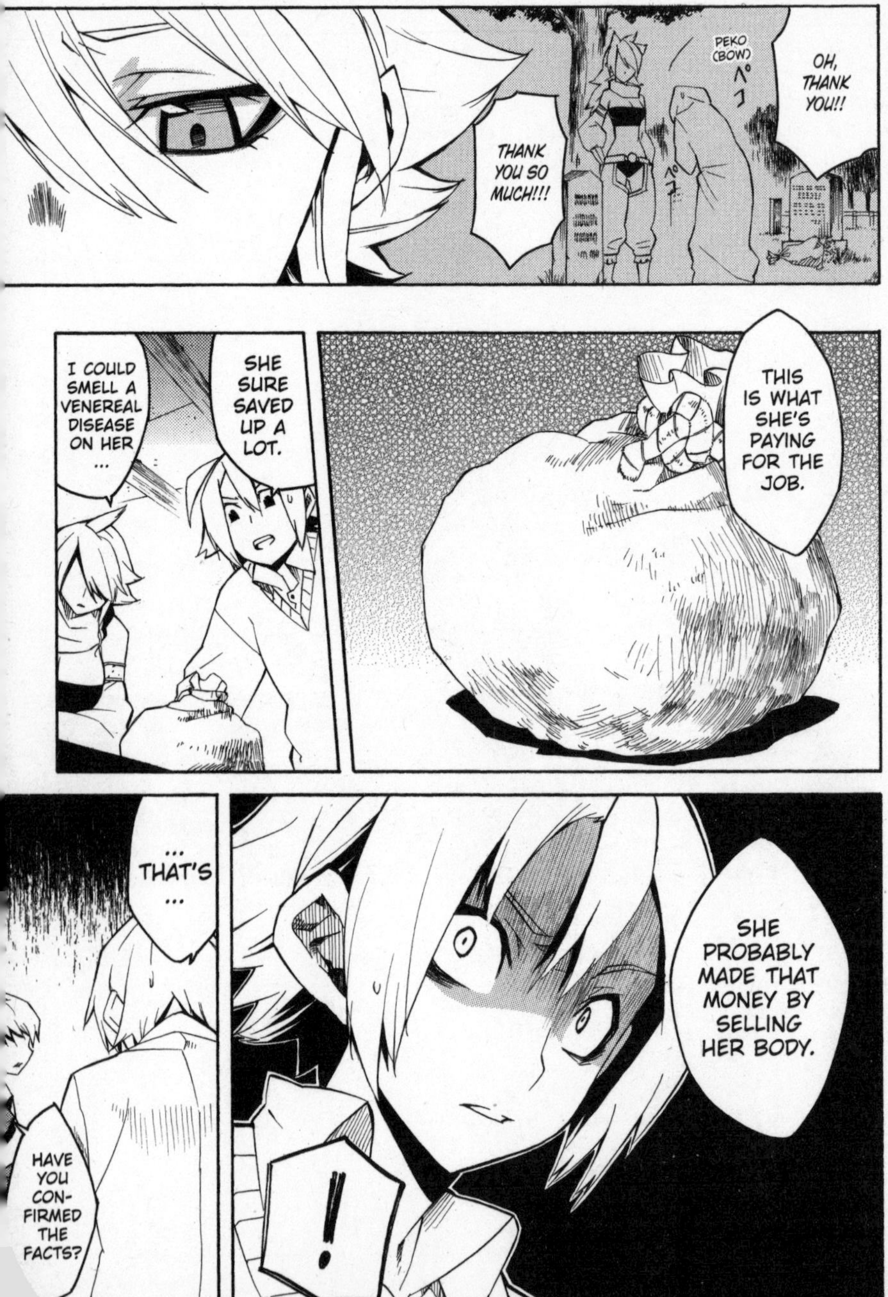
OH, THANK YOU!!
PEKO (BOW)
THANK YOU SO MUCH!!!
THIS IS WHAT SHE'S PAYING FOR THE JOB.
SHE SURE SAVED UP A LOT.
I COULD SMELL A VENEREAL DISEASE ON HER ...
SHE PROBABLY MADE THAT MONEY BY SELLING HER BODY.
!
... THAT'S ...
HAVE YOU CON-FIRMED THE FACTS?

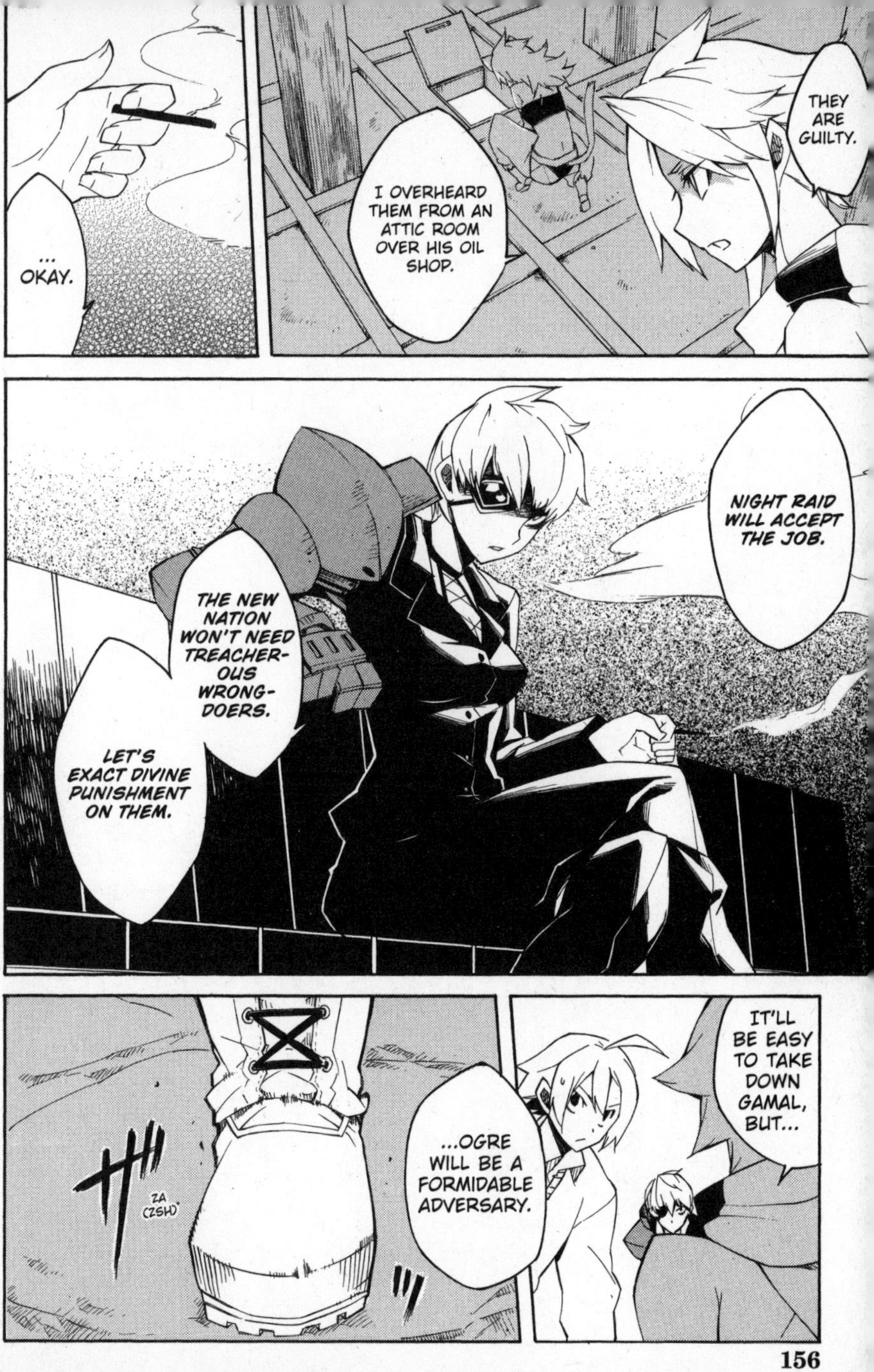
THEY ARE GUILTY.
I OVERHEARD THEM FROM AN ATTIC ROOM OVER HIS OIL SHOP.
...OKAY.
NIGHT RAID WILL ACCEPT THE JOB.
THE NEW NATION WON'T NEED TREACHER-OUS WRONG-DOERS.
LET'S EXACT DIVINE PUNISHMENT ON THEM.
IT'LL BE EASY TO TAKE DOWN GAMAL, BUT...
...OGRE WILL BE A FORMIDABLE ADVERSARY.
ZA (ZSH)

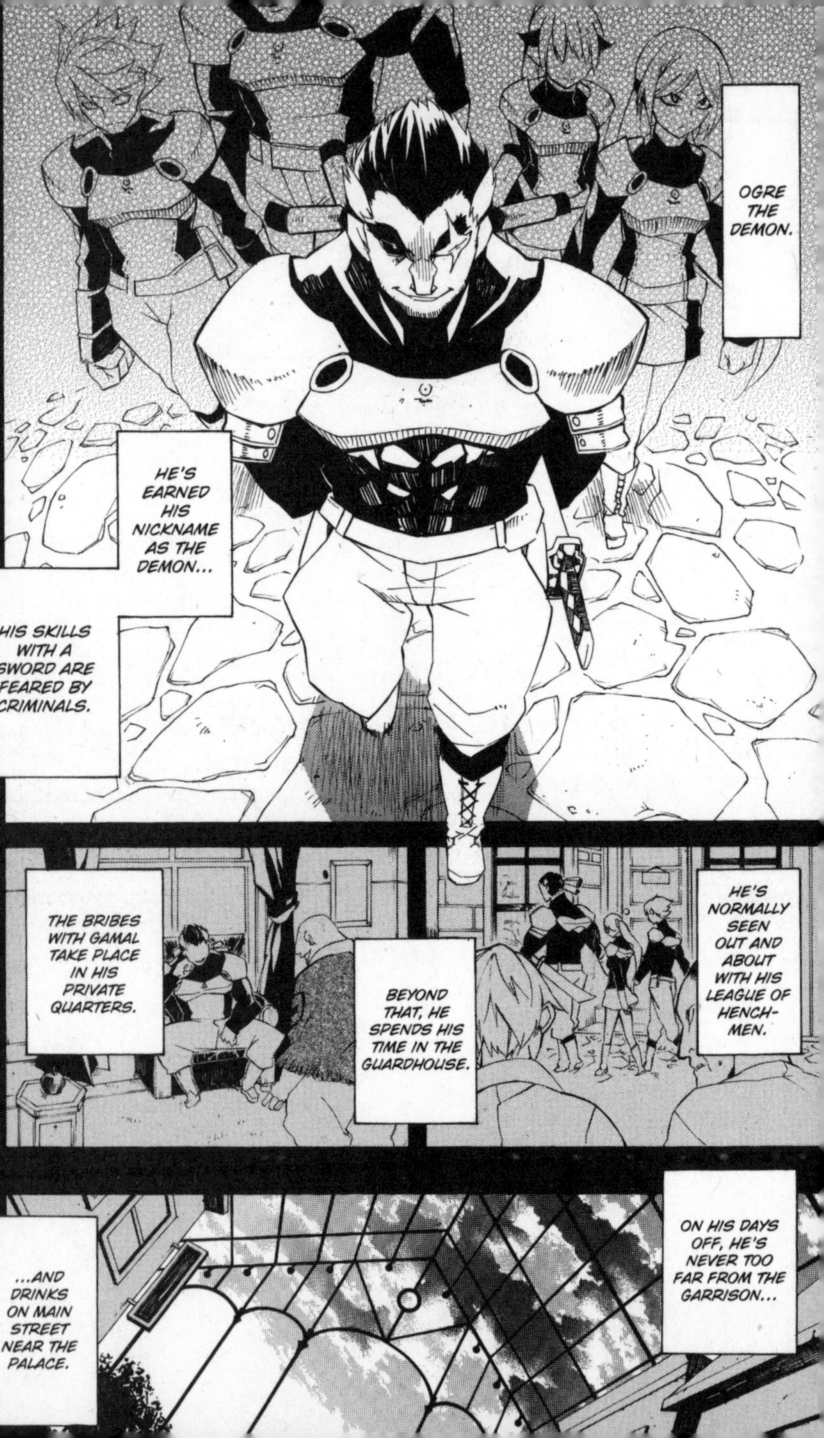
OGRE THE DEMON.
HE'S EARNED HIS NICKNAME AS THE DEMON...
HIS SKILLS WITH A SWORD ARE FEARED BY CRIMINALS.
HE'S NORMALLY SEEN OUT AND ABOUT WITH HIS LEAGUE OF HENCH-MEN.
BEYOND THAT, HE SPENDS HIS TIME IN THE GUARDHOUSE.
THE BRIBES WITH GAMAL TAKE PLACE IN HIS PRIVATE QUARTERS.
ON HIS DAYS OFF, HE'S NEVER TOO FAR FROM THE GARRISON...
...AND DRINKS ON MAIN STREET NEAR THE PALACE.

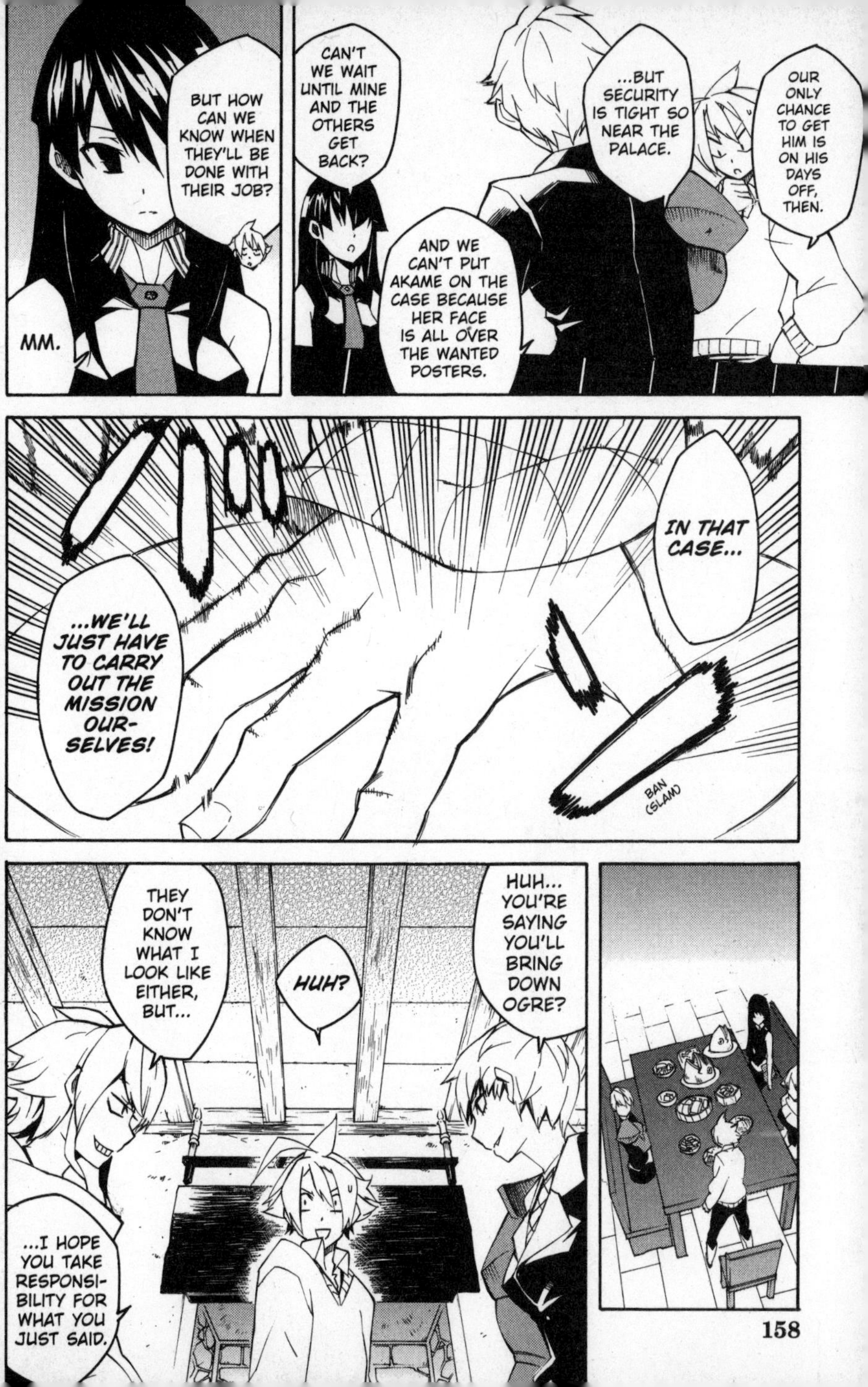
OUR ONLY CHANCE TO GET HIM IS ON HIS DAYS OFF, THEN.
...BUT SECURITY IS TIGHT SO NEAR THE PALACE.
AND WE CAN'T PUT AKAME ON THE CASE BECAUSE HER FACE IS ALL OVER THE WANTED POSTERS.
CAN'T WE WAIT UNTIL MINE AND THE OTHERS GET BACK?
BUT HOW CAN WE KNOW WHEN THEY'LL BE DONE WITH THEIR JOB?
MM.
IN THAT CASE...
...WE'LL JUST HAVE TO CARRY OUT THE MISSION OUR-SELVES!
BAN (SLAM)
HUH... YOU'RE SAYING YOU'LL BRING DOWN OGRE?
HUH?
THEY DON'T KNOW WHAT I LOOK LIKE EITHER, BUT...
...I HOPE YOU TAKE RESPONSI-BILITY FOR WHAT YOU JUST SAID.

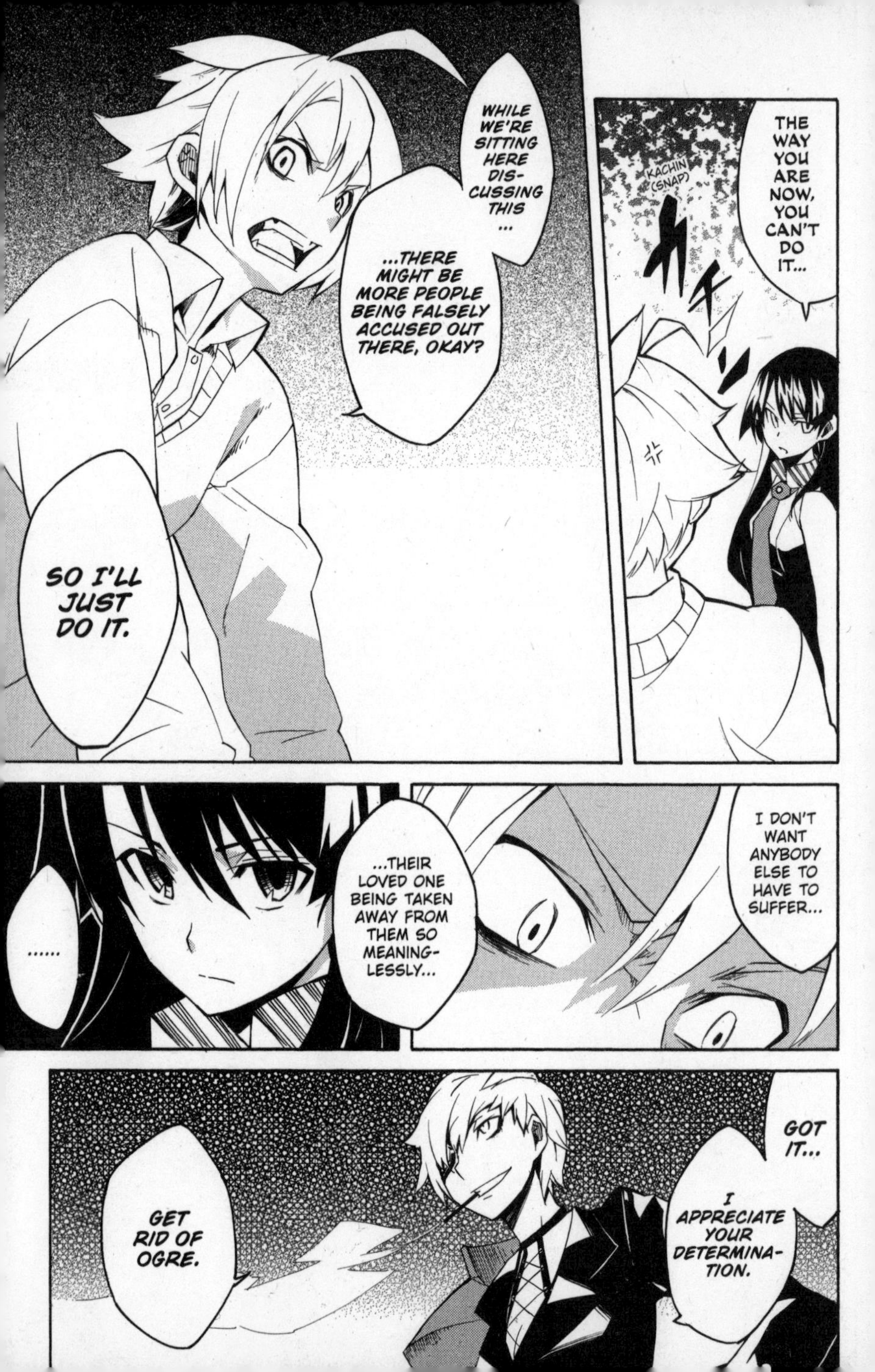
THE WAY YOU ARE NOW, YOU CAN'T DO IT...
KACHIN (SNAP)
WHILE WE'RE SITTING HERE DIS-CUSSING THIS ...
...THERE MIGHT BE MORE PEOPLE BEING FALSELY ACCUSED OUT THERE, OKAY?
SO I'LL JUST DO IT.
I DON'T WANT ANYBODY ELSE TO HAVE TO SUFFER...
...THEIR LOVED ONE BEING TAKEN AWAY FROM THEM SO MEANING-LESSLY...
......
GOT IT...
I APPRECIATE YOUR DETERMINA-TION.
GET RID OF OGRE.

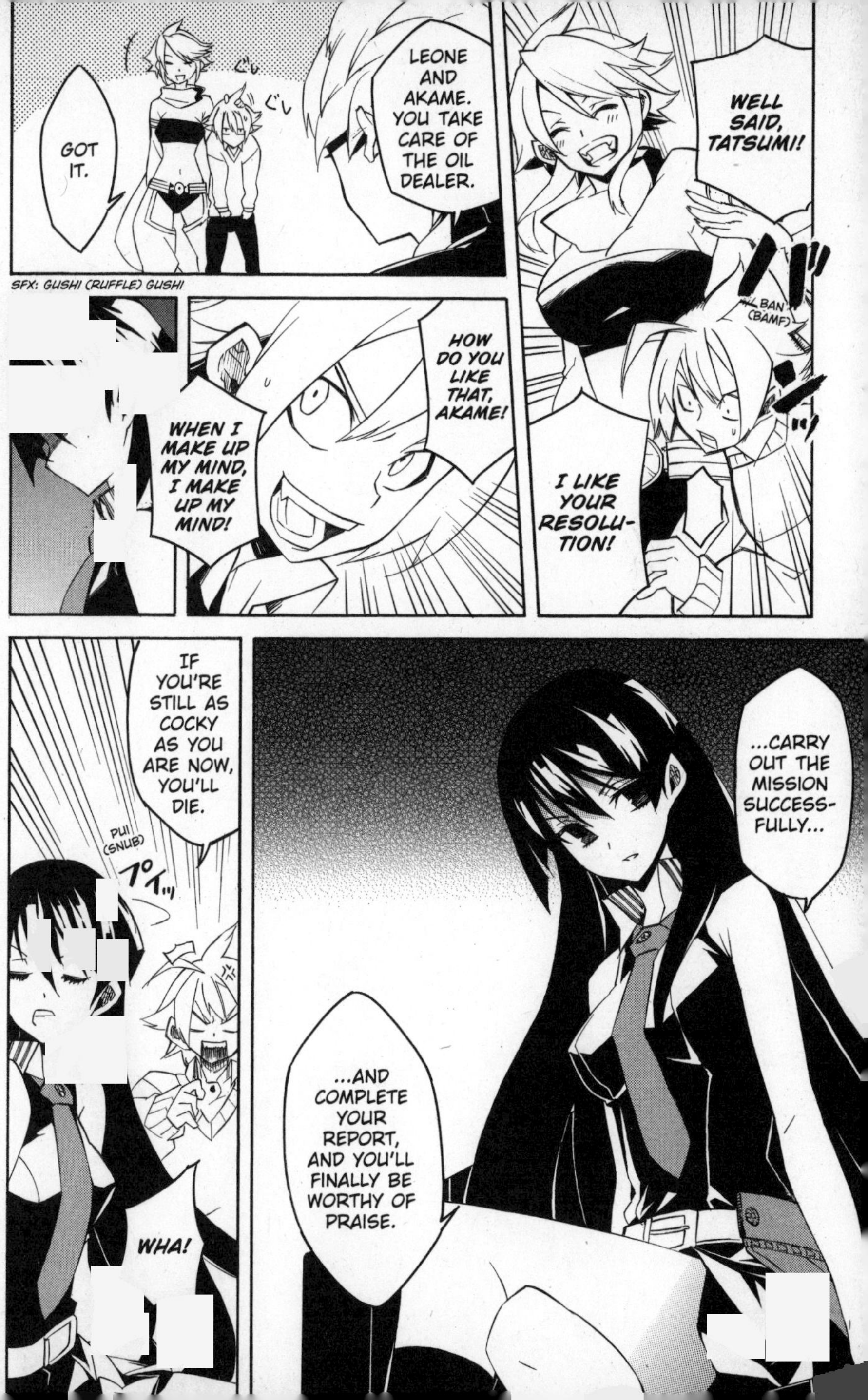
WELL SAID, TATSUMI!
BAN (BAMF)
I LIKE YOUR RESOLUTION!
LEONE AND AKAME. YOU TAKE CARE OF THE OIL DEALER.
GOT IT.
SFX: GUSHI (RUFFLE) GUSHI
HOW DO YOU LIKE THAT, AKAME!
WHEN I MAKE UP MY MIND, I MAKE UP MY MIND!
...CARRY OUT THE MISSION SUCCESSFULLY...
...AND COMPLETE YOUR REPORT, AND YOU'LL FINALLY BE WORTHY OF PRAISE.
IF YOU'RE STILL AS COCKY AS YOU ARE NOW, YOU'LL DIE.
PUI (SNUB)
WHA!

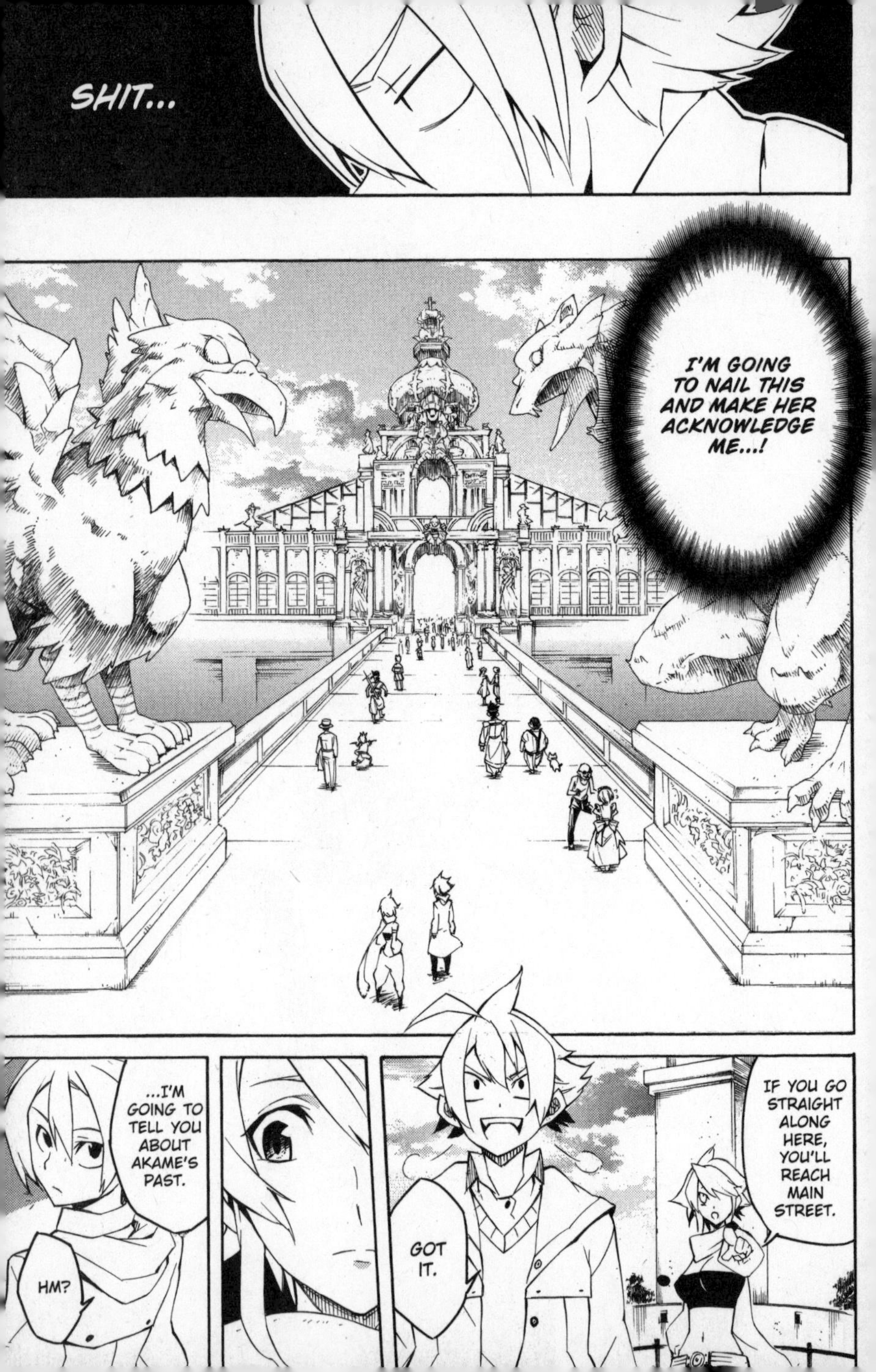
SHIT...
I'M GOING TO NAIL THIS AND MAKE HER ACKNOWLEDGE ME...!
...I'M GOING TO TELL YOU ABOUT AKAME'S PAST.
HM?
GOT IT.
IF YOU GO STRAIGHT ALONG HERE, YOU'LL REACH MAIN STREET.

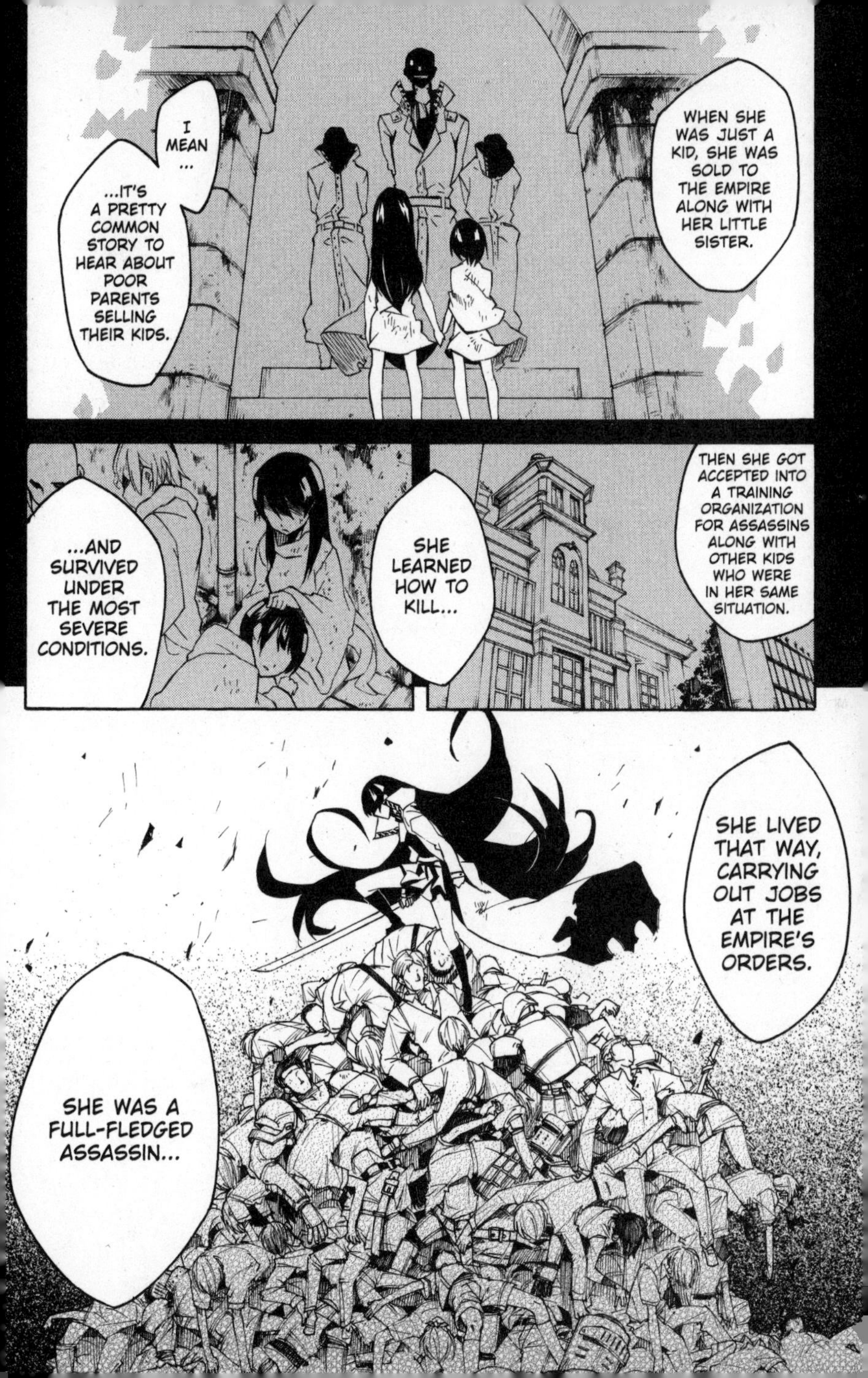
WHEN SHE WAS JUST A KID, SHE WAS SOLD TO THE EMPIRE ALONG WITH HER LITTLE SISTER.
I MEAN ...
...IT'S A PRETTY COMMON STORY TO HEAR ABOUT POOR PARENTS SELLING THEIR KIDS.
THEN SHE GOT ACCEPTED INTO A TRAINING ORGANIZATION FOR ASSASSINS ALONG WITH OTHER KIDS WHO WERE IN HER SAME SITUATION.
SHE LEARNED HOW TO KILL...
...AND SURVIVED UNDER THE MOST SEVERE CONDITIONS.
SHE LIVED THAT WAY, CARRYING OUT JOBS AT THE EMPIRE'S ORDERS.
SHE WAS A FULL-FLEDGED ASSASSIN...

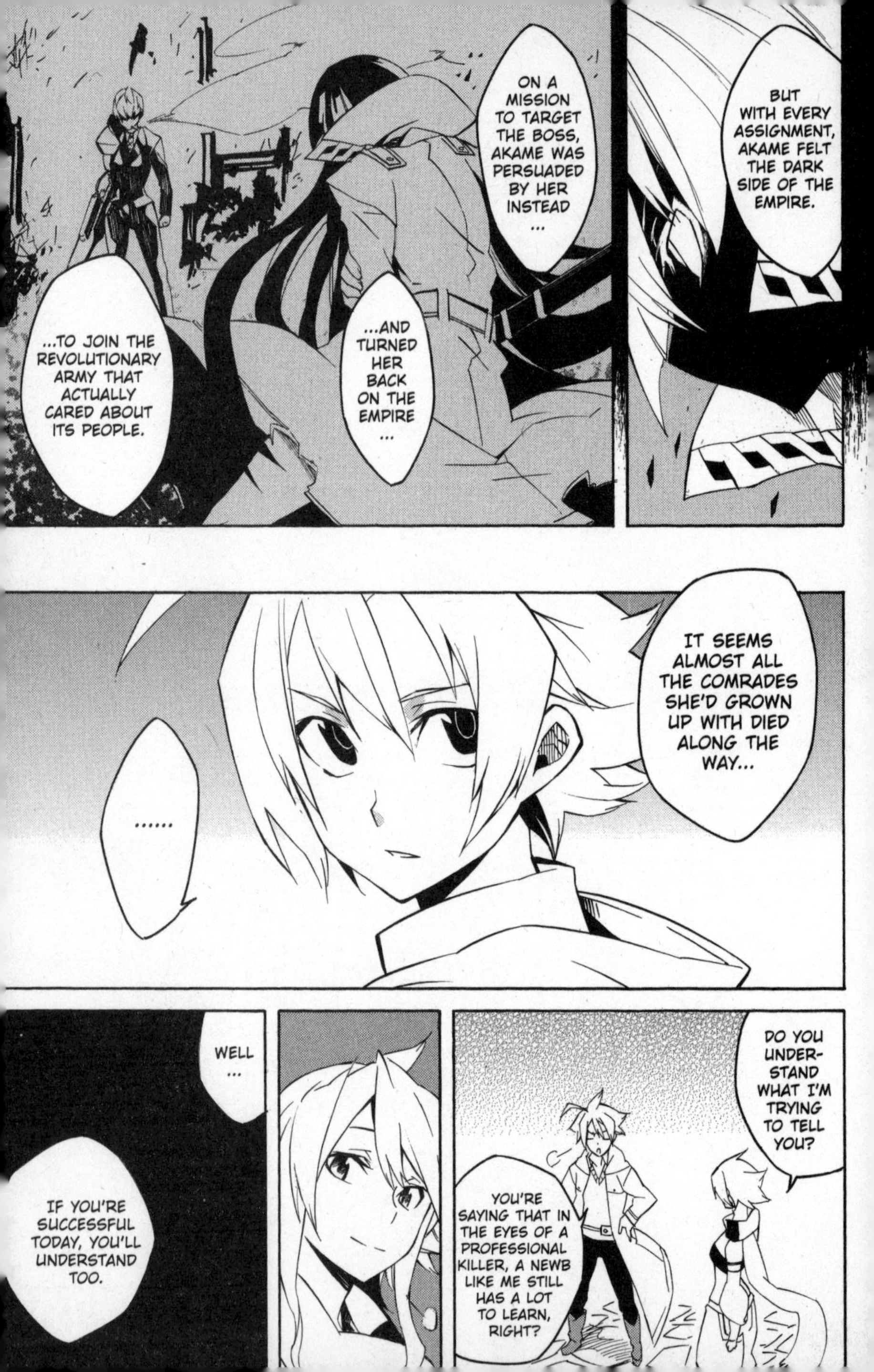
BUT WITH EVERY ASSIGNMENT, AKAME FELT THE DARK SIDE OF THE EMPIRE.
ON A MISSION TO TARGET THE BOSS, AKAME WAS PERSUADED BY HER INSTEAD ...
...AND TURNED HER BACK ON THE EMPIRE ...
...TO JOIN THE REVOLUTIONARY ARMY THAT ACTUALLY CARED ABOUT ITS PEOPLE.
IT SEEMS ALMOST ALL THE COMRADES SHE'D GROWN UP WITH DIED ALONG THE WAY...
......
DO YOU UNDER-STAND WHAT I'M TRYING TO TELL YOU?
YOU'RE SAYING THAT IN THE EYES OF A PROFESSIONAL KILLER, A NEWB LIKE ME STILL HAS A LOT TO LEARN, RIGHT?
WELL ...
IF YOU'RE SUCCESSFUL TODAY, YOU'LL UNDERSTAND TOO.

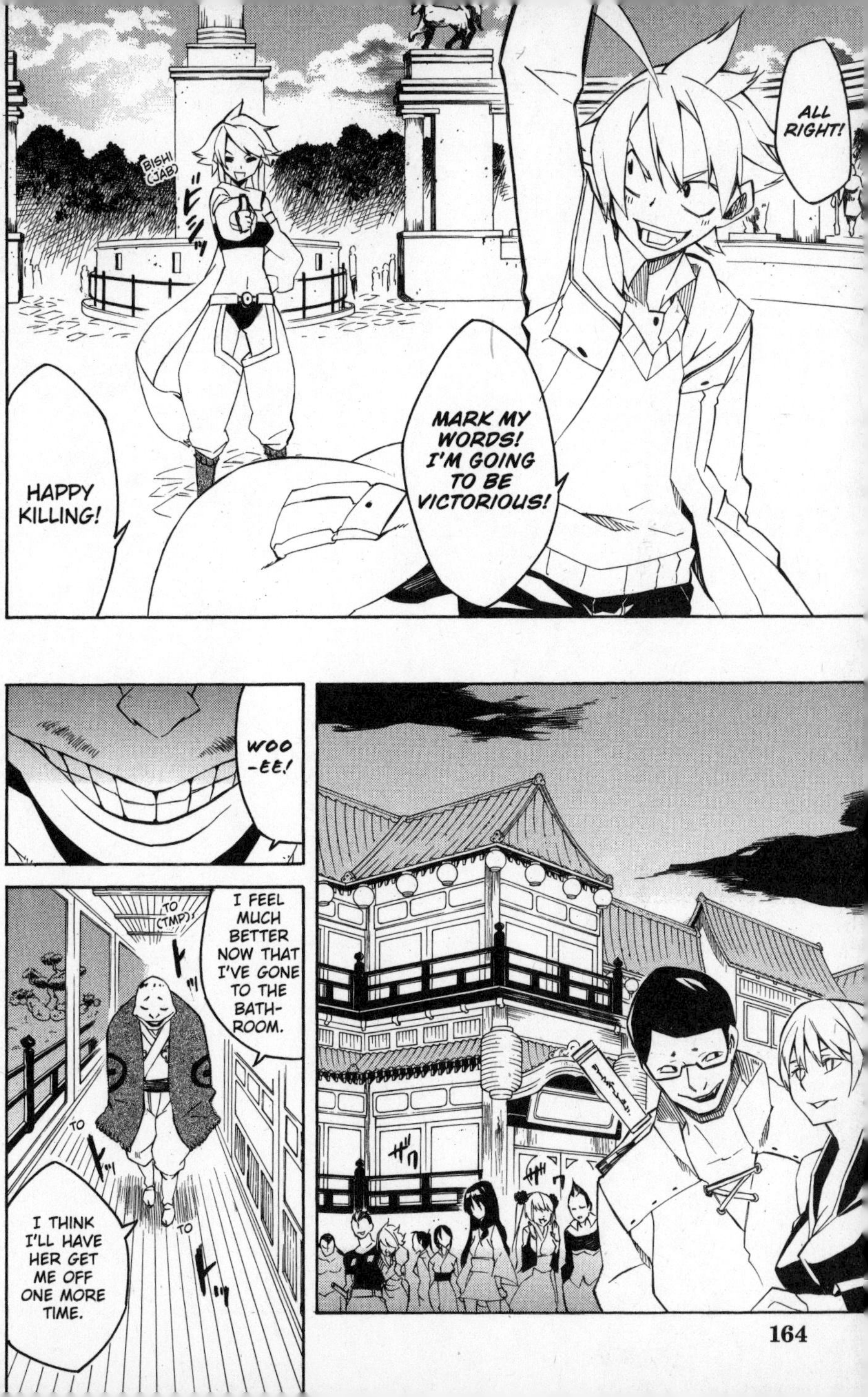

ALL RIGHT!
MARK MY WORDS! I'M GOING TO BE VICTORIOUS!
BISHI (JAB)
HAPPY KILLING!
WOO-EE!
TO (TMP)
I FEEL MUCH BETTER NOW THAT I'VE GONE TO THE BATH-ROOM.
TO
TO
I THINK I'LL HAVE HER GET ME OFF ONE MORE TIME.

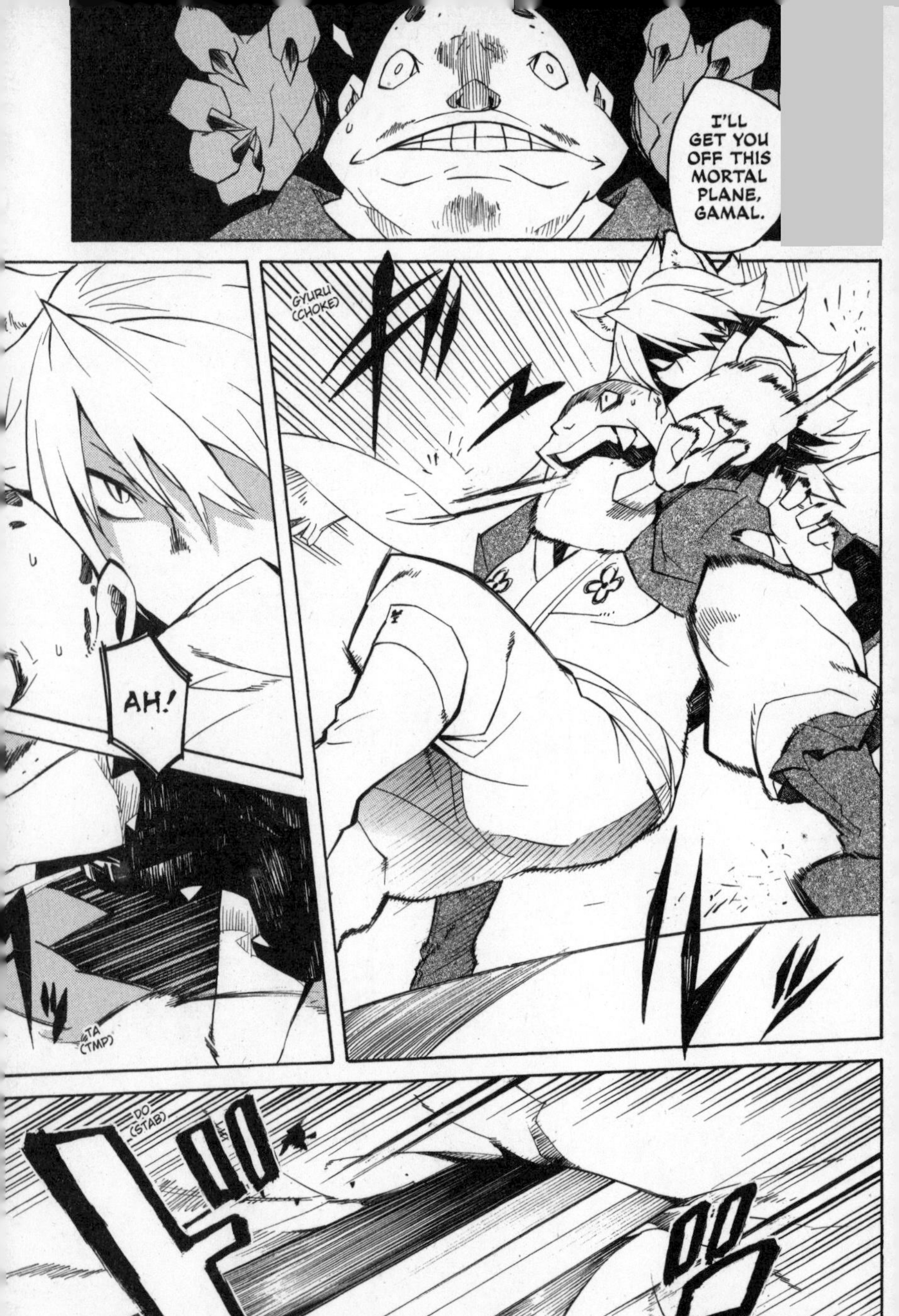
I'LL GET YOU OFF THIS MORTAL PLANE, GAMAL.
GYURU (CHOKE)
AH!
TA (TMP)
DO (STAB)

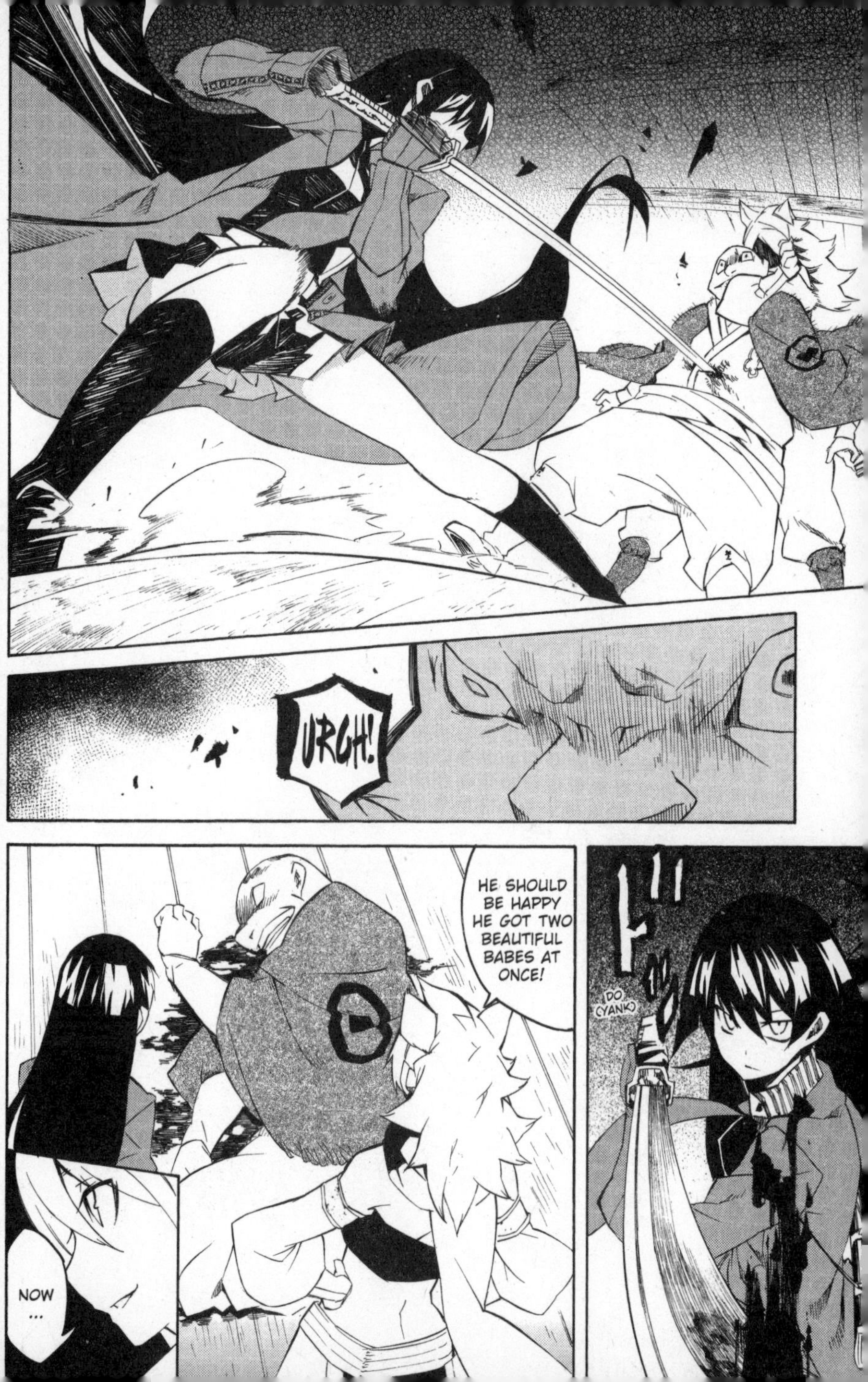
URGH!
DO (YANK)
HE SHOULD BE HAPPY HE GOT TWO BEAUTIFUL BABES AT ONCE!
NOW ...

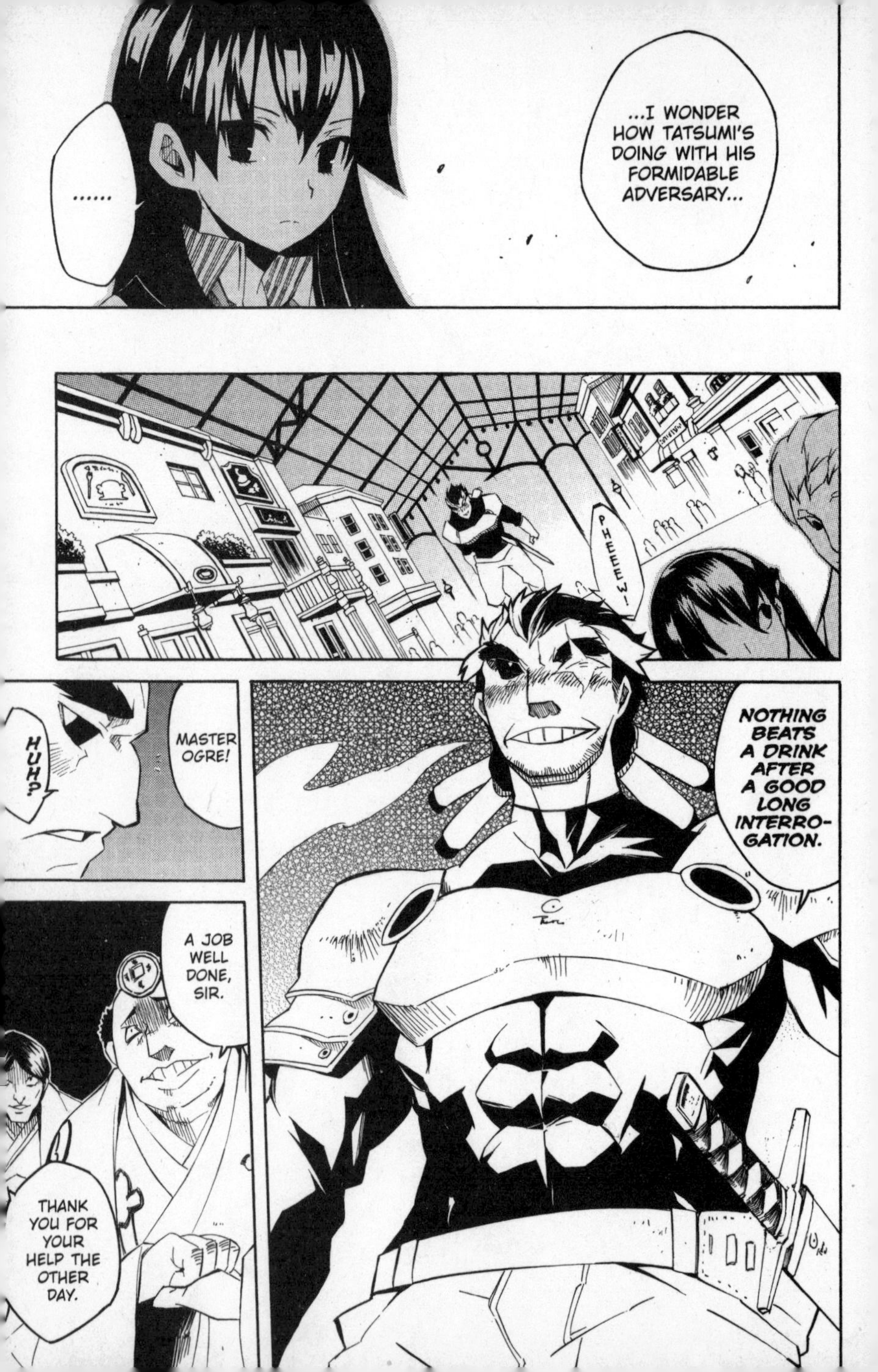
...I WONDER HOW TATSUMI'S DOING WITH HIS FORMIDABLE ADVERSARY...
......
PHEEEW!
NOTHING BEATS A DRINK AFTER A GOOD LONG INTERROGATION.
MASTER OGRE!
HUH?
A JOB WELL DONE, SIR.
THANK YOU FOR YOUR HELP THE OTHER DAY.

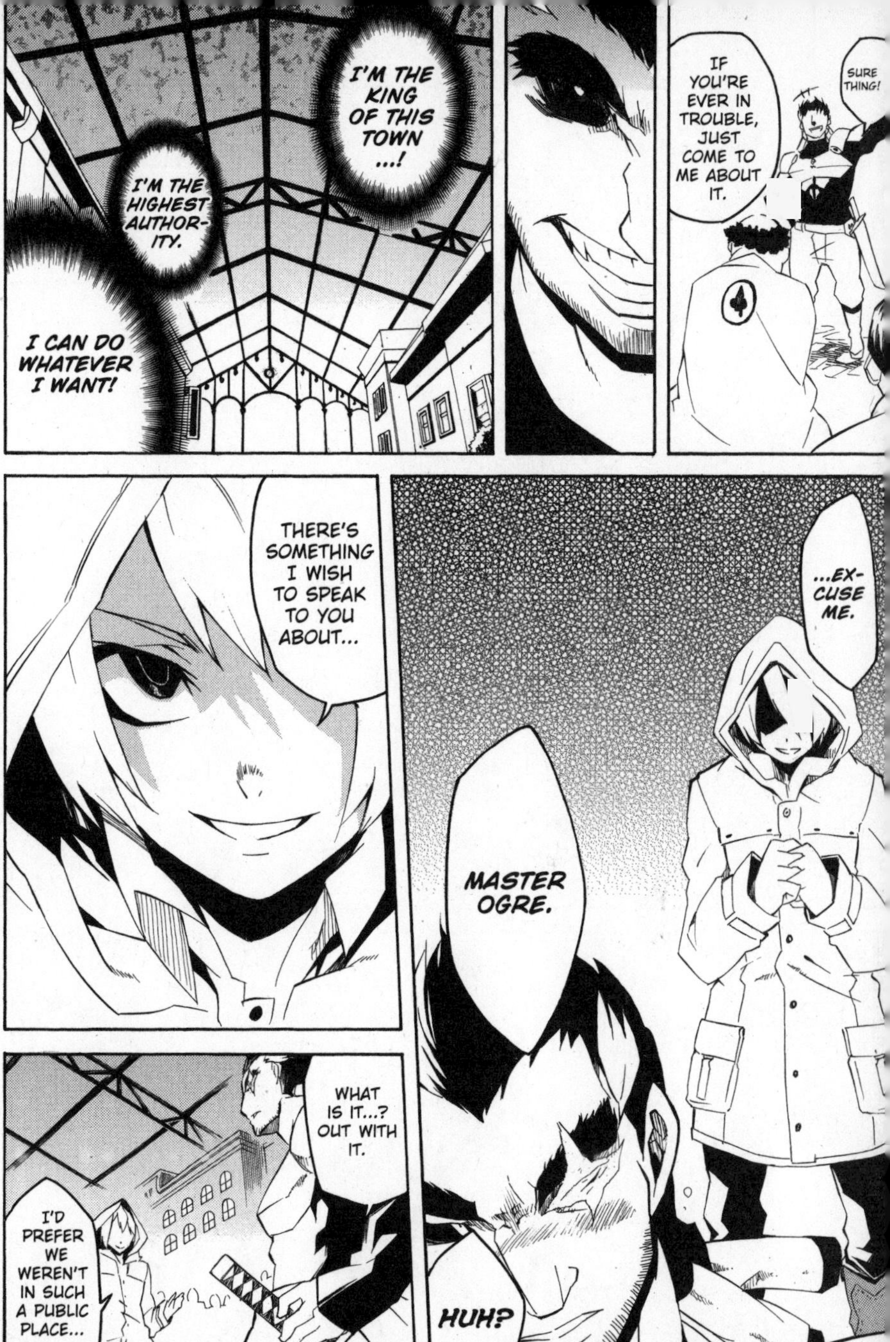
IF YOU'RE EVER IN TROUBLE, JUST COME TO ME ABOUT IT.
SURE THING!
I'M THE KING OF THIS TOWN ...!
I'M THE HIGHEST AUTHORITY.
I CAN DO WHATEVER I WANT!
...EXCUSE ME.
MASTER OGRE.
HUH?
THERE'S SOMETHING I WISH TO SPEAK TO YOU ABOUT...
WHAT IS IT...? OUT WITH IT.
I'D PREFER WE WEREN'T IN SUCH A PUBLIC PLACE...

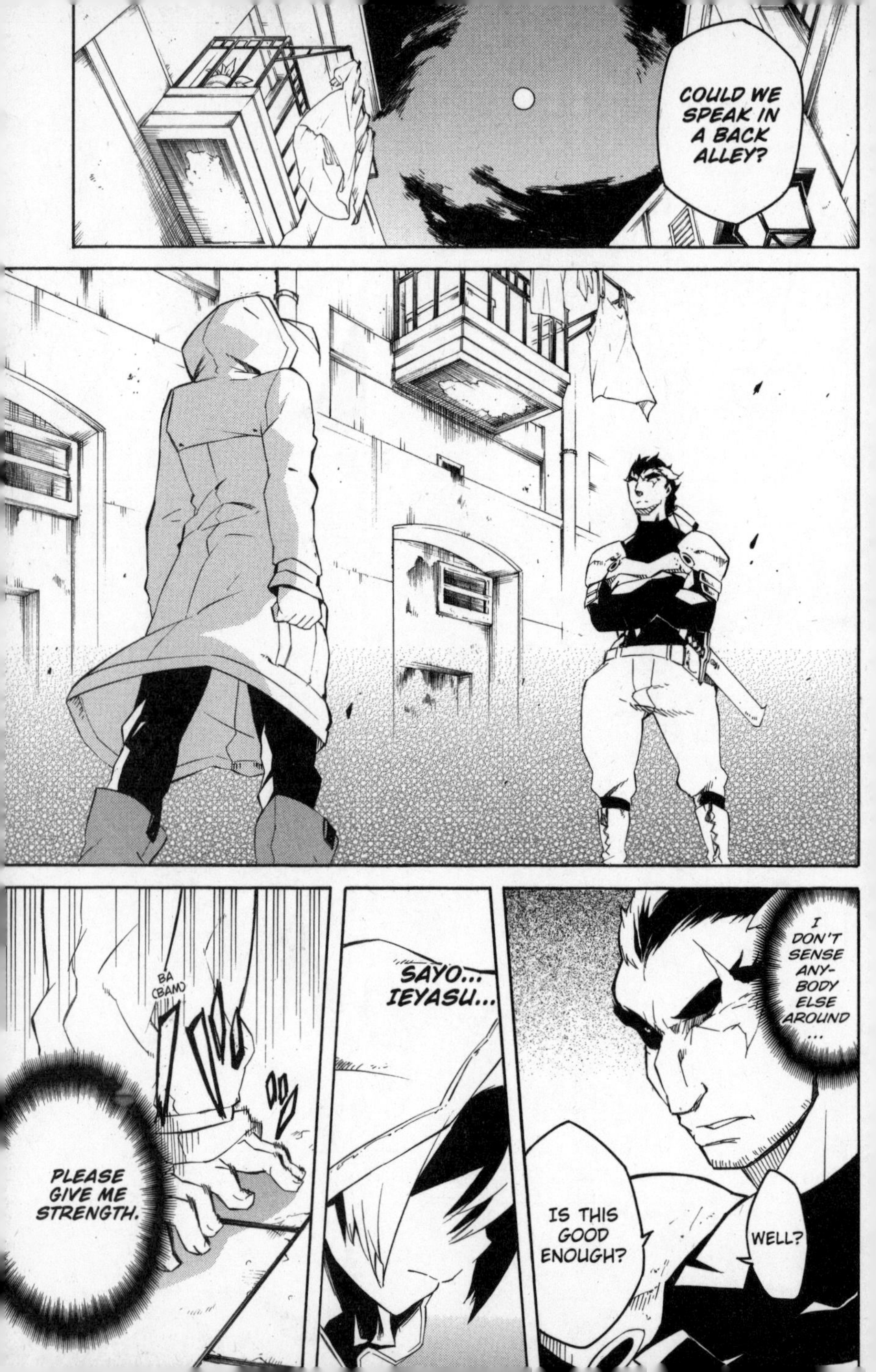
COULD WE SPEAK IN A BACK ALLEY?
I DON'T SENSE ANY-BODY ELSE AROUND...
WELL?
IS THIS GOOD ENOUGH?
SAYO... IEYASU...
BA (BAM)
PLEASE GIVE ME STRENGTH.

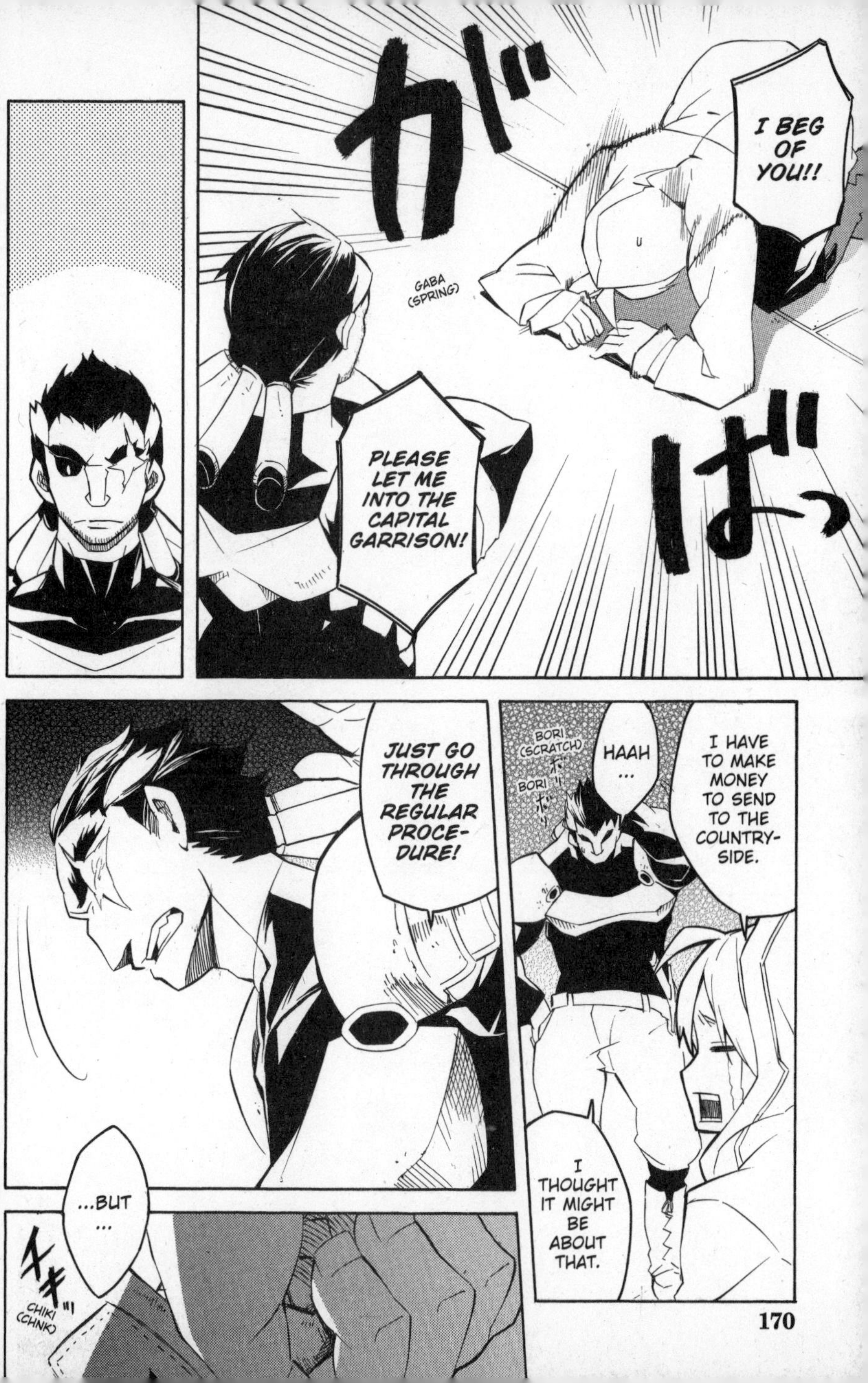
I BEG OF YOU!!
GABA (SPRING)
PLEASE LET ME INTO THE CAPITAL GARRISON!
I HAVE TO MAKE MONEY TO SEND TO THE COUNTRY-SIDE.
HAAH ...
BORI (SCRATCH) BORI
I THOUGHT IT MIGHT BE ABOUT THAT.
JUST GO THROUGH THE REGULAR PROCE-DURE!
...BUT ...
CHIKI (CHNK)

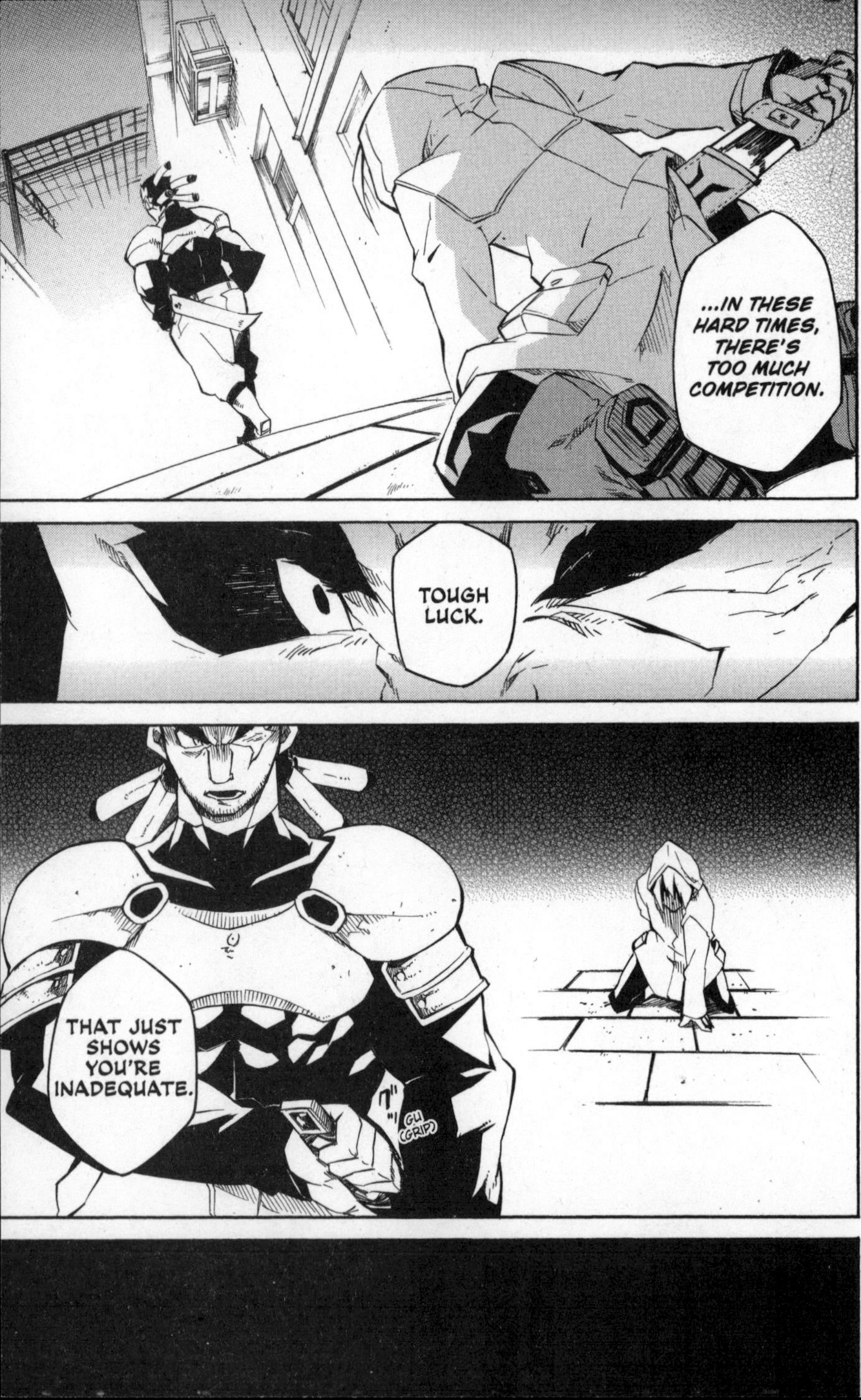
...IN THESE HARD TIMES, THERE'S TOO MUCH COMPETITION.
TOUGH LUCK.
THAT JUST SHOWS YOU'RE INADEQUATE.
GU (GRIP)

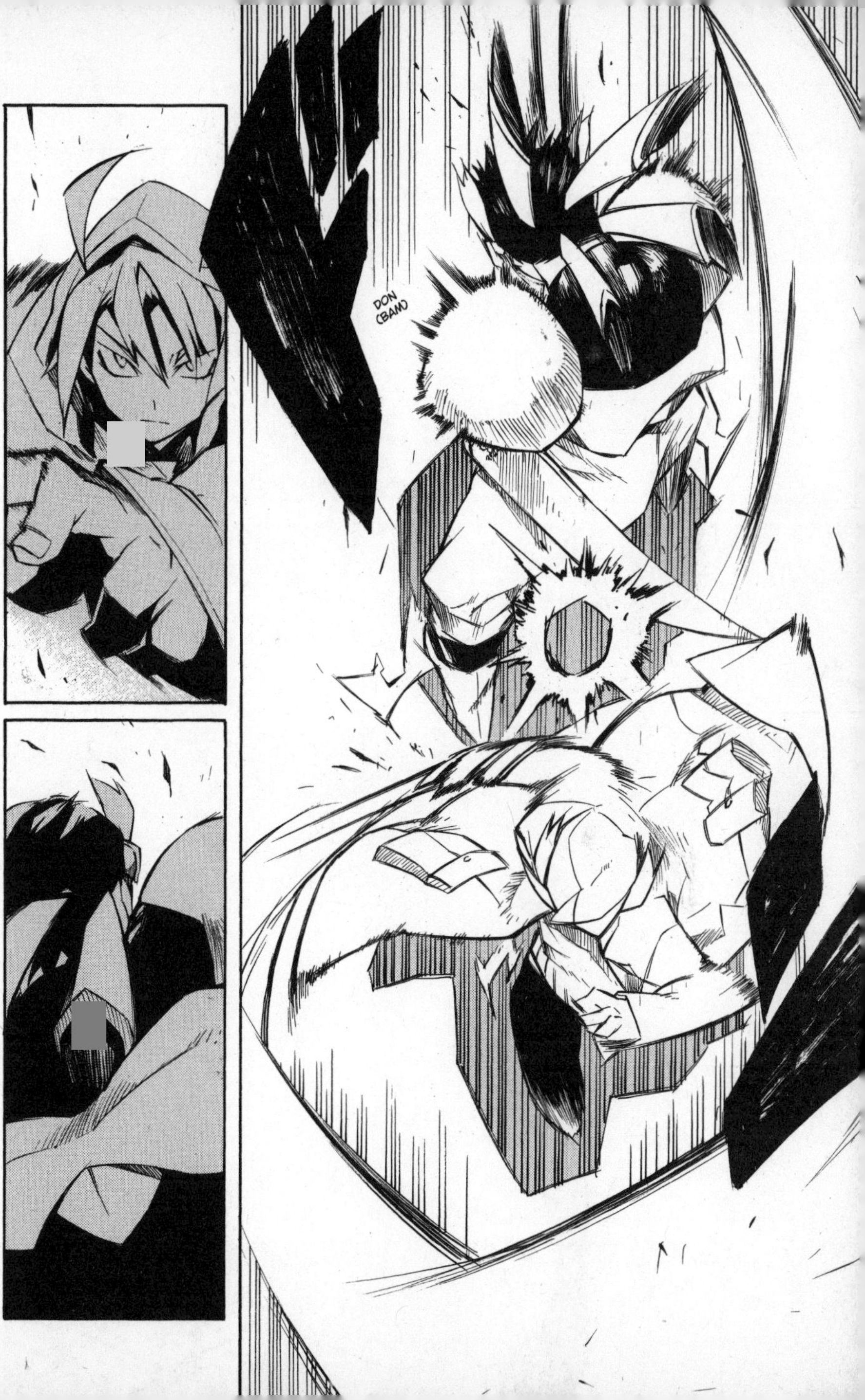
DON
(BAM)

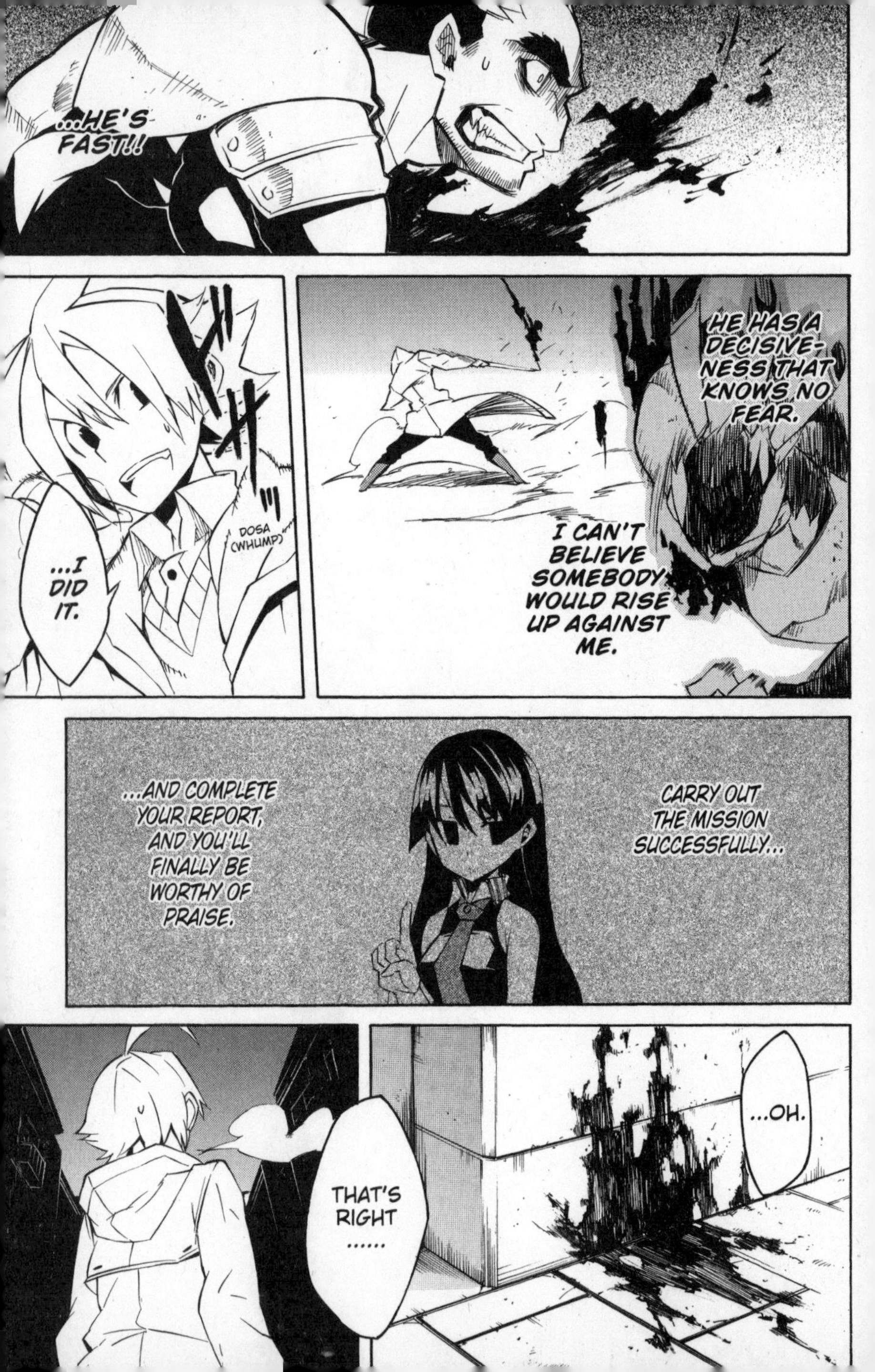
...HE'S FAST!!
HE HAS A DECISIVE-NESS THAT KNOWS NO FEAR.
I CAN'T BELIEVE SOMEBODY WOULD RISE UP AGAINST ME.
DOSA (WHUMP)
...I DID IT.
CARRY OUT THE MISSION SUCCESSFULLY...
...AND COMPLETE YOUR REPORT, AND YOU'LL FINALLY BE WORTHY OF PRAISE.
...OH.
THAT'S RIGHT ......

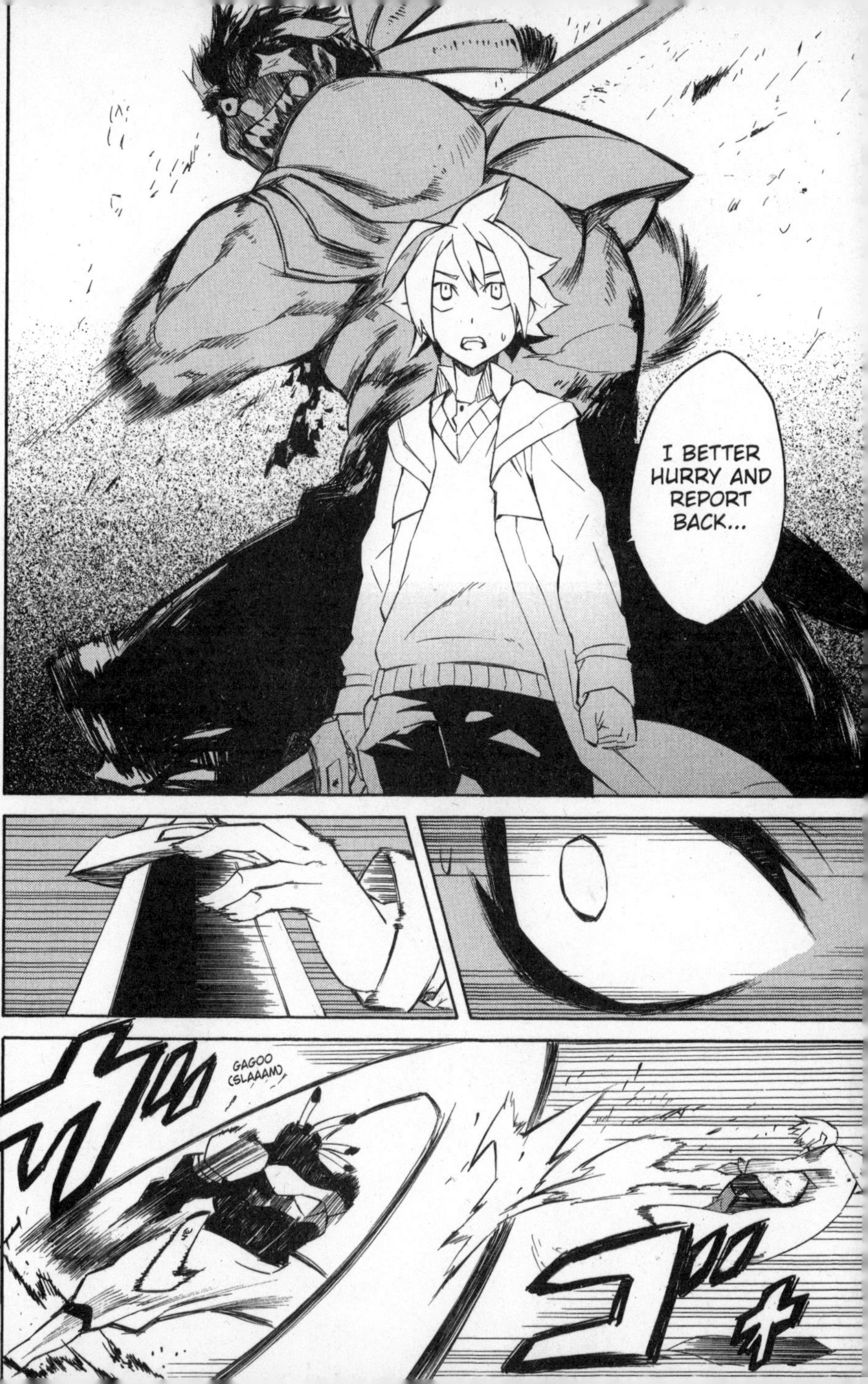
I BETTER HURRY AND REPORT BACK...
GAGOO (SLAAAM)

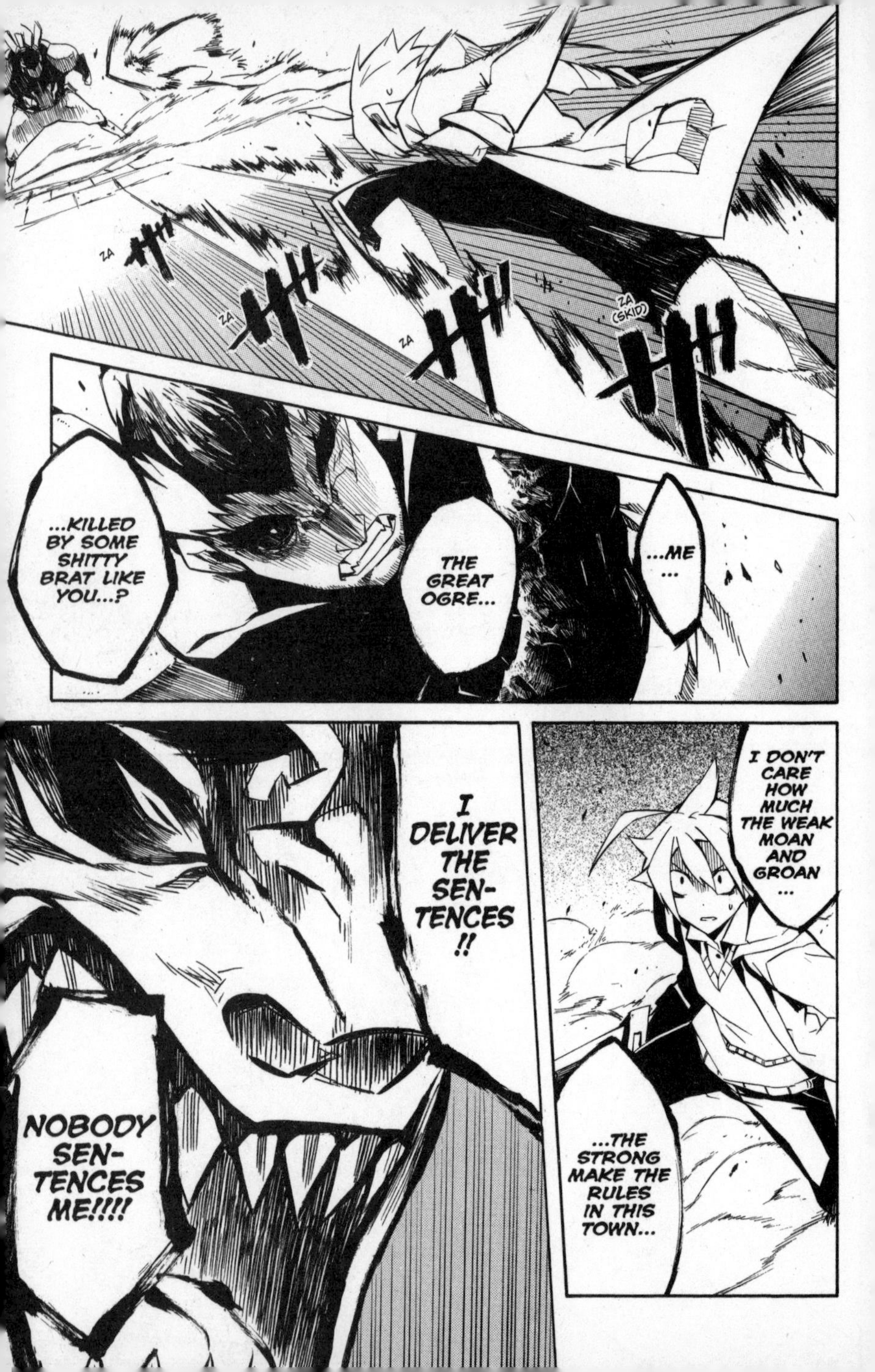
ZA (SKID)
ZA
ZA
ZA
...ME ...
THE GREAT OGRE...
...KILLED BY SOME SHITTY BRAT LIKE YOU...?
I DON'T CARE HOW MUCH THE WEAK MOAN AND GROAN ...
...THE STRONG MAKE THE RULES IN THIS TOWN...
I DELIVER THE SEN-TENCES !!
NOBODY SEN-TENCES ME!!!!

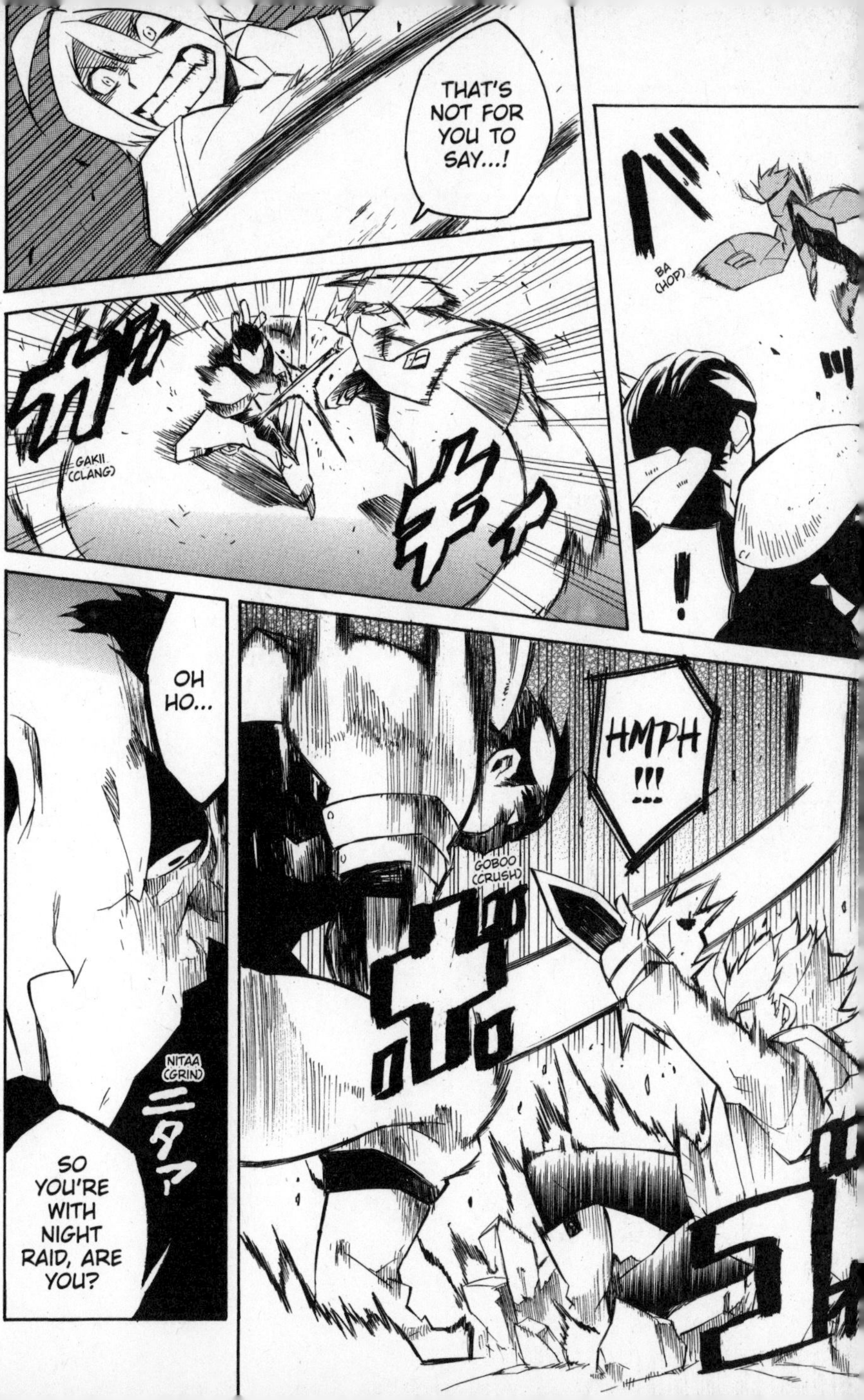
THAT'S NOT FOR YOU TO SAY...!
GAKII (CLANG)
BA (HOP)
!
HMPH!!!
GOBOO (CRUSH)
OH HO...
NITAA (GRIN)
SO YOU'RE WITH NIGHT RAID, ARE YOU?

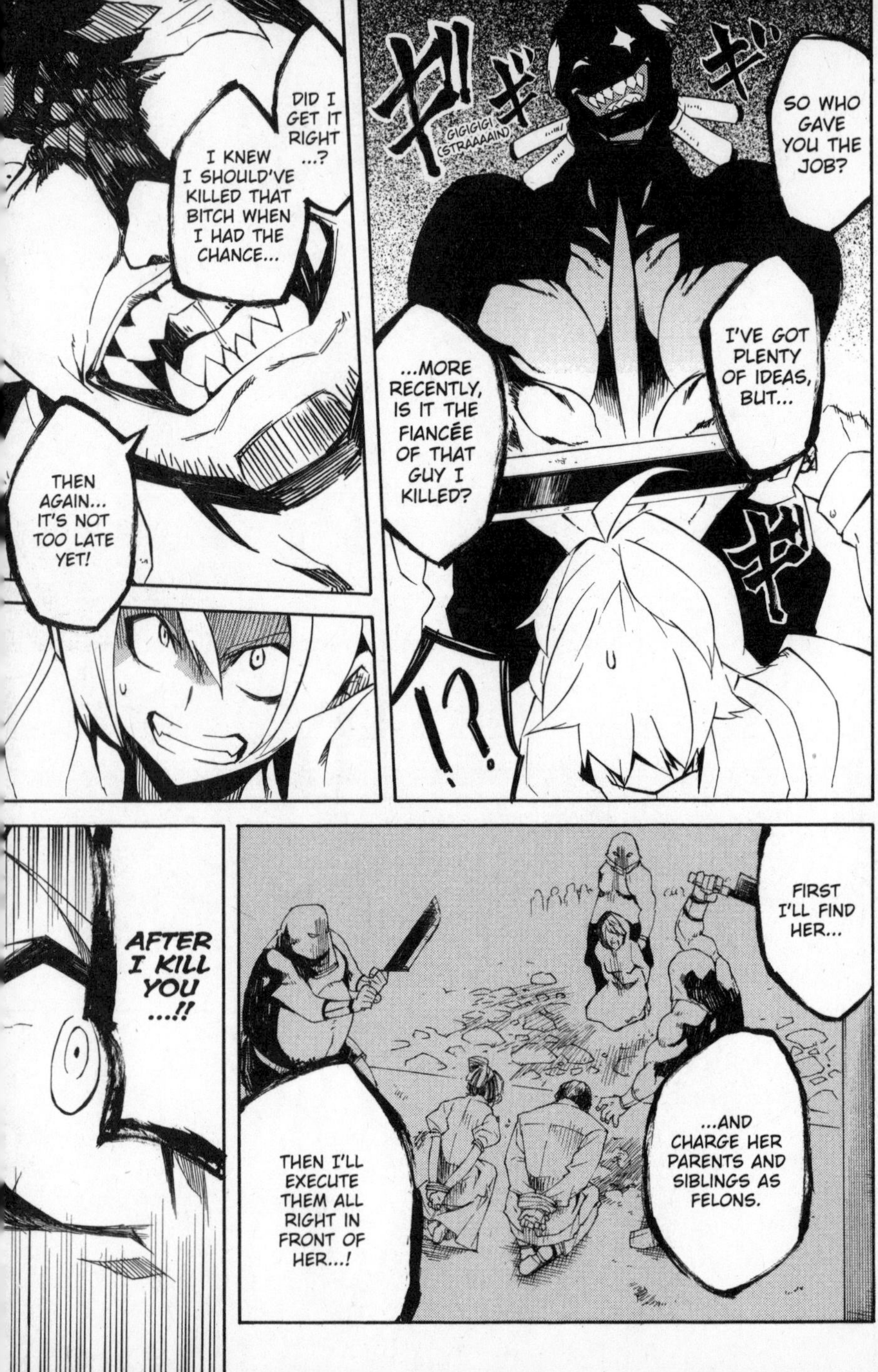
SO WHO GAVE YOU THE JOB?
GIGIGIGI (STRAAAAIN)
I'VE GOT PLENTY OF IDEAS, BUT...
...MORE RECENTLY, IS IT THE FIANCÉE OF THAT GUY I KILLED?
!?
DID I GET IT RIGHT ...?
I KNEW I SHOULD'VE KILLED THAT BITCH WHEN I HAD THE CHANCE...
THEN AGAIN... IT'S NOT TOO LATE YET!
FIRST I'LL FIND HER...
...AND CHARGE HER PARENTS AND SIBLINGS AS FELONS.
THEN I'LL EXECUTE THEM ALL RIGHT IN FRONT OF HER...!
AFTER I KILL YOU ...!!

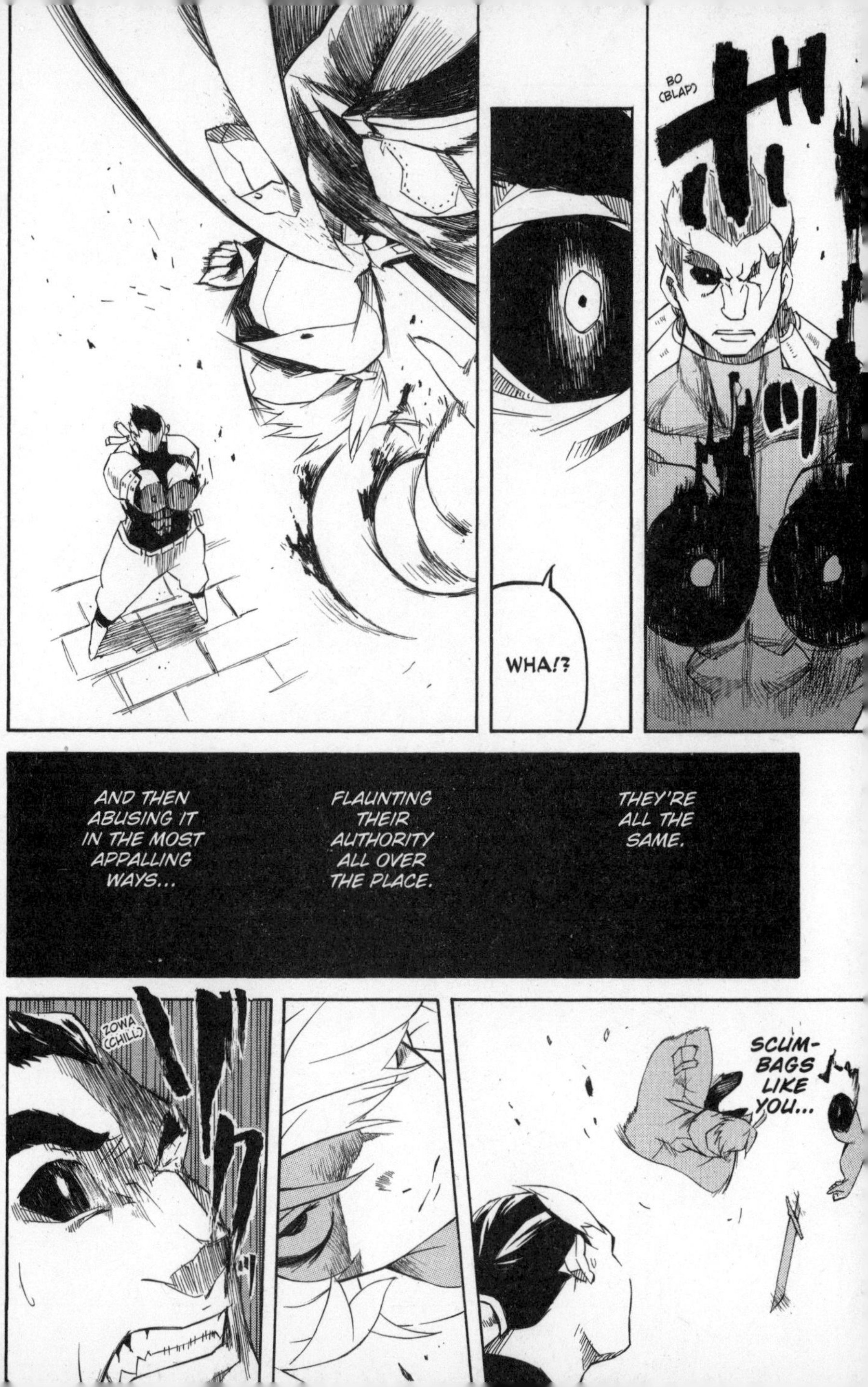
BO (BLAP)
WHA!?
AND THEN ABUSING IT IN THE MOST APPALLING WAYS...
FLAUNTING THEIR AUTHORITY ALL OVER THE PLACE.
THEY'RE ALL THE SAME.
SCUM-BAGS LIKE YOU...
ZOWA (CHILL)

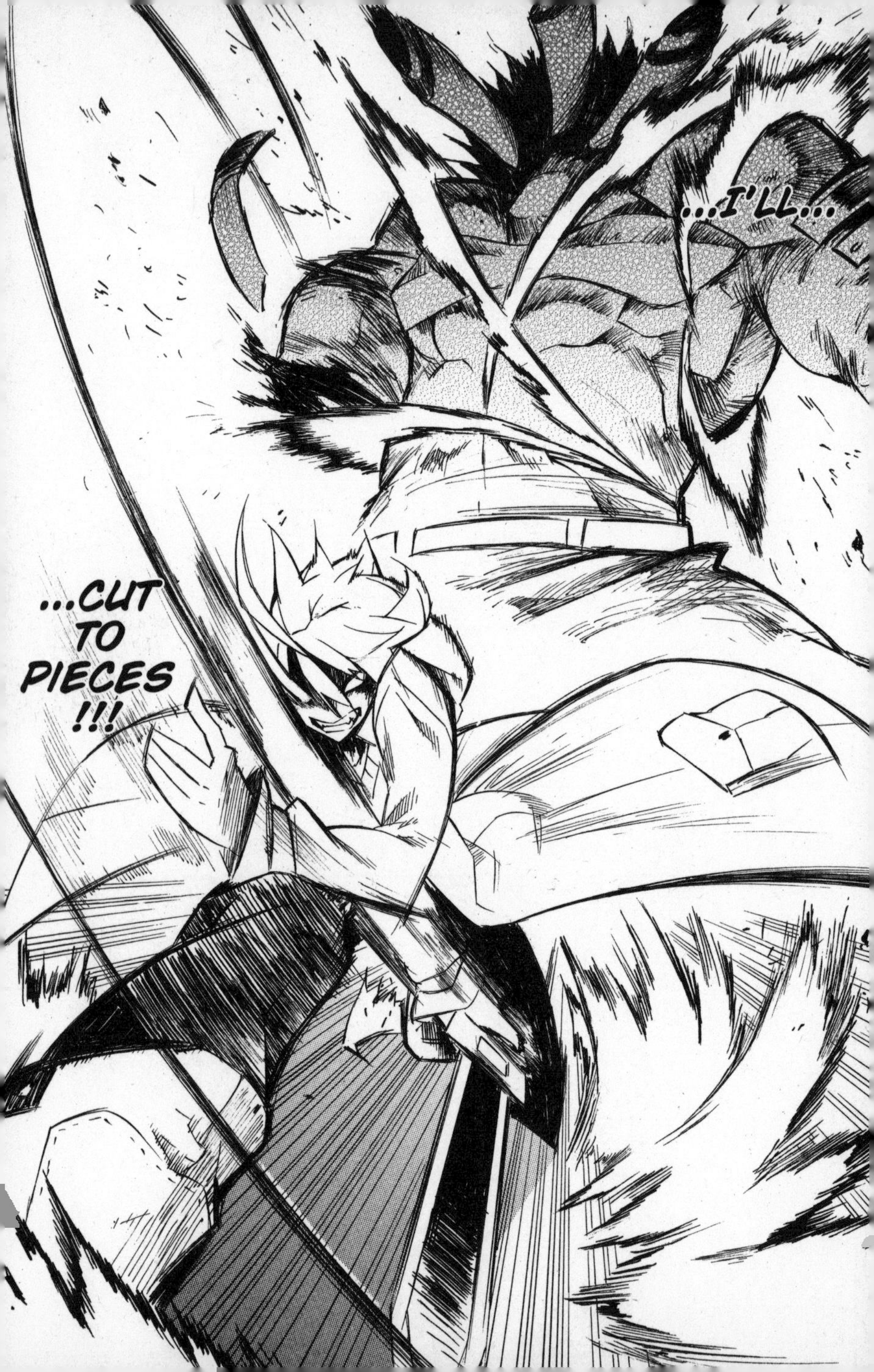
...I'LL...
...CUT TO PIECES !!!

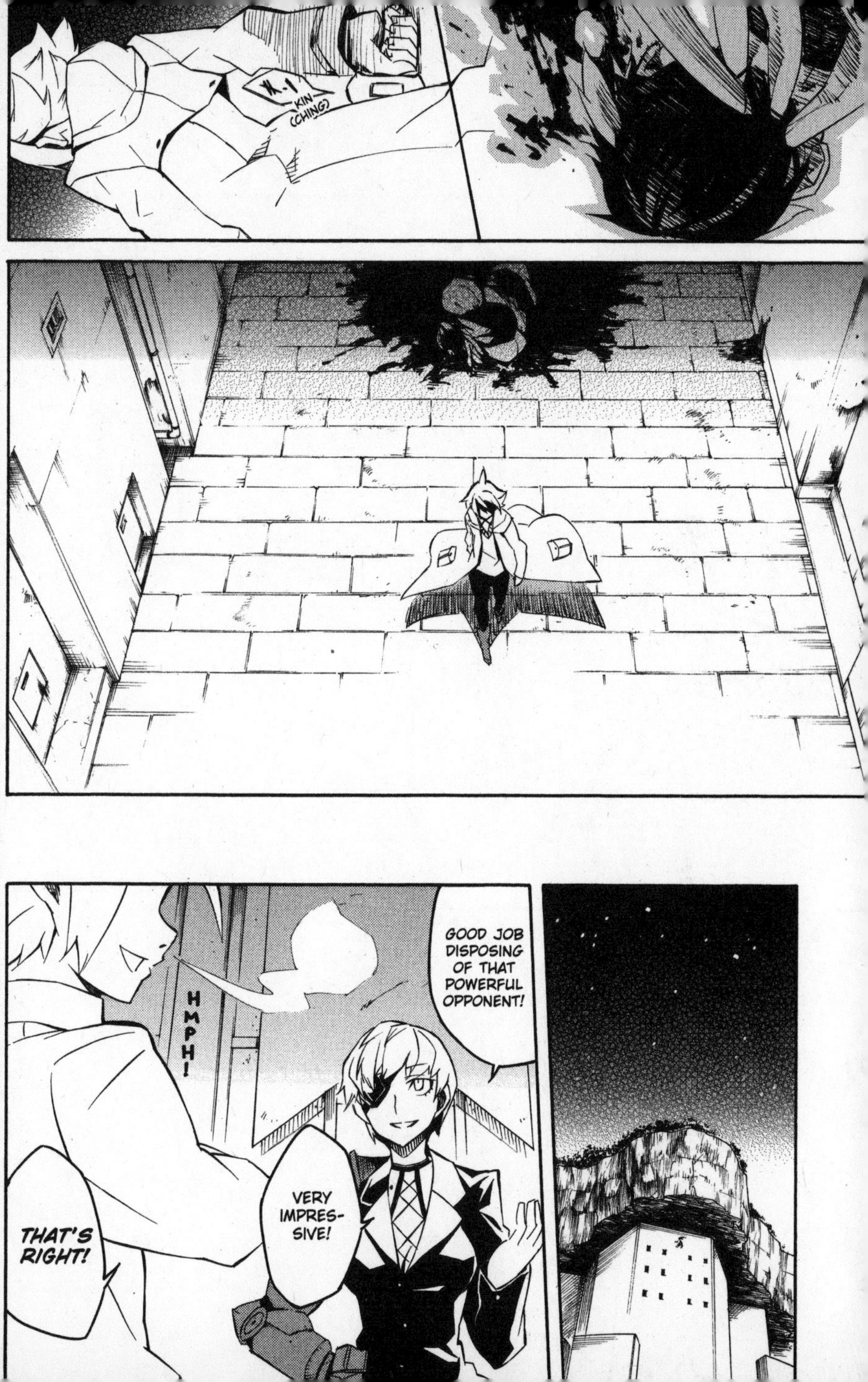
KIN (CHING)
GOOD JOB DISPOSING OF THAT POWERFUL OPPONENT!
HMPH!
VERY IMPRES-SIVE!
THAT'S RIGHT!

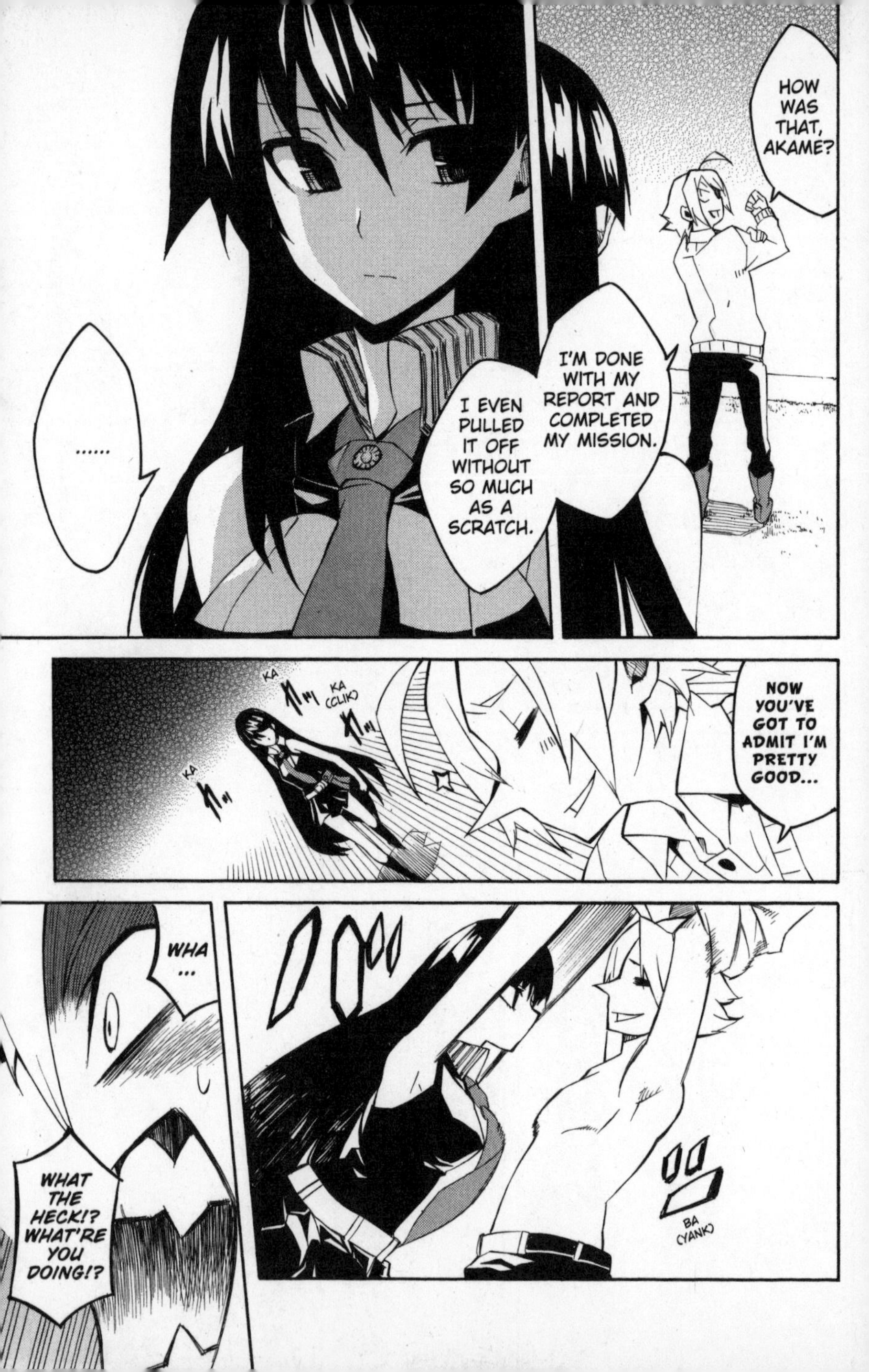
HOW WAS THAT, AKAME?
I'M DONE WITH MY REPORT AND COMPLETED MY MISSION.
I EVEN PULLED IT OFF WITHOUT SO MUCH AS A SCRATCH.
......
NOW YOU'VE GOT TO ADMIT I'M PRETTY GOOD...
KA (CLIK)
KA
KA
BA (YANK)
WHA ...
WHAT THE HECK!? WHAT'RE YOU DOING!?

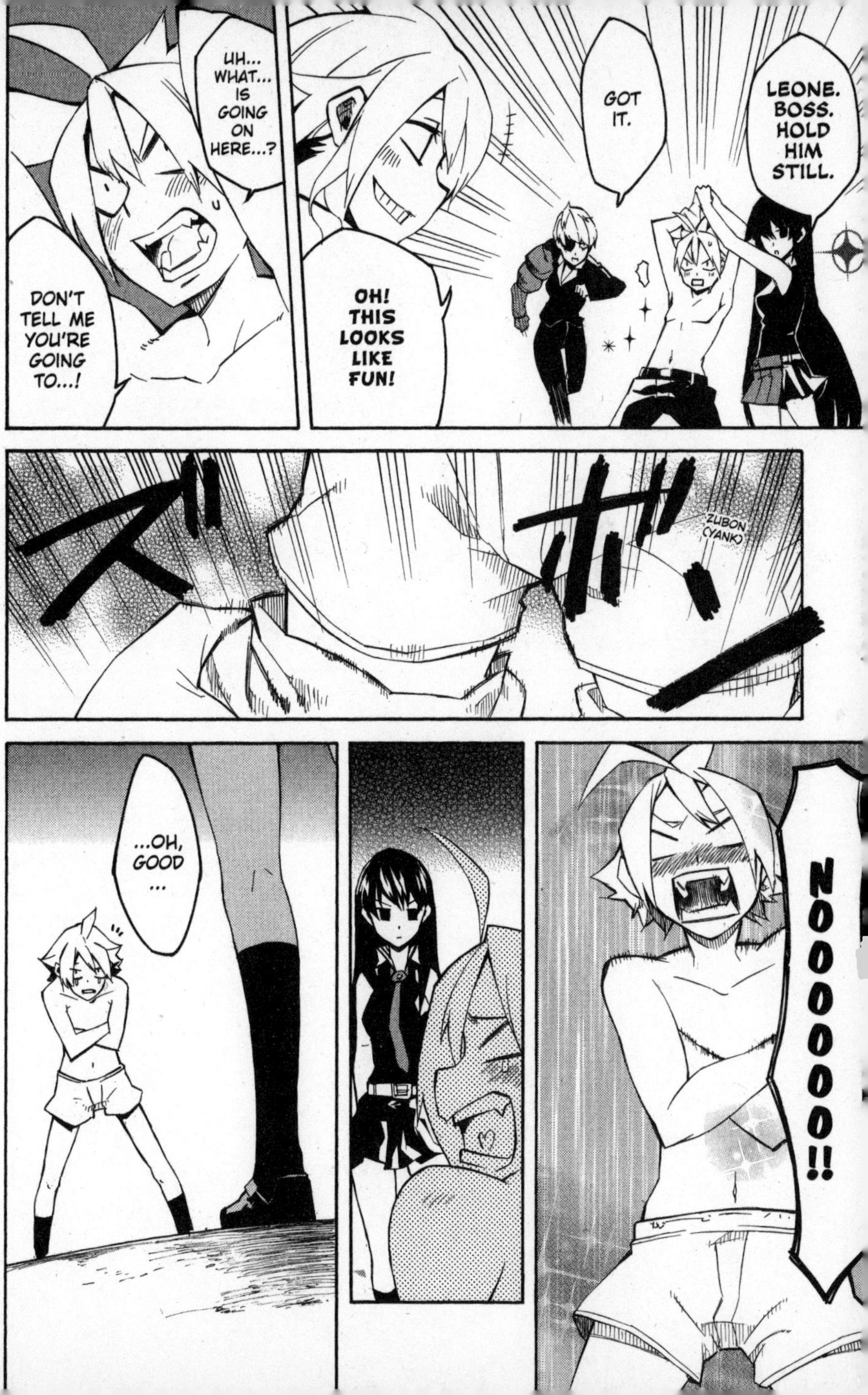
LEONE. BOSS. HOLD HIM STILL.
GOT IT.
OH! THIS LOOKS LIKE FUN!
UH... WHAT... IS GOING ON HERE...?
DON'T TELL ME YOU'RE GOING TO...!
ZUBON (YANK)
NOOOOOOO!!
...OH, GOOD ...

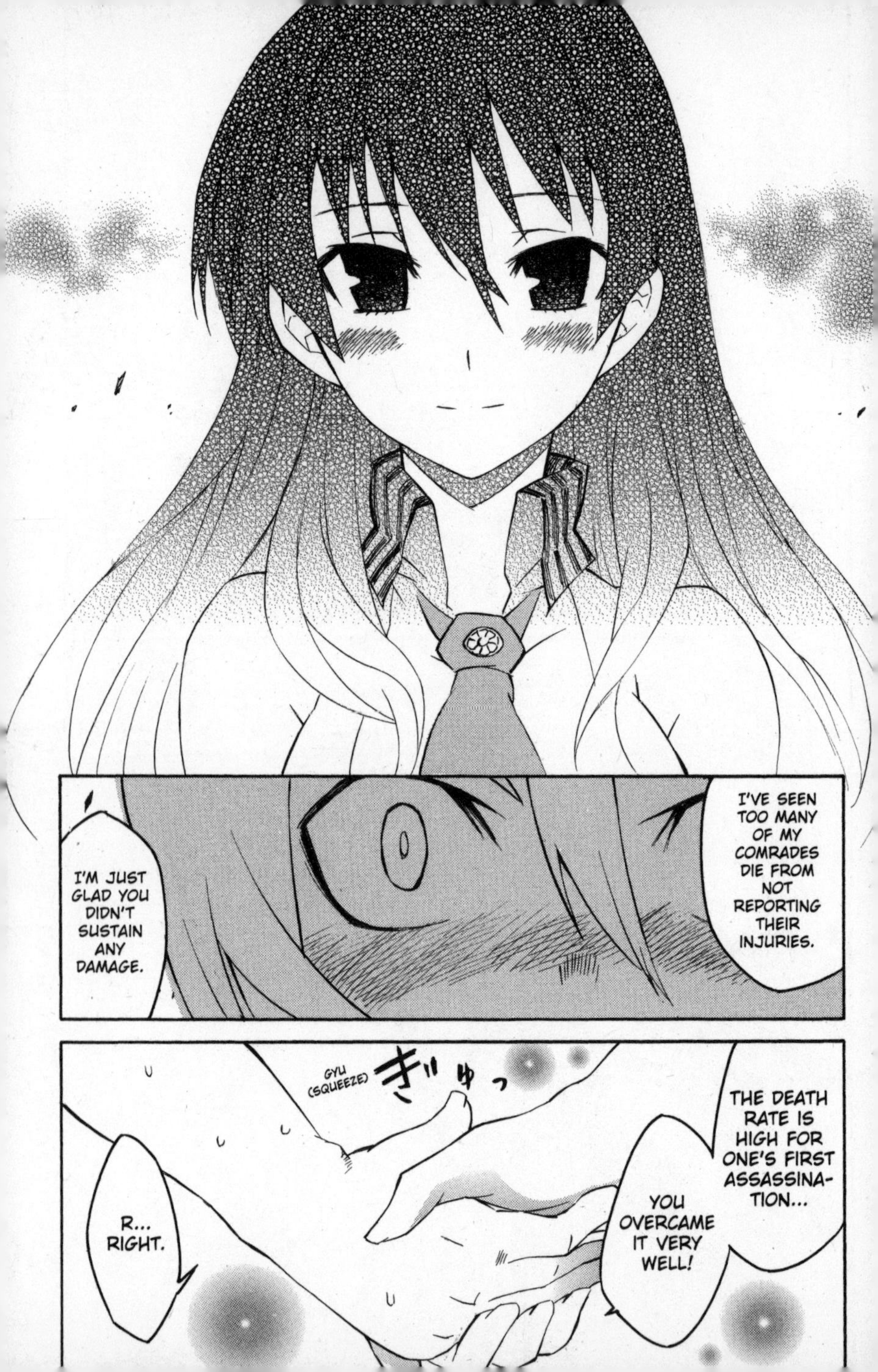
I'VE SEEN TOO MANY OF MY COMRADES DIE FROM NOT REPORTING THEIR INJURIES.
I'M JUST GLAD YOU DIDN'T SUSTAIN ANY DAMAGE.
THE DEATH RATE IS HIGH FOR ONE'S FIRST ASSASSINA-TION...
GYU (SQUEEZE)
YOU OVERCAME IT VERY WELL!
R... RIGHT.

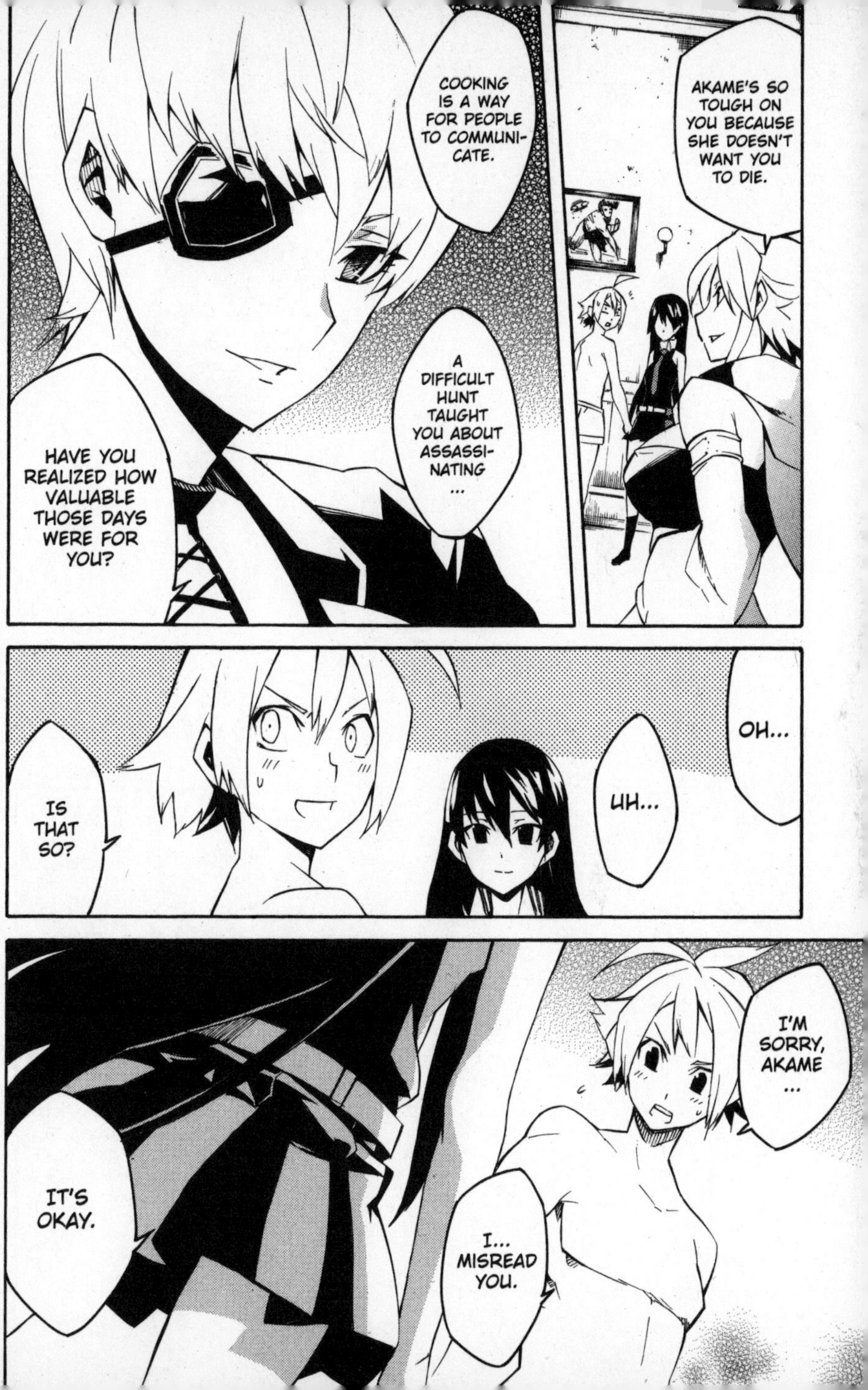
AKAME'S SO TOUGH ON YOU BECAUSE SHE DOESN'T WANT YOU TO DIE.
COOKING IS A WAY FOR PEOPLE TO COMMUNI-CATE.
A DIFFICULT HUNT TAUGHT YOU ABOUT ASSASSI-NATING ...
HAVE YOU REALIZED HOW VALUABLE THOSE DAYS WERE FOR YOU?
OH...
UH...
IS THAT SO?
I'M SORRY, AKAME ...
I... MISREAD YOU.
IT'S OKAY.

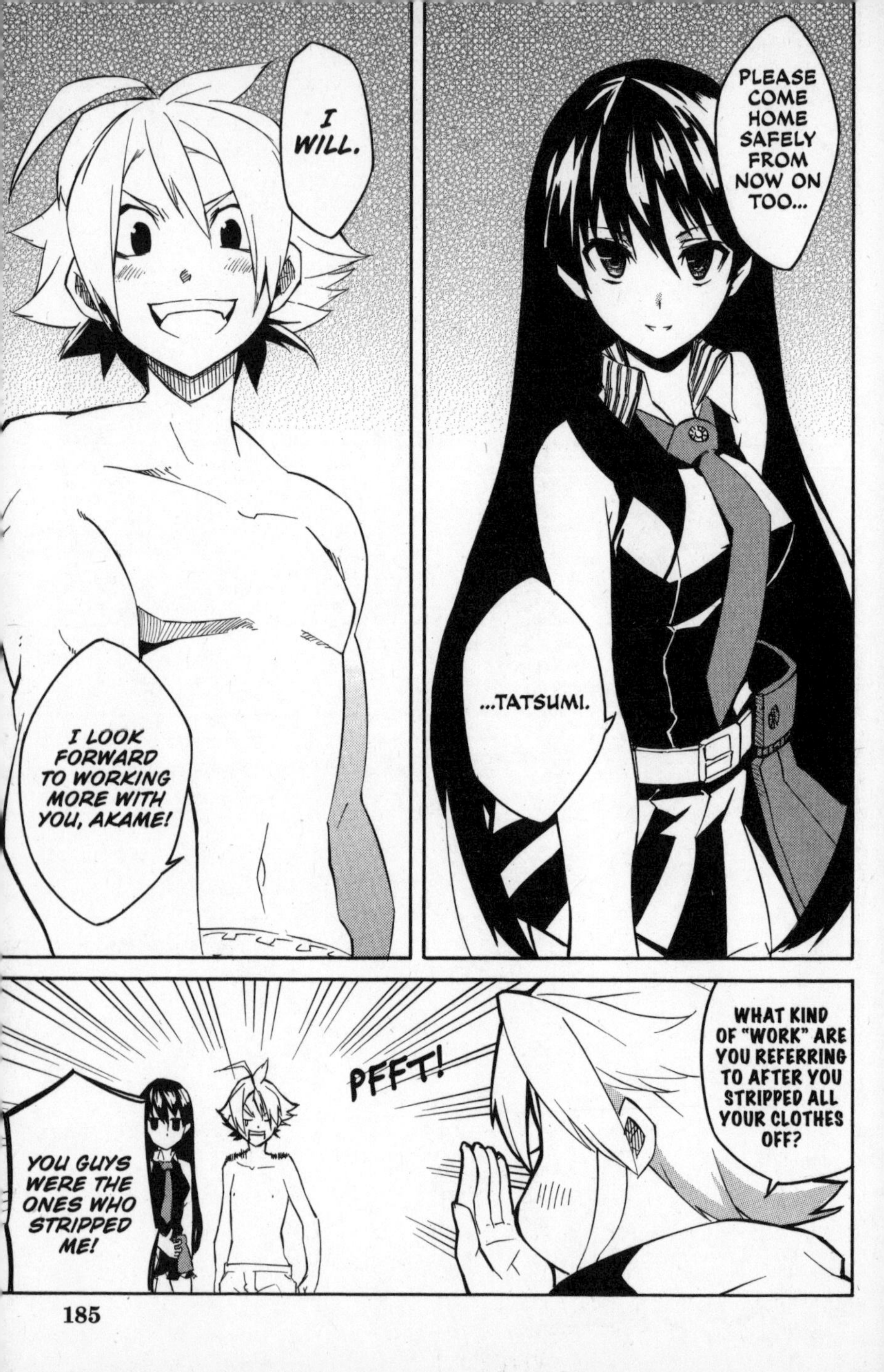
PLEASE COME HOME SAFELY FROM NOW ON TOO...
...TATSUMI.
I WILL.
I LOOK FORWARD TO WORKING MORE WITH YOU, AKAME!
WHAT KIND OF "WORK" ARE YOU REFERRING TO AFTER YOU STRIPPED ALL YOUR CLOTHES OFF?
PFFT!
YOU GUYS WERE THE ONES WHO STRIPPED ME!

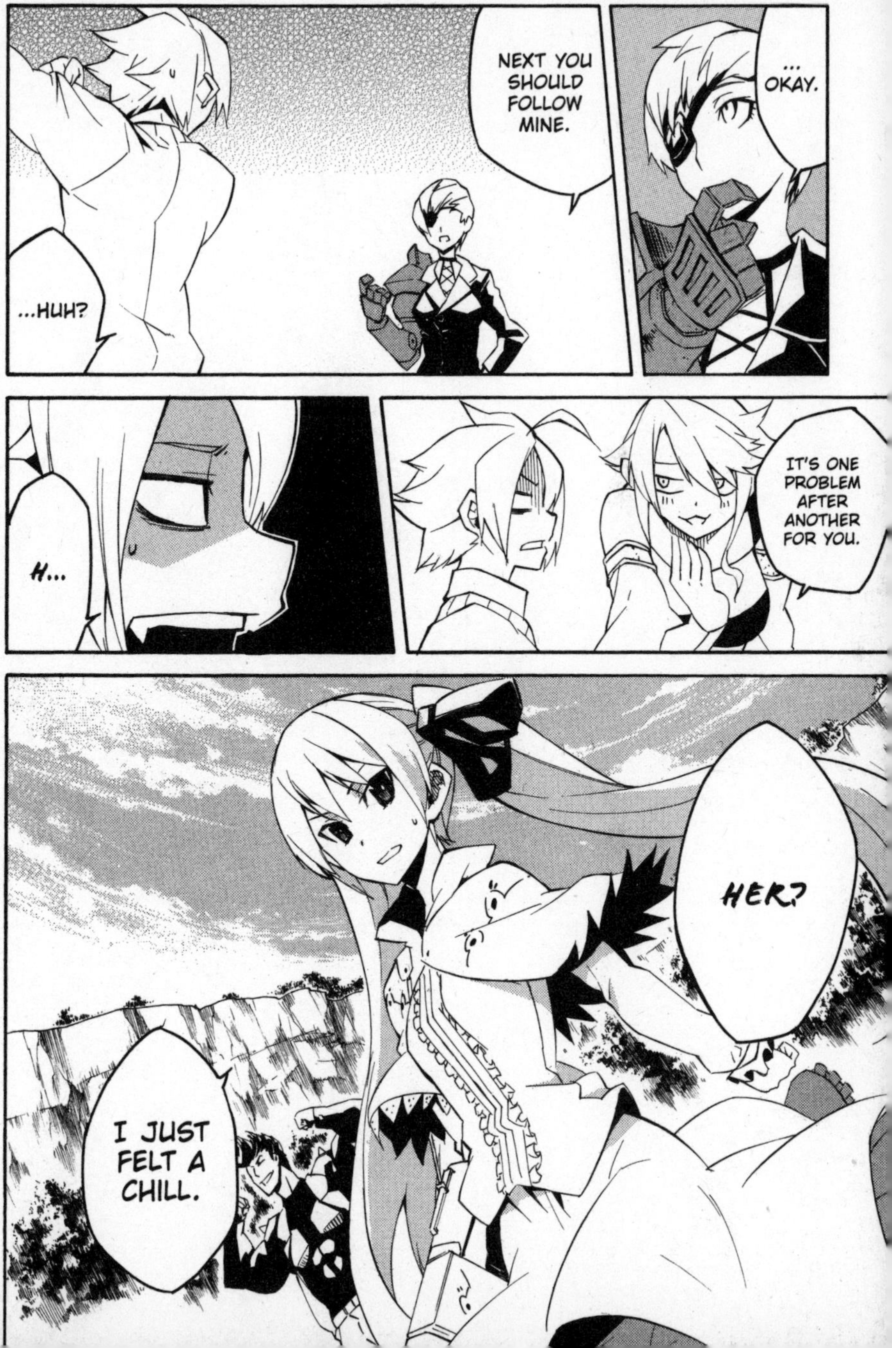
... OKAY.
NEXT YOU SHOULD FOLLOW MINE.
...HUH?
IT'S ONE PROBLEM AFTER ANOTHER FOR YOU.
H...
HER?
I JUST FELT A CHILL.

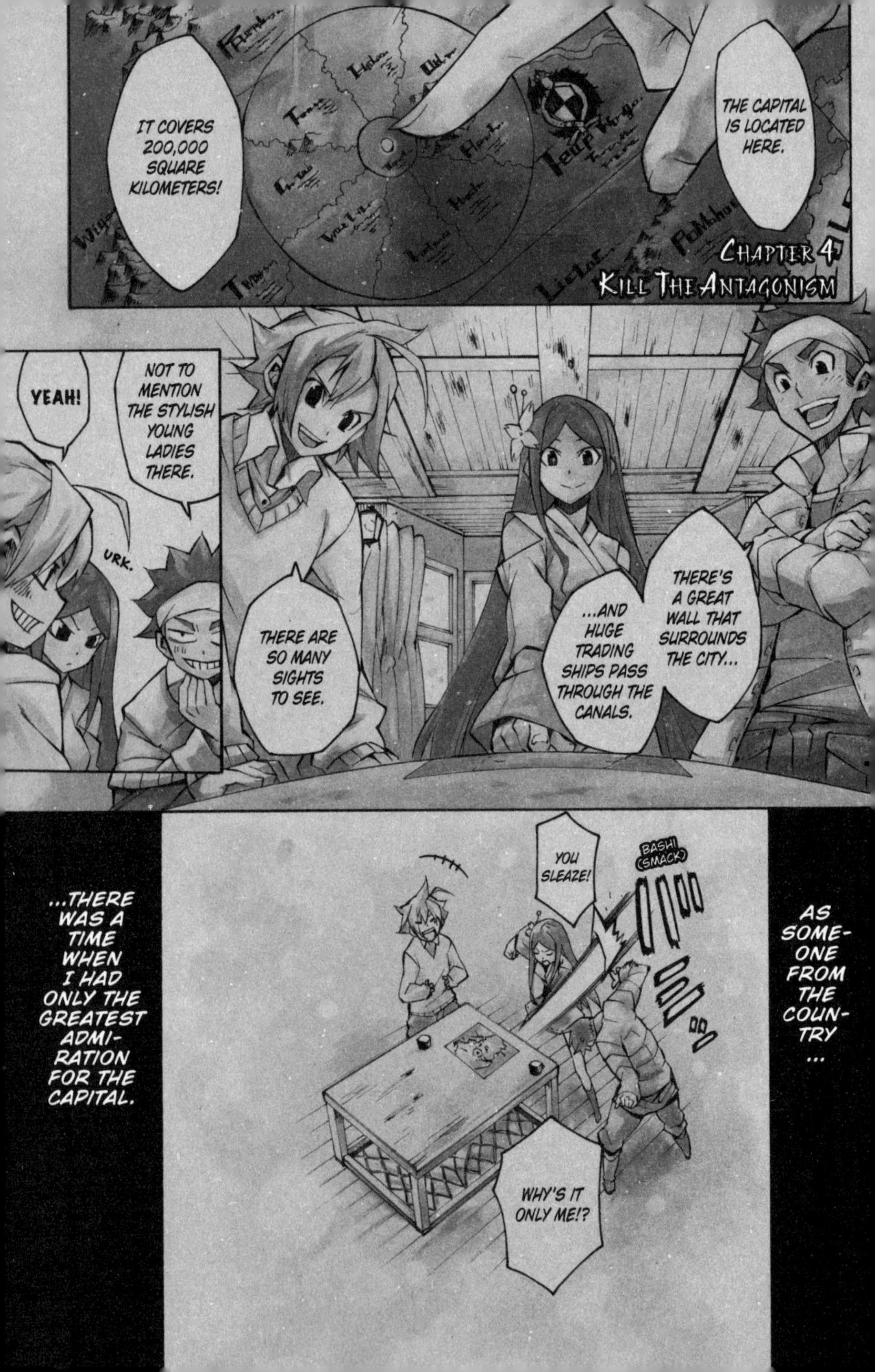
THE CAPITAL IS LOCATED HERE.
IT COVERS 200,000 SQUARE KILOMETERS!
CHAPTER 4
KILL THE ANTAGONISM
THERE'S A GREAT WALL THAT SURROUNDS THE CITY...
...AND HUGE TRADING SHIPS PASS THROUGH THE CANALS.
THERE ARE SO MANY SIGHTS TO SEE.
NOT TO MENTION THE STYLISH YOUNG LADIES THERE.
YEAH!
URK.
AS SOMEONE FROM THE COUNTRY...
BASHI (SMACK)
YOU SLEAZE!
WHY'S IT ONLY ME!?
...THERE WAS A TIME WHEN I HAD ONLY THE GREATEST ADMIRATION FOR THE CAPITAL.

Chapter 4
Kill the Antagonism

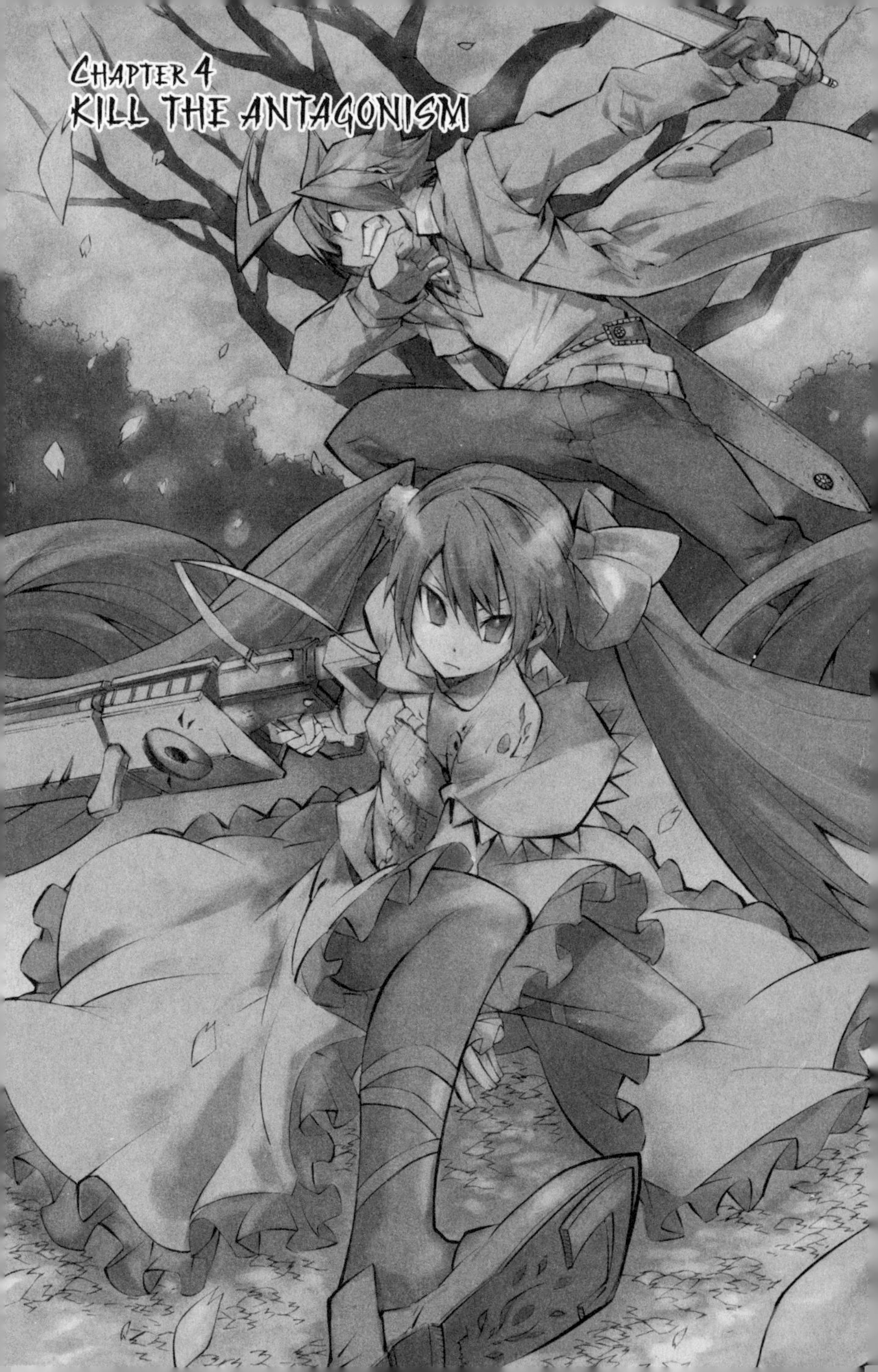

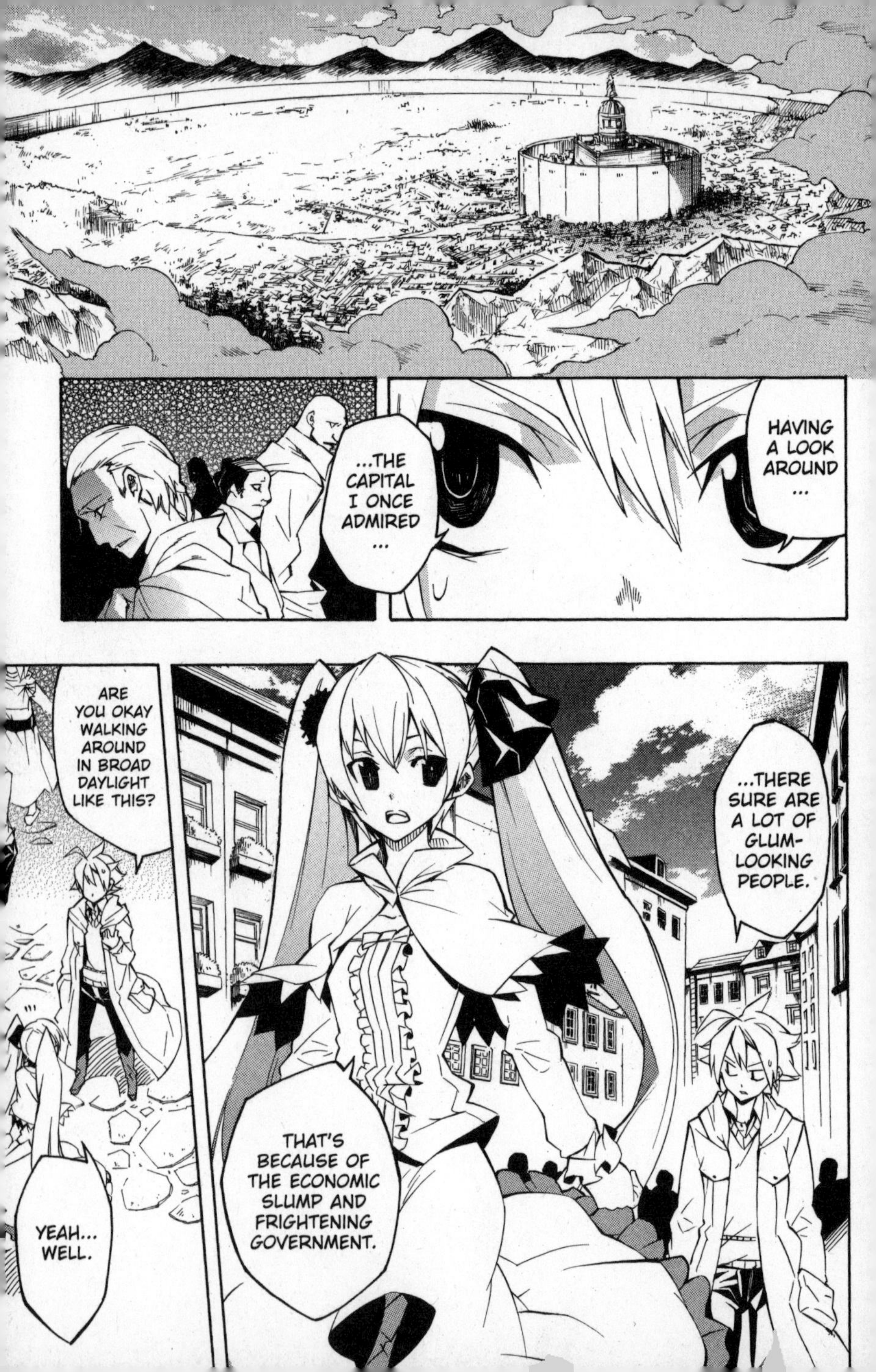
HAVING A LOOK AROUND ...
...THE CAPITAL I ONCE ADMIRED ...
...THERE SURE ARE A LOT OF GLUM-LOOKING PEOPLE.
THAT'S BECAUSE OF THE ECONOMIC SLUMP AND FRIGHTENING GOVERNMENT.
ARE YOU OKAY WALKING AROUND IN BROAD DAYLIGHT LIKE THIS?
YEAH... WELL.

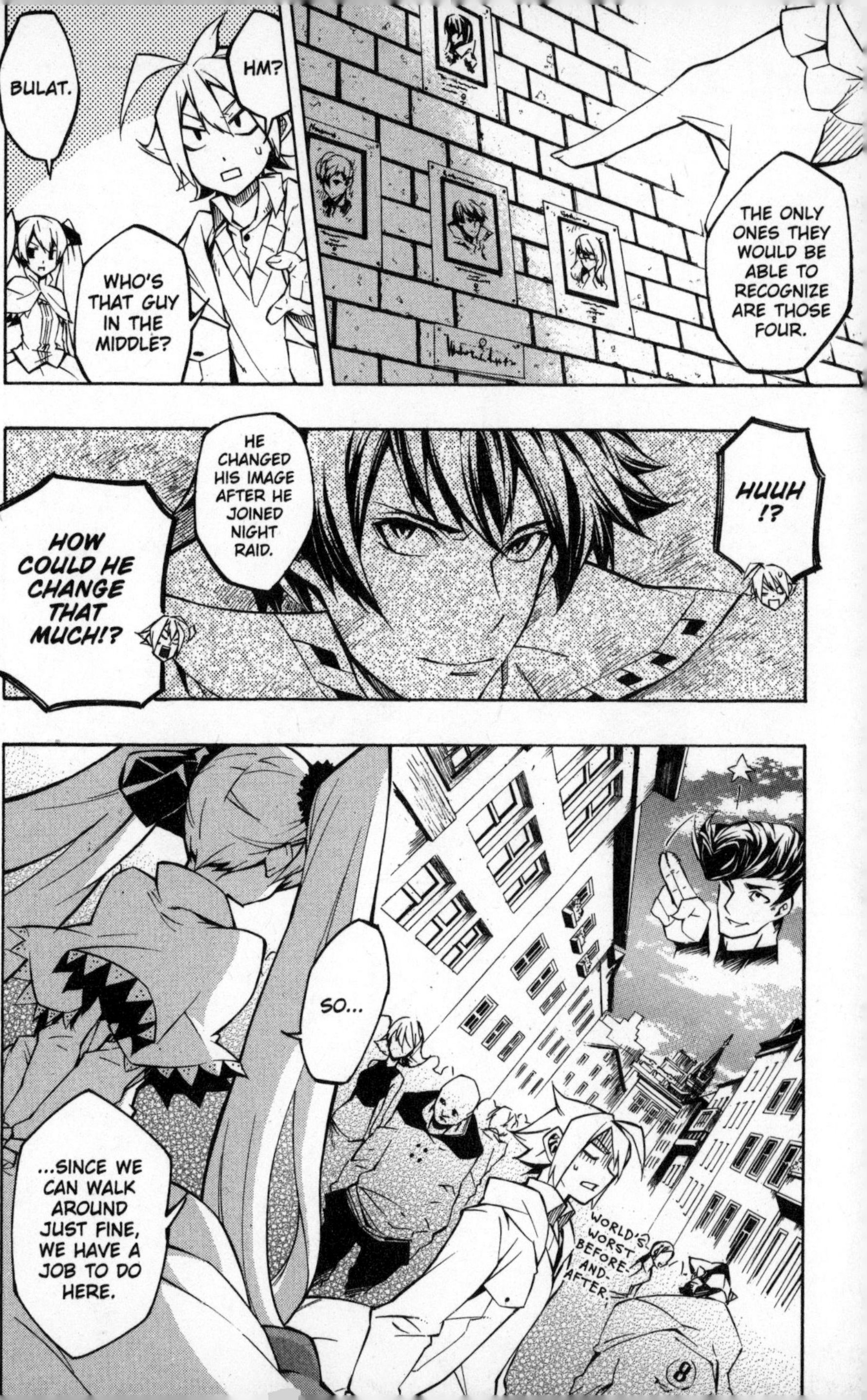
THE ONLY ONES THEY WOULD BE ABLE TO RECOGNIZE ARE THOSE FOUR.
HM?
BULAT.
WHO'S THAT GUY IN THE MIDDLE?
HUUH!?
HE CHANGED HIS IMAGE AFTER HE JOINED NIGHT RAID.
HOW COULD HE CHANGE THAT MUCH!?
SO...
...SINCE WE CAN WALK AROUND JUST FINE, WE HAVE A JOB TO DO HERE.
WORLD'S WORST BEFORE-AND-AFTER.

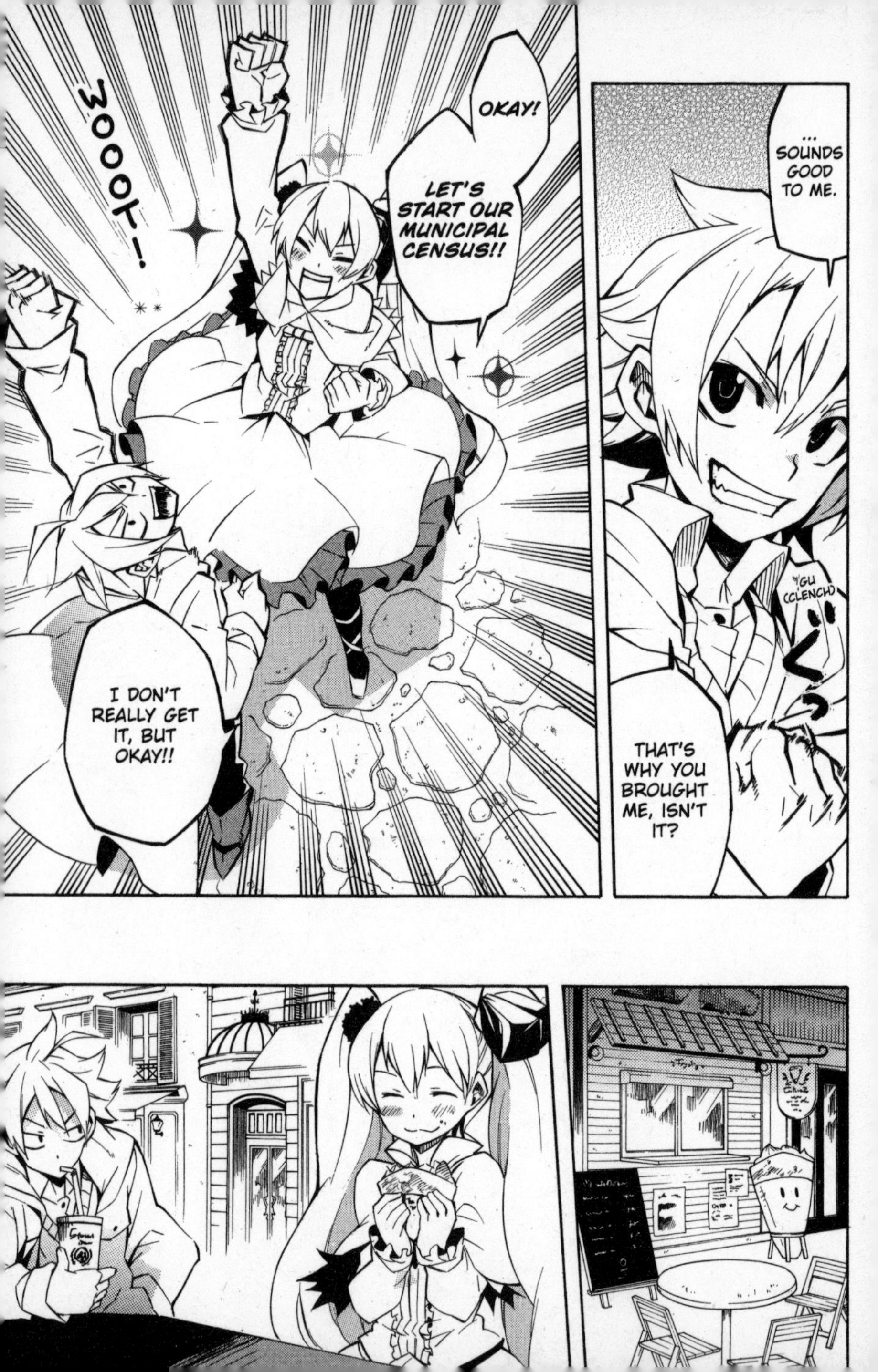

... SOUNDS GOOD TO ME.
*GU (CLENCH)
THAT'S WHY YOU BROUGHT ME, ISN'T IT?
OKAY!
LET'S START OUR MUNICIPAL CENSUS!!
WOOOT!!
I DON'T REALLY GET IT, BUT OKAY!!

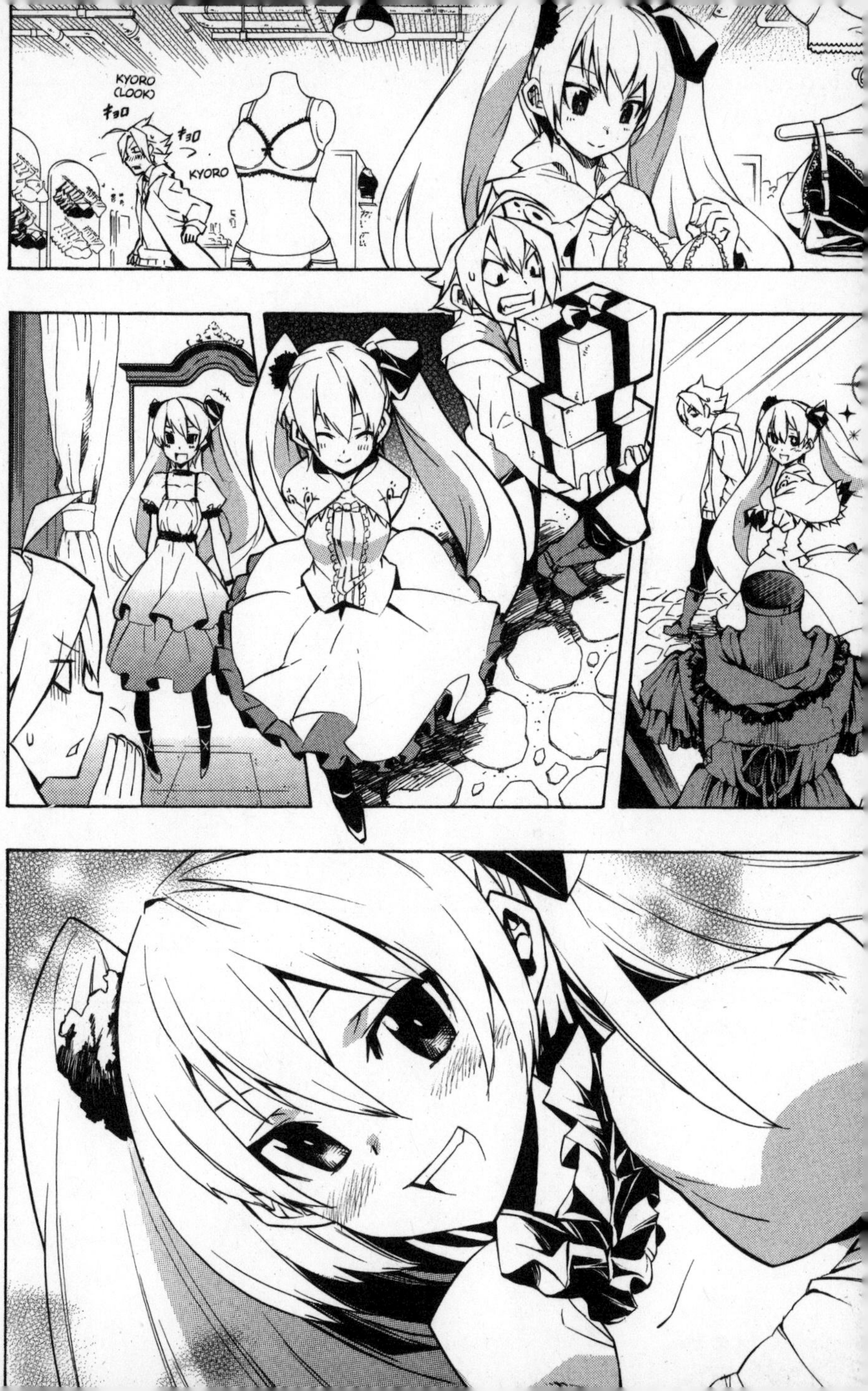
KYORO (LOOK)
キョロ
キョロ
KYORO

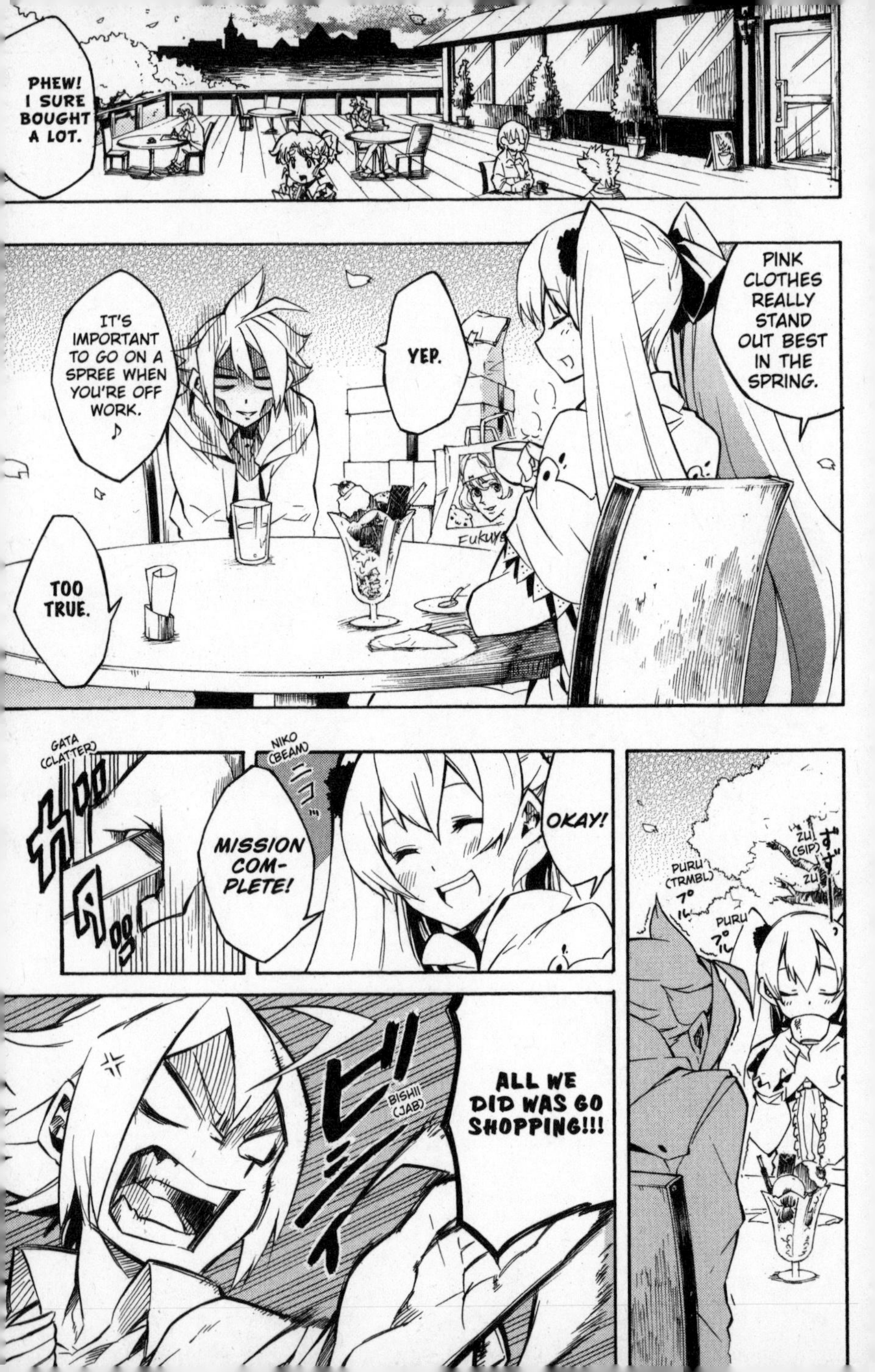
PHEW! I SURE BOUGHT A LOT.
PINK CLOTHES REALLY STAND OUT BEST IN THE SPRING.
YEP.
IT'S IMPORTANT TO GO ON A SPREE WHEN YOU'RE OFF WORK. ♪
TOO TRUE.
ZU (SIP)
ZU
PURU (TRMBL)
PURU
NIKO (BEAM)
OKAY!
MISSION COM-PLETE!
GATA (CLATTER)
ALL WE DID WAS GO SHOPPING!!!
BISHII (JAB)

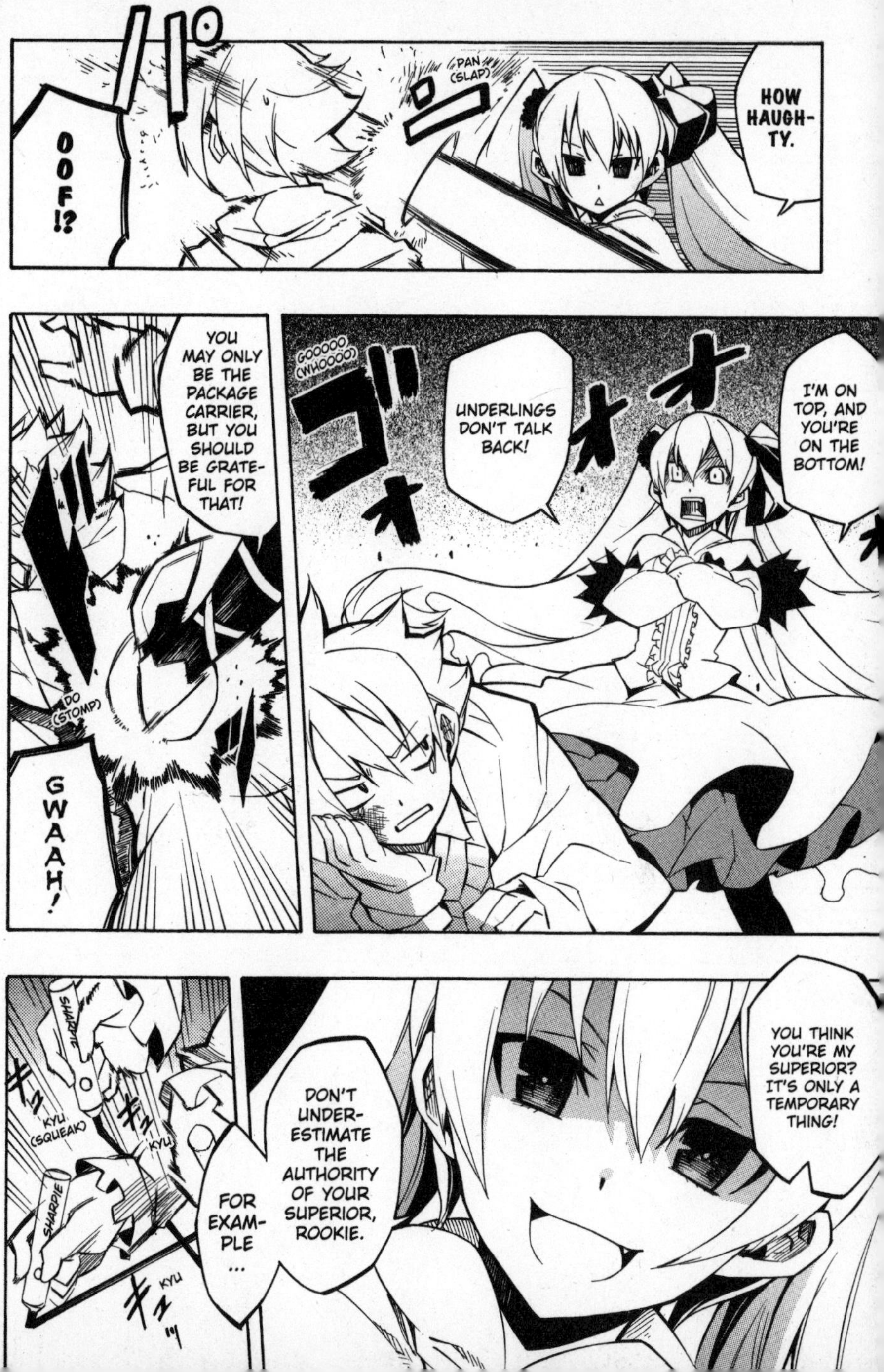
HOW HAUGHTY.
PAN (SLAP)
OOF!?
I'M ON TOP, AND YOU'RE ON THE BOTTOM!
UNDERLINGS DON'T TALK BACK!
GOOOOO (WHOOOO)
YOU MAY ONLY BE THE PACKAGE CARRIER, BUT YOU SHOULD BE GRATEFUL FOR THAT!
DO (STOMP)
GWAAH!
YOU THINK YOU'RE MY SUPERIOR? IT'S ONLY A TEMPORARY THING!
DON'T UNDERESTIMATE THE AUTHORITY OF YOUR SUPERIOR, ROOKIE.
FOR EXAMPLE...
SHARPIE
KYU (SQUEAK)
KYU
SHARPIE
KYU

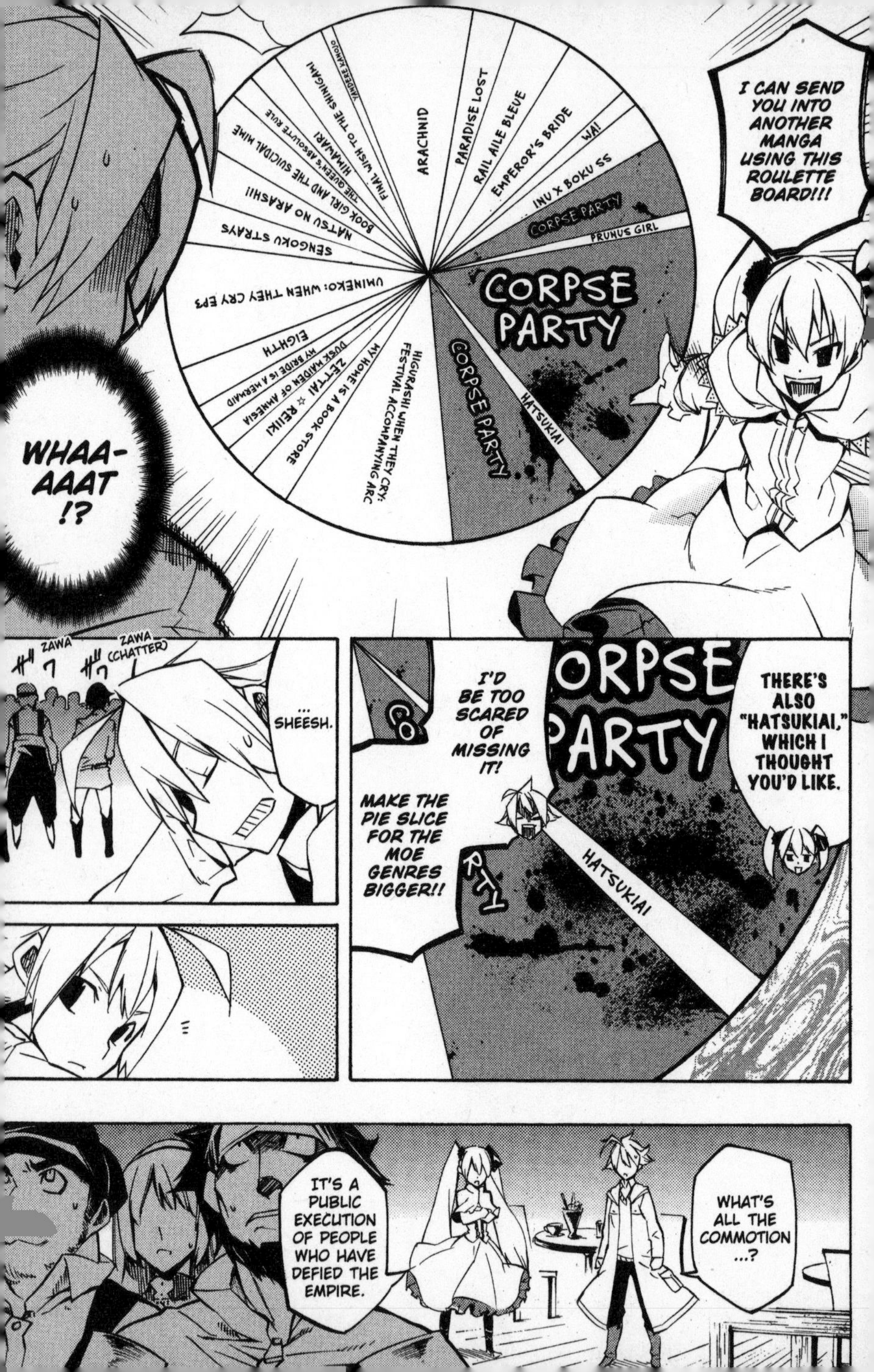
I CAN SEND YOU INTO ANOTHER MANGA USING THIS ROULETTE BOARD!!!
ARACHNID
PARADISE LOST
RAIL AILE BLEUE
EMPEROR'S BRIDE
WA!
INU X BOKU SS
CORPSE PARTY
PRUNUS GIRL
CORPSE PARTY
HATSUKIAI
CORPSE PARTY
HIGURASHI WHEN THEY CRY: FESTIVAL ACCOMPANYING ARC
MY HOME IS A BOOK STORE
ZETTAI ☆ REIIKI
DUSK MAIDEN OF AMNESIA
MY BRIDE IS A MERMAID
EIGHTH
UMINEKO: WHEN THEY CRY EP3
SENGOKU STRAYS
NATSU NO ARASHI!!
BOOK GIRL AND THE SUICIDAL MIME
THE QUEEN'S ABSOLUTE RULE
HIMAWARI
FINAL WISH TO THE SHINIGAMI
YANDERE KANOJO
WHAA-AAAT!?
THERE'S ALSO "HATSUKIAI," WHICH I THOUGHT YOU'D LIKE.
CORPSE PARTY
HATSUKIAI
I'D BE TOO SCARED OF MISSING IT!
MAKE THE PIE SLICE FOR THE MOE GENRES BIGGER!!
ZAWA ZAWA (CHATTER)
...SHEESH.
WHAT'S ALL THE COMMOTION ...?
IT'S A PUBLIC EXECUTION OF PEOPLE WHO HAVE DEFIED THE EMPIRE.

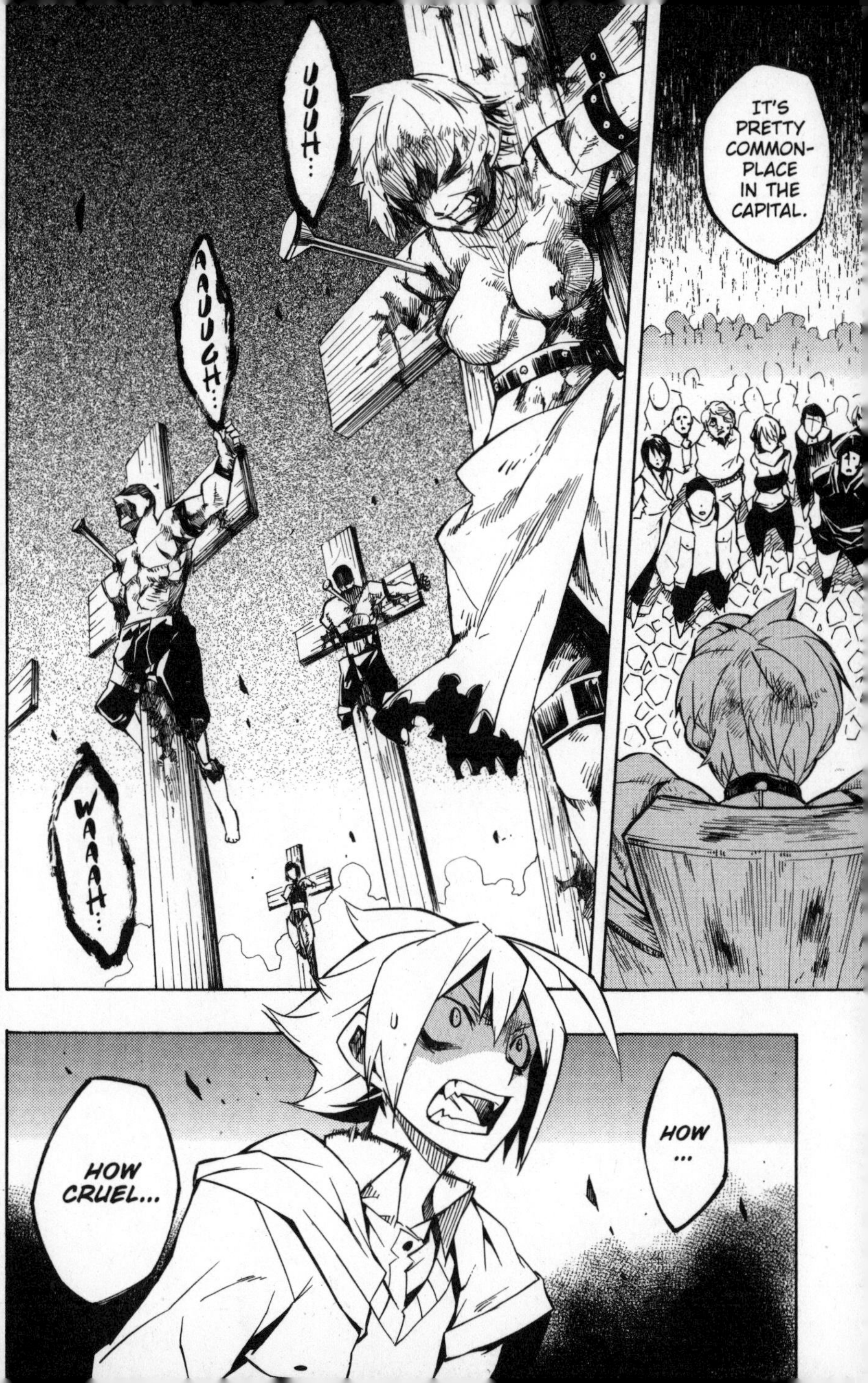
IT'S PRETTY COMMONPLACE IN THE CAPITAL.
UUUH...
AAUUCH...
WAAAH...
HOW ...
HOW CRUEL...

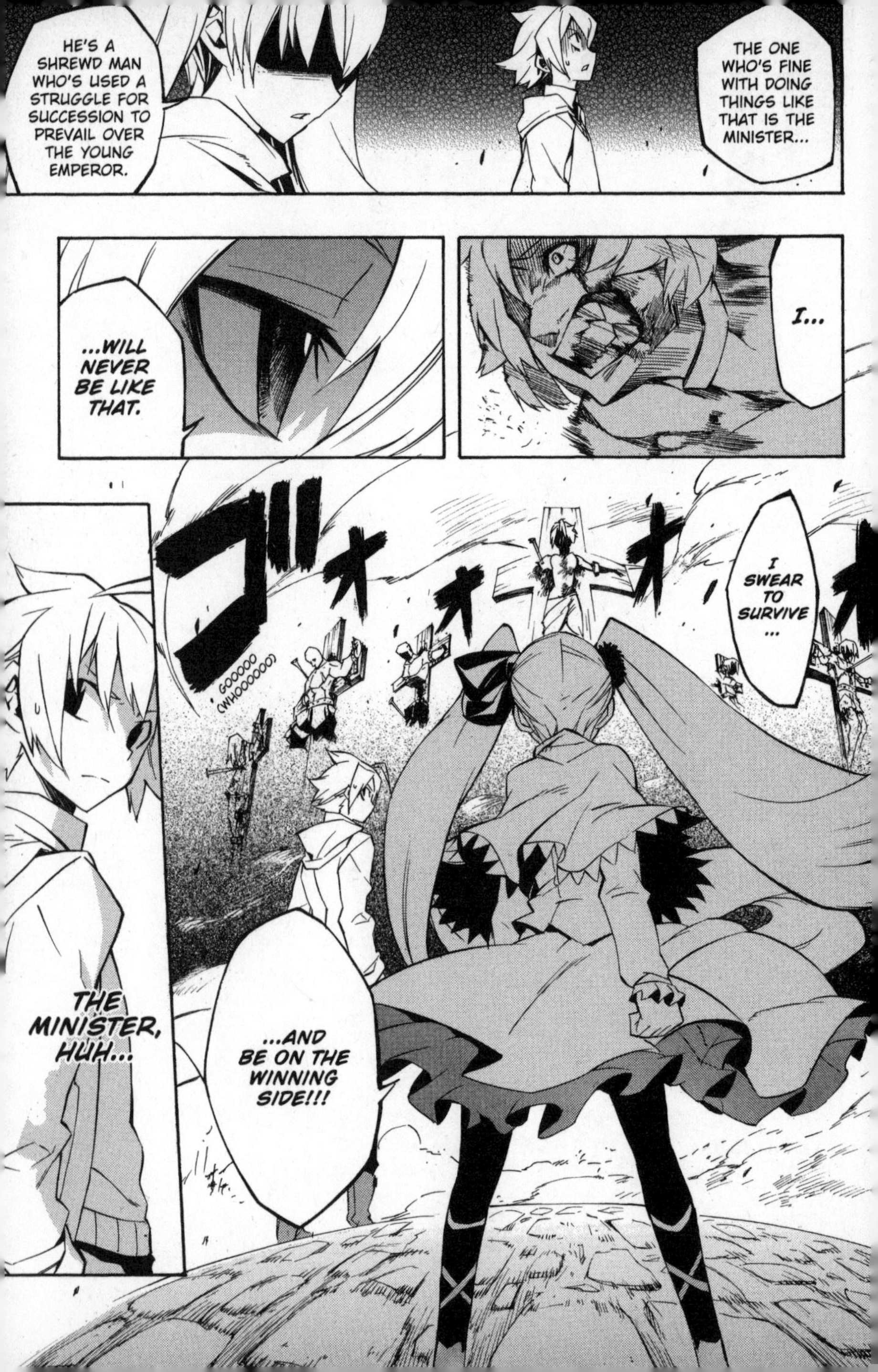
THE ONE WHO'S FINE WITH DOING THINGS LIKE THAT IS THE MINISTER...
HE'S A SHREWD MAN WHO'S USED A STRUGGLE FOR SUCCESSION TO PREVAIL OVER THE YOUNG EMPEROR.
I...
...WILL NEVER BE LIKE THAT.
ゴォォォ
GOOOOO (WHOOOOOO)
I SWEAR TO SURVIVE...
...AND BE ON THE WINNING SIDE!!!
THE MINISTER, HUH...

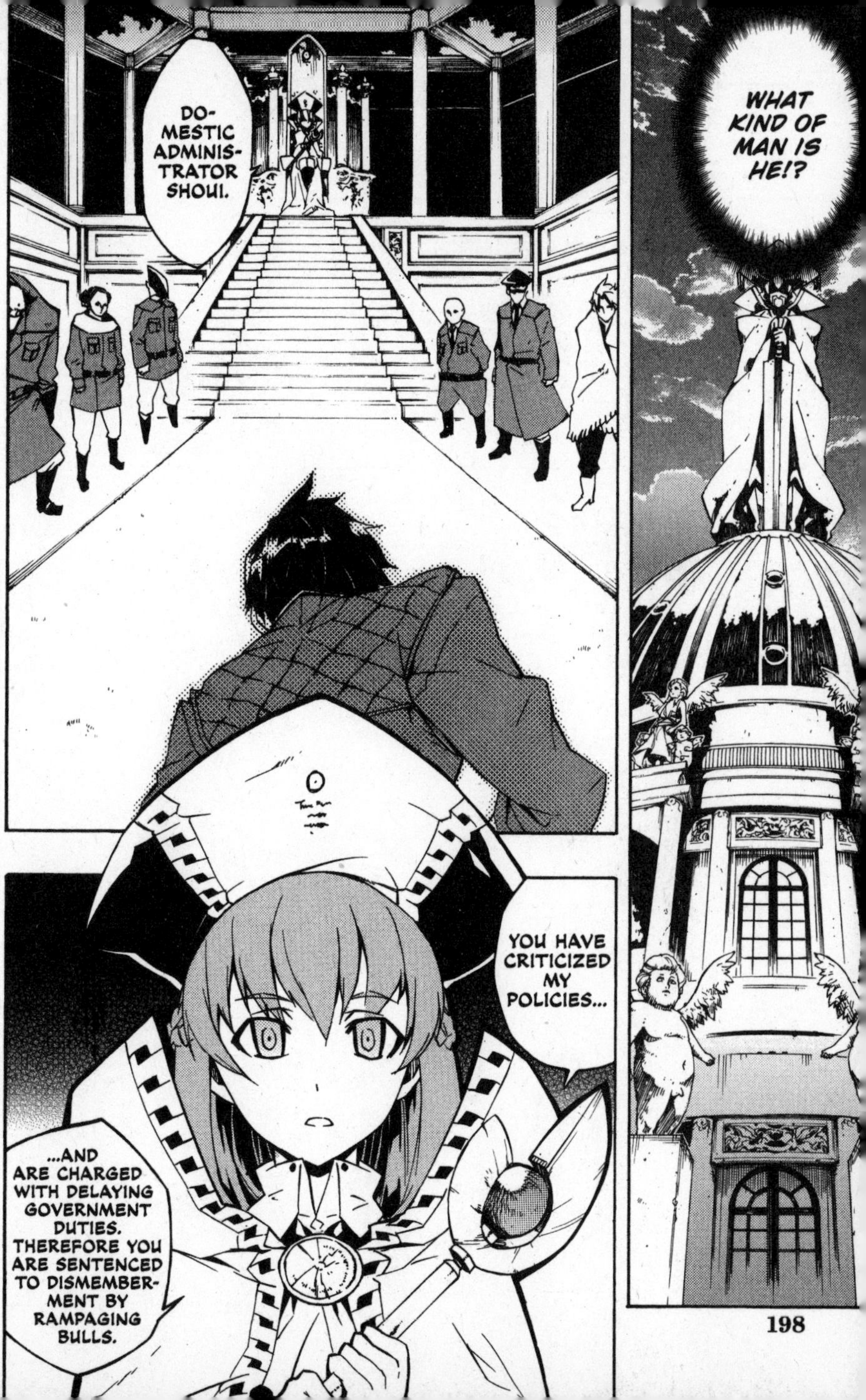
WHAT KIND OF MAN IS HE!?
DO-MESTIC ADMINIS-TRATOR SHOUI.
YOU HAVE CRITICIZED MY POLICIES...
...AND ARE CHARGED WITH DELAYING GOVERNMENT DUTIES. THEREFORE YOU ARE SENTENCED TO DISMEMBER-MENT BY RAMPAGING BULLS.

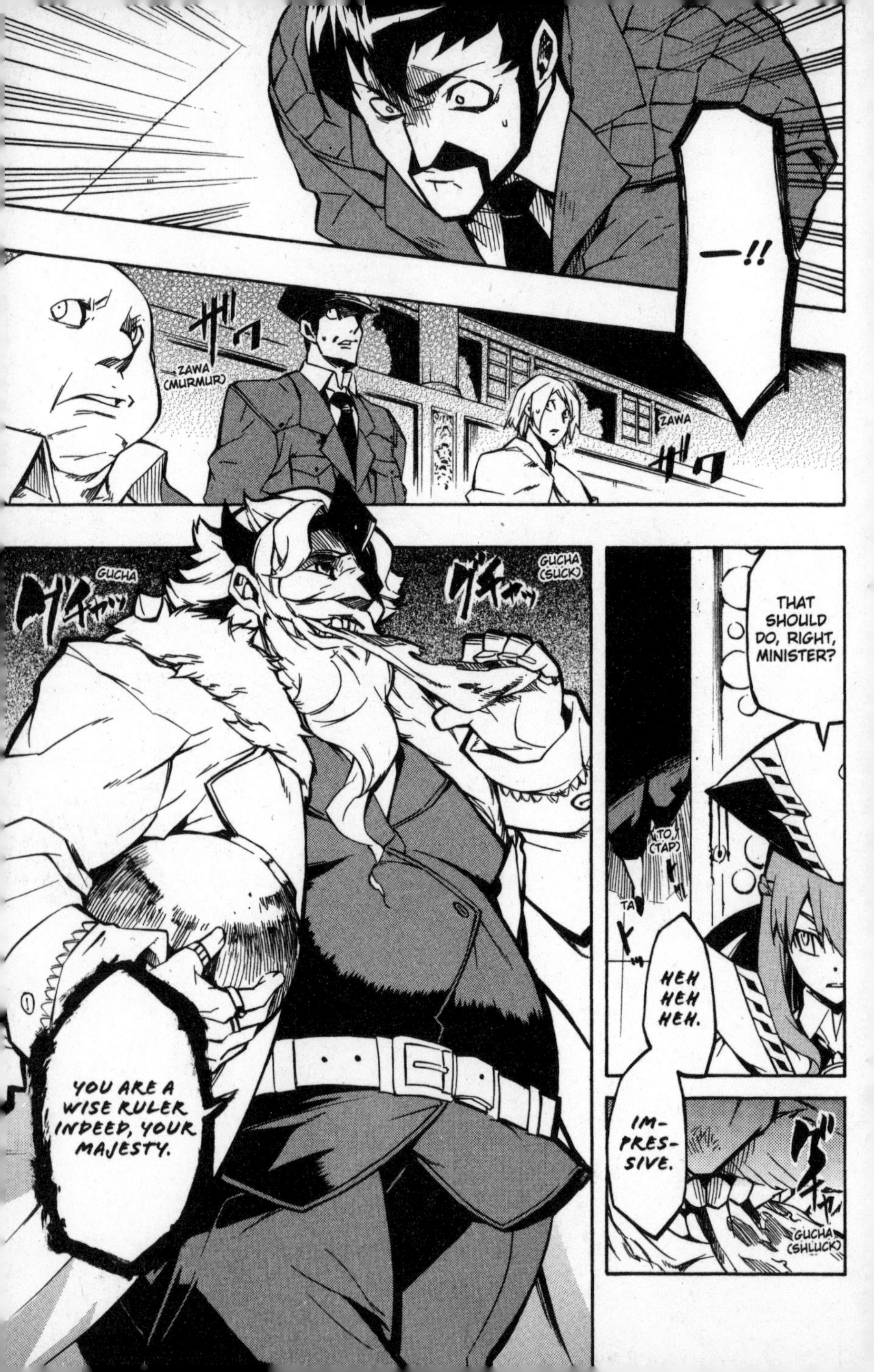
—!!
ZAWA
ZAWA (MURMUR)
THAT SHOULD DO, RIGHT, MINISTER?
TO (TAP)
TA
HEH HEH HEH.
IM-PRES-SIVE.
GUCHA (SHLUCK)
GUCHA (SUCK)
GUCHA
YOU ARE A WISE RULER INDEED, YOUR MAJESTY.

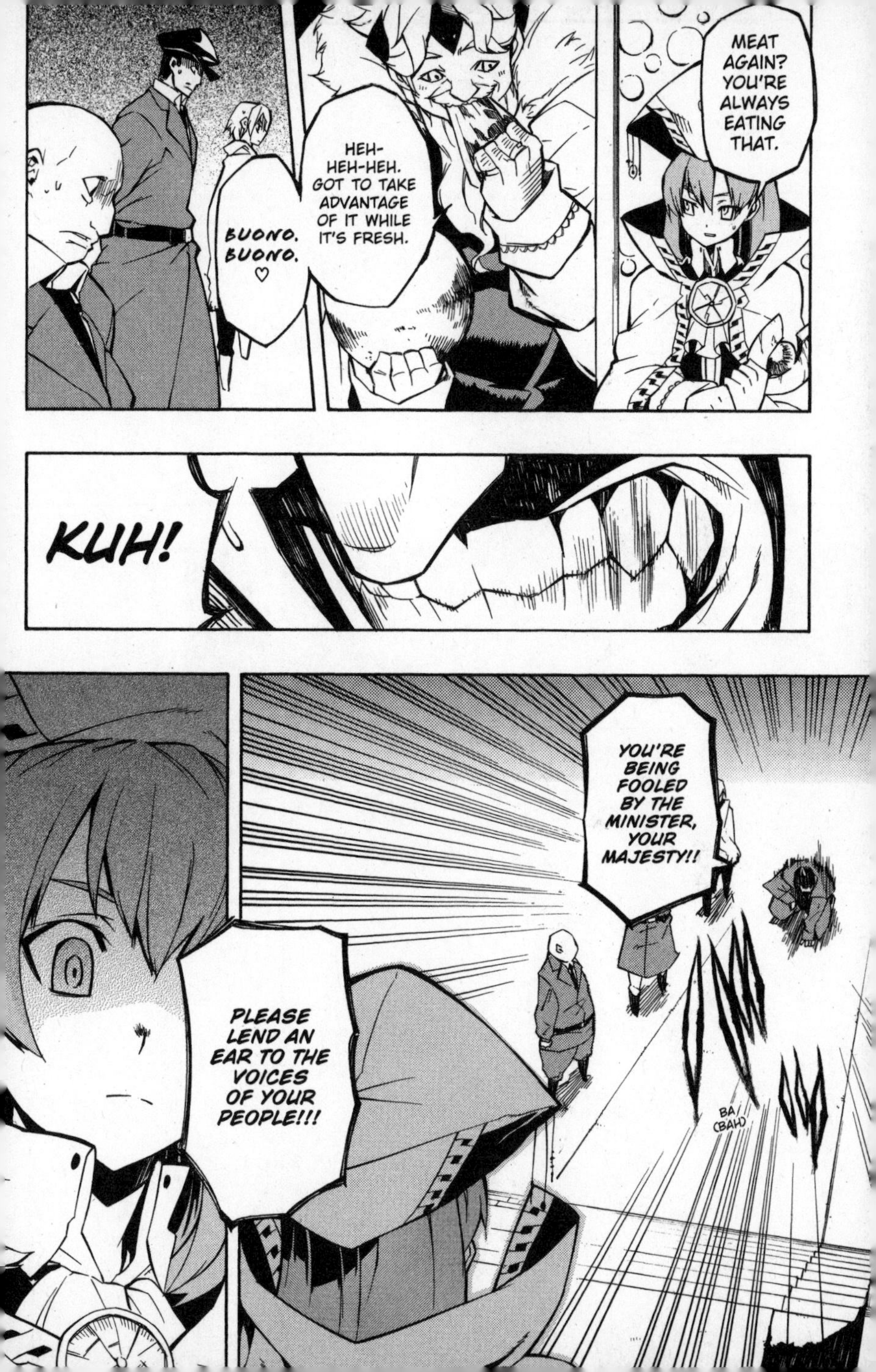
MEAT AGAIN? YOU'RE ALWAYS EATING THAT.
HEH-HEH-HEH. GOT TO TAKE ADVANTAGE OF IT WHILE IT'S FRESH.
BUONO. BUONO. ♡
KUH!
YOU'RE BEING FOOLED BY THE MINISTER, YOUR MAJESTY!!
PLEASE LEND AN EAR TO THE VOICES OF YOUR PEOPLE!!!
BA (BAH)

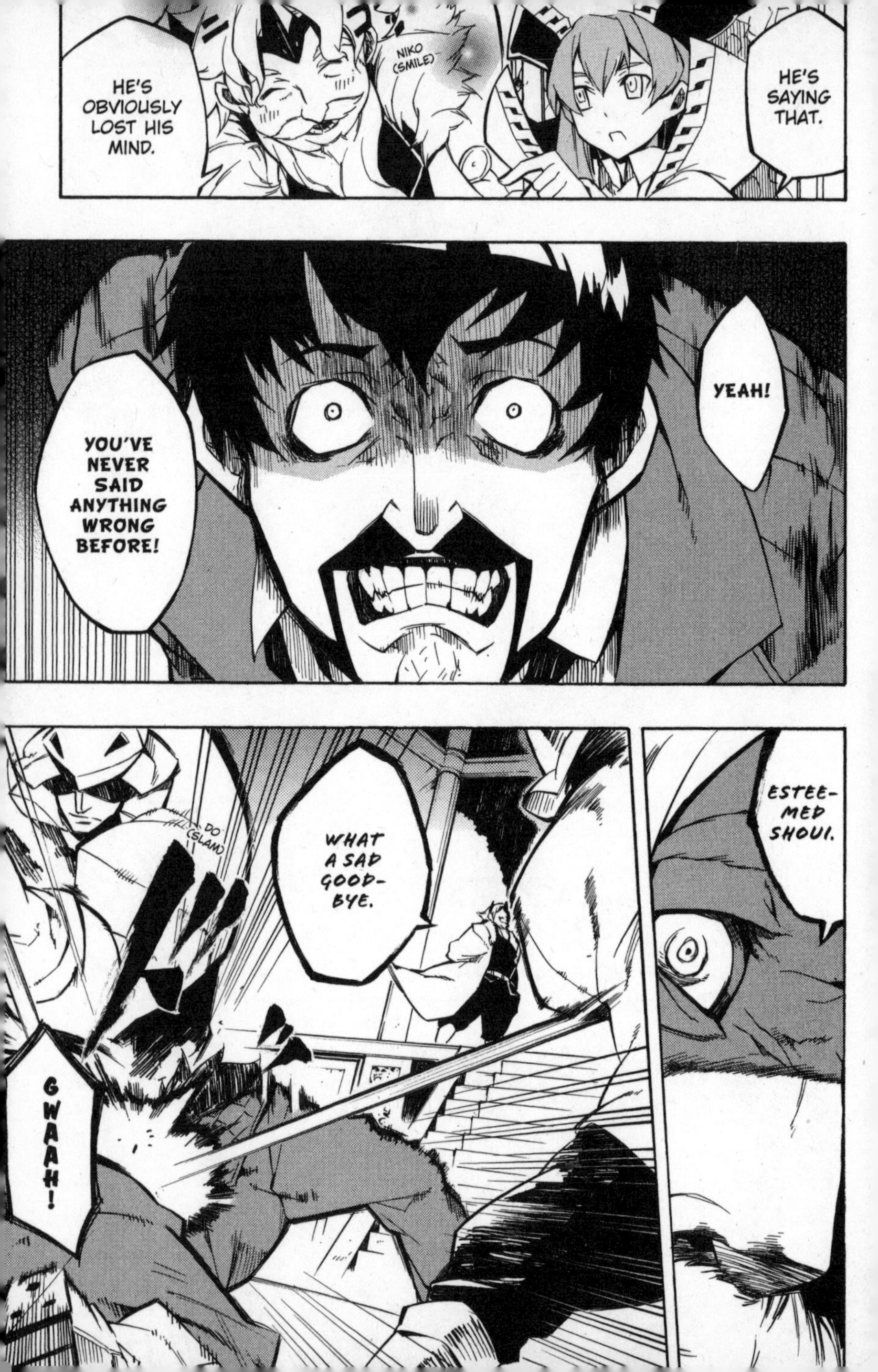
HE'S SAYING THAT.
NIKO (SMILE)
HE'S OBVIOUSLY LOST HIS MIND.
YEAH!
YOU'VE NEVER SAID ANYTHING WRONG BEFORE!
ESTEE-MED SHOUI.
WHAT A SAD GOOD-BYE.
DO (SLAM)
GWAAH!

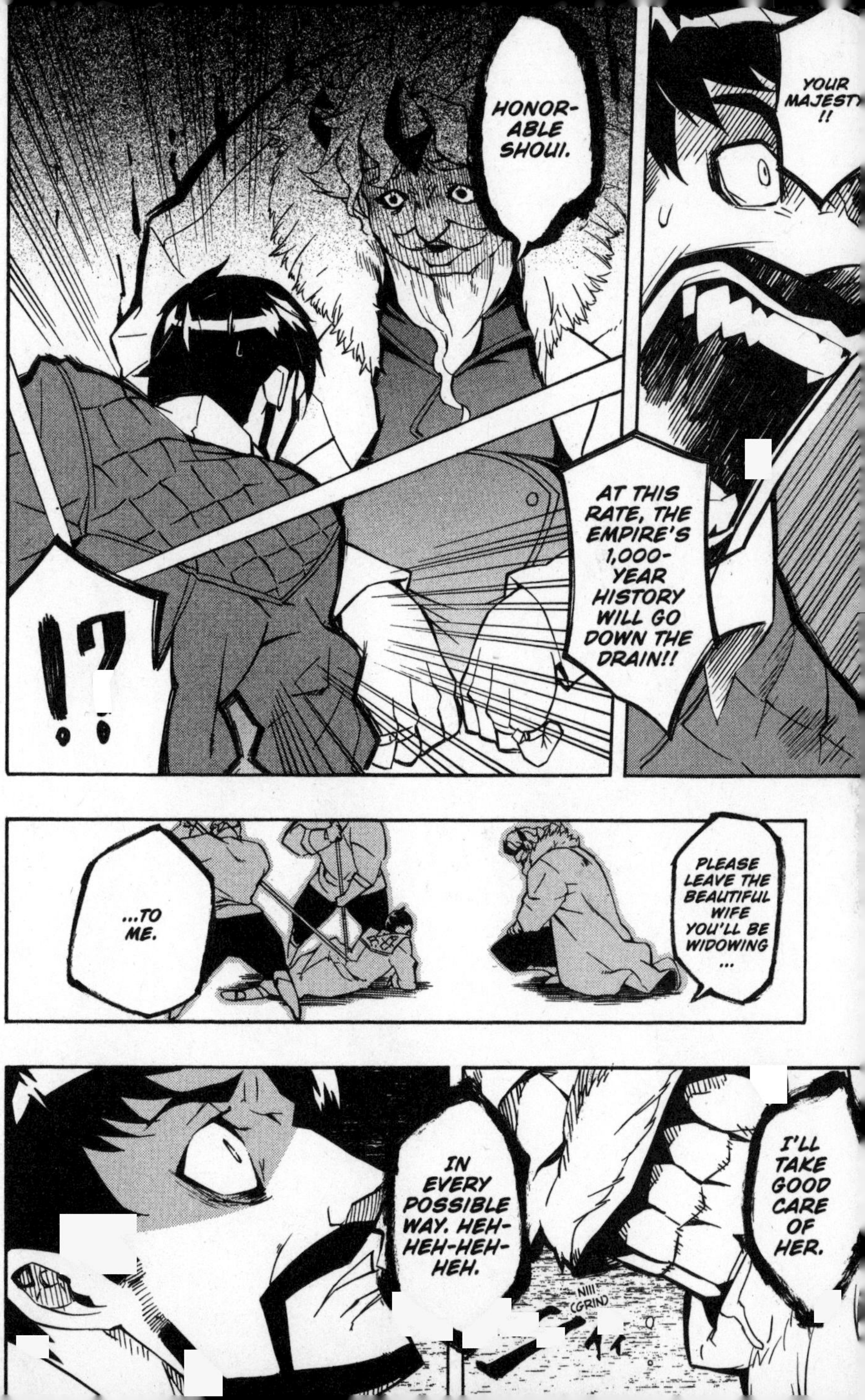
YOUR MAJESTY!!
AT THIS RATE, THE EMPIRE'S 1,000-YEAR HISTORY WILL GO DOWN THE DRAIN!!
HONOR-ABLE SHOUI.
!?
PLEASE LEAVE THE BEAUTIFUL WIFE YOU'LL BE WIDOWING...
...TO ME.
I'LL TAKE GOOD CARE OF HER.
IN EVERY POSSIBLE WAY. HEH-HEH-HEH-HEH.
NIII! (GRIND

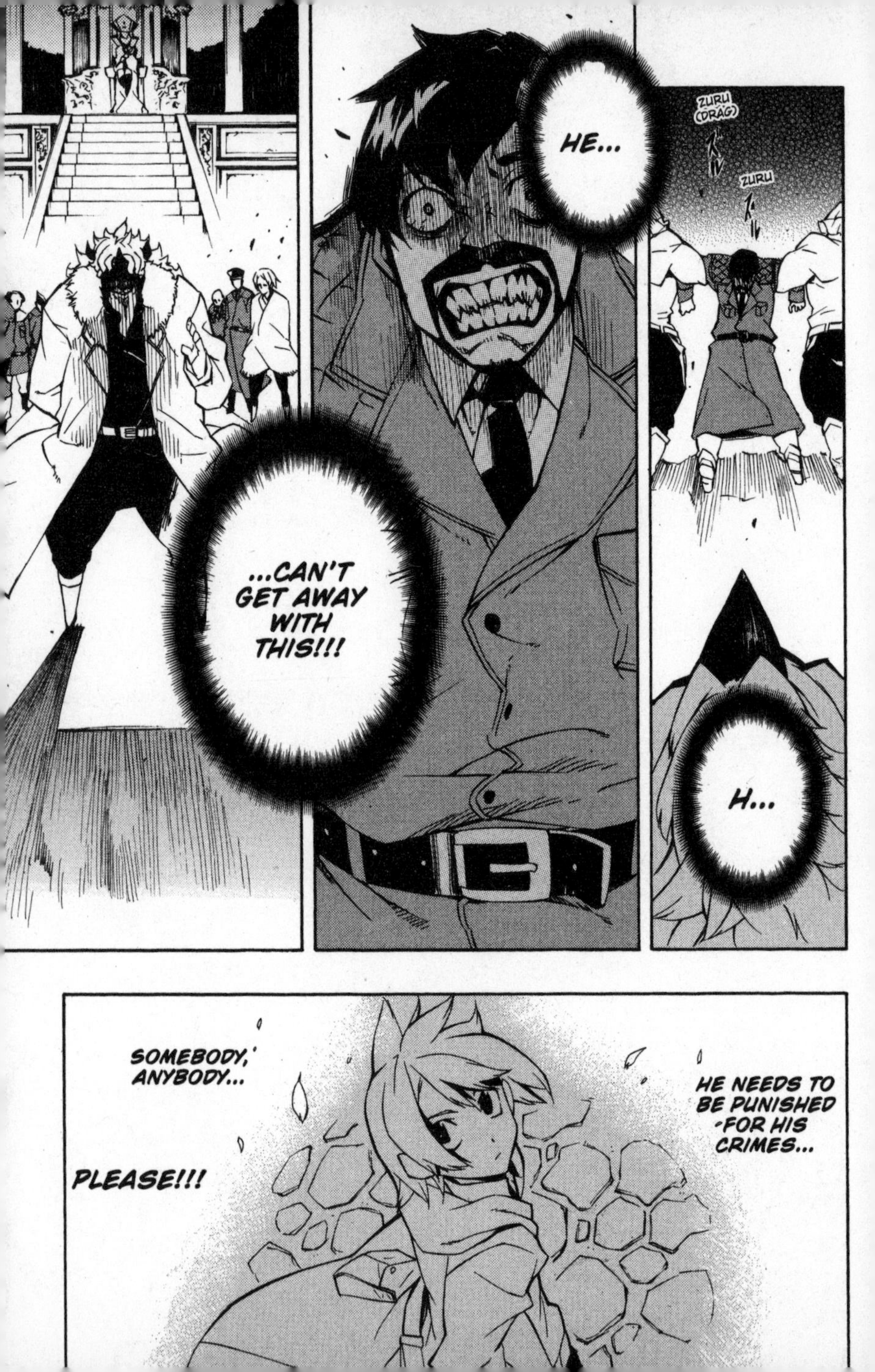
ZURU (DRAG)
ZURU
H...
HE...
...CAN'T GET AWAY WITH THIS!!!
HE NEEDS TO BE PUNISHED FOR HIS CRIMES...
SOMEBODY, ANYBODY...
PLEASE!!!

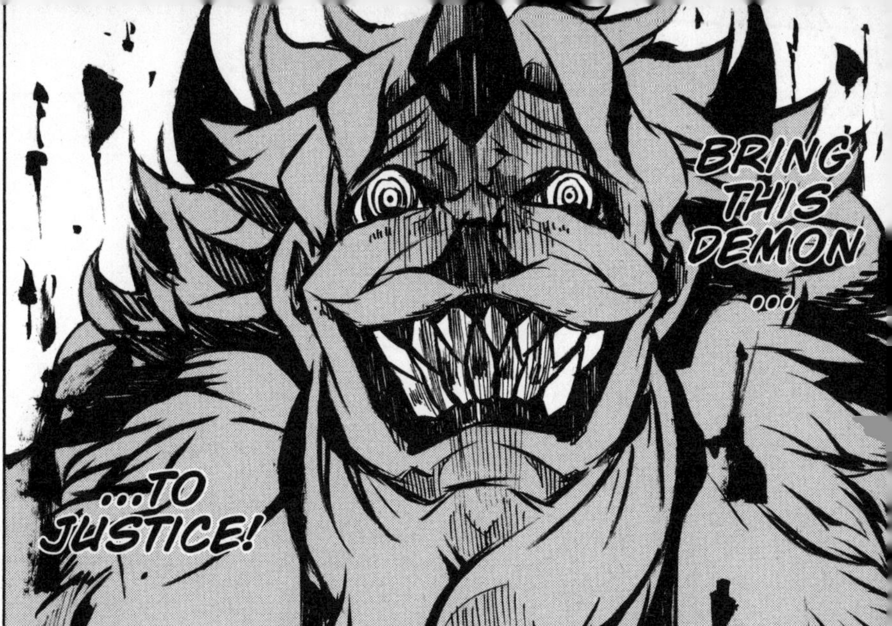
BRING THIS DEMON...
...TO JUSTICE!

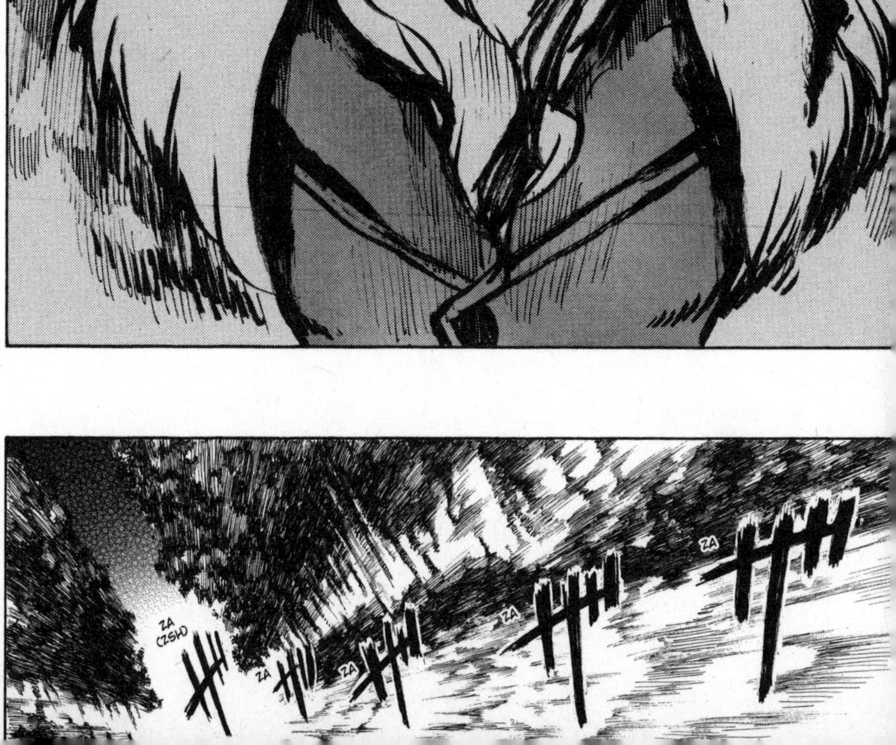
ZA
ZA
ZA
ZA
ZA (ZSH)

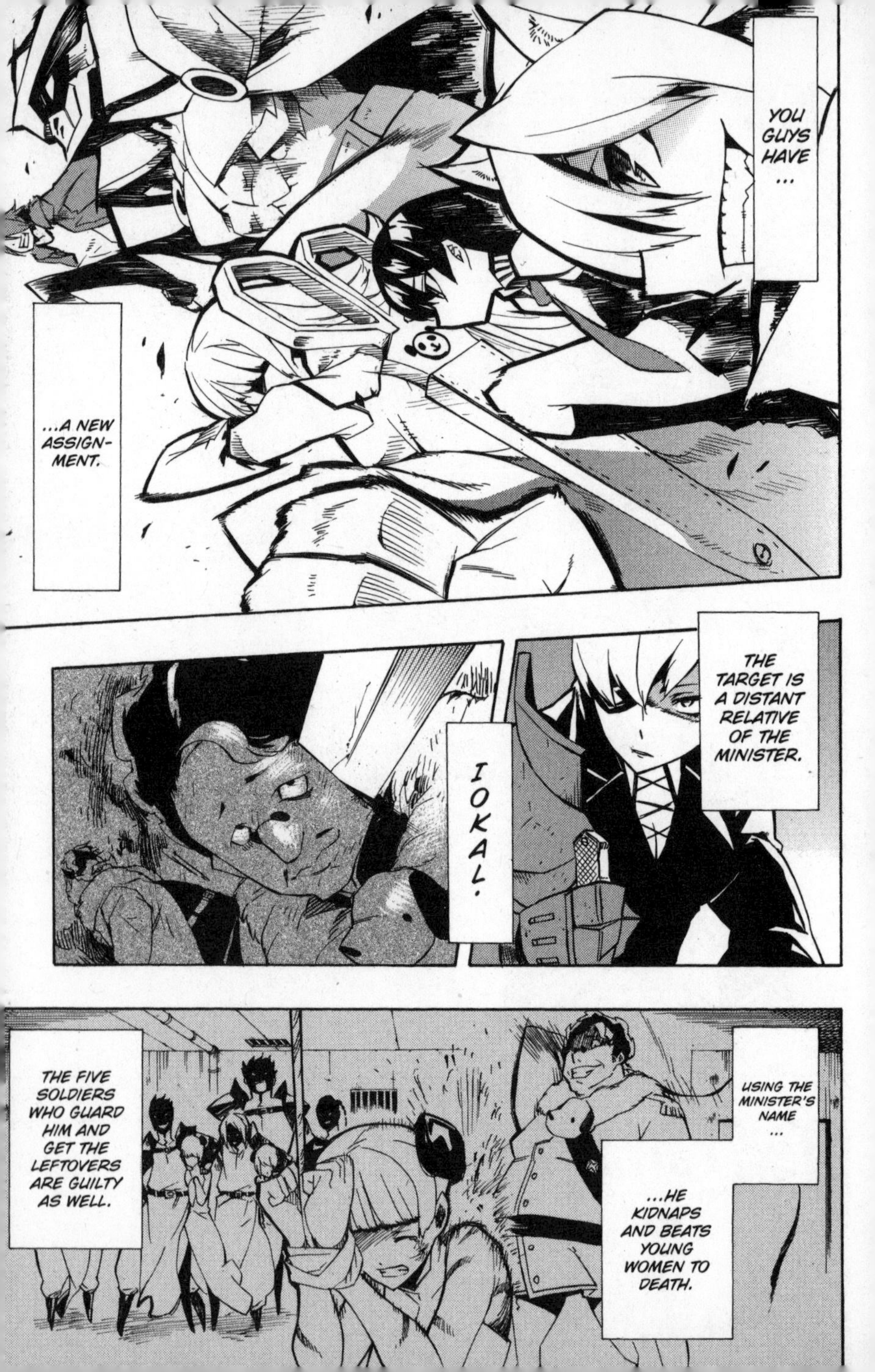
YOU GUYS HAVE ...
...A NEW ASSIGN-MENT.
THE TARGET IS A DISTANT RELATIVE OF THE MINISTER.
IOKAL.
USING THE MINISTER'S NAME ...
...HE KIDNAPS AND BEATS YOUNG WOMEN TO DEATH.
THE FIVE SOLDIERS WHO GUARD HIM AND GET THE LEFTOVERS ARE GUILTY AS WELL.

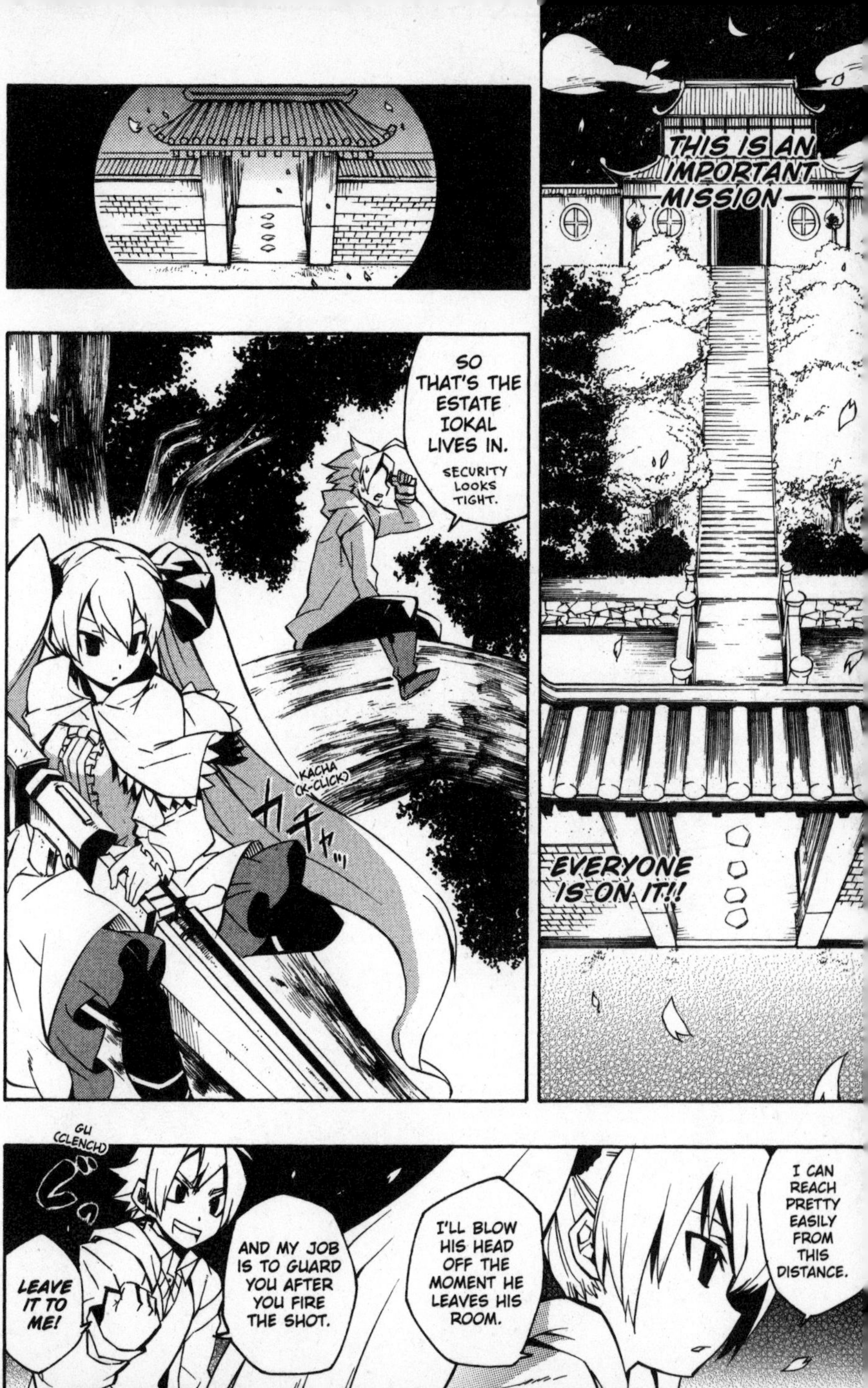
THIS IS AN IMPORTANT MISSION
EVERYONE IS ON IT!!
SO THAT'S THE ESTATE IOKAL LIVES IN.
SECURITY LOOKS TIGHT.
KACHA (K-CLICK)
I CAN REACH PRETTY EASILY FROM THIS DISTANCE.
I'LL BLOW HIS HEAD OFF THE MOMENT HE LEAVES HIS ROOM.
AND MY JOB IS TO GUARD YOU AFTER YOU FIRE THE SHOT.
LEAVE IT TO ME!
GU (CLENCH)

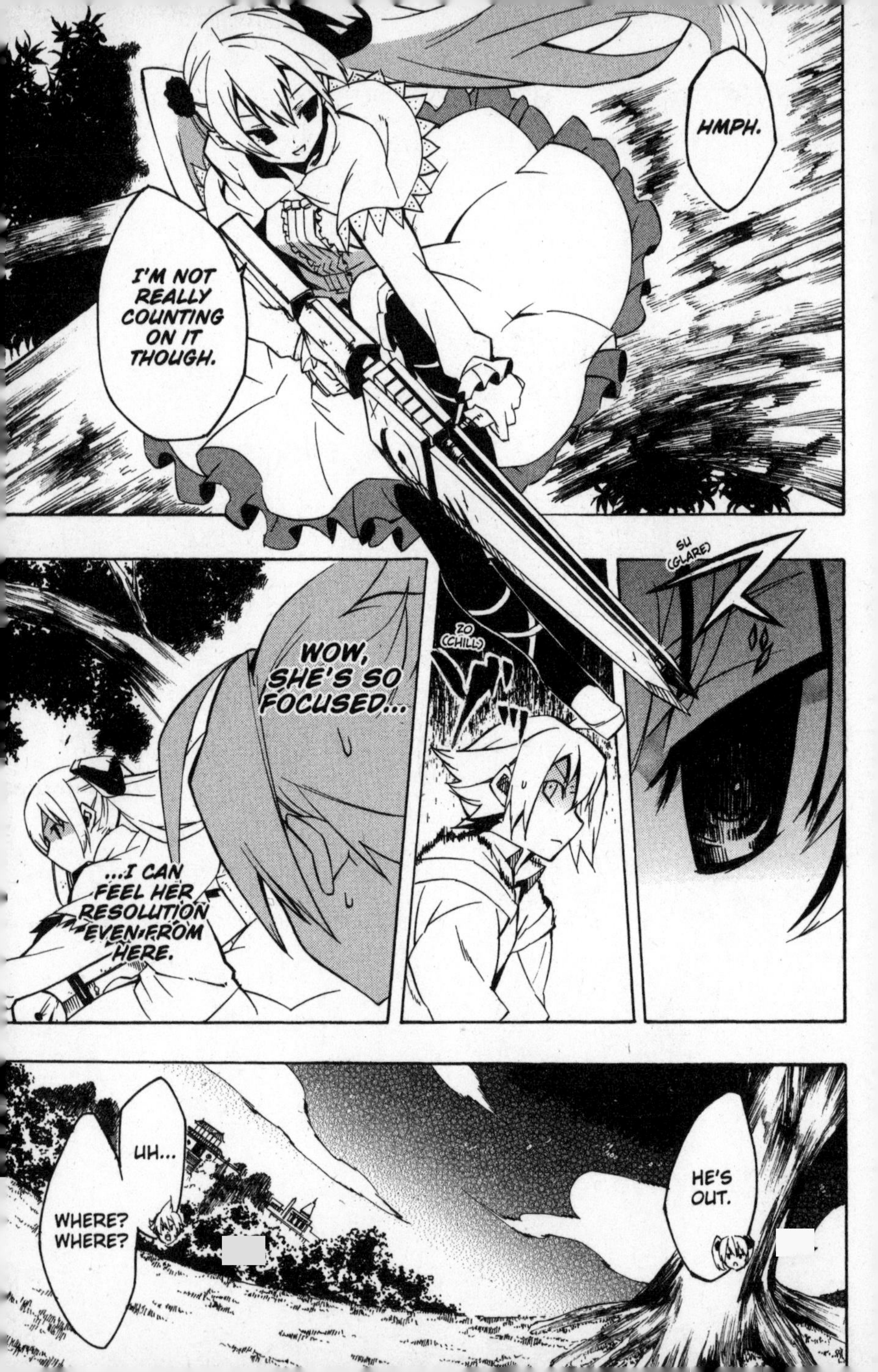
HMPH.
I'M NOT REALLY COUNTING ON IT THOUGH.
SU (GLARE)
ZO (CHILL)
WOW, SHE'S SO FOCUSED...
...I CAN FEEL HER RESOLUTION EVEN FROM HERE.
HE'S OUT.
UH...
WHERE? WHERE?

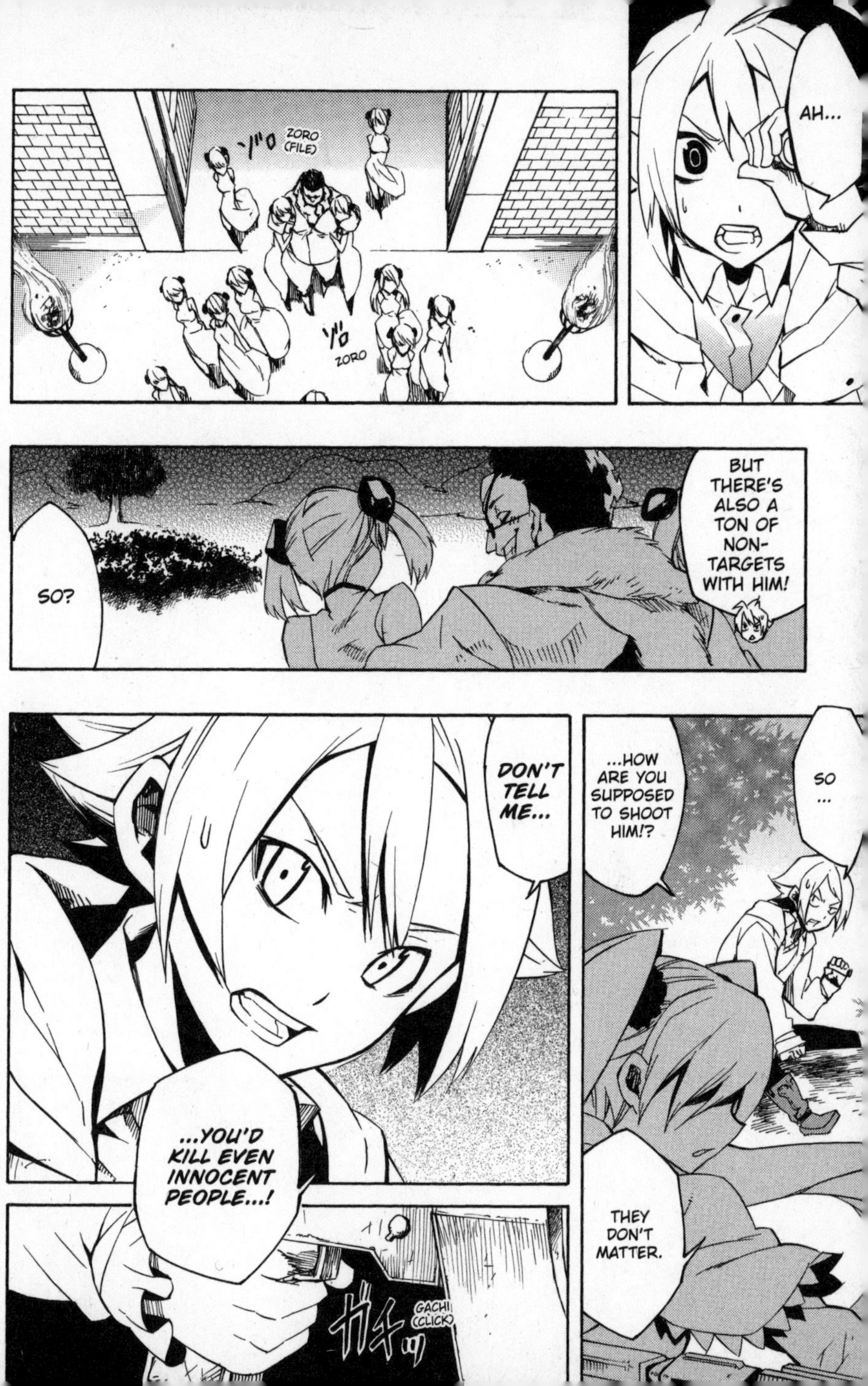
AH...
ゾロ
ZORO (FILE)
ゾロ
ZORO
BUT THERE'S ALSO A TON OF NON-TARGETS WITH HIM!
SO?
SO ...
...HOW ARE YOU SUPPOSED TO SHOOT HIM!?
THEY DON'T MATTER.
DON'T TELL ME...
...YOU'D KILL EVEN INNOCENT PEOPLE...!
ガチ
GACHI (CLICK)

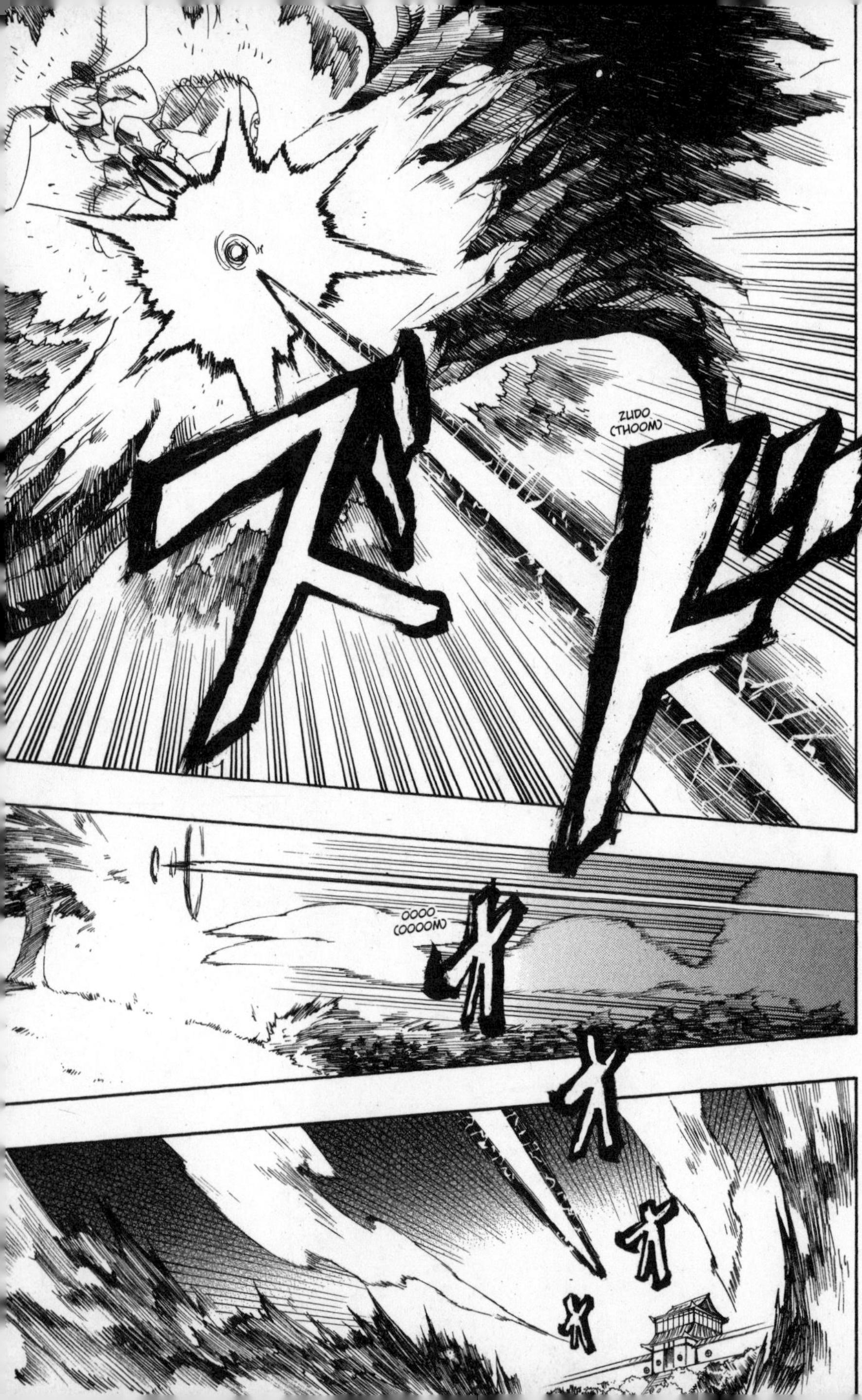
ZUDO
(THOOM)
OOOO
(OOOOM)

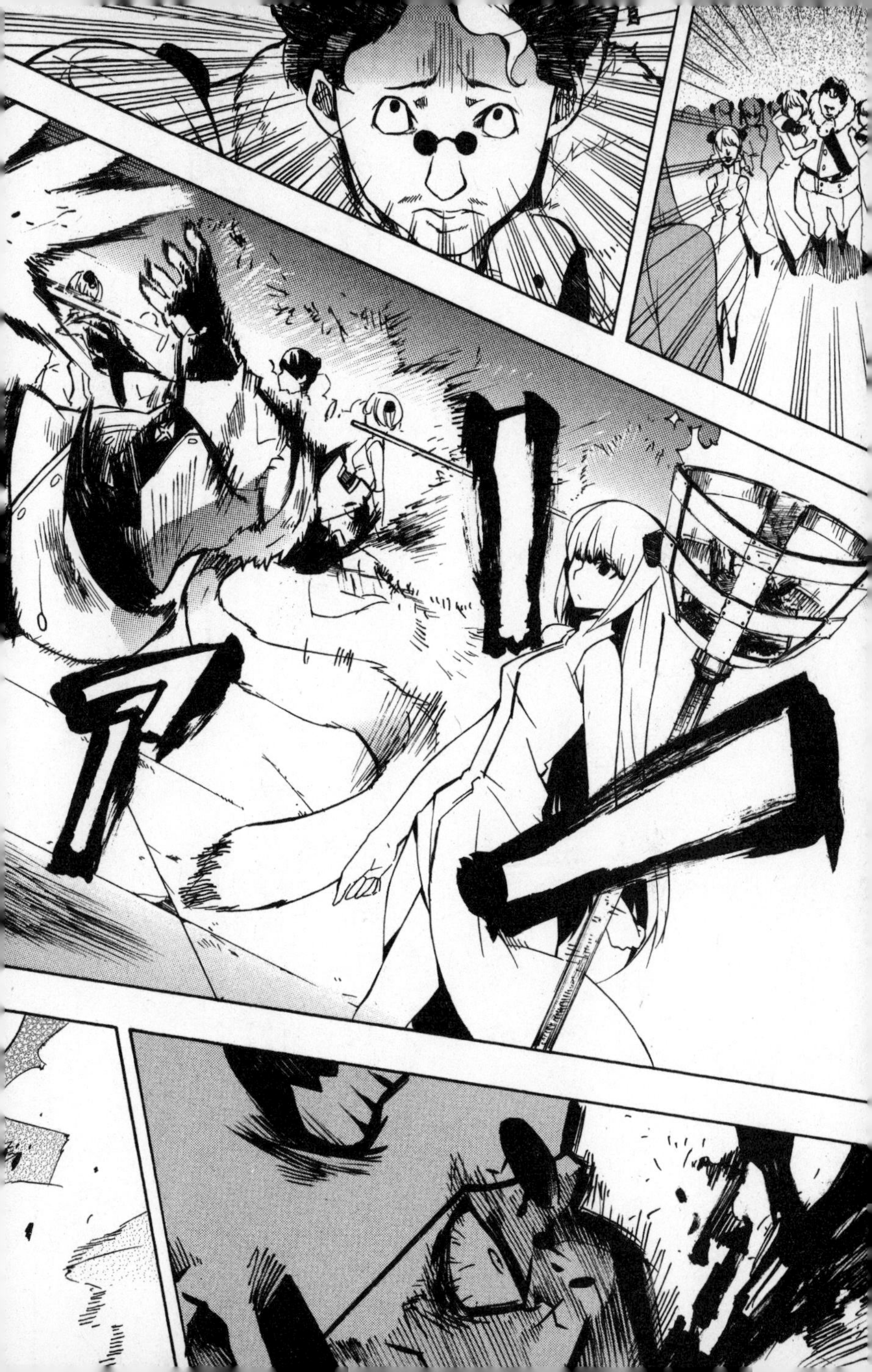

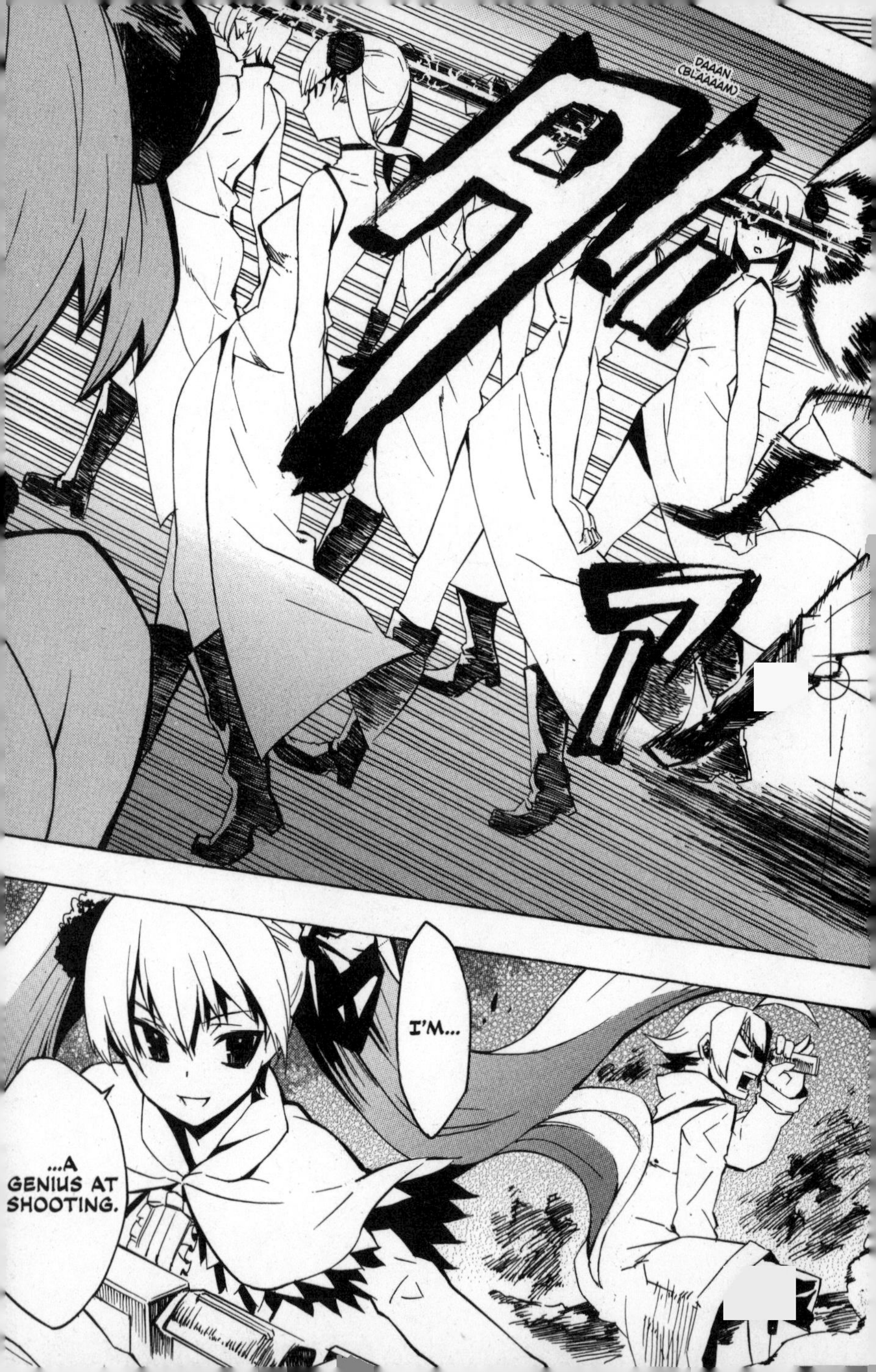
DAAAN
(BLAAAAM)
I'M...
...A GENIUS AT SHOOTING.

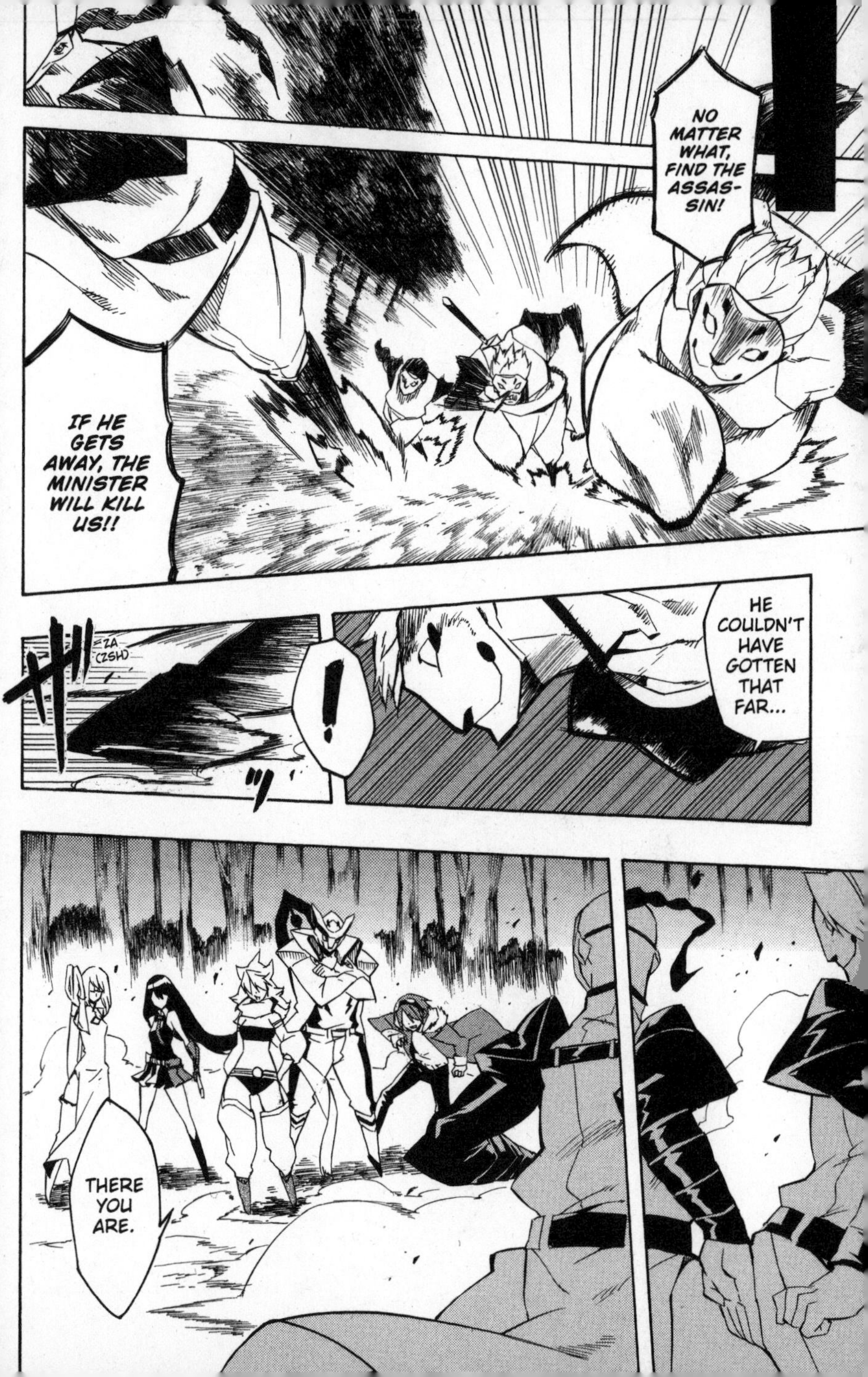
NO MATTER WHAT, FIND THE ASSAS-SIN!
IF HE GETS AWAY, THE MINISTER WILL KILL US!!
HE COULDN'T HAVE GOTTEN THAT FAR...
!
ZA (ZSH)
THERE YOU ARE.

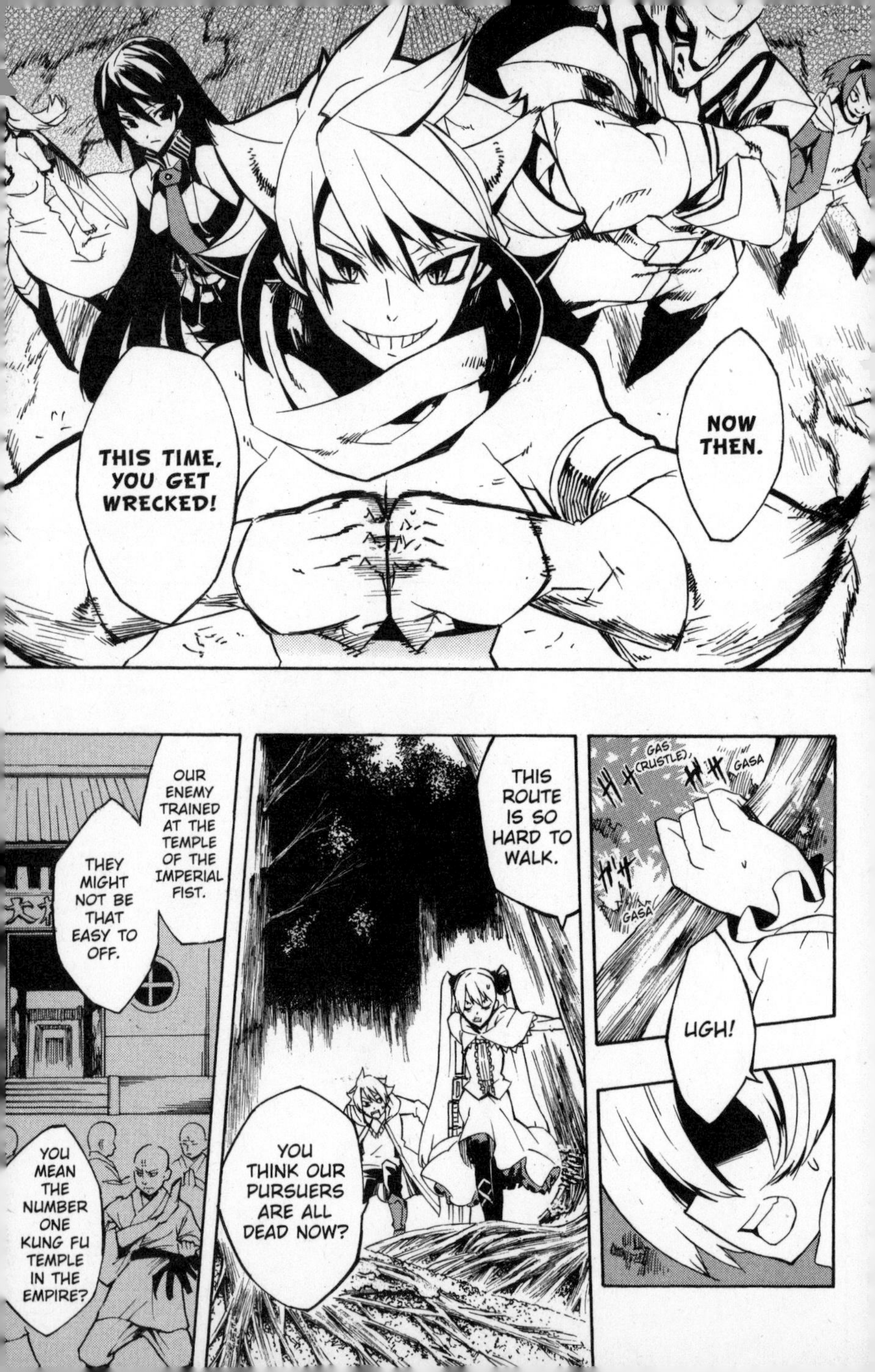
NOW THEN.
THIS TIME, YOU GET WRECKED!
GAS (RUSTLE), GASA
GASA
UGH!
THIS ROUTE IS SO HARD TO WALK.
YOU THINK OUR PURSUERS ARE ALL DEAD NOW?
OUR ENEMY TRAINED AT THE TEMPLE OF THE IMPERIAL FIST.
THEY MIGHT NOT BE THAT EASY TO OFF.
YOU MEAN THE NUMBER ONE KUNG FU TEMPLE IN THE EMPIRE?

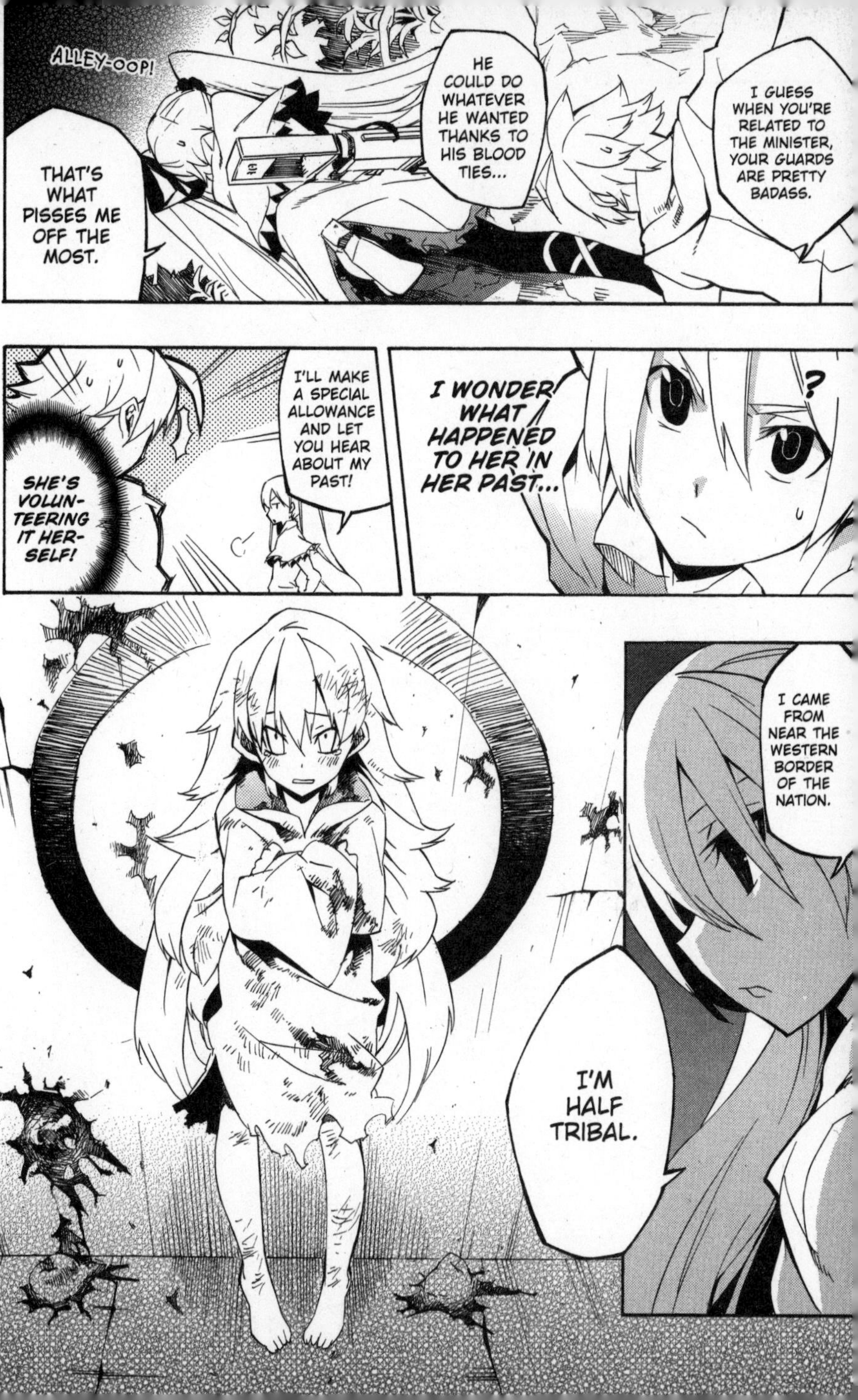
I GUESS WHEN YOU'RE RELATED TO THE MINISTER, YOUR GUARDS ARE PRETTY BADASS.
HE COULD DO WHATEVER HE WANTED THANKS TO HIS BLOOD TIES...
ALLEY-OOP!
THAT'S WHAT PISSES ME OFF THE MOST.
?
I WONDER WHAT HAPPENED TO HER IN HER PAST...
I'LL MAKE A SPECIAL ALLOWANCE AND LET YOU HEAR ABOUT MY PAST!
SHE'S VOLUN-TEERING IT HER-SELF!
I CAME FROM NEAR THE WESTERN BORDER OF THE NATION.
I'M HALF TRIBAL.

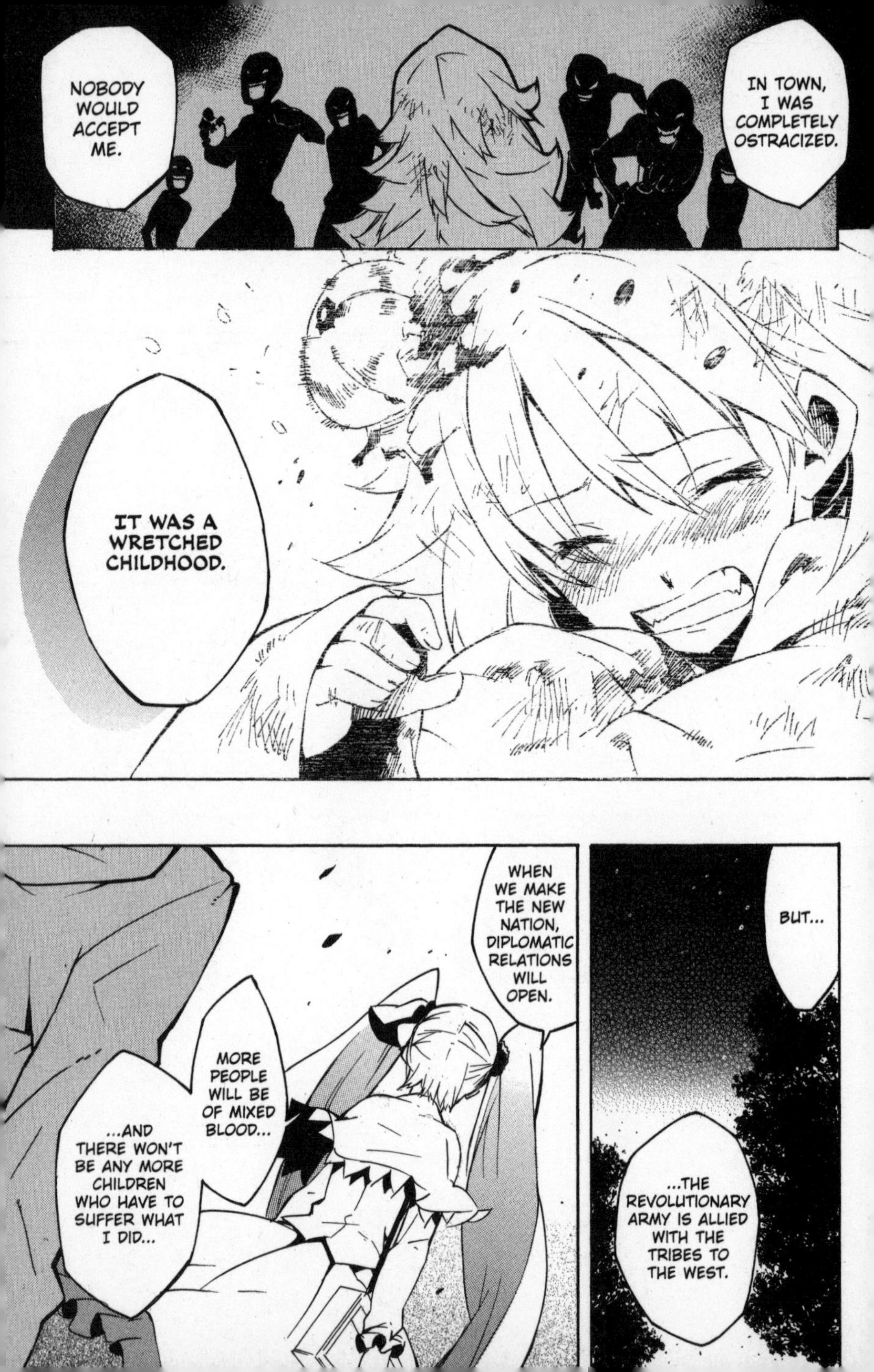
IN TOWN, I WAS COMPLETELY OSTRACIZED.
NOBODY WOULD ACCEPT ME.
IT WAS A WRETCHED CHILDHOOD.
BUT...
...THE REVOLUTIONARY ARMY IS ALLIED WITH THE TRIBES TO THE WEST.
WHEN WE MAKE THE NEW NATION, DIPLOMATIC RELATIONS WILL OPEN.
MORE PEOPLE WILL BE OF MIXED BLOOD...
...AND THERE WON'T BE ANY MORE CHILDREN WHO HAVE TO SUFFER WHAT I DID...

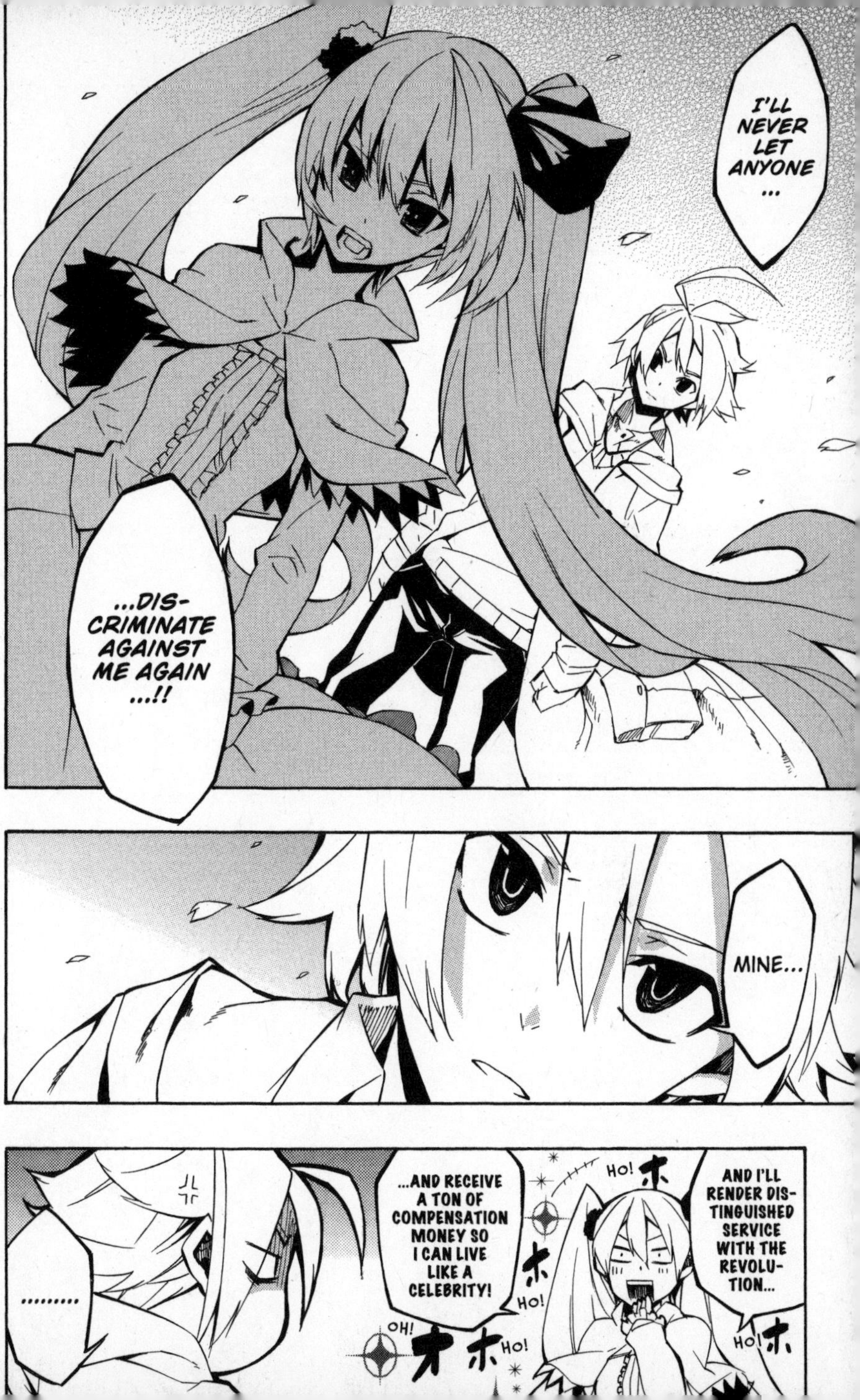
I'LL NEVER LET ANYONE ...
...DIS-CRIMINATE AGAINST ME AGAIN ...!!
MINE...
AND I'LL RENDER DIS-TINGUISHED SERVICE WITH THE REVOLU-TION...
...AND RECEIVE A TON OF COMPENSATION MONEY SO I CAN LIVE LIKE A CELEBRITY!
HO! ホ
HO! ホ
HO! ホ
OH! オ
HO! ホ
....

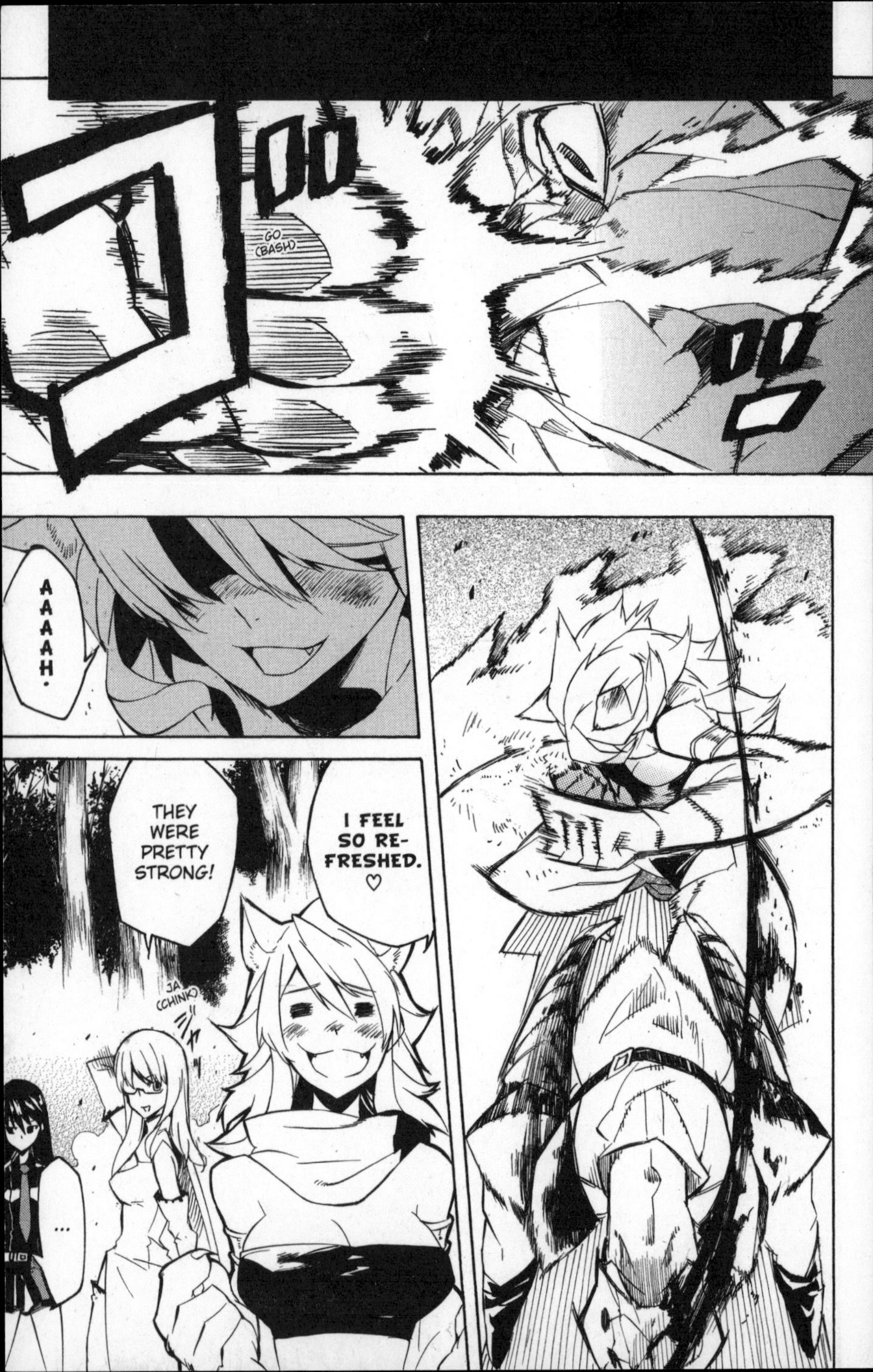
GO (BASH)
AAAAAH.
I FEEL SO RE-FRESHED. ♡
THEY WERE PRETTY STRONG!
JA (CHINK)
...

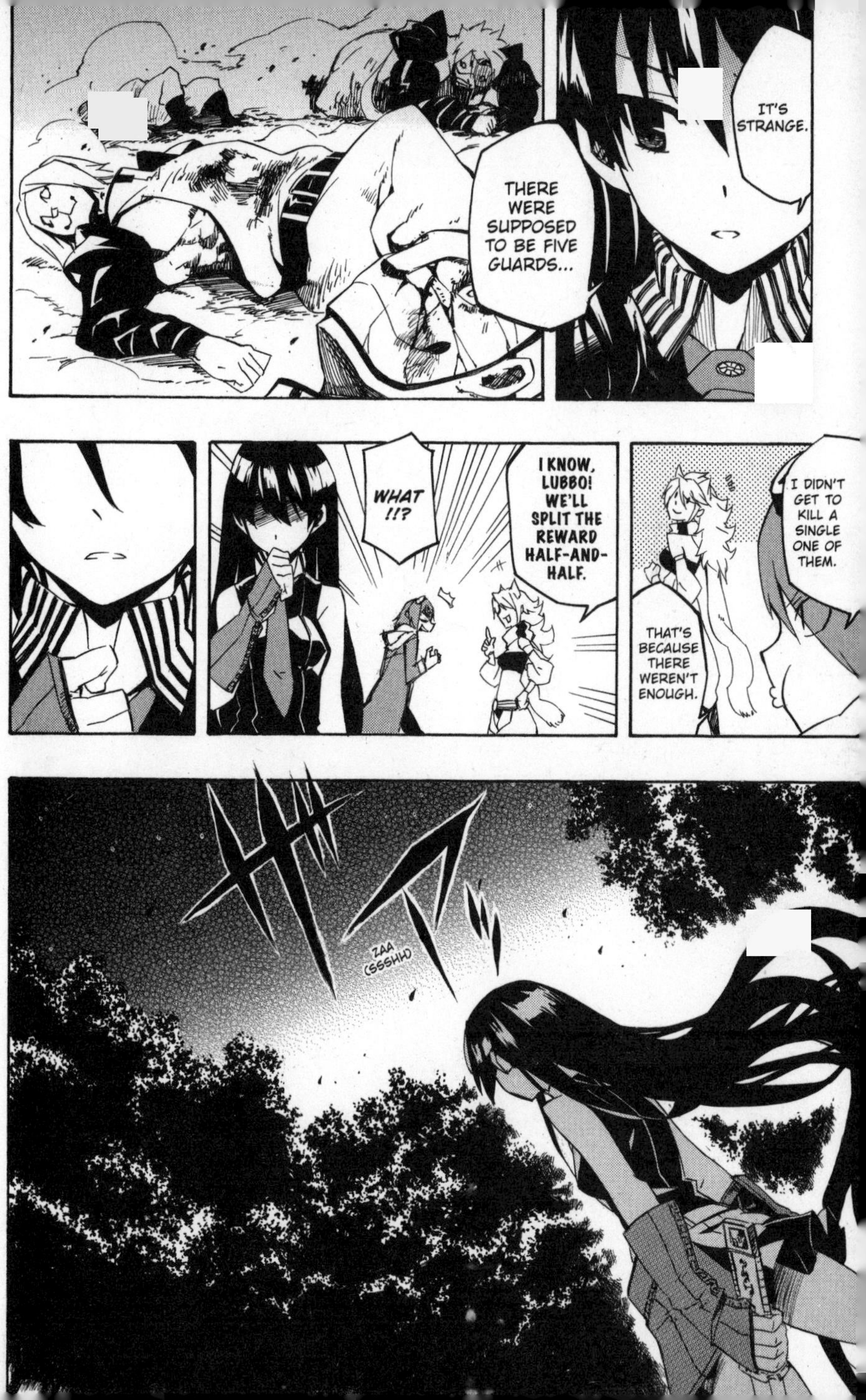
IT'S STRANGE.
THERE WERE SUPPOSED TO BE FIVE GUARDS...
I DIDN'T GET TO KILL A SINGLE ONE OF THEM.
THAT'S BECAUSE THERE WEREN'T ENOUGH.
I KNOW, LUBBO! WE'LL SPLIT THE REWARD HALF-AND-HALF.
WHAT !!?
ZAA (SSSHH)

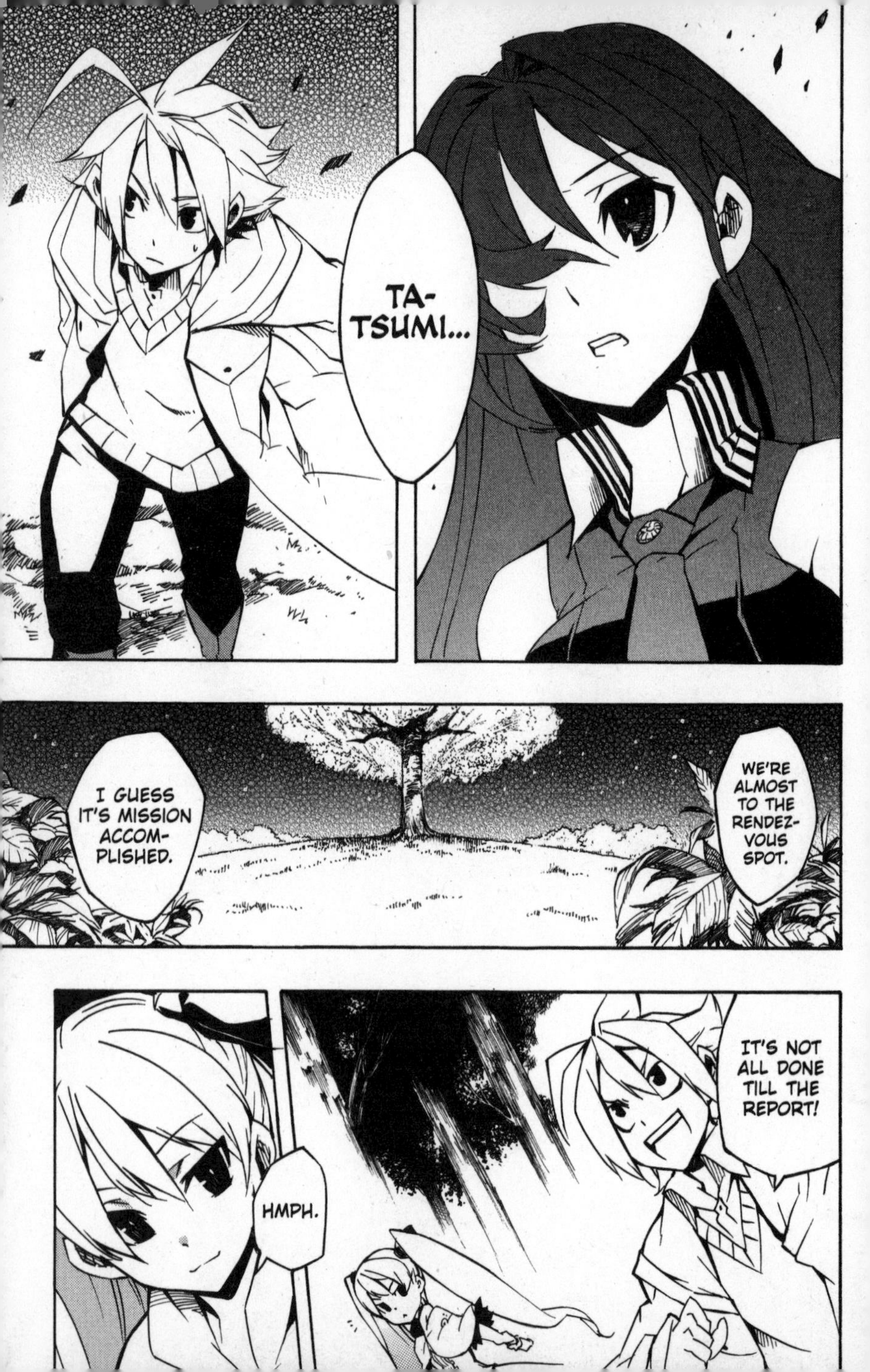
TA-TSUMI...
WE'RE ALMOST TO THE RENDEZ-VOUS SPOT.
I GUESS IT'S MISSION ACCOM-PLISHED.
IT'S NOT ALL DONE TILL THE REPORT!
HMPH.

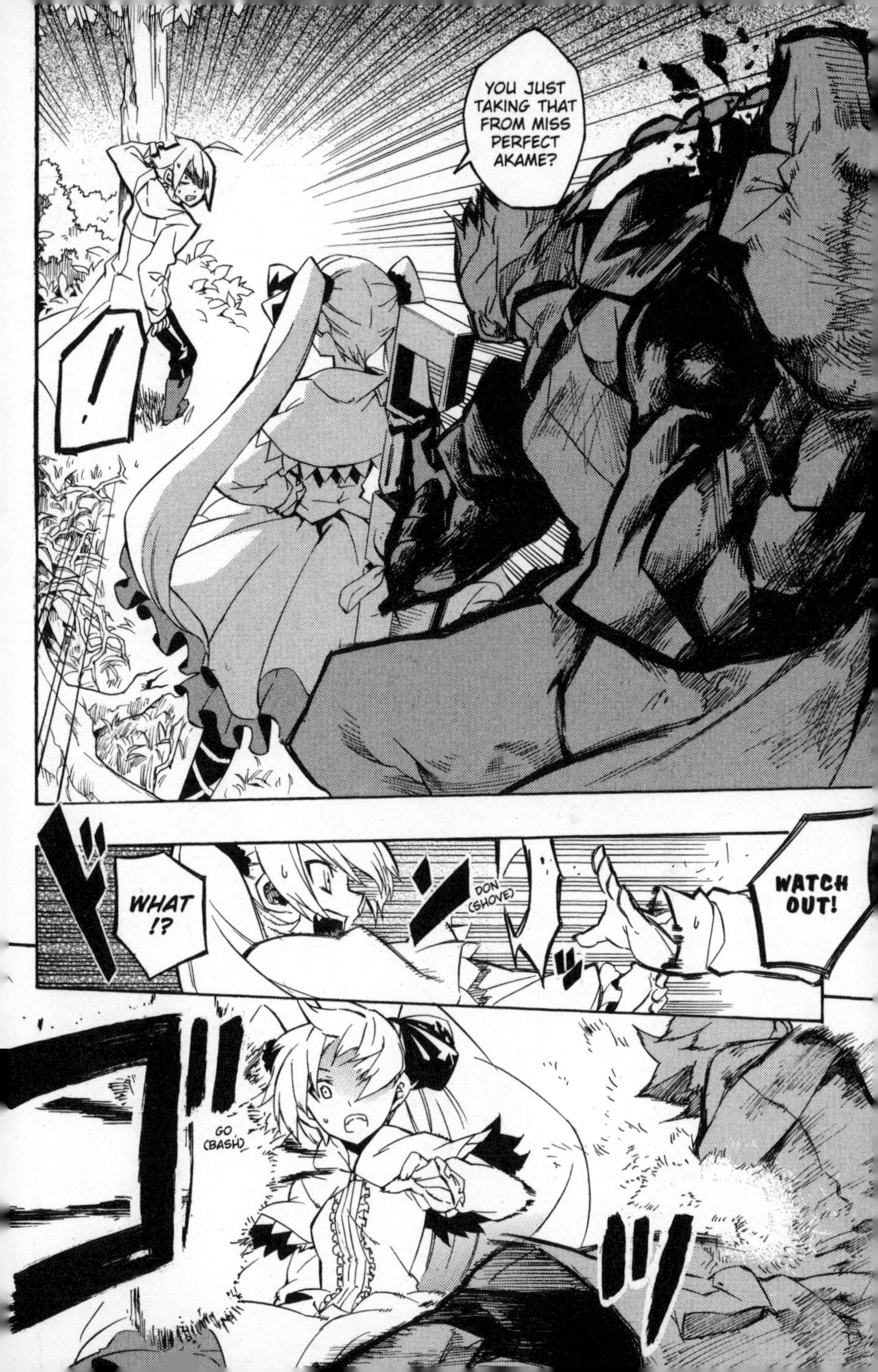
YOU JUST TAKING THAT FROM MISS PERFECT AKAME?
WATCH OUT!
DON (SHOVE)
WHAT !?
GO (BASH)

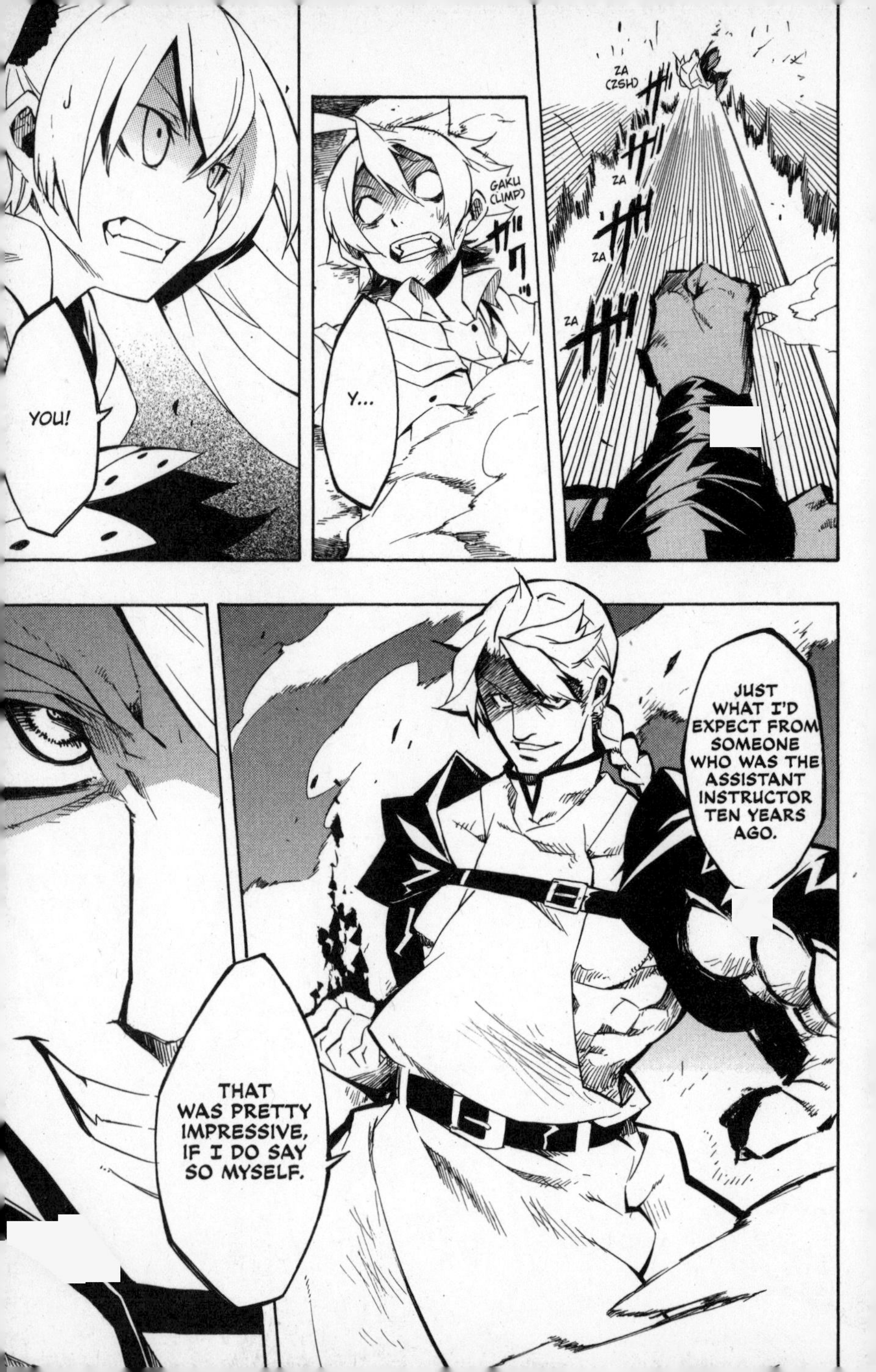
ZA (ZSH)
ZA
ZA
ZA
GAKU (LIMP)
Y...
YOU!
JUST WHAT I'D EXPECT FROM SOMEONE WHO WAS THE ASSISTANT INSTRUCTOR TEN YEARS AGO.
THAT WAS PRETTY IMPRESSIVE, IF I DO SAY SO MYSELF.

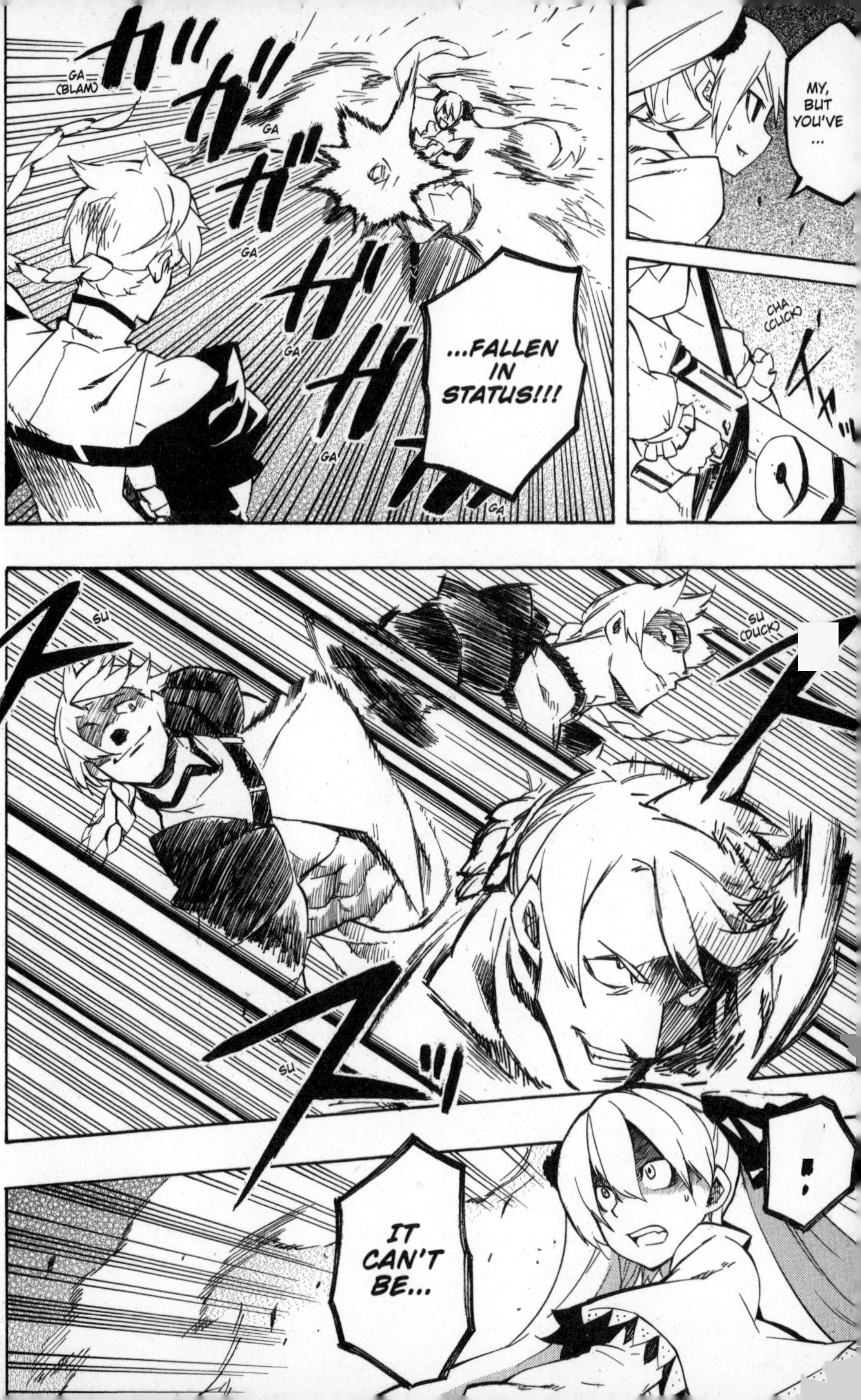
MY, BUT YOU'VE ...
CHA (CLICK)
GA (BLAM)
GA
GA
GA
GA
GA
...FALLEN IN STATUS!!!
SU (DUCK)
SU
SU
!
IT CAN'T BE...

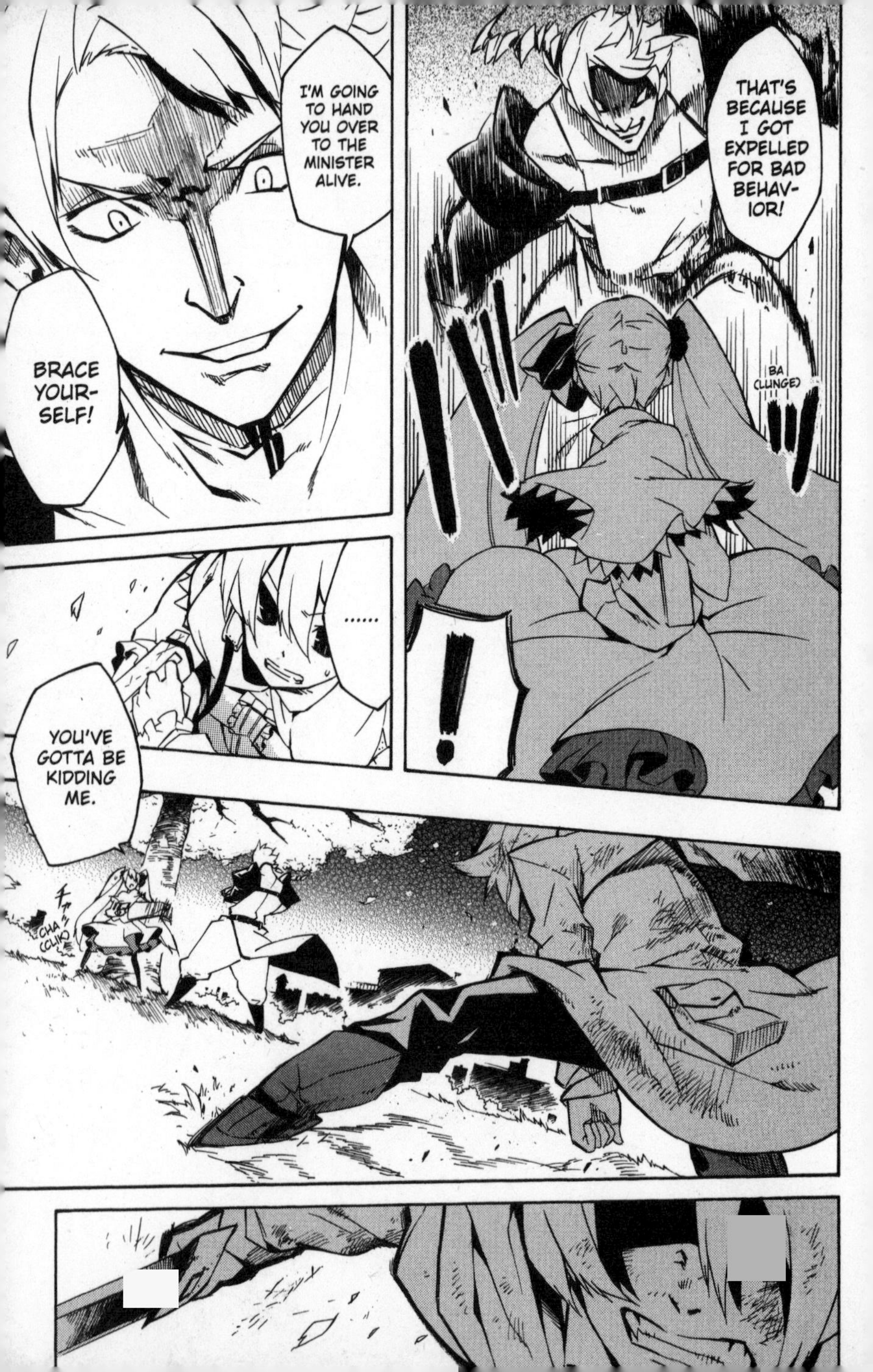
THAT'S BECAUSE I GOT EXPELLED FOR BAD BEHAV-IOR!
BA (LUNGE)
!
I'M GOING TO HAND YOU OVER TO THE MINISTER ALIVE.
BRACE YOUR-SELF!
......
YOU'VE GOTTA BE KIDDING ME.
CHA (CLIK)

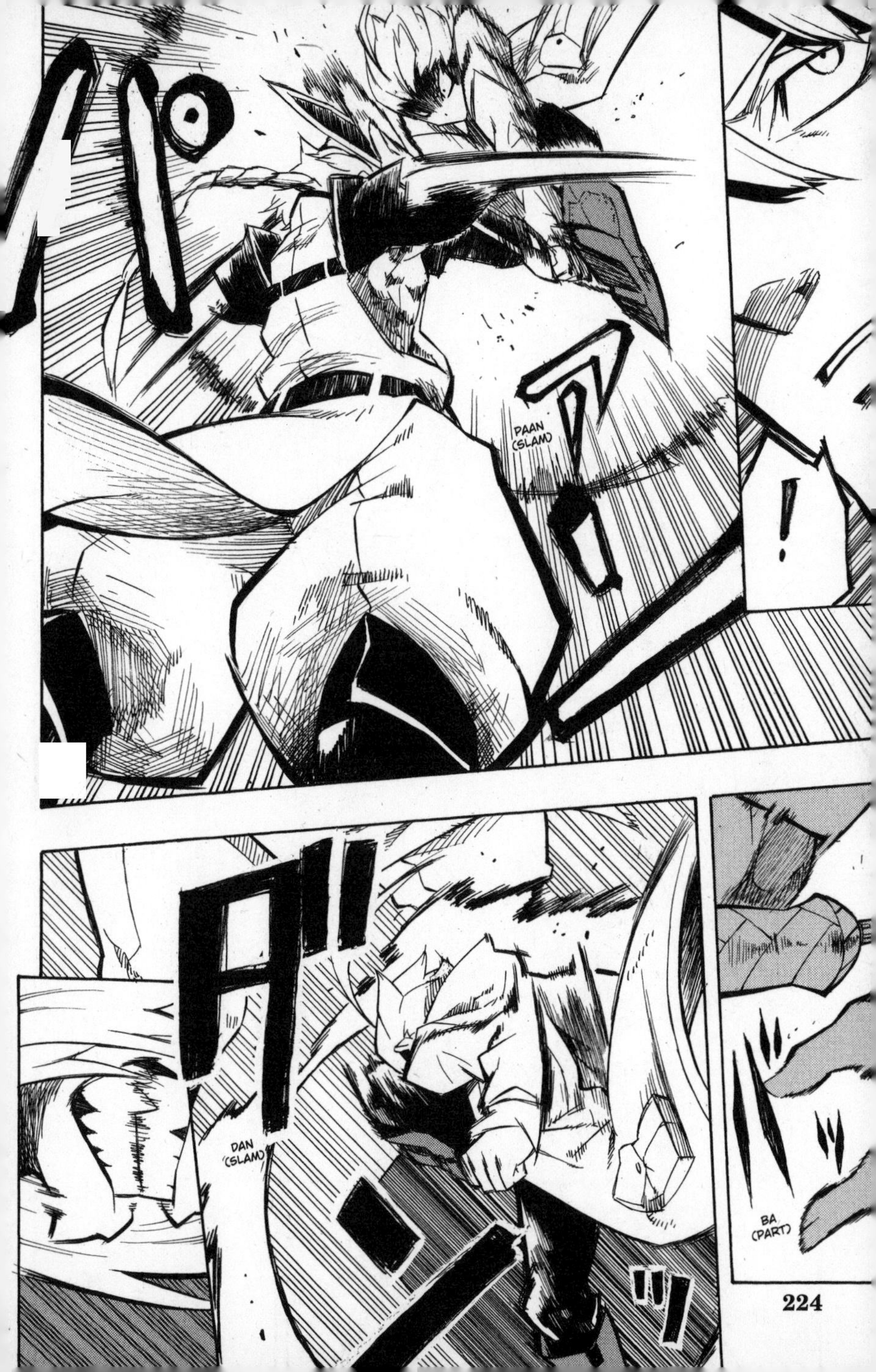
PAAN
(SLAM)
BA
(PART)
DAN
(SLAM)

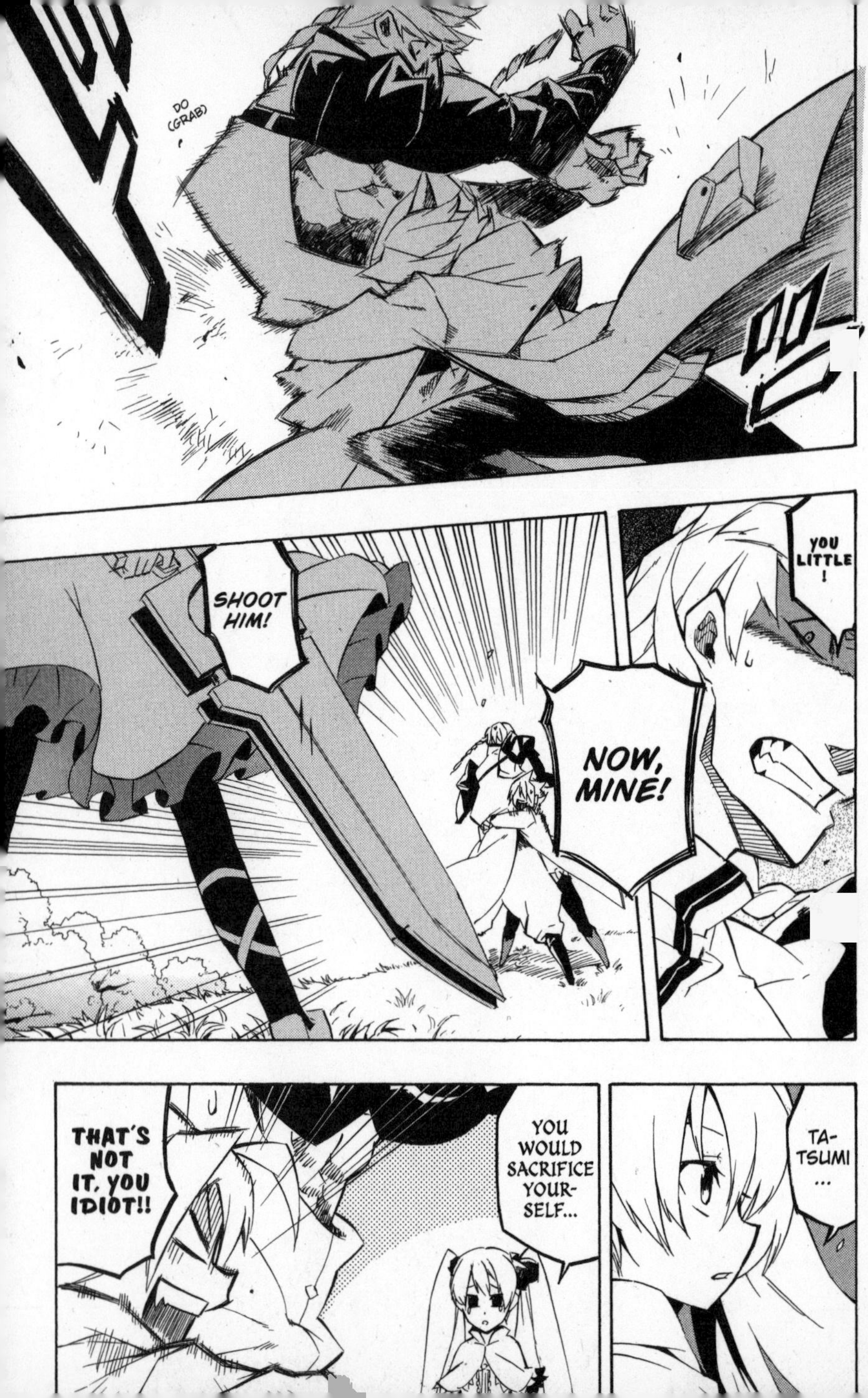
DO (GRAB)
YOU LITTLE!
SHOOT HIM!
NOW, MINE!
TA-TSUMI...
YOU WOULD SACRIFICE YOUR-SELF...
THAT'S NOT IT, YOU IDIOT!!

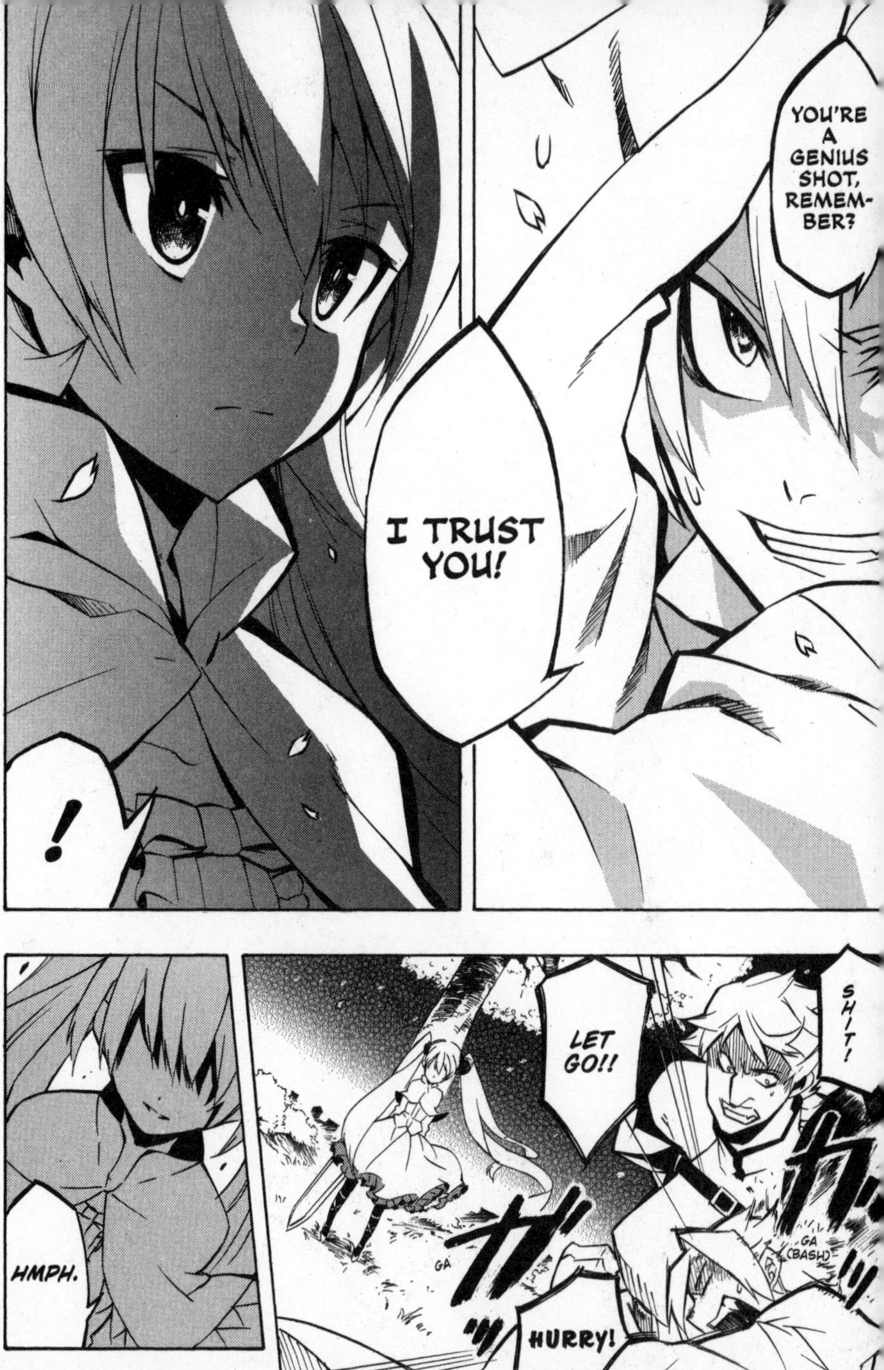
YOU'RE A GENIUS SHOT, REMEMBER?
I TRUST YOU!
!
SHIT!
LET GO!!
GA (BASH)
GA
HURRY!
HMPH.

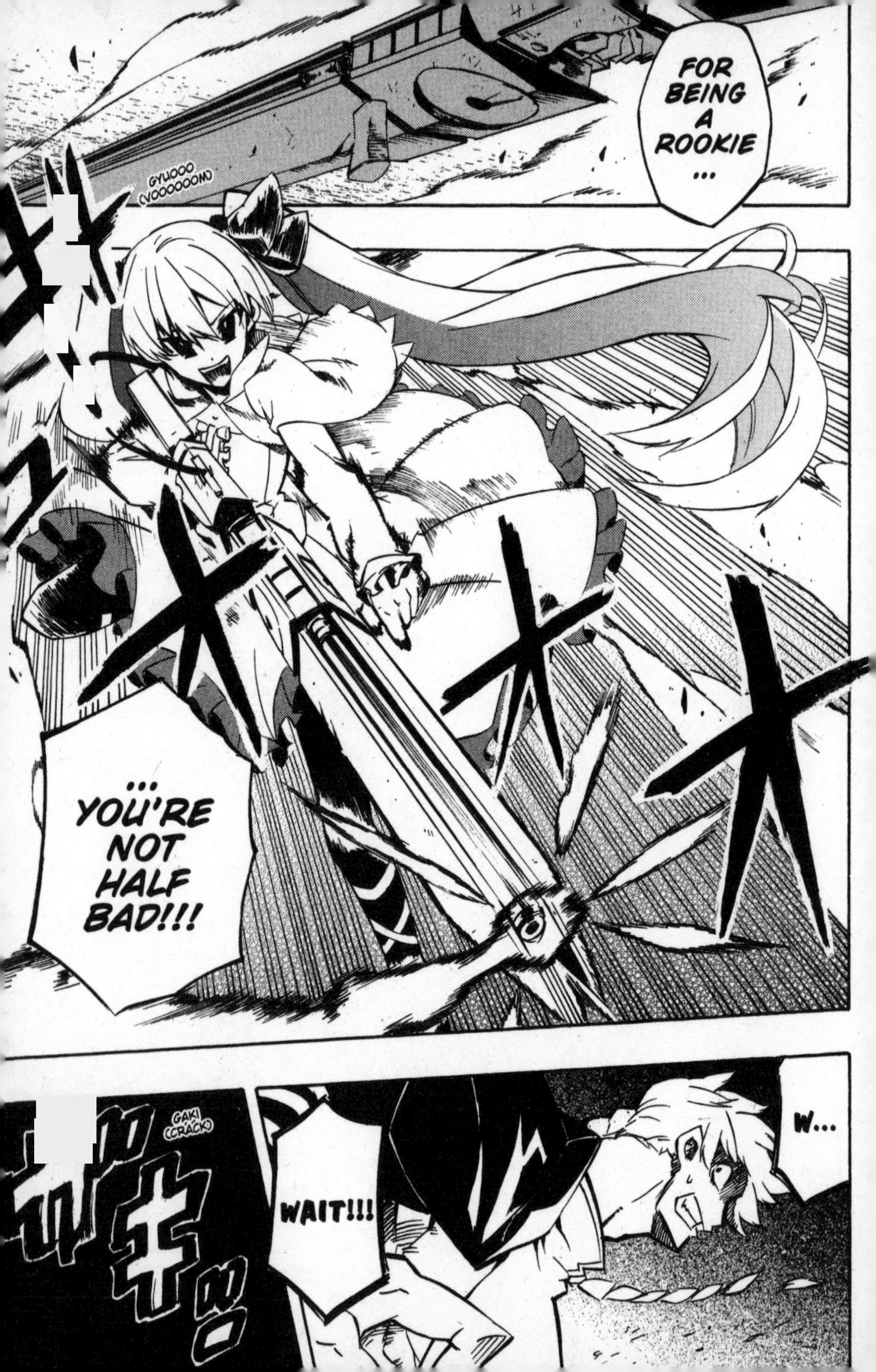
FOR BEING A ROOKIE ...
GYUOOO (VOOOOOOW)
... YOU'RE NOT HALF BAD!!!
W...
WAIT!!!
GAKI (CRACK)

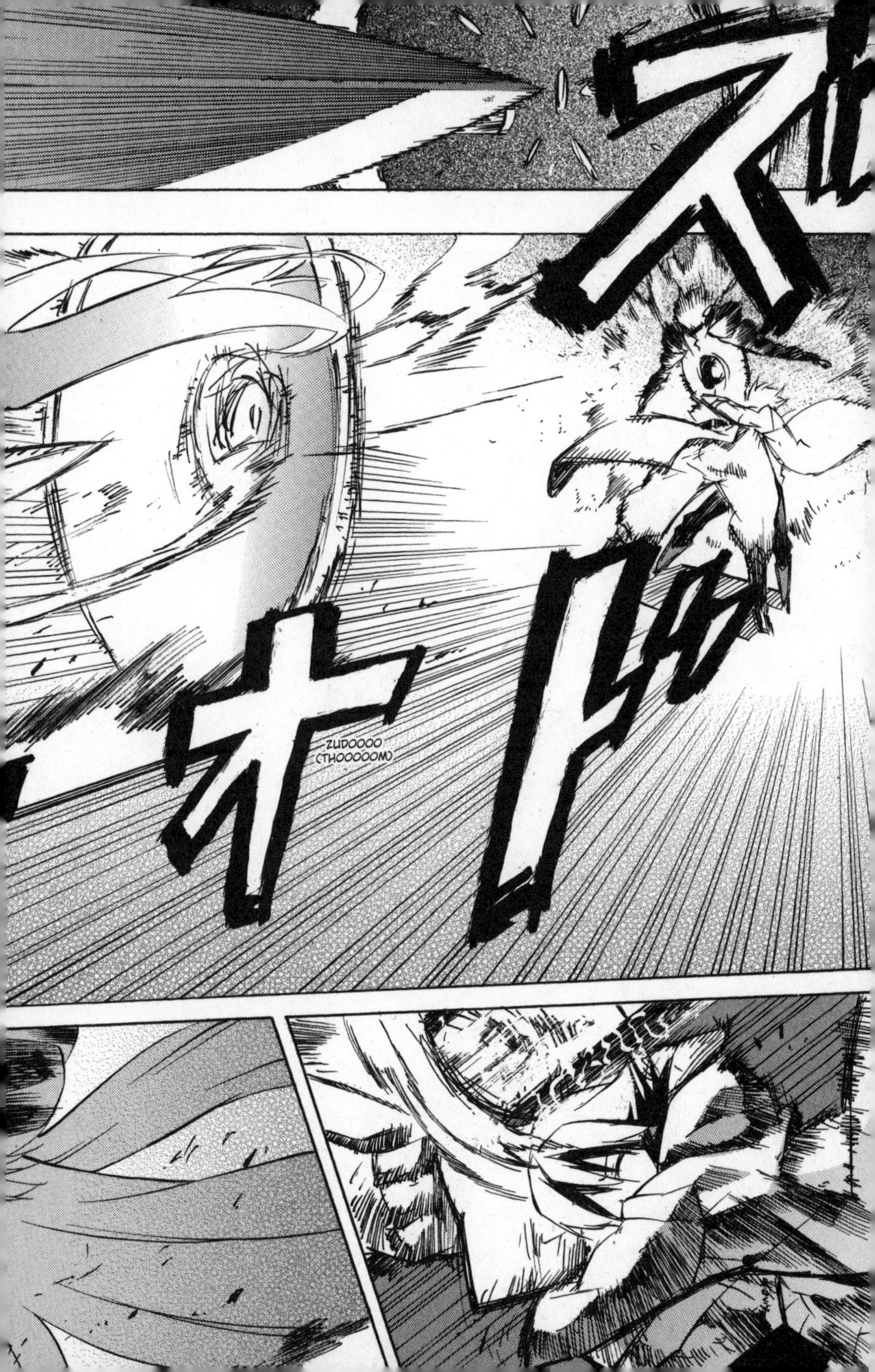
ZUDOOOO
(THOOOOOM)

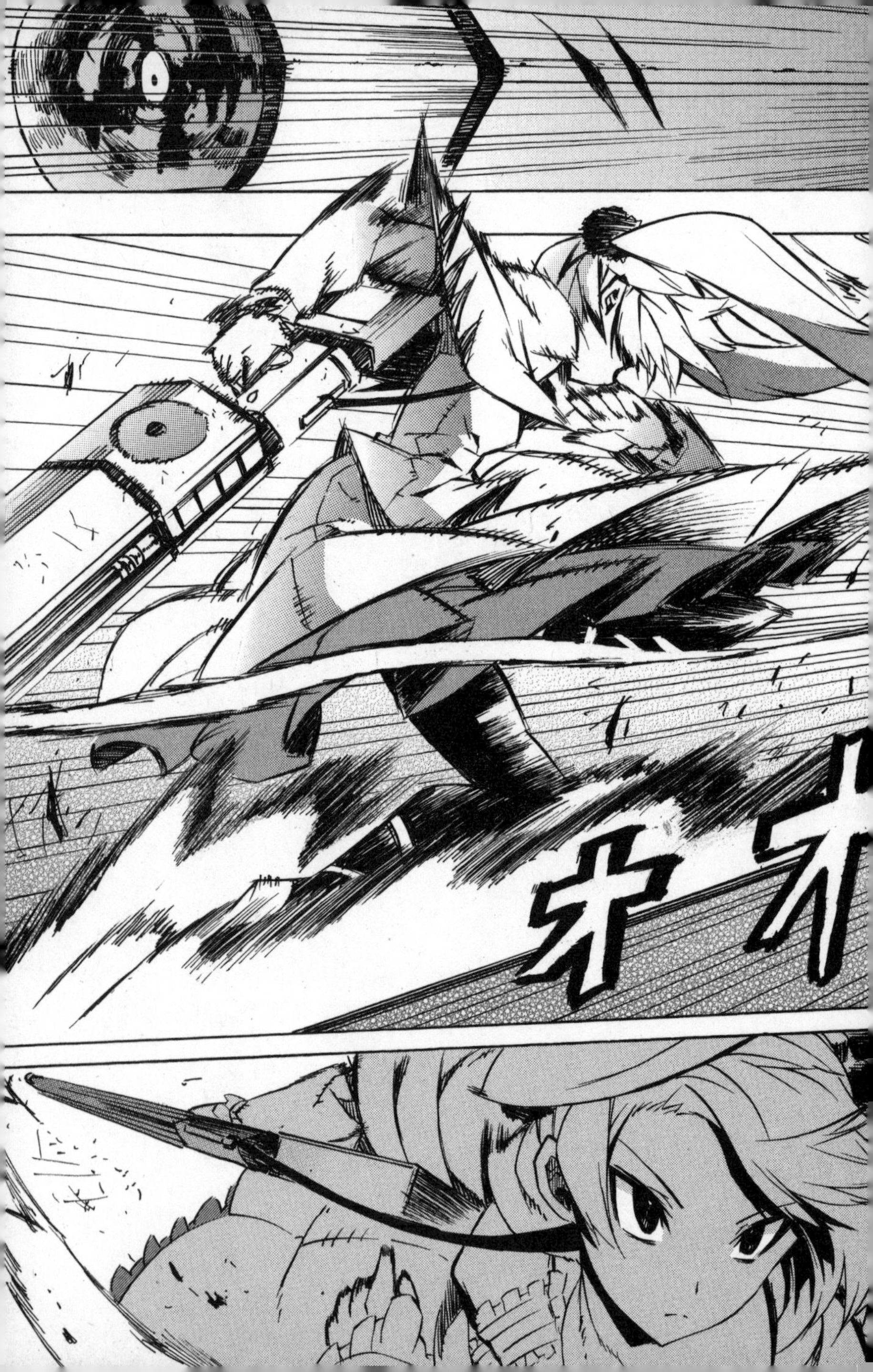
オオ

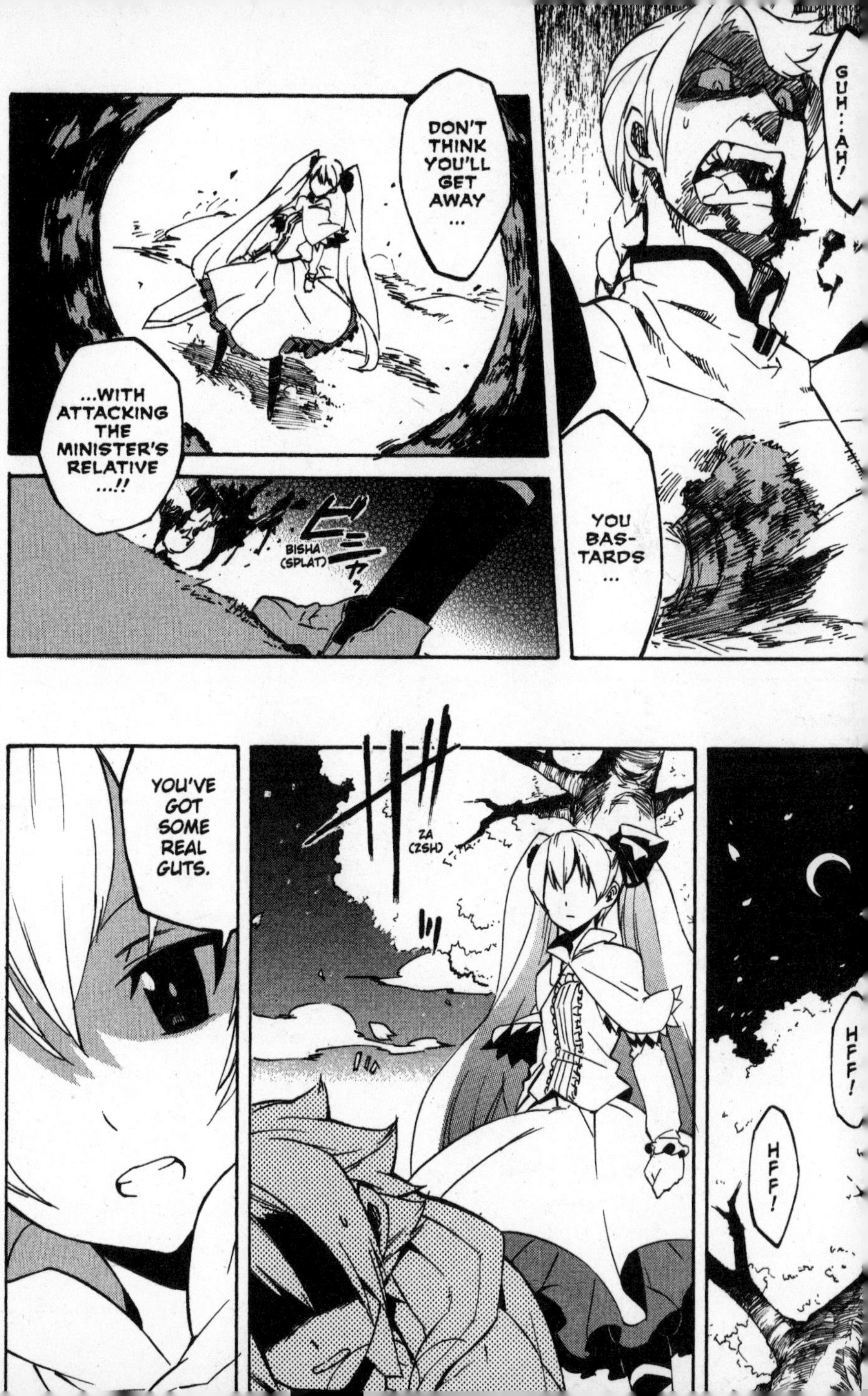
GUH...AH!
YOU BASTARDS...
DON'T THINK YOU'LL GET AWAY...
...WITH ATTACKING THE MINISTER'S RELATIVE...!!
BISHA (SPLAT)
HFF!
HFF!
ZA (ZSH)
YOU'VE GOT SOME REAL GUTS.

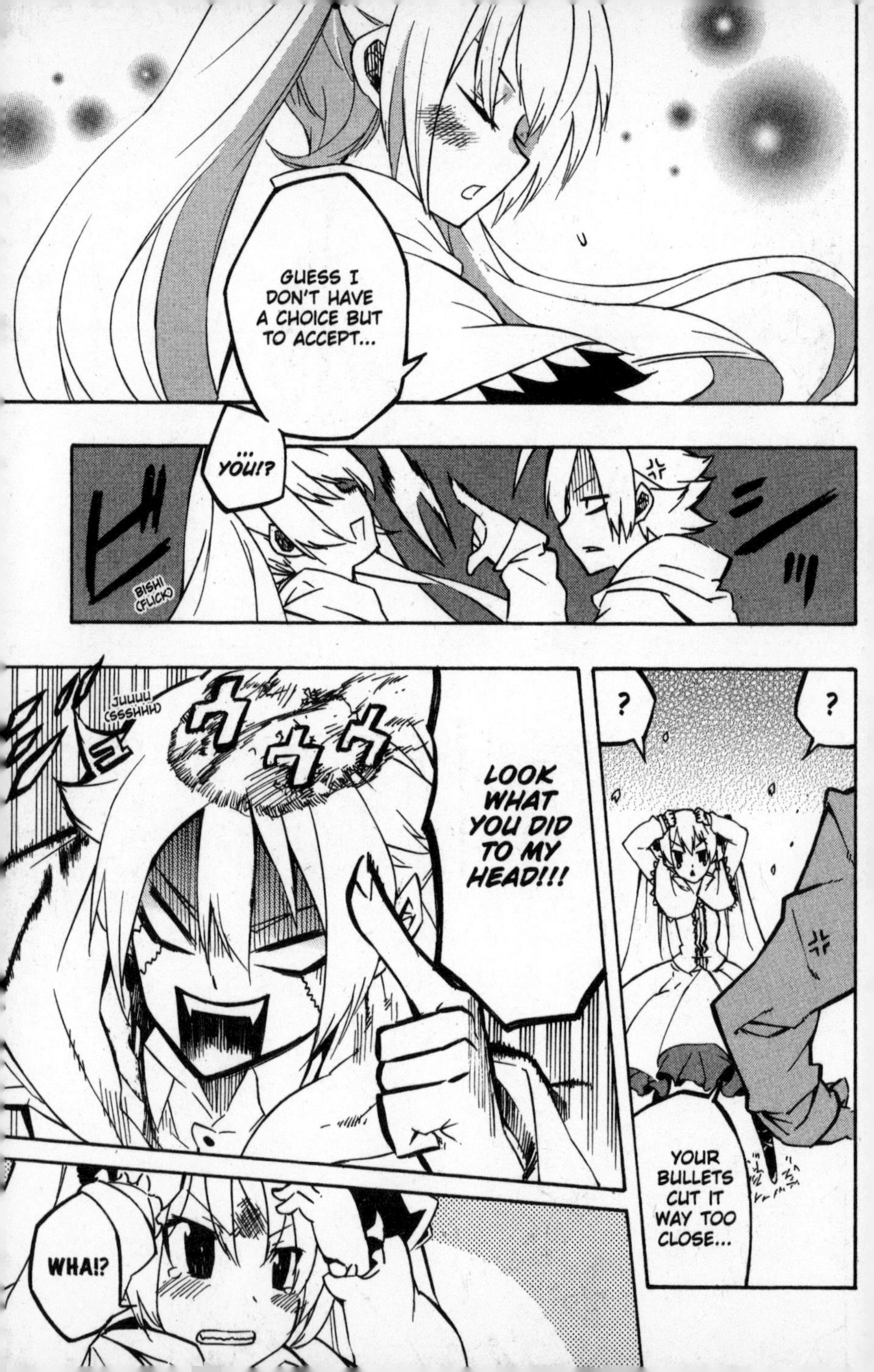
GUESS I DON'T HAVE A CHOICE BUT TO ACCEPT...
...YOU!?
BISHI (FLICK)
?
?
YOUR BULLETS CUT IT WAY TOO CLOSE...
LOOK WHAT YOU DID TO MY HEAD!!!
JUUUU (SSSHHH)
WHA!?

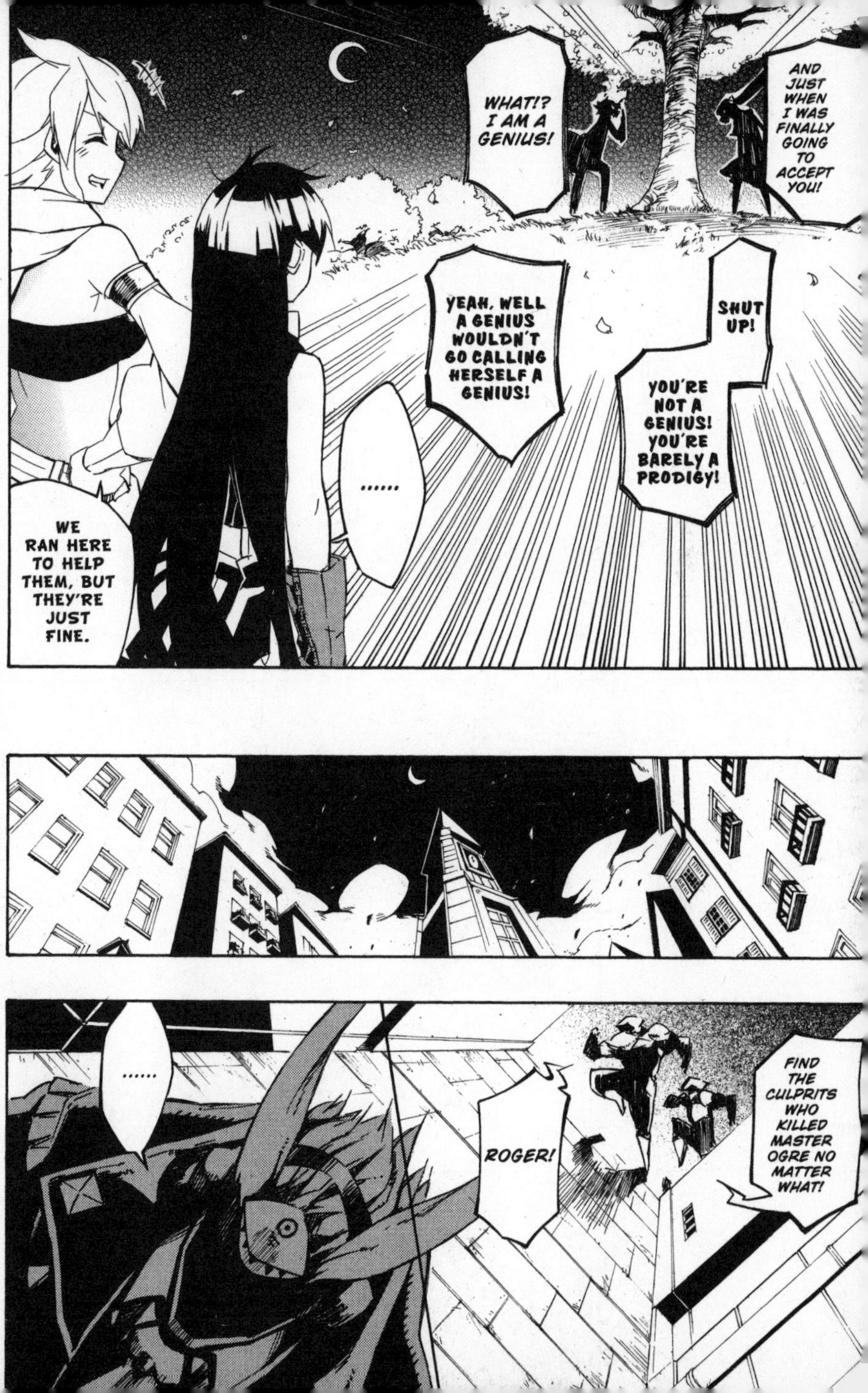
AND JUST WHEN I WAS FINALLY GOING TO ACCEPT YOU!
WHAT!? I AM A GENIUS!
SHUT UP!
YEAH, WELL A GENIUS WOULDN'T GO CALLING HERSELF A GENIUS!
YOU'RE NOT A GENIUS! YOU'RE BARELY A PRODIGY!
......
WE RAN HERE TO HELP THEM, BUT THEY'RE JUST FINE.
FIND THE CULPRITS WHO KILLED MASTER OGRE NO MATTER WHAT!
ROGER!
......

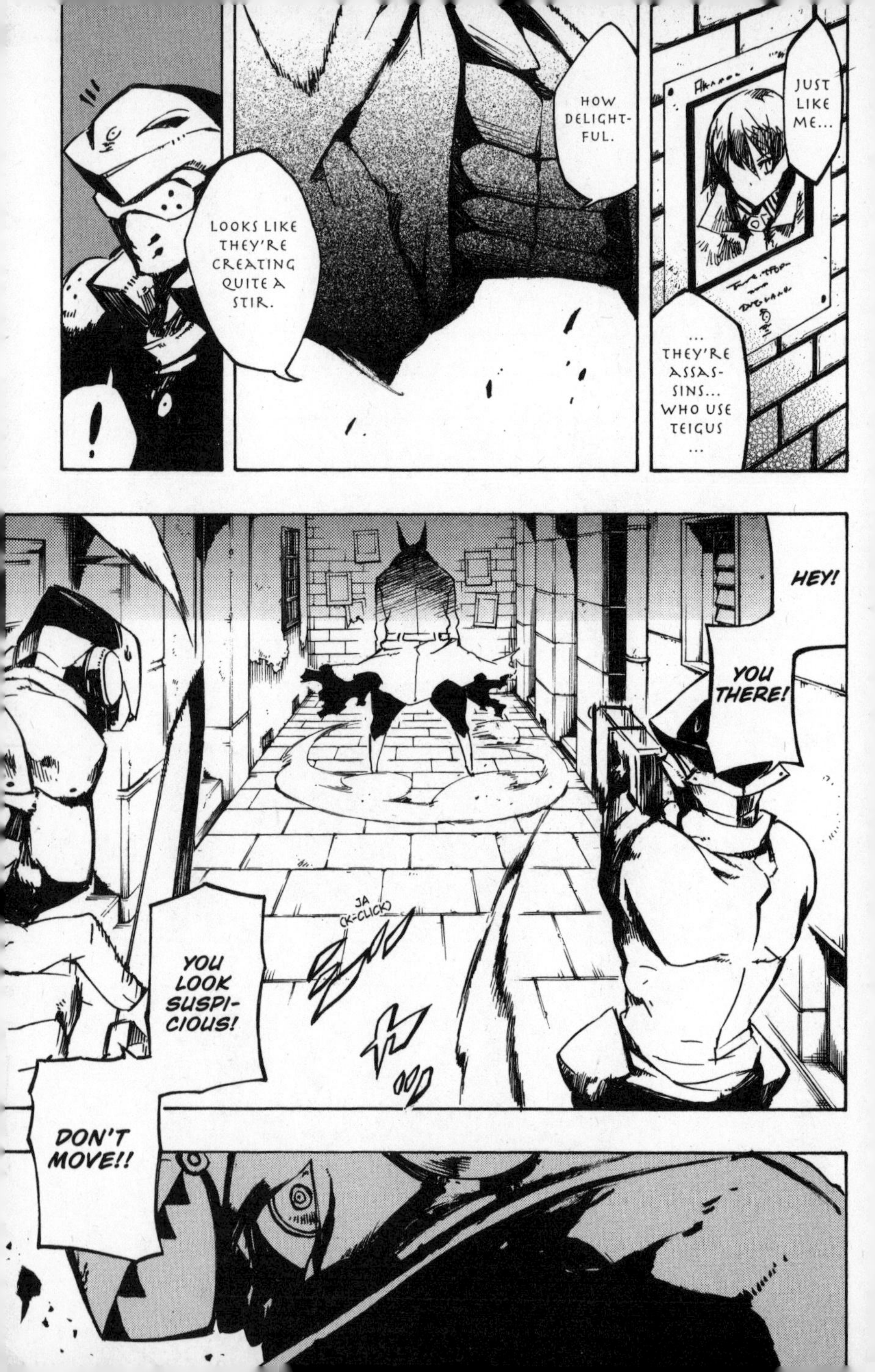
JUST LIKE ME...
... THEY'RE ASSAS-SINS... WHO USE TEIGUS ...
HOW DELIGHT-FUL.
LOOKS LIKE THEY'RE CREATING QUITE A STIR.
HEY!
YOU THERE!
YOU LOOK SUSPICI-CIOUS!
JA (K-CLICK)
DON'T MOVE!!

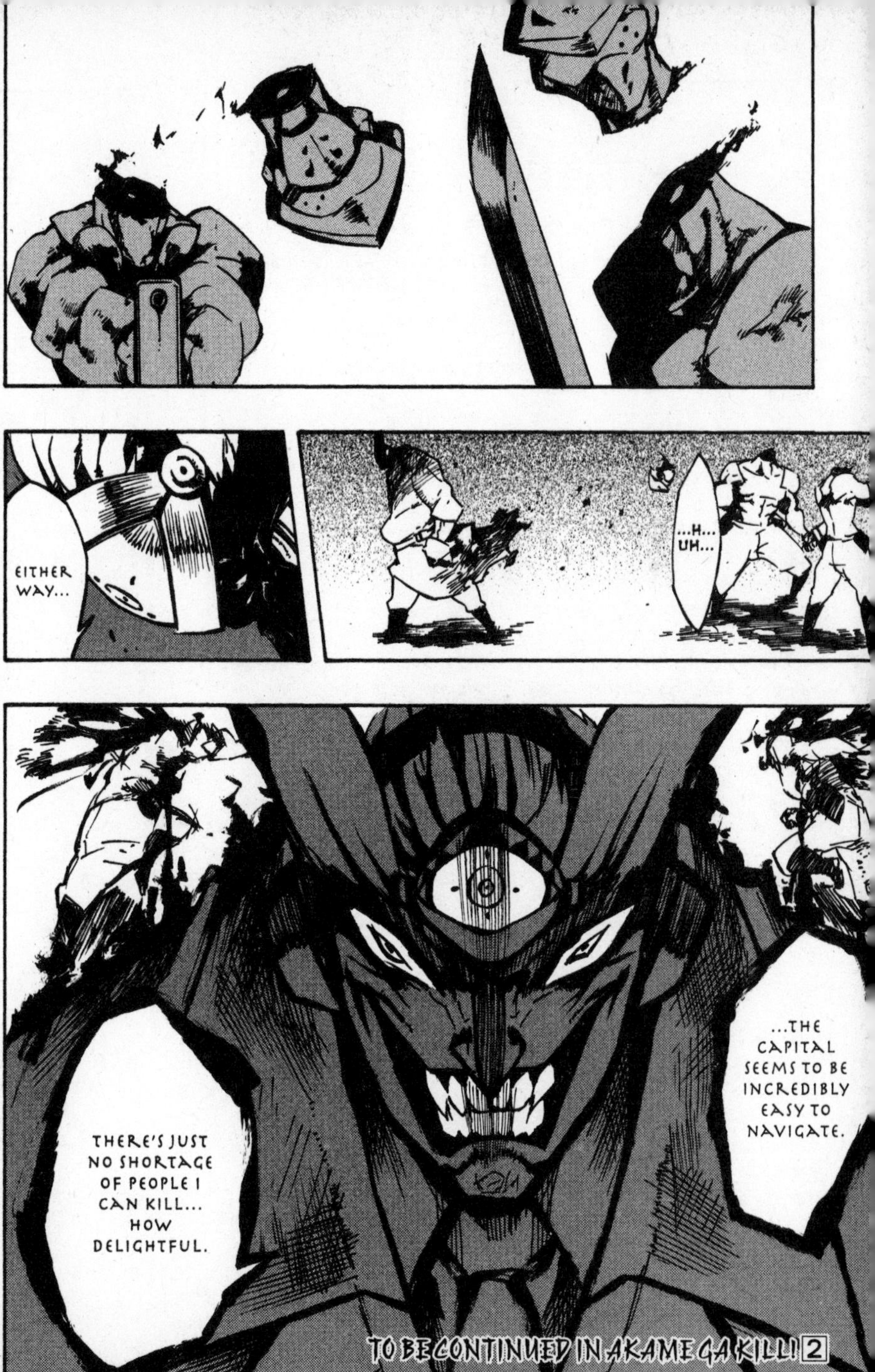
...H...
UH...
EITHER WAY...
...THE CAPITAL SEEMS TO BE INCREDIBLY EASY TO NAVIGATE.
THERE'S JUST NO SHORTAGE OF PEOPLE I CAN KILL... HOW DELIGHTFUL.
TO BE CONTINUED IN AKAME GA KILL! 2

TAKAHIRO's PostScript

Thank you to everyone who bought this book.
This is Takahiro from Minato Soft who headed this work.

I'm now going to explain how *Akame ga KILL!* came about.

In 2007, I received an e-mail from an editor.
They asked me if I'd like to do a manga for a Square Enix magazine. Being a lover of manga, I immediately agreed to do it. First we held a meeting, and he got to hear my idea for the project.

I said to them, "So it's about an all-female band of assassins, and the protagonist is a boy who is captured by them and has to work for them."
Hearing that, the editor grinned at me and said, "I love it!" and I got the immediate okay. It really was a conference held by two obvious masochists.
As for the timing of the manga's serialization, I had just gone independent, so I asked them to wait until my company had released two titles first and got stabilized, and they did. During that time, I thought up the characters, story, and world.

In August of 2009, "Majikoi - Oh! Samurai Girls" was released, so I wanted to start nailing down the artist for the serialization. That's when I got to meet Tashiro-san. His action scenes were particularly eye-catching, so I knew he'd do a great job pulling off the fast-paced scenes. Not to mention he draws cute girls!

I hope I get to write to you all again in volume 2.
Until then~

Takahiro

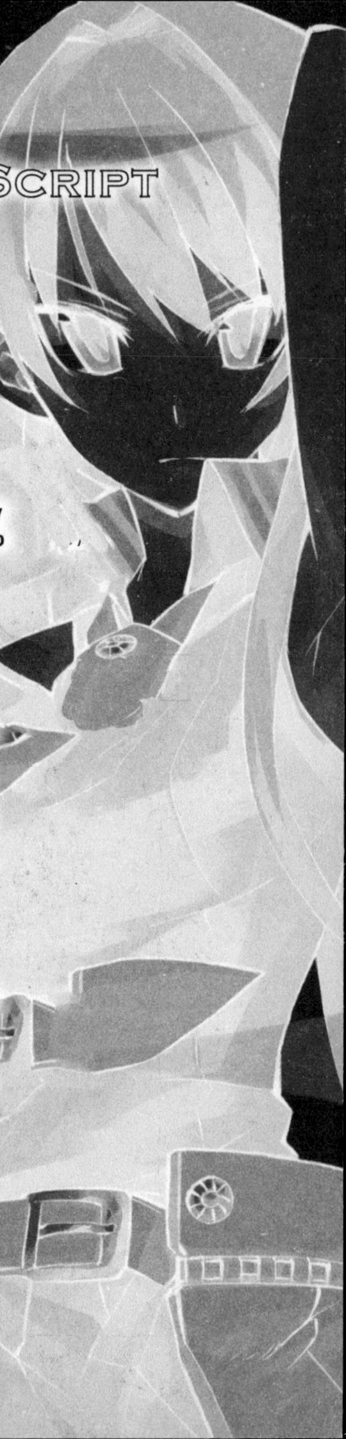

AKAME GA KILL!

ORIGINAL STORY BY

TAKAHIRO-SAMA

EDITOR

KOZUMI-SAMA

EVERYONE WHO HELPED WITH THIS PROJECT

KAGETSU-SAN

TAKAGI-SAN

YAMASHITA-KUN

FUJINO-SAN

NOZUE-SAN

AOYAMA-SAN

IMAI-SAN

YAMAGIYWA-SAN

SUZUKI-SAN

YAMAMOTO-SAN

PINE-SAN

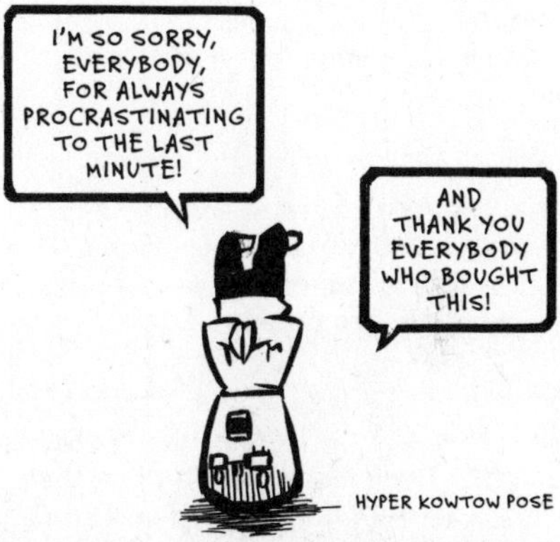
I'M SO SORRY, EVERYBODY, FOR ALWAYS PROCRASTINATING TO THE LAST MINUTE!
AND THANK YOU EVERYBODY WHO BOUGHT THIS!
HYPER KOWTOW POSE

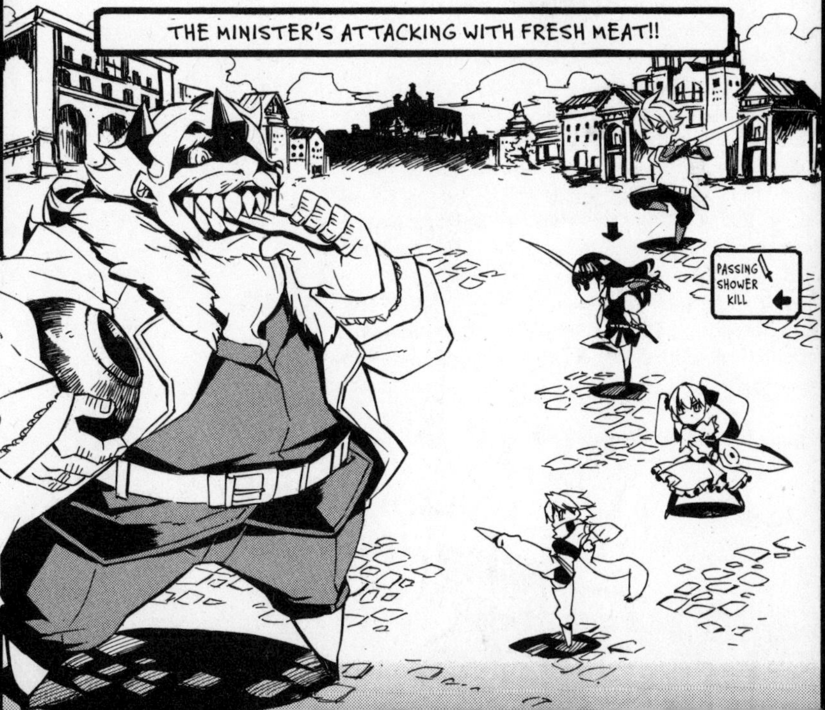
THE MINISTER'S ATTACKING WITH FRESH MEAT!!
PASSING SHOWER KILL

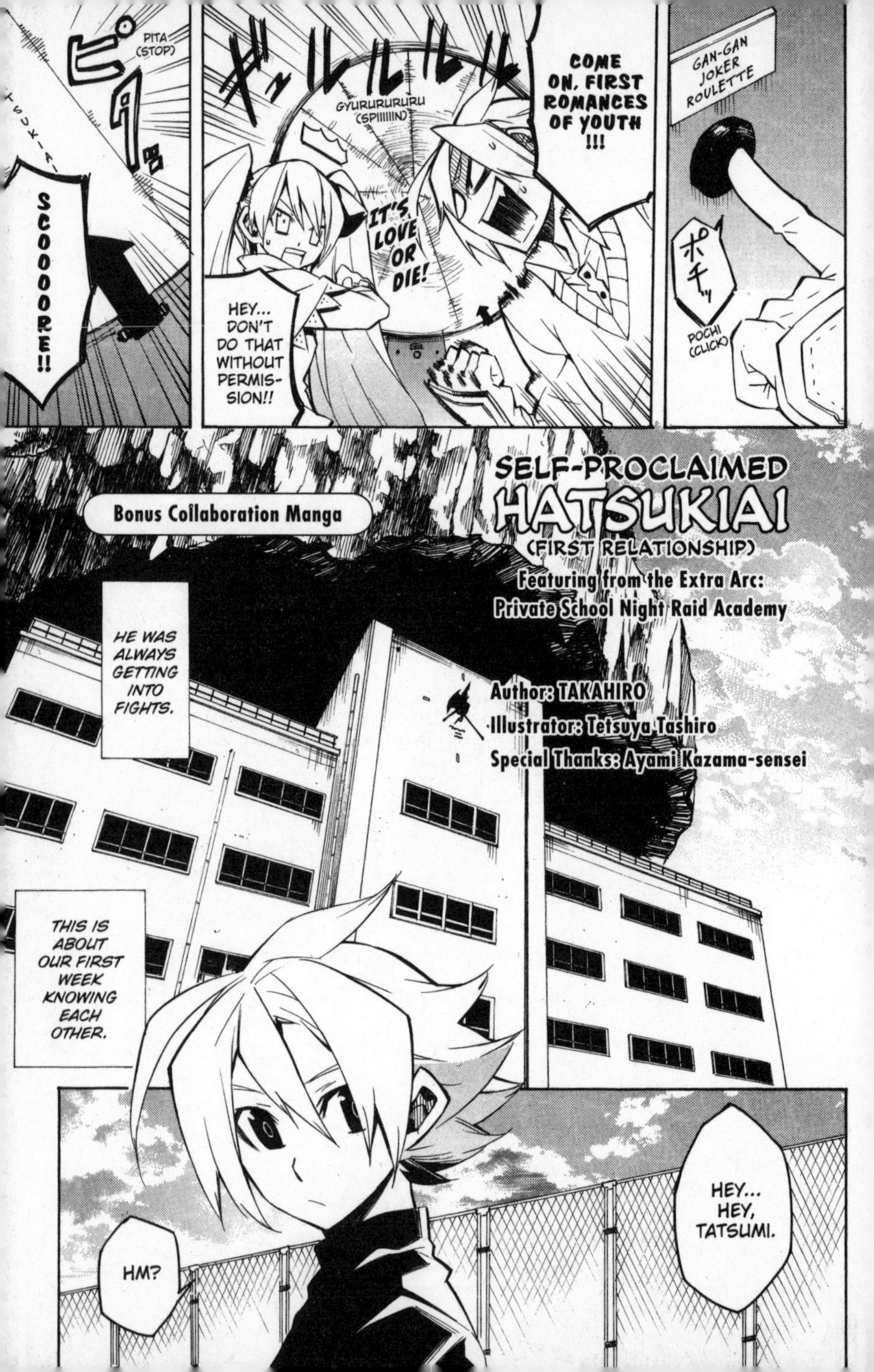
GAN-GAN JOKER ROULETTE
ポチッ
POCHI (CLICK)
COME ON, FIRST ROMANCES OF YOUTH !!!
GYURURURURU (SPIIIIIIN)
IT'S LOVE OR DIE!
HEY... DON'T DO THAT WITHOUT PERMISSION!!
PITA (STOP)
TSUKIAI
SCOOOOORE!!
SELF-PROCLAIMED HATSUKIAI (FIRST RELATIONSHIP)
Featuring from the Extra Arc: Private School Night Raid Academy
Author: TAKAHIRO
Illustrator: Tetsuya Tashiro
Special Thanks: Ayami Kazama-sensei
Bonus Collaboration Manga
HE WAS ALWAYS GETTING INTO FIGHTS.
THIS IS ABOUT OUR FIRST WEEK KNOWING EACH OTHER.
HEY... HEY, TATSUMI.
HM?

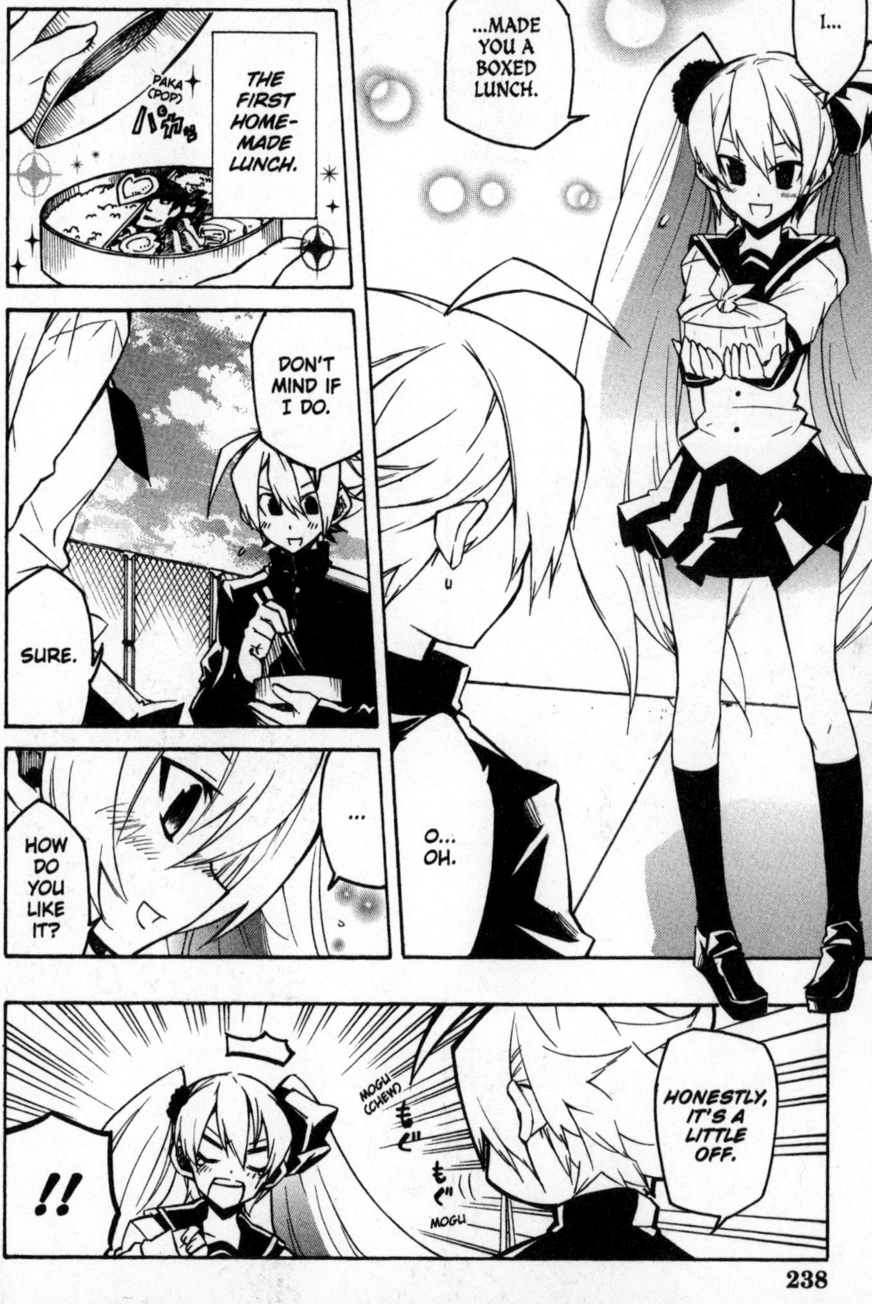
I...
...MADE YOU A BOXED LUNCH.
O... OH.
PAKA (POP)
パカ
THE FIRST HOME-MADE LUNCH.
DON'T MIND IF I DO.
SURE.
...
HOW DO YOU LIKE IT?
HONESTLY, IT'S A LITTLE OFF.
MOGU (CHEW)
もぐ
もぐ
MOGU
!!

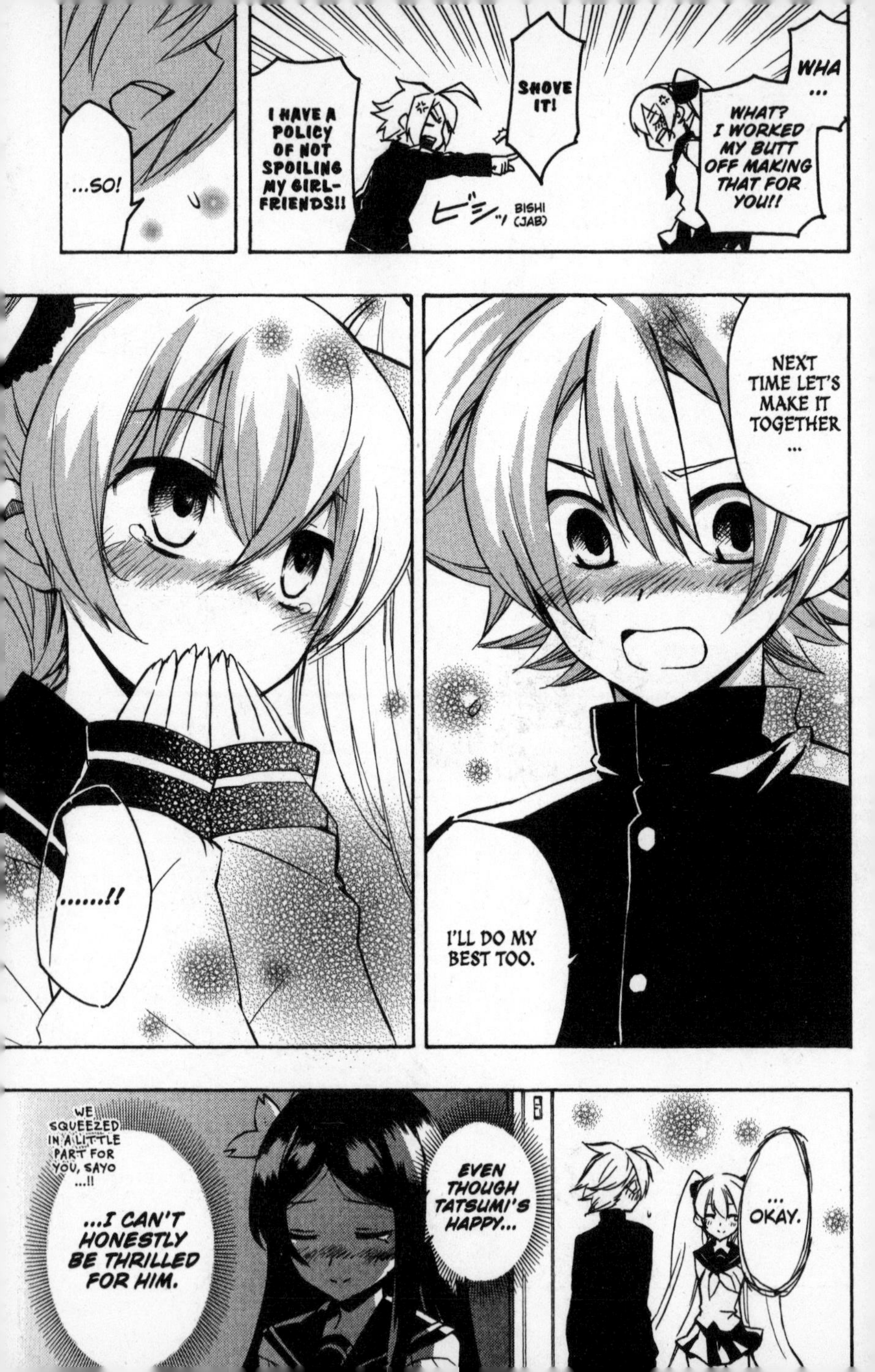
WHA...
WHAT? I WORKED MY BUTT OFF MAKING THAT FOR YOU!!
SHOVE IT!
I HAVE A POLICY OF NOT SPOILING MY GIRL-FRIENDS!!
BISHI (JAB)
...SO!
NEXT TIME LET'S MAKE IT TOGETHER...
I'LL DO MY BEST TOO.
......!!
...OKAY.
EVEN THOUGH TATSUMI'S HAPPY...
...I CAN'T HONESTLY BE THRILLED FOR HIM.
WE SQUEEZED IN A LITTLE PART FOR YOU, SAYO...!!

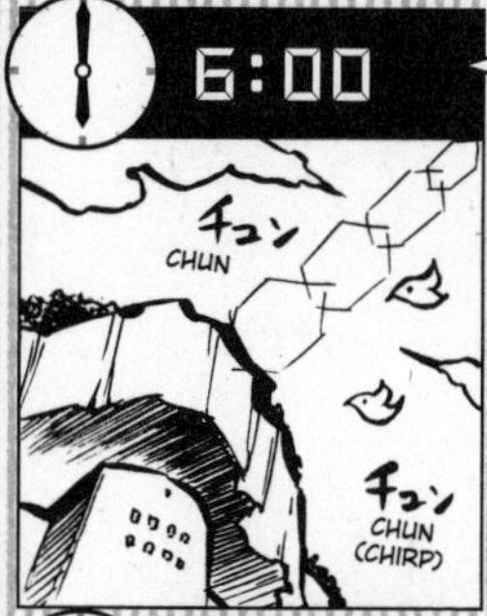
6:00
チュン
CHUN
チュン
CHUN (CHIRP)

Mornings are early on the mountain. Today will be another full day of learning how to get by in the hideout.

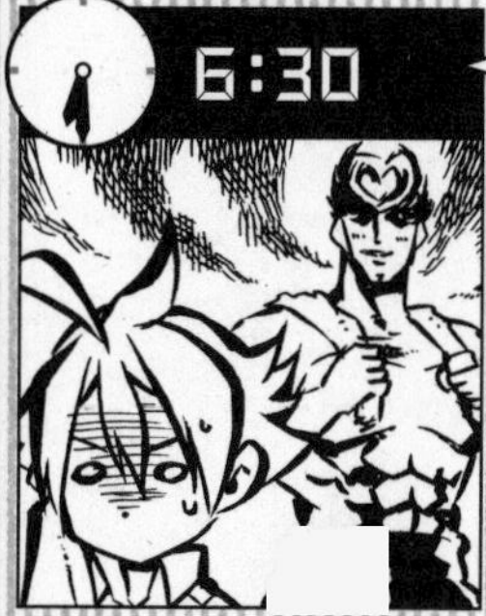
6:30

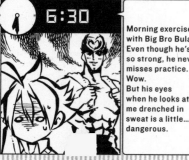

Morning exercise with Big Bro Bulat. Even though he's so strong, he never misses practice. Wow.
But his eyes when he looks at me drenched in sweat is a little... dangerous.

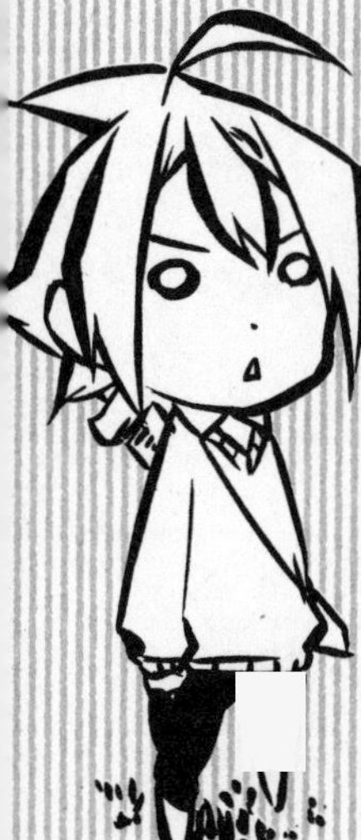

TATSUMI'S JOURNAL

~MY DAYS WITH THE ASSASSINS~

STORY:
TAKAHIRO

ILLUSTRATIONS:
TETSUYA TASHIRO

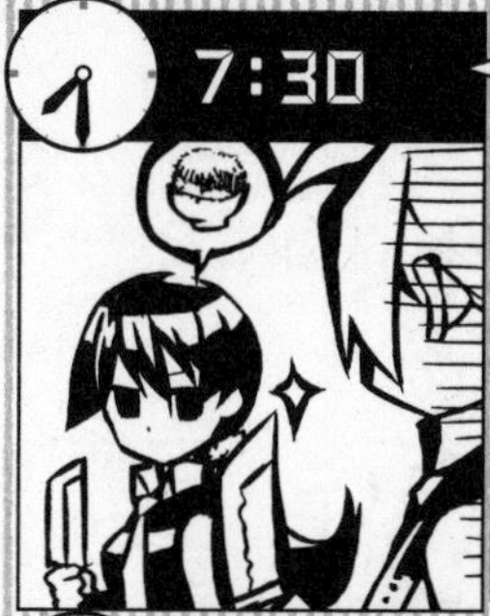
7:30

Prepare breakfast with Akame.
Tatsumi: "What should we make for breakfast today?"
Akame: "Croquettes over rice."
So it's croquettes over rice first thing in the morning.
She really is an assassin. Dicey.

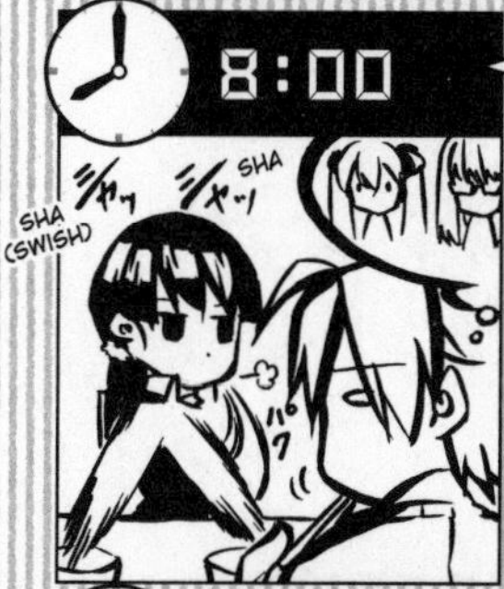
8:00
SHA (SWISH)
SHA

Breakfast. Sheele and Mine aren't morning people and haven't woken up yet. Akame says that's typical and eats their croquettes over rice portions. This girl is bad news.

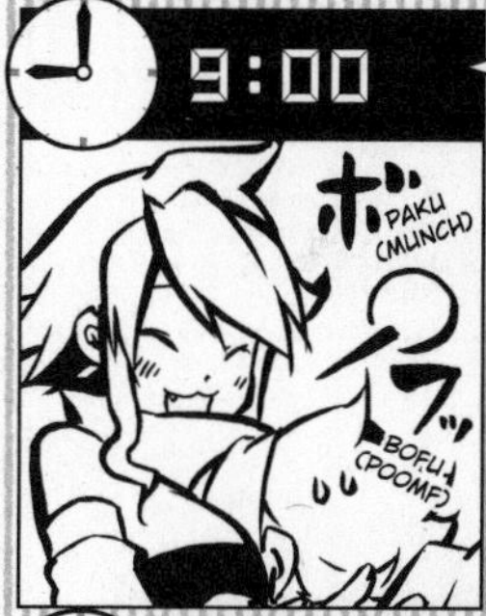
9:00
PAKU (MUNCH)
BOFU (POOMF)

Leone was out gathering information at the capital and comes home in the morning.
Tatsumi: "Give me back the money you swindled out of me when we first met."
Leone: "But that was your tuition fee. You'll just have to put up with this. ♪"
My face gets buried in her bosom.
What a huge rack... Yikes.

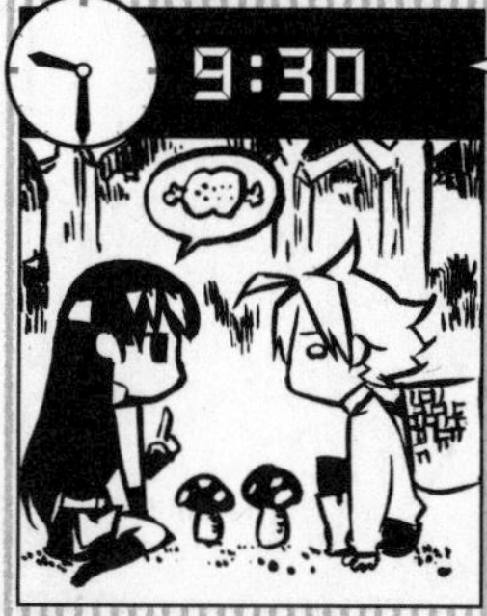
9:30

Go to collect ingredients with Akame in the mountain.
Search for a subject of conversation.
Tatsumi: "Akame, what type of men do you like?"
Akame: "I don't really know. I like my grilled meat to be dripping with juices."
For some reason the conversation always goes back to food... Danger.

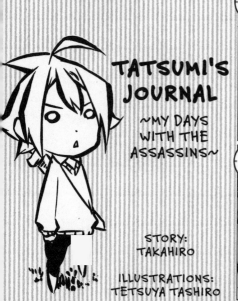

12:30

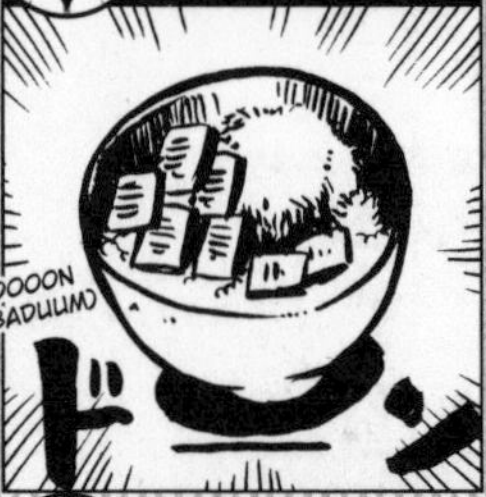
DOOON (BADUUM)
ドーン

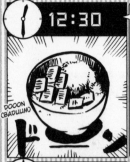

Lunch is Elegant Tuna over rice. Everyone's stomachs after all these heavy foods must be... in trouble.

2:00

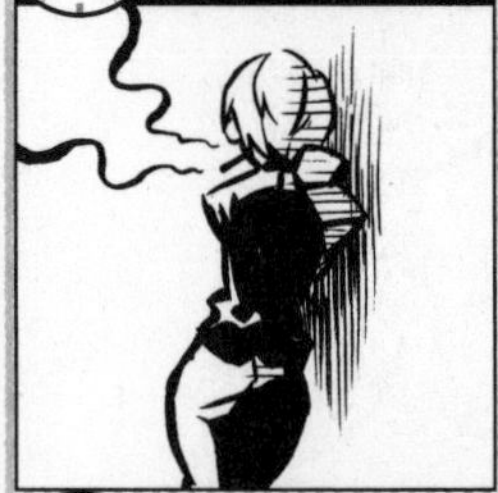

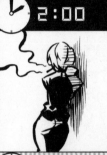

The boss goes through several cigarettes. She must like them.
Najenda: "So, Tatsumi. You smoke?"
I think she wants a smoking buddy.
Akame: "Najenda. Don't force him to smoke."
Mine: "It's smoky enough in here as it is."
The boss's sad look when she smiles wryly at her scolding underlings... That's assassins for you. They're outspoken even against their own boss... Dangerous.

4:00

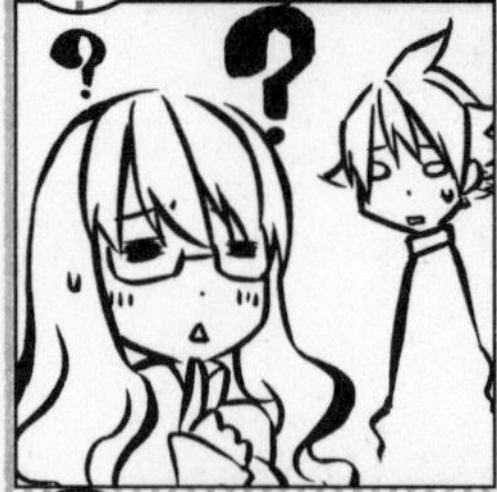
?
?

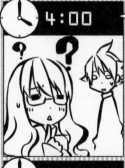

While training, Sheele was zoning out.
I asked her what she was doing.
Sheele: "Actually, I was just wondering the same thing. What was I going to do after lunch?"
...Typical assassin. They're so liberal with how they spend their time. Not good.

6:00

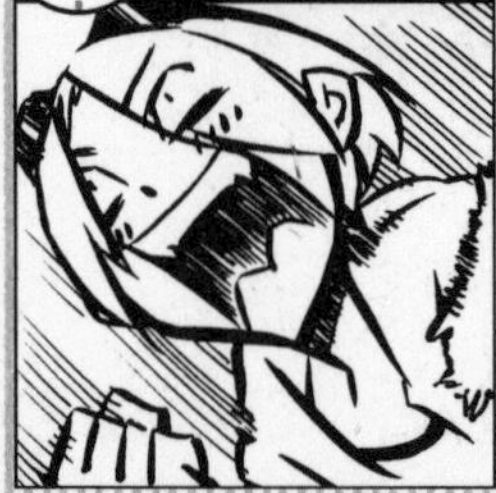

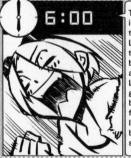

This time of day is when the boss takes her bath.
Lubbo invited me to peek with him, but I was scared and declined.
Lubbock: "I'm going. Even if they bust me in the jaw for it!"
I admire his zeal, but he's in for some trouble.

6:10

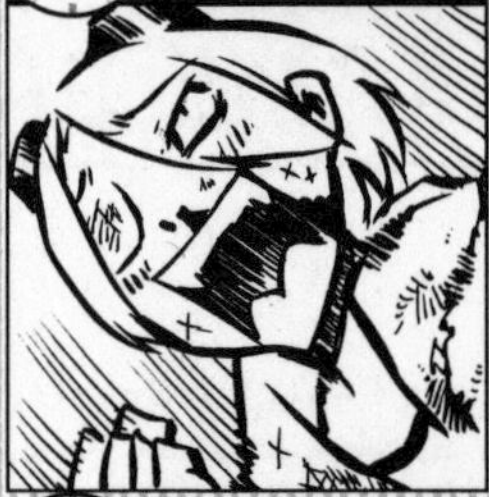

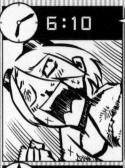

Lubbo failed and got sent home beat up.
Next it's Akame's turn to bathe.
The fact that Lubbo is gutsy enough to want to peek again is dubious.

7:00

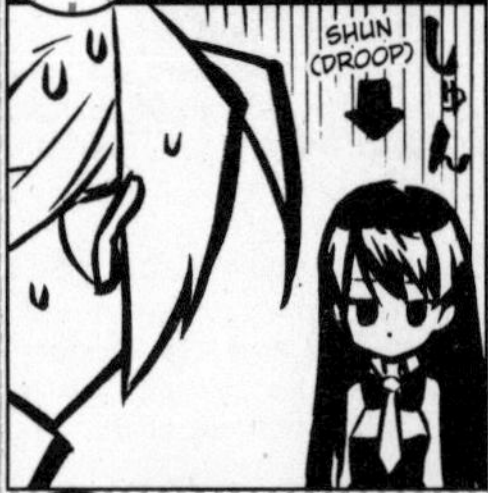
SHUN (DROOP)
しゅん

Tatsumi: "Let's not have grilled kalbi over rice for dinner tonight."
Akame: "Why not?"
Tatsumi: "We've got to serve something a little lighter and more refreshing!"
Akame: "......Okay."
She told me with a glum expression.
Man, my conscience is at risk.

9:00

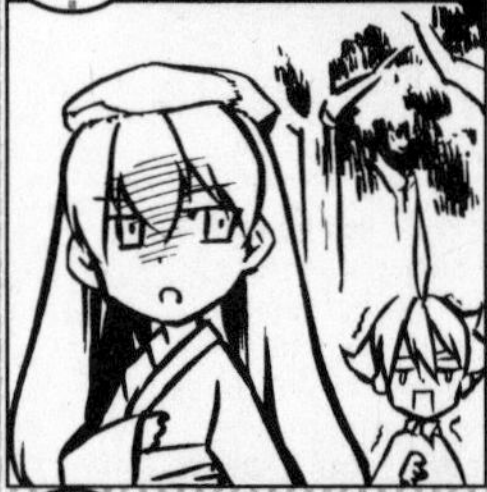

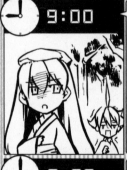

It's my time to bathe. Because Mine went overtime for her bath, we almost bumped into one another.
Mine: "If you caught me naked, I'd just blast you away."
She really would do it. I'm constantly one step away from death here...
Scary.

0:00

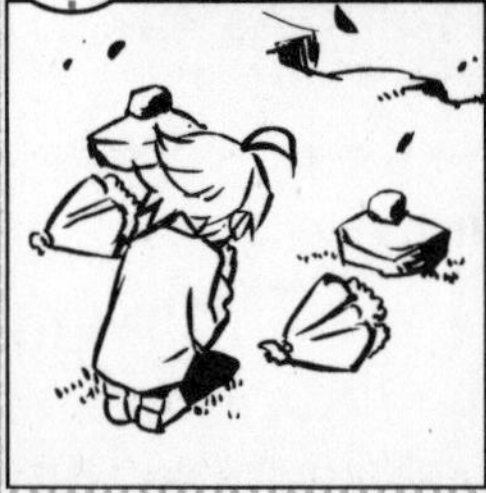

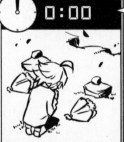

After training, and before going to sleep, I visit Sayo's and Ieyasu's graves. Sheele's left flowers for them.
It seems she wanted to do that first thing this afternoon.
She's a good person.
Sayo, Ieyasu. I'm going to do my best tomorrow as well.

AKAME GA

TAKAHIRO
TETSUYA TASHIRO

Translation: Christine Dashiell • Lettering: James Dashiell

AKAME GA KILL! Vol. 1
© 2010 Takahiro, Tetsuya Tashiro / SQUARE ENIX CO., LTD. First published in Japan in 2010 by SQUARE ENIX CO., LTD. English translation rights arranged with SQUARE ENIX CO., LTD. and Yen Press, LLC through Tuttle-Mori Agency, Inc., Tokyo.

English translation © 2015 by SQUARE ENIX CO., LTD.

Yen Press
1290 Avenue of the Americas
New York, NY 10104

Visit us at yenpress.com
facebook.com/yenpress
twitter.com/yenpress
yenpress.tumblr.com
instagram.com/yenpress

First Yen Press Edition: January 2015

Yen Press is an imprint of Yen Press, LLC.
The Yen Press name and logo are trademarks of Yen Press, LLC.

The publisher is not responsible for websites (or their content) that are not owned by the publisher.

Library of Congress Control Number: 2015373812

ISBN: 978-0-316-25946-0

14

WOR

Printed in the United States of America